# STRIP JOINT

by CAROL LAY

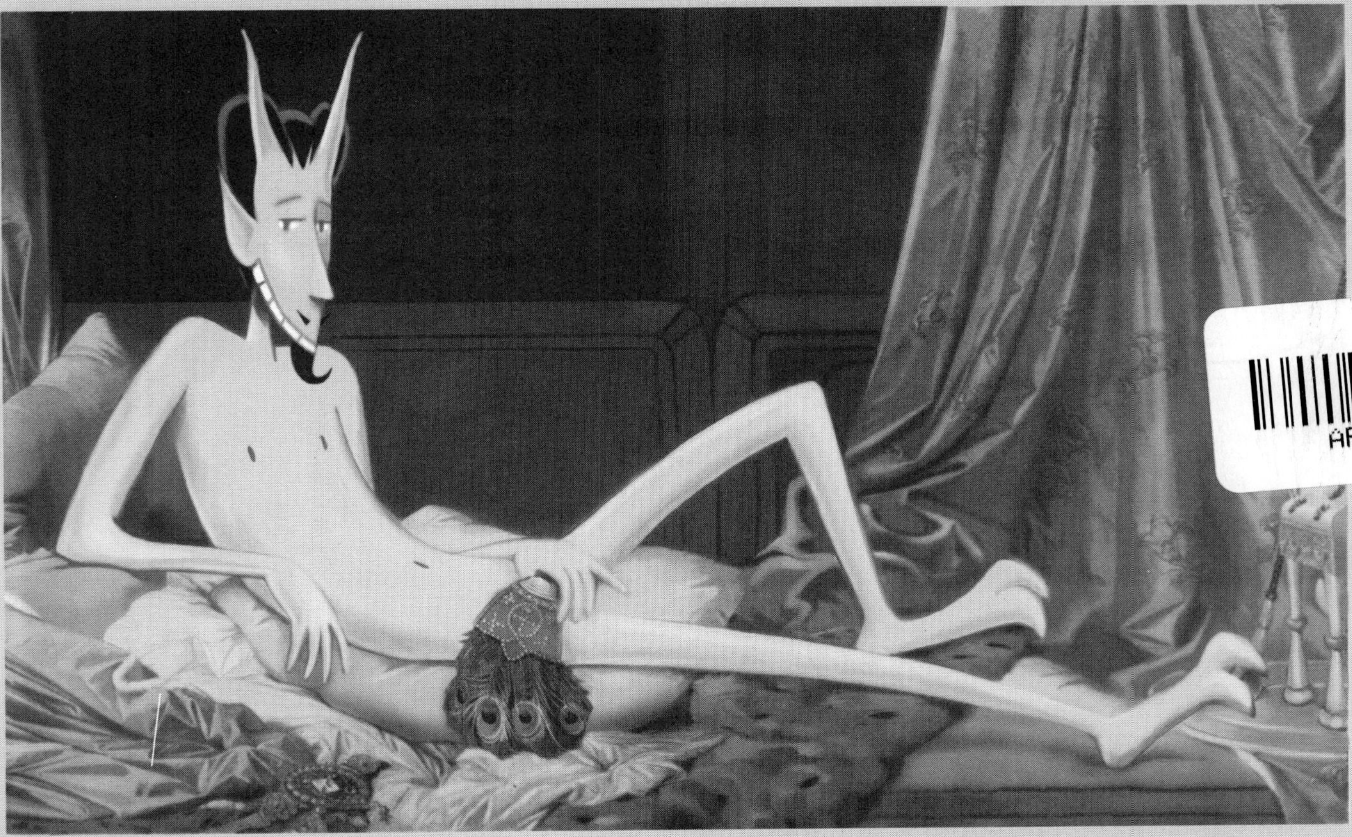

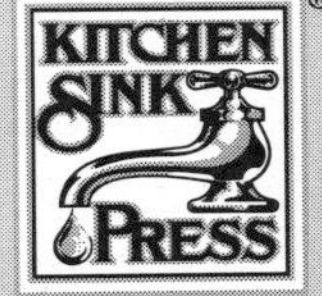


Northampton, Massachusetts

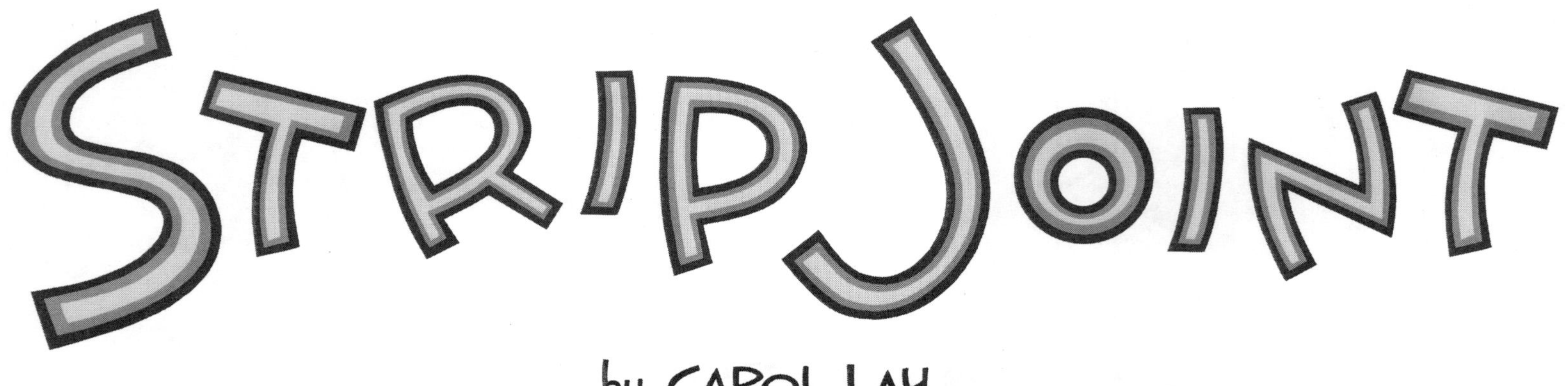


by CAROL LAY


publisher
Denis Kitchen

editor
Christopher Couch

art director
C. Evan Metcalf

designer
Chris Shadoian

art intern
Tom Martin

vice president
James Kitchen

senior director, sales and marketing
Jamie Riehle

national sales director
Ryan D. Eagan

director of customer service
Karen Lowman

production manager
John Wills

warehouse manager
Dwight Jackson

Library of Congress Cataloging-In-Publication Data

Lay, Carol.
Strip joint / by Carol Lay.
p. cm.
ISBN 0-87816-578-9
I. Title
PN6727.L37S77 1998 98-35925
741.5'973–dc21

First Printing, September 1998 5 4 3 2 1

# Introduction

The following is the most unbelievable *Story Minute* of them all. It's the tale of a woman who almost disappeared off the face of the planet. To protect her identity, let's call her "Carol L."

Carol L. was a young and talented cartoonist and, like so many young and talented cartoonists, she didn't know what she wanted to be when she didn't go grow. (Not growing up is key to being a cartoonist. If you grow up, you might as well go work at H&R Block filling out 1040s.)

Oh, she knew she'd do something involved with her artwork . . . but what? Her problem was that she was too versatile. Buddy Rich once said that settling on his life's work was easy: "I was brilliant at playing drums, rotten at everything else. So what was there to decide?"

Carol L. couldn't play the drums. At least, I don't think she could play the drums. But she could do just about everything else, especially if it involved drawing, so she had way too many options of form and style. Her sketchbook looked like eighteen illustrators (no two from the same planet) had jammed to fill up pages. What to do, what to do, what to do?

In the mid-seventies, she started lettering Marvel Comics, which was a little like Dunkin' Donuts hiring the young Wolfgang Puck to twist crullers. Soon after, a brilliant and insightful editor[1] over at Hanna-Barbera employed her to letter for him and then gave her a chance to ink some comics. She did it so well that this wise and perceptive editor[2] assigned her to try penciling a few of the stories. This she did so well that the discerning and clear-sighted editor[3] bowed to the inevitable and let her start writing as well.

From lettering to doing whole stories on her own; this is an ascent that can take years. Decades, even.

In the matter of Carol L., it took maybe three months, maybe less. (The editor was worried that she'd soon have his job, plus she'd start running the printing presses, plus she'd probably kick Bill and Joe out and start running the studio.)

She didn't do any of that, but soon she was everywhere and in every style—doing advertising design, drawing underground and mainstream comics, and doing storyboards for commercials, rock videos, movies, and animation. Everyone wanted to hire her.

So what was the problem? Well, if she'd been a little less talented, that could have been a Happy Ending right there. But she wasn't and it wasn't.

Back in the sixties, George Carlin was a successful comedian . . . one everyone wanted to hire. But he woke up one morning and made an amazing discovery: he wasn't in his own act.

That was how he described it. His act was very funny, but in it he was a game show host and he was an Indian drill sergeant and he was an anchorman and he was the hippie-dippy weatherman, Al Sleet. At no point was he George Carlin. And the material, though written by him and hilarious, did not particularly reflect his point of view. Or anyone's.

So he made a change. He grew his hair and beard long, and started dressing on-stage the way he dressed off-stage. He retired the cast of characters and found his own voice and, in so doing, became maybe the most important stand-up comedian of his generation. He certainly took what he was doing to a whole new level.

Carol L. had much the same problem; she was successful, but she was drawing like everyone. Which meant she wasn't drawing like Carol L. She'd mastered every style but her own. She didn't have one . . . yet.

So instead of looking at other artists, she started looking into herself, seeking out her own voice and bringing it to the surface. Before long, it was heard loud and clear throughout the cartooning community, for she had plenty to say and all the skills to say it.

A few, at first, wondered about the odd people she was concocting—characters sporting heads that were comprised of teeth from the upper lip down. Most looked like they could have gone through a crate of Colgate after every meal. "Why is she drawing like that?" they asked.

Soon, about the time she created her splendid, self-syndicated *Story Minute*, they got it; she wasn't redesigning the human face . . . she was reconfiguring the entire world, filtering reality through a unique (but wicked) sense o' humor.

The teeth? That's merely the way people look in the reality of Carol L. Once you migrate to her plane of existence, it doesn't seem that odd. In fact, after you finish reading this, her latest collection, you'll probably decide that her world makes more sense than your so-called "real" one. You'll find yourself looking at people with chins and wondering why their overbites don't extend down to their collars.

The answer, of course, is that it's more interesting her way. Everything is. For Carol L. has proven to be not only an incredible stylist, but a born storyteller as well. As her biggest fan[4] puts it, "There are published, best-selling authors who can't tell as fine a story in seventeen hours as she can in sixty seconds." Those who knew her when she was starting out[5] are thrilled to see her produce a strip as special as its creator. In fact, one of her first employers[6] thinks one *Story Minute* is worth a few hours of any other comic.

The End.

—Mark Evanier

1. Me.
2. Me.
3. Still me. And really, it didn't take any of those discerning qualities, which I've never had anyway. Even a dense and near-sighted editorial troglodyte can look at gold and tell it glistens.
4. Me.
5. Me.
6. Still me. And really, even a dense and near-sighted editorial troglodyte can look at gold . . . .

# Foreword

I sometimes get email from people who wonder if I'm doing all right. This is because, like many cartoonists, I tell stories that may or may not have something to do with what is going on in my life at the time. For instance, when I moved into a dark apartment already occupied by a destructive black cat, I wrote a couple of stories—one about shadow goblins in a windowless house, and another about living with a destructive black cat. But just because the women in those stories came to unhappy ends doesn't mean that's what happened to me—in reality we ended up moving into a place with nice, big windows after we got the cat declawed. Sometimes, though, hard times are reflected more literally in my stories. That's life.

But more often, story ideas come from watching people, reading the news, or from staring at the ceiling. Because my sense of humor is on the dark side, there are many murders, broken hearts, and mass extinctions in these pages, but there are also a fair number of absurd or happy endings.

And don't be misled by the quaintly racy title and cover art. There is exactly one four-letter word in this collection of strips and only one naked lady cavorting through the woods.

Caveat emptor.

Carol Lay
New York City

For my brother, John.

Also for my
husband, Allen Murdock—my
sounding board, contributor, spell-checker,
grammarian, Macintosh repairman,
and dive buddy.

# THE STRIPS

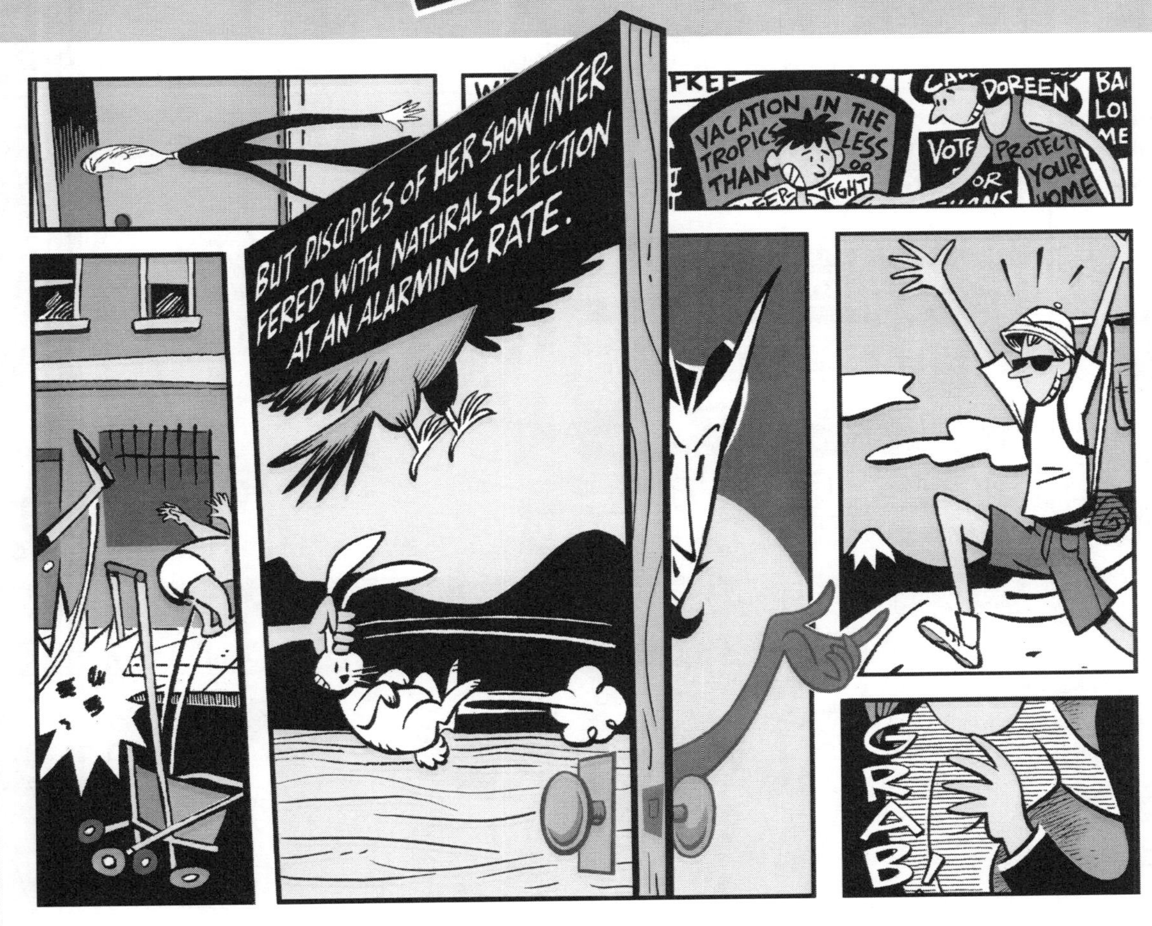

VACATION IN THE TROPICS
LESS
THAN
TIGHT
DOREEN
VOTE
PROTECT YOUR HOME
BUT DISCIPLES OF HER SHOW INTERFERED WITH NATURAL SELECTION AT AN ALARMING RATE.
GRAB!

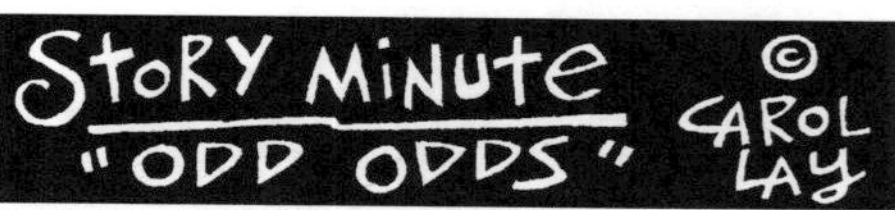

Story Minute
"ODD ODDS"
© CAROL LAY

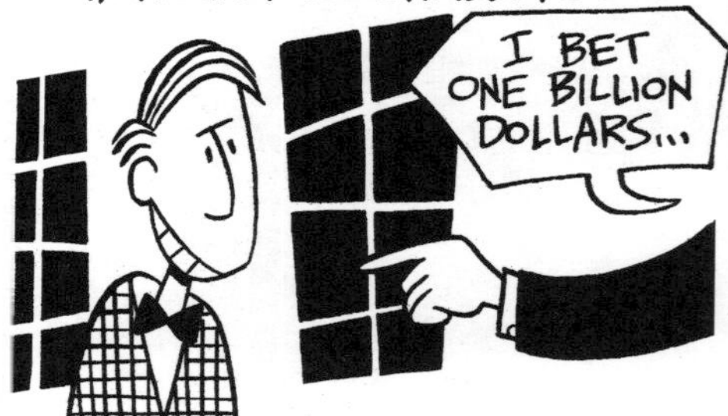

THE MAN ACCEPTED AN INTRIGUING CHALLENGE.
I BET ONE BILLION DOLLARS...

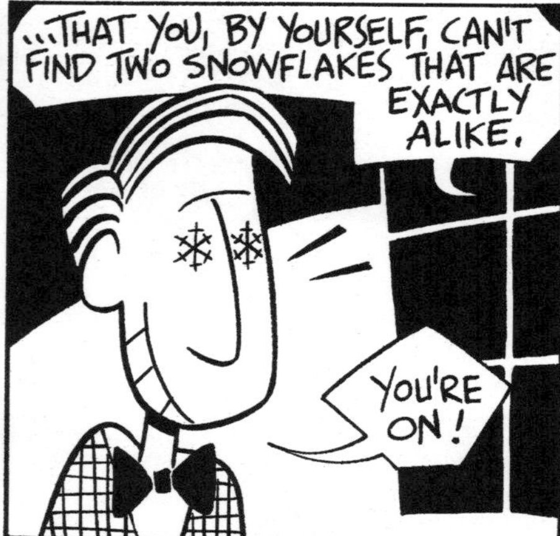

...THAT YOU, BY YOURSELF, CAN'T FIND TWO SNOWFLAKES THAT ARE EXACTLY ALIKE.
YOU'RE ON!

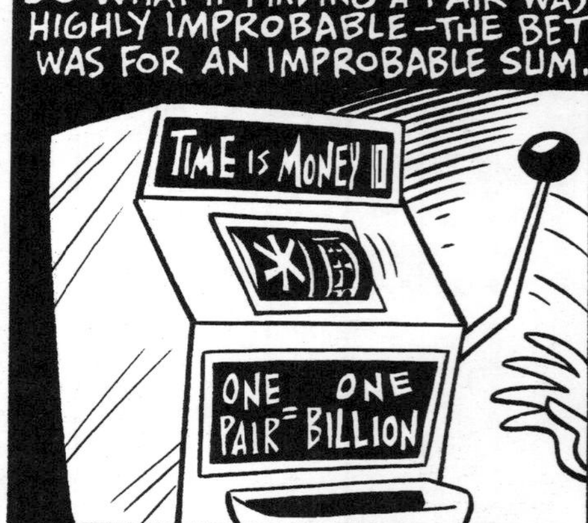

SO WHAT IF FINDING A PAIR WAS HIGHLY IMPROBABLE—THE BET WAS FOR AN IMPROBABLE SUM.
TIME IS MONEY
ONE PAIR = ONE BILLION

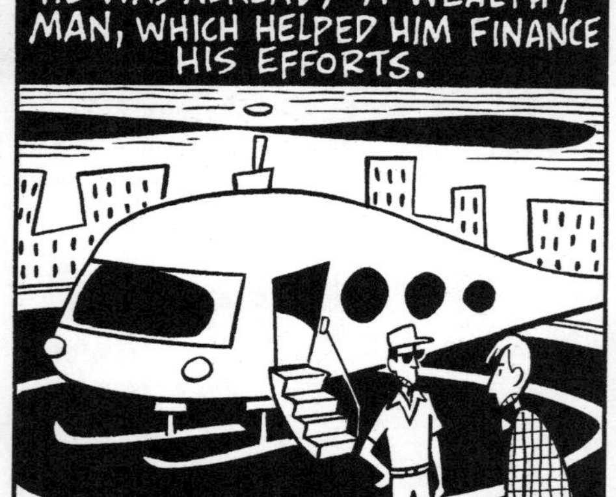

HE WAS ALREADY A WEALTHY MAN, WHICH HELPED HIM FINANCE HIS EFFORTS.

SO, WITH DOGGED DETERMINATION, HE EXAMINED THOUSANDS OF SNOWFLAKES A DAY.

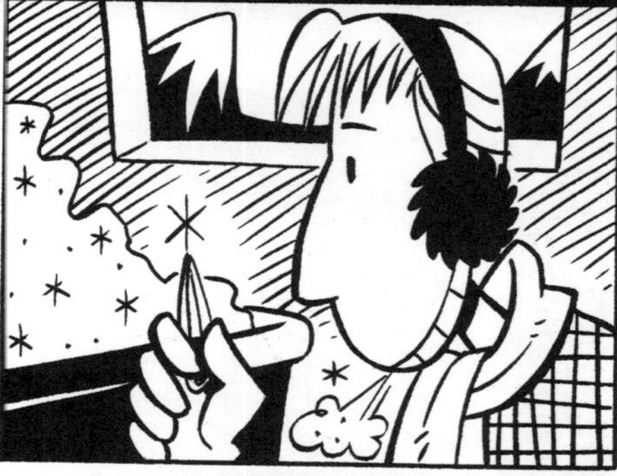
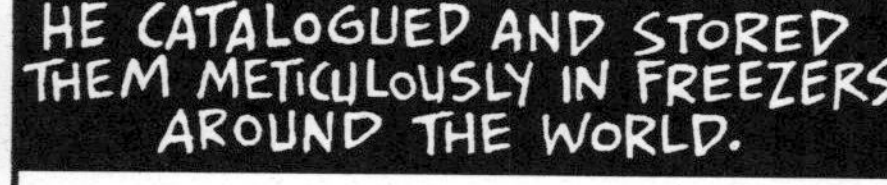

HE CATALOGUED AND STORED THEM METICULOUSLY IN FREEZERS AROUND THE WORLD.

1BUZ3K7
1BUZ3K8
1BUZ3K9

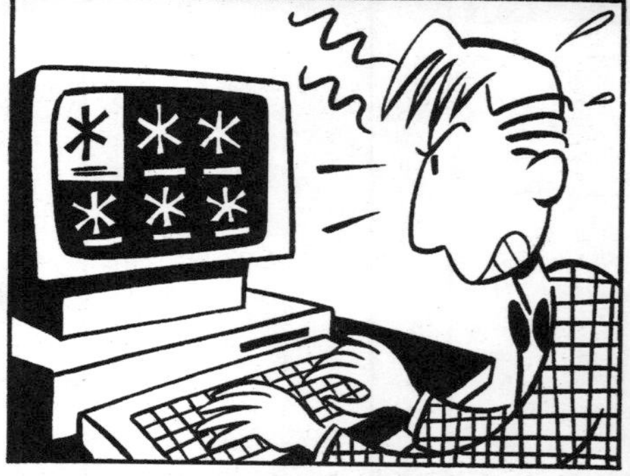

HE COULD NOT BELIEVE THAT EACH FLAKE FROM THIS ENDLESS SUPPLY COULD BE UNIQUE.

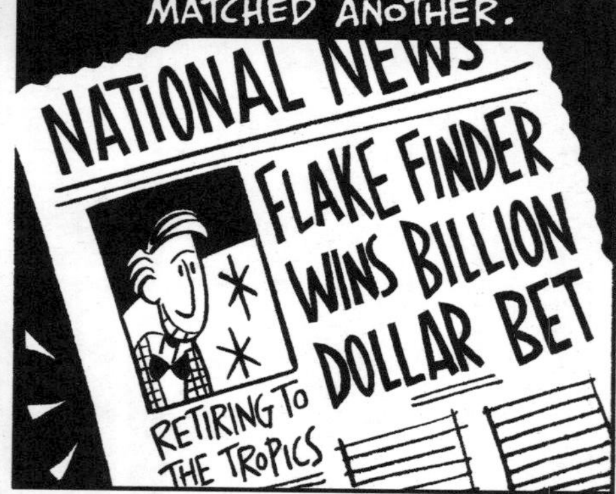

MANY YEARS LATER, HE FINALLY FOUND ONE FLAKE THAT EXACTLY MATCHED ANOTHER.
NATIONAL NEWS
FLAKE FINDER WINS BILLION DOLLAR BET
RETIRING TO THE TROPICS

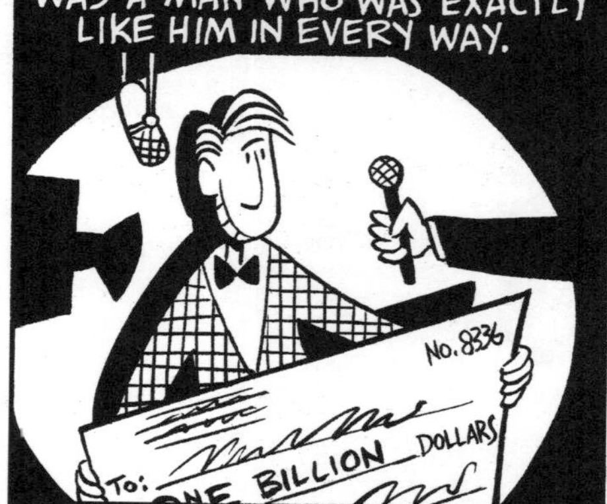

ACROSS THE UNIVERSE, THERE WAS A MAN WHO WAS EXACTLY LIKE HIM IN EVERY WAY.
No. 8336
ONE BILLION DOLLARS
TO:

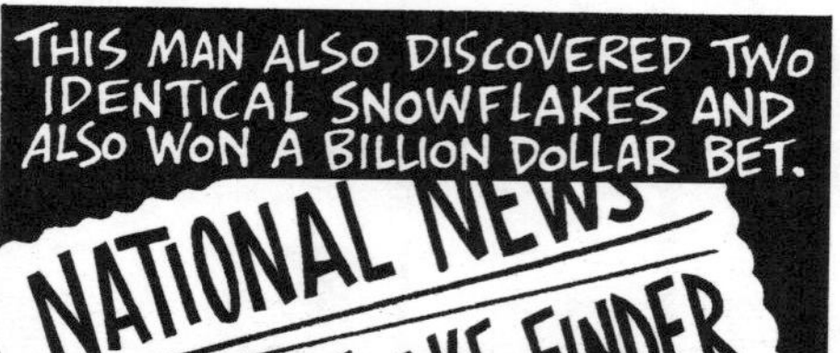

THIS MAN ALSO DISCOVERED TWO IDENTICAL SNOWFLAKES AND ALSO WON A BILLION DOLLAR BET.

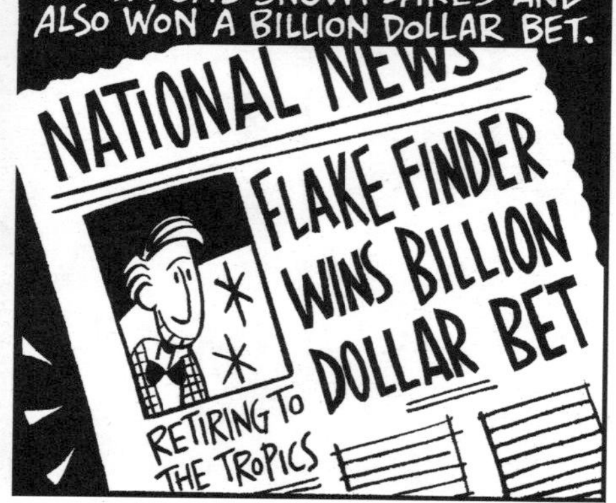

NATIONAL NEWS
FLAKE FINDER WINS BILLION DOLLAR BET
RETIRING TO THE TROPICS

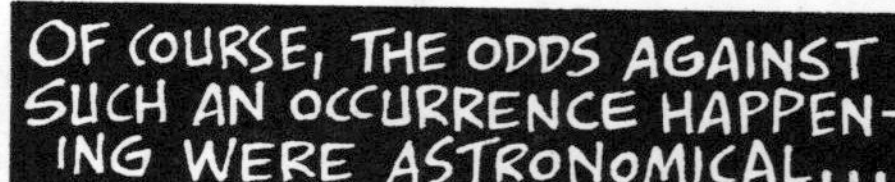

OF COURSE, THE ODDS AGAINST SUCH AN OCCURRENCE HAPPENING WERE ASTRONOMICAL...

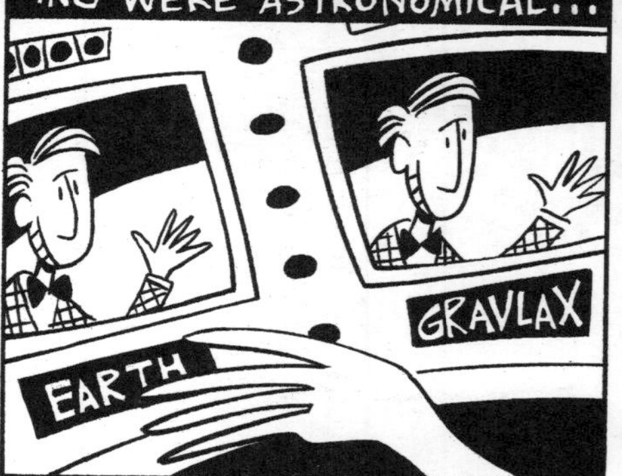

GRAVLAX
EARTH

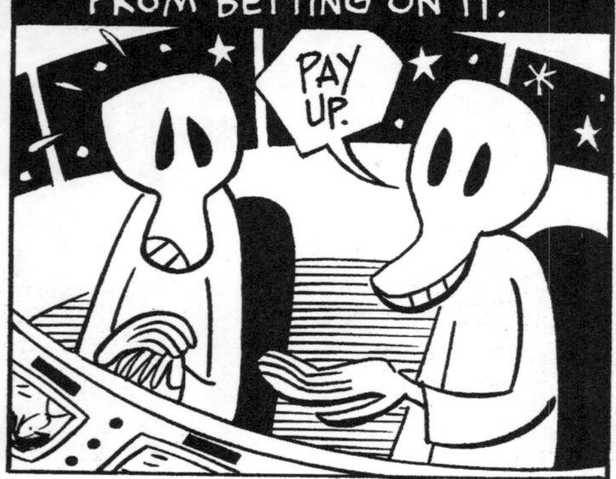

...BUT THAT HADN'T STOPPED A COUPLE OF SPORTING TYPES FROM BETTING ON IT.
PAY UP.

Story Minute © Carol Lay

"Multiple Choice"

SHE HAD A COUPLE OF DOZEN PERSONALITIES.

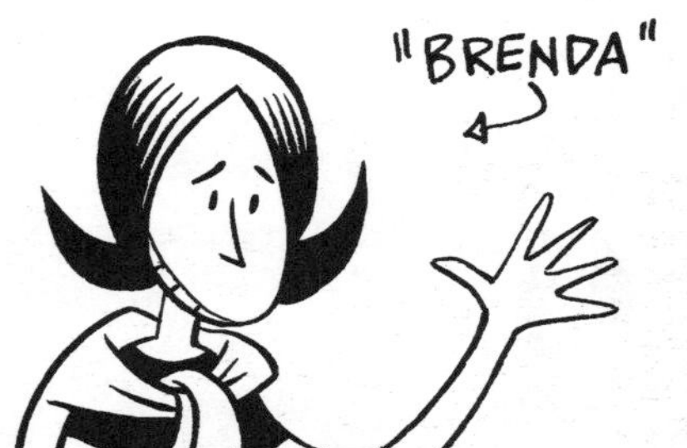


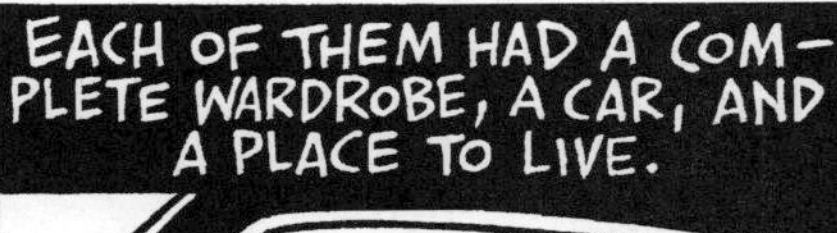


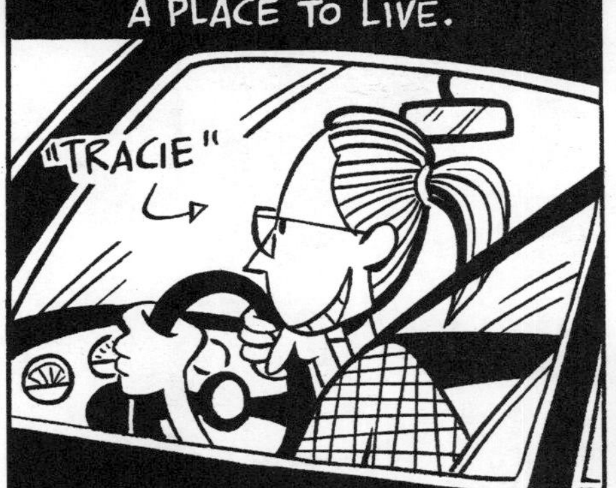


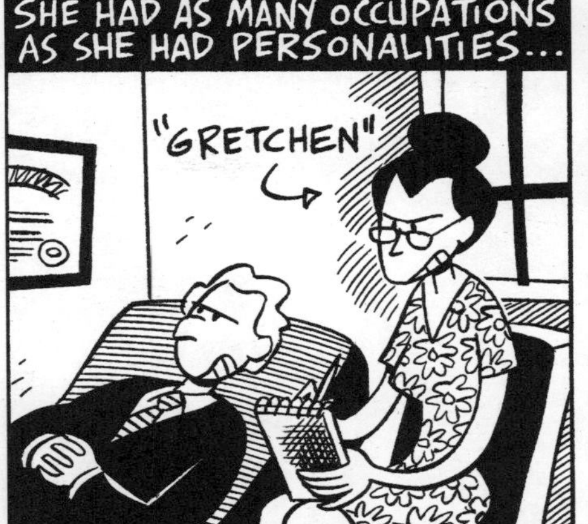


...BUT THE WORKLOAD CRAMPED HER MULTIPLE LIFE-STYLES.

"LOIS"

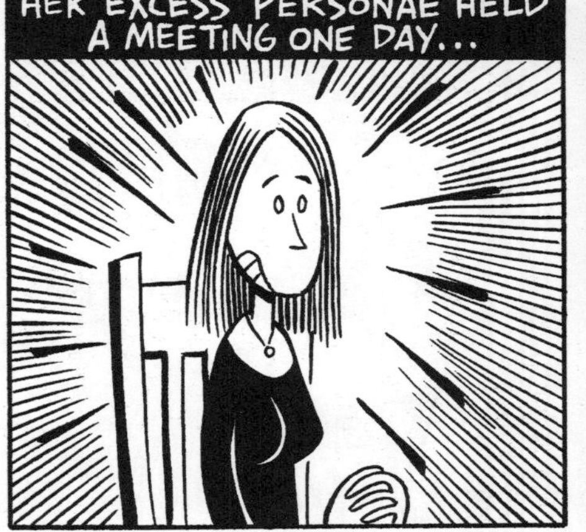


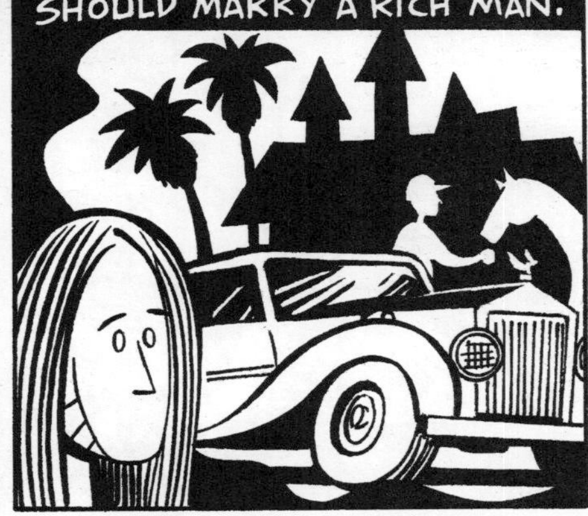


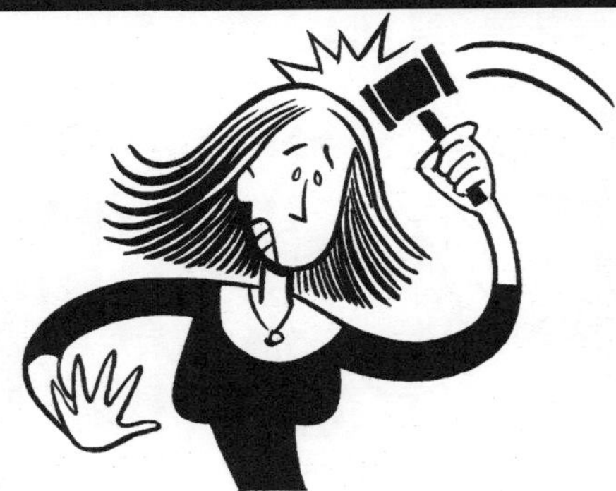


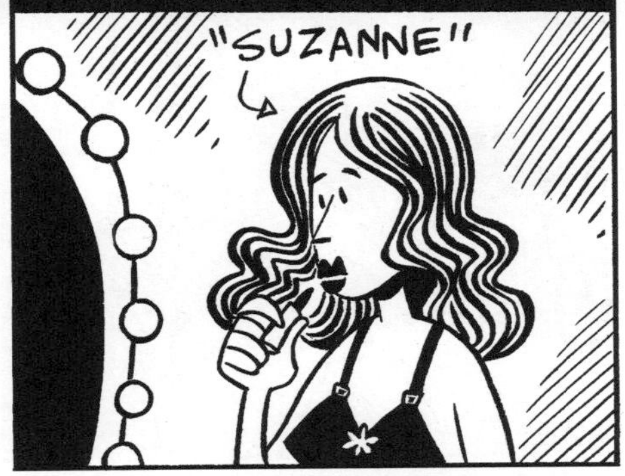


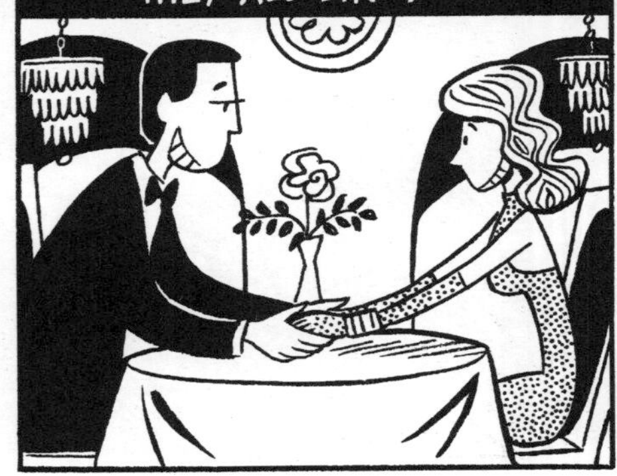


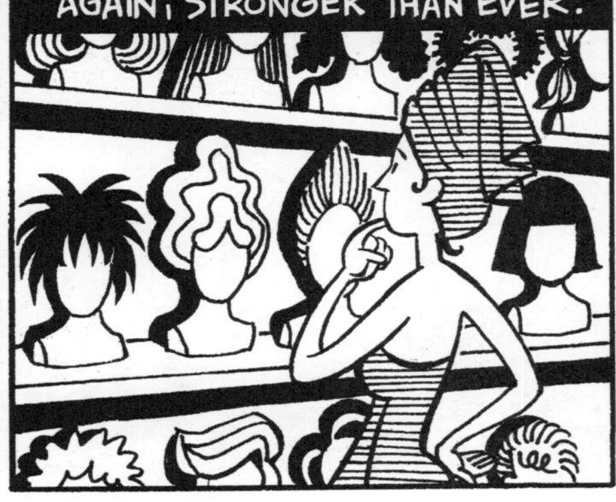


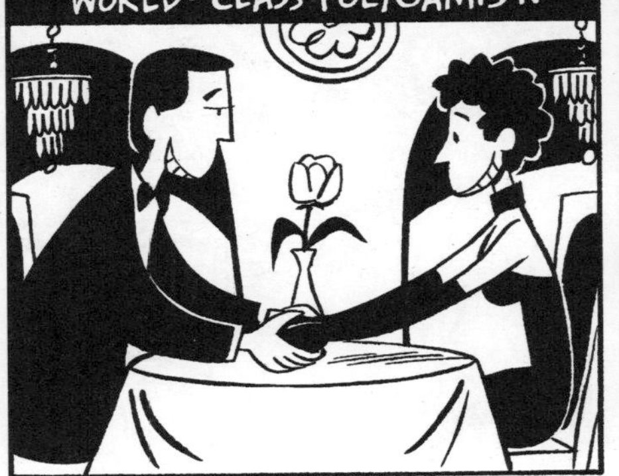


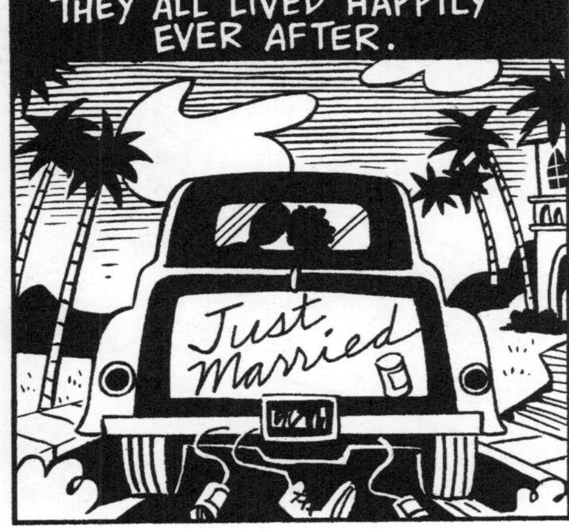

STORY MINUTE © CAROL LAY
"NO TIME TO KILL"

THE FIERCEST RIVALS ARE ALWAYS OF THE SAME SEX.

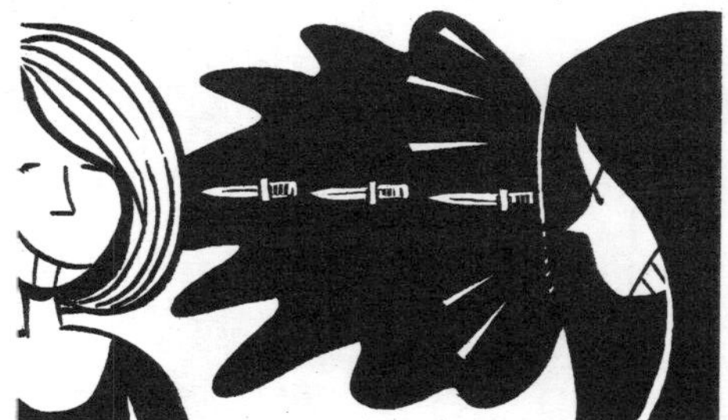

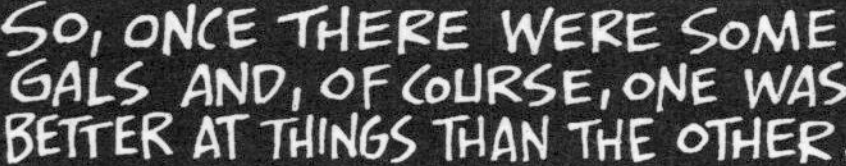


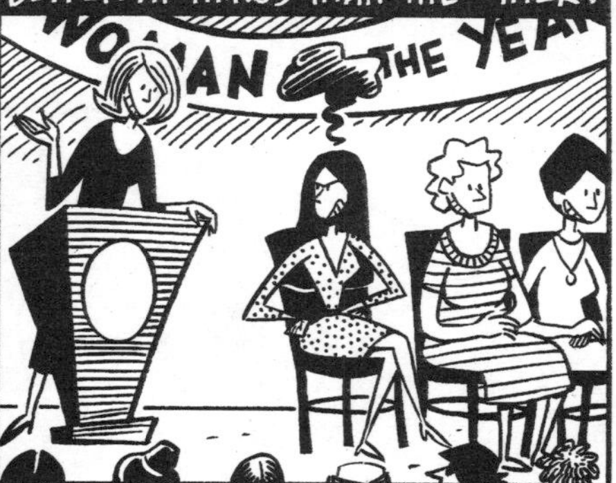

THE LESS GIFTED ONE HAD CHOSEN THE RIVALRY, NOT HAVING ENOUGH TO DO.

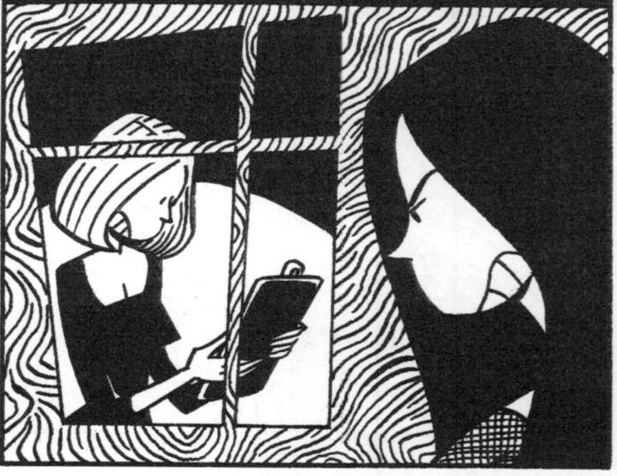

WHEN HER RIVAL "STOLE" THE MAN SHE WANTED, SHE DECIDED TO TAKE HER OUT—PERMANENTLY.

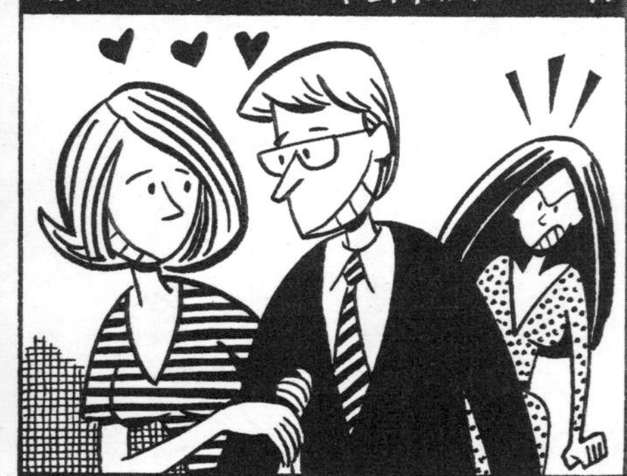

SHE DEVISED A PLAN THAT WOULD MAKE HER RIVAL'S DEATH APPEAR ACCIDENTAL.

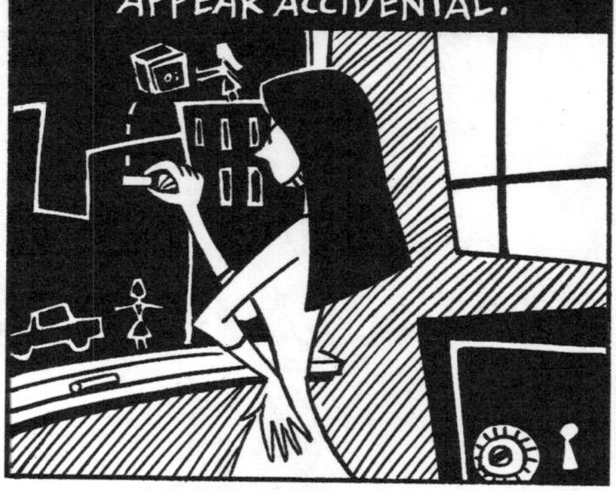

FORTUNATELY, THE INTENDED VICTIM CAUGHT WIND OF THIS AND ACTED QUICKLY.

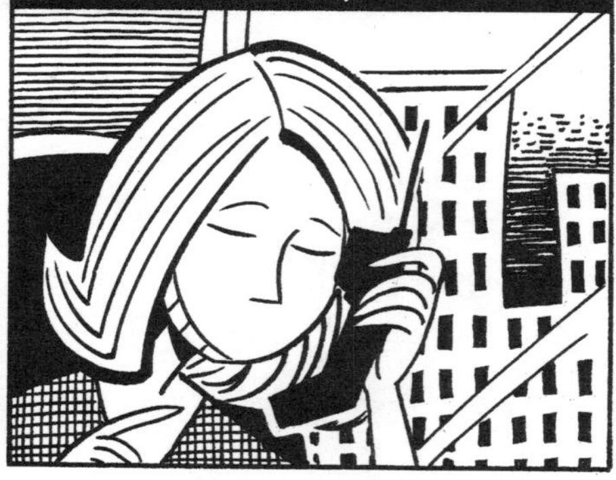

SHE GAVE THE JEALOUS RIVAL A TOP JOB IN HER FIRM.

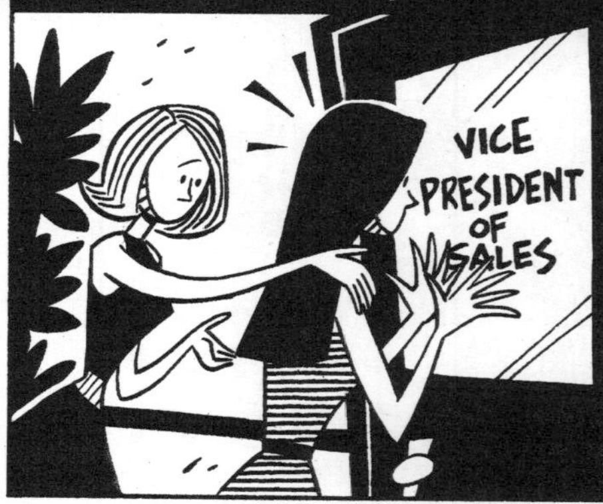


THE WORK INVOLVED LONG HOURS OUT OF TOWN WHICH LEFT HER WITH NO TIME TO PLOT MURDER.

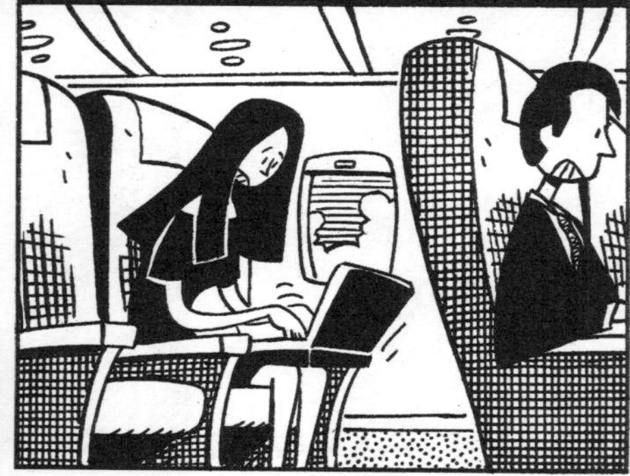

TAKING HER OPPONENT'S MONEY ONLY MADE HER WANT EVEN MORE TO COMMIT THE CRIME...

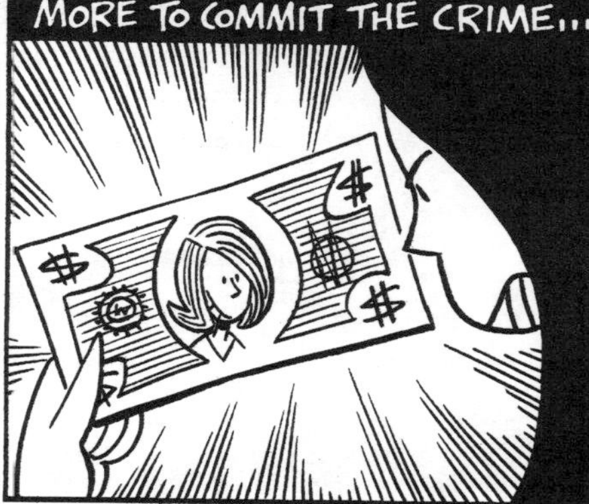

...BUT, SOMEHOW, SHE JUST NEVER GOT AROUND TO IT.

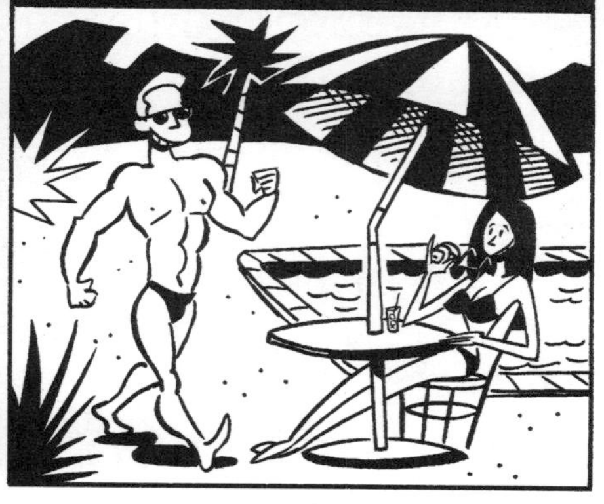

THE LONG HOURS AND HECTIC PACE EVENTUALLY CAUSED HER TO HAVE A HEART ATTACK...

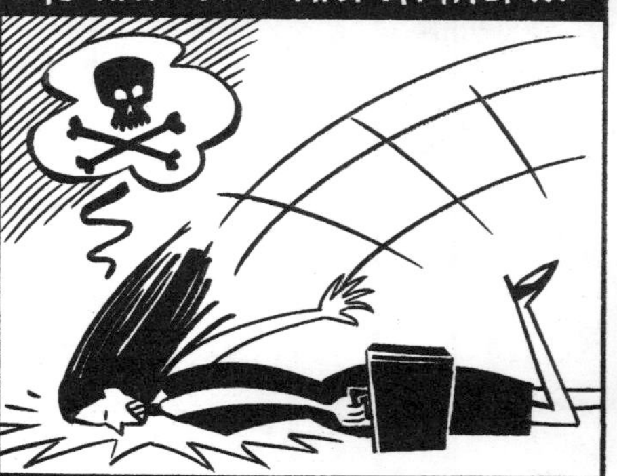

...PROVING, IN THE END, WHICH ONE OF THEM WAS BETTER AT PLOTTING MURDER, TOO.

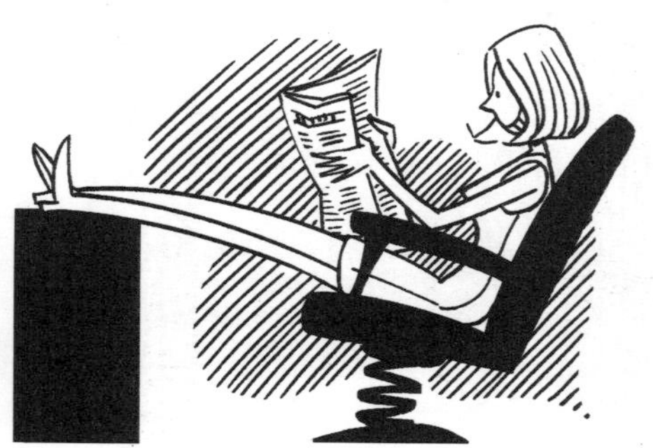

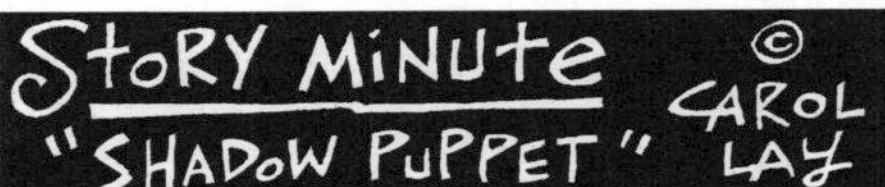
STORY MINUTE
"SHADOW PUPPET"
© CAROL LAY

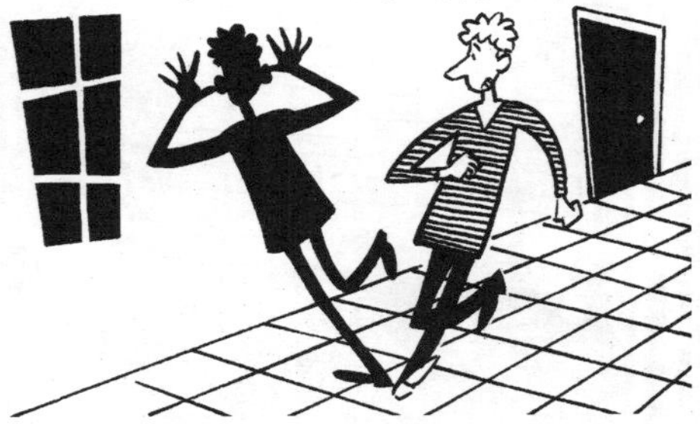
HE FOUND HIS SHADOW DEVELOPING A LIFE OF ITS OWN.

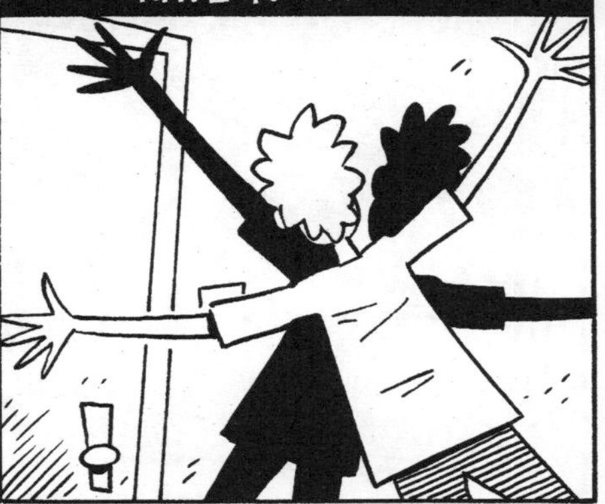
IT ROCKED WHEN IT SHOULD HAVE ROLLED...

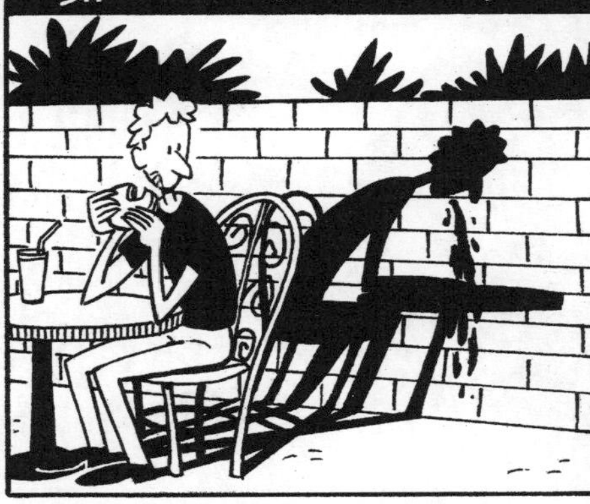
...AND SPEWED WHEN IT SHOULD HAVE CHEWED.

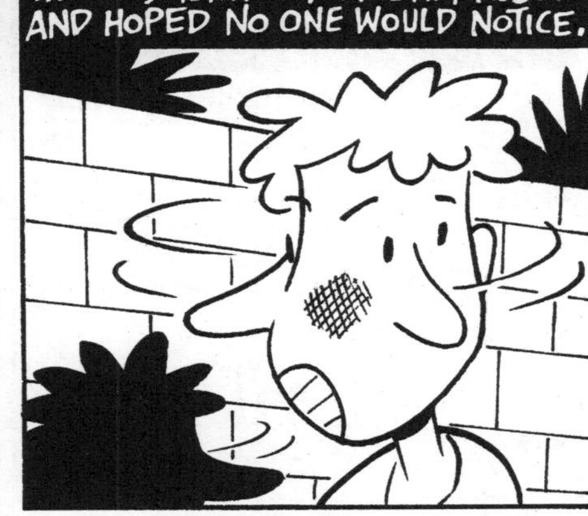
HE WAS TERRIBLY EMBARRASSED AND HOPED NO ONE WOULD NOTICE.

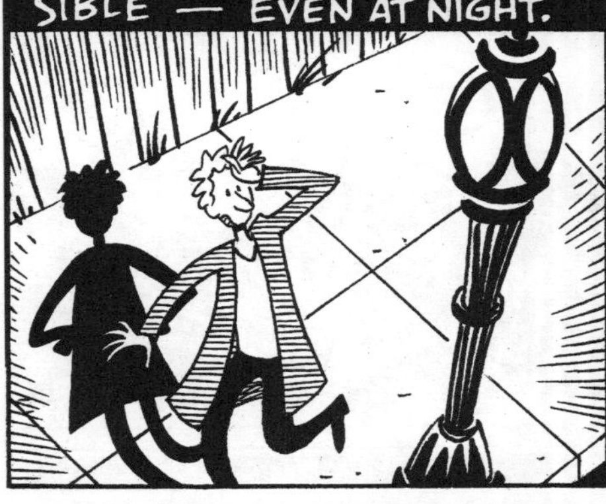
HE TRIED TO AVOID STRONG LIGHT, BUT THAT WAS IMPOSSIBLE — EVEN AT NIGHT.

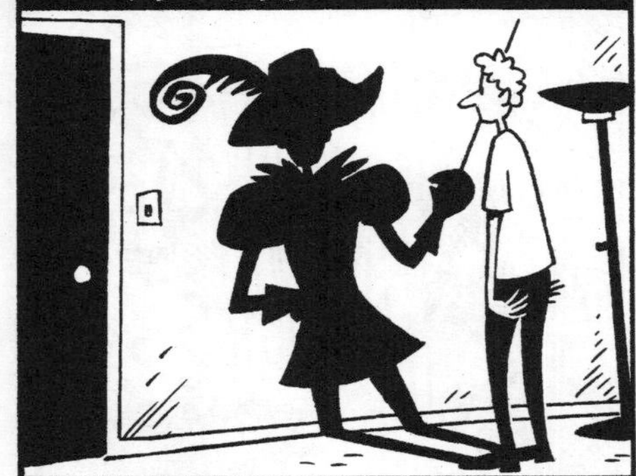
THINGS TOOK A BAD TURN WHEN THE SHADOW STARTED WEARING PECULIAR OUTFITS.

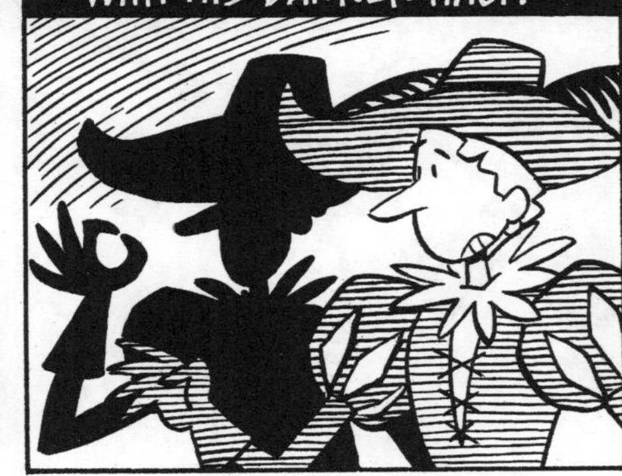
TO DISGUISE ITS ECCENTRICITIES, HE DRESSED TO BE COMPATIBLE WITH HIS DARKER HALF.

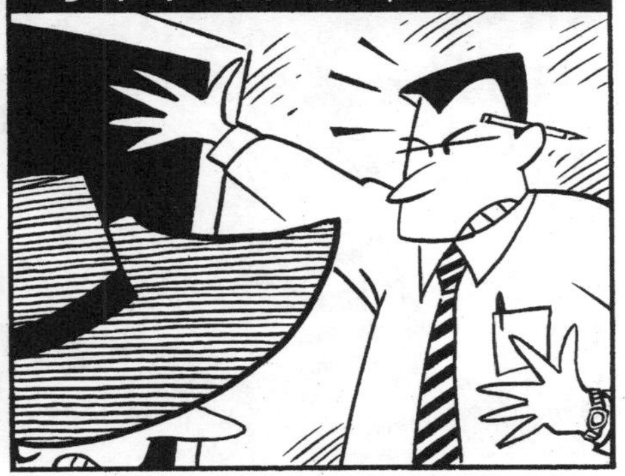
THIS SEEMED TO PLEASE HIS SHADOW, BUT NOT HIS SUPERIORS AT WORK.

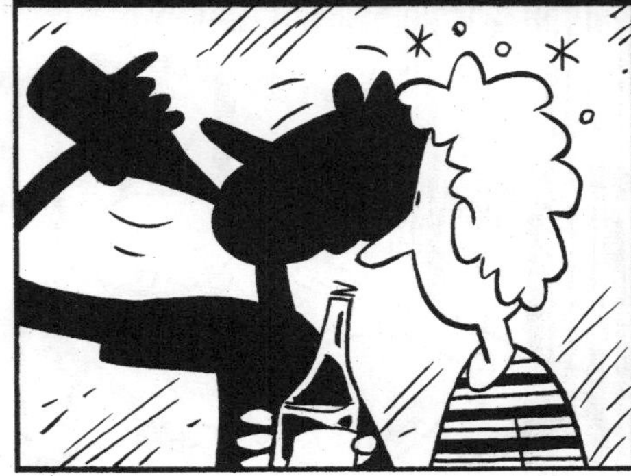
WHEN HIS SHADOW BEGAN DRINKING HEAVILY, IT SEEMED LIKE A GOOD IDEA.

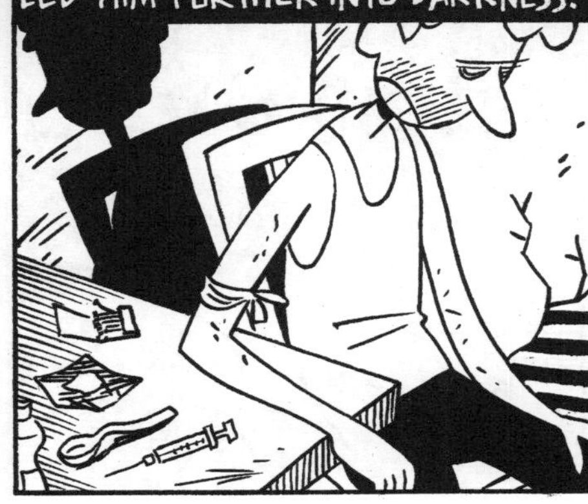
KEEPING UP WITH HIS SHADE LED HIM FURTHER INTO DARKNESS.

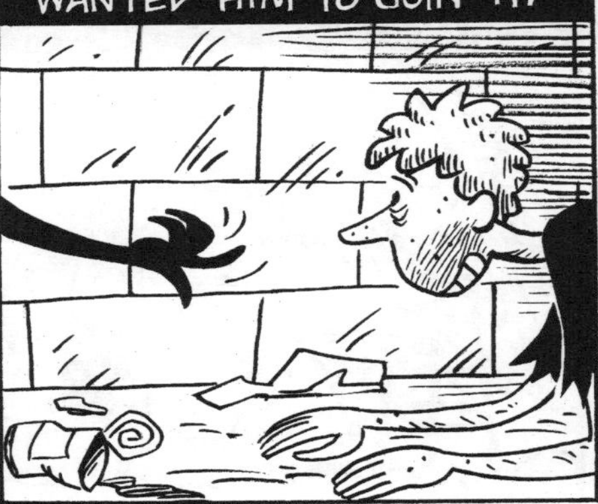
IT WAS AS IF HIS SHADOW WANTED HIM TO JOIN IT.

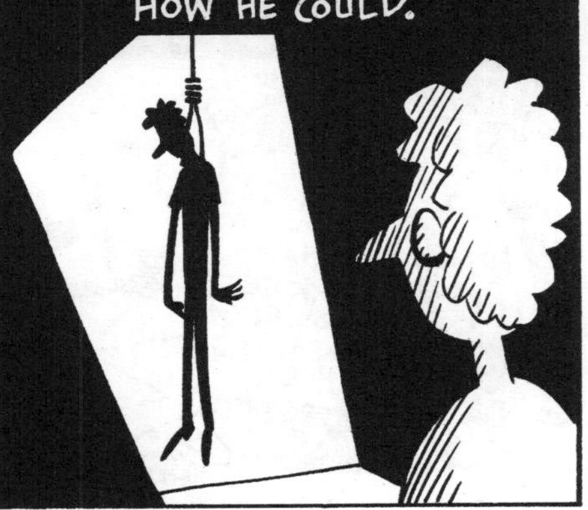
AND, ONE DAY, HE WAS SHOWN HOW HE COULD.

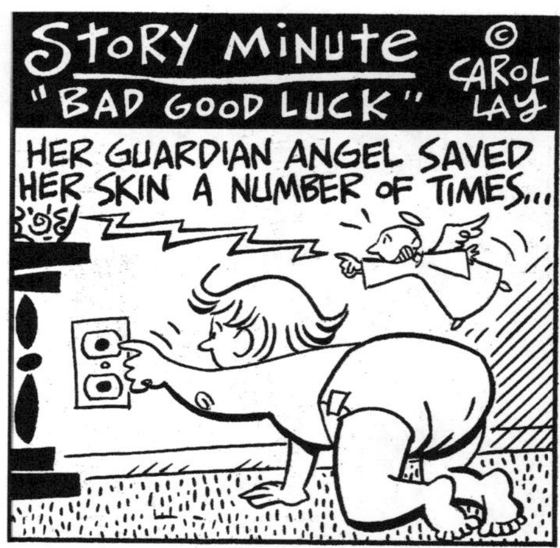
STORY MINUTE
"BAD GOOD LUCK"
© CAROL LAY
HER GUARDIAN ANGEL SAVED HER SKIN A NUMBER OF TIMES...

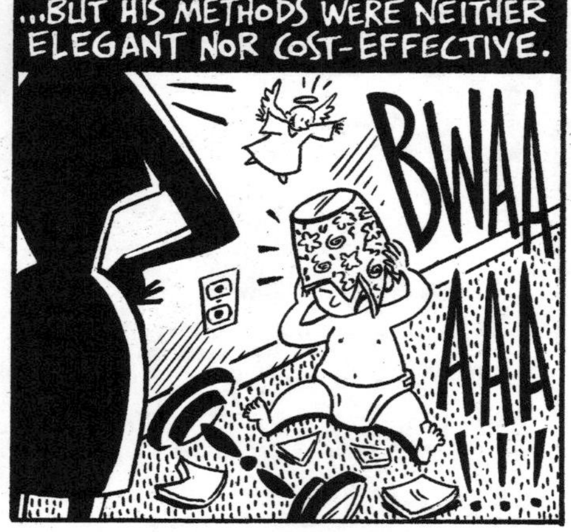
...BUT HIS METHODS WERE NEITHER ELEGANT NOR COST-EFFECTIVE.
BWAAAAAA!!!

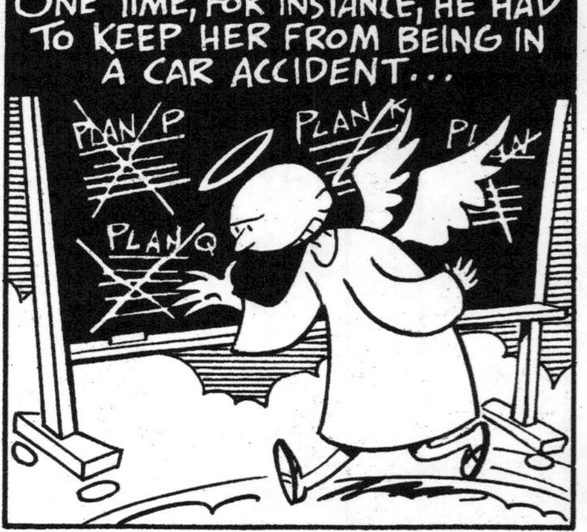
ONE TIME, FOR INSTANCE, HE HAD TO KEEP HER FROM BEING IN A CAR ACCIDENT...
PLAN P
PLAN Q

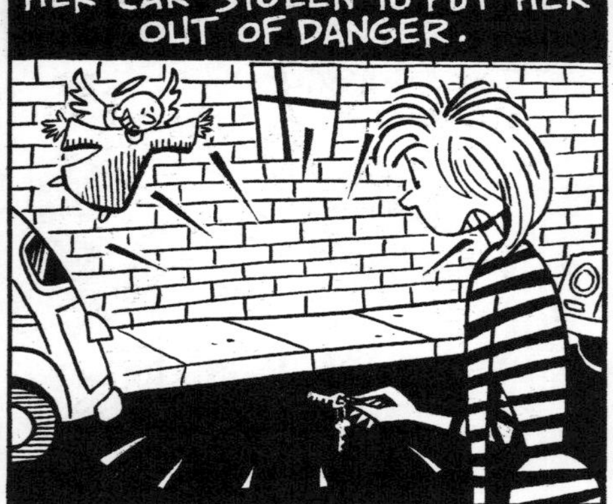
...SO HE ARRANGED TO HAVE HER CAR STOLEN TO PUT HER OUT OF DANGER.

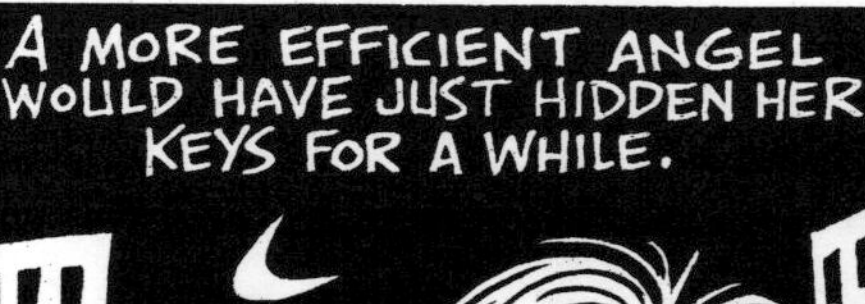
A MORE EFFICIENT ANGEL WOULD HAVE JUST HIDDEN HER KEYS FOR A WHILE.

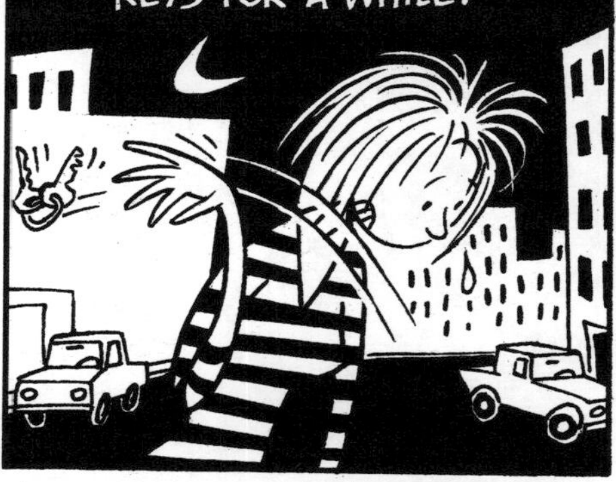

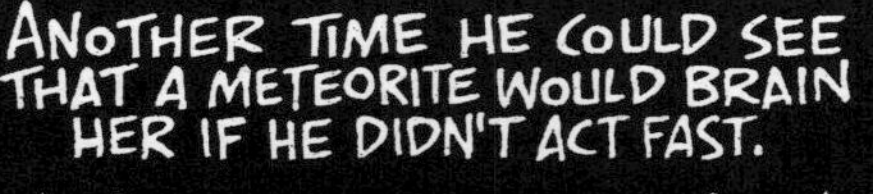
ANOTHER TIME HE COULD SEE THAT A METEORITE WOULD BRAIN HER IF HE DIDN'T ACT FAST.

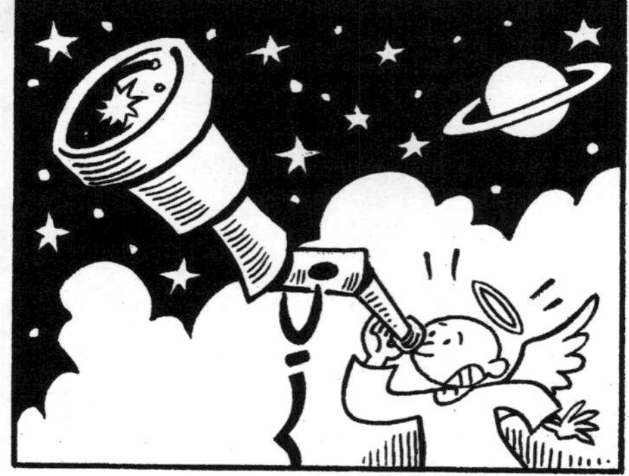

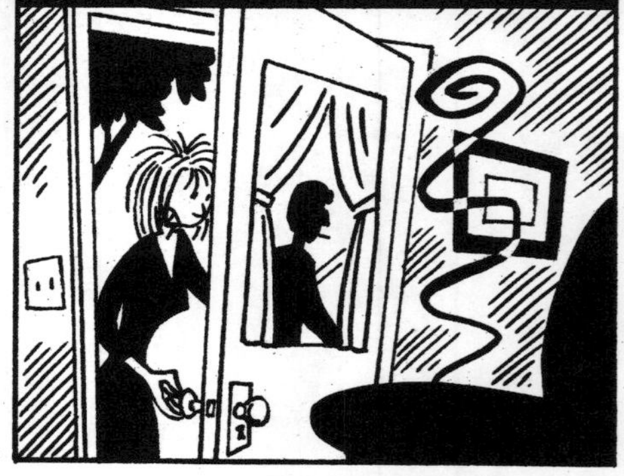
HE HAD A VISITOR DROP A LIT CIGARETTE IN HER SOFA WITH DISASTROUS CONSEQUENCES.

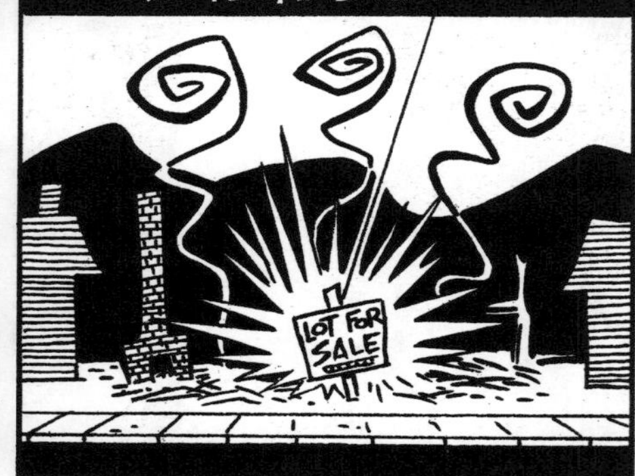
SHE MOVED TO A SHELTER AND NEVER EVEN NOTICED WHEN THE METEORITE HIT.
LOT FOR SALE

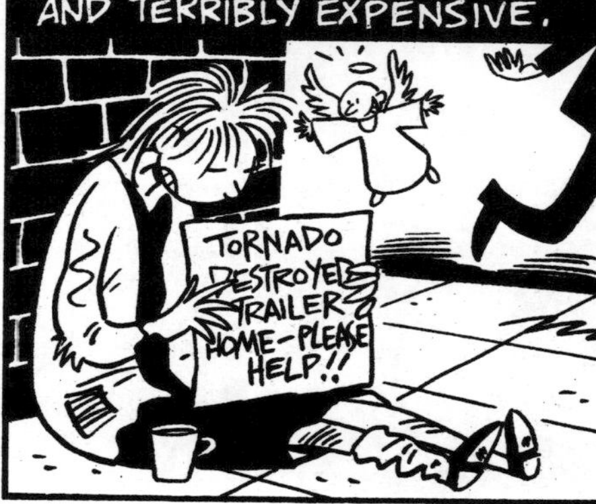
THESE FREQUENT RESCUES WERE PAINFULLY DISRUPTIVE AND TERRIBLY EXPENSIVE.
TORNADO DESTROYED TRAILER HOME-PLEASE HELP!!

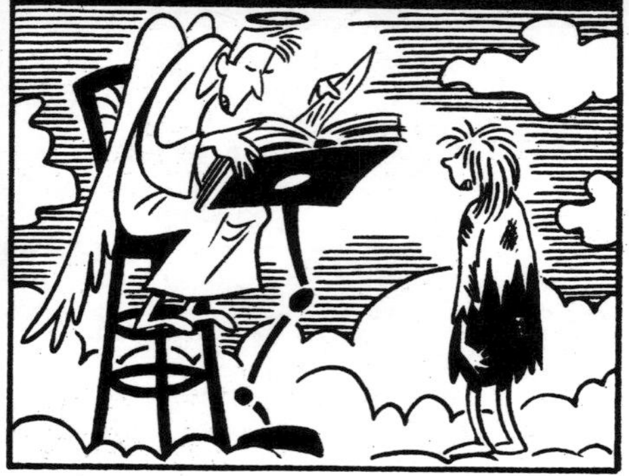
WHEN SHE FINALLY PASSED ON, SAINT PETER READ THE ACCOUNT OF HER TRAGIC GOOD LUCK.

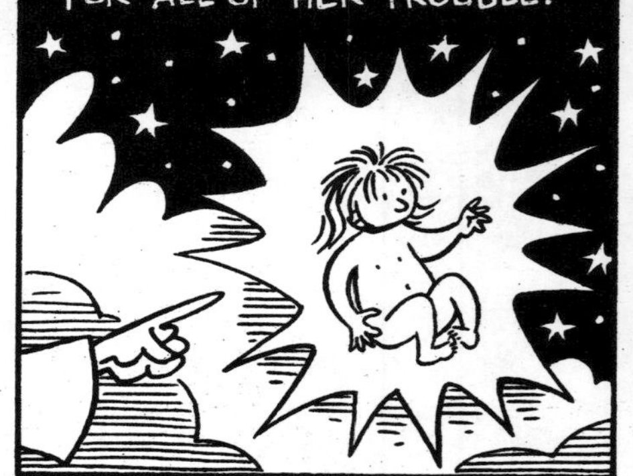
HE GAVE THE OLD DEAR A REBATE OF EIGHTY GOOD YEARS FOR ALL OF HER TROUBLE.

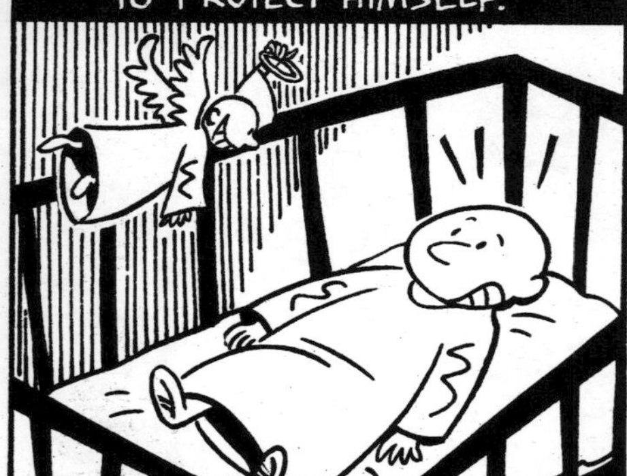
THEN HE HAD THE ANGEL REIN-CARNATED AND REASSIGNED TO PROTECT HIMSELF.

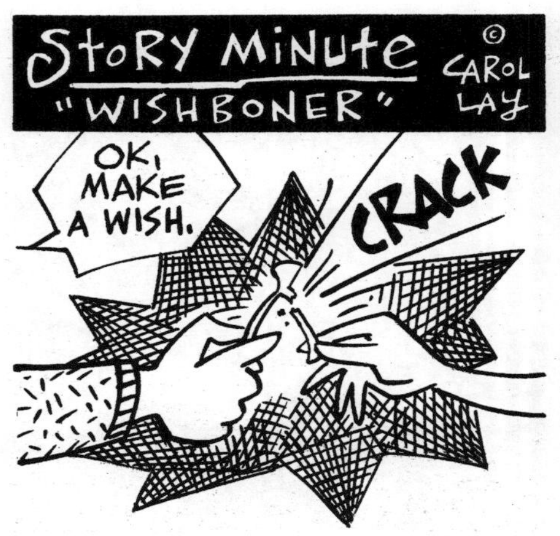
Story Minute
"WISHBONER"
© CAROL LAY
OK, MAKE A WISH.
CRACK

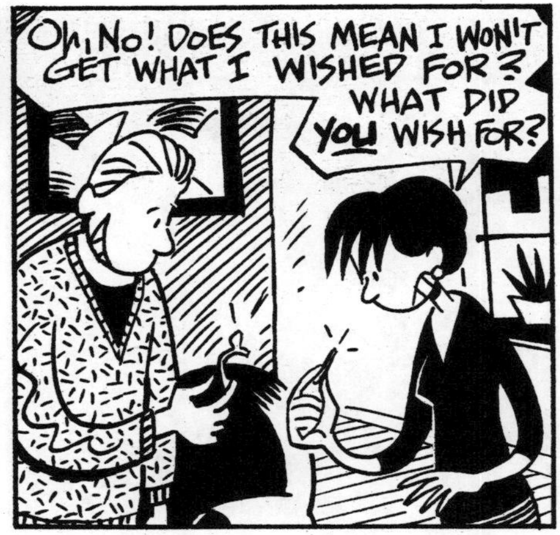
OH, NO! DOES THIS MEAN I WON'T GET WHAT I WISHED FOR?
WHAT DID YOU WISH FOR?

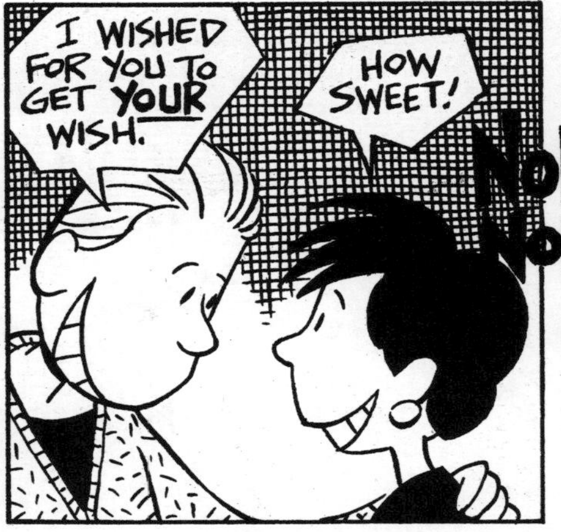
I WISHED FOR YOU TO GET YOUR WISH.
HOW SWEET!
NOK NOK!

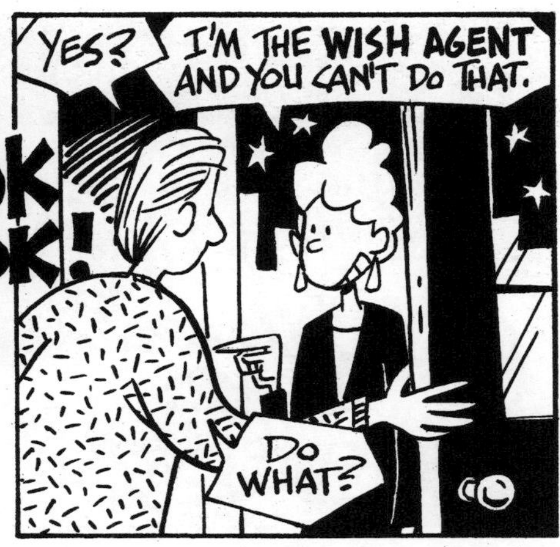
YES?
I'M THE WISH AGENT AND YOU CAN'T DO THAT.
DO WHAT?

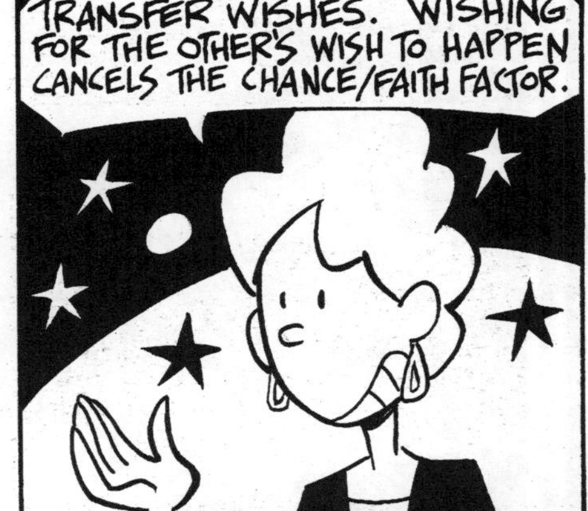
TRANSFER WISHES. WISHING FOR THE OTHER'S WISH TO HAPPEN CANCELS THE CHANCE/FAITH FACTOR.

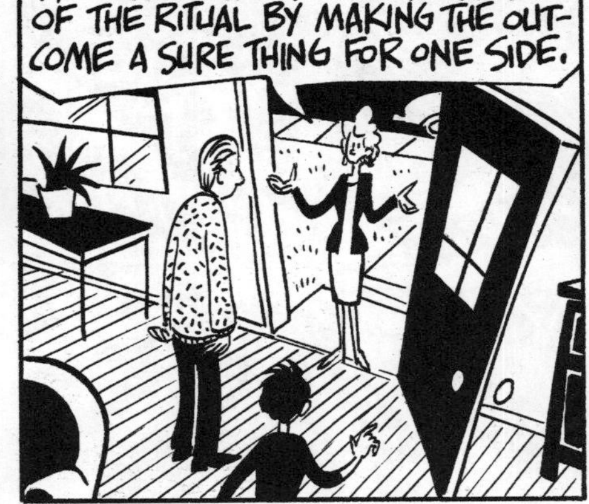
IT TAKES AWAY THE ROMANCE OF THE RITUAL BY MAKING THE OUTCOME A SURE THING FOR ONE SIDE.

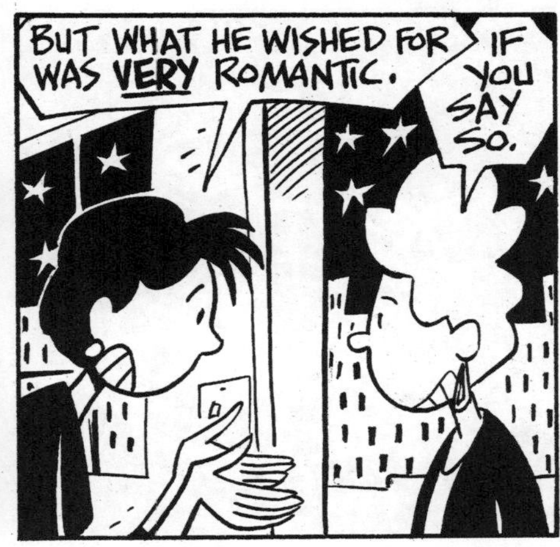
BUT WHAT HE WISHED FOR WAS VERY ROMANTIC.
IF YOU SAY SO.

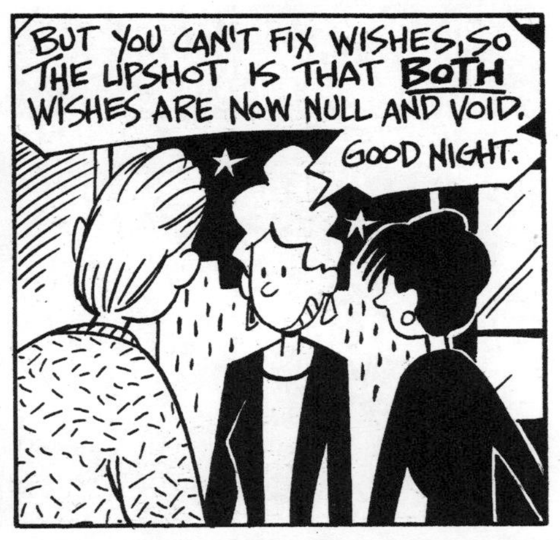
BUT YOU CAN'T FIX WISHES, SO THE UPSHOT IS THAT BOTH WISHES ARE NOW NULL AND VOID.
GOOD NIGHT.

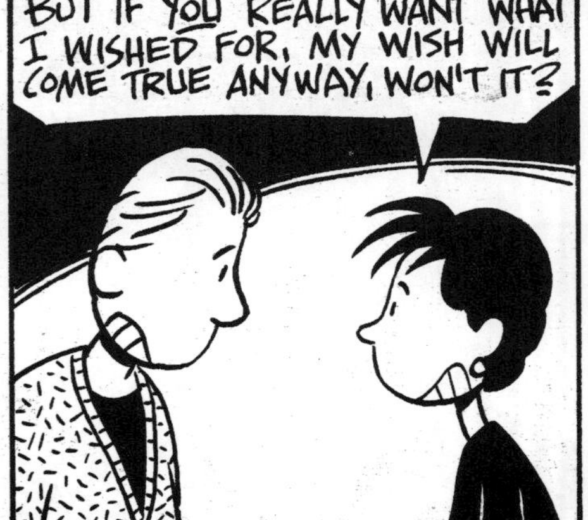
BUT IF YOU REALLY WANT WHAT I WISHED FOR, MY WISH WILL COME TRUE ANYWAY, WON'T IT?

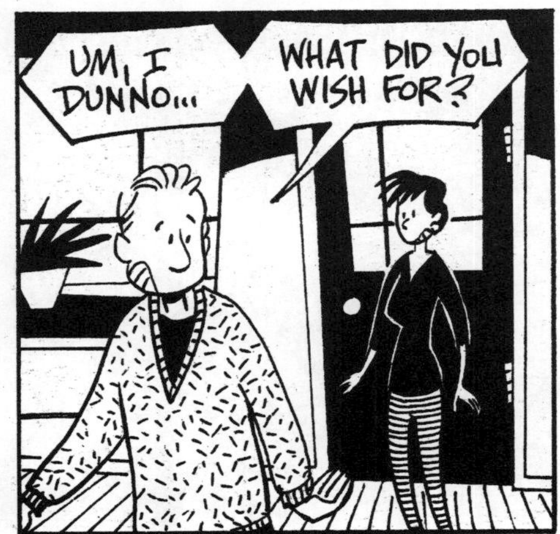
UM, I DUNNO...
WHAT DID YOU WISH FOR?

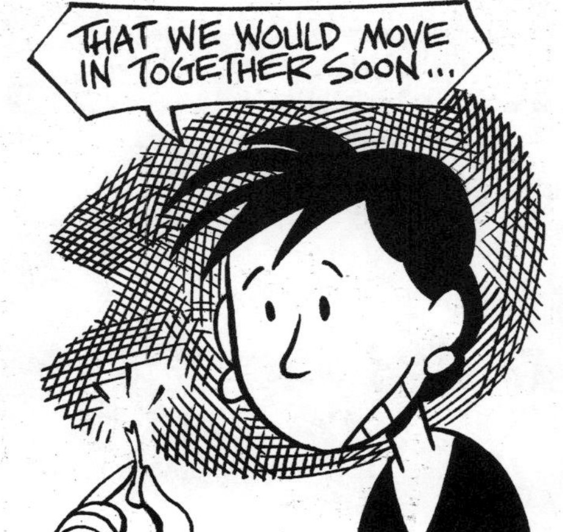
THAT WE WOULD MOVE IN TOGETHER SOON...

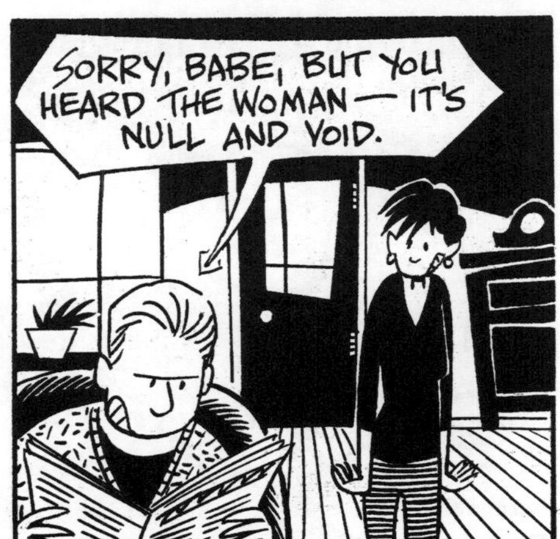
SORRY, BABE, BUT YOU HEARD THE WOMAN — IT'S NULL AND VOID.

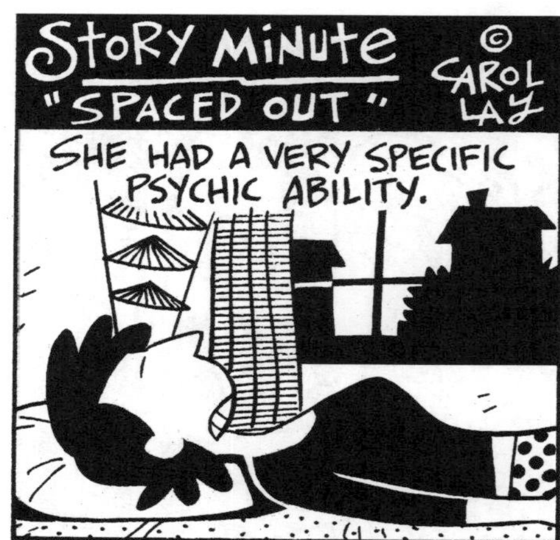
Story Minute
"Spaced Out"
© Carol Lay
She had a very specific psychic ability.

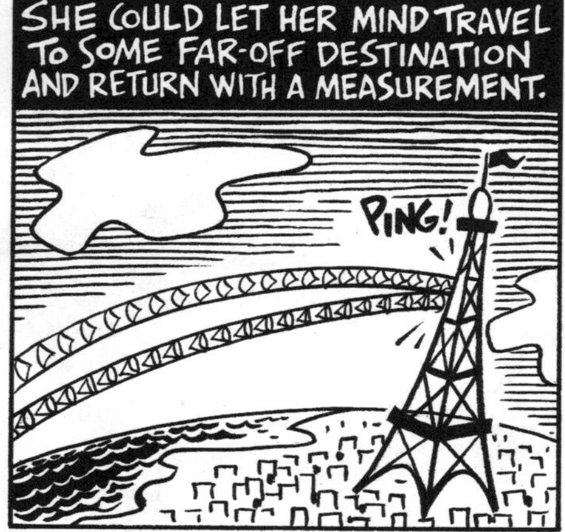
She could let her mind travel to some far-off destination and return with a measurement.
PING!

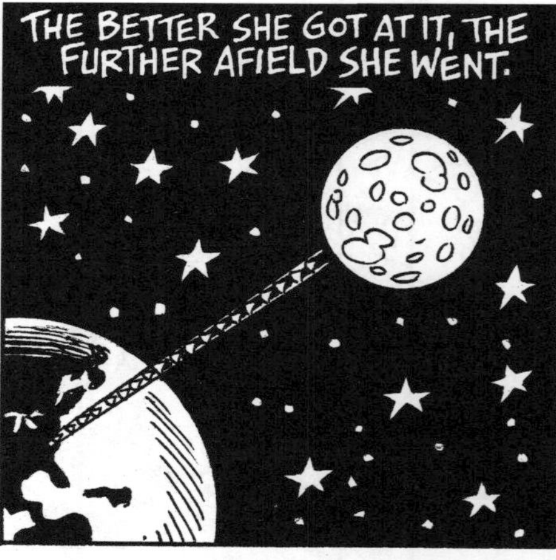
The better she got at it, the further afield she went.

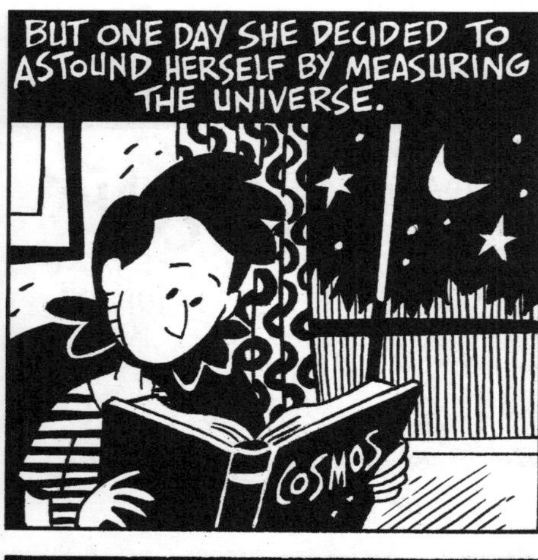
But one day she decided to astound herself by measuring the universe.
Cosmos

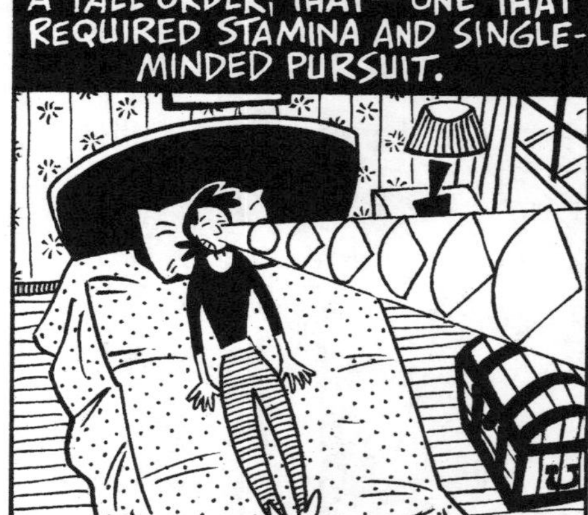
A tall order, that—one that required stamina and single-minded pursuit.

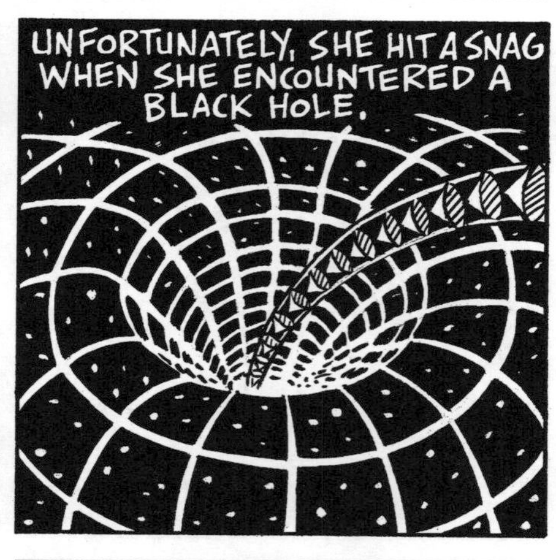
Unfortunately, she hit a snag when she encountered a black hole.

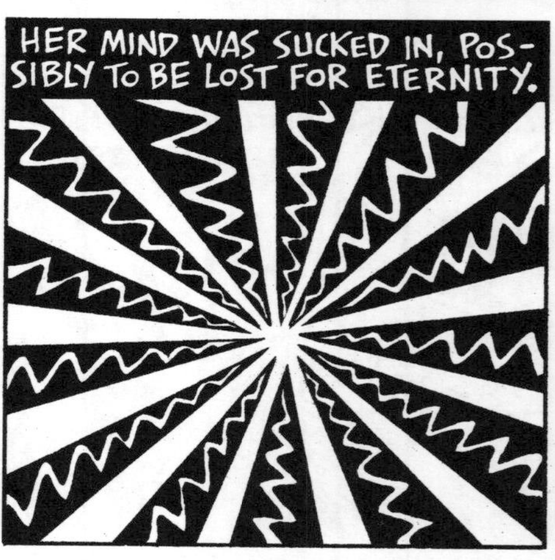
Her mind was sucked in, possibly to be lost for eternity.

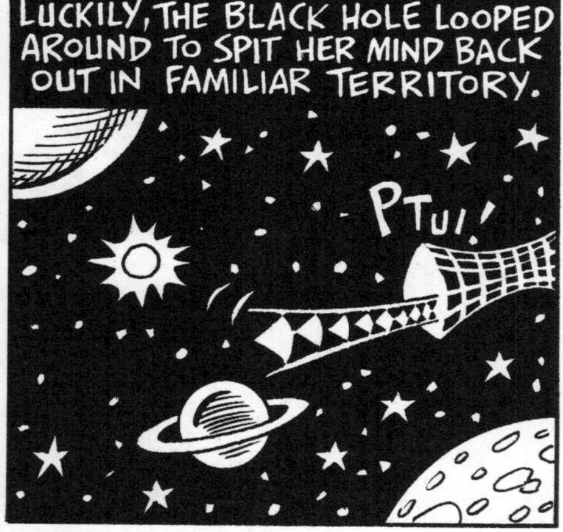
Luckily, the black hole looped around to spit her mind back out in familiar territory.
PTUI!

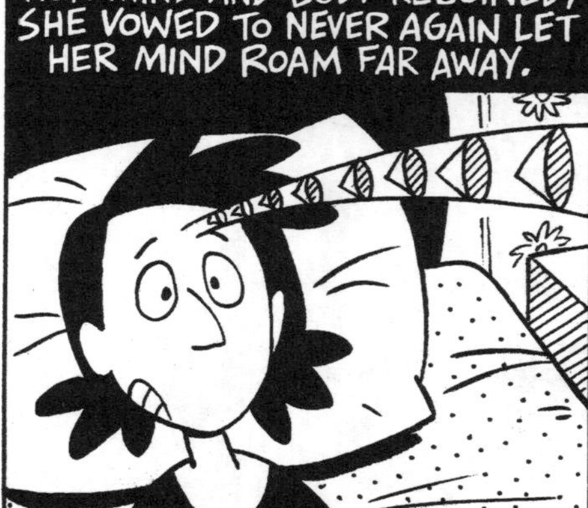
Her mind and body rejoined, she vowed to never again let her mind roam far away.

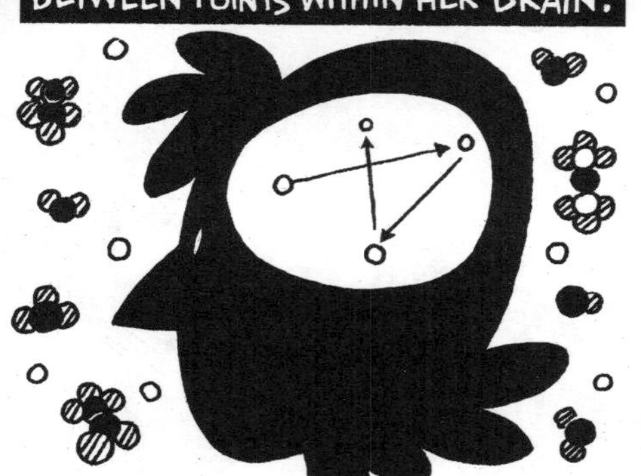
She would content herself with measuring small distances between points within her brain.

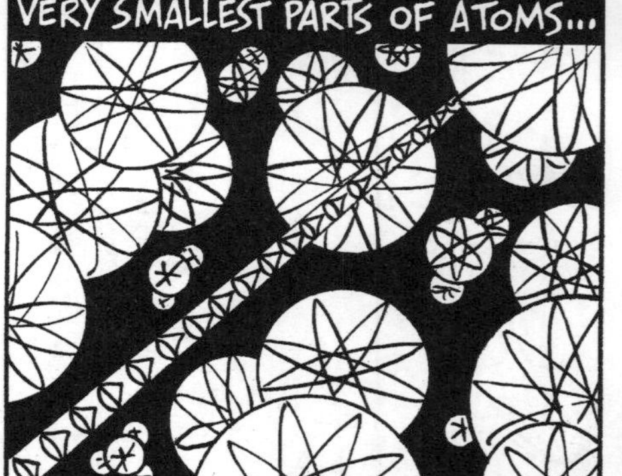
So eventually, her mind got lost again while gauging the very smallest parts of atoms...

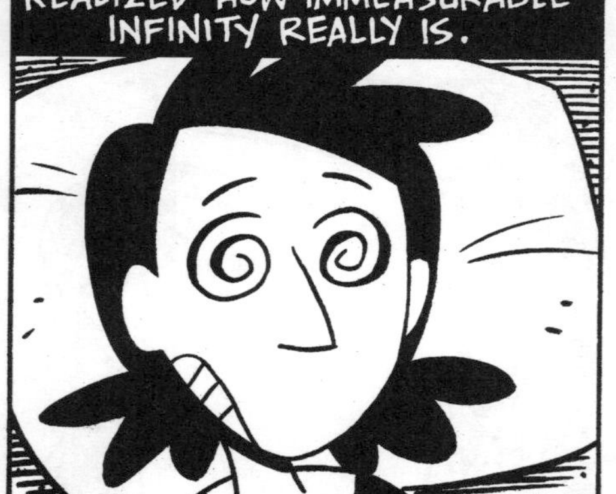
...which was when she finally realized how immeasurable infinity really is.

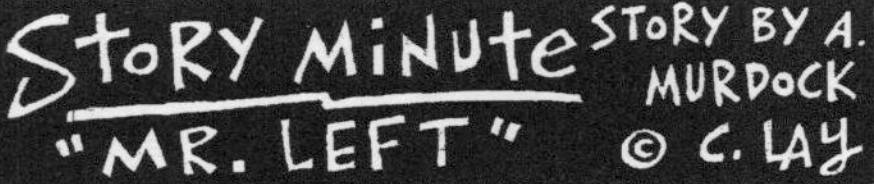


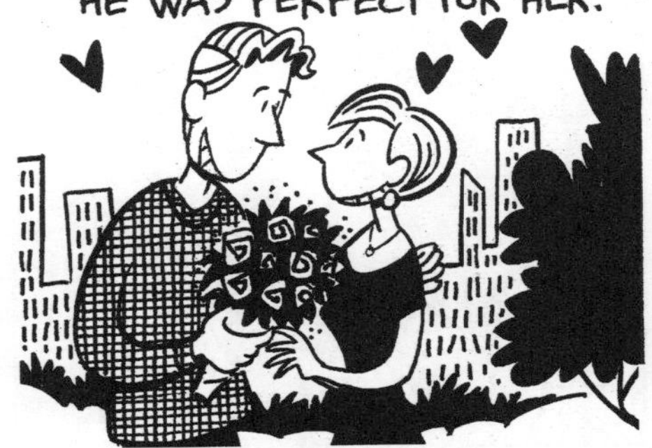


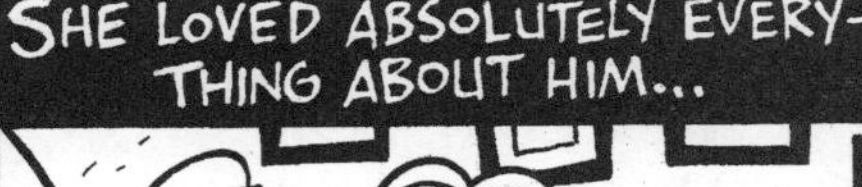


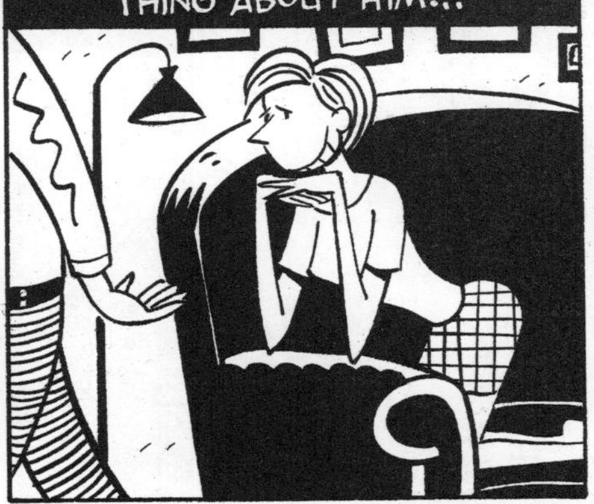

...Except his taste in music.

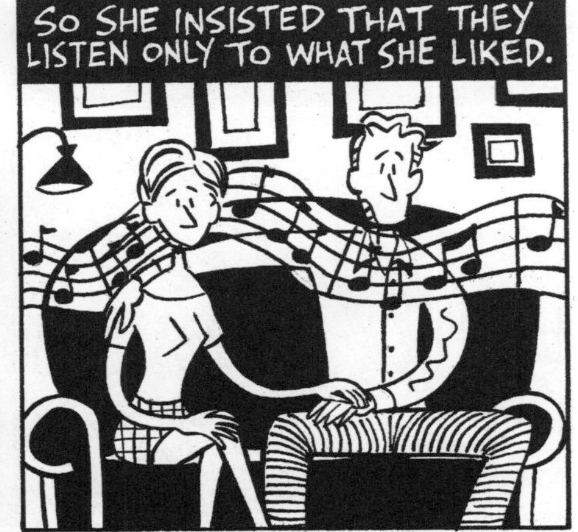


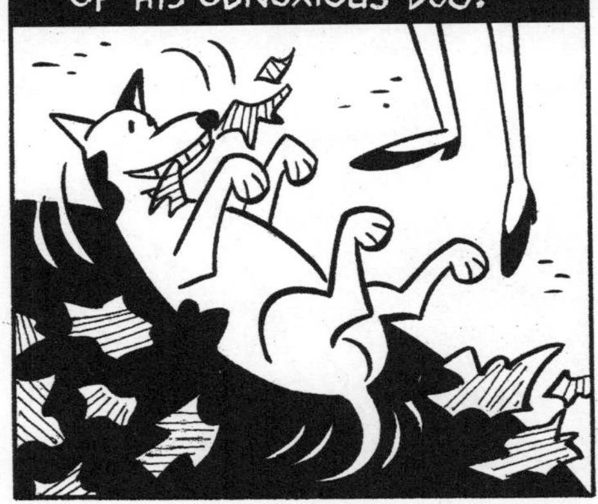

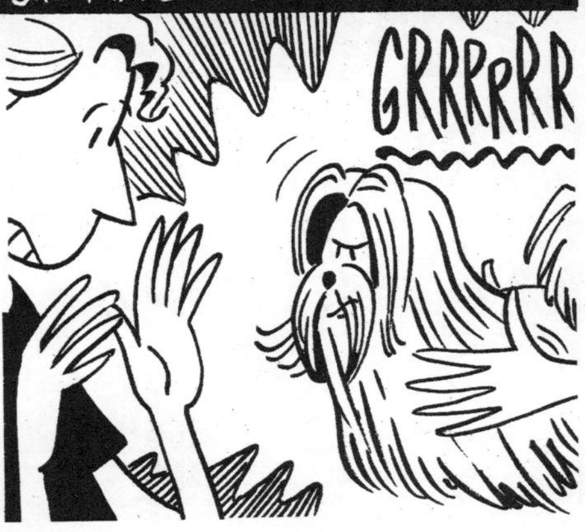


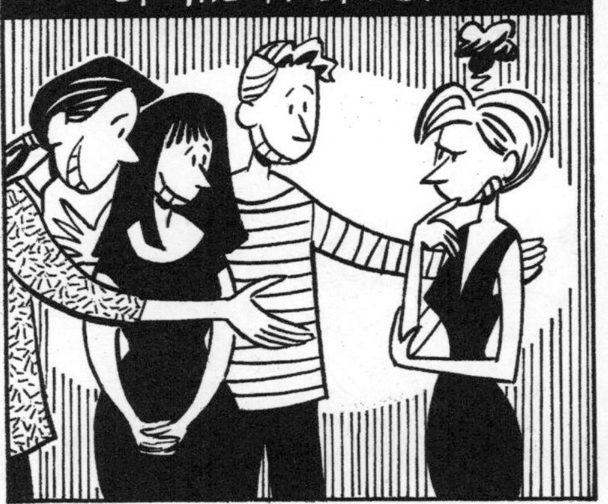


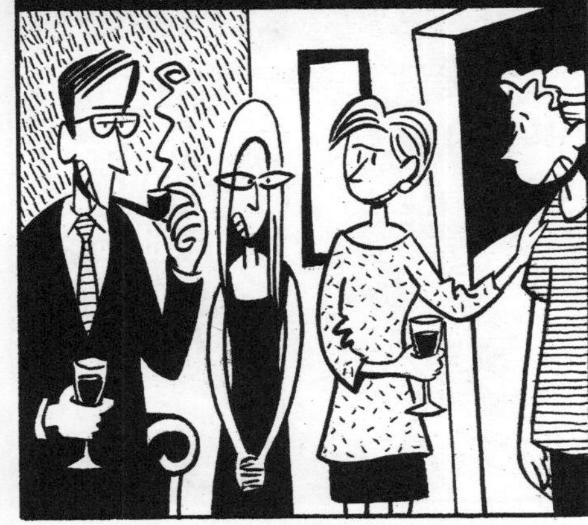


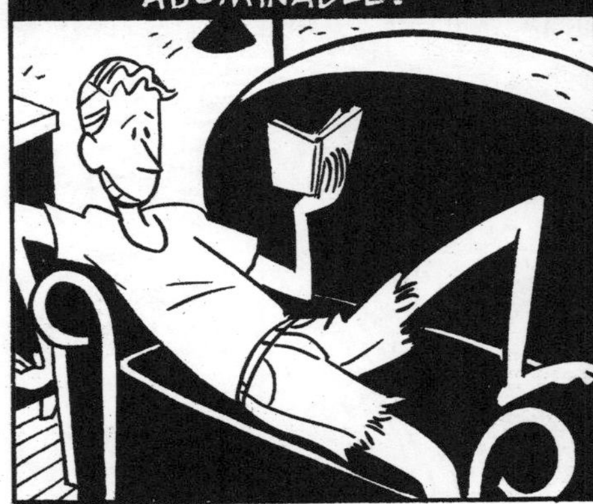


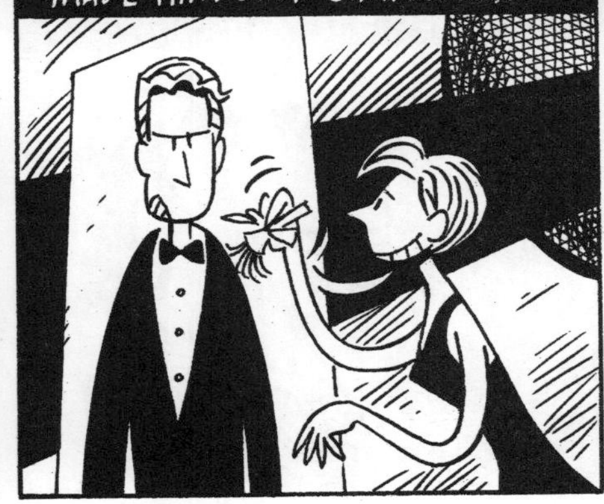


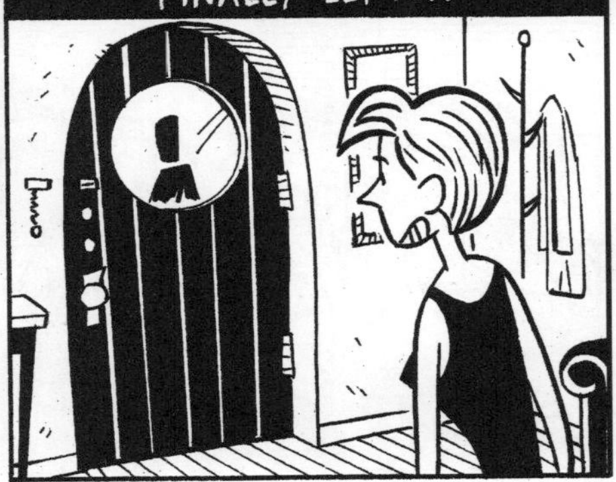


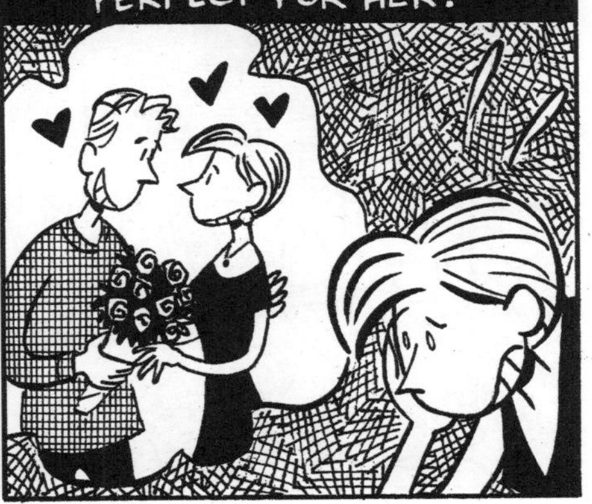

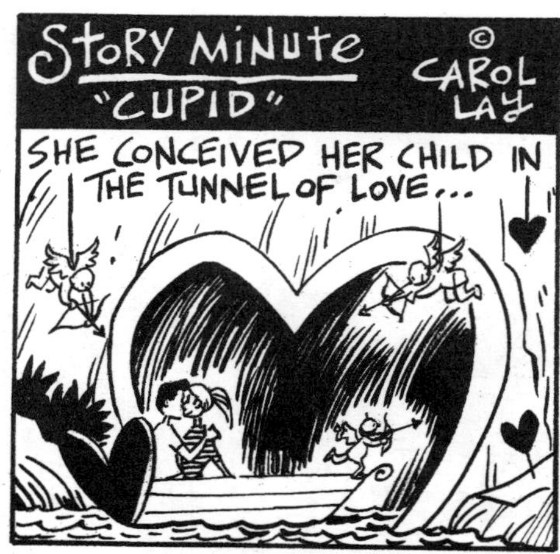
STORY MINUTE
"CUPID"
© CAROL LAY
SHE CONCEIVED HER CHILD IN THE TUNNEL OF LOVE...

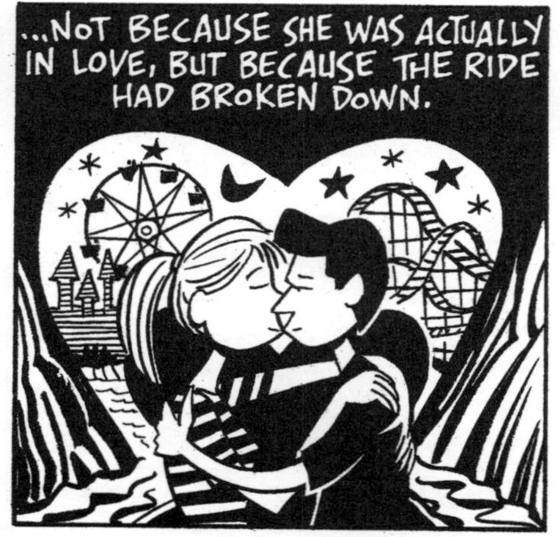
...NOT BECAUSE SHE WAS ACTUALLY IN LOVE, BUT BECAUSE THE RIDE HAD BROKEN DOWN.

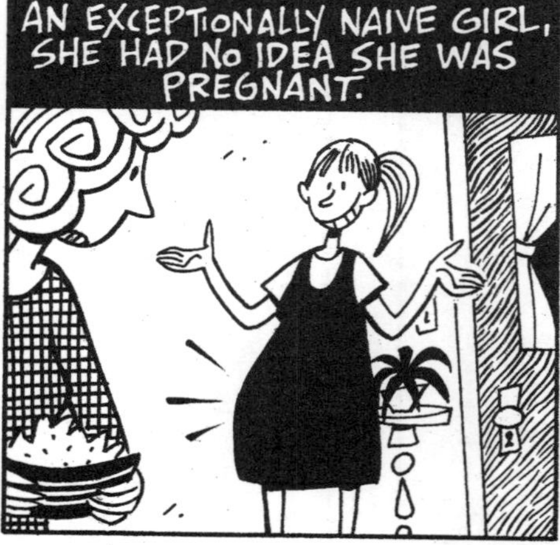
AN EXCEPTIONALLY NAIVE GIRL, SHE HAD NO IDEA SHE WAS PREGNANT.

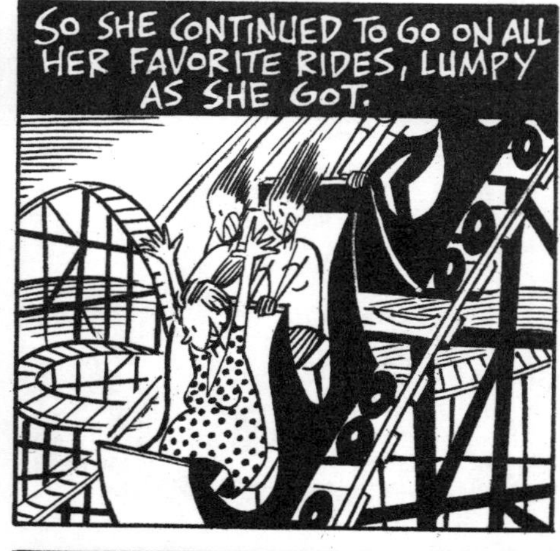
SO SHE CONTINUED TO GO ON ALL HER FAVORITE RIDES, LUMPY AS SHE GOT.

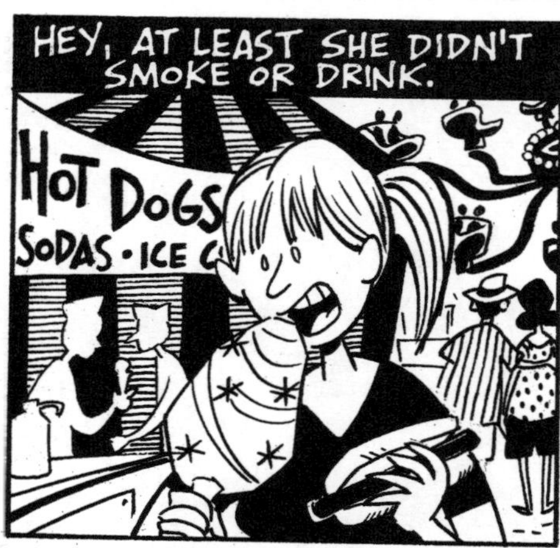
HEY, AT LEAST SHE DIDN'T SMOKE OR DRINK.
HOT DOGS
SODAS • ICE C

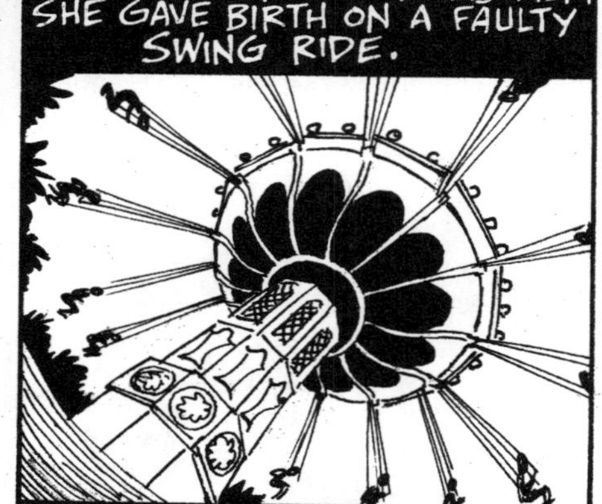
BUT ANYWAY, NINE MONTHS LATER, SHE GAVE BIRTH ON A FAULTY SWING RIDE.

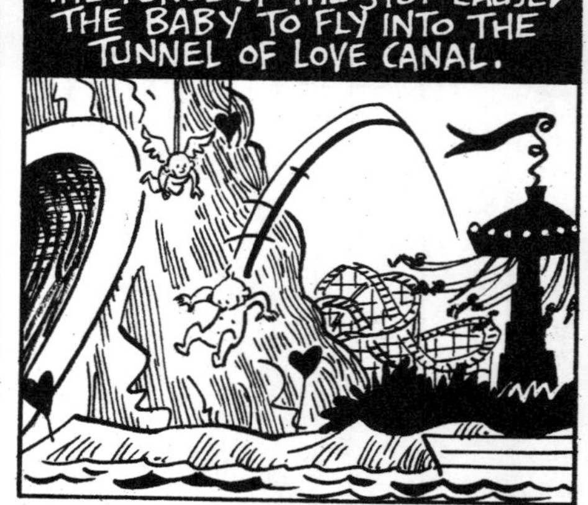
THE FORCE OF THE STOP CAUSED THE BABY TO FLY INTO THE TUNNEL OF LOVE CANAL.

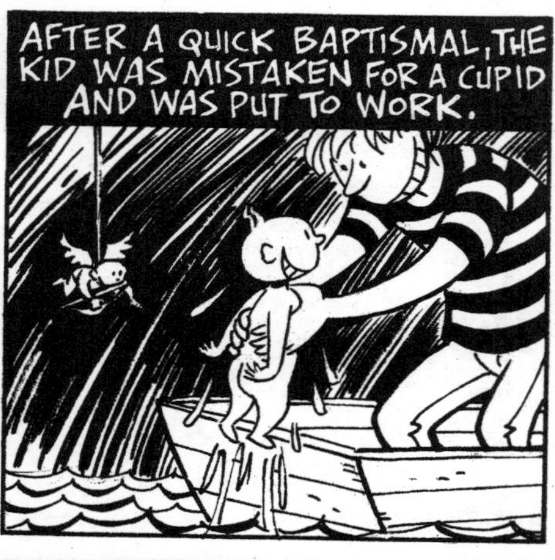
AFTER A QUICK BAPTISMAL, THE KID WAS MISTAKEN FOR A CUPID AND WAS PUT TO WORK.

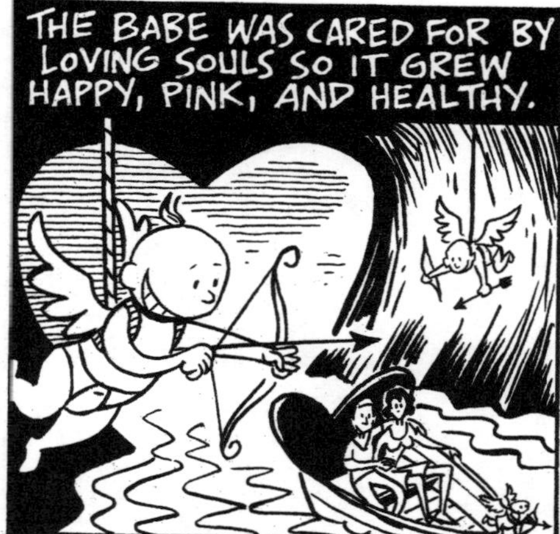
THE BABE WAS CARED FOR BY LOVING SOULS SO IT GREW HAPPY, PINK, AND HEALTHY.

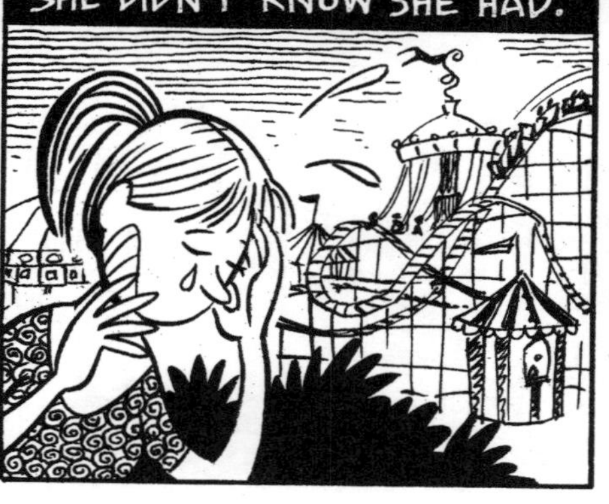
THE MOTHER, THOUGH, FELT DEEP LOSS FOR THE CHILD SHE DIDN'T KNOW SHE HAD.

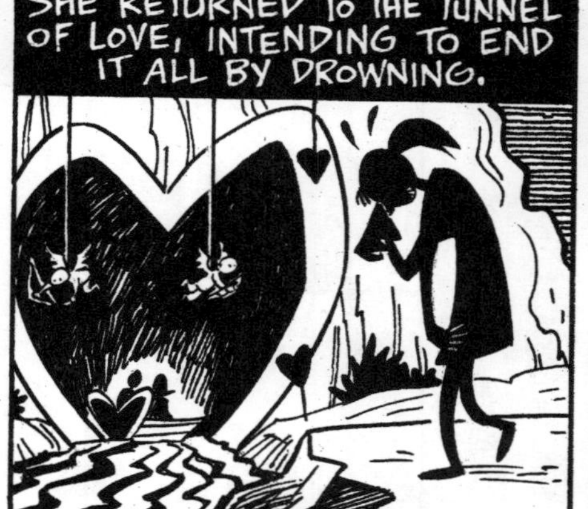
SHE RETURNED TO THE TUNNEL OF LOVE, INTENDING TO END IT ALL BY DROWNING.

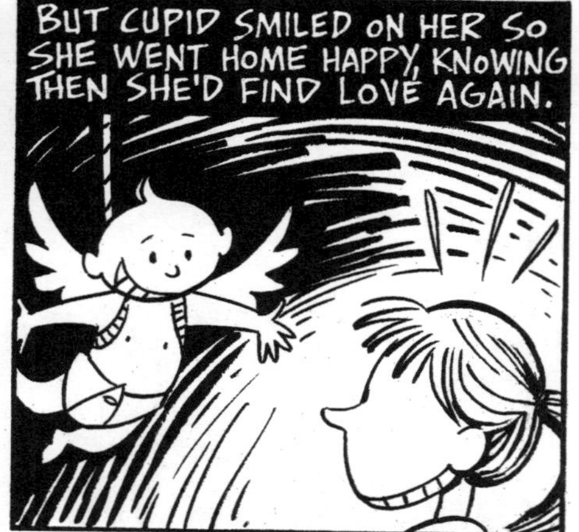
BUT CUPID SMILED ON HER SO SHE WENT HOME HAPPY, KNOWING THEN SHE'D FIND LOVE AGAIN.

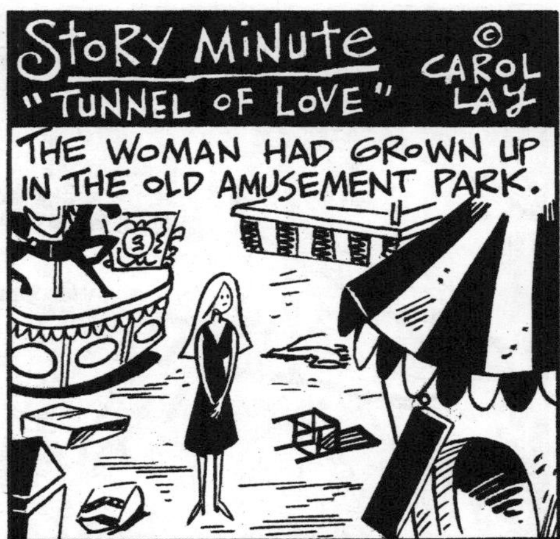
STORY MINUTE
"TUNNEL OF LOVE"
© CAROL LAY
THE WOMAN HAD GROWN UP IN THE OLD AMUSEMENT PARK.

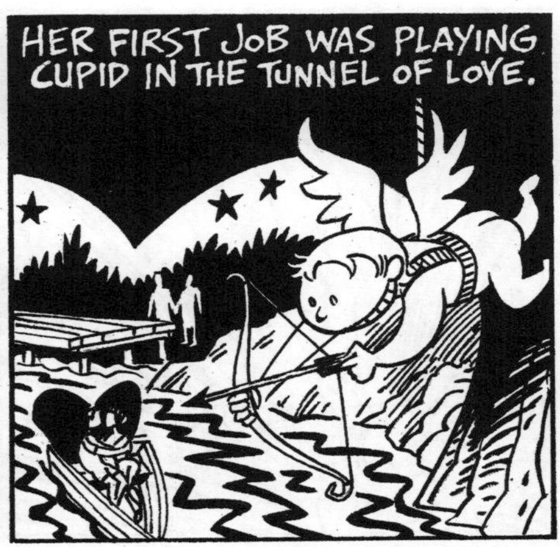
HER FIRST JOB WAS PLAYING CUPID IN THE TUNNEL OF LOVE.

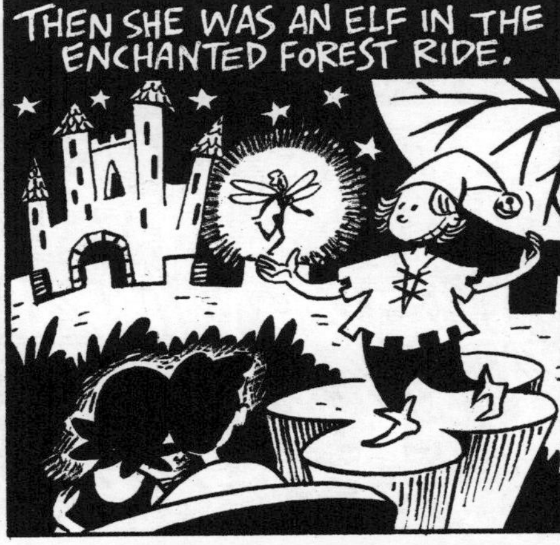
THEN SHE WAS AN ELF IN THE ENCHANTED FOREST RIDE.

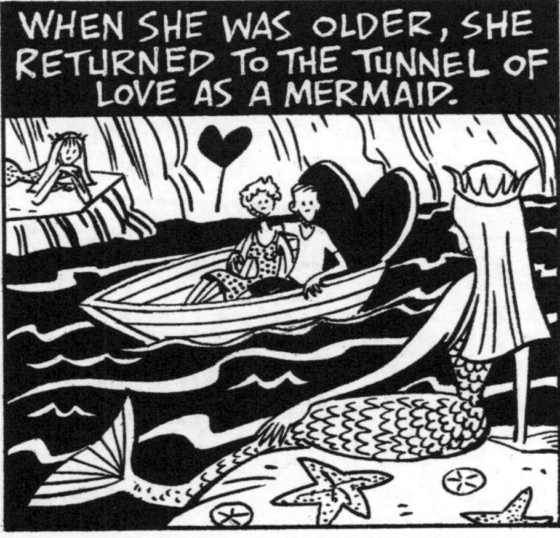
WHEN SHE WAS OLDER, SHE RETURNED TO THE TUNNEL OF LOVE AS A MERMAID.

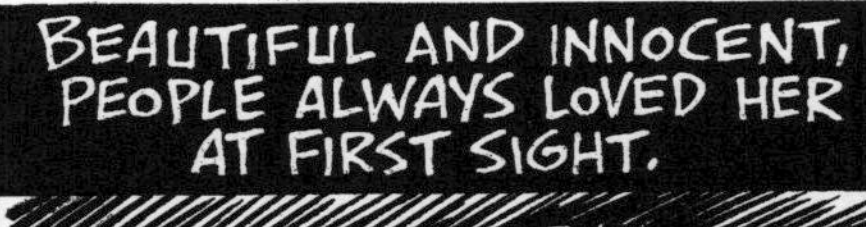
BEAUTIFUL AND INNOCENT, PEOPLE ALWAYS LOVED HER AT FIRST SIGHT.

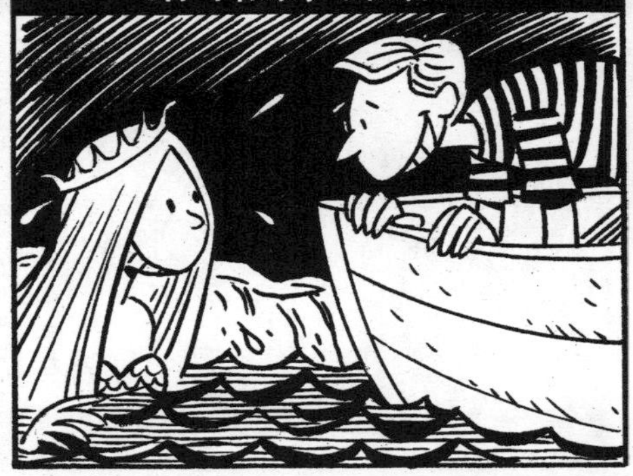

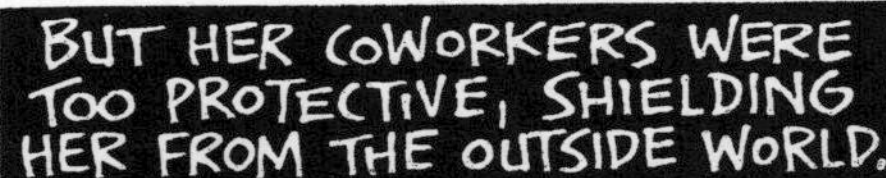
BUT HER COWORKERS WERE TOO PROTECTIVE, SHIELDING HER FROM THE OUTSIDE WORLD.

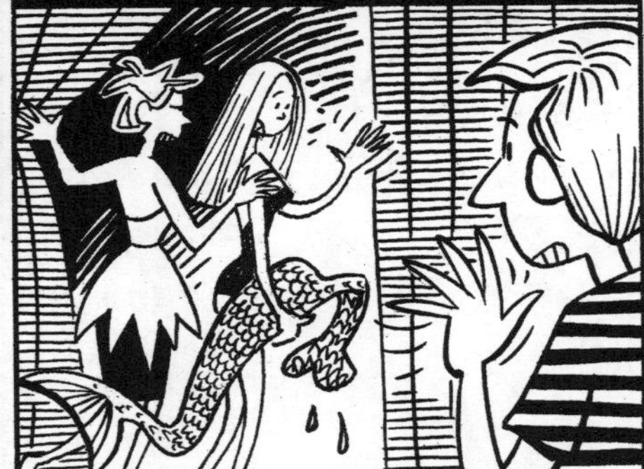

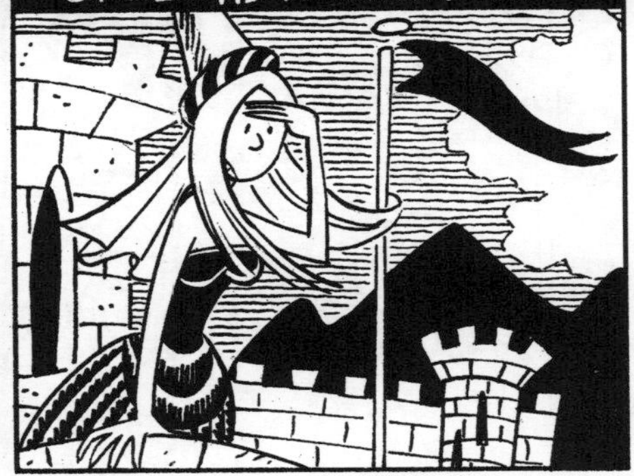
BUT, STILL, SHE LONGED TO DISCOVER THE REAL WORLD, CRUEL AS IT MIGHT BE.

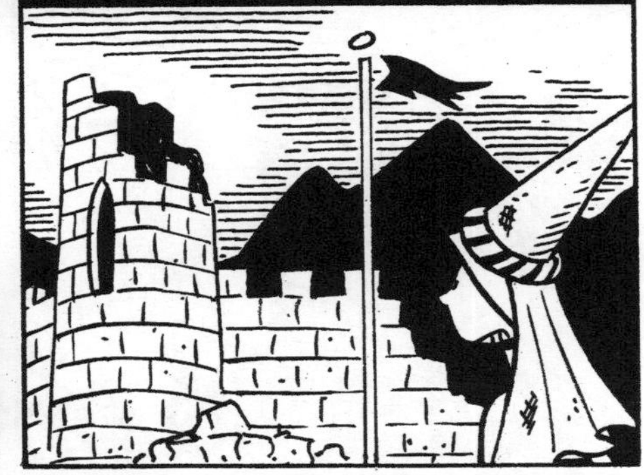
SHE GREW OLDER AND THE PARK AROUND HER STARTED TO FALL APART.

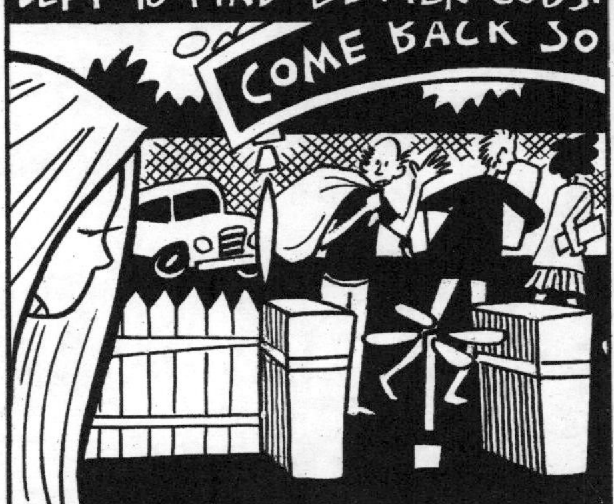
ONE BY ONE, HER COWORKERS LEFT TO FIND BETTER JOBS.
COME BACK SO

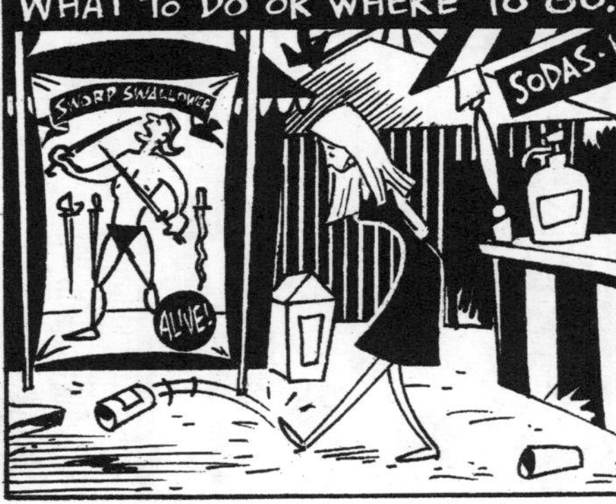
WHEN THE PARK WAS FINALLY CONDEMNED SHE DIDN'T KNOW WHAT TO DO OR WHERE TO GO.
SWORD SWALLOWER
ALIVE!
SODAS

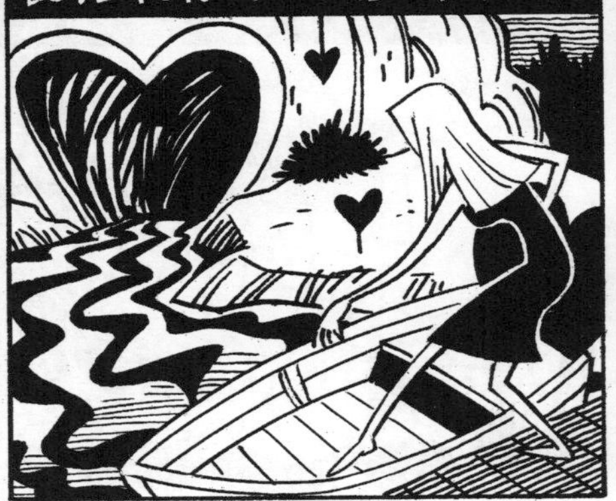
SHE WENT TO THE TUNNEL OF LOVE FOR ONE LAST RIDE...

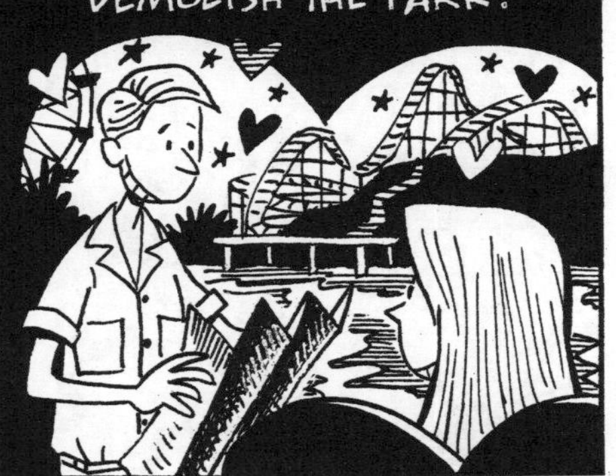
...AND FELL IN LOVE WITH THE MAN WHOSE JOB IT WAS TO DEMOLISH THE PARK.

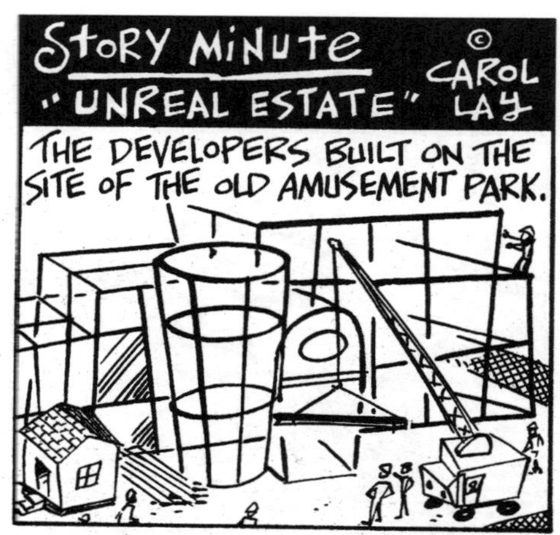
STORY MINUTE
"UNREAL ESTATE"
© CAROL LAY
THE DEVELOPERS BUILT ON THE SITE OF THE OLD AMUSEMENT PARK.

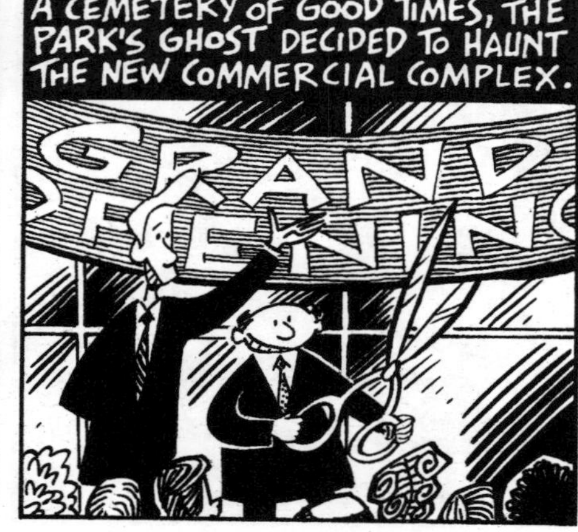
A CEMETERY OF GOOD TIMES, THE PARK'S GHOST DECIDED TO HAUNT THE NEW COMMERCIAL COMPLEX.
GRAND

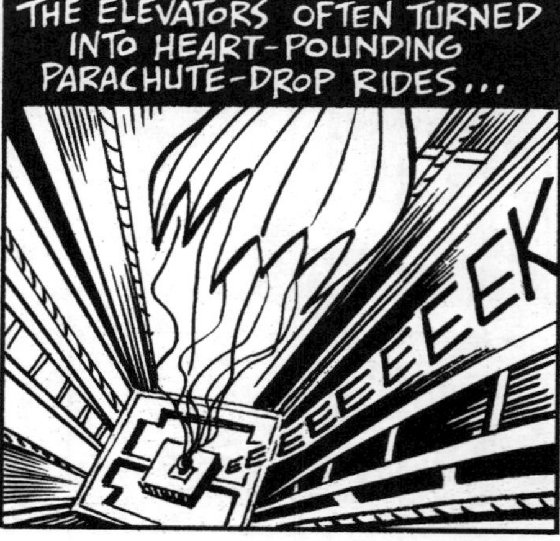
THE ELEVATORS OFTEN TURNED INTO HEART-POUNDING PARACHUTE-DROP RIDES...
EEEEEEEEEEEK

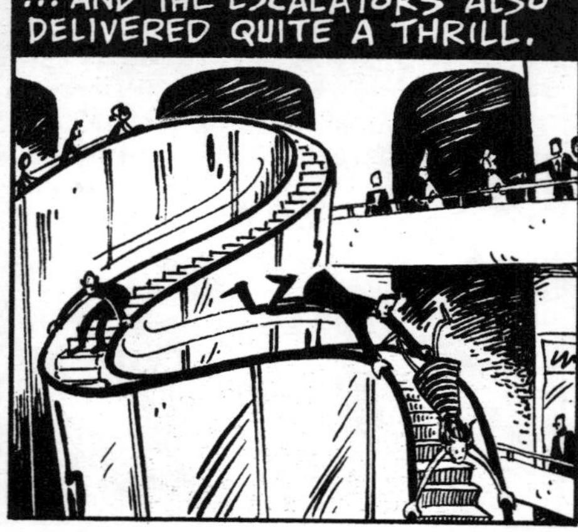
...AND THE ESCALATORS ALSO DELIVERED QUITE A THRILL.

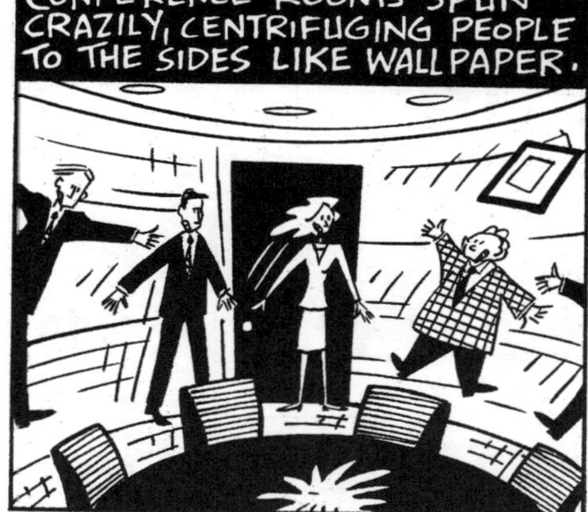
CONFERENCE ROOMS SPUN CRAZILY, CENTRIFUGING PEOPLE TO THE SIDES LIKE WALLPAPER.

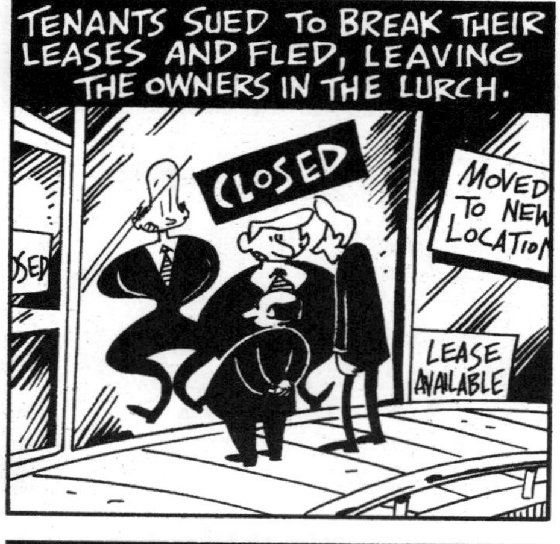
TENANTS SUED TO BREAK THEIR LEASES AND FLED, LEAVING THE OWNERS IN THE LURCH.
CLOSED
MOVED TO NEW LOCATION
LEASE AVAILABLE

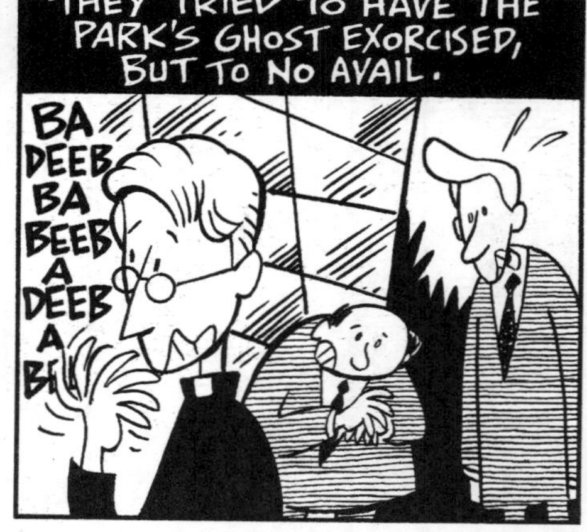
THEY TRIED TO HAVE THE PARK'S GHOST EXORCISED, BUT TO NO AVAIL.
BA DEEB BA BEEB A DEEB A

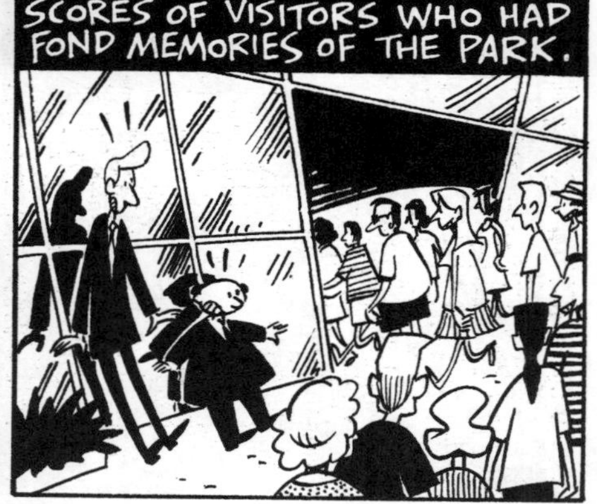
WORD OF MOUTH, HOWEVER, BROUGHT SCORES OF VISITORS WHO HAD FOND MEMORIES OF THE PARK.

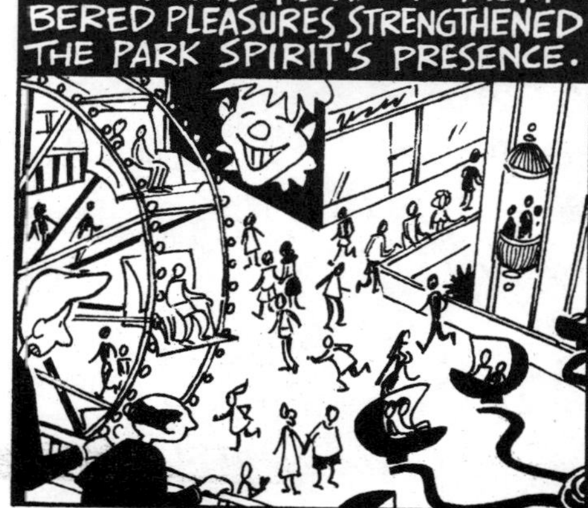
THEIR NUMBERS AND REMEMBERED PLEASURES STRENGTHENED THE PARK SPIRIT'S PRESENCE.

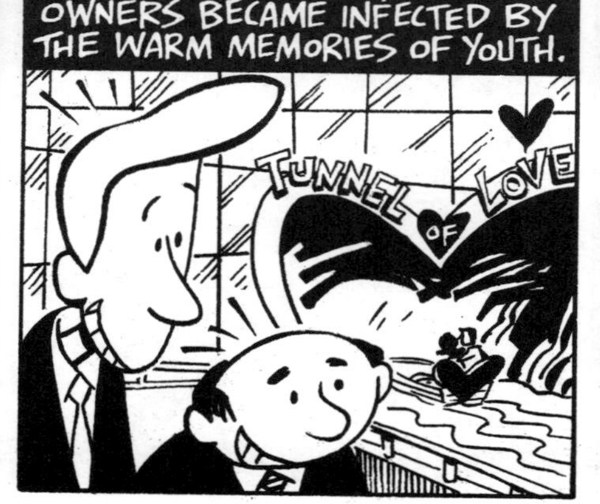
EVEN THE FINANCIALLY-STRAPPED OWNERS BECAME INFECTED BY THE WARM MEMORIES OF YOUTH.
TUNNEL OF LOVE

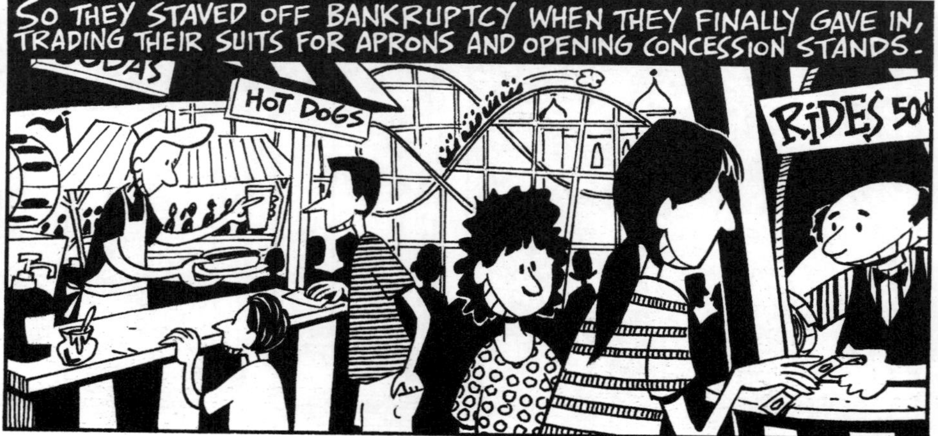
SO THEY STAVED OFF BANKRUPTCY WHEN THEY FINALLY GAVE IN, TRADING THEIR SUITS FOR APRONS AND OPENING CONCESSION STANDS.
HOT DOGS
RIDES 50¢

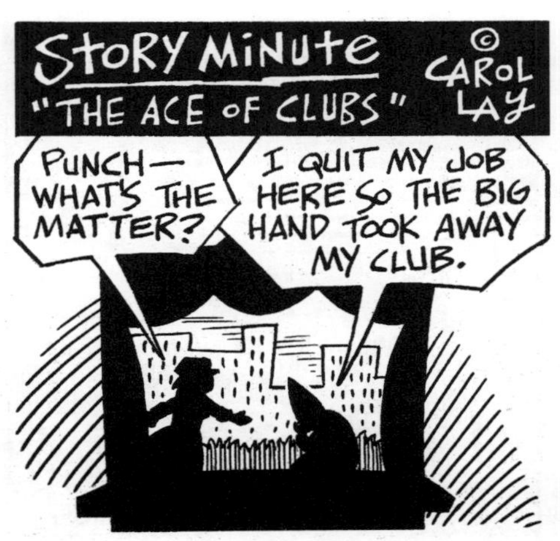
STORY MINUTE
"THE ACE OF CLUBS"
© CAROL LAY
PUNCH— WHAT'S THE MATTER?
I QUIT MY JOB HERE SO THE BIG HAND TOOK AWAY MY CLUB.
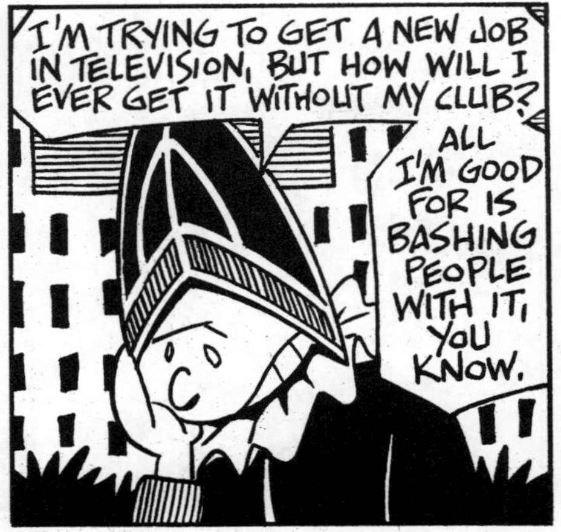
I'M TRYING TO GET A NEW JOB IN TELEVISION, BUT HOW WILL I EVER GET IT WITHOUT MY CLUB?
ALL I'M GOOD FOR IS BASHING PEOPLE WITH IT, YOU KNOW.
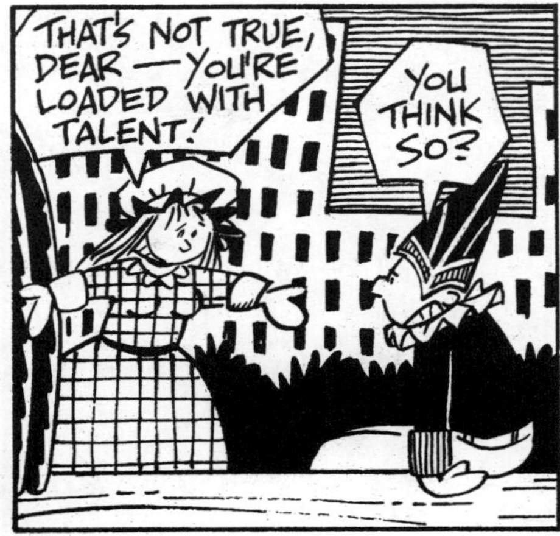
THAT'S NOT TRUE, DEAR — YOU'RE LOADED WITH TALENT!
YOU THINK SO?
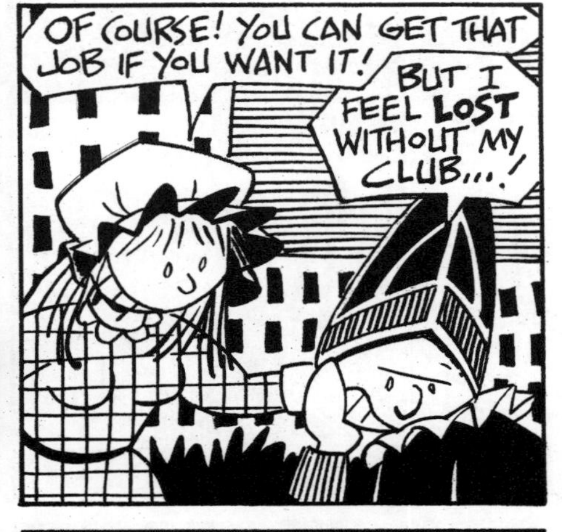
OF COURSE! YOU CAN GET THAT JOB IF YOU WANT IT!
BUT I FEEL LOST WITHOUT MY CLUB...!
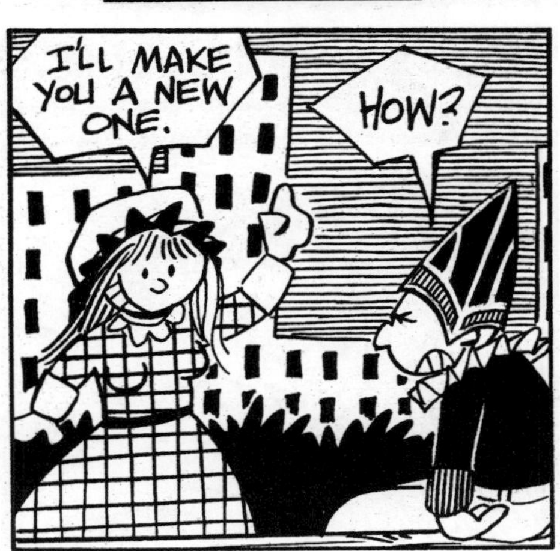
I'LL MAKE YOU A NEW ONE.
HOW?
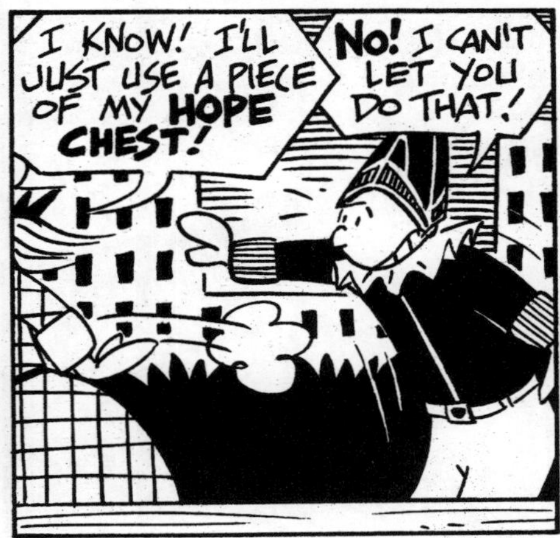
I KNOW! I'LL JUST USE A PIECE OF MY HOPE CHEST!
NO! I CAN'T LET YOU DO THAT!
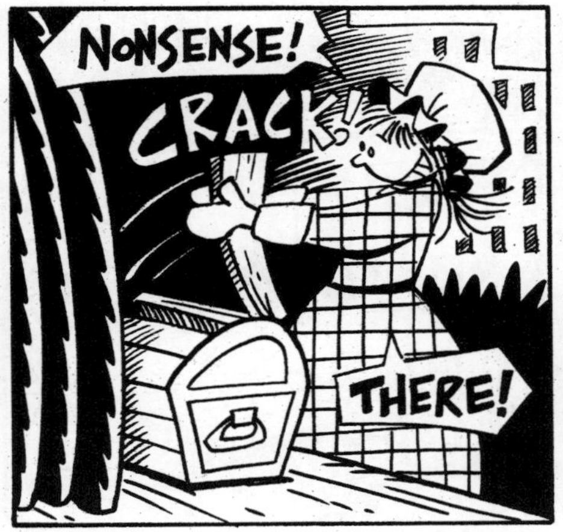
NONSENSE!
CRACK!
THERE!
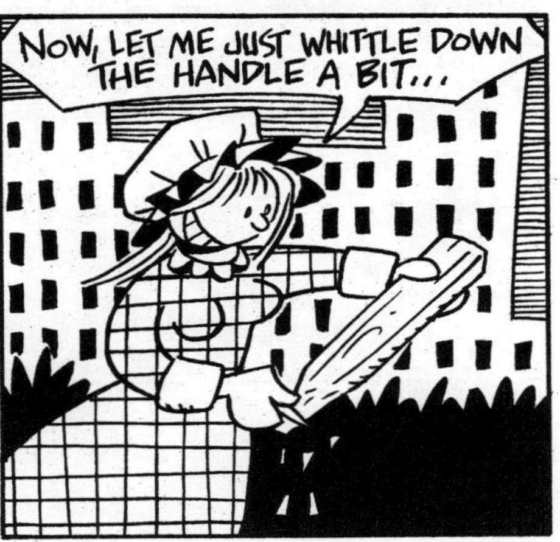
NOW, LET ME JUST WHITTLE DOWN THE HANDLE A BIT...
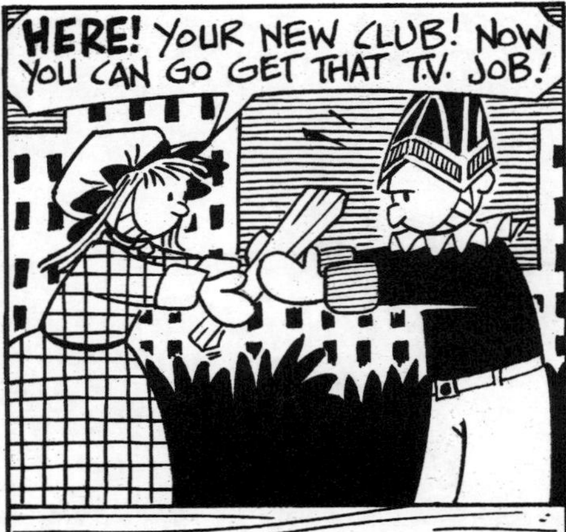
HERE! YOUR NEW CLUB! NOW YOU CAN GO GET THAT T.V. JOB!
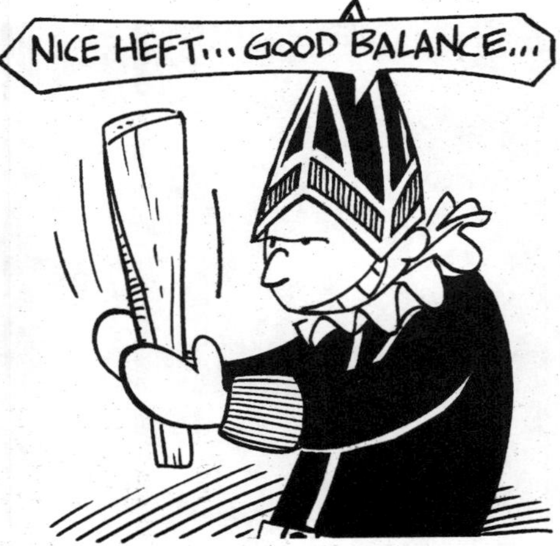
NICE HEFT... GOOD BALANCE...
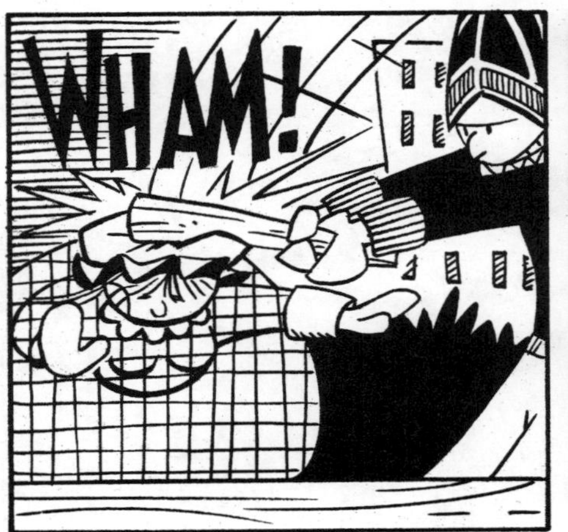
WHAM!
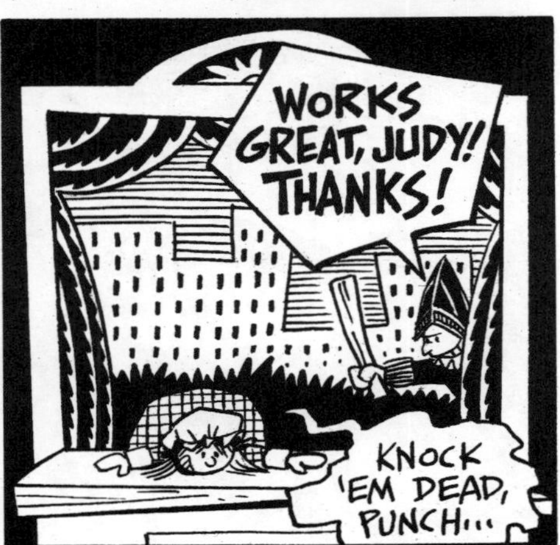
WORKS GREAT, JUDY! THANKS!
KNOCK 'EM DEAD, PUNCH...

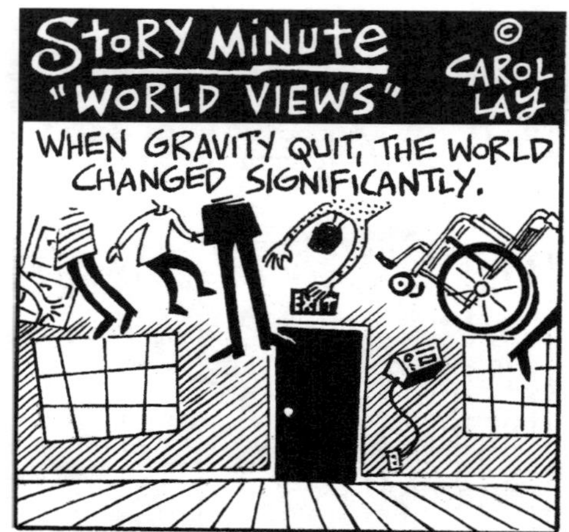
STORY MINUTE
"WORLD VIEWS"
© CAROL LAY
WHEN GRAVITY QUIT, THE WORLD CHANGED SIGNIFICANTLY.
EXIT

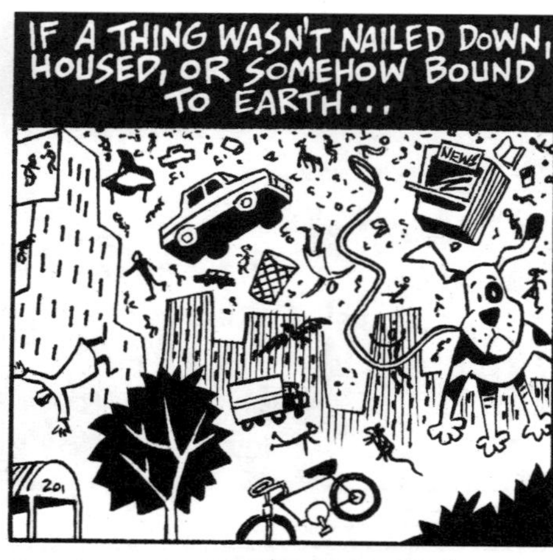
IF A THING WASN'T NAILED DOWN, HOUSED, OR SOMEHOW BOUND TO EARTH...
NEWS

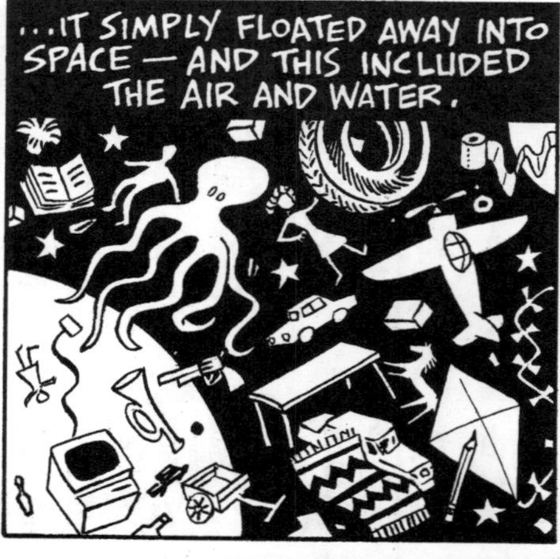
...IT SIMPLY FLOATED AWAY INTO SPACE — AND THIS INCLUDED THE AIR AND WATER.

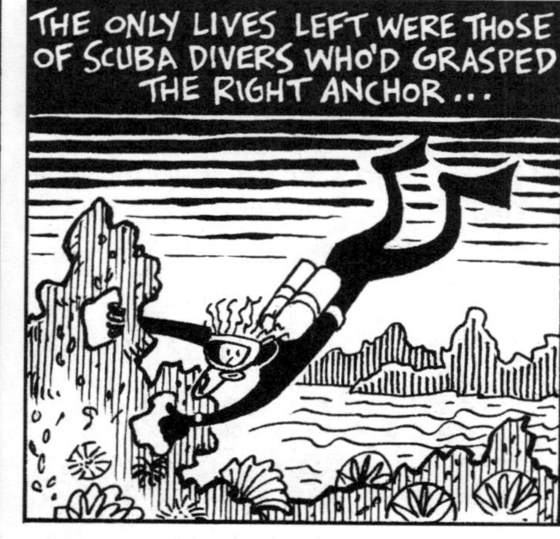
THE ONLY LIVES LEFT WERE THOSE OF SCUBA DIVERS WHO'D GRASPED THE RIGHT ANCHOR...

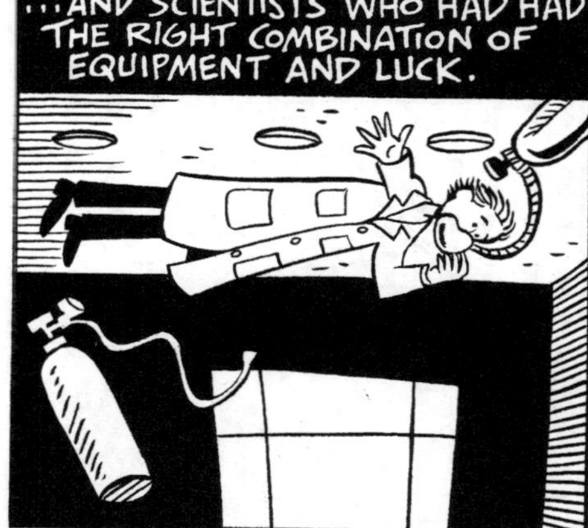
...AND SCIENTISTS WHO HAD HAD THE RIGHT COMBINATION OF EQUIPMENT AND LUCK.

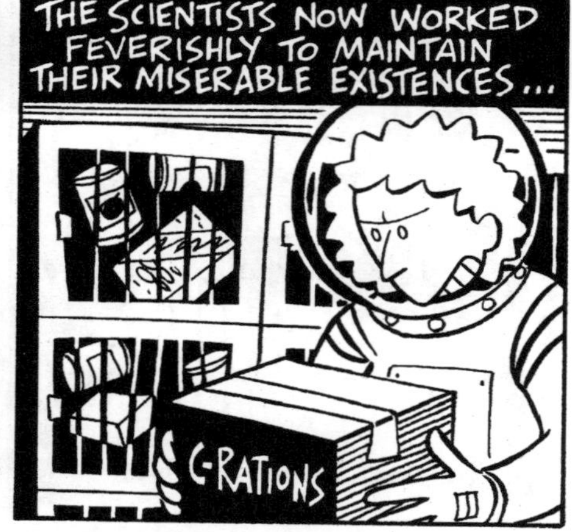
THE SCIENTISTS NOW WORKED FEVERISHLY TO MAINTAIN THEIR MISERABLE EXISTENCES...
C-RATIONS

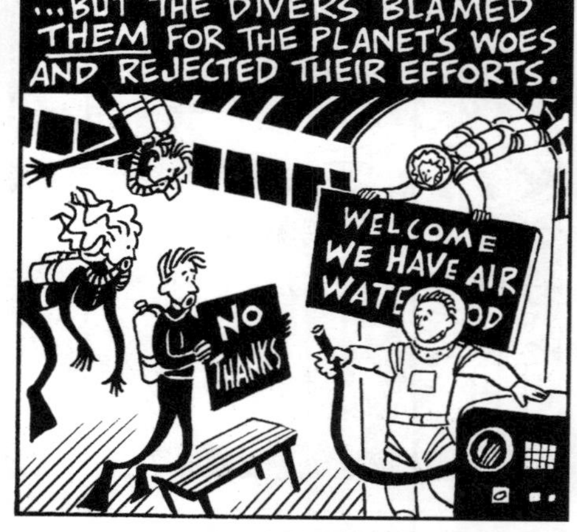
...BUT THE DIVERS BLAMED THEM FOR THE PLANET'S WOES AND REJECTED THEIR EFFORTS.
WELCOME
WE HAVE AIR
NO THANKS

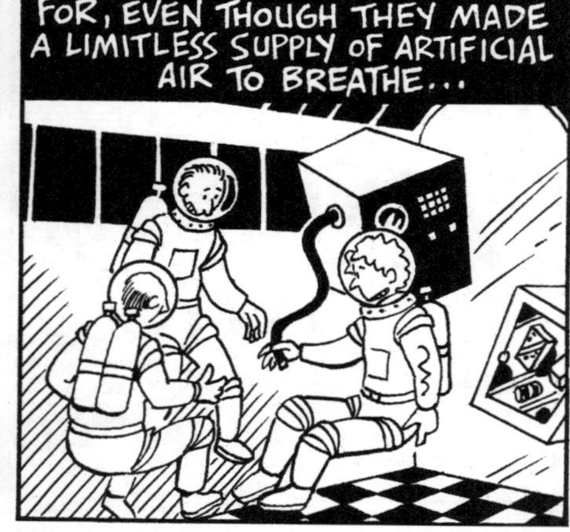
FOR, EVEN THOUGH THEY MADE A LIMITLESS SUPPLY OF ARTIFICIAL AIR TO BREATHE...

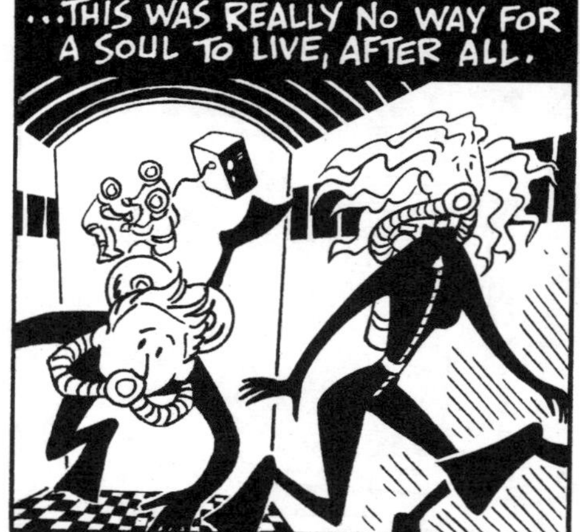
...THIS WAS REALLY NO WAY FOR A SOUL TO LIVE, AFTER ALL.

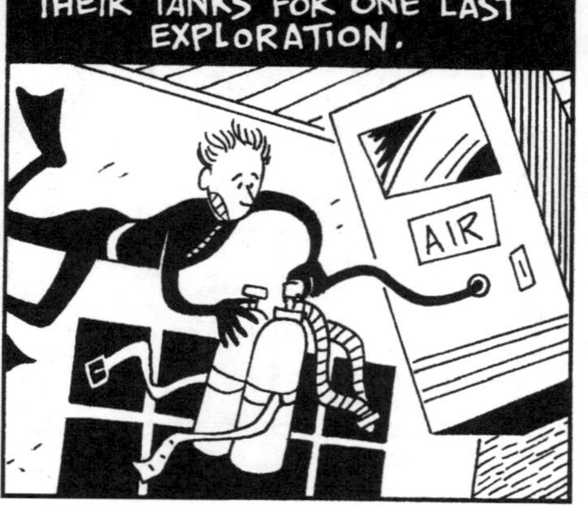
ONE BY ONE, THE DIVERS FILLED THEIR TANKS FOR ONE LAST EXPLORATION.
AIR

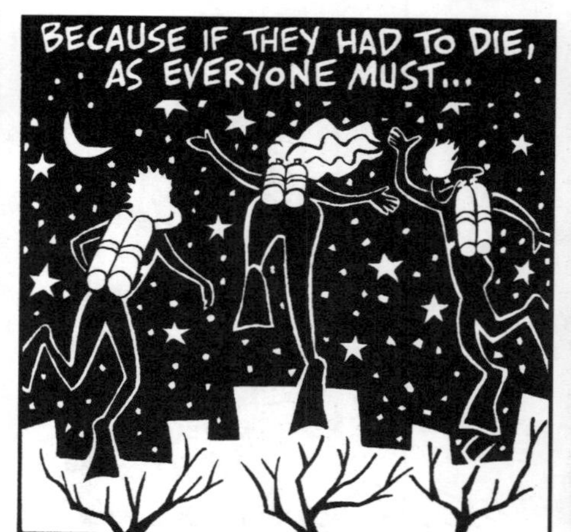
BECAUSE IF THEY HAD TO DIE, AS EVERYONE MUST...

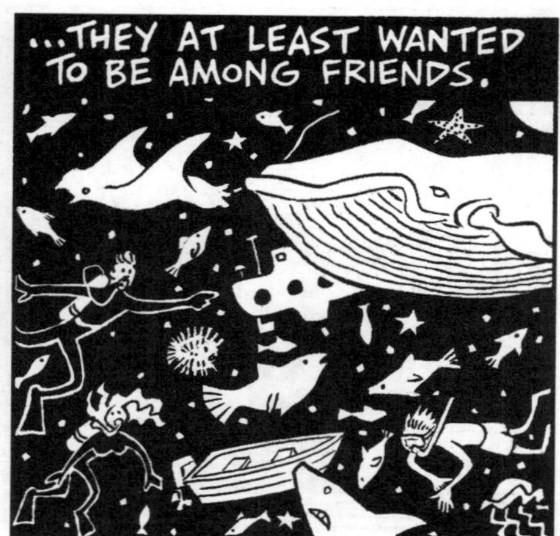
...THEY AT LEAST WANTED TO BE AMONG FRIENDS.

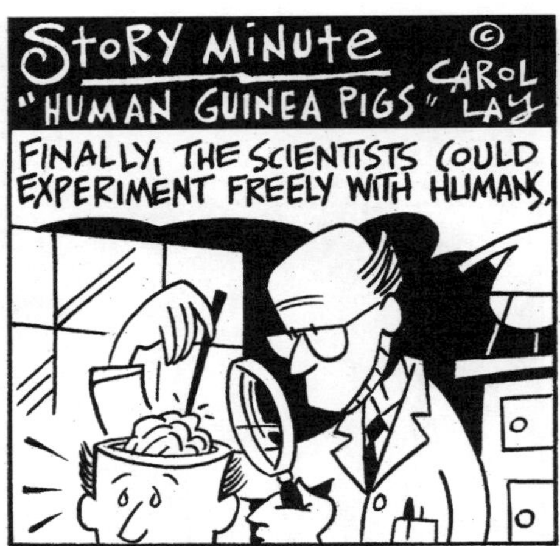
STORY MINUTE
"HUMAN GUINEA PIGS"
© CAROL LAY
FINALLY, THE SCIENTISTS COULD EXPERIMENT FREELY WITH HUMANS,

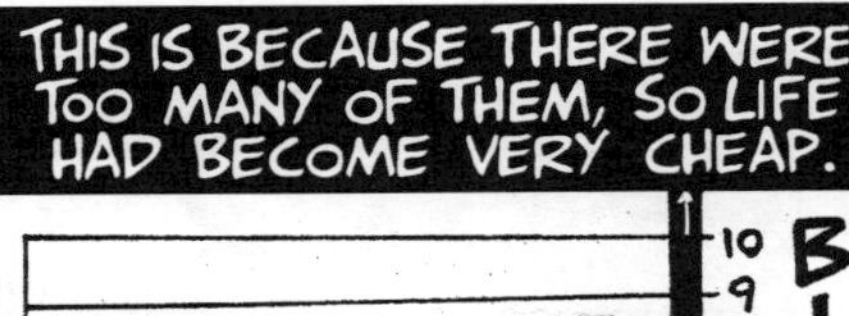
THIS IS BECAUSE THERE WERE TOO MANY OF THEM, SO LIFE HAD BECOME VERY CHEAP.

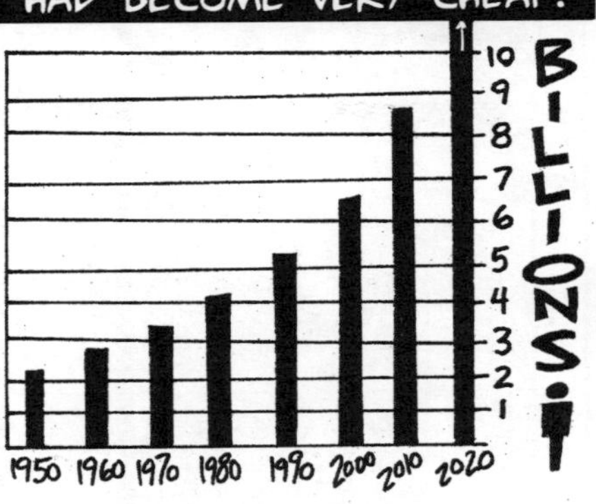
10
9
8
7
6
5
4
3
2
1
BILLIONS
1950 1960 1970 1980 1990 2000 2010 2020

THE SCIENTISTS PREYED ON MEMBERS OF THE LOWER CLASS WHO HAD NO LEGAL RECOURSE.

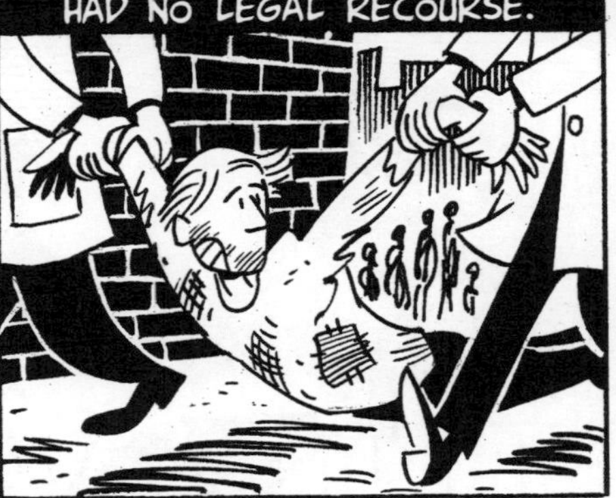

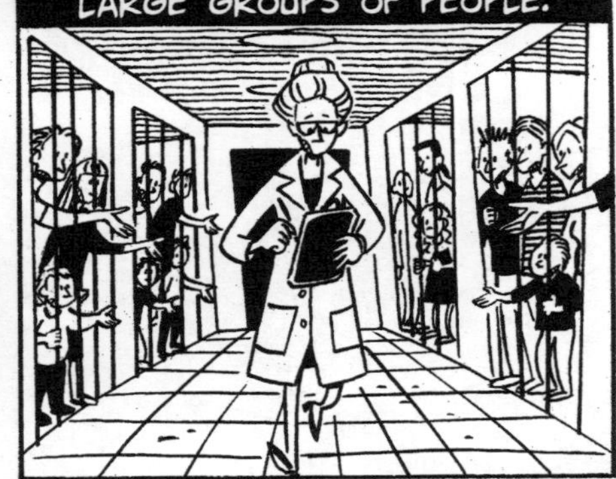
ONE BEHAVIORAL SCIENTIST STUDIED SELECTIVE ELIMINATION AMONG LARGE GROUPS OF PEOPLE.

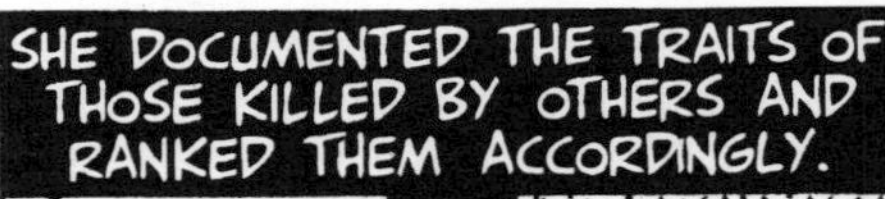
SHE DOCUMENTED THE TRAITS OF THOSE KILLED BY OTHERS AND RANKED THEM ACCORDINGLY.

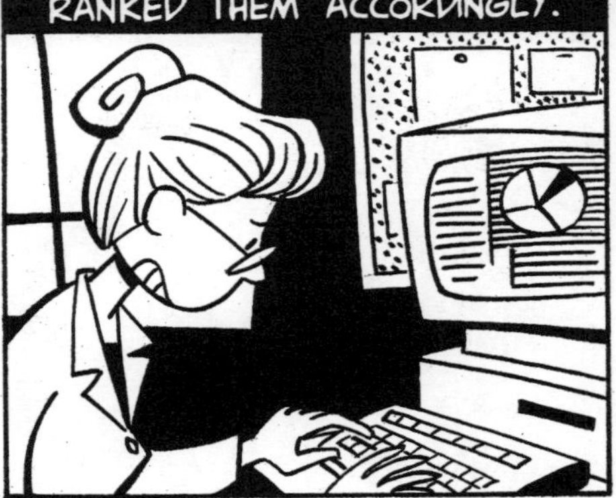

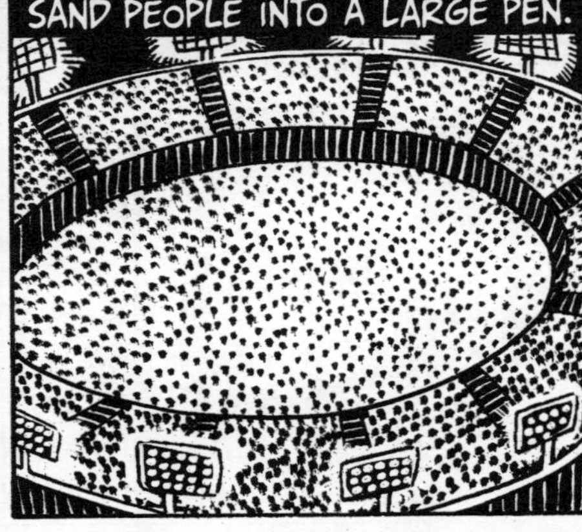
TO DO THIS, SHE GATHERED A THOUSAND PEOPLE INTO A LARGE PEN.

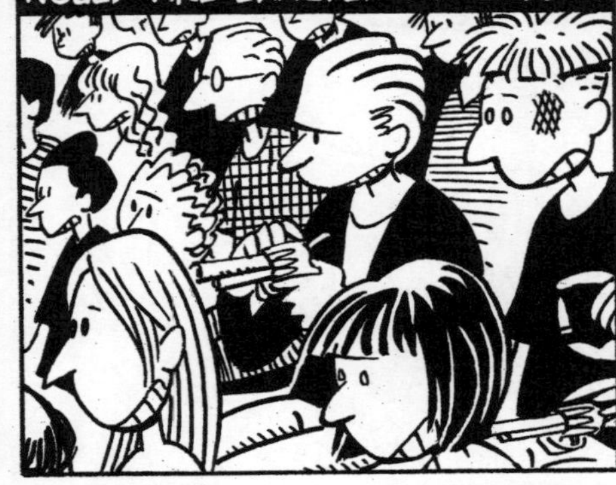
IN THE STANDS WERE ANOTHER THOUSAND WHO EACH HAD A GUN THAT WOULD FIRE EXACTLY ONE BULLET.

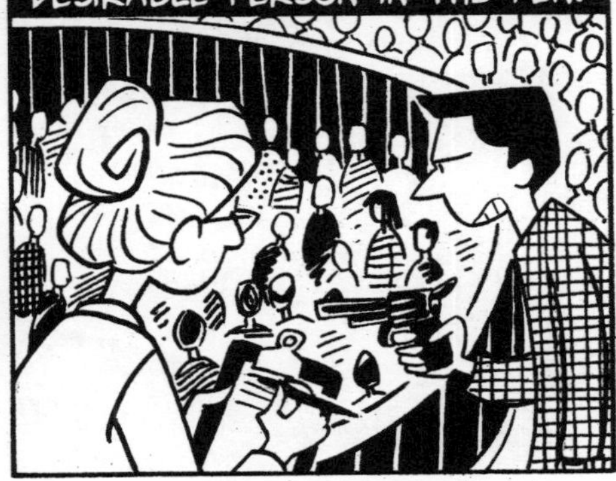
ONE BY ONE, THEY WERE GIVEN INSTRUCTIONS TO KILL THE LEAST DESIRABLE PERSON IN THE PEN.

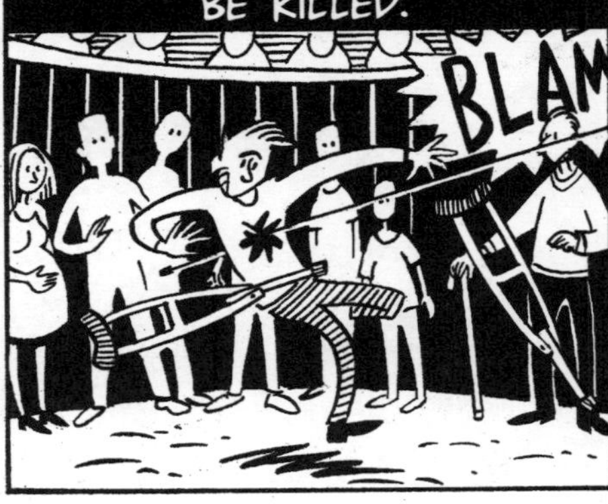
THE INFIRM AND MENTALLY ILL WERE ALWAYS THE FIRST TO BE KILLED.
BLAM

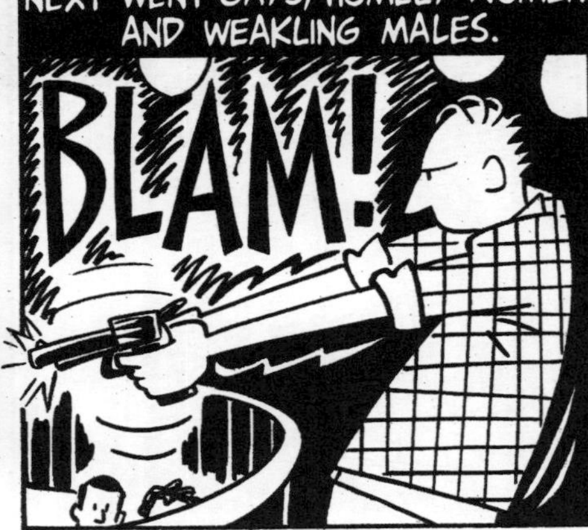
NEXT WENT GAYS, HOMELY WOMEN AND WEAKLING MALES.
BLAM!

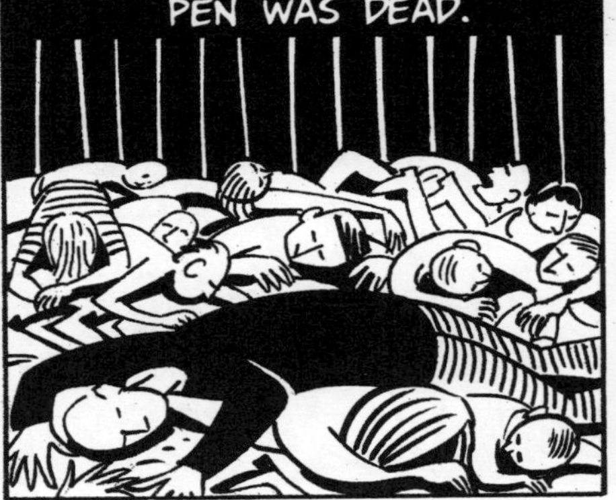
THIS CONTINUED UNTIL EVERY WOMAN, MAN, AND CHILD IN THE PEN WAS DEAD.

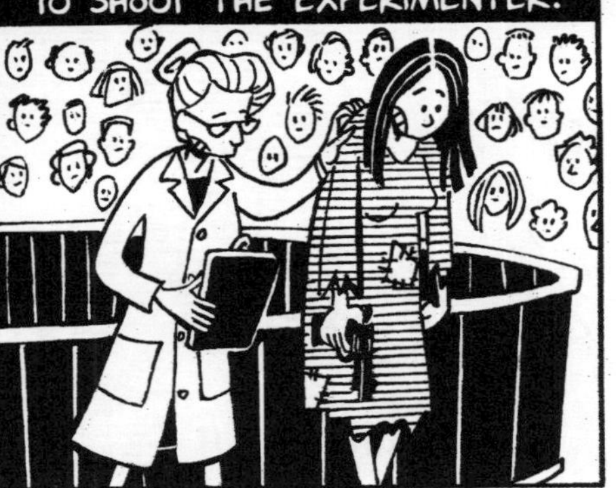
THE REALLY TRAGIC THING, THOUGH, WAS THAT NO ONE EVER THOUGHT TO SHOOT THE EXPERIMENTER.

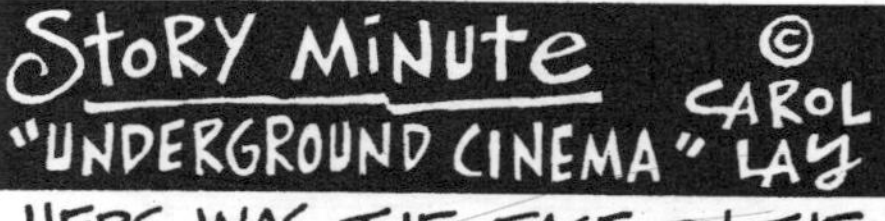
STORY MINUTE
"UNDERGROUND CINEMA"
© CAROL LAY
HERS WAS THE FACE ON THE CUTTING ROOM FLOOR.

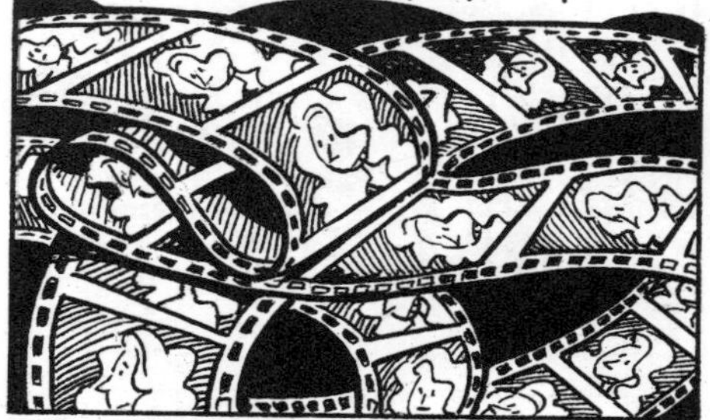

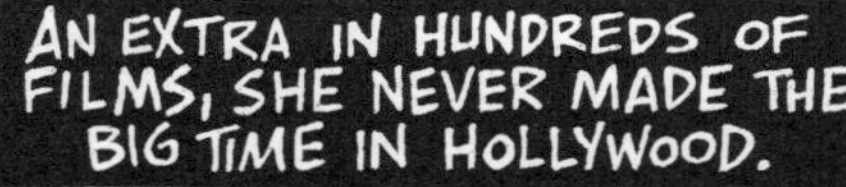
AN EXTRA IN HUNDREDS OF FILMS, SHE NEVER MADE THE BIG TIME IN HOLLYWOOD.

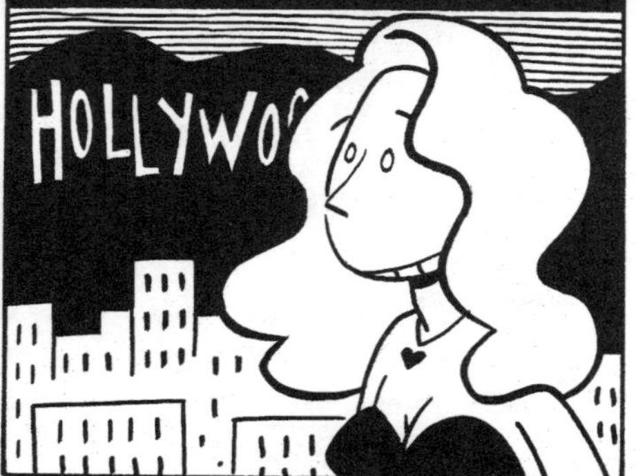
HOLLYWOO

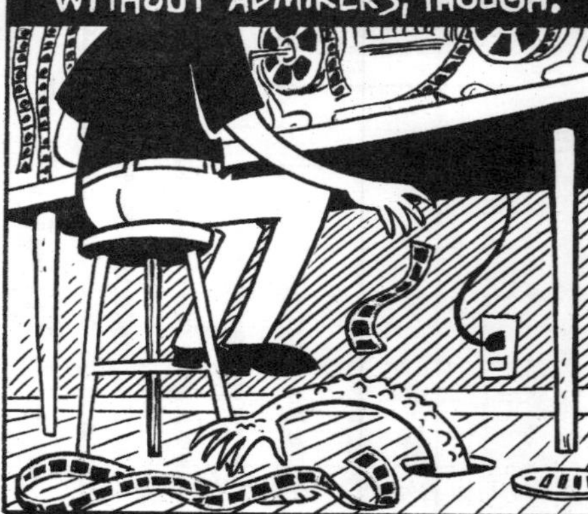
THAT DIDN'T MEAN SHE WAS WITHOUT ADMIRERS, THOUGH.

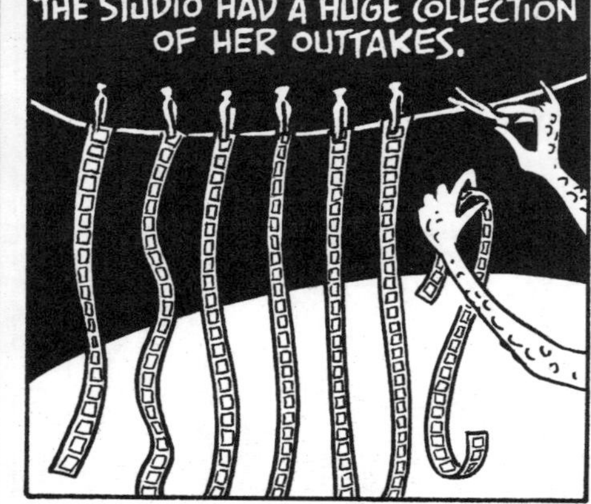
THE CREATURES WHO LIVED UNDER THE STUDIO HAD A HUGE COLLECTION OF HER OUTTAKES.

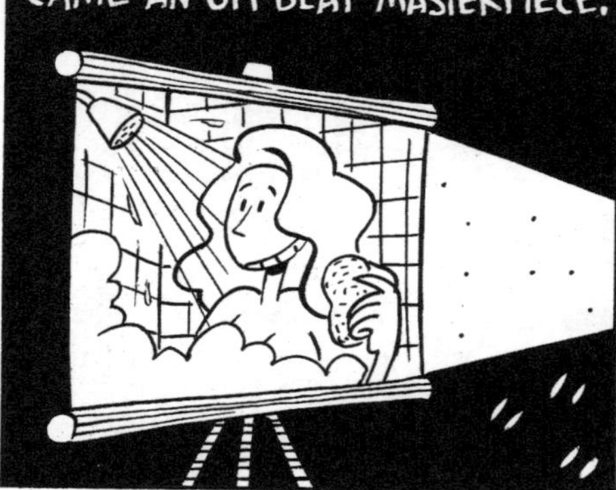
WITH CREATIVE SNIPPING AND SPLICING, THESE OUTTAKES BECAME AN OFFBEAT MASTERPIECE.

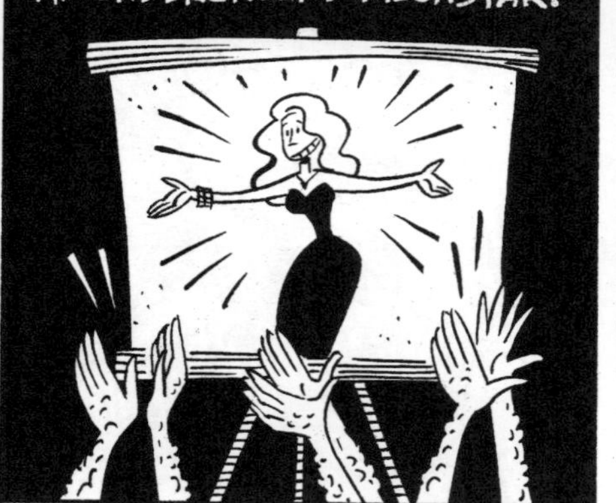
THE WOULD-BE ACTRESS WAS SOON AN UNDERGROUND MEGASTAR.

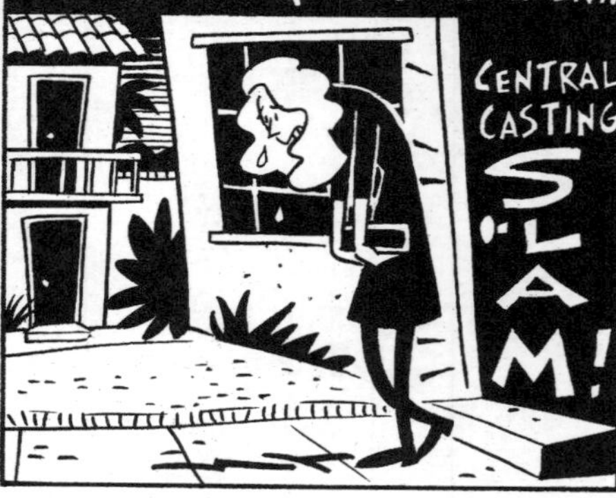
ON THE SURFACE, THOUGH, THE POOR ACTRESS WAS STILL VERY UNDISCOVERED AND QUITE DESPONDENT.
CENTRAL CASTING
SLAM!

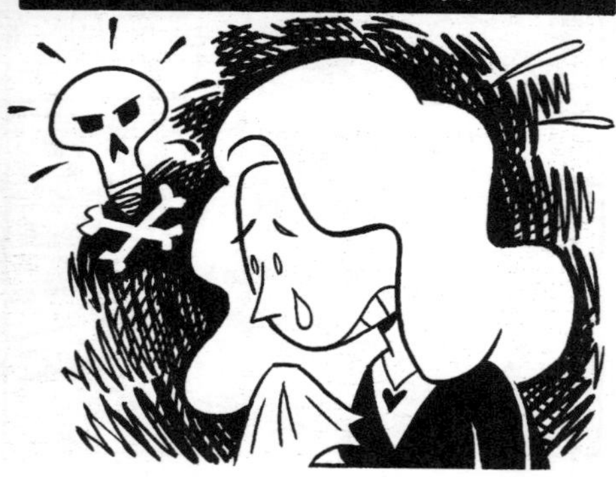
RATHER THAN SUFFER THE HUMILIATION OF FAILURE, SHE DECIDED TO GO OUT WITH A BANG.

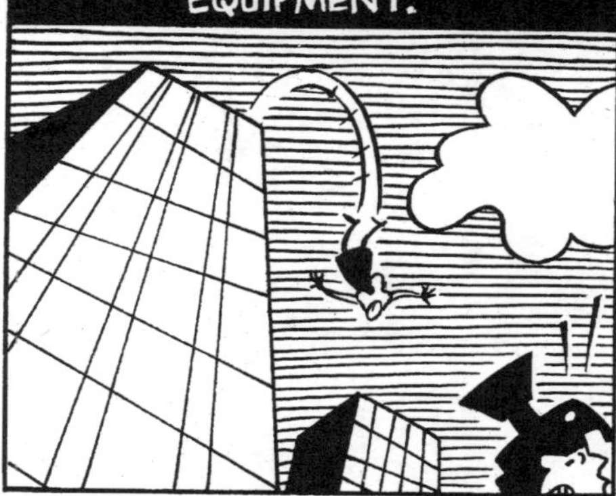
SHE DID A STUNT WOMAN'S JOB, BUT WITHOUT THE REQUIRED EQUIPMENT.

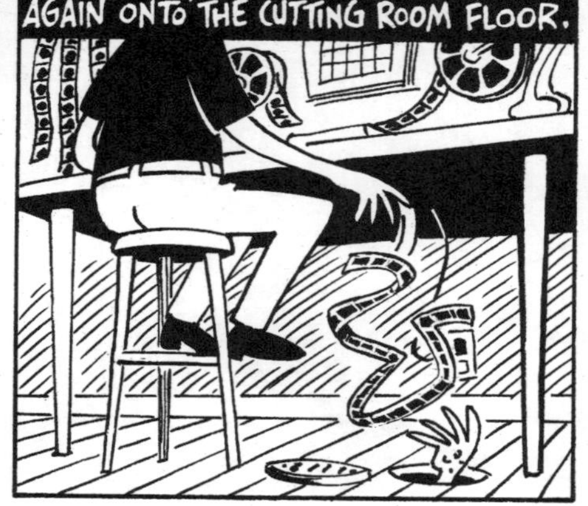
NATURALLY, HER SCENE WAS SNIPPED AGAIN ONTO THE CUTTING ROOM FLOOR.

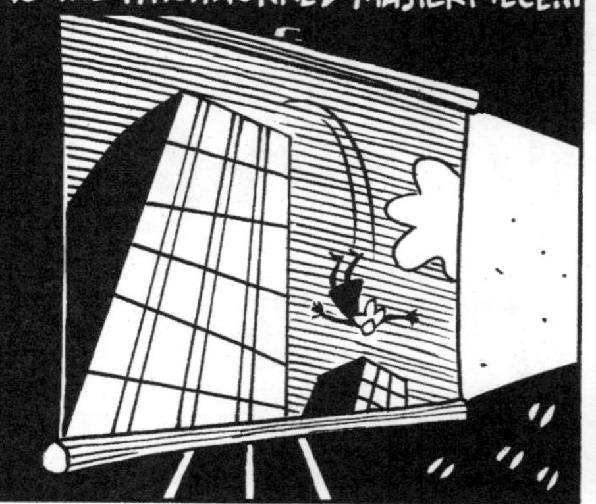
IT MADE, HOWEVER, A SOCKO ENDING TO THE PATCHWORKED MASTERPIECE...

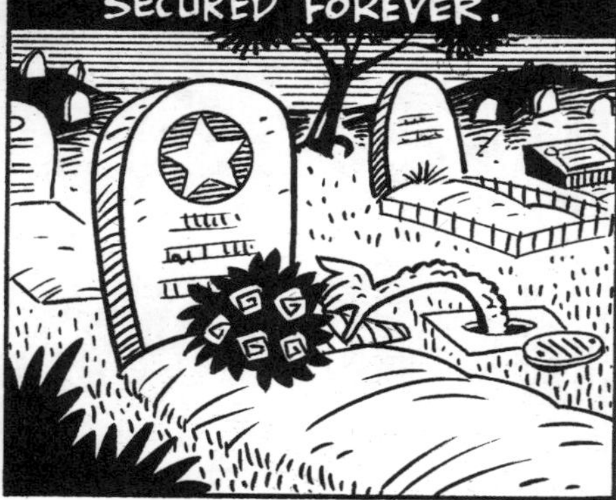
...AND HER STAR STATUS IN THE UNDERGROUND CINEMA WAS SECURED FOREVER.

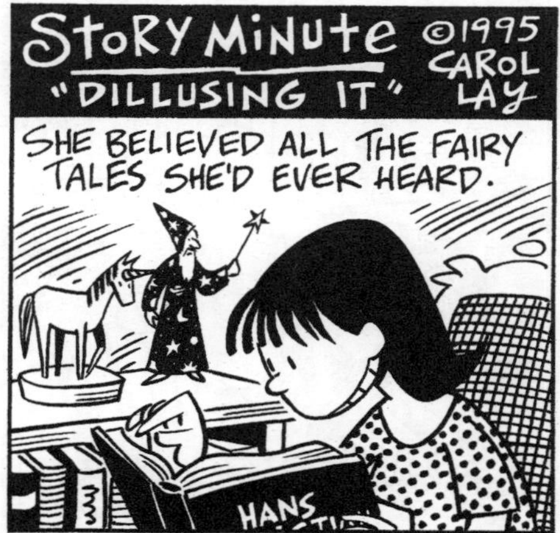
STORY MINUTE ©1995 CAROL LAY
"DILLUSING IT"
SHE BELIEVED ALL THE FAIRY TALES SHE'D EVER HEARD.
HANS

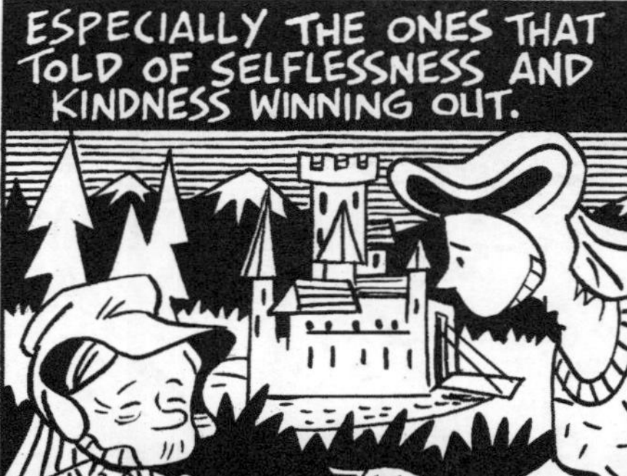
ESPECIALLY THE ONES THAT TOLD OF SELFLESSNESS AND KINDNESS WINNING OUT.

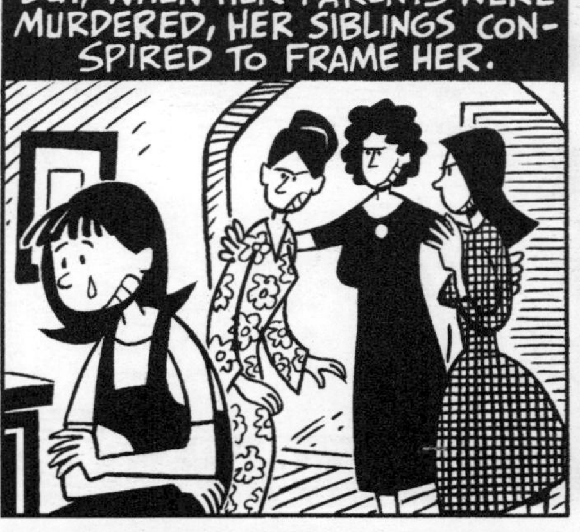
BUT, WHEN HER PARENTS WERE MURDERED, HER SIBLINGS CONSPIRED TO FRAME HER.

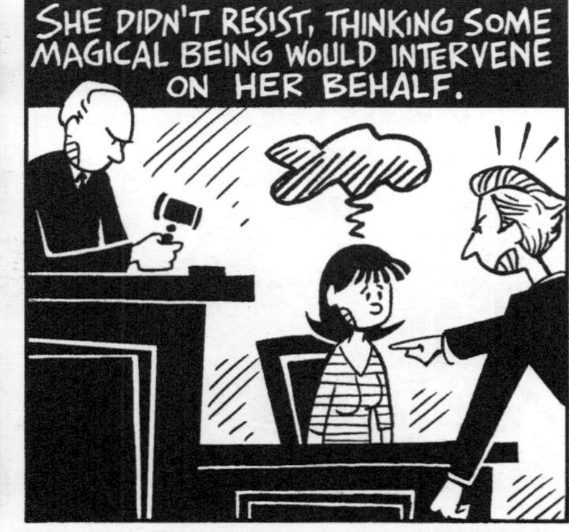
SHE DIDN'T RESIST, THINKING SOME MAGICAL BEING WOULD INTERVENE ON HER BEHALF.

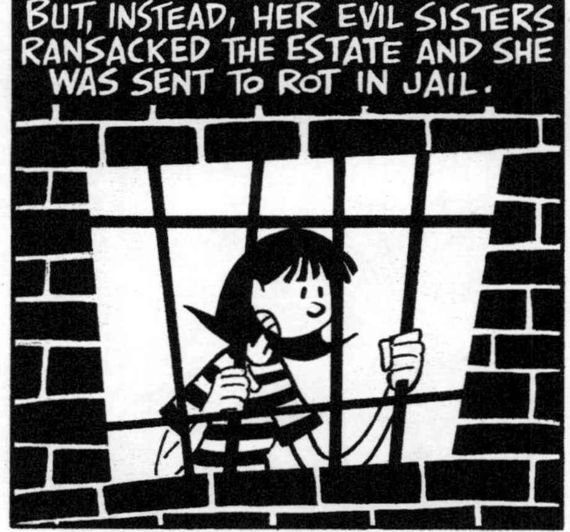
BUT, INSTEAD, HER EVIL SISTERS RANSACKED THE ESTATE AND SHE WAS SENT TO ROT IN JAIL.

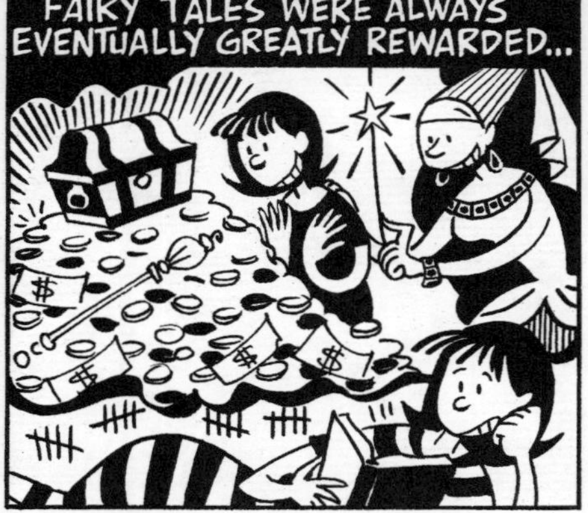
SHE KNEW THAT INNOCENTS IN FAIRY TALES WERE ALWAYS EVENTUALLY GREATLY REWARDED...

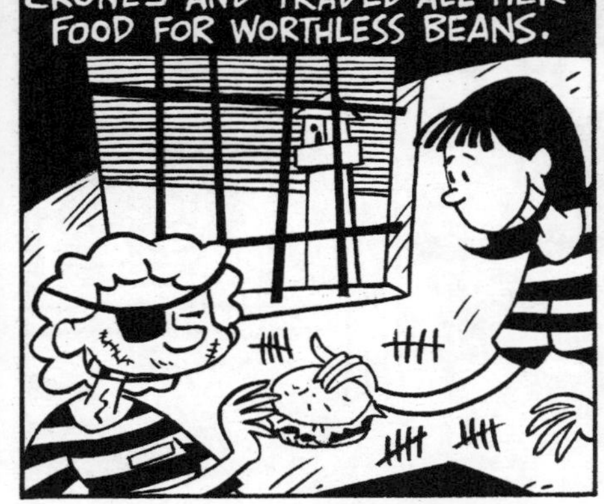
...SO SHE WAS GENEROUS TO OLD CRONES AND TRADED ALL HER FOOD FOR WORTHLESS BEANS.

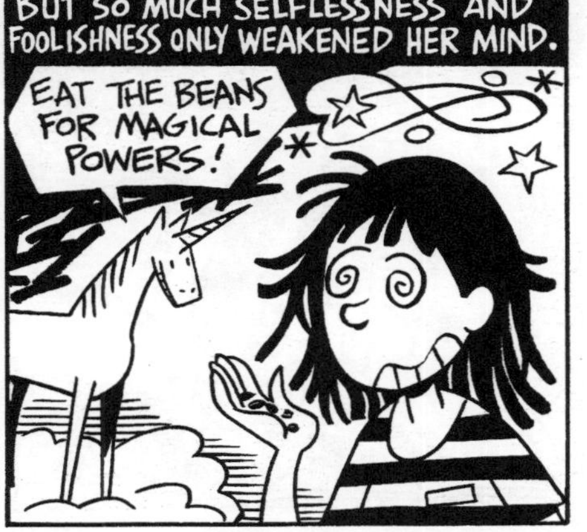
BUT SO MUCH SELFLESSNESS AND FOOLISHNESS ONLY WEAKENED HER MIND.
EAT THE BEANS FOR MAGICAL POWERS!

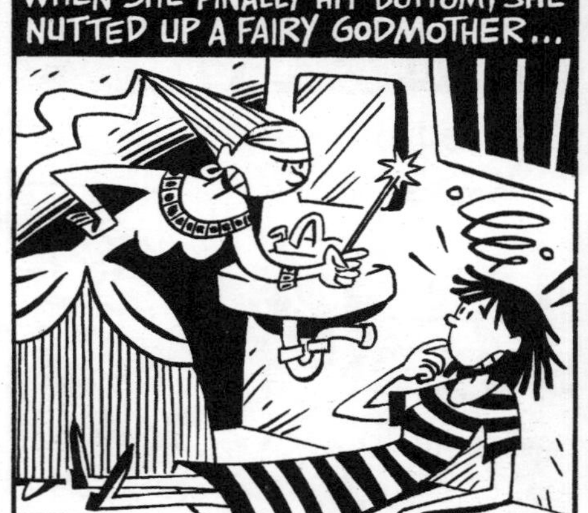
WHEN SHE FINALLY HIT BOTTOM, SHE NUTTED UP A FAIRY GODMOTHER...

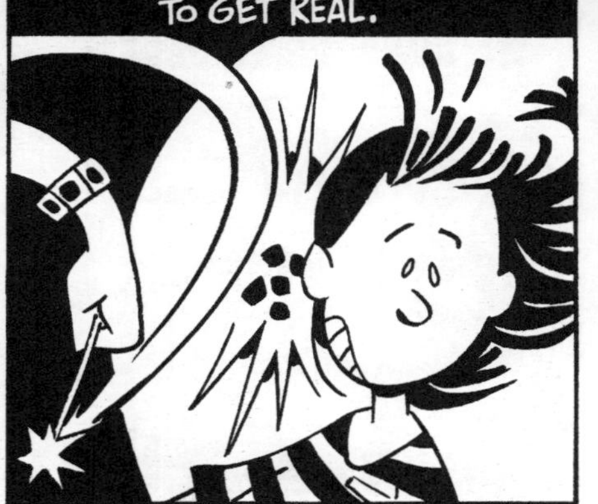
...WHO STRONGLY ADVISED HER TO GET REAL.

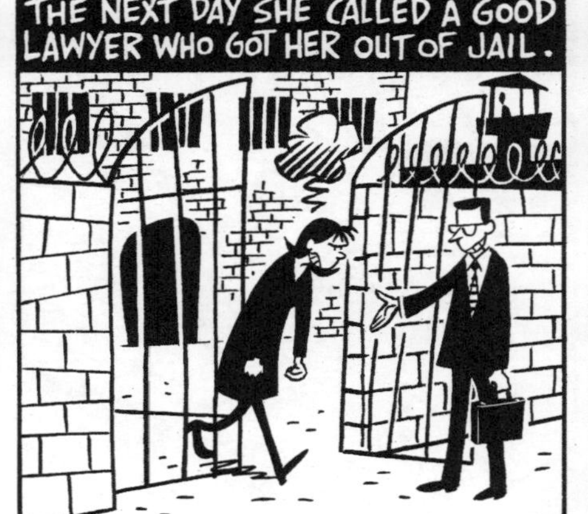
THE NEXT DAY SHE CALLED A GOOD LAWYER WHO GOT HER OUT OF JAIL.

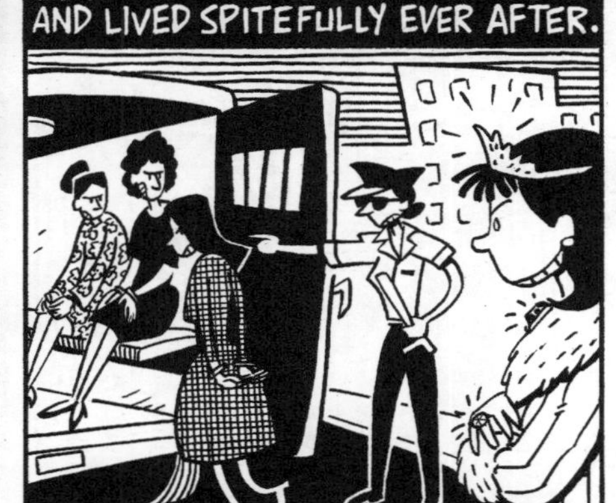
THEN SHE SICKED HIM ON HER SISTERS AND LIVED SPITEFULLY EVER AFTER.

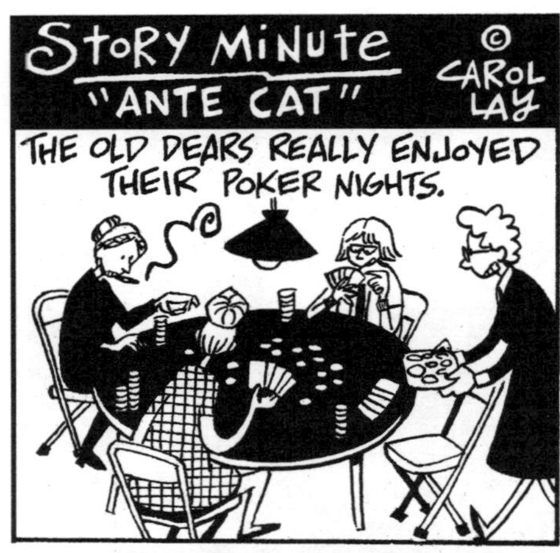
STORY MINUTE
"ANTE CAT"
© CAROL LAY
THE OLD DEARS REALLY ENJOYED THEIR POKER NIGHTS.

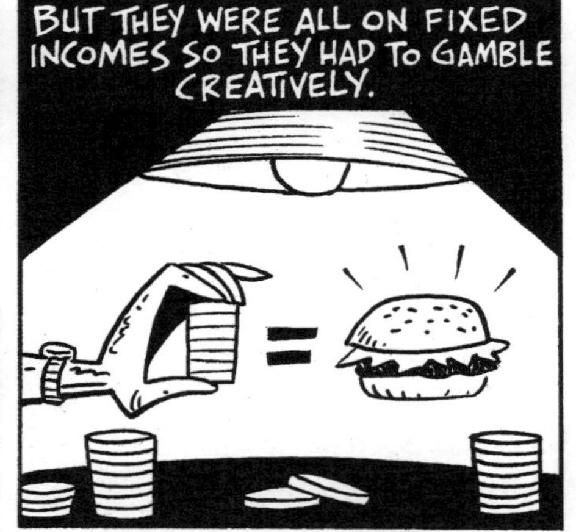
BUT THEY WERE ALL ON FIXED INCOMES SO THEY HAD TO GAMBLE CREATIVELY.

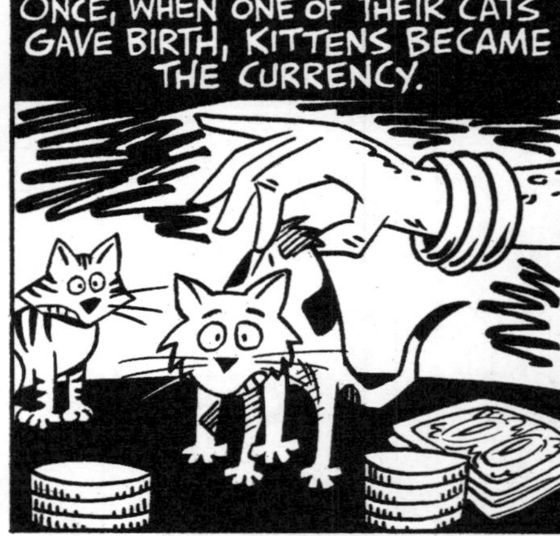
ONCE, WHEN ONE OF THEIR CATS GAVE BIRTH, KITTENS BECAME THE CURRENCY.

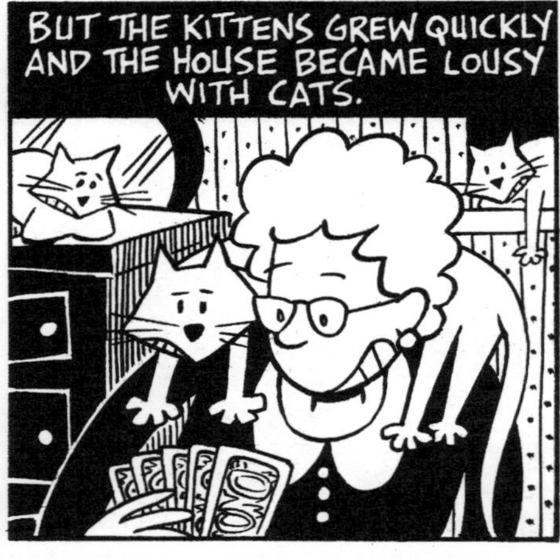
BUT THE KITTENS GREW QUICKLY AND THE HOUSE BECAME LOUSY WITH CATS.

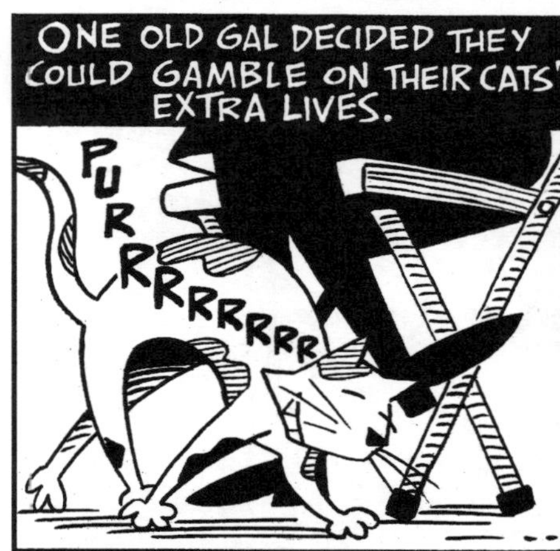
ONE OLD GAL DECIDED THEY COULD GAMBLE ON THEIR CATS' EXTRA LIVES.
PURRRRRRRRR

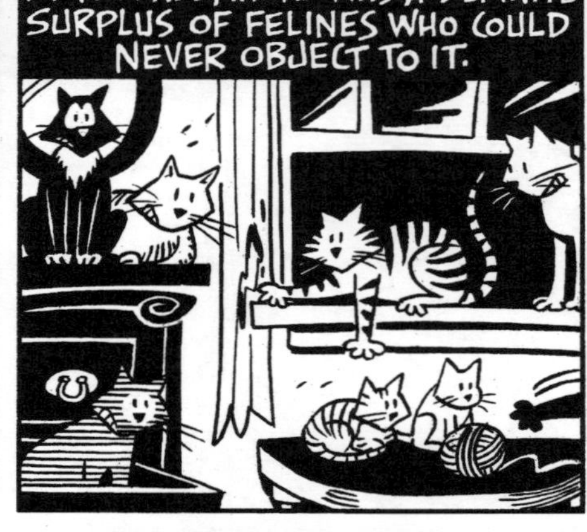
AFTER ALL, THERE WAS A DEFINITE SURPLUS OF FELINES WHO COULD NEVER OBJECT TO IT.

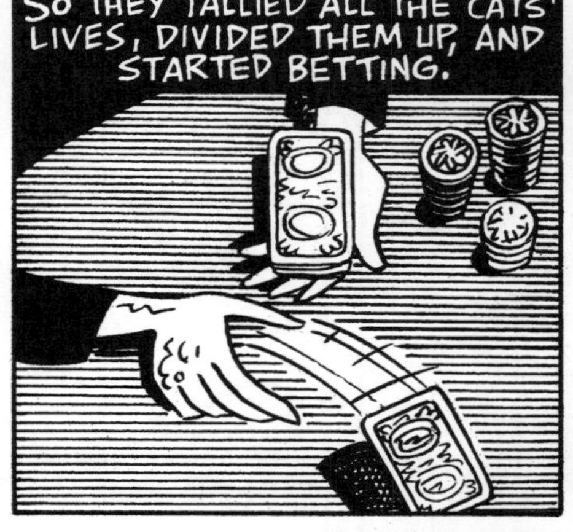
SO THEY TALLIED ALL THE CATS' LIVES, DIVIDED THEM UP, AND STARTED BETTING.

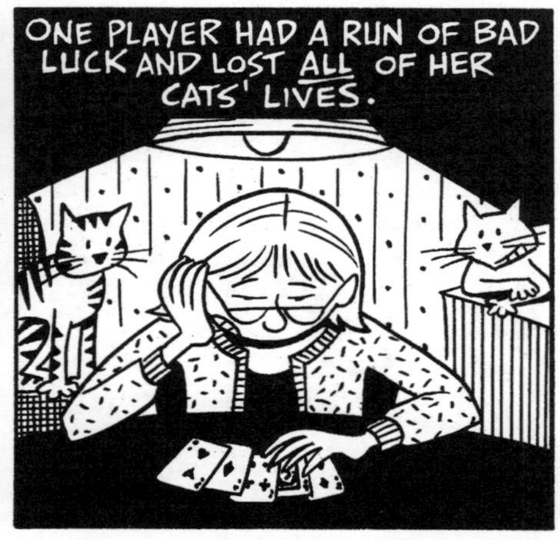
ONE PLAYER HAD A RUN OF BAD LUCK AND LOST ALL OF HER CATS' LIVES.

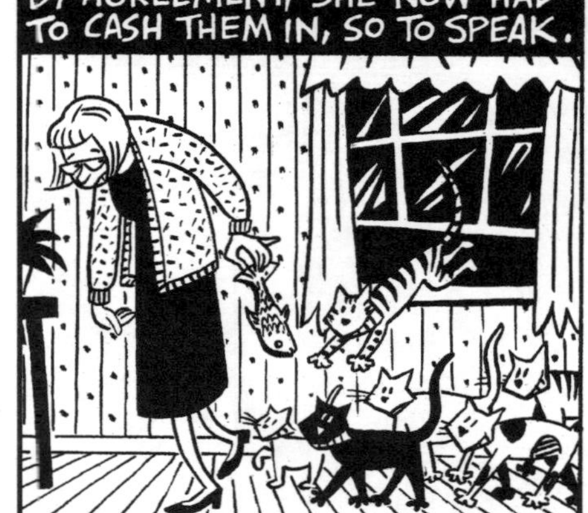
BY AGREEMENT, SHE NOW HAD TO CASH THEM IN, SO TO SPEAK.

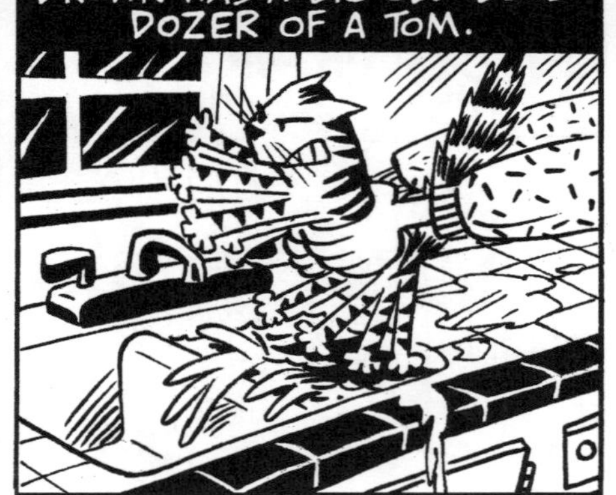
THE FIRST ONE SHE TRIED TO DROWN WAS A BIG OLD BULL-DOZER OF A TOM.

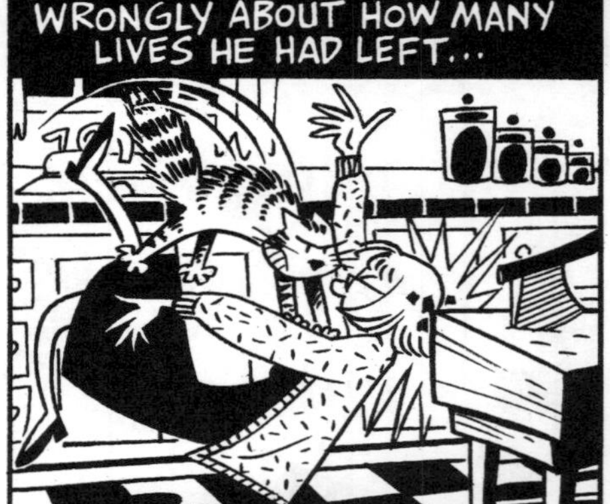
BUT THE OLD GAL HAD FIGURED WRONGLY ABOUT HOW MANY LIVES HE HAD LEFT...

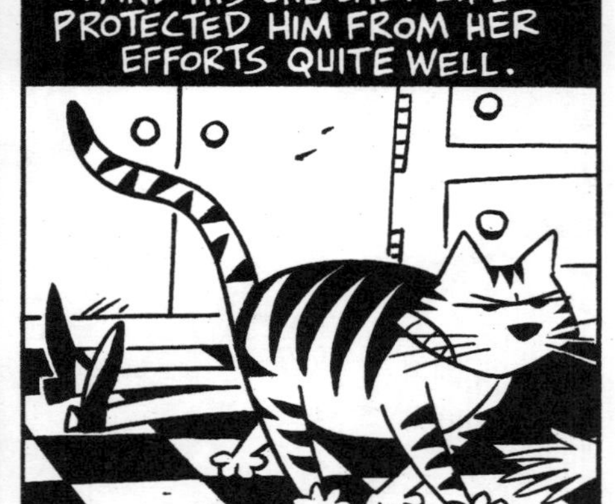
...AND HIS ONE LAST LIFE PROTECTED HIM FROM HER EFFORTS QUITE WELL.

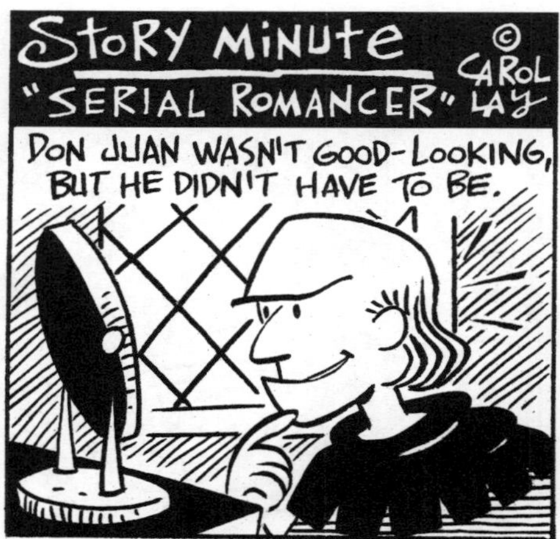
STORY MINUTE
"SERIAL ROMANCER"
© CAROL LAY
DON JUAN WASN'T GOOD-LOOKING, BUT HE DIDN'T HAVE TO BE.

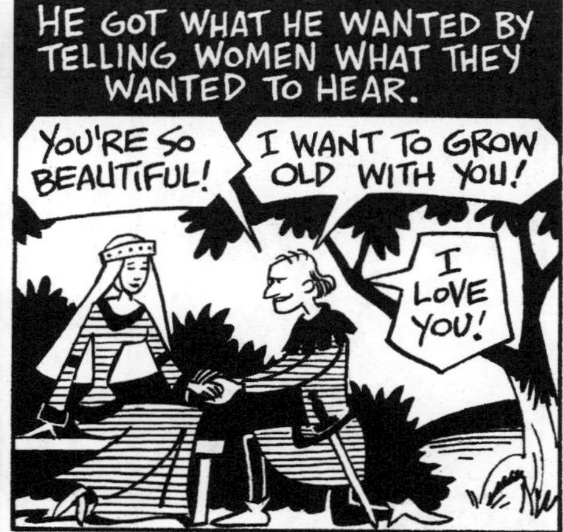
HE GOT WHAT HE WANTED BY TELLING WOMEN WHAT THEY WANTED TO HEAR.
YOU'RE SO BEAUTIFUL!
I WANT TO GROW OLD WITH YOU!
I LOVE YOU!

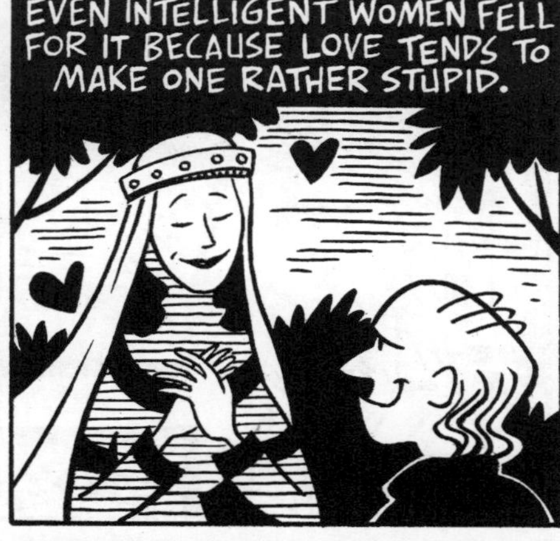
EVEN INTELLIGENT WOMEN FELL FOR IT BECAUSE LOVE TENDS TO MAKE ONE RATHER STUPID.

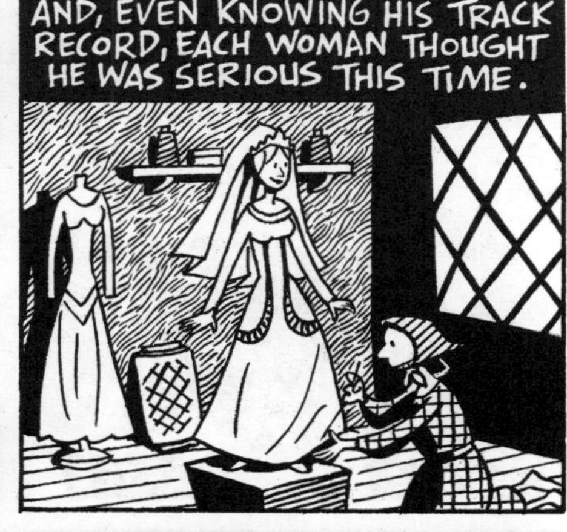
AND, EVEN KNOWING HIS TRACK RECORD, EACH WOMAN THOUGHT HE WAS SERIOUS THIS TIME.

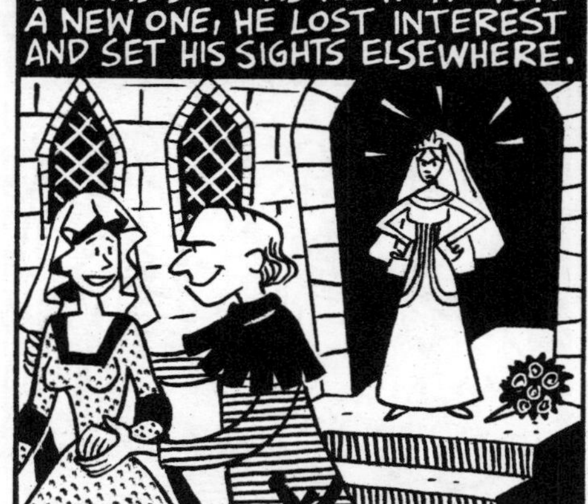
BUT AS SOON AS HE WON OVER A NEW ONE, HE LOST INTEREST AND SET HIS SIGHTS ELSEWHERE.

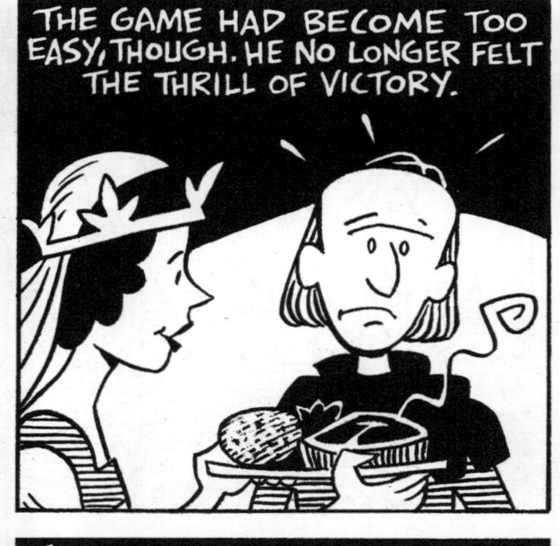
THE GAME HAD BECOME TOO EASY, THOUGH. HE NO LONGER FELT THE THRILL OF VICTORY.

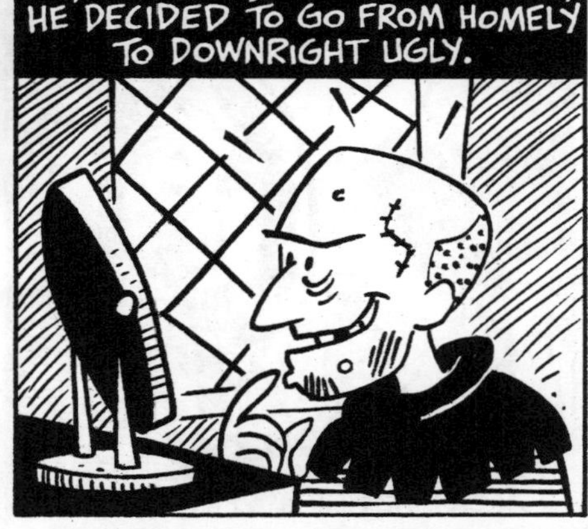
SO, TO INCREASE THE CHALLENGE, HE DECIDED TO GO FROM HOMELY TO DOWNRIGHT UGLY.

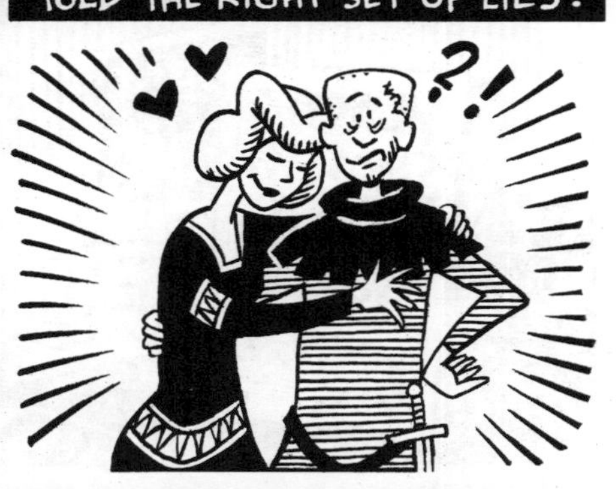
BUT EVEN THIS DIDN'T TURN OFF HIS TARGETS AS LONG AS HE TOLD THE RIGHT SET OF LIES.
?!

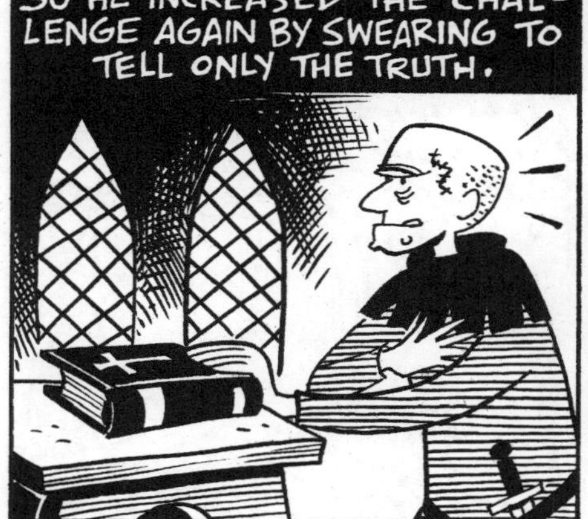
SO HE INCREASED THE CHALLENGE AGAIN BY SWEARING TO TELL ONLY THE TRUTH.

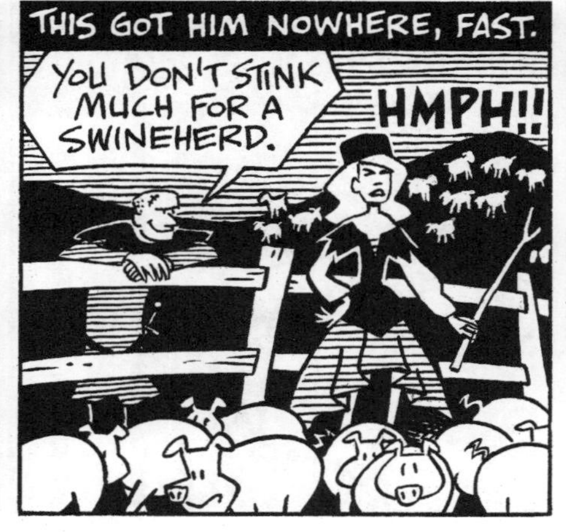
THIS GOT HIM NOWHERE, FAST.
YOU DON'T STINK MUCH FOR A SWINEHERD.
HMPH!!

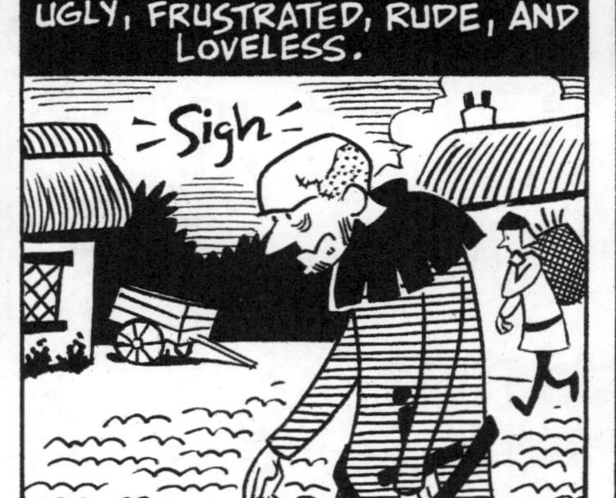
SO THERE HE WAS—ALONE, UGLY, FRUSTRATED, RUDE, AND LOVELESS.
Sigh

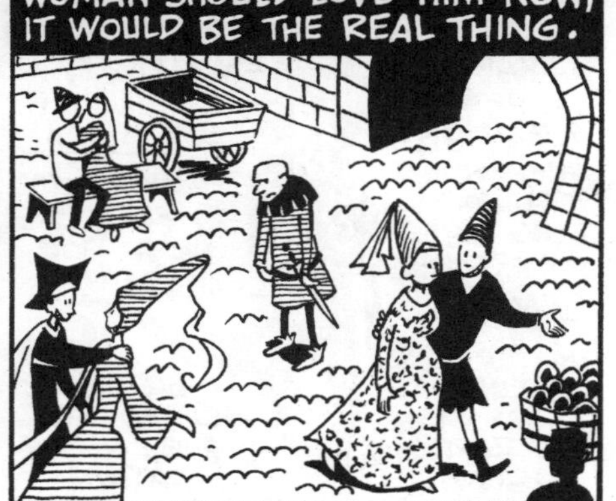
...BUT AT LEAST HE KNEW IF A WOMAN SHOULD LOVE HIM NOW, IT WOULD BE THE REAL THING.

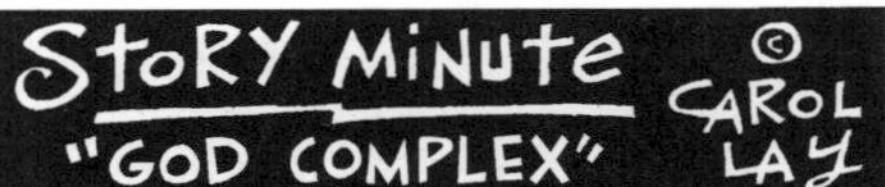


THERE HAD BEEN ENORMOUS ADVANCES MADE IN PLASTIC SURGERY.

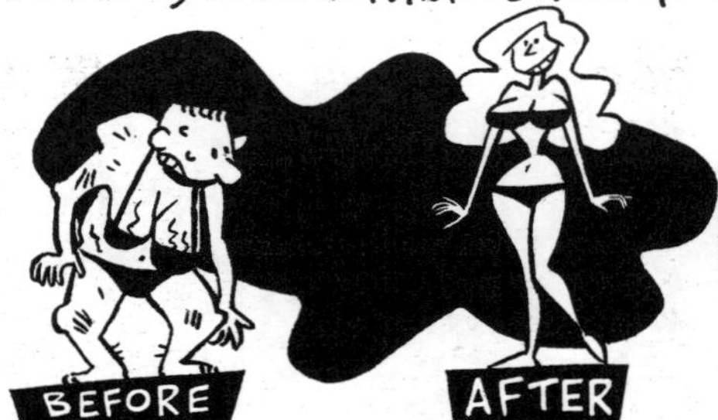


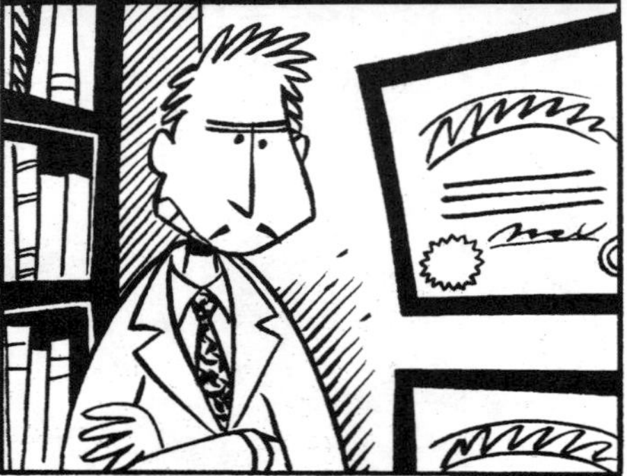


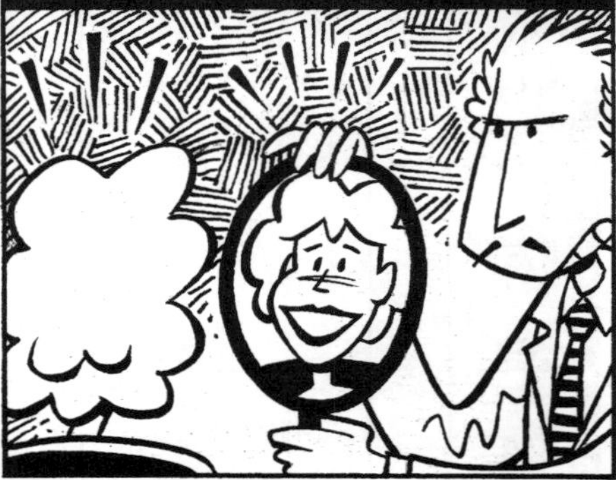


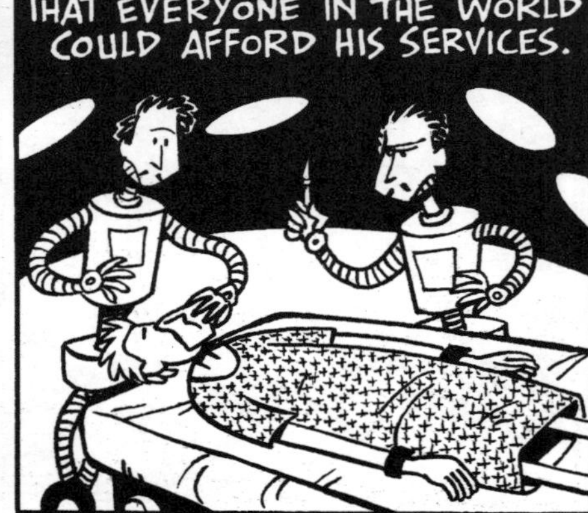


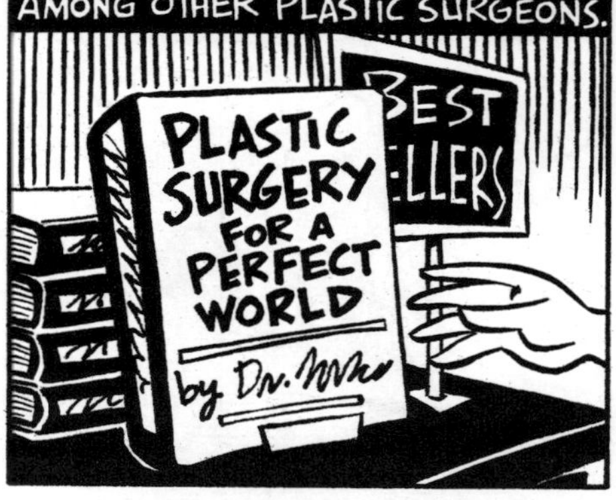


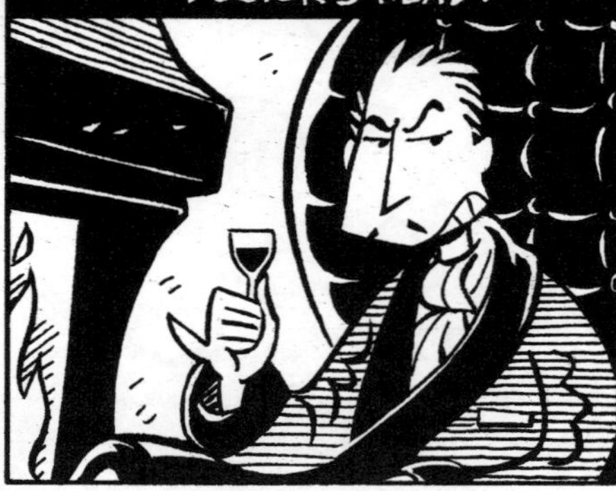


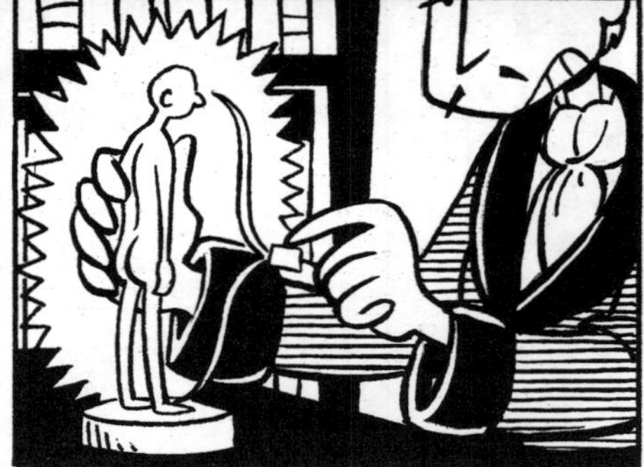


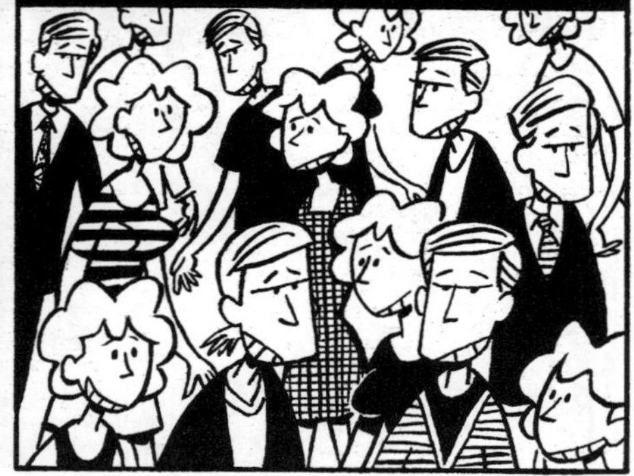


THE EARTH WOULD TAKE A GIANT STEP FORWARD BY MANKIND TAKING A MAJOR LEAP BACK.

LARGE EARS TO DETECT PREDATORS

PREHENSILE TAIL AND LONG ARMS FOR ARBOREAL TRANSPORT

SEX NEUTERING TO CURB AGGRESSION AND REPRODUCTION

SMALLER BRAIN FOR HAPPIER EXISTENCE

HAIRY BODY TO PRECLUDE NEED FOR CLOTHING

SHORT TORSO AND LEGS FOR FUEL CONSERVATION

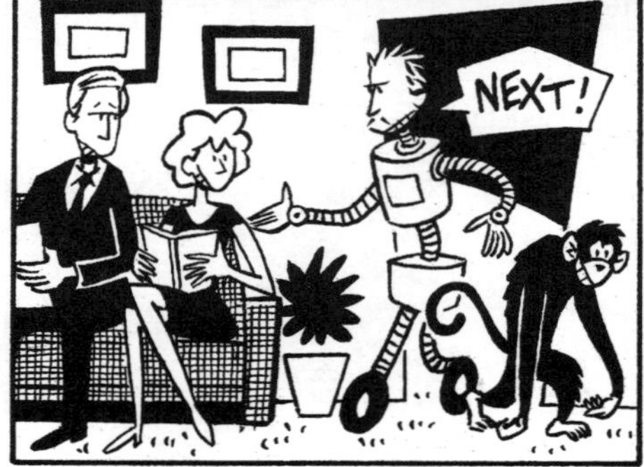


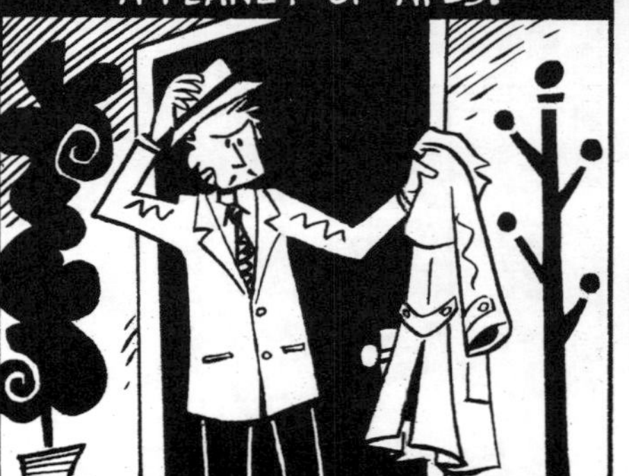


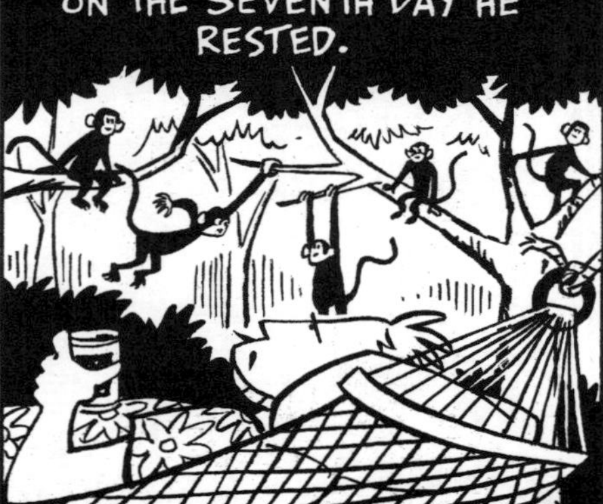

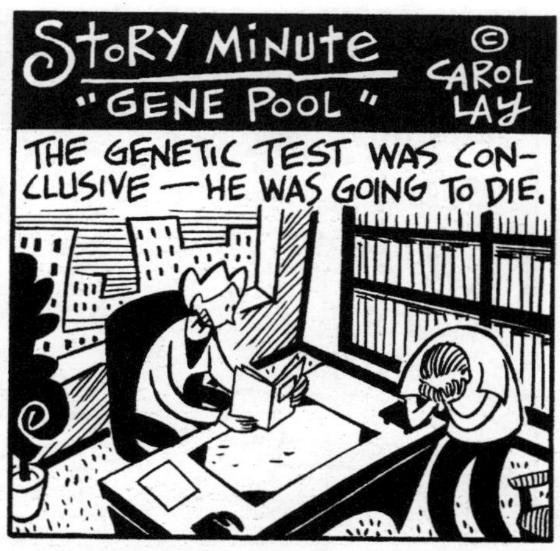
STORY MINUTE
"GENE POOL"
© CAROL LAY
THE GENETIC TEST WAS CONCLUSIVE — HE WAS GOING TO DIE.

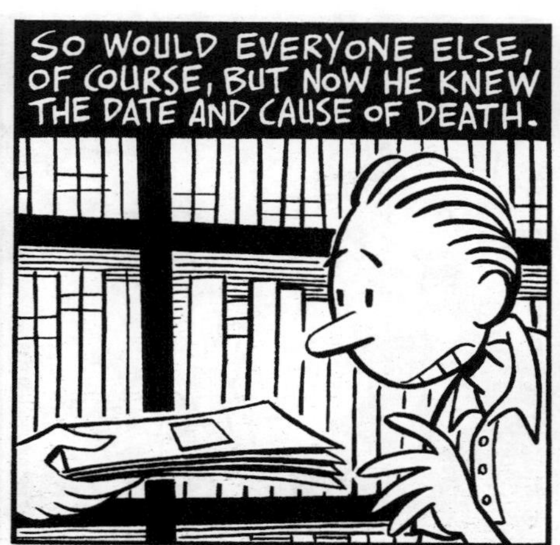
SO WOULD EVERYONE ELSE, OF COURSE, BUT NOW HE KNEW THE DATE AND CAUSE OF DEATH.

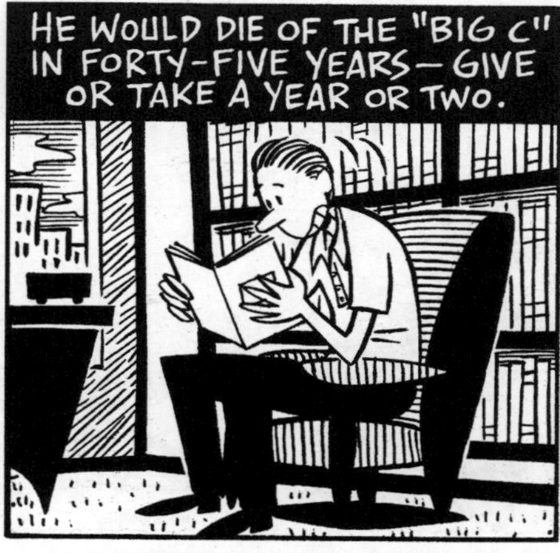
HE WOULD DIE OF THE "BIG C" IN FORTY-FIVE YEARS — GIVE OR TAKE A YEAR OR TWO.

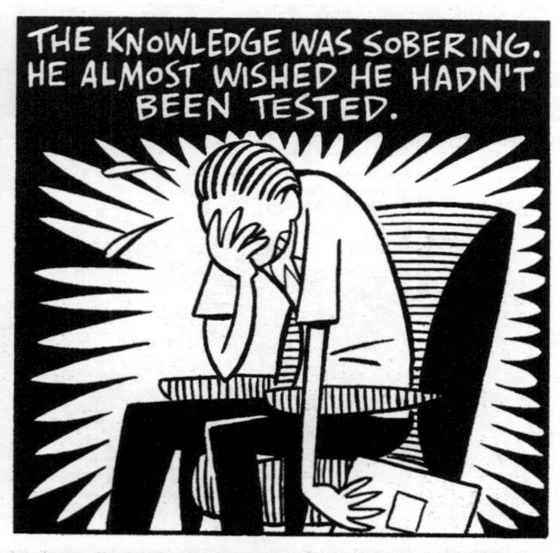
THE KNOWLEDGE WAS SOBERING. HE ALMOST WISHED HE HADN'T BEEN TESTED.

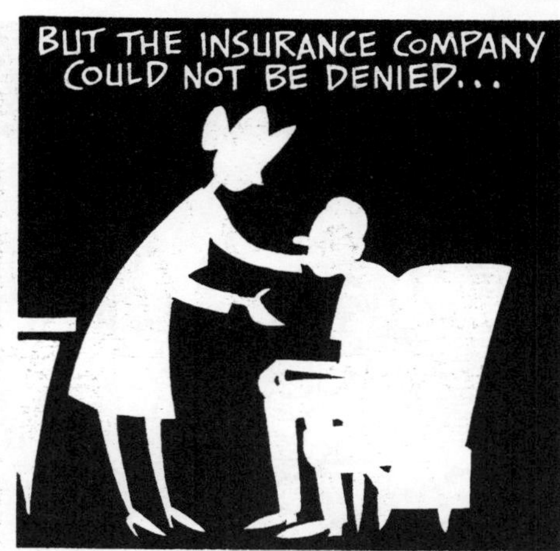
BUT THE INSURANCE COMPANY COULD NOT BE DENIED...

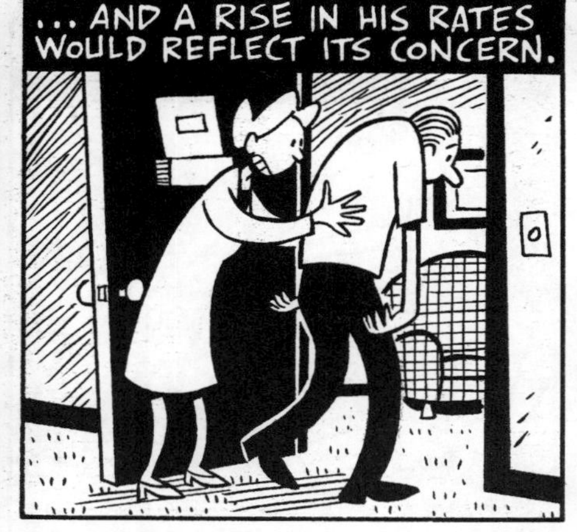
... AND A RISE IN HIS RATES WOULD REFLECT ITS CONCERN.

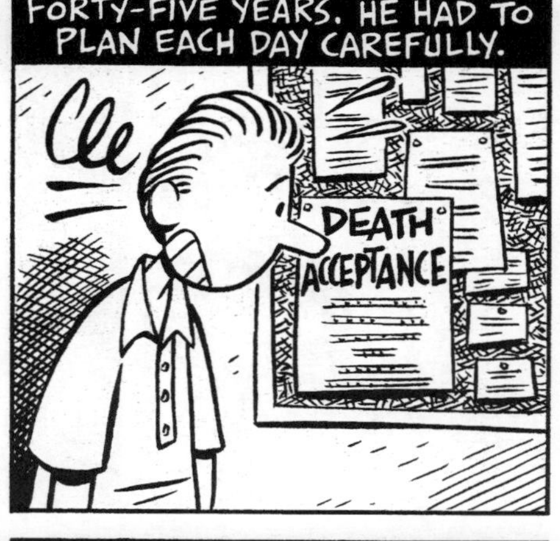
FORTY-FIVE YEARS. HE HAD TO PLAN EACH DAY CAREFULLY.
DEATH ACCEPTANCE

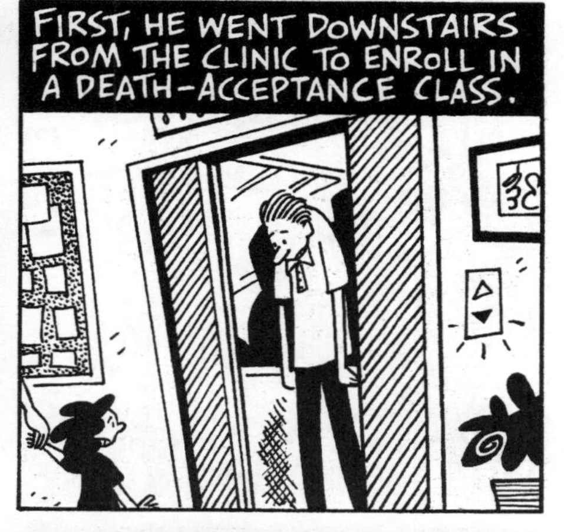
FIRST, HE WENT DOWNSTAIRS FROM THE CLINIC TO ENROLL IN A DEATH-ACCEPTANCE CLASS.

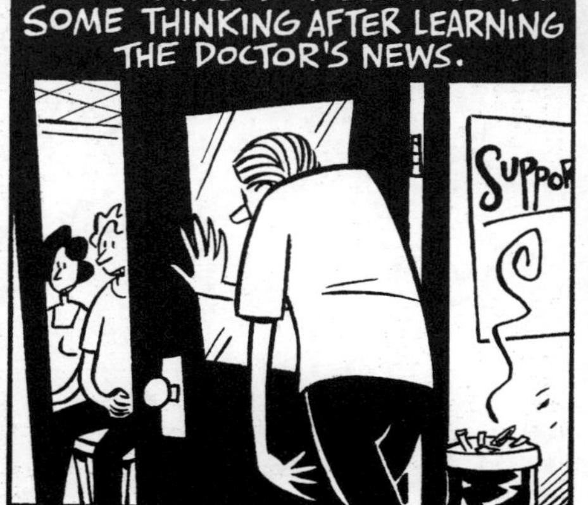
HE DEFINITELY NEEDED TO DO SOME THINKING AFTER LEARNING THE DOCTOR'S NEWS.

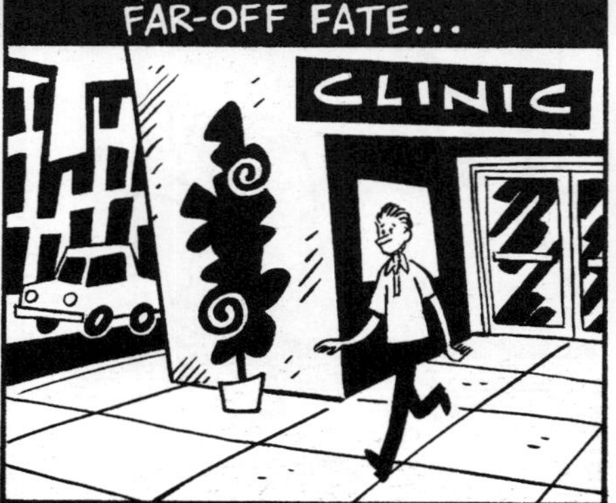
BUT AS HE WAS LEAVING THE CLASS, HAVING ACCEPTED HIS FAR-OFF FATE...
CLINIC

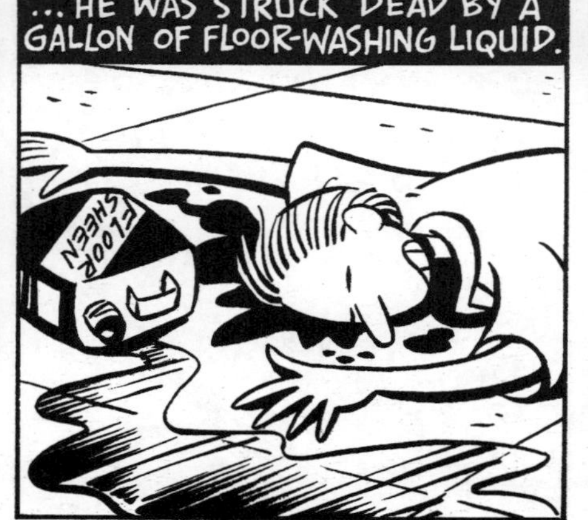
... HE WAS STRUCK DEAD BY A GALLON OF FLOOR-WASHING LIQUID.
FLOOR SHEEN

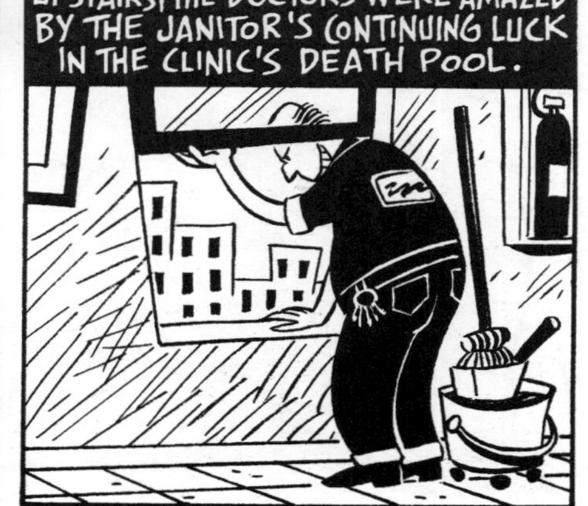
UPSTAIRS, THE DOCTORS WERE AMAZED BY THE JANITOR'S CONTINUING LUCK IN THE CLINIC'S DEATH POOL.

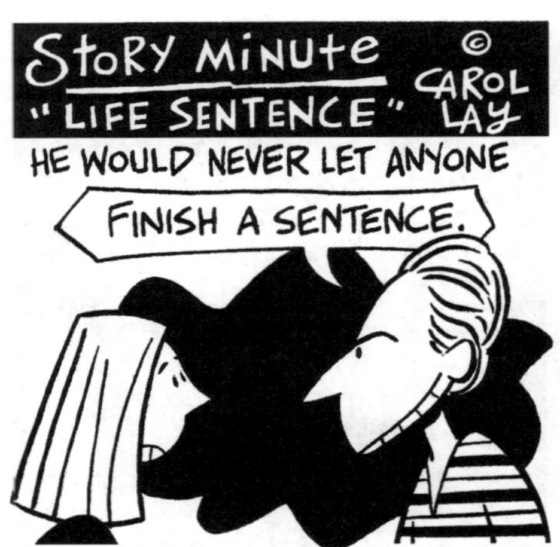

Story Minute © Carol Lay
"Life Sentence"
HE WOULD NEVER LET ANYONE
FINISH A SENTENCE.


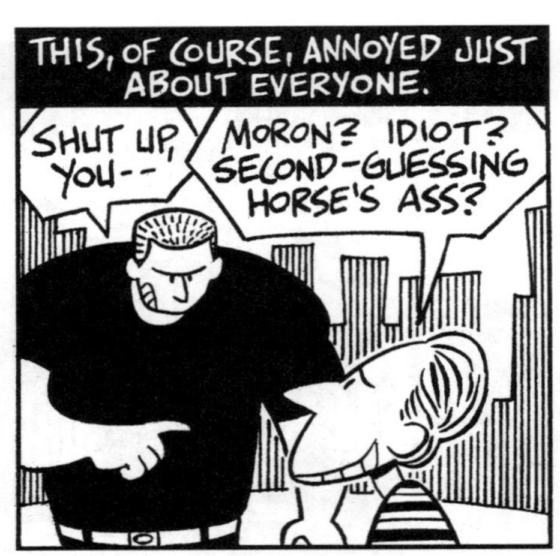

THIS, OF COURSE, ANNOYED JUST ABOUT EVERYONE.
SHUT UP, YOU--
MORON? IDIOT? SECOND-GUESSING HORSE'S ASS?


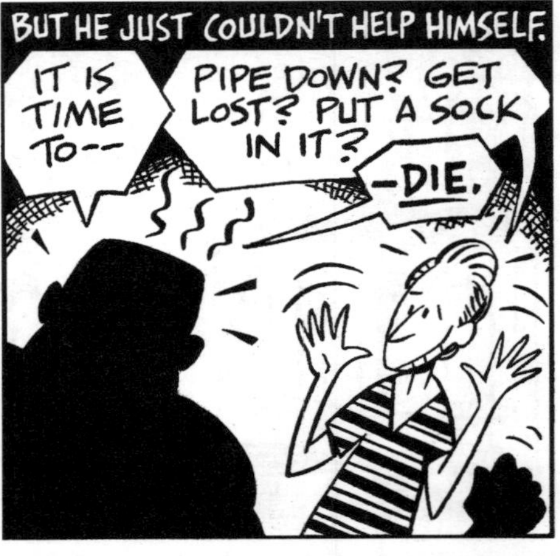

BUT HE JUST COULDN'T HELP HIMSELF.
IT IS TIME TO--
PIPE DOWN? GET LOST? PUT A SOCK IN IT?
—DIE.


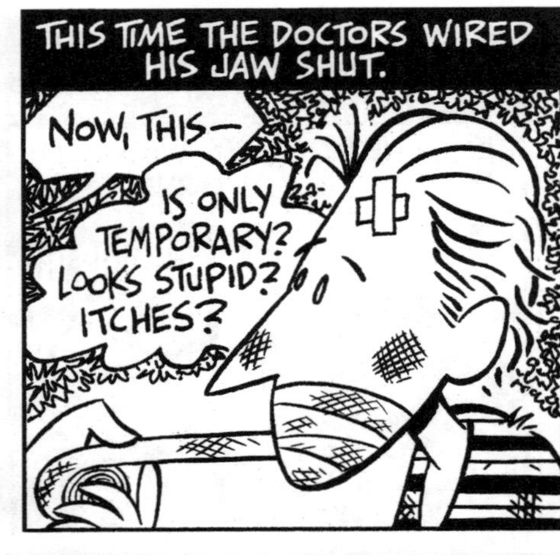

THIS TIME THE DOCTORS WIRED HIS JAW SHUT.
NOW, THIS—
IS ONLY TEMPORARY? LOOKS STUPID? ITCHES?


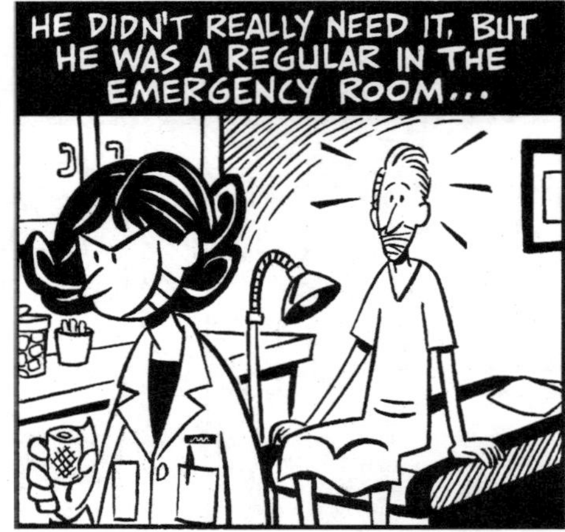

HE DIDN'T REALLY NEED IT, BUT HE WAS A REGULAR IN THE EMERGENCY ROOM...


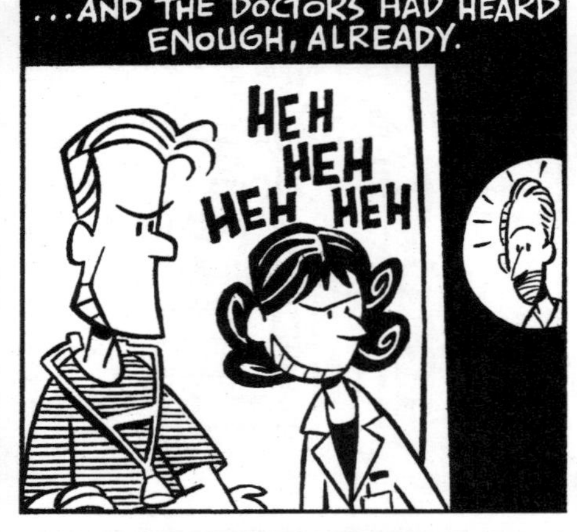

...AND THE DOCTORS HAD HEARD ENOUGH, ALREADY.
HEH HEH HEH HEH


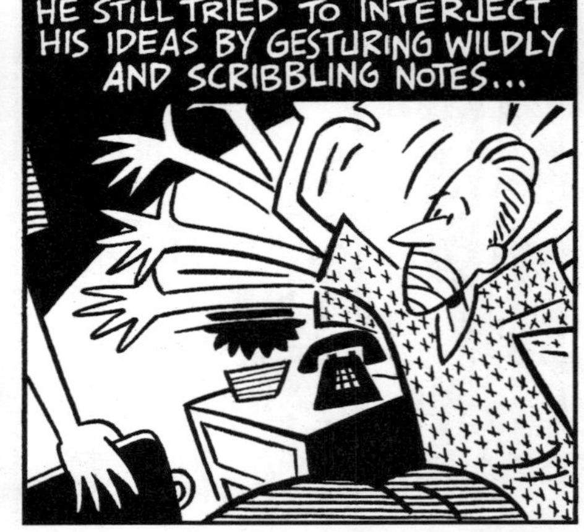

HE STILL TRIED TO INTERJECT HIS IDEAS BY GESTURING WILDLY AND SCRIBBLING NOTES...


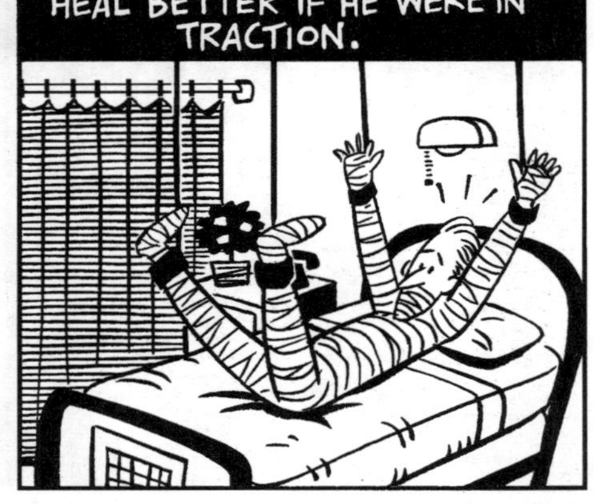

...SO THE DOCTORS DECIDED HE'D HEAL BETTER IF HE WERE IN TRACTION.


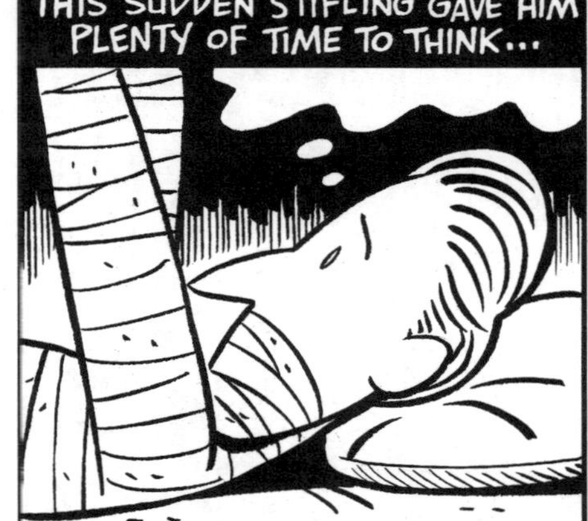

THIS SUDDEN STIFLING GAVE HIM PLENTY OF TIME TO THINK...


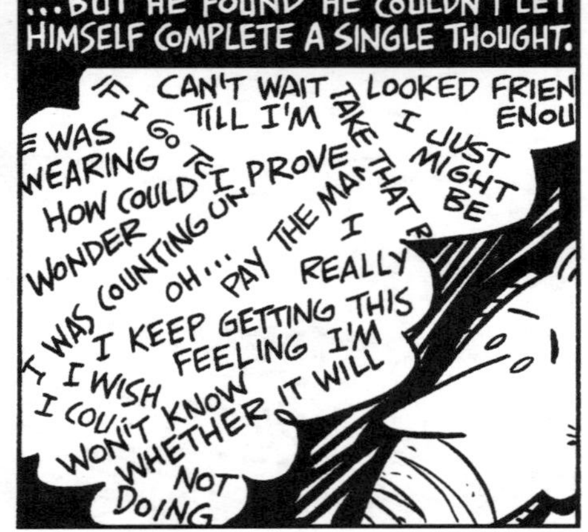

...BUT HE FOUND HE COULDN'T LET HIMSELF COMPLETE A SINGLE THOUGHT.
IF I GO TO
CAN'T WAIT TILL I'M
LOOKED FRIEN ENOU
TAKE THAT R
I JUST MIGHT BE
WAS WEARING
HOW COULD I PROVE
WONDER
I WAS COUNTING ON
OH...
PAY THE MA
I REALLY
I KEEP GETTING THIS FEELING I'M
I WISH
I COU
WON'T KNOW WHETHER IT WILL
NOT DOING


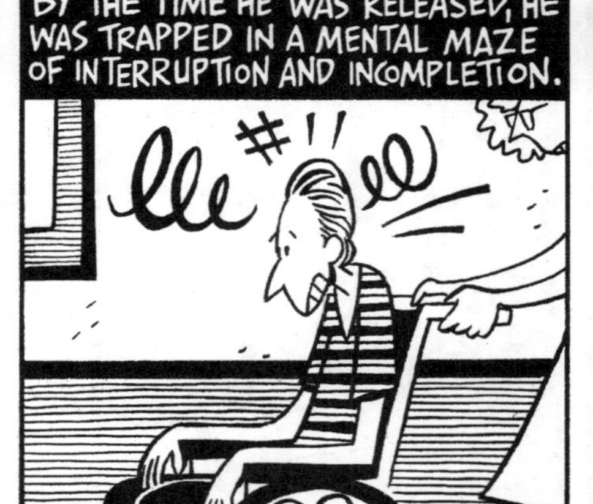

BY THE TIME HE WAS RELEASED, HE WAS TRAPPED IN A MENTAL MAZE OF INTERRUPTION AND INCOMPLETION.


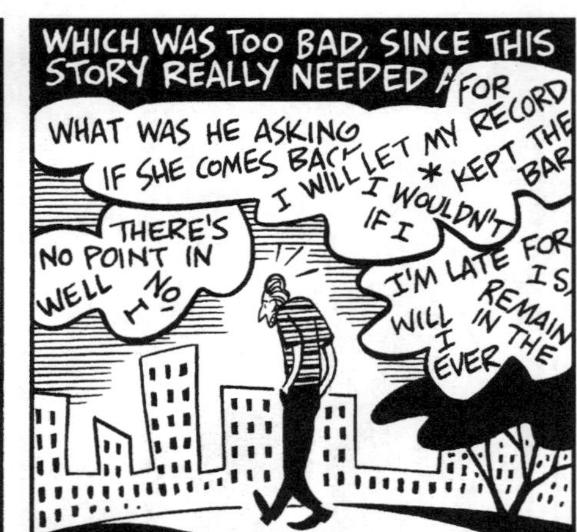

WHICH WAS TOO BAD, SINCE THIS STORY REALLY NEEDED A
WHAT WAS HE ASKING
IF SHE COMES BACK
I WILL
FOR
LET MY RECORD
* KEPT THE BAR
I WOULDN'T
IF I
THERE'S NO POINT IN
WELL
NO
I
I'M LATE FOR
IS
REMAIN IN THE
WILL
I
EVER

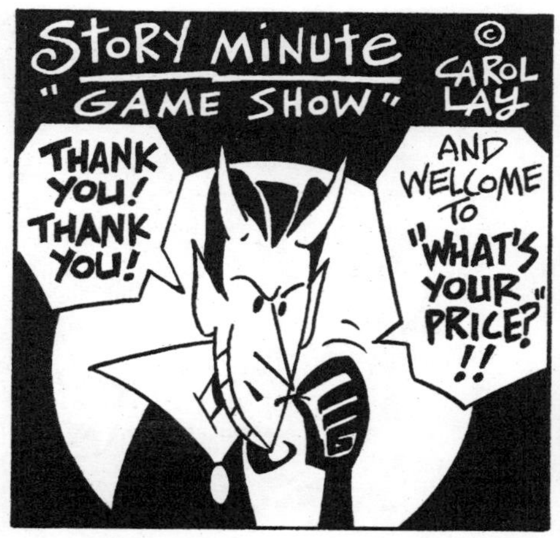
STORY MINUTE
"GAME SHOW"
© CAROL LAY
THANK YOU! THANK YOU!
AND WELCOME TO "WHAT'S YOUR PRICE?" !!
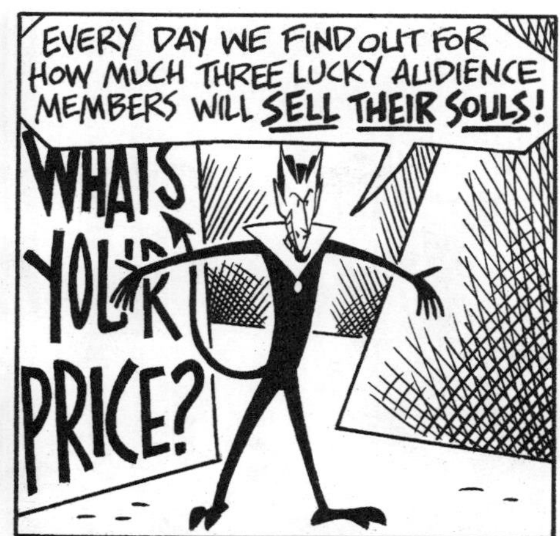
EVERY DAY WE FIND OUT FOR HOW MUCH THREE LUCKY AUDIENCE MEMBERS WILL SELL THEIR SOULS!
WHAT'S YOUR PRICE?
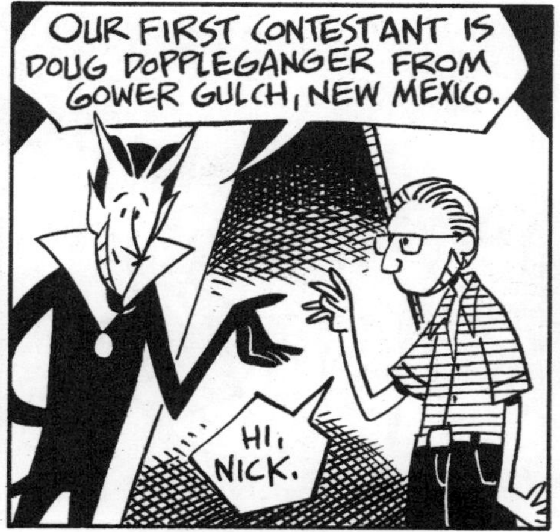
OUR FIRST CONTESTANT IS DOUG DOPPLEGANGER FROM GOWER GULCH, NEW MEXICO.
HI, NICK.
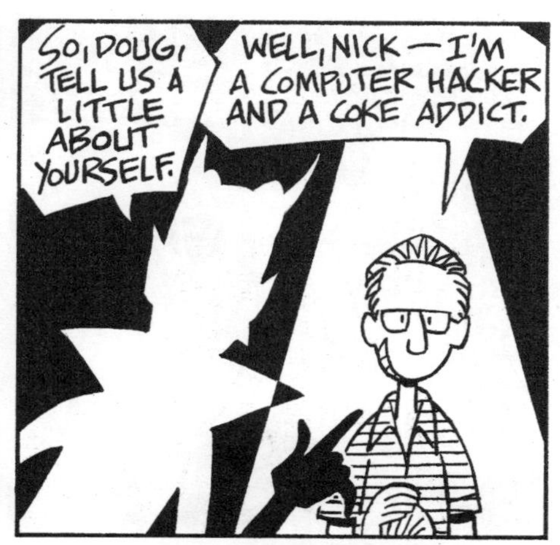
SO, DOUG, TELL US A LITTLE ABOUT YOURSELF.
WELL, NICK — I'M A COMPUTER HACKER AND A COKE ADDICT.
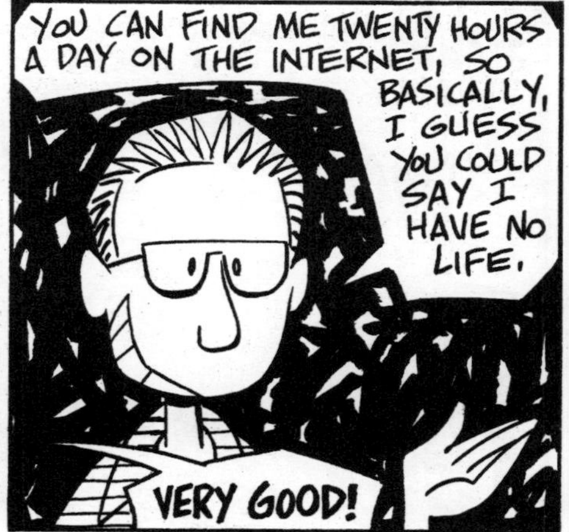
YOU CAN FIND ME TWENTY HOURS A DAY ON THE INTERNET, SO BASICALLY, I GUESS YOU COULD SAY I HAVE NO LIFE.
VERY GOOD!
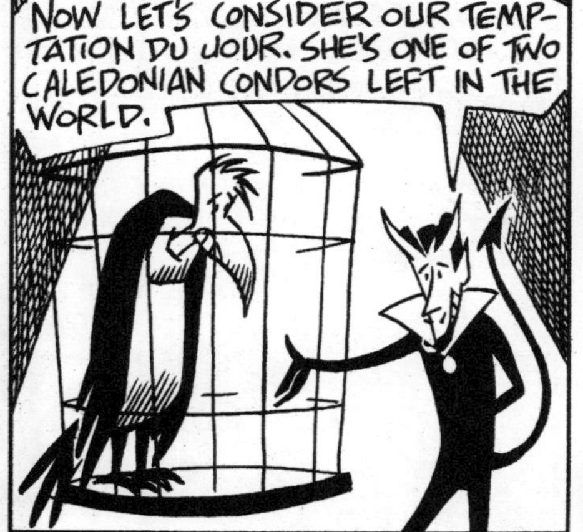
NOW LET'S CONSIDER OUR TEMPTATION DU JOUR. SHE'S ONE OF TWO CALEDONIAN CONDORS LEFT IN THE WORLD.
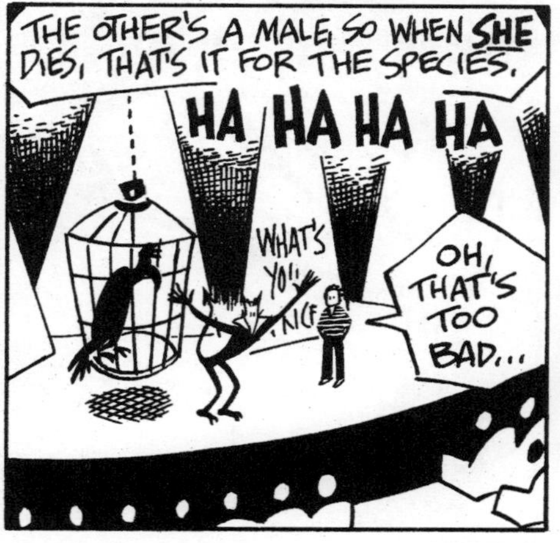
THE OTHER'S A MALE, SO WHEN SHE DIES, THAT'S IT FOR THE SPECIES.
HA HA HA HA
OH, THAT'S TOO BAD...
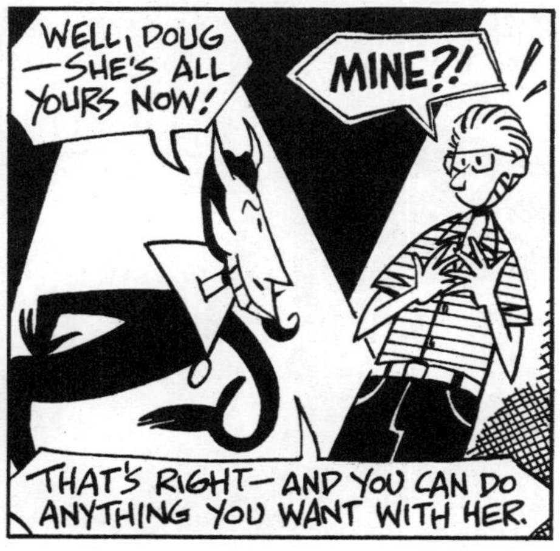
WELL, DOUG — SHE'S ALL YOURS NOW!
MINE?!
THAT'S RIGHT — AND YOU CAN DO ANYTHING YOU WANT WITH HER.
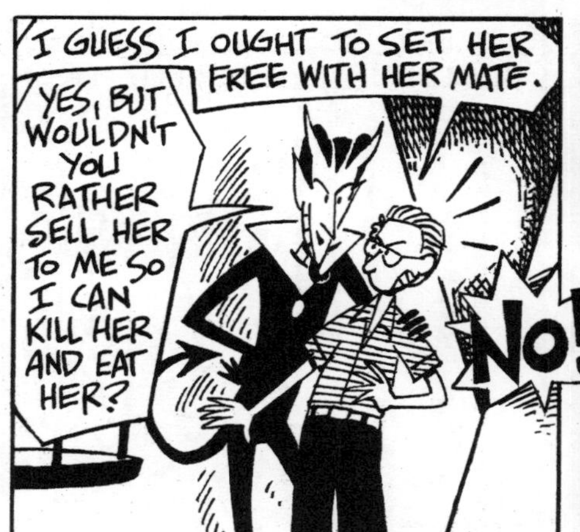
I GUESS I OUGHT TO SET HER FREE WITH HER MATE.
YES, BUT WOULDN'T YOU RATHER SELL HER TO ME SO I CAN KILL HER AND EAT HER?
NO!
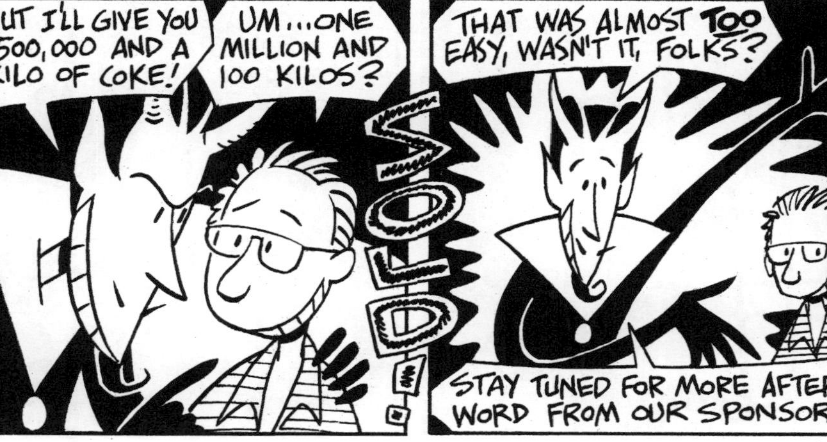
BUT I'LL GIVE YOU $500,000 AND A KILO OF COKE!
UM... ONE MILLION AND 100 KILOS?
SOLD!
THAT WAS ALMOST TOO EASY, WASN'T IT, FOLKS?
STAY TUNED FOR MORE AFTER A WORD FROM OUR SPONSOR.
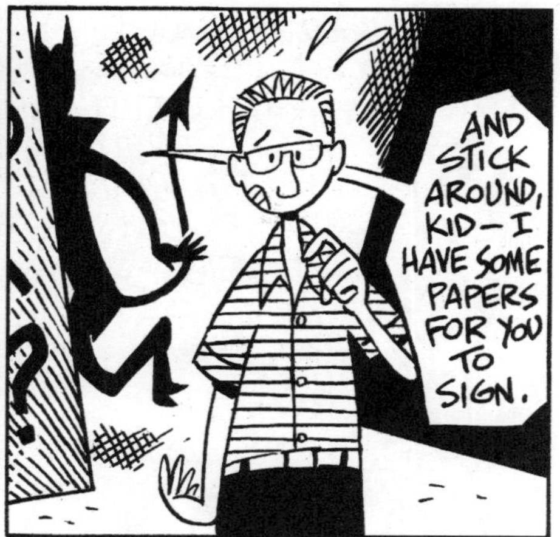
AND STICK AROUND, KID — I HAVE SOME PAPERS FOR YOU TO SIGN.

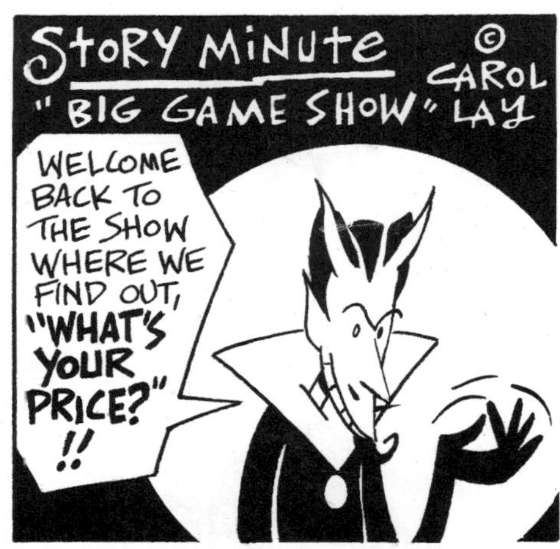
STORY MINUTE
"BIG GAME SHOW"
© CAROL LAY
WELCOME BACK TO THE SHOW WHERE WE FIND OUT, "WHAT'S YOUR PRICE?" !!

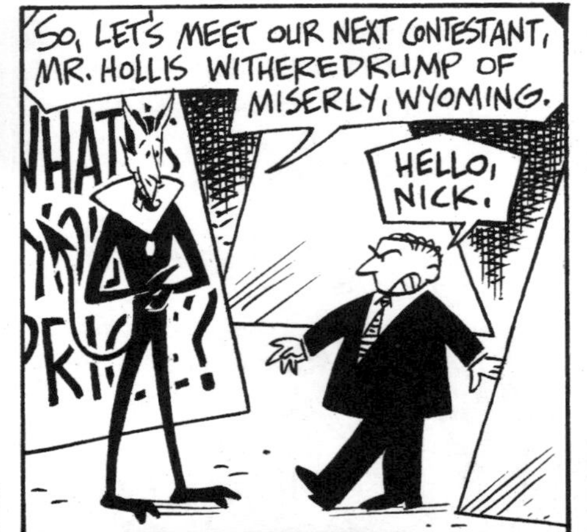
SO, LET'S MEET OUR NEXT CONTESTANT, MR. HOLLIS WITHEREDRUMP OF MISERLY, WYOMING.
HELLO, NICK.

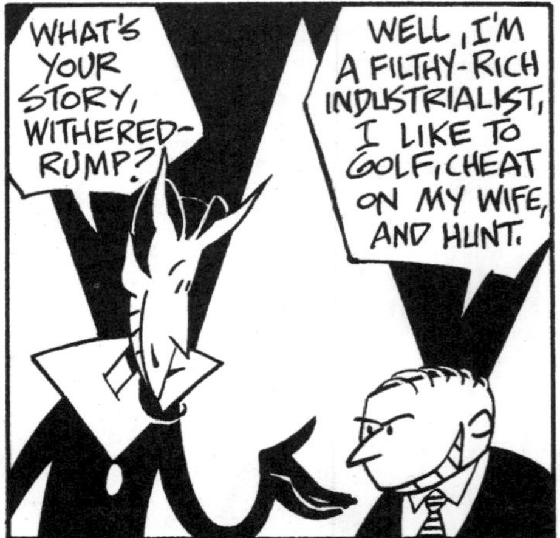
WHAT'S YOUR STORY, WITHERED-RUMP?
WELL, I'M A FILTHY-RICH INDUSTRIALIST, I LIKE TO GOLF, CHEAT ON MY WIFE, AND HUNT.

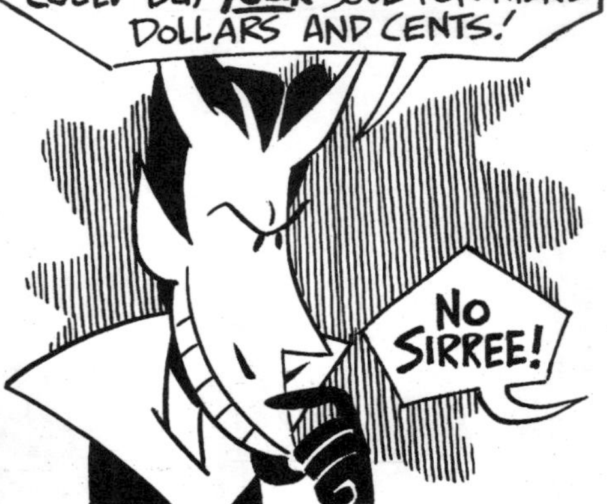
VERY INTERESTING! I SEE NO ONE COULD BUY YOUR SOUL FOR MERE DOLLARS AND CENTS!
NO SIRREE!

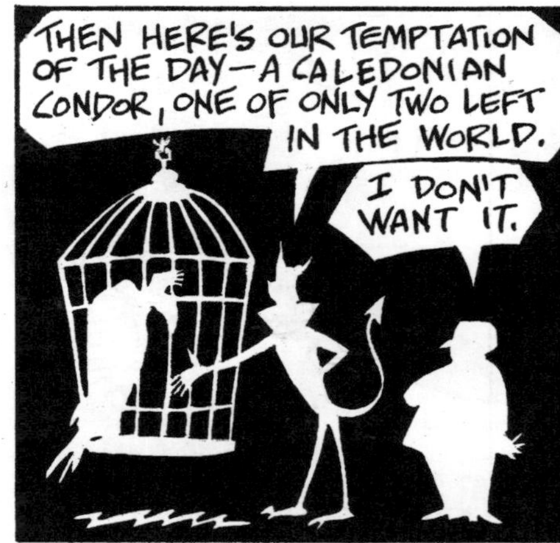
THEN HERE'S OUR TEMPTATION OF THE DAY—A CALEDONIAN CONDOR, ONE OF ONLY TWO LEFT IN THE WORLD.
I DON'T WANT IT.

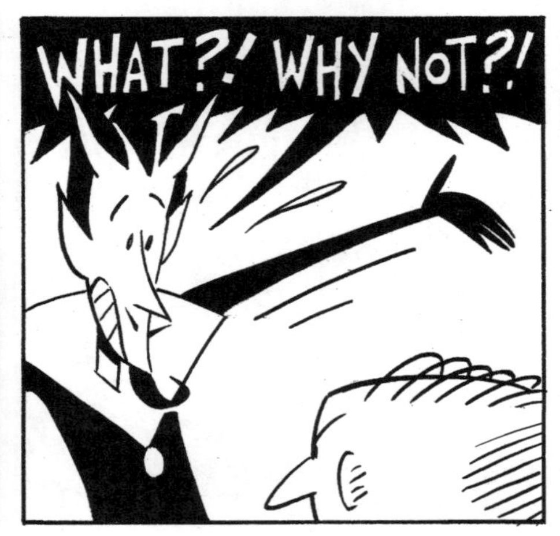
WHAT?! WHY NOT?!

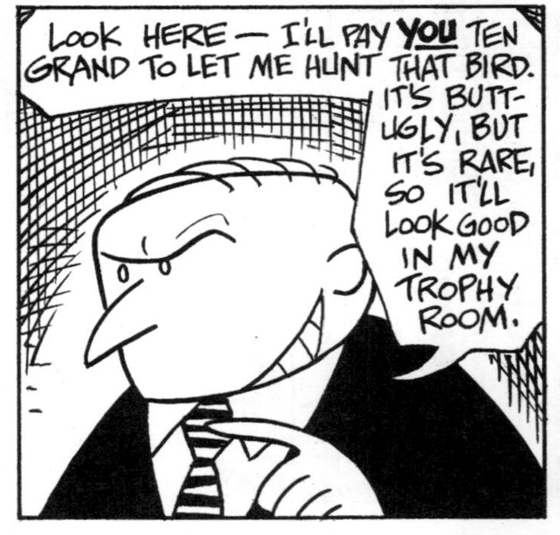
LOOK HERE— I'LL PAY YOU TEN GRAND TO LET ME HUNT THAT BIRD. IT'S BUTT-UGLY, BUT IT'S RARE, SO IT'LL LOOK GOOD IN MY TROPHY ROOM.

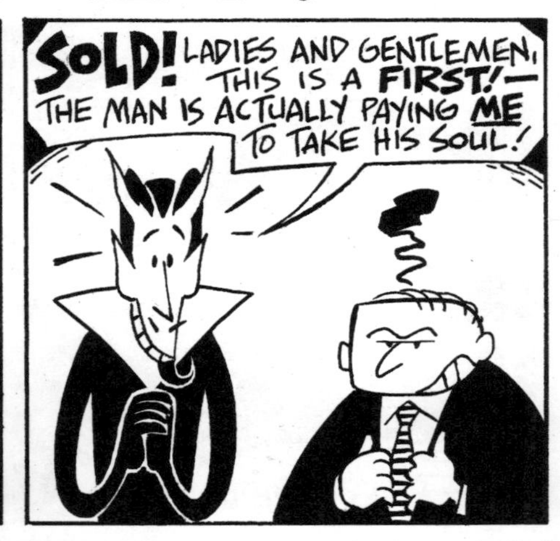
SOLD! LADIES AND GENTLEMEN, THIS IS A FIRST!— THE MAN IS ACTUALLY PAYING ME TO TAKE HIS SOUL!

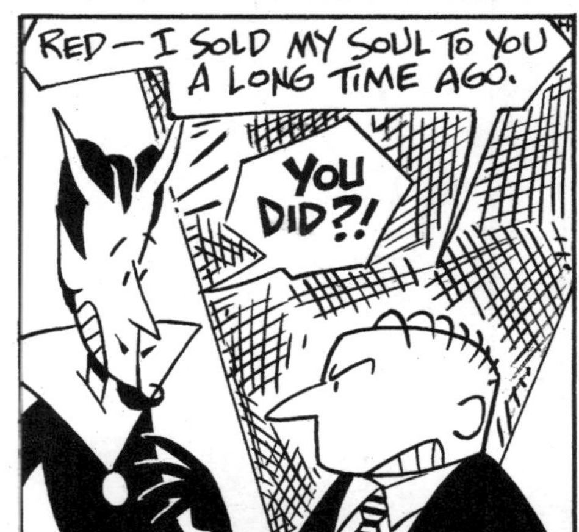
RED— I SOLD MY SOUL TO YOU A LONG TIME AGO.
YOU DID?!

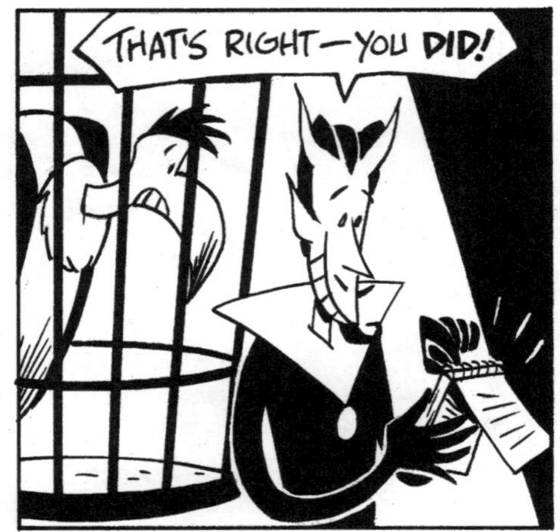
THAT'S RIGHT—YOU DID!

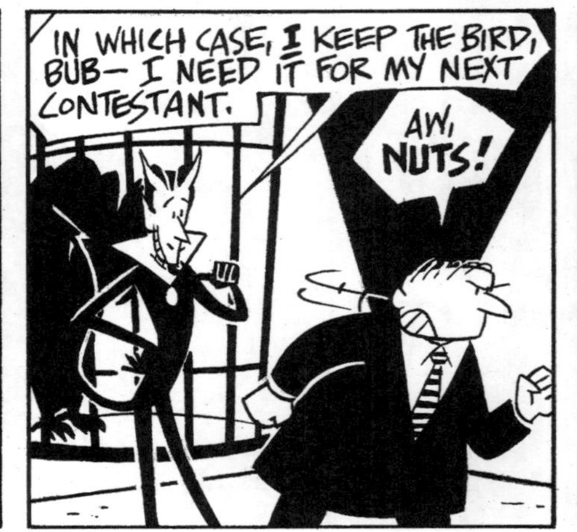
IN WHICH CASE, I KEEP THE BIRD, BUB— I NEED IT FOR MY NEXT CONTESTANT.
AW, NUTS!

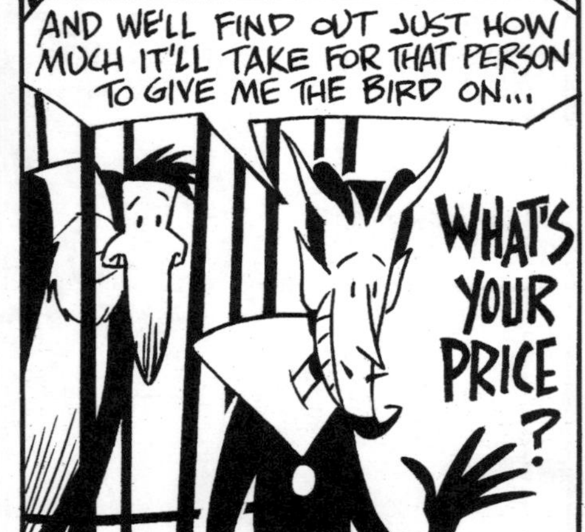
AND WE'LL FIND OUT JUST HOW MUCH IT'LL TAKE FOR THAT PERSON TO GIVE ME THE BIRD ON...
WHAT'S YOUR PRICE?

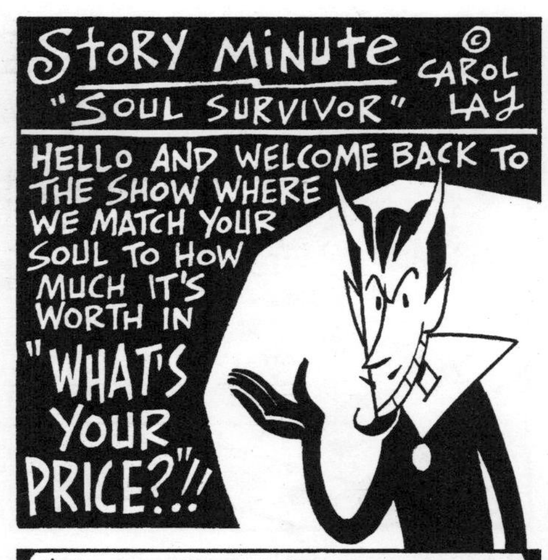
STORY MINUTE
© CAROL LAY
"SOUL SURVIVOR"
HELLO AND WELCOME BACK TO THE SHOW WHERE WE MATCH YOUR SOUL TO HOW MUCH IT'S WORTH IN "WHAT'S YOUR PRICE?"!!
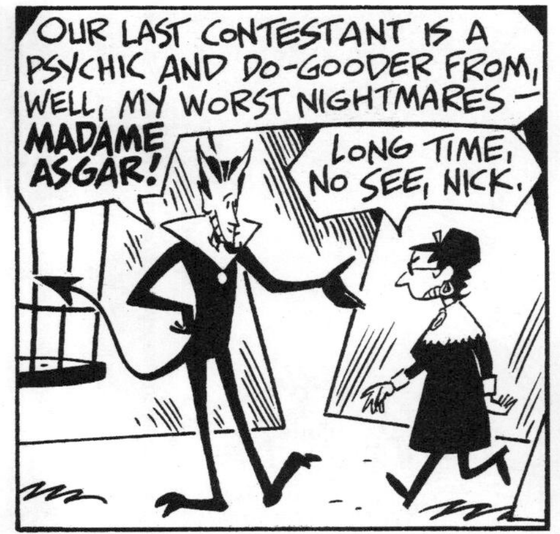
OUR LAST CONTESTANT IS A PSYCHIC AND DO-GOODER FROM, WELL, MY WORST NIGHTMARES — MADAME ASGAR!
LONG TIME, NO SEE, NICK.
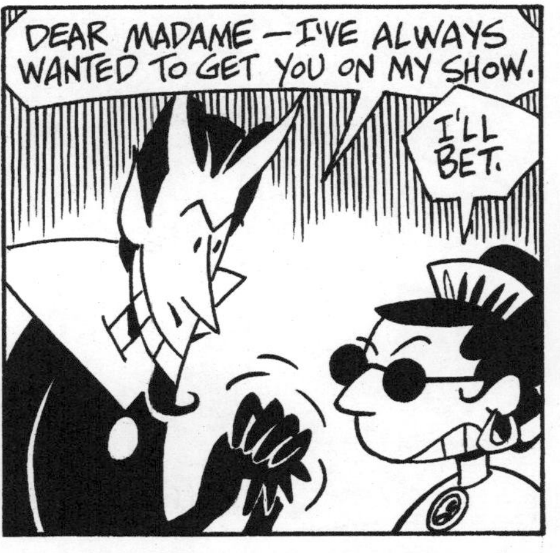
DEAR MADAME — I'VE ALWAYS WANTED TO GET YOU ON MY SHOW.
I'LL BET.
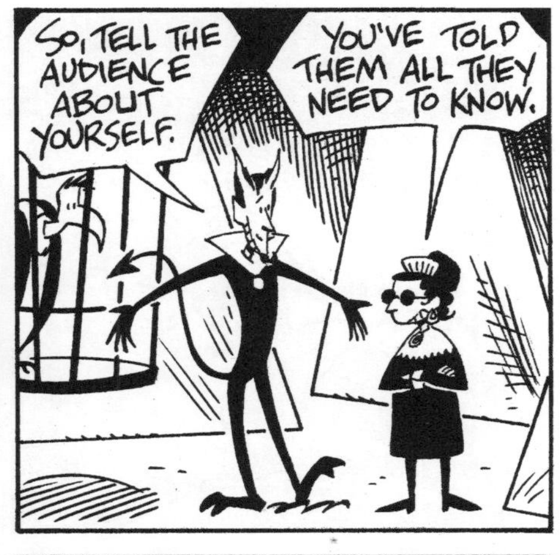
SO, TELL THE AUDIENCE ABOUT YOURSELF.
YOU'VE TOLD THEM ALL THEY NEED TO KNOW.
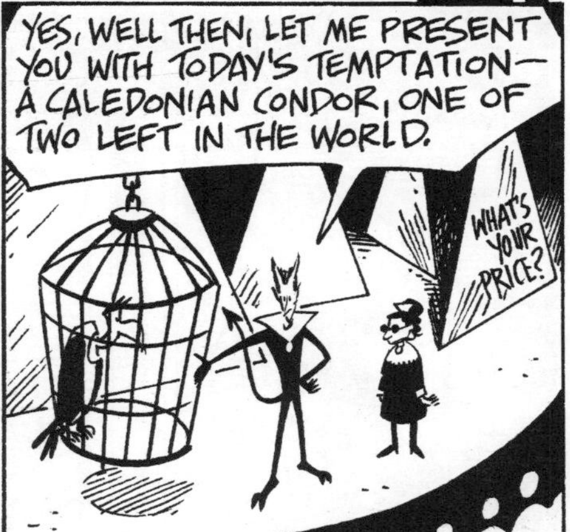
YES, WELL THEN, LET ME PRESENT YOU WITH TODAY'S TEMPTATION — A CALEDONIAN CONDOR, ONE OF TWO LEFT IN THE WORLD.
WHAT'S YOUR PRICE?
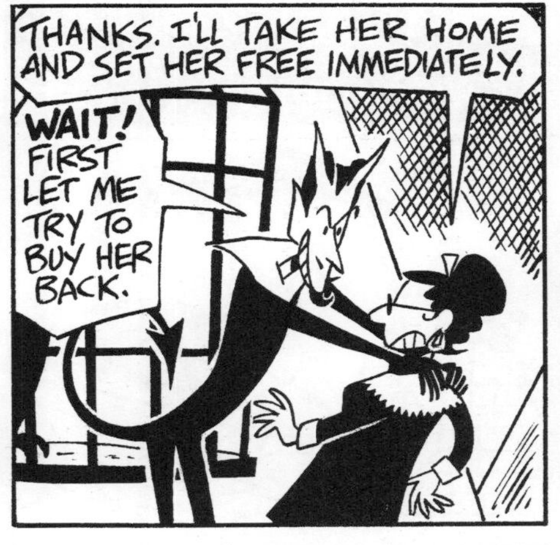
THANKS. I'LL TAKE HER HOME AND SET HER FREE IMMEDIATELY.
WAIT! FIRST LET ME TRY TO BUY HER BACK.
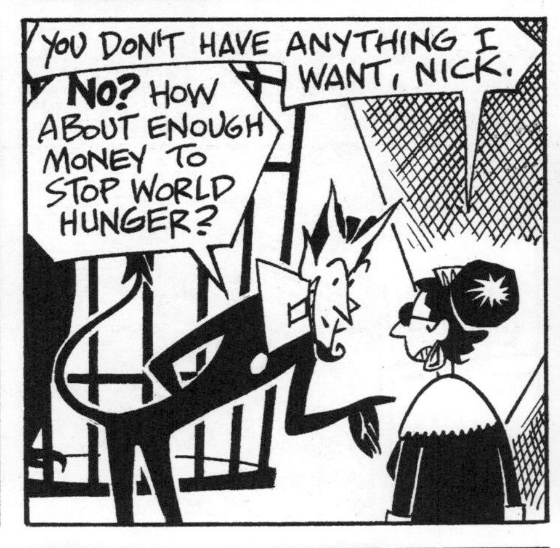
YOU DON'T HAVE ANYTHING I WANT, NICK.
NO? HOW ABOUT ENOUGH MONEY TO STOP WORLD HUNGER?
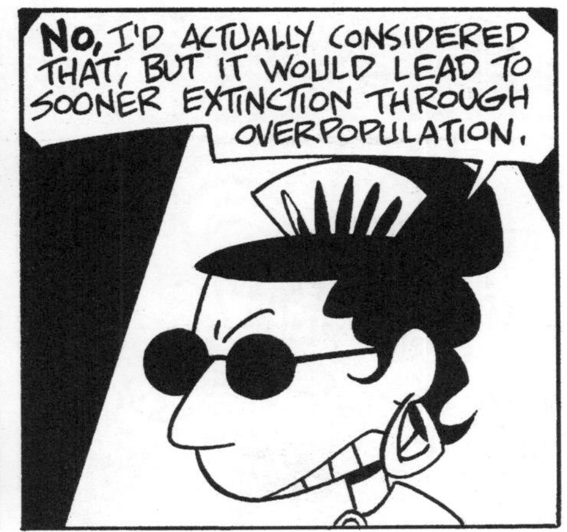
NO, I'D ACTUALLY CONSIDERED THAT, BUT IT WOULD LEAD TO SOONER EXTINCTION THROUGH OVERPOPULATION.
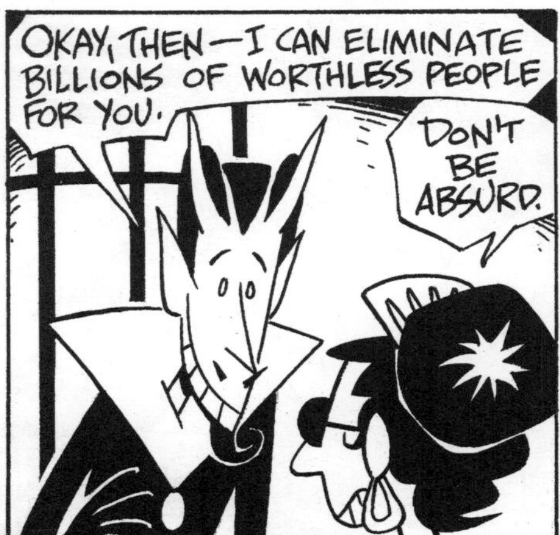
OKAY, THEN — I CAN ELIMINATE BILLIONS OF WORTHLESS PEOPLE FOR YOU.
DON'T BE ABSURD.
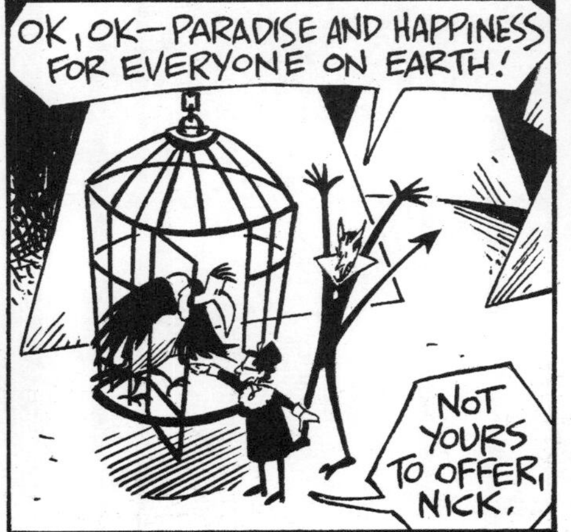
OK, OK — PARADISE AND HAPPINESS FOR EVERYONE ON EARTH!
NOT YOURS TO OFFER, NICK.
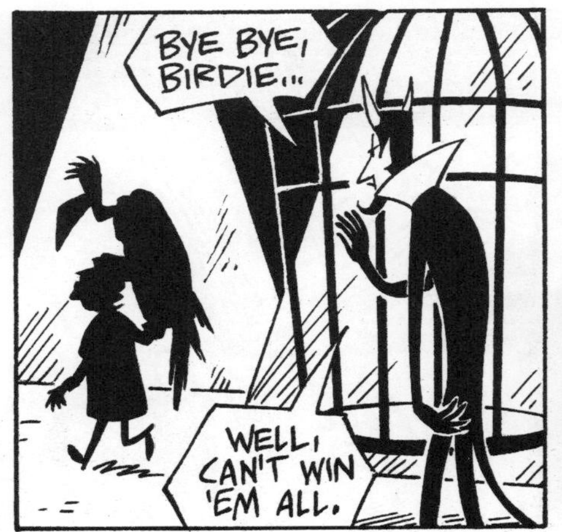
BYE BYE, BIRDIE...
WELL, CAN'T WIN 'EM ALL.
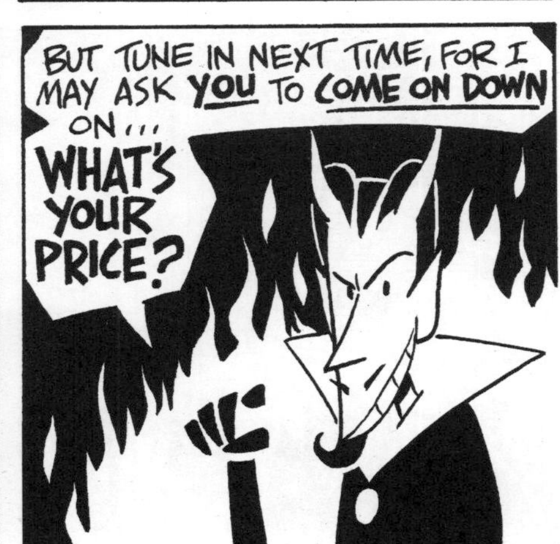
BUT TUNE IN NEXT TIME, FOR I MAY ASK YOU TO COME ON DOWN ON... WHAT'S YOUR PRICE?

THOSE WHO SENT IT TO TWENTY FRIENDS WERE PROMISED FANTASTIC LUCK...

$62,000,000 WINNER!

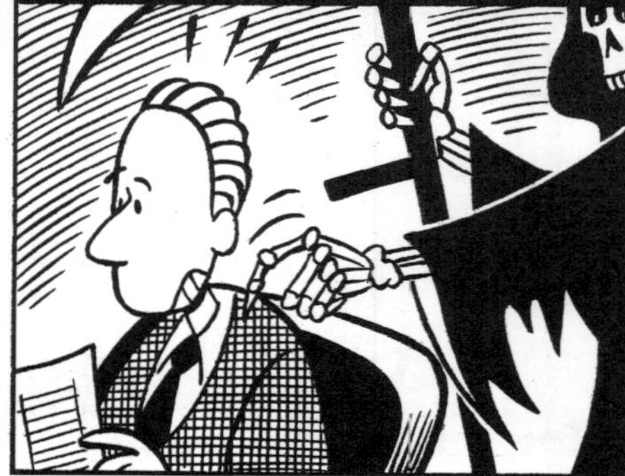


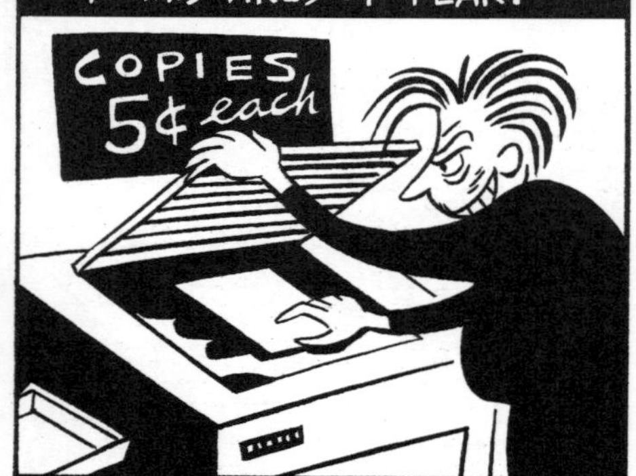


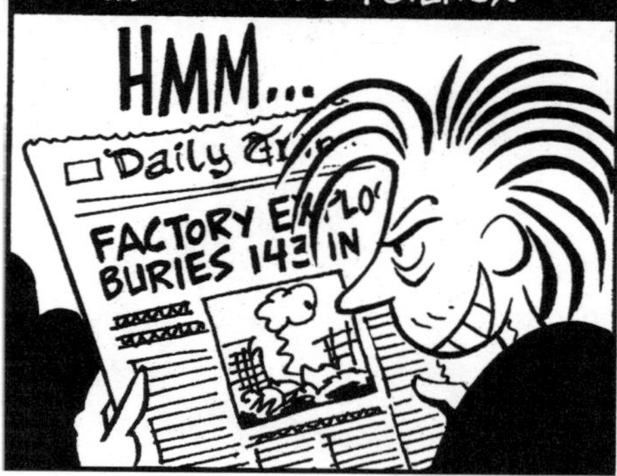


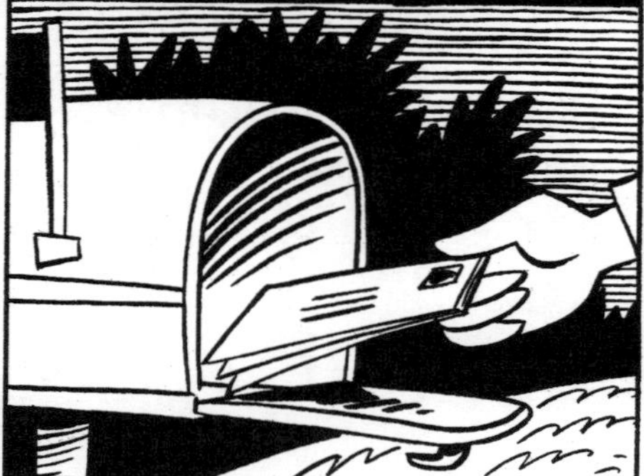


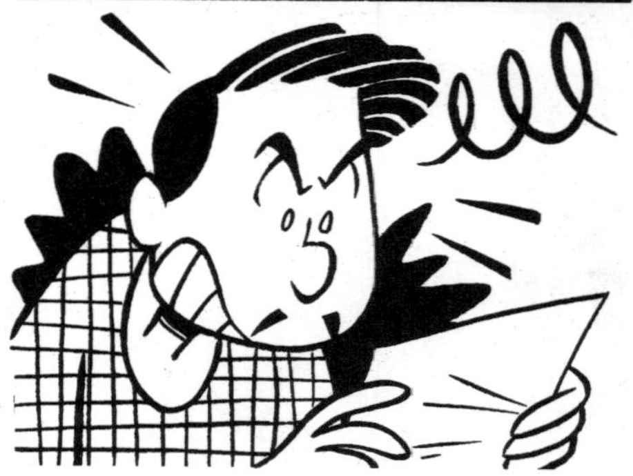


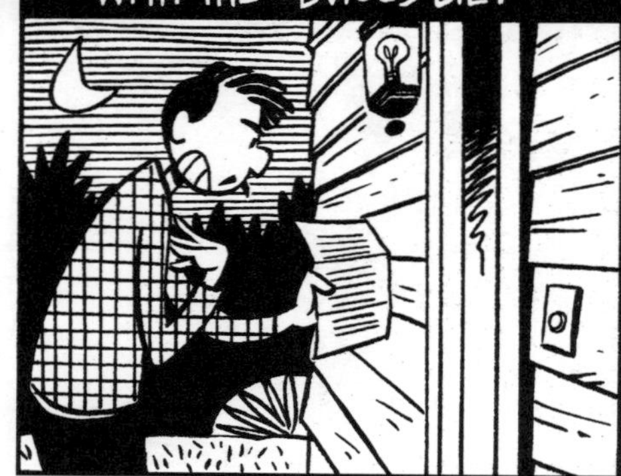


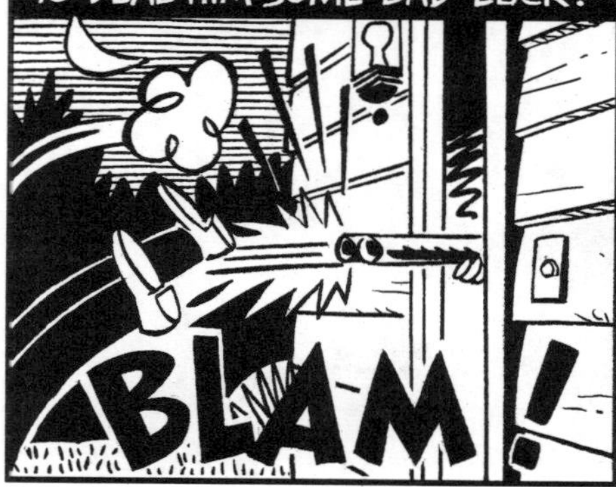


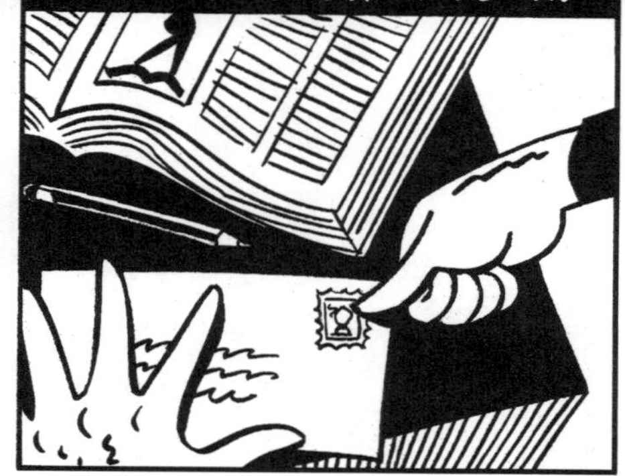


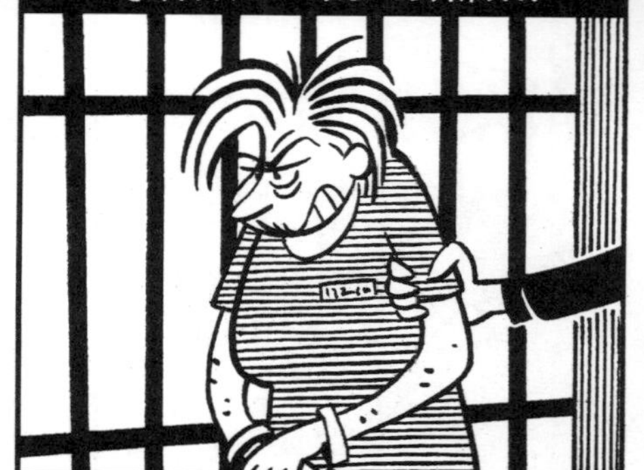


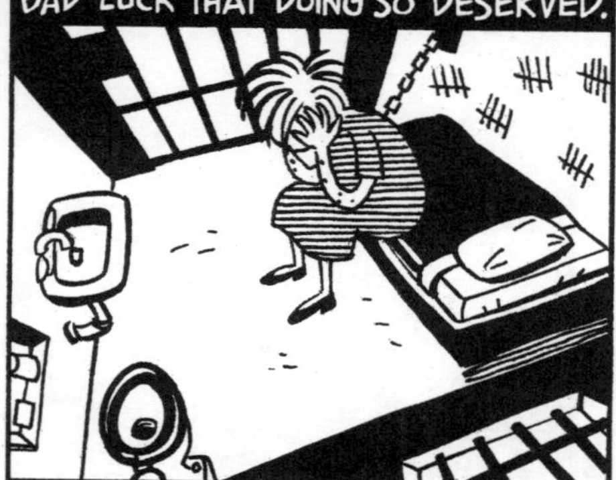

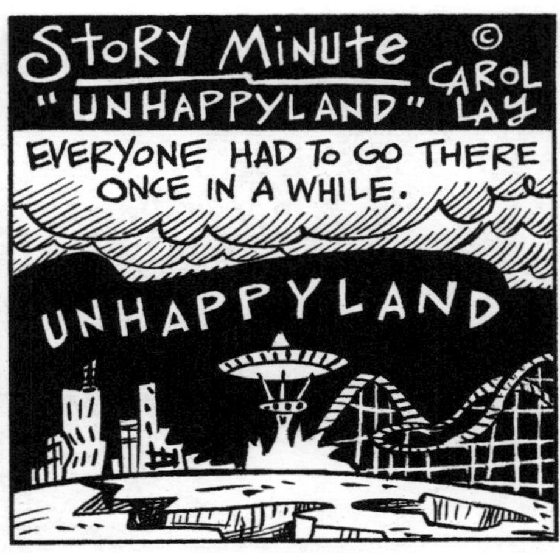
STORY MINUTE © CAROL LAY
"UNHAPPYLAND"
EVERYONE HAD TO GO THERE ONCE IN A WHILE.
UNHAPPYLAND

IT WAS PART OF THE DEAL ONE MADE IN ORDER TO PLAY THE GAME.
UNHAPPYLAND
WHEEL OF MISFORTUNE
DEEP PIT
CASTLE MOROSO

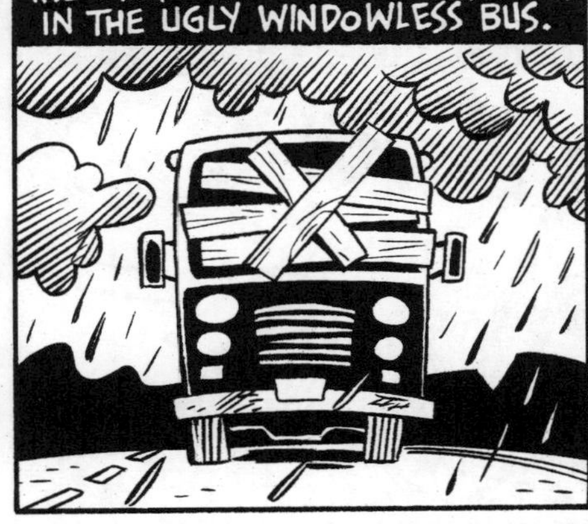
THE ONLY WAY TO GET THERE WAS IN THE UGLY WINDOWLESS BUS.

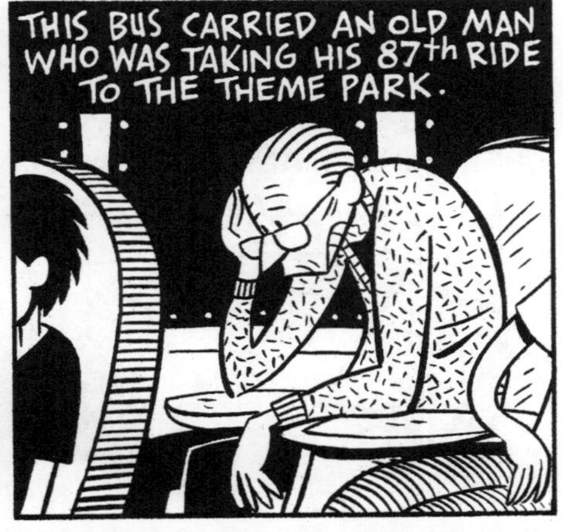
THIS BUS CARRIED AN OLD MAN WHO WAS TAKING HIS 87th RIDE TO THE THEME PARK.

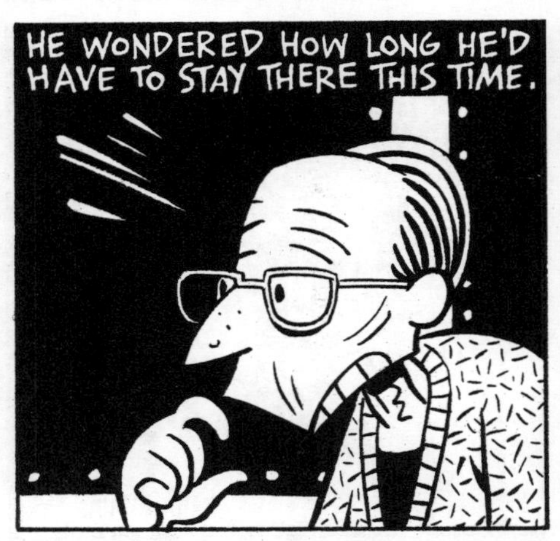
HE WONDERED HOW LONG HE'D HAVE TO STAY THERE THIS TIME.

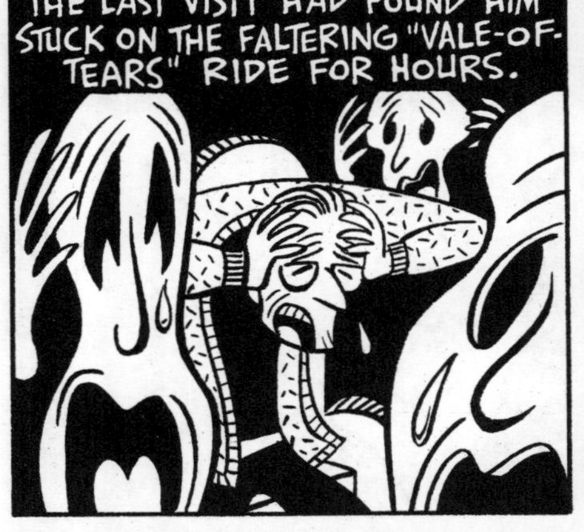
THE LAST VISIT HAD FOUND HIM STUCK ON THE FALTERING "VALE-OF-TEARS" RIDE FOR HOURS.

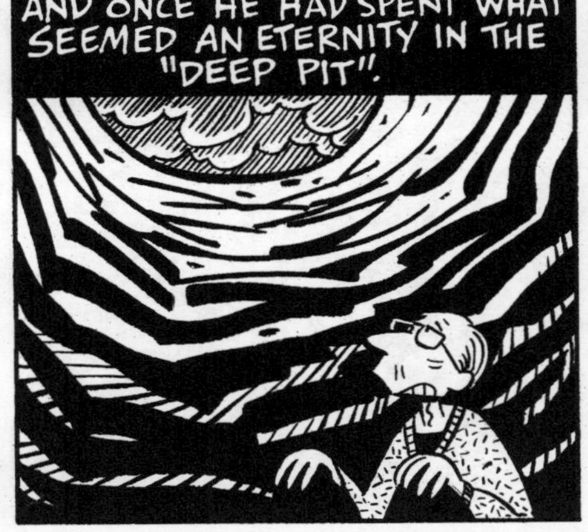
AND ONCE HE HAD SPENT WHAT SEEMED AN ETERNITY IN THE "DEEP PIT".

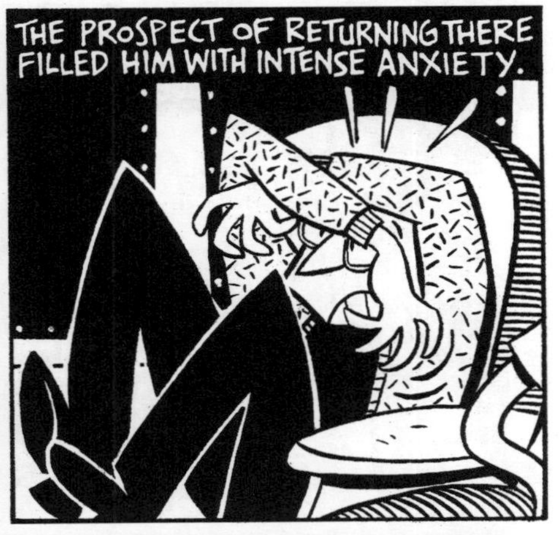
THE PROSPECT OF RETURNING THERE FILLED HIM WITH INTENSE ANXIETY.

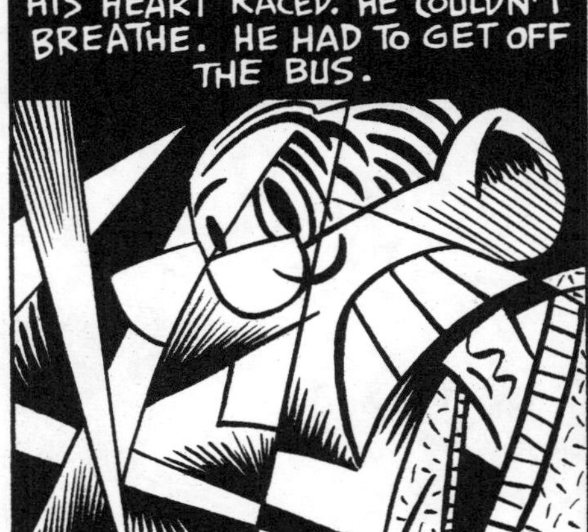
HIS HEART RACED. HE COULDN'T BREATHE. HE HAD TO GET OFF THE BUS.

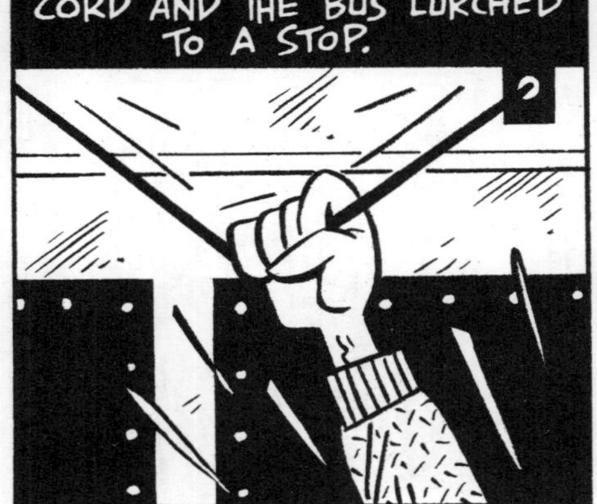
HE PULLED THE EMERGENCY CORD AND THE BUS LURCHED TO A STOP.

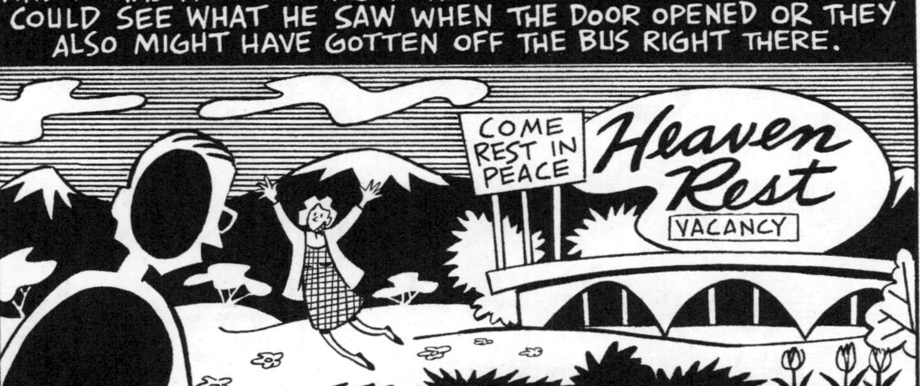
AND IT WAS A GOOD THING NONE OF THE OTHER PASSENGERS COULD SEE WHAT HE SAW WHEN THE DOOR OPENED OR THEY ALSO MIGHT HAVE GOTTEN OFF THE BUS RIGHT THERE.
COME REST IN PEACE
Heaven Rest
VACANCY

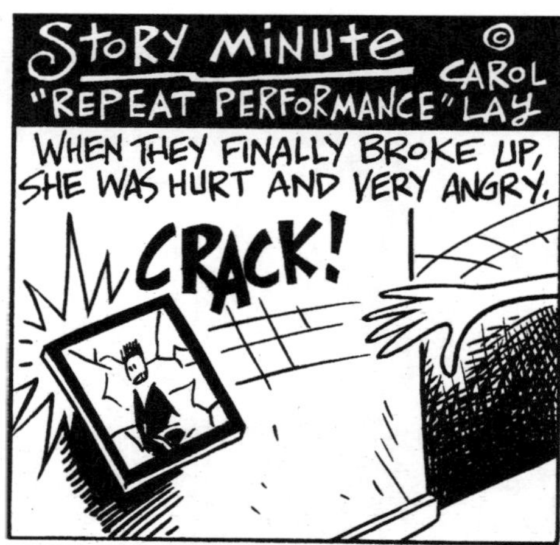
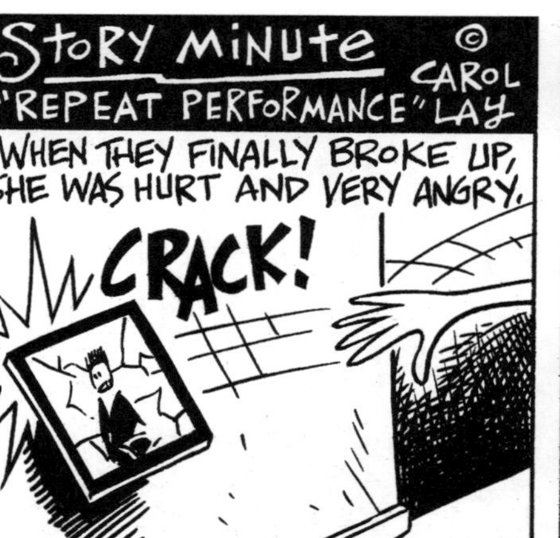
STORY MINUTE ©
CAROL LAY
"REPEAT PERFORMANCE"
WHEN THEY FINALLY BROKE UP, SHE WAS HURT AND VERY ANGRY.
CRACK!
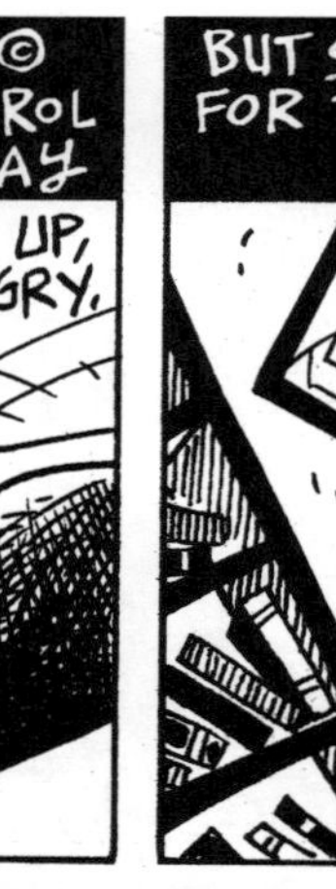
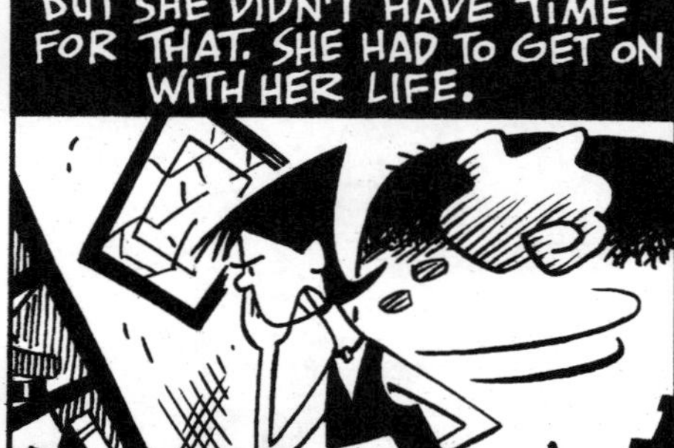
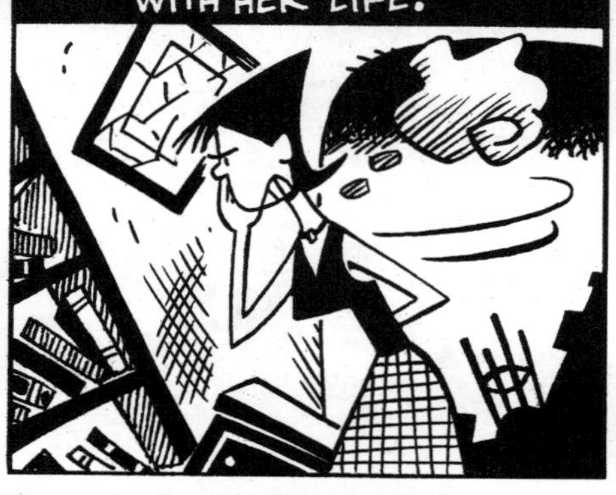
BUT SHE DIDN'T HAVE TIME FOR THAT. SHE HAD TO GET ON WITH HER LIFE.
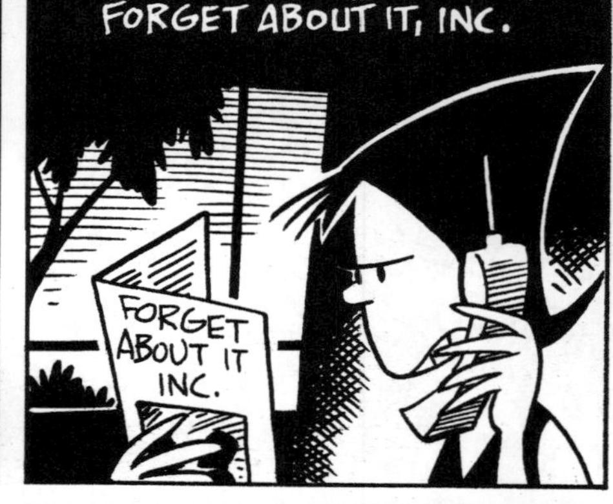
SO SHE SAVED HER MONEY AND MADE AN APPOINTMENT AT FORGET ABOUT IT, INC.
FORGET ABOUT IT INC.
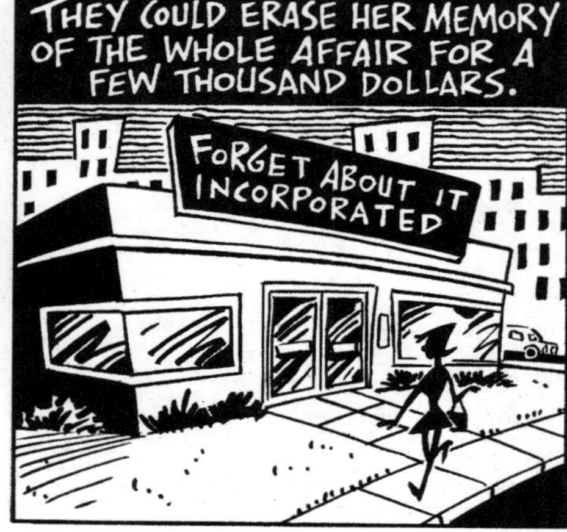
THEY COULD ERASE HER MEMORY OF THE WHOLE AFFAIR FOR A FEW THOUSAND DOLLARS.
FORGET ABOUT IT INCORPORATED
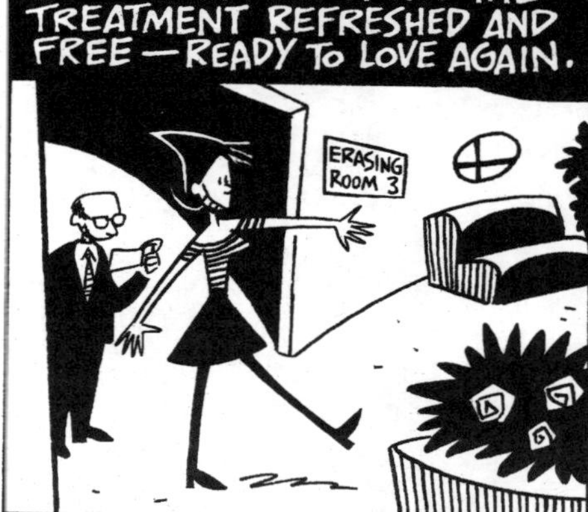
SHE EMERGED FROM THE TREATMENT REFRESHED AND FREE—READY TO LOVE AGAIN.
ERASING ROOM 3
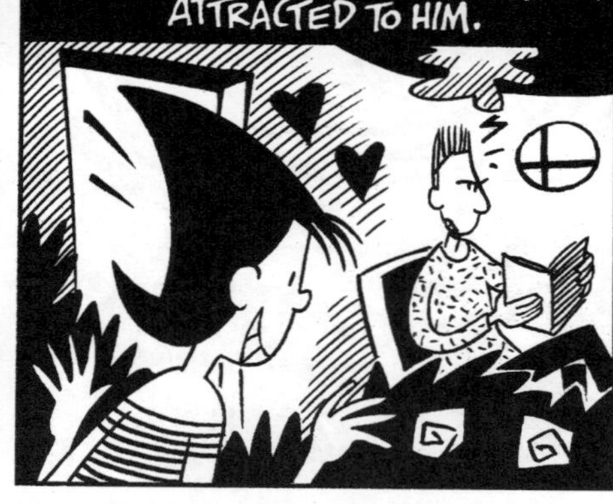
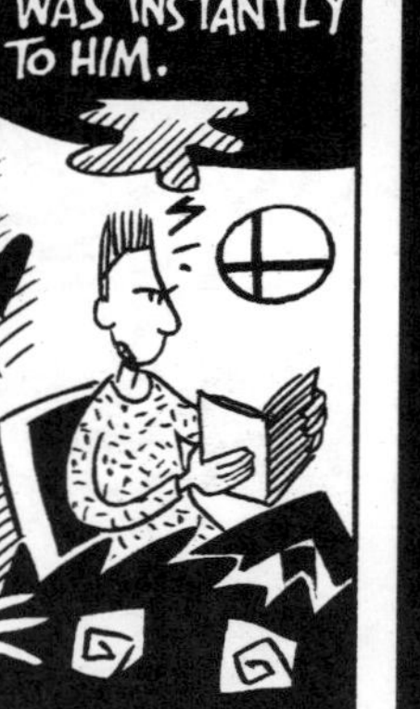
SHE SPIED A MAN IN THE WAITING ROOM AND WAS INSTANTLY ATTRACTED TO HIM.
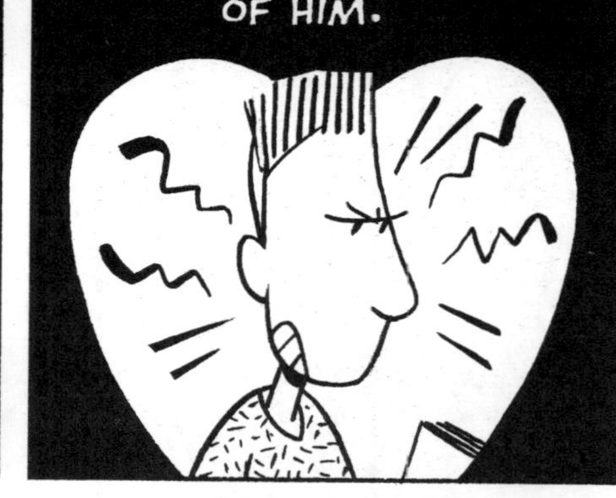
IT WAS HER NEWLY-PARTED LOVER, ALTHOUGH SHE HAD NO MEMORY OF HIM.
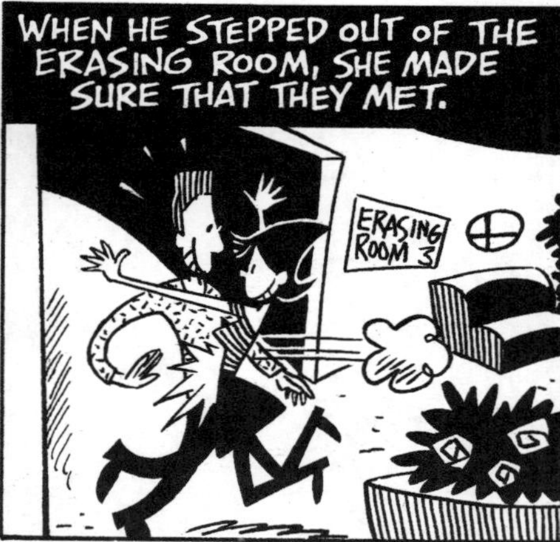
WHEN HE STEPPED OUT OF THE ERASING ROOM, SHE MADE SURE THAT THEY MET.
ERASING ROOM 3
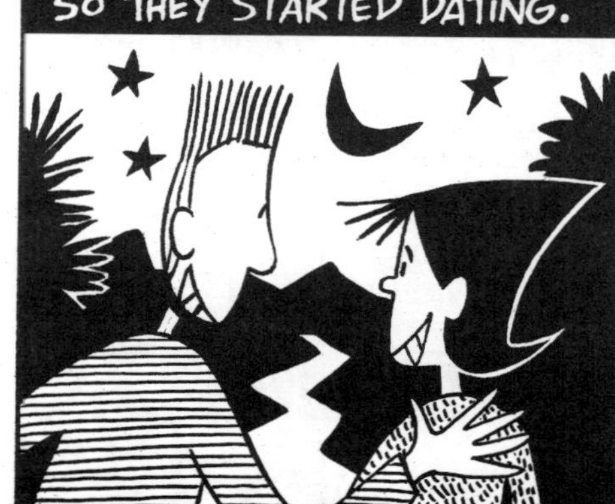
THE ATTRACTION WAS MUTUAL SO THEY STARTED DATING.
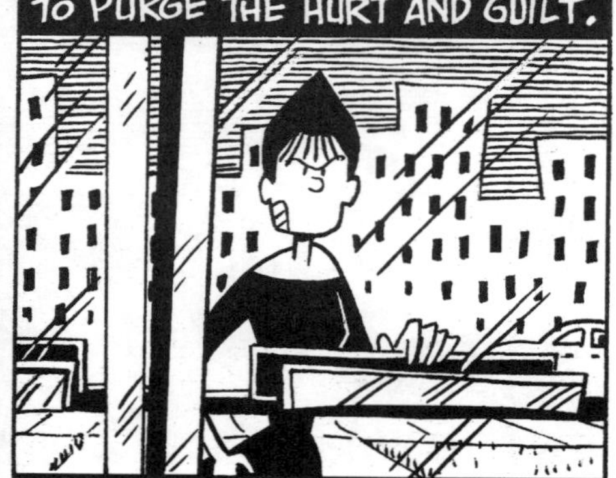
A YEAR LATER THEY BROKE UP AND RETURNED SEPARATELY TO PURGE THE HURT AND GUILT.
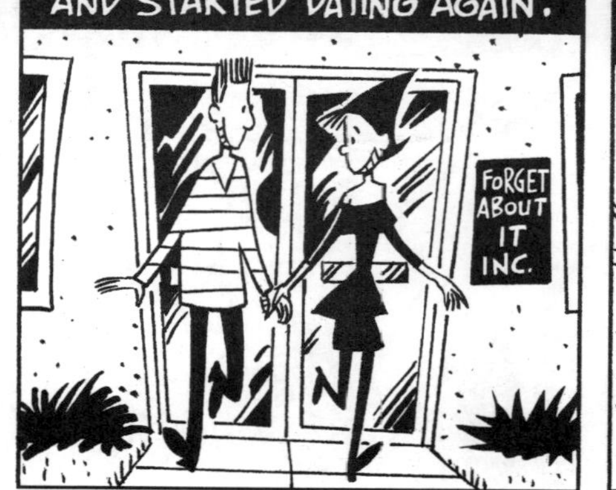
NATURALLY, THEY MET AGAIN AND STARTED DATING AGAIN.
FORGET ABOUT IT INC.
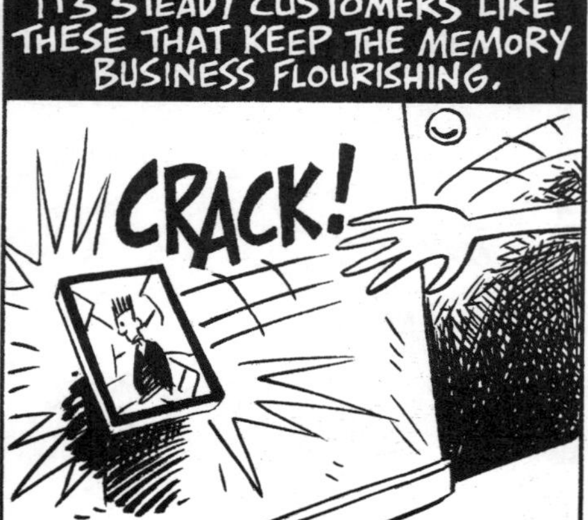
IT'S STEADY CUSTOMERS LIKE THESE THAT KEEP THE MEMORY BUSINESS FLOURISHING.
CRACK!

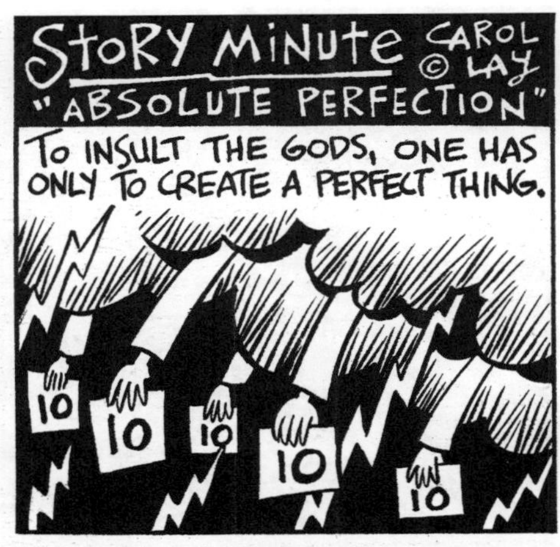
Story Minute
Carol © Lay
"Absolute Perfection"
To insult the gods, one has only to create a perfect thing.
10
10
10
10
10

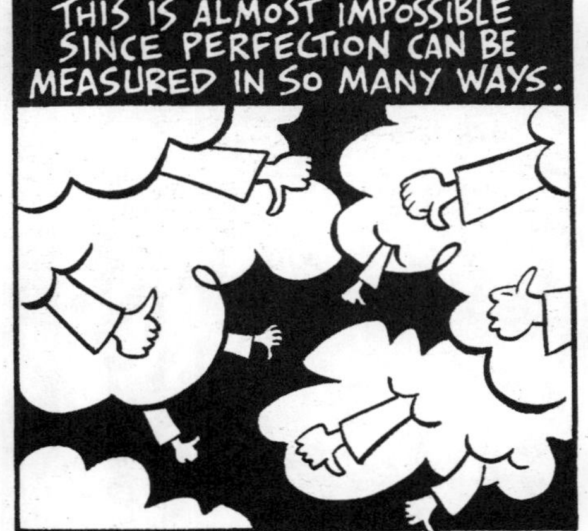
This is almost impossible since perfection can be measured in so many ways.

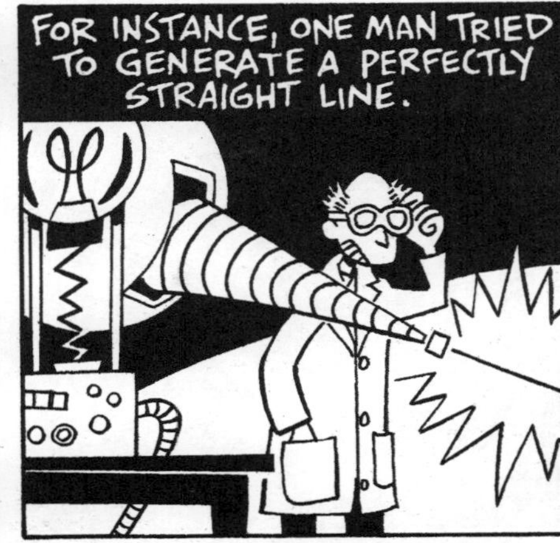
For instance, one man tried to generate a perfectly straight line.

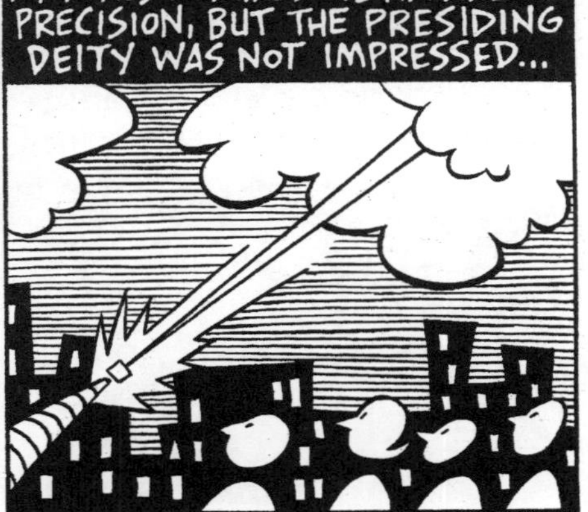
Mortals admired its apparent precision, but the presiding deity was not impressed...

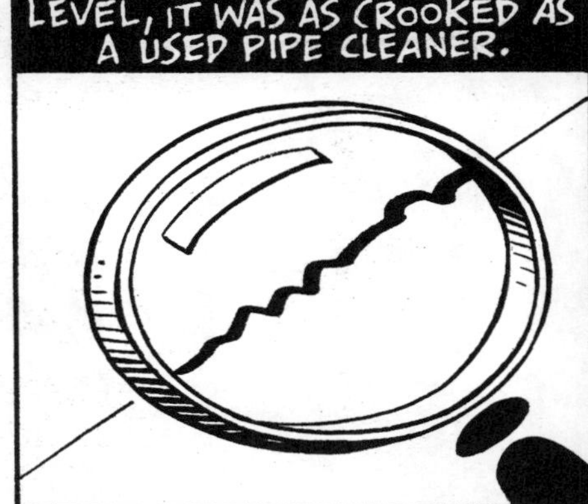
...because, on a microscopic level, it was as crooked as a used pipe cleaner.

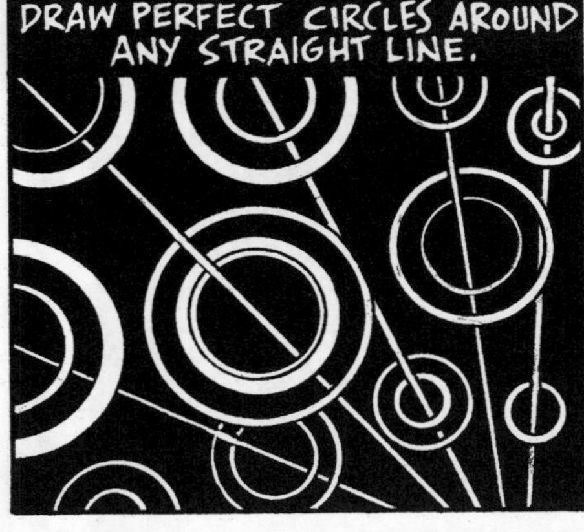
And so what? This god could draw perfect circles around any straight line.

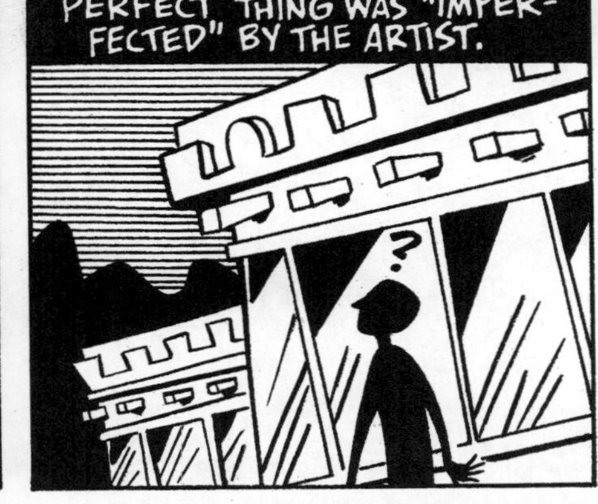
In some cultures, a so-called perfect thing was "imperfected" by the artist.
?

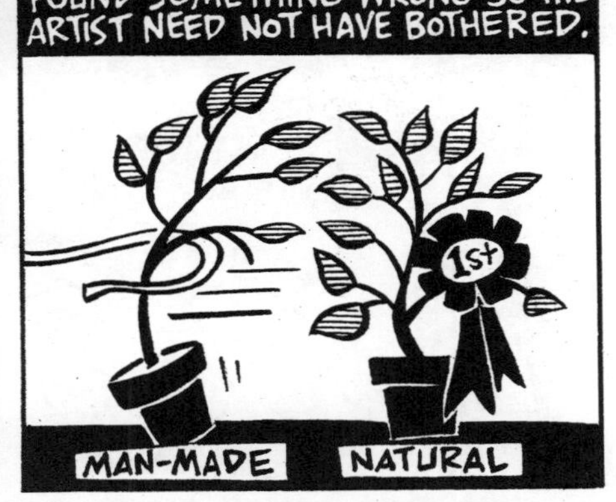
But the gods could have always found something wrong so the artist need not have bothered.
1st
Man-made
Natural

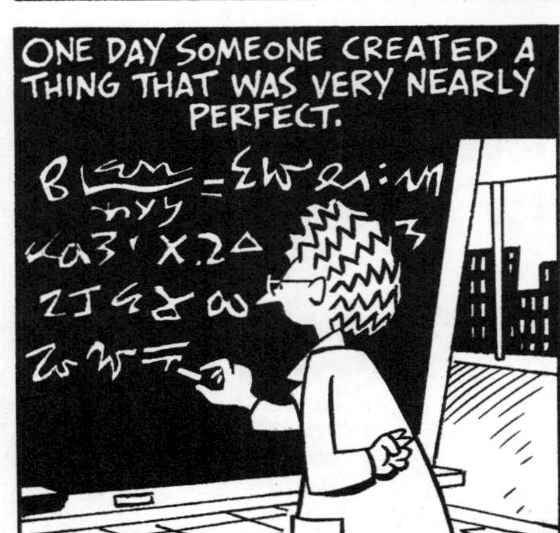
One day someone created a thing that was very nearly perfect.

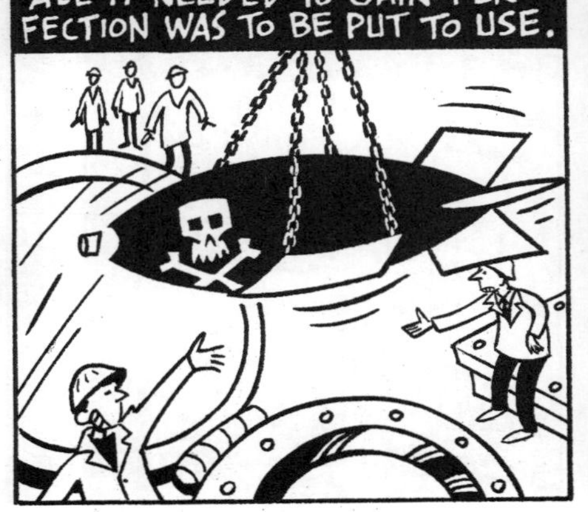
All it needed to gain perfection was to be put to use.

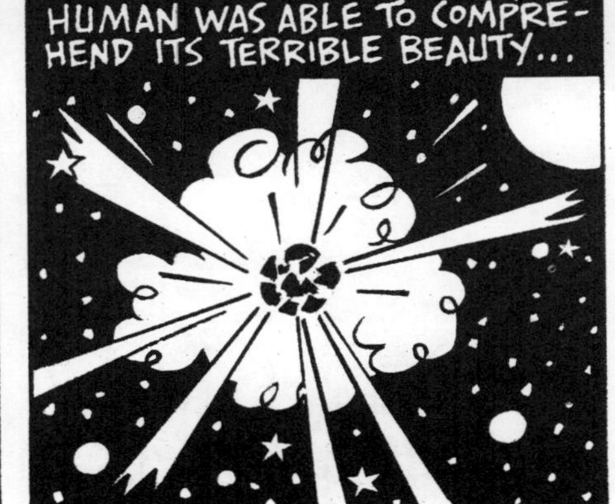
When it was finally used, no human was able to comprehend its terrible beauty...

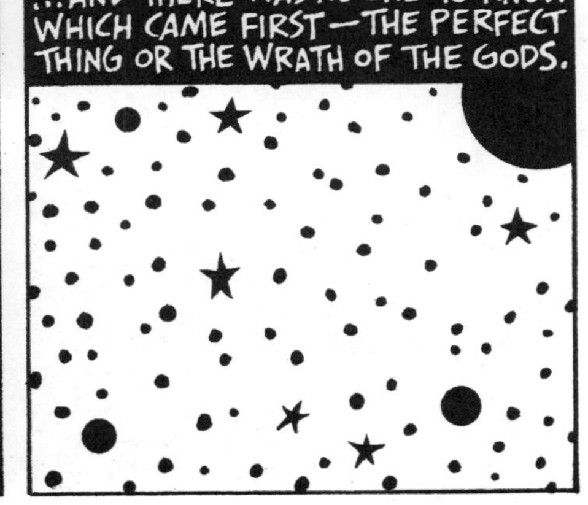
...and there was no one to know which came first—the perfect thing or the wrath of the gods.

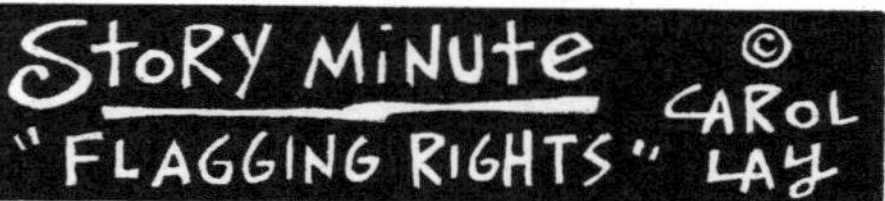
STORY MINUTE
"FLAGGING RIGHTS"
© CAROL LAY

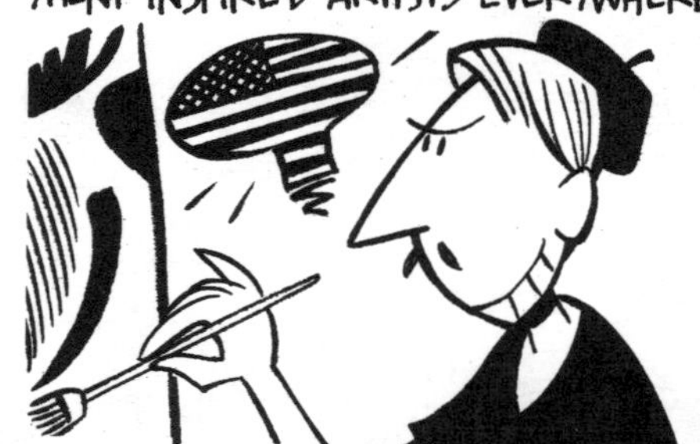
THE FLAG-DESECRATION AMENDMENT INSPIRED ARTISTS EVERYWHERE.

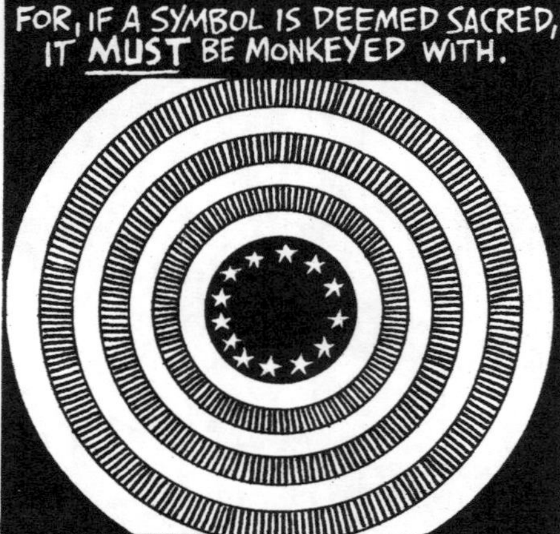
FOR, IF A SYMBOL IS DEEMED SACRED, IT MUST BE MONKEYED WITH.

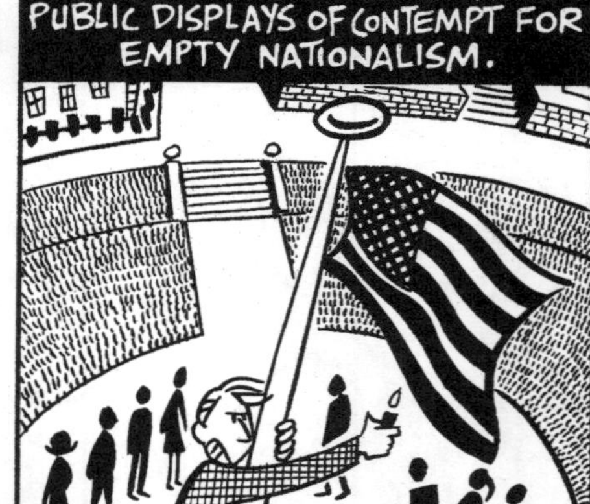
AMATEURS WERE OBVIOUS WITH PUBLIC DISPLAYS OF CONTEMPT FOR EMPTY NATIONALISM.

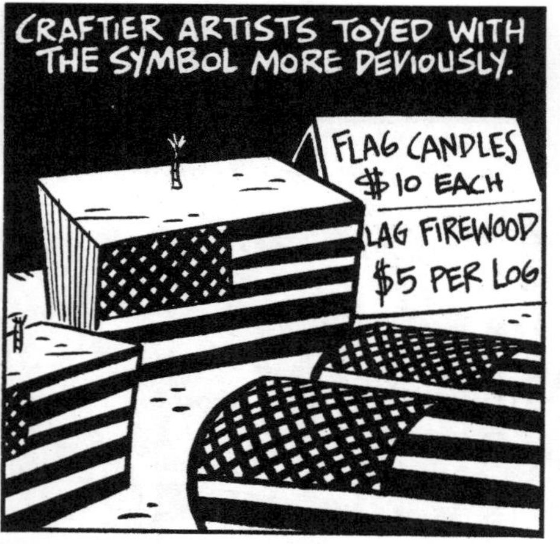
CRAFTIER ARTISTS TOYED WITH THE SYMBOL MORE DEVIOUSLY.
FLAG CANDLES $10 EACH
LAG FIREWOOD $5 PER LOG

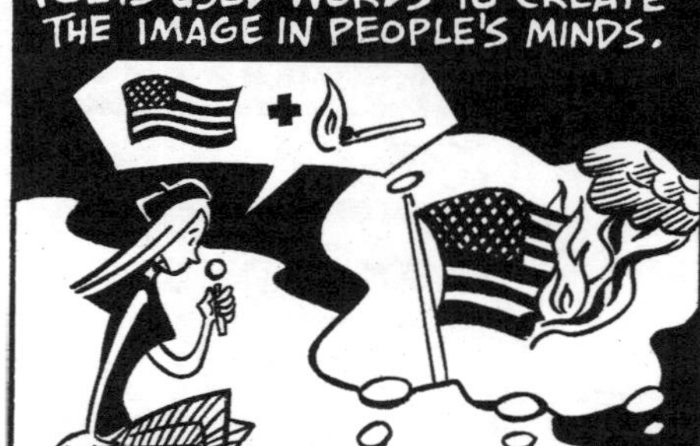
POETS USED WORDS TO CREATE THE IMAGE IN PEOPLE'S MINDS.

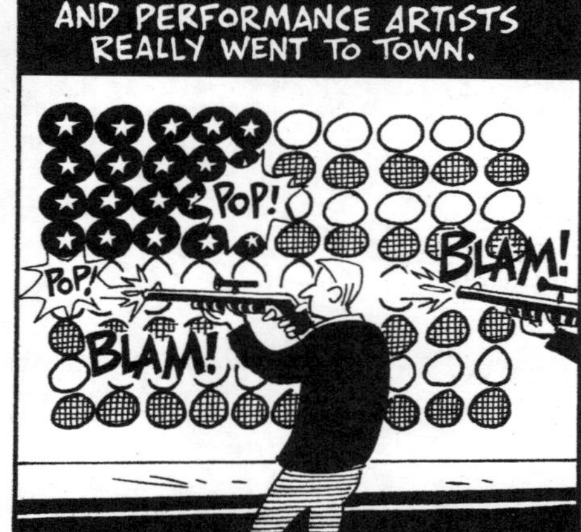
AND PERFORMANCE ARTISTS REALLY WENT TO TOWN.
POP!
POP!
BLAM!
BLAM!

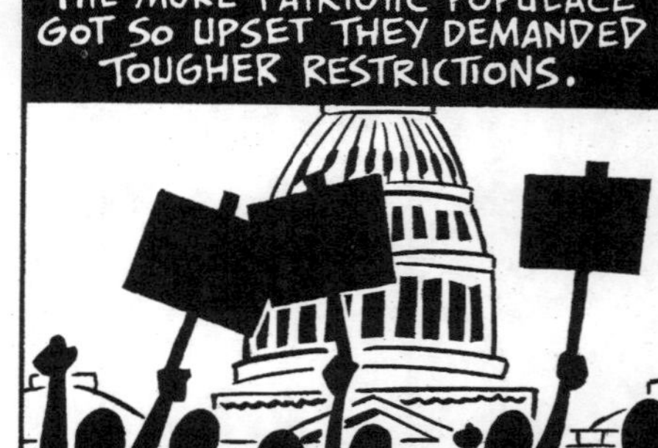
THE MORE PATRIOTIC POPULACE GOT SO UPSET THEY DEMANDED TOUGHER RESTRICTIONS.

SOON, ANYONE WHO "INSULTED" THOSE WHO DEFENDED THE COUNTRY WAS ON DEATH ROW.

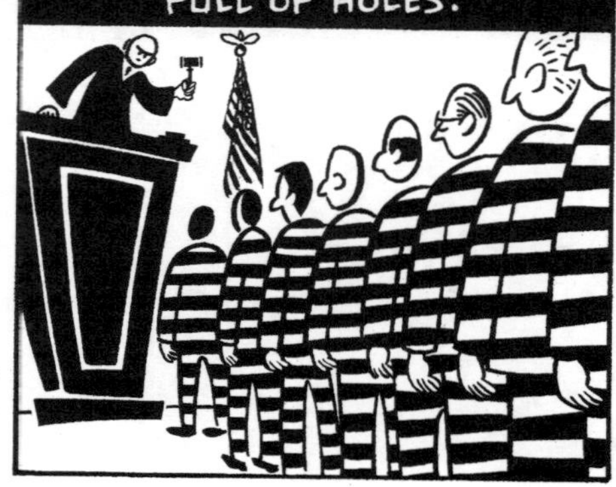
THEY WERE ALL FATED TO BE BURNED, TROD UPON, OR SHOT FULL OF HOLES.

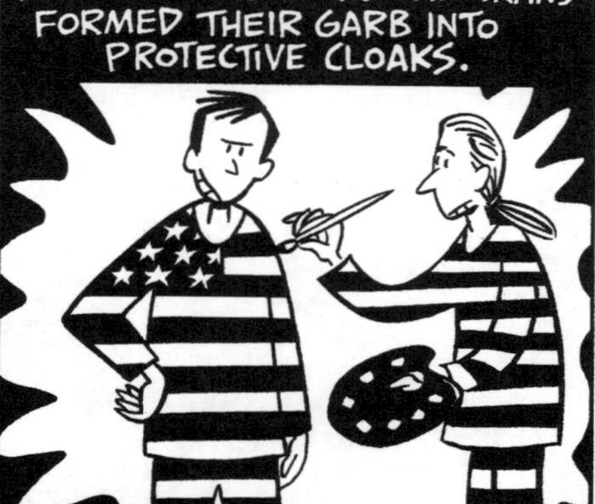
BUT THE PRISONERS HAD TRANSFORMED THEIR GARB INTO PROTECTIVE CLOAKS.

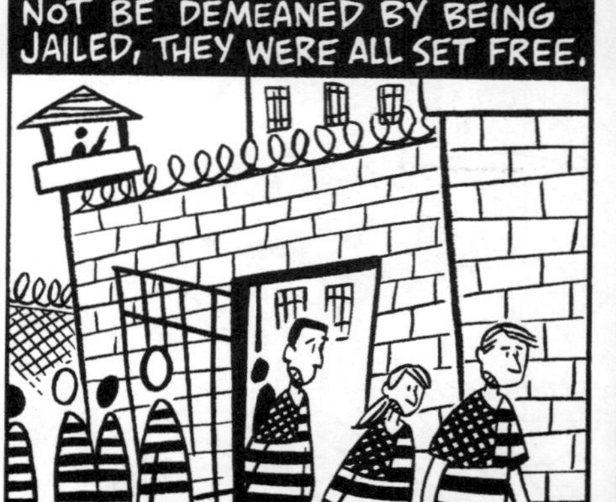
AND SINCE THE FLAG COULD NOT BE DEMEANED BY BEING JAILED, THEY WERE ALL SET FREE.

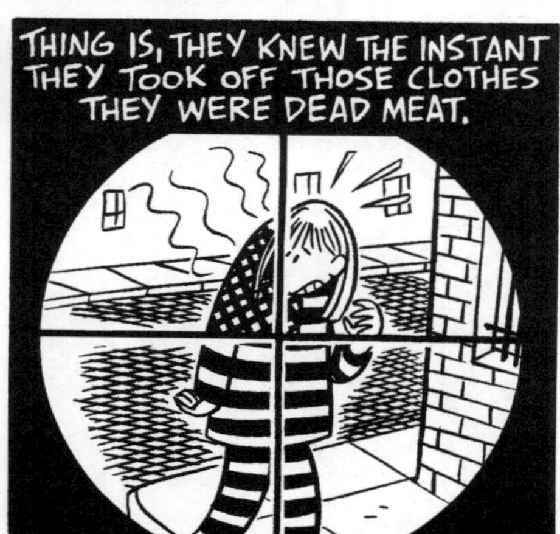
THING IS, THEY KNEW THE INSTANT THEY TOOK OFF THOSE CLOTHES THEY WERE DEAD MEAT.

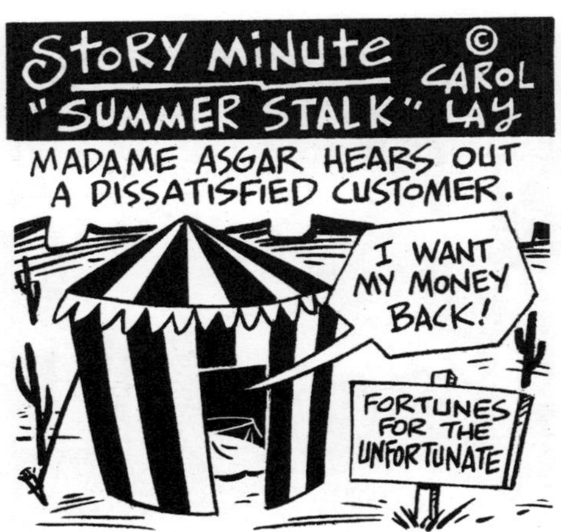
STORY MINUTE © CAROL LAY
"SUMMER STALK"
MADAME ASGAR HEARS OUT A DISSATISFIED CUSTOMER.
I WANT MY MONEY BACK!
FORTUNES FOR THE UNFORTUNATE

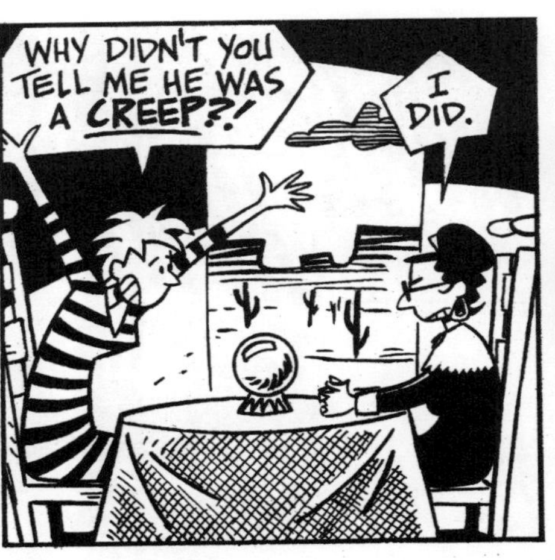
WHY DIDN'T YOU TELL ME HE WAS A CREEP?!
I DID.

I SHOWED YOU A COPY OF HIS POLICE RECORD AND NEWS CLIPPINGS OF HIS CRIMES.
BAD MAN

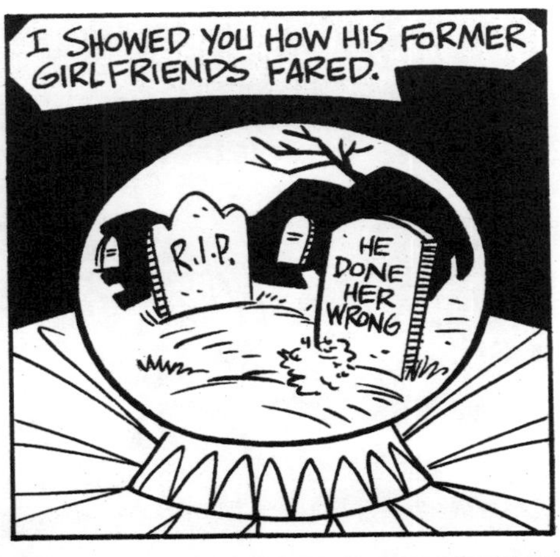
I SHOWED YOU HOW HIS FORMER GIRLFRIENDS FARED.
R.I.P.
HE DONE HER WRONG

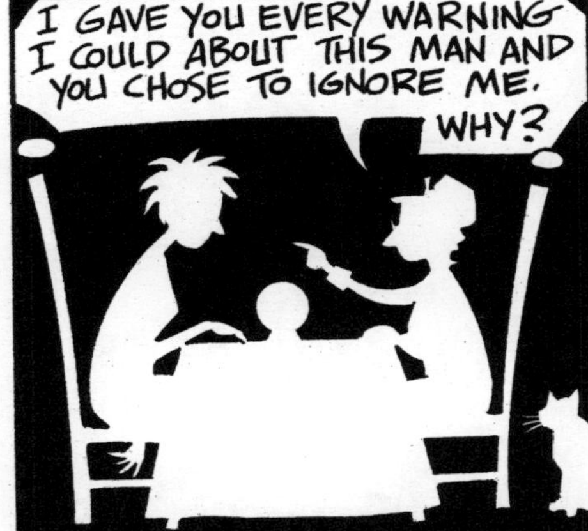
I GAVE YOU EVERY WARNING I COULD ABOUT THIS MAN AND YOU CHOSE TO IGNORE ME.
WHY?

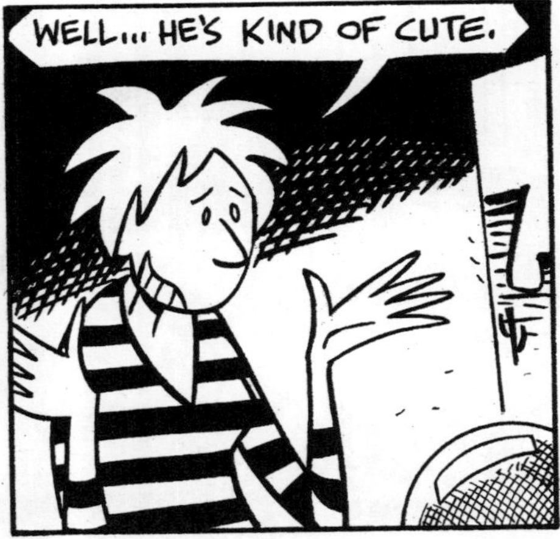
WELL... HE'S KIND OF CUTE.

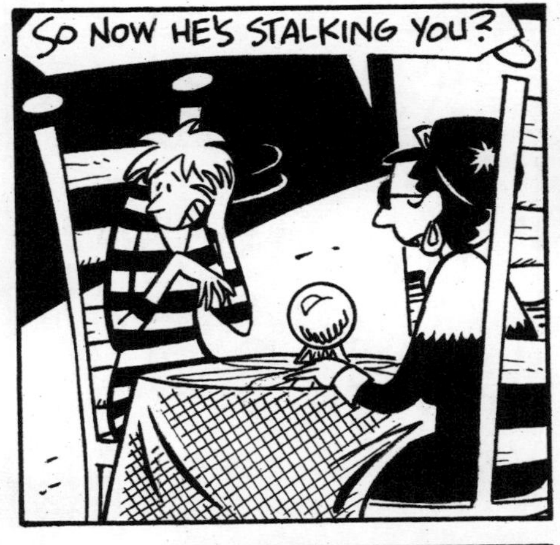
SO NOW HE'S STALKING YOU?

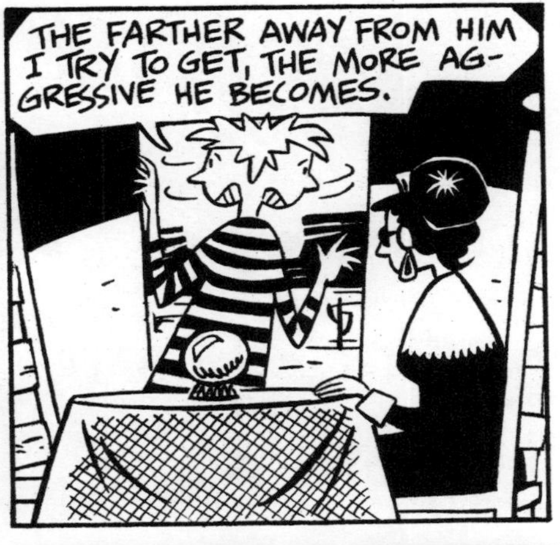
THE FARTHER AWAY FROM HIM I TRY TO GET, THE MORE AG-GRESSIVE HE BECOMES.

FARTHER AWAY?! YOU MOVED FROM THE BEDROOM TO THE LIVINGROOM SOFA. WHY DON'T YOU LEAVE?

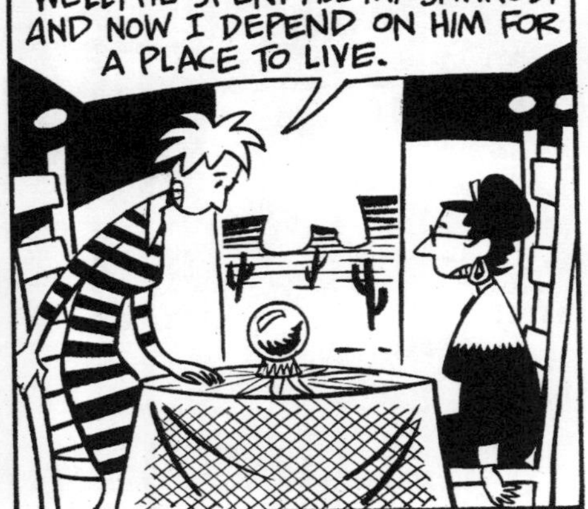
WELL, HE SPENT ALL MY SAVINGS, AND NOW I DEPEND ON HIM FOR A PLACE TO LIVE.

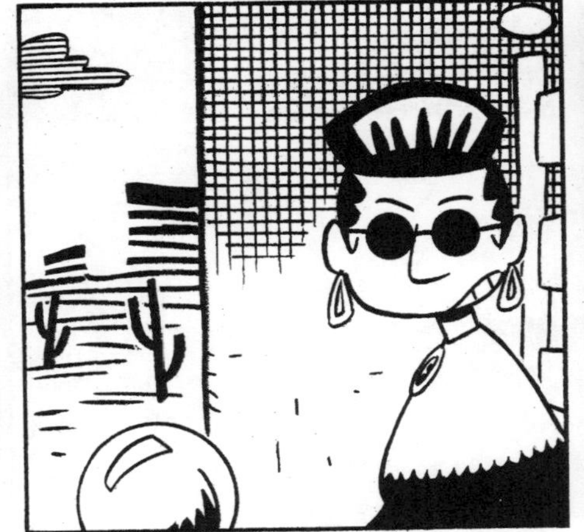

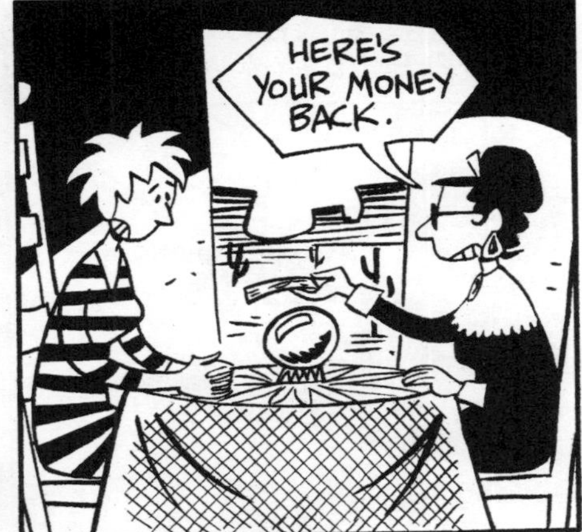
HERE'S YOUR MONEY BACK.

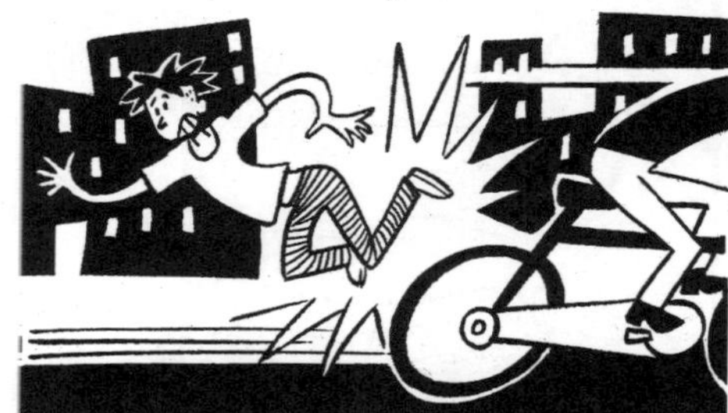
Story Minute ©
"MISFORTUNE HUNTER"
CAROL LAY
THINKING POSITIVELY COMES NATURALLY TO SOME PEOPLE...

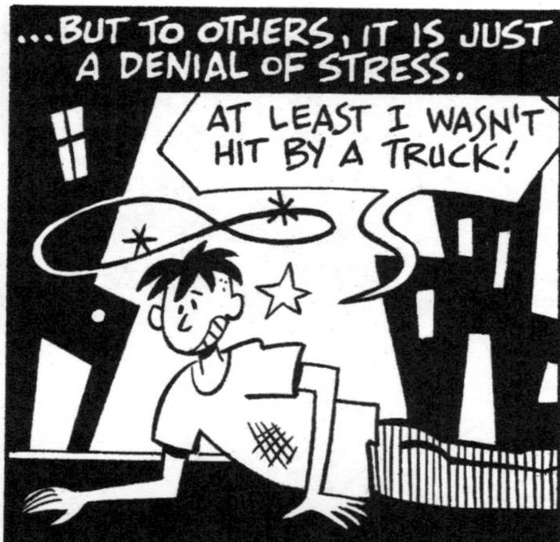
...BUT TO OTHERS, IT IS JUST A DENIAL OF STRESS.
AT LEAST I WASN'T HIT BY A TRUCK!

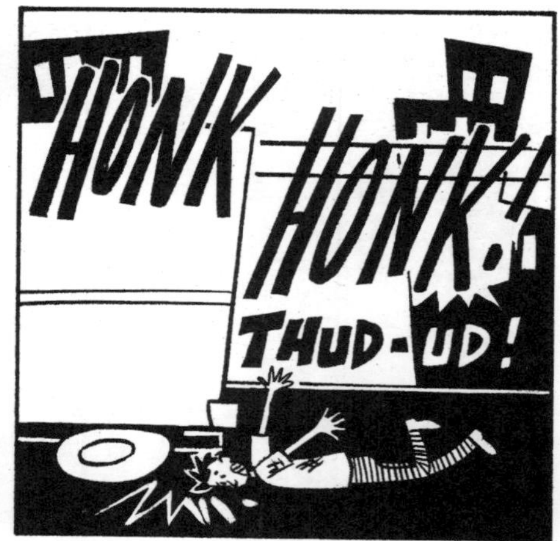
HONK
HONK!
THUD-UD!

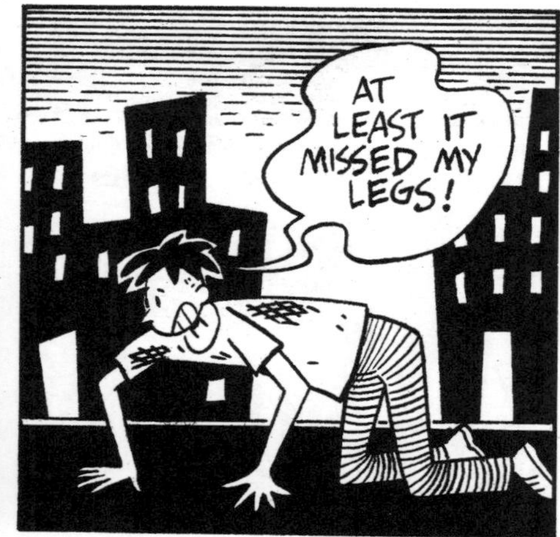
AT LEAST IT MISSED MY LEGS!

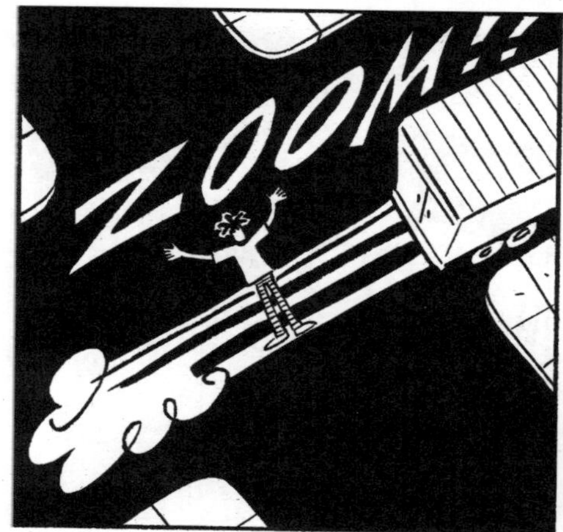
ZOOM!!

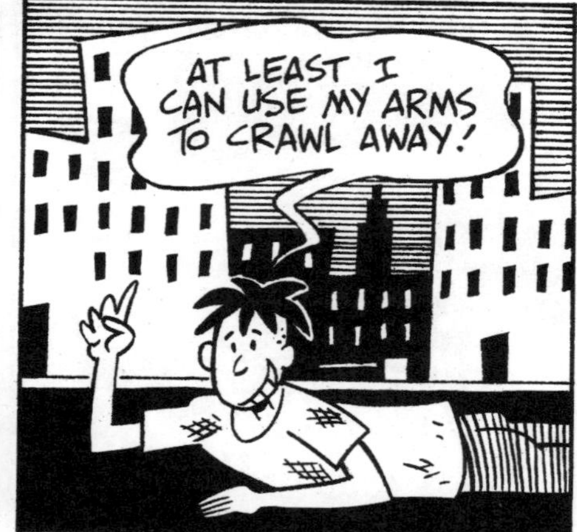
AT LEAST I CAN USE MY ARMS TO CRAWL AWAY!

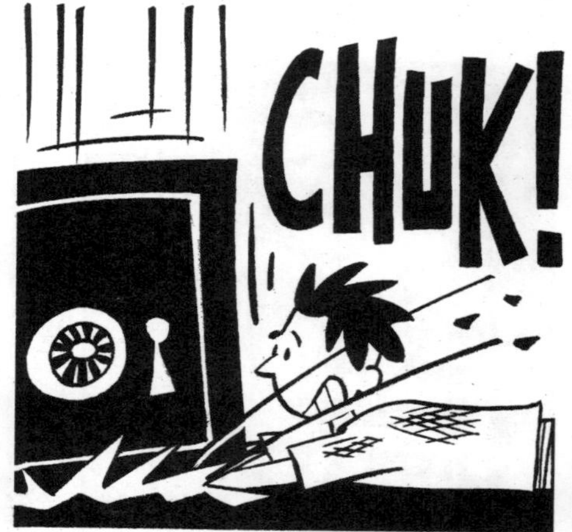
CHUK!

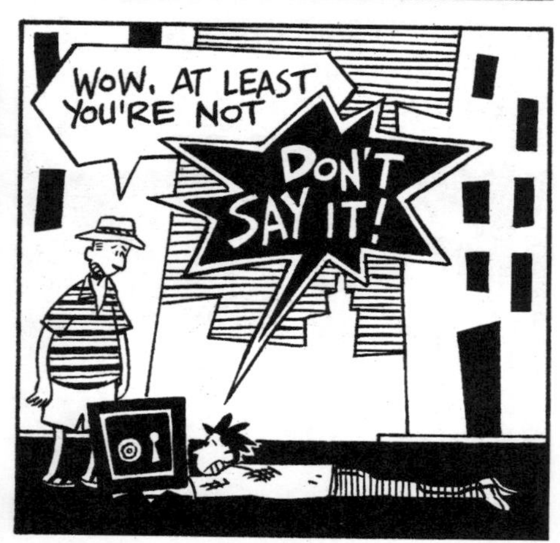
WOW, AT LEAST YOU'RE NOT
DON'T SAY IT!

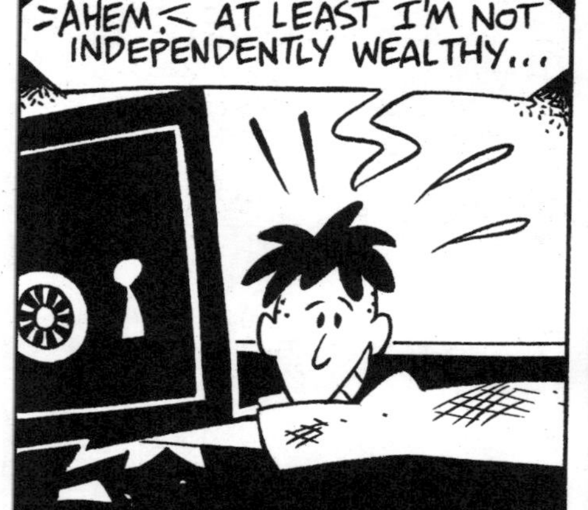
>AHEM< AT LEAST I'M NOT INDEPENDENTLY WEALTHY...

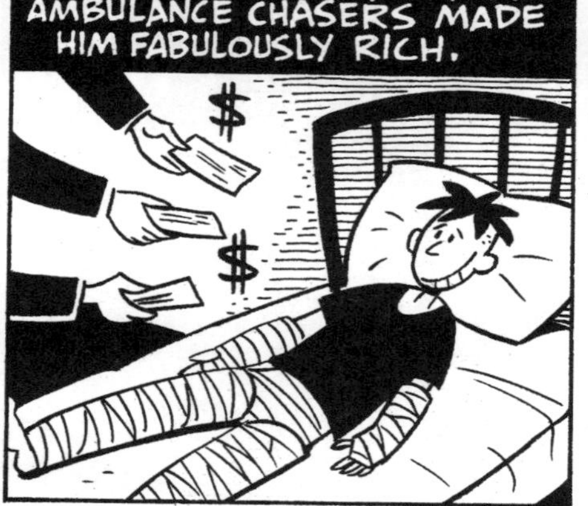
BEFORE HE KNEW IT, SEVERAL AMBULANCE CHASERS MADE HIM FABULOUSLY RICH.
$
$

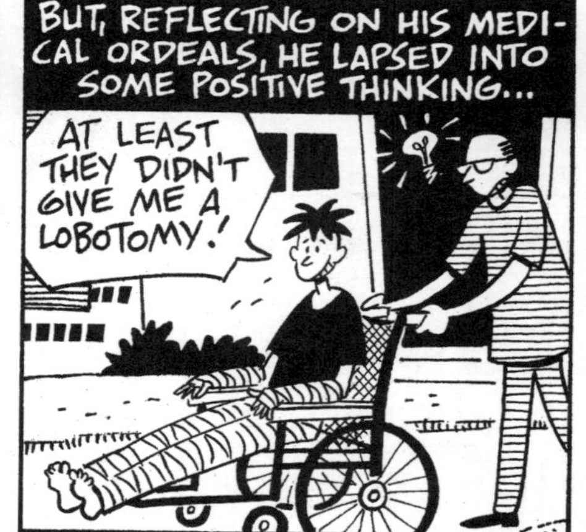
BUT, REFLECTING ON HIS MEDICAL ORDEALS, HE LAPSED INTO SOME POSITIVE THINKING...
AT LEAST THEY DIDN'T GIVE ME A LOBOTOMY!

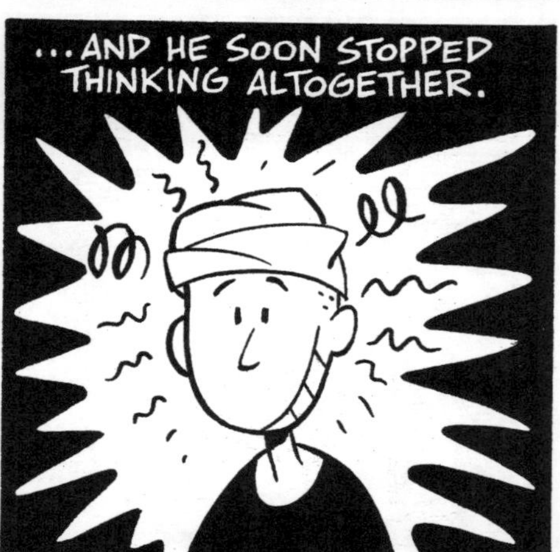
...AND HE SOON STOPPED THINKING ALTOGETHER.

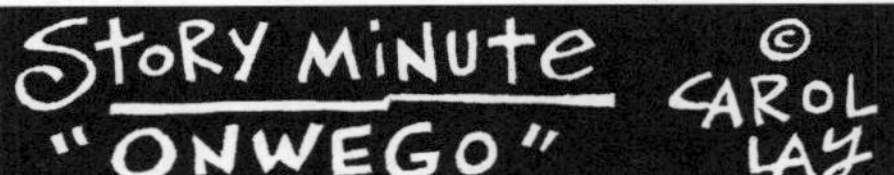


NOTHING MUCH HAPPENED IN THE LITTLE TOWN ANYMORE.

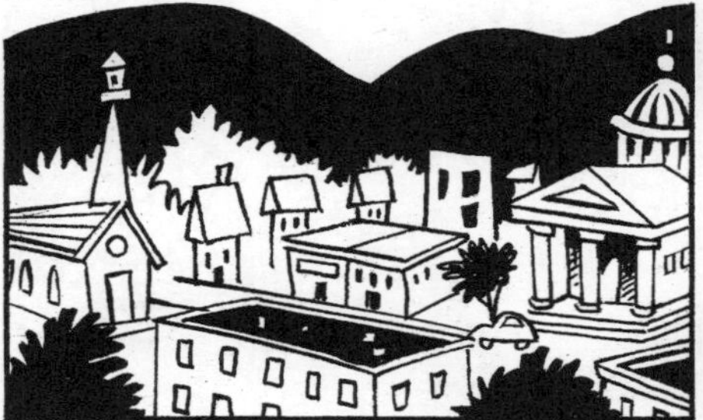

THE ENNUI WAS CONTAGIOUS SO ONE RESIDENT KEPT HER SANITY BY BUILDING A MODEL OF IT.

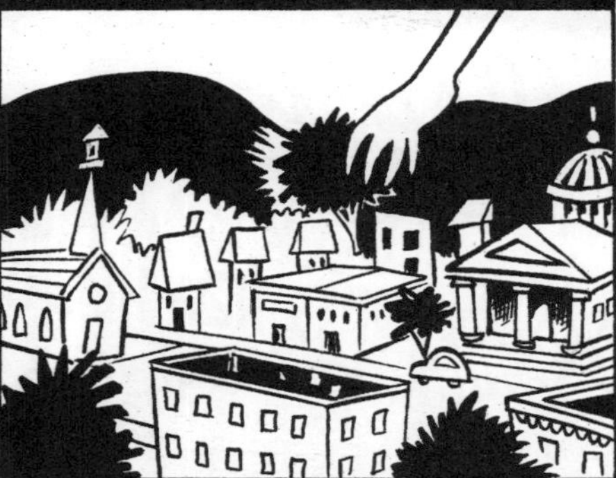

SHE FIGURED IT WOULD BE EASY TO COMPLETE SINCE NOTHING EVER CHANGED.

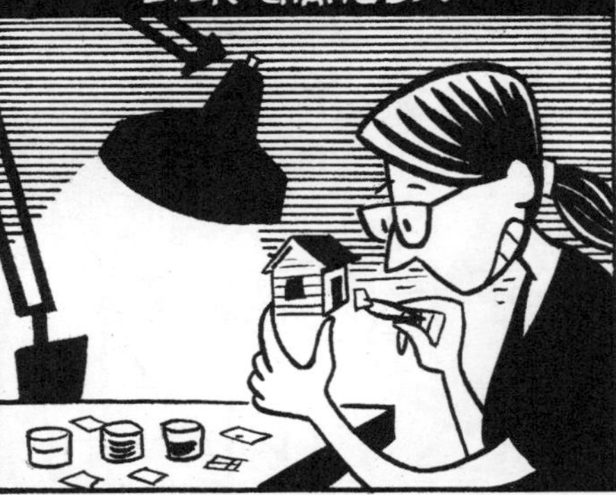

WHEN SHE WAS DONE, THOUGH, IT BORED HER SO MUCH THAT SHE MOVED IT OUTSIDE.

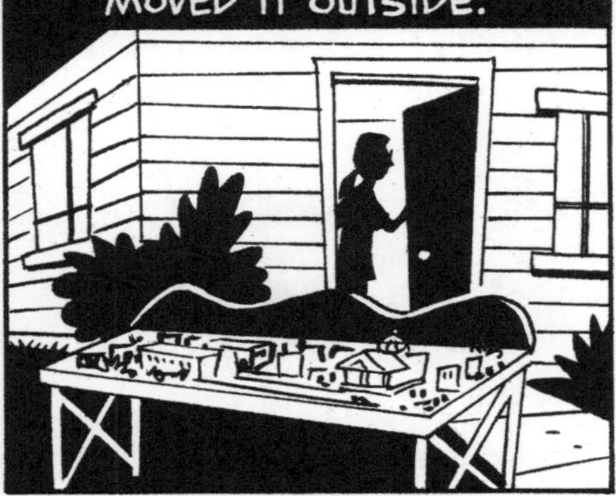

PASSERSBY ADMIRED ITS FAITHFULNESS BUT WERE DISMAYED BY ITS LACK OF EXCITEMENT.

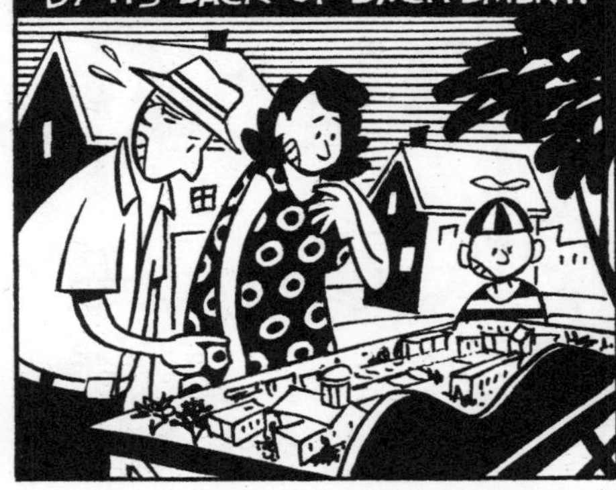

SOMEONE PLACED THE BUTCHER MODEL IN A FIGHT WITH THE BAKER MODEL.

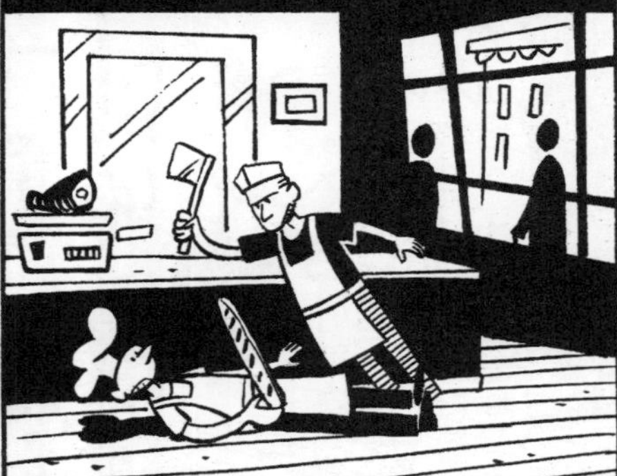

AND SOMEHOW THE MAYOR MODEL ENDED UP IN BED WITH THE HOSPITAL ADMINISTRATOR MODEL.

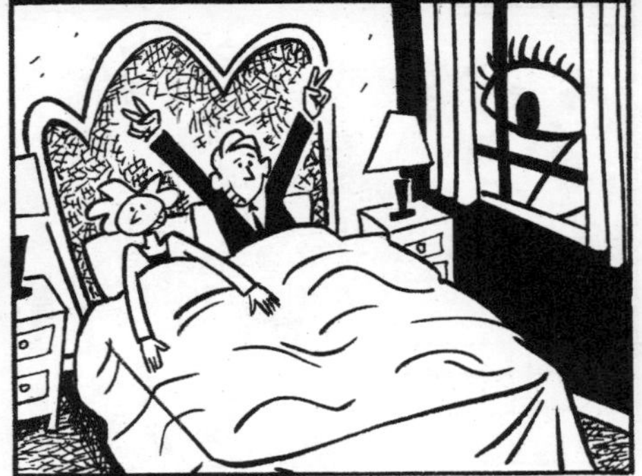

ON VIEWING THEMSELVES IN THESE SCENES, THE PARTICIPANTS WERE GIVEN GOOD IDEAS.

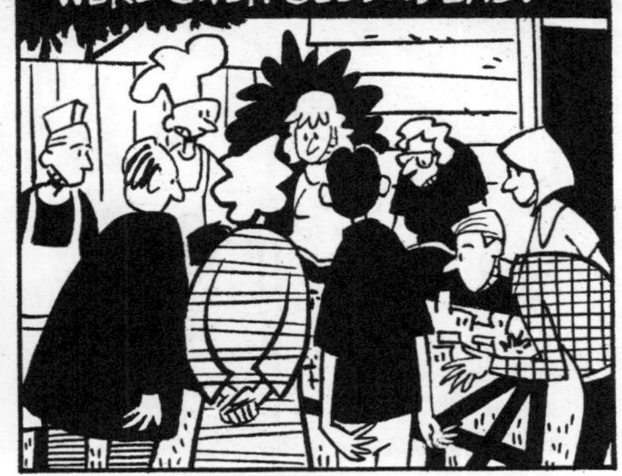

SOME WENT OUT AND DID WHATEVER THE MODEL "ALLOWED" THEM TO DO...

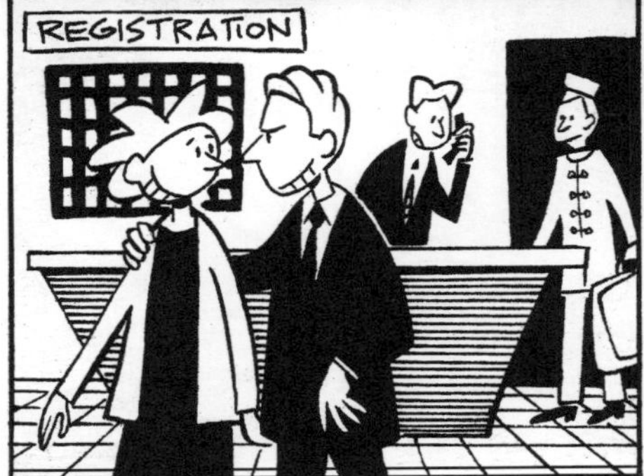


...WHILE OTHERS DID SOMETHING COMPLETELY DIFFERENT TO ASSERT THEIR FREE WILLS.

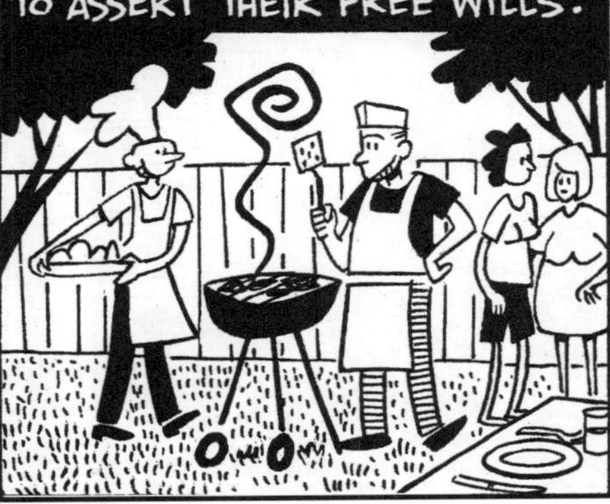

BUT THE TOWN'S REBIRTH WENT UNNOTICED BY ONE OF ITS OWN...

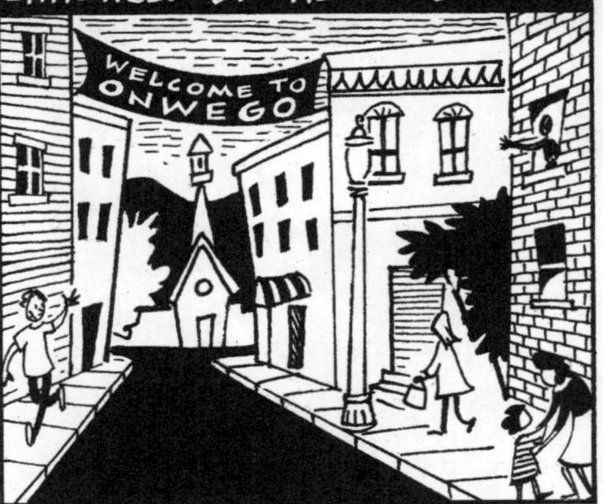


...WHO WAS TOO BUSY BEING DISMAYED BY A VERY ACCURATE MODEL SHE'D MADE OF HERSELF.

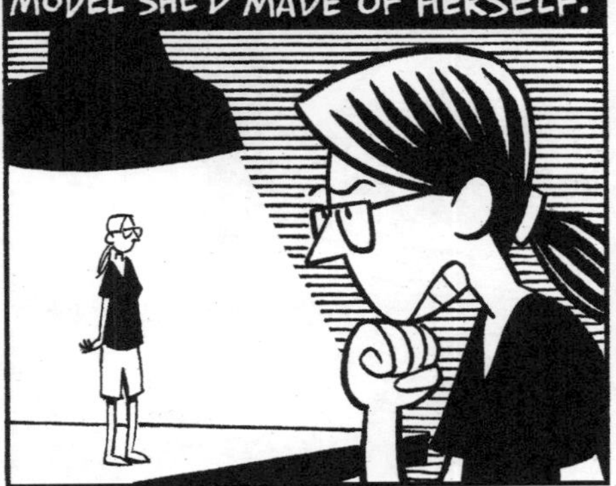

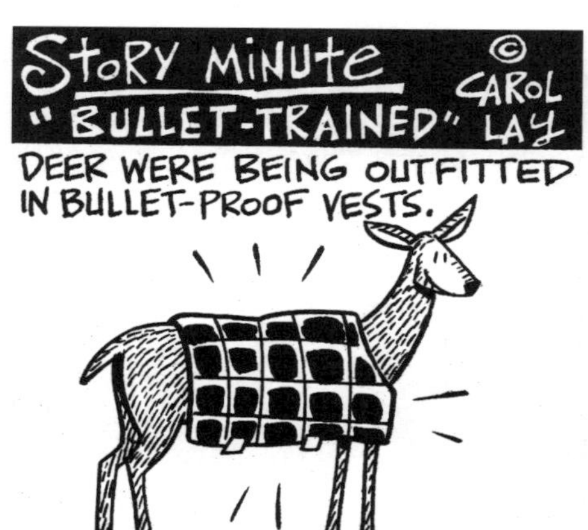
Story Minute
"Bullet-Trained"
© Carol Lay
Deer were being outfitted in bullet-proof vests.

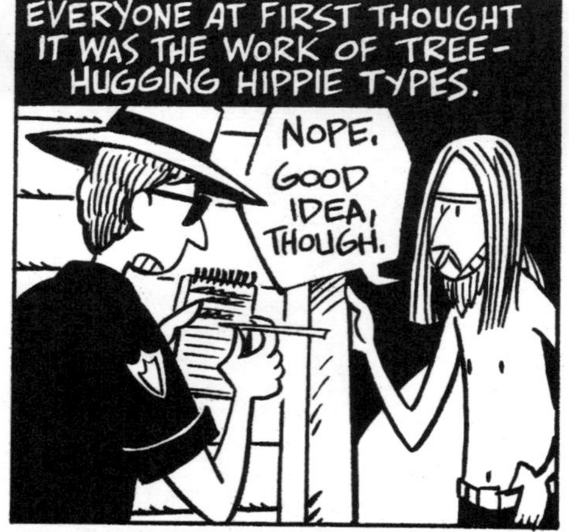
Everyone at first thought it was the work of tree-hugging hippie types.
Nope. Good idea, though.

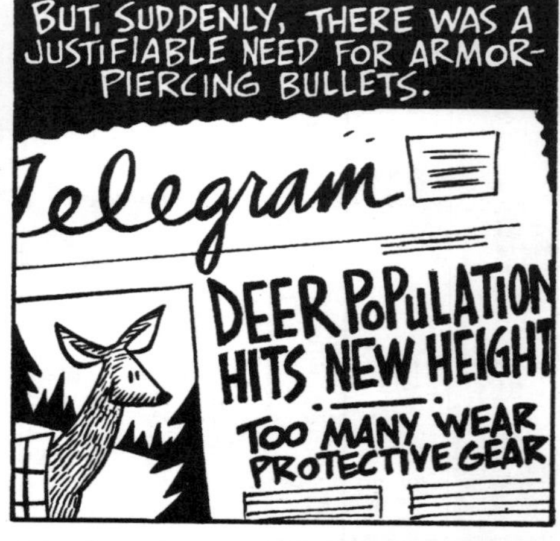
But, suddenly, there was a justifiable need for armor-piercing bullets.
Telegram
Deer Population Hits New Height
Too many wear protective gear

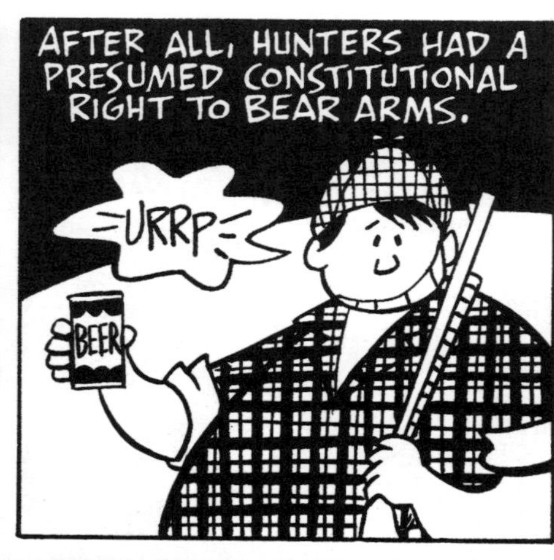
After all, hunters had a presumed constitutional right to bear arms.
URRP
Beer

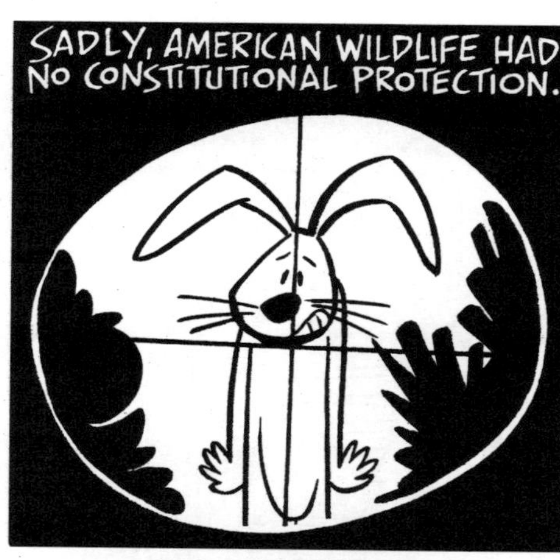
Sadly, American wildlife had no constitutional protection.

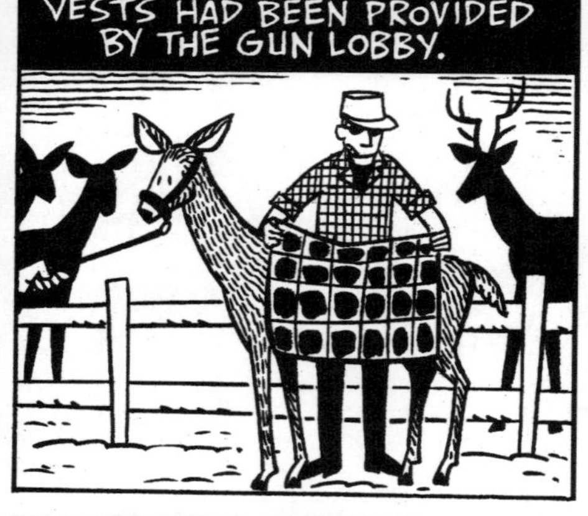
But it turned out that the vests had been provided by the gun lobby.

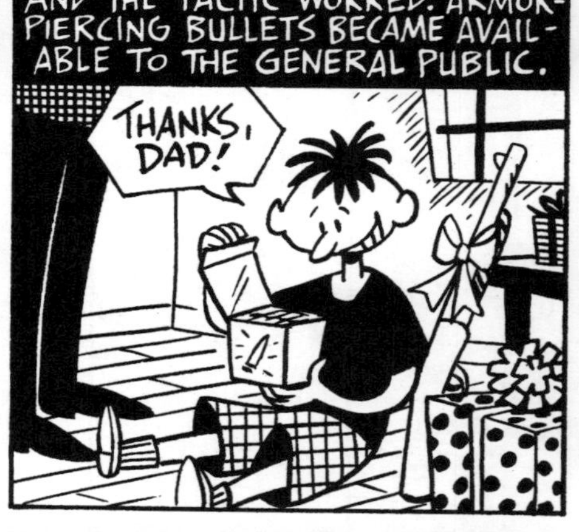
And the tactic worked. Armor-piercing bullets became available to the general public.
Thanks, Dad!

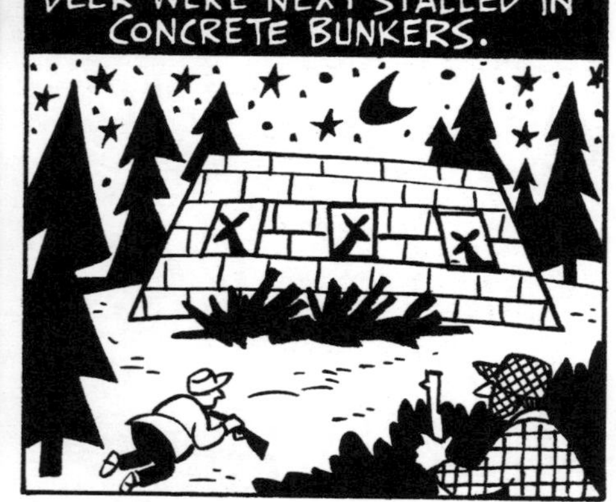
But why stop there? Deer were next stalled in concrete bunkers.

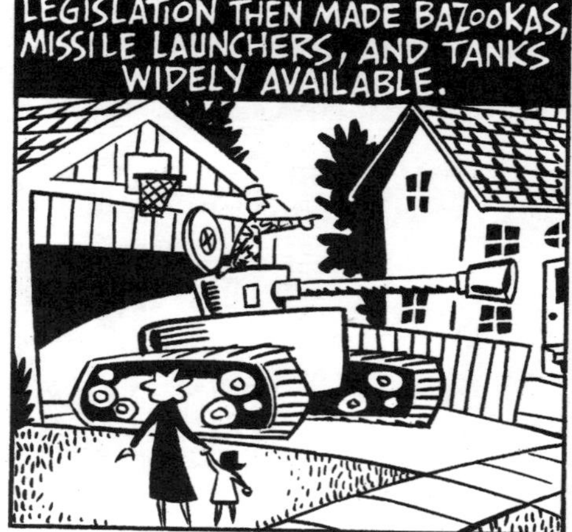
Legislation then made bazookas, missile launchers, and tanks widely available.

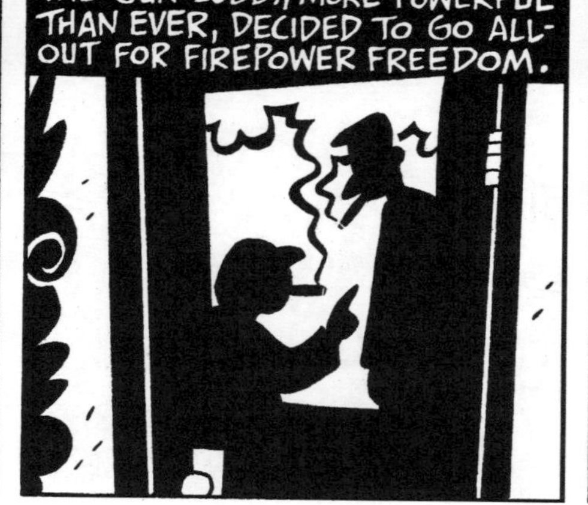
The gun lobby, more powerful than ever, decided to go all-out for firepower freedom.

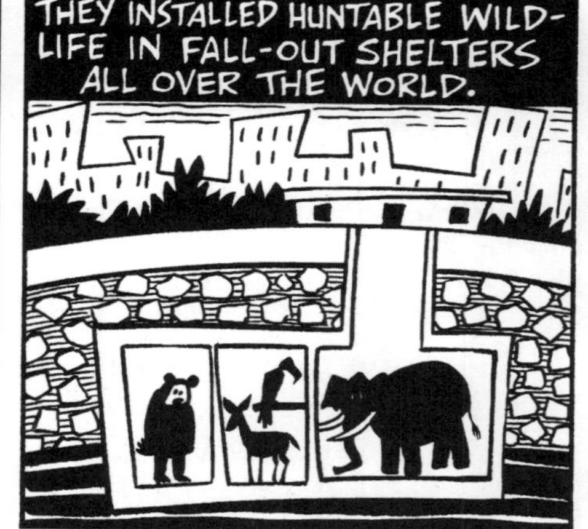
They installed huntable wildlife in fall-out shelters all over the world.

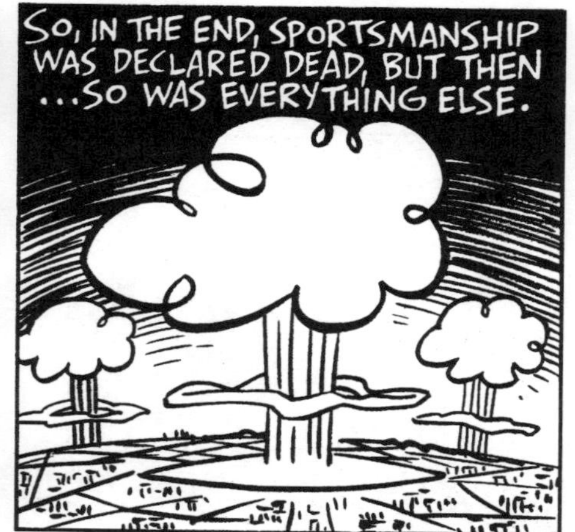
So, in the end, sportsmanship was declared dead, but then ...so was everything else.

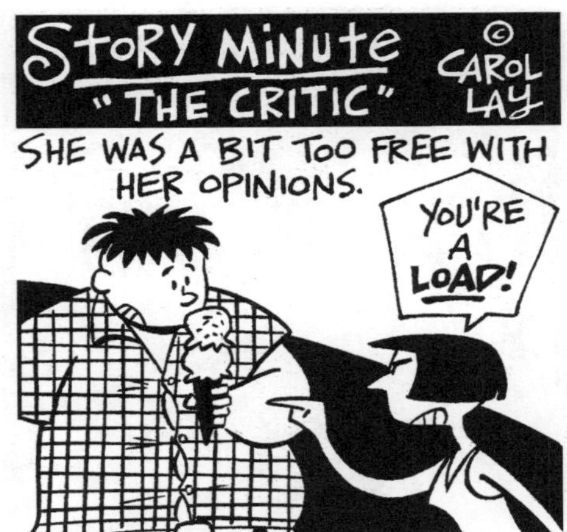
Story Minute
"THE CRITIC"
© CAROL LAY
SHE WAS A BIT TOO FREE WITH HER OPINIONS.
YOU'RE A LOAD!

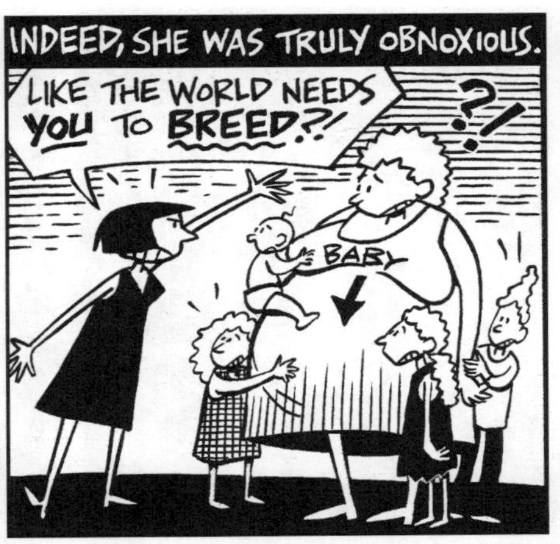
INDEED, SHE WAS TRULY OBNOXIOUS.
LIKE THE WORLD NEEDS YOU TO BREED?!
?!
BABY

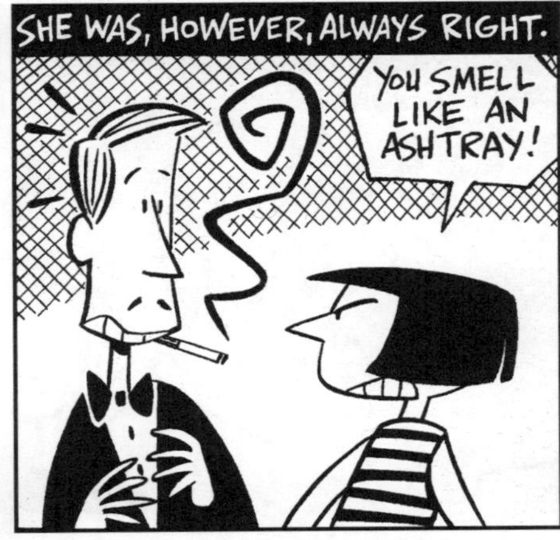
SHE WAS, HOWEVER, ALWAYS RIGHT.
YOU SMELL LIKE AN ASHTRAY!

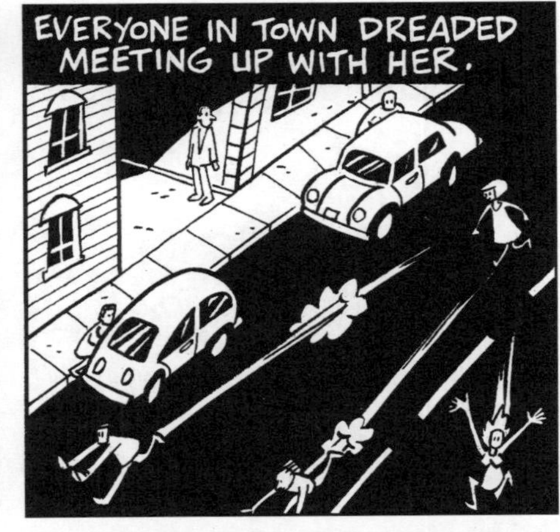
EVERYONE IN TOWN DREADED MEETING UP WITH HER.

MANY BECAME PRISONERS IN THEIR OWN HOMES.
TRAILER TRASH!

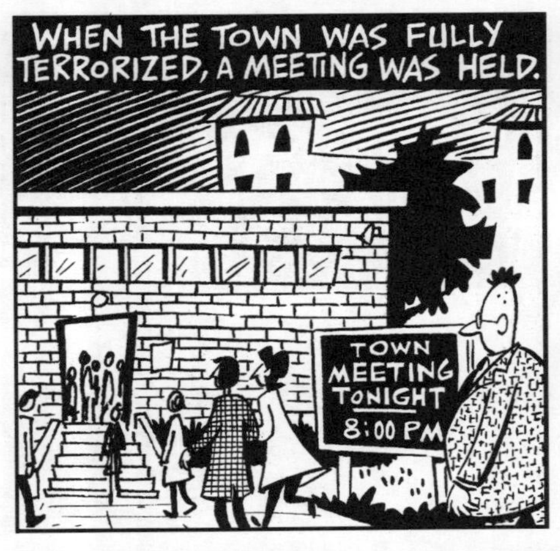
WHEN THE TOWN WAS FULLY TERRORIZED, A MEETING WAS HELD.
TOWN MEETING TONIGHT 8:00 PM

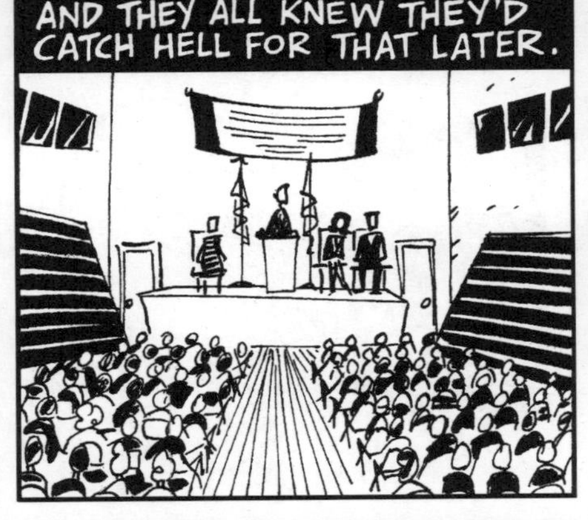
THEY DIDN'T INVITE THEIR CRITIC AND THEY ALL KNEW THEY'D CATCH HELL FOR THAT LATER.

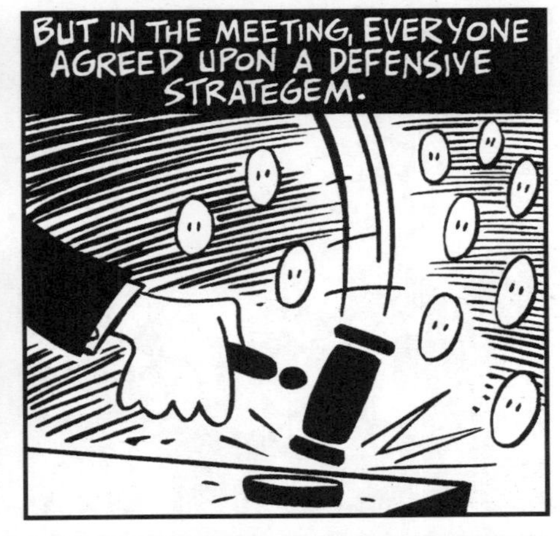
BUT IN THE MEETING, EVERYONE AGREED UPON A DEFENSIVE STRATEGEM.

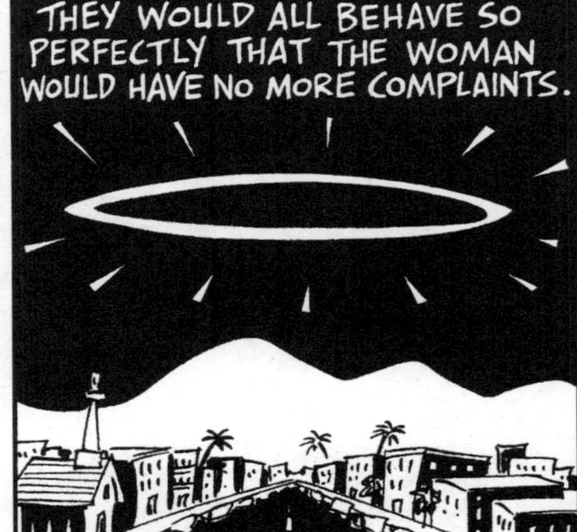
THEY WOULD ALL BEHAVE SO PERFECTLY THAT THE WOMAN WOULD HAVE NO MORE COMPLAINTS.

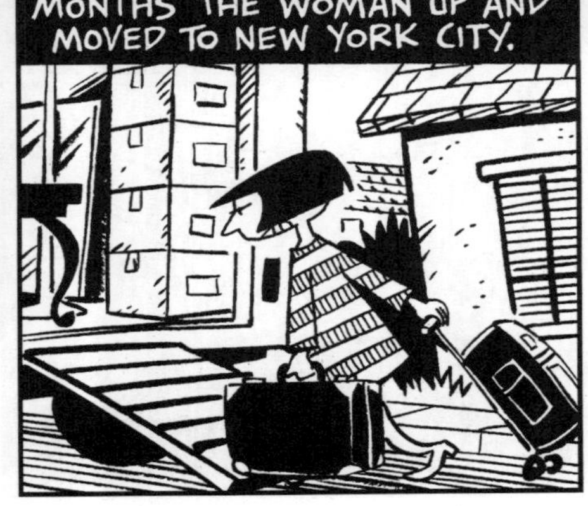
IT WORKED. AFTER THREE MONTHS THE WOMAN UP AND MOVED TO NEW YORK CITY.

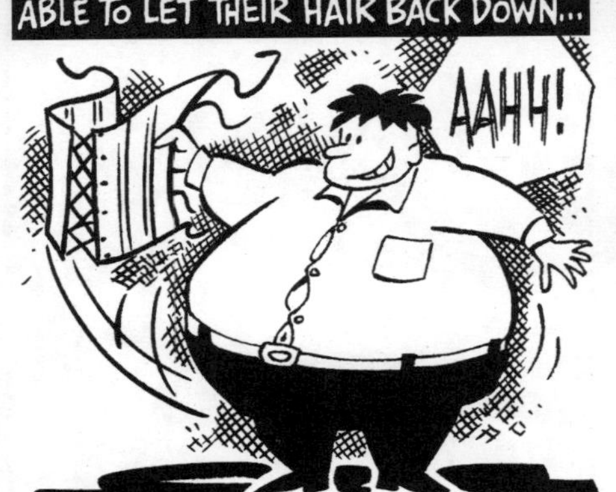
HER FORMER NEIGHBORS WERE ABLE TO LET THEIR HAIR BACK DOWN...
AAHH!

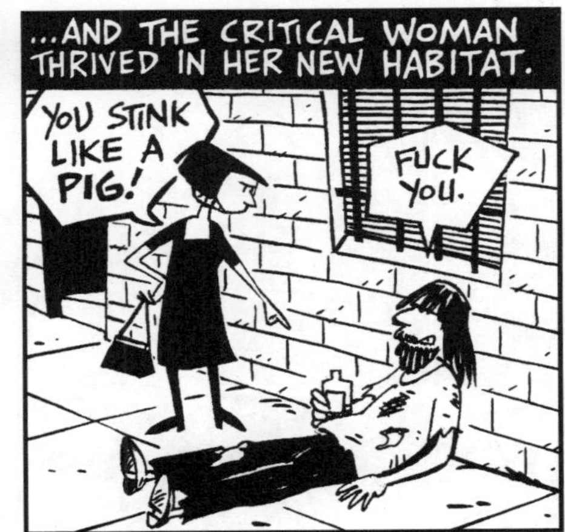
...AND THE CRITICAL WOMAN THRIVED IN HER NEW HABITAT.
YOU STINK LIKE A PIG!
FUCK YOU.

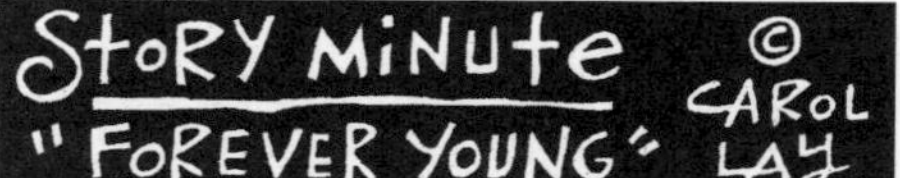
Story Minute
"Forever Young"
© Carol Lay

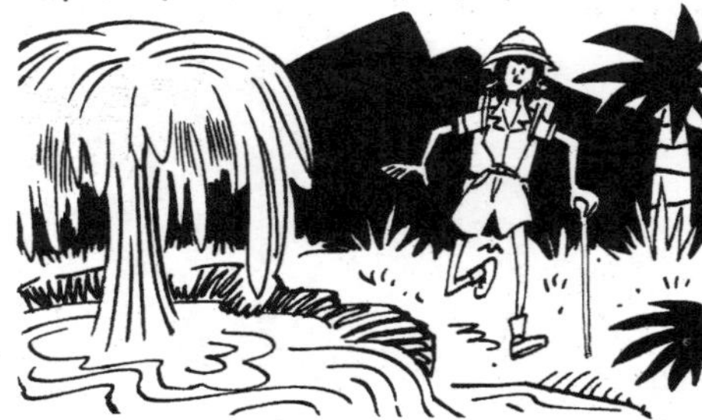
THE EXPLORER STUMBLED UPON THE FOUNTAIN OF YOUTH...

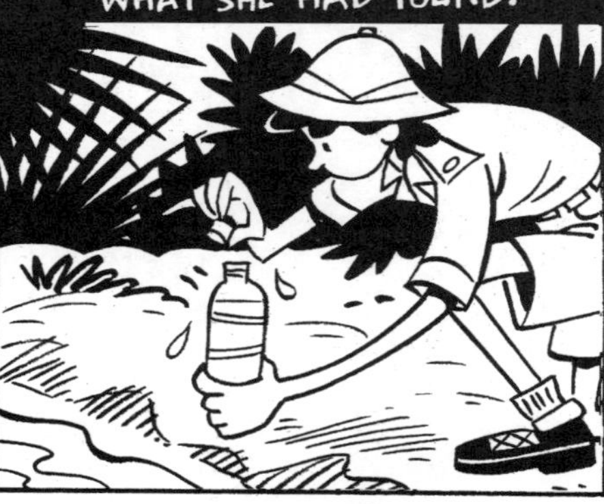
...BUT IT WOULD BE MANY YEARS BEFORE SHE WOULD REALIZE WHAT SHE HAD FOUND.

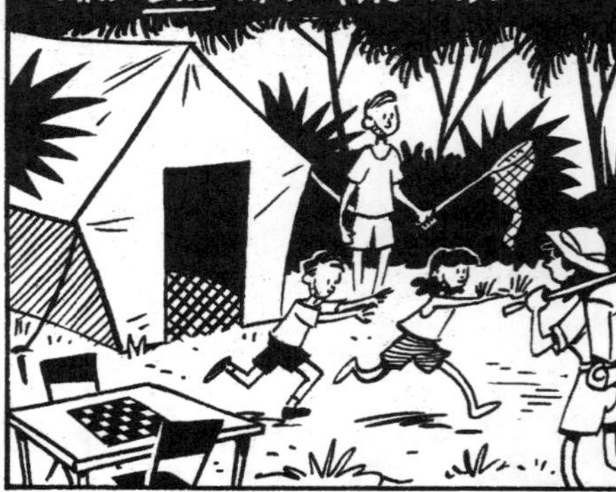
THIS IS BECAUSE THE ELIXIR ONLY WORKED ON VIRGINS AND SHE HAD TWO KIDS.

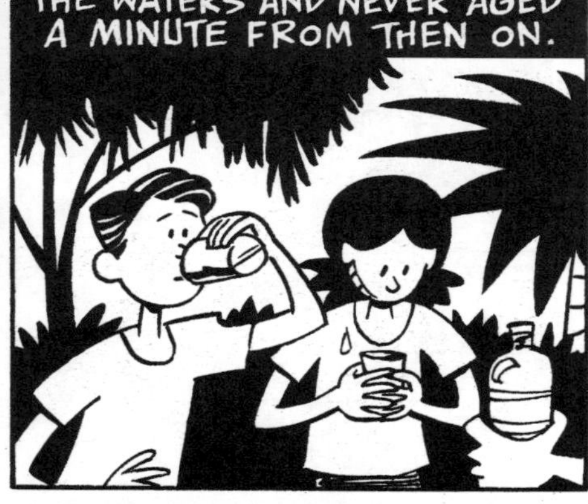
HER CHILDREN, THOUGH, SAMPLED THE WATERS AND NEVER AGED A MINUTE FROM THEN ON.

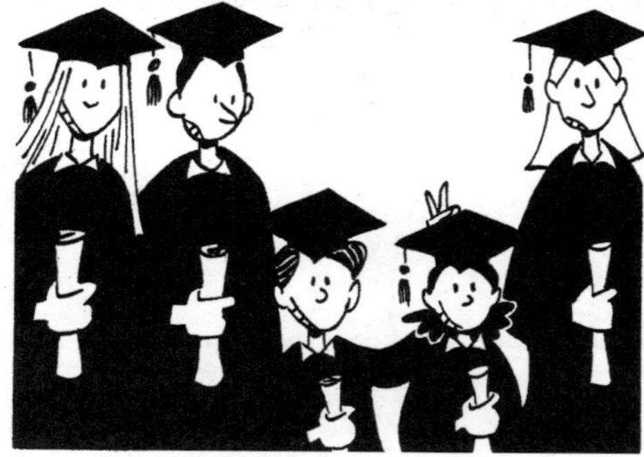
WHEN THEY WERE IN THEIR TWENTIES, THEY STILL LOOKED AND ACTED LIKE YOUNGSTERS.

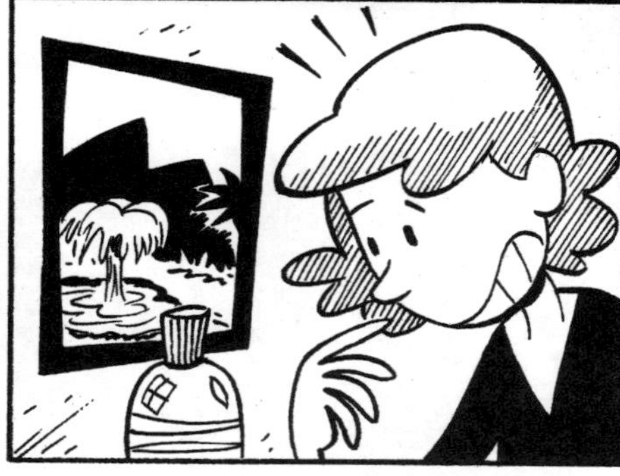
THAT'S WHEN THE EXPLORER FINALLY REALIZED WHAT SHE'D FOUND SO MANY YEARS BEFORE.

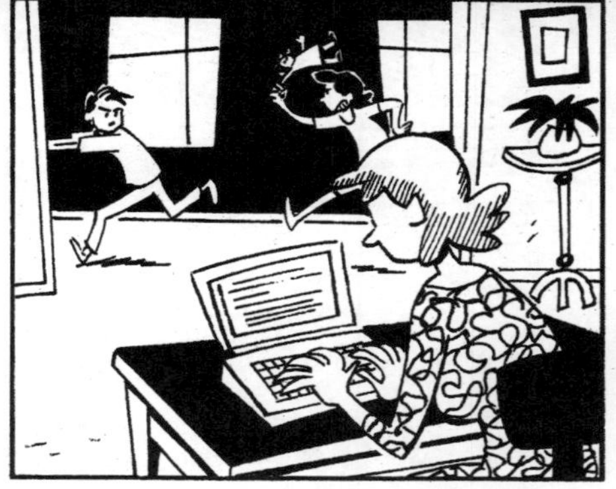
SHE WROTE ABOUT HER DISCOVERY IN A SCIENTIFIC JOURNAL...

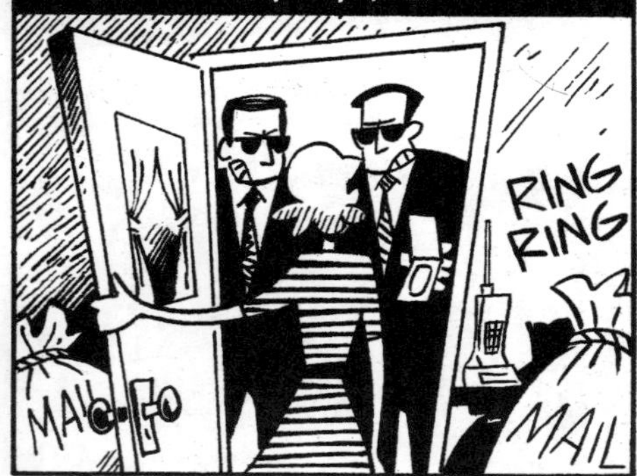
...AND WAS SWAMPED BY DEMANDS TO REVEAL THE WHEREABOUTS OF THE FOUNTAIN.
RING RING
MAIL
MAIL

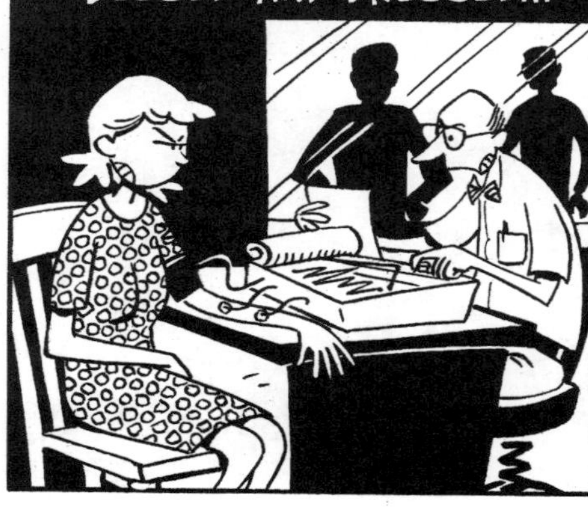
SHE WAS THREATENED, TEMPTED, BUGGED AND DRUGGED...

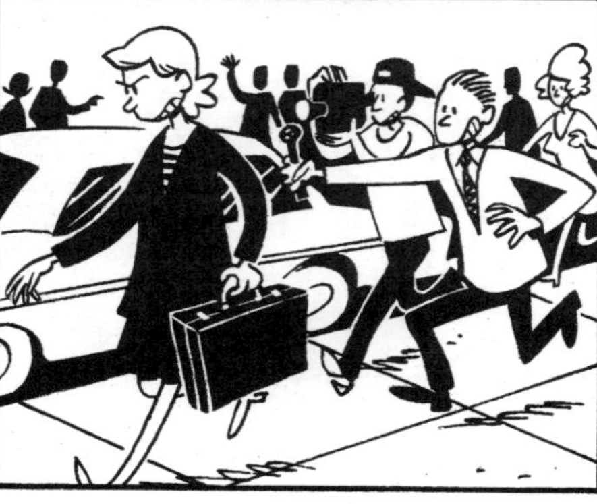
...BUT SHE NEVER TOLD ANYONE WHERE TO FIND THE FOUNTAIN.

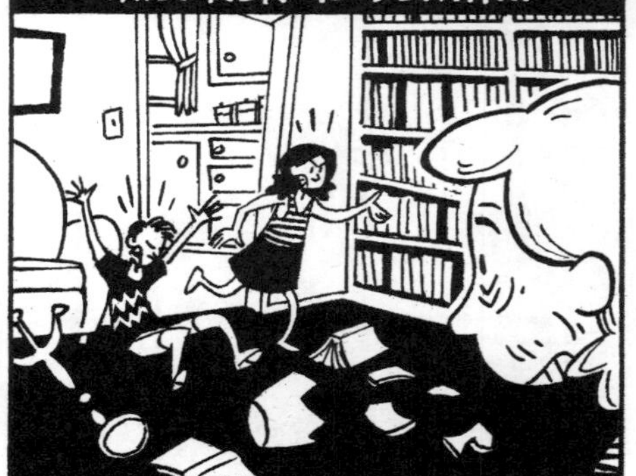
BECAUSE EVEN THOUGH SHE STILL LOVED HER OWN YOUNG CHILDREN TO DEATH...

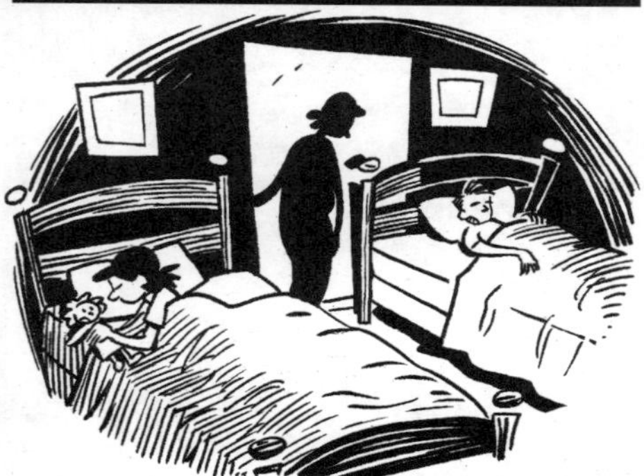
...SHE MOURNED THE LOSS OF THE GRANDCHILDREN SHE KNEW SHE WOULD NEVER HAVE.

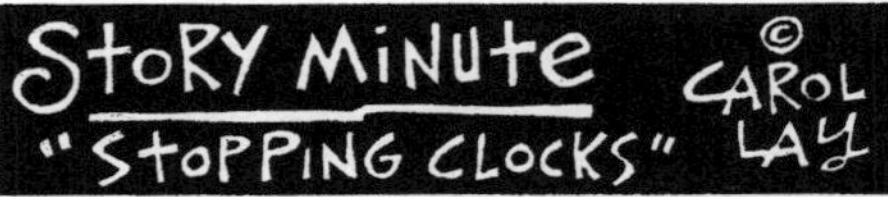


THE EXPLORER NEVER TOLD WHERE SHE'D FOUND THE FOUNTAIN OF YOUTH...

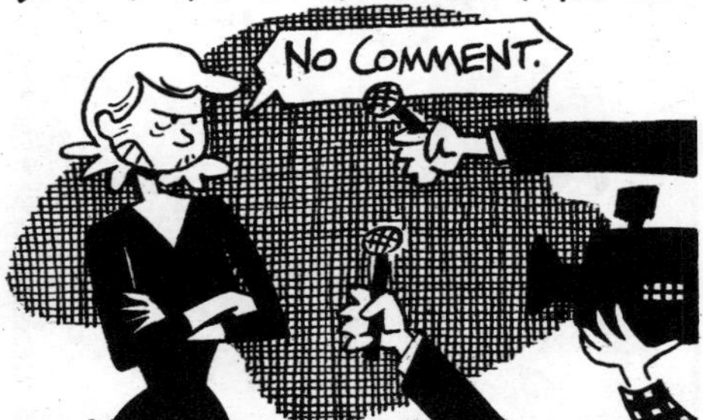


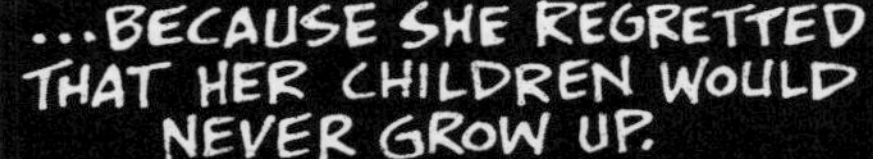


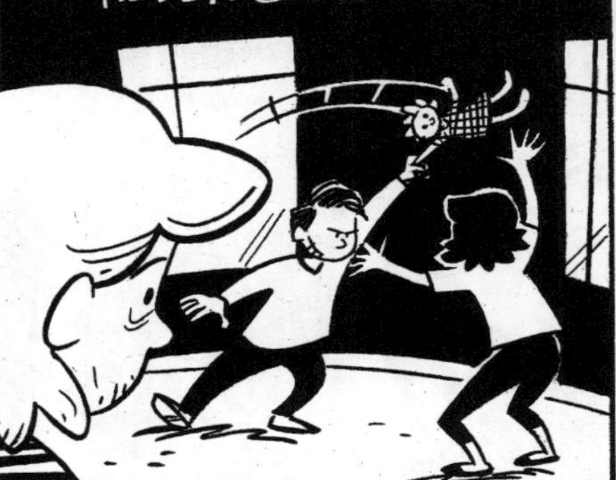

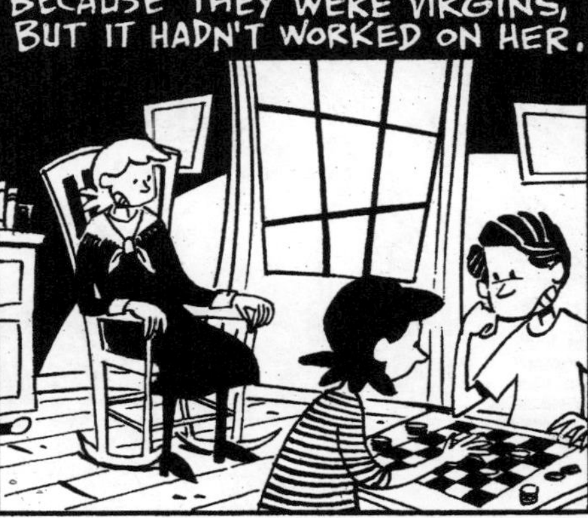


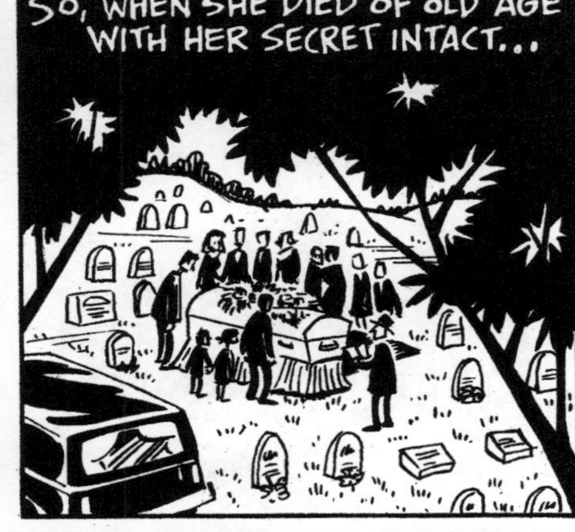


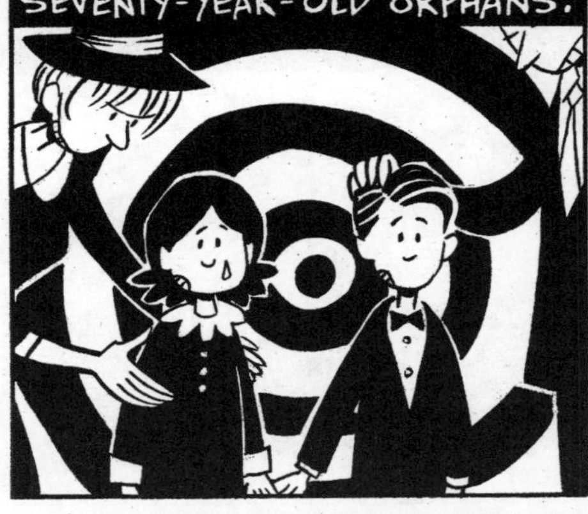


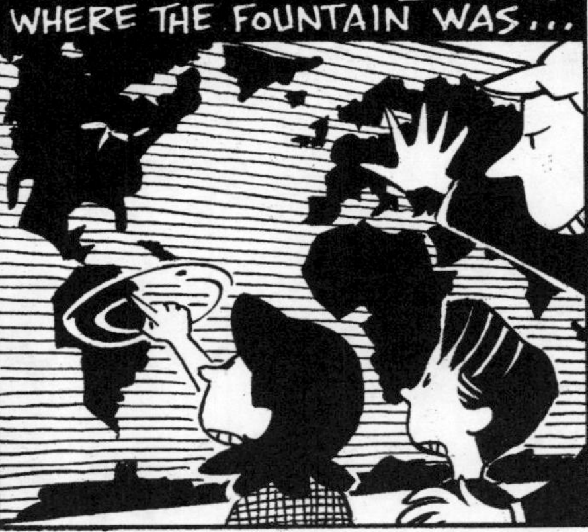


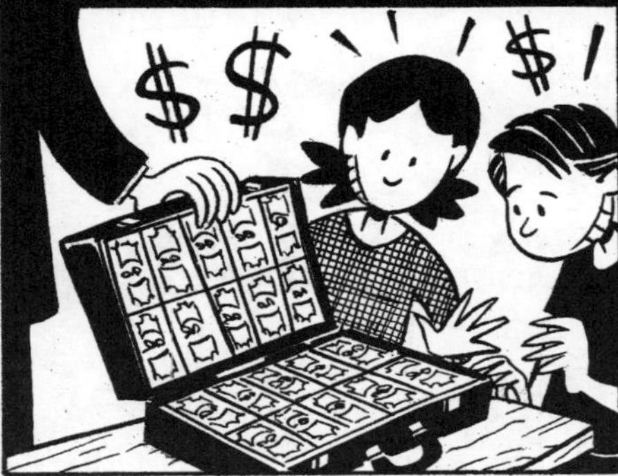


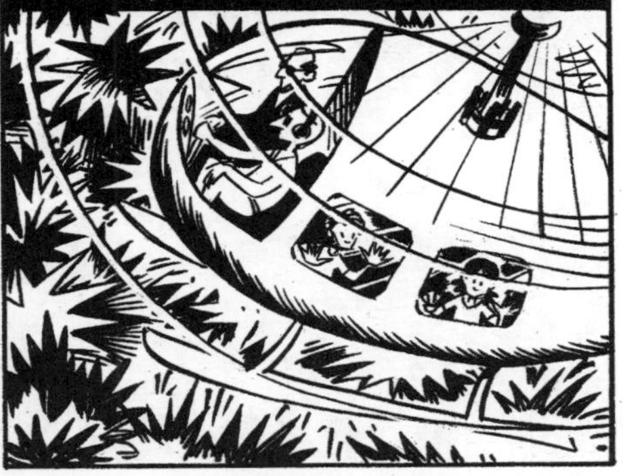


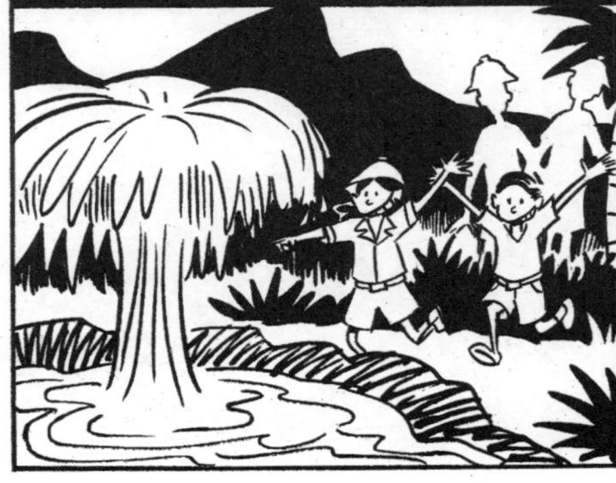


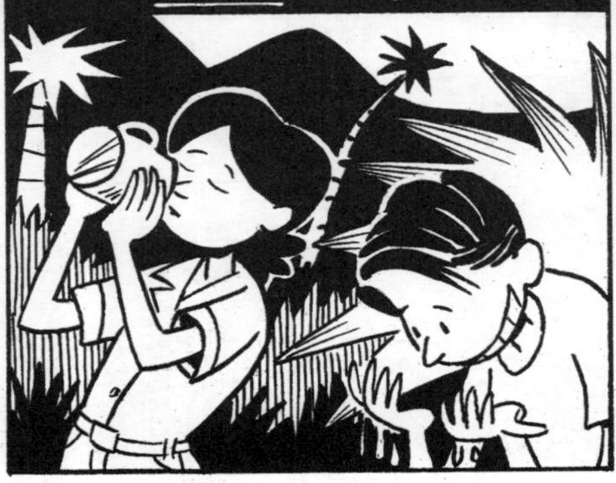


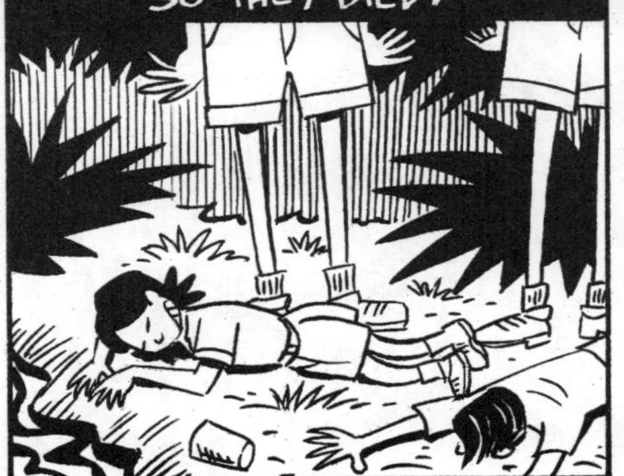


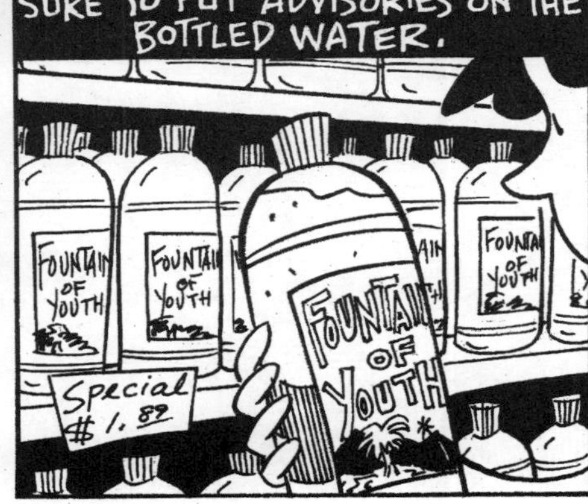

STORY MINUTE © CAROL LAY
"THE AGE OF ESSENCES"
GREEDY PEOPLE BOTTLED THE WATERS OF THE FOUNTAIN OF YOUTH...

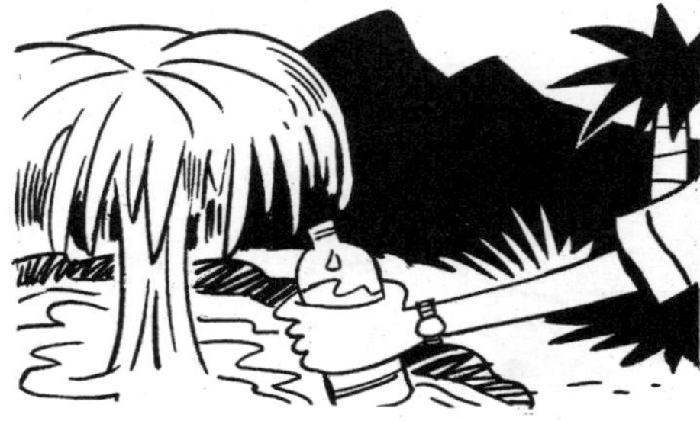

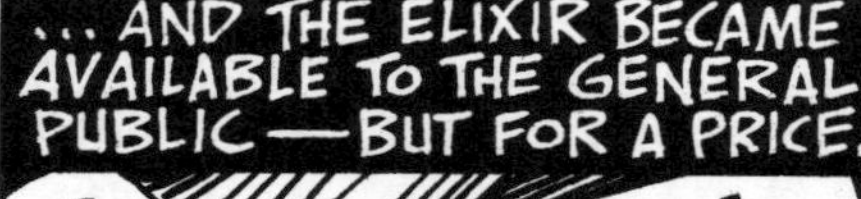
...AND THE ELIXIR BECAME AVAILABLE TO THE GENERAL PUBLIC — BUT FOR A PRICE.

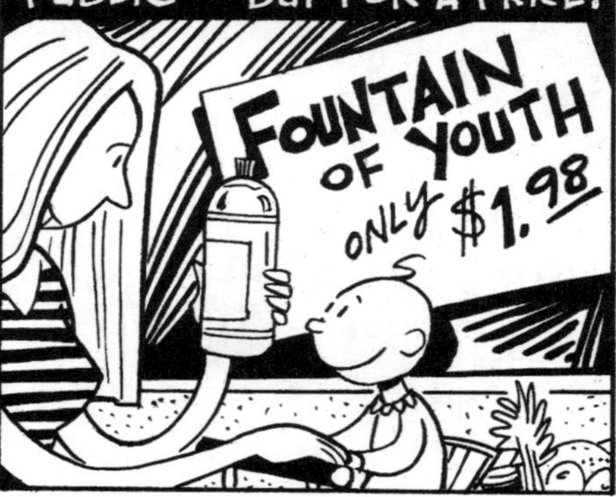
FOUNTAIN OF YOUTH
ONLY $1.98

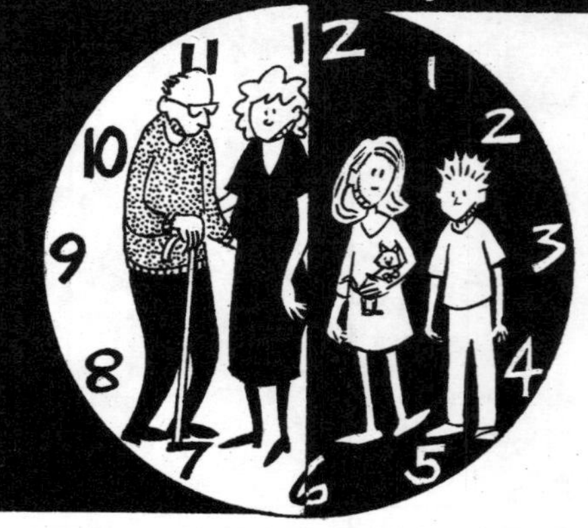
IT ONLY STOPPED THE AGING PROCESS IN VIRGINS...

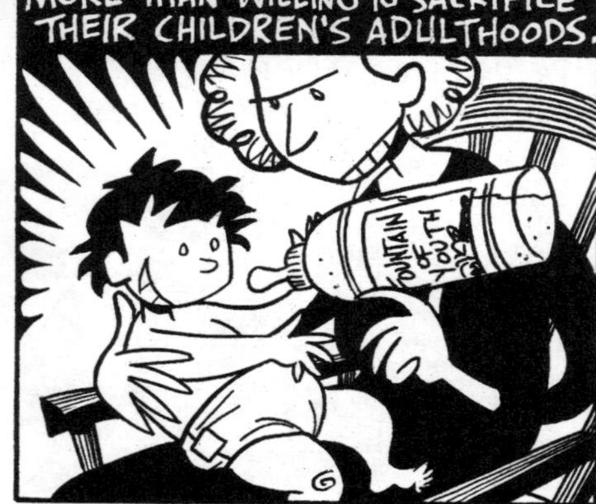
...BUT PLENTY OF PARENTS WERE MORE THAN WILLING TO SACRIFICE THEIR CHILDREN'S ADULTHOODS.

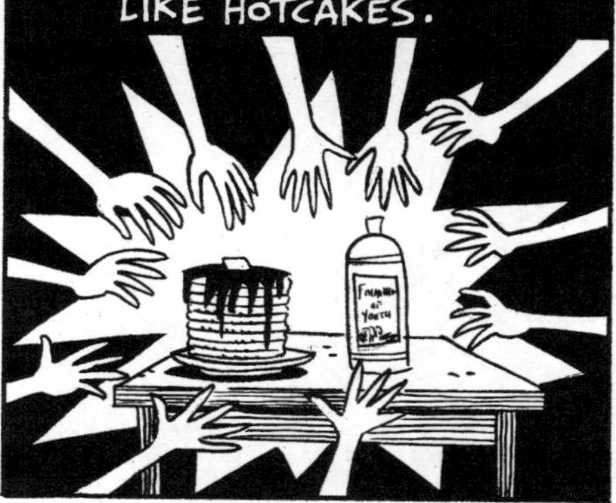
YOUTH WAS PRIZED TOO HIGHLY, IT SEEMED, SO THE ELIXIR SOLD LIKE HOTCAKES.

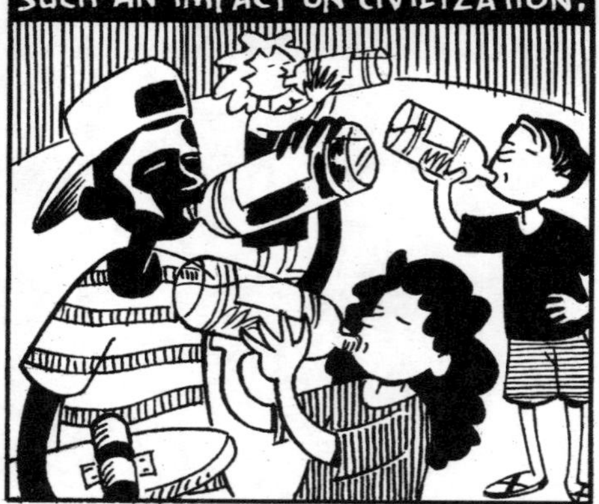
HOT CAKES, HOWEVER, NEVER HAD SUCH AN IMPACT ON CIVILIZATION.

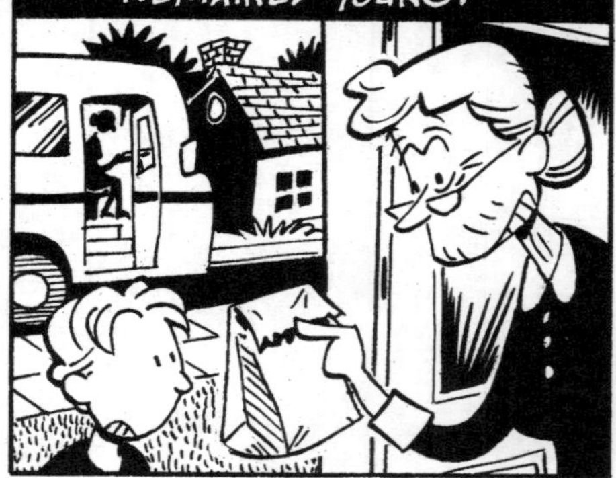
THOSE WHO HAD TO, AGED AS USUAL, BUT THEIR CHILDREN REMAINED YOUNG.

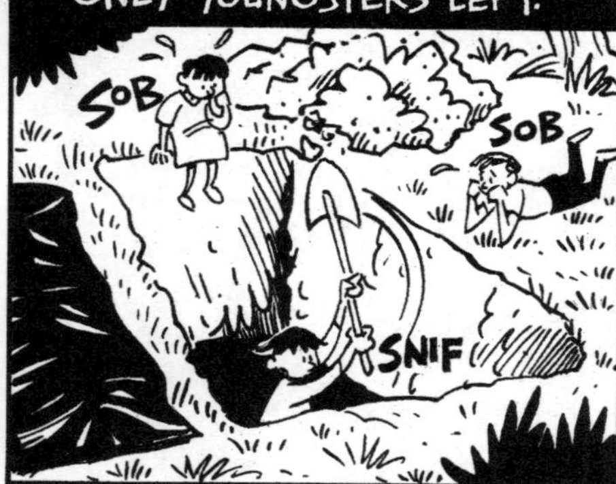
THE OLD ONES DIED OFF ONE BY ONE UNTIL THERE WERE ONLY YOUNGSTERS LEFT.
SOB
SOB
SNIF

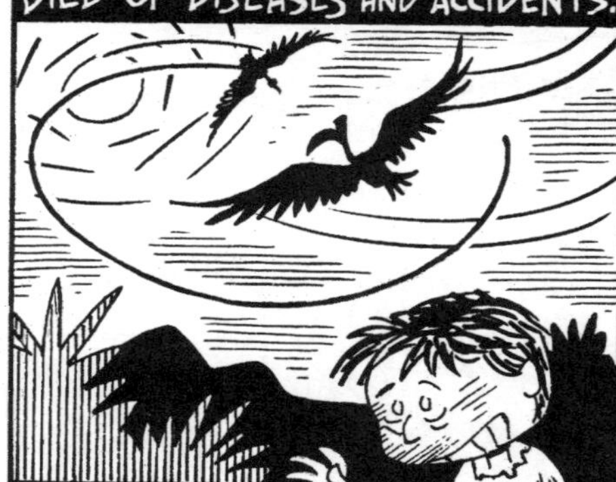
AND, HAVING NO ONE TO LOOK AFTER THEM, THE CHILDREN DIED OF DISEASES AND ACCIDENTS.

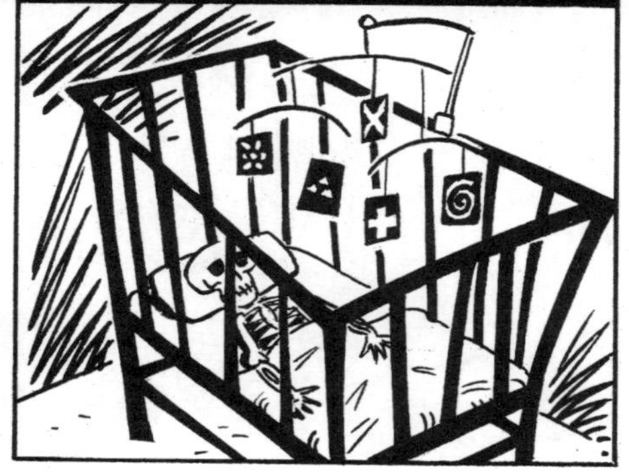
WITH NO HEIRS TO INHERIT THE EARTH, THE HUMAN RACE BECAME EXTINCT.

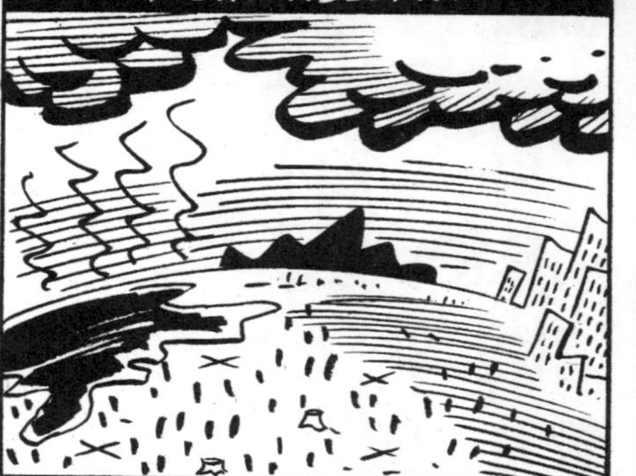
EDEN RESEMBLED A JUNKYARD, BUT EVENTUALLY IT WOULD RIGHT ITSELF...

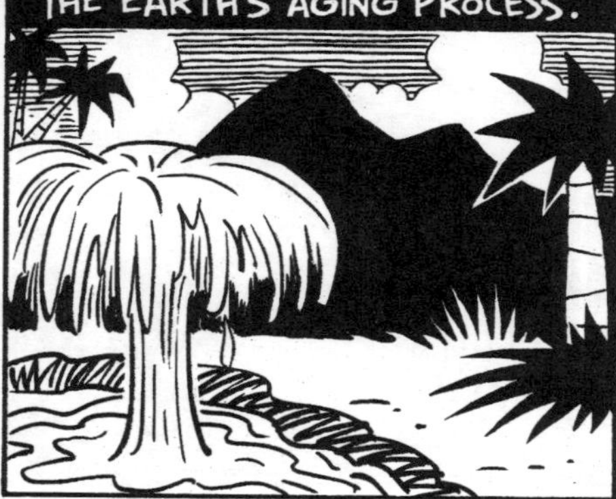
...FOR THE FOUNTAIN OF YOUTH HAD DONE ITS JOB IN STOPPING THE EARTH'S AGING PROCESS.

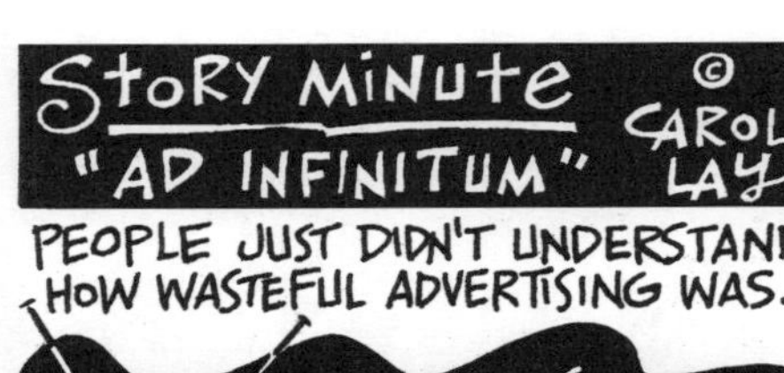
Story Minute
"Ad Infinitum"
© Carol Lay
People just didn't understand how wasteful advertising was.

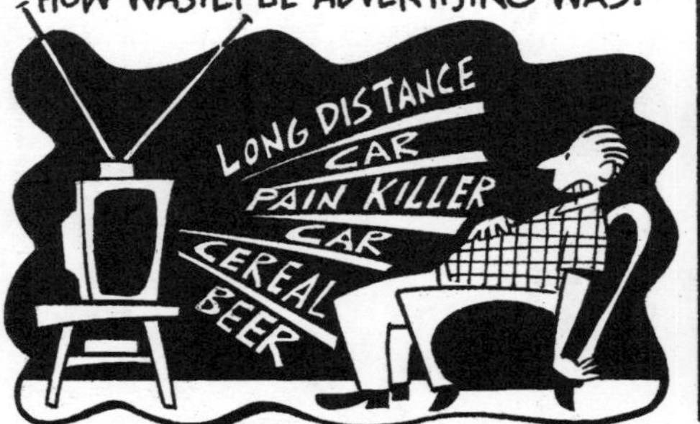
Long distance
Car
Pain killer
Car
Cereal
Beer

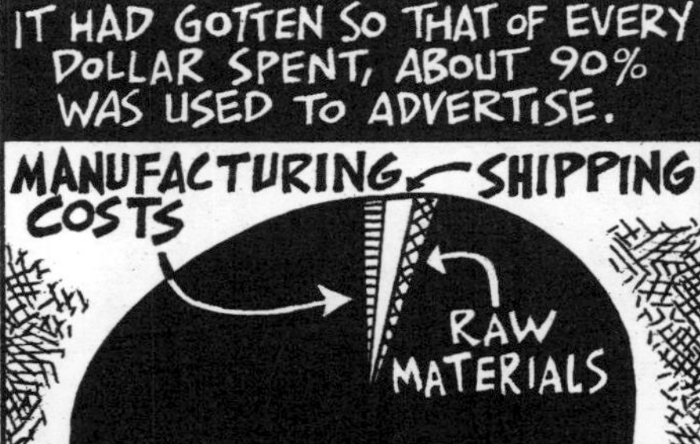
It had gotten so that of every dollar spent, about 90% was used to advertise.
Manufacturing costs
Shipping
Raw materials
Promotional costs

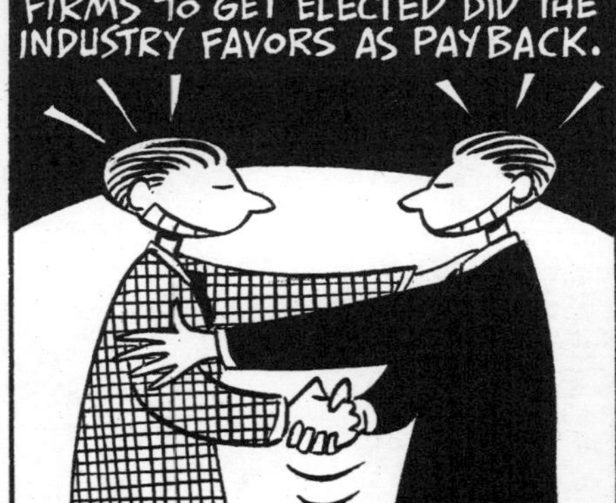
Politicians who had used ad firms to get elected did the industry favors as payback.

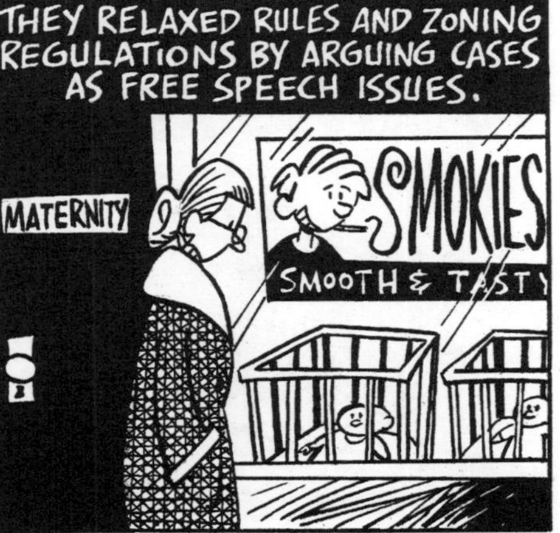
They relaxed rules and zoning regulations by arguing cases as free speech issues.
Maternity
Smokies
Smooth & Tasty

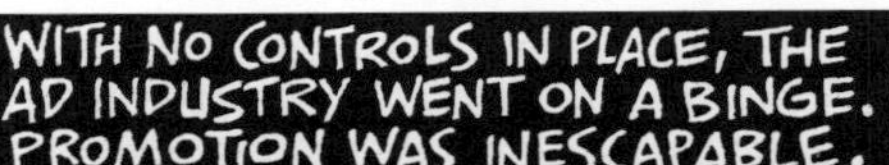
With no controls in place, the ad industry went on a binge. Promotion was inescapable.

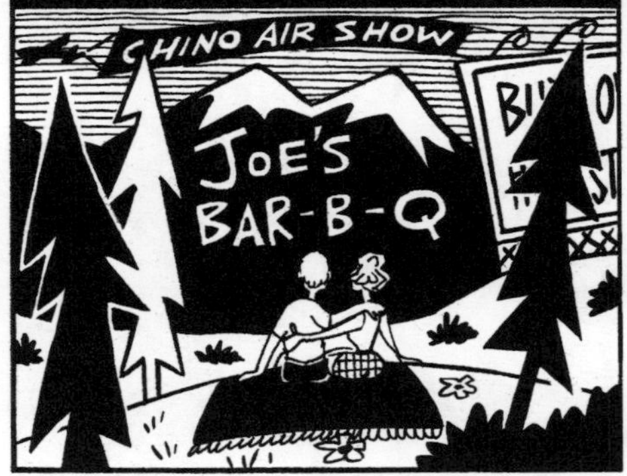
Chino Air Show
Joe's Bar-B-Q

When landscapes became over-saturated, personal product placement came into vogue.

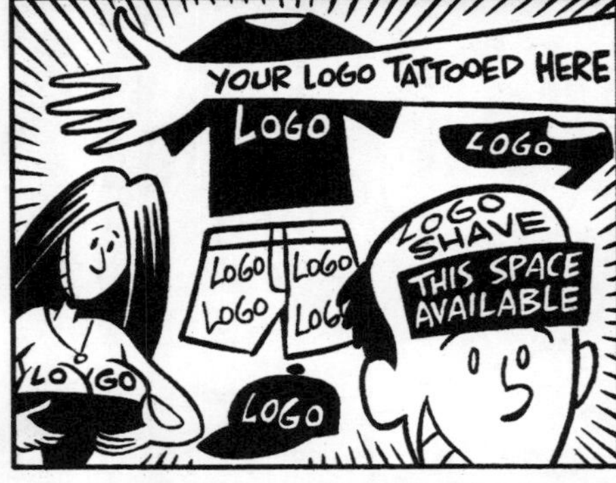
Your logo tattooed here
Logo
Logo
Logo shave
This space available
Logo Logo Logo
Logo
Logo

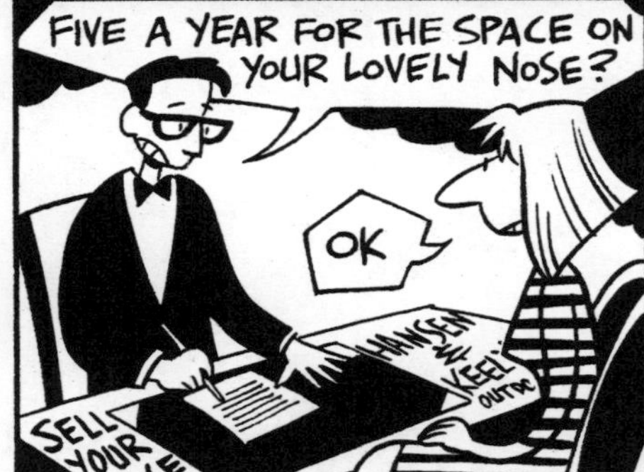
For an annual stipend, a person could lease him or herself out for ad space.
Five a year for the space on your lovely nose?
OK

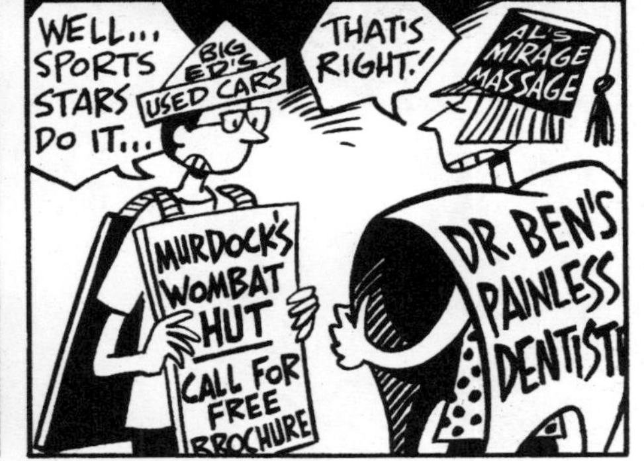
Because ad budgets inflated retail prices enormously, people needed the extra cash.
Well... sports stars do it...
That's right!
Big Ed's Used Cars
Al's Mirage Massage
Murdock's Wombat Hut
Call for free brochure
Dr. Ben's Painless

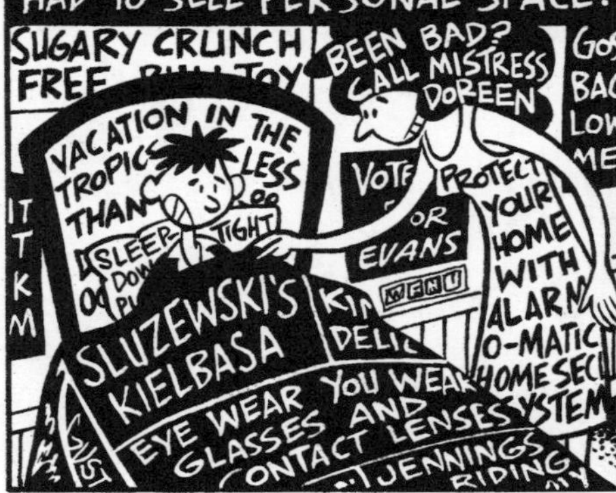
And the more the companies advertised, the more folks had to sell personal space.
Sugary Crunch
Been bad? Call Mistress Doreen
Vacation in the tropics less than
Vote for Evans
Protect your home with Alarm-O-Matic
Sluzewski's Kielbasa
Eye wear you wear
Glasses and contact lenses

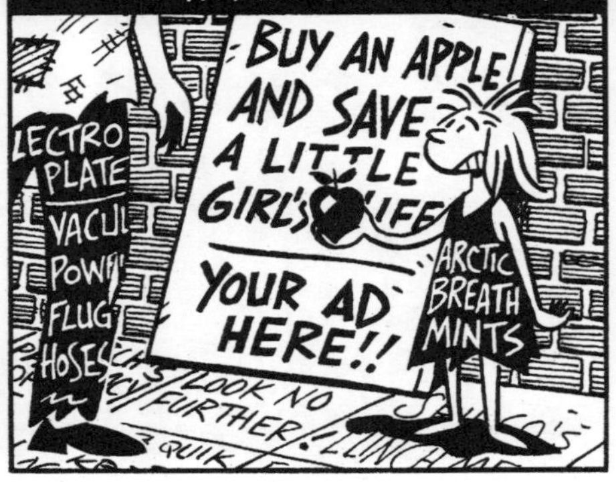
The whole business spiraled out of control into a world-wide economic depression.
Buy an apple and save a little girl's life
Your ad here!!
Arctic Breath Mints
Look no further

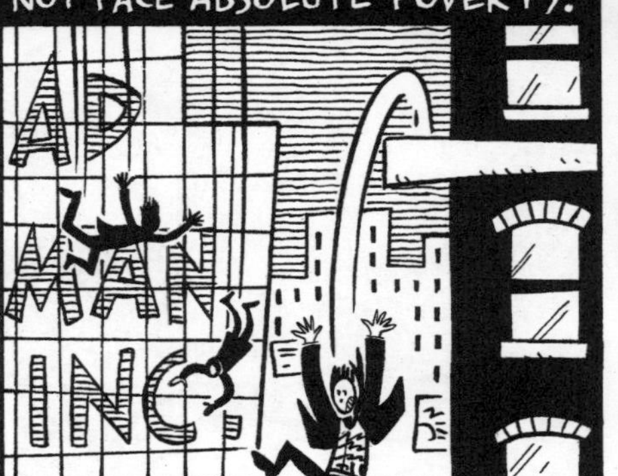
Having adapted to maximum materialism, most folks could not face absolute poverty.
Ad Man Inc.

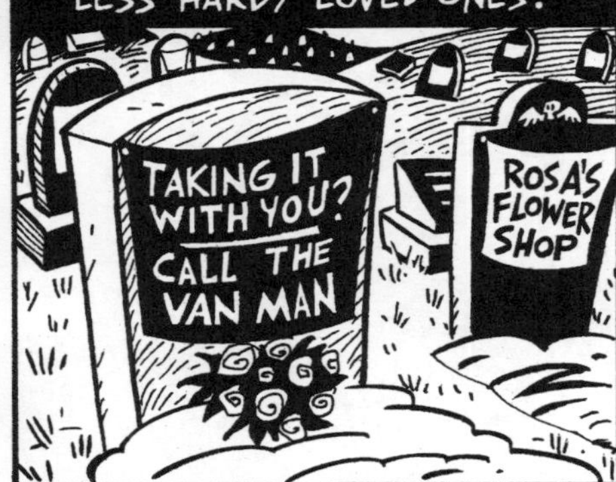
But those who survived learned to deal with the loss of their less hardy loved ones.
Taking it with you? Call the Van Man
Rosa's Flower Shop

STORY MINUTE
"ATAVISION"
© CAROL LAY

THE WOMAN WAS A DEDICATED PSYCHIC EXPLORER.

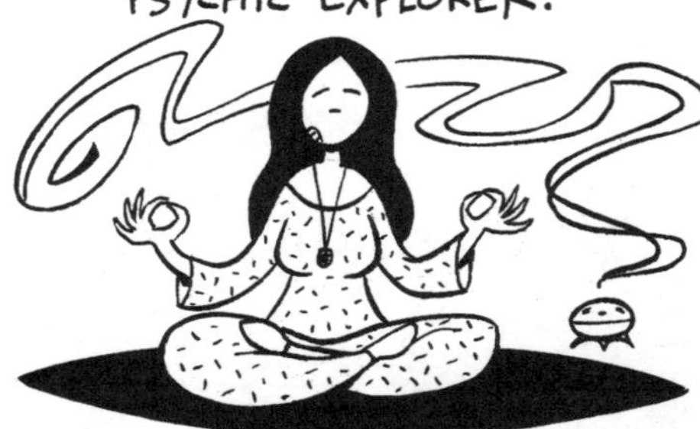

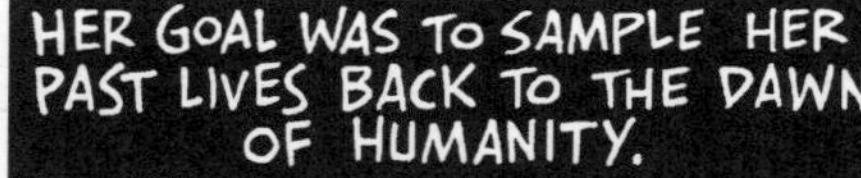


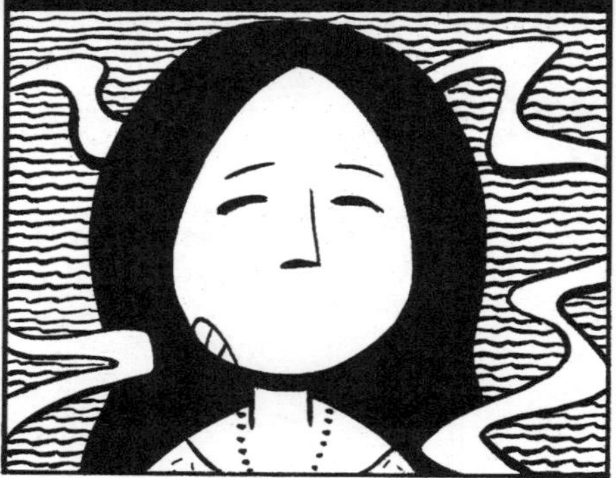

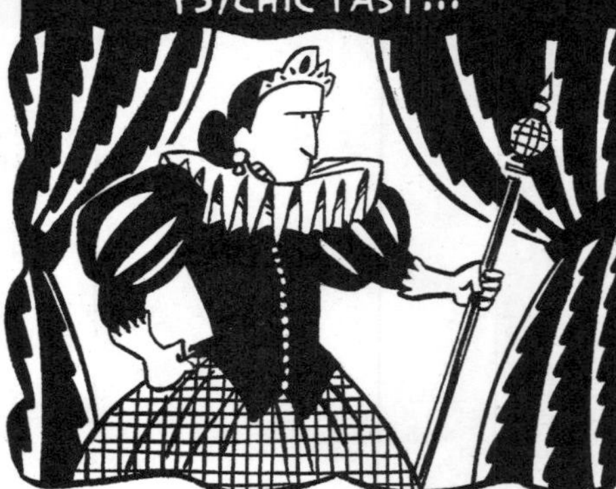


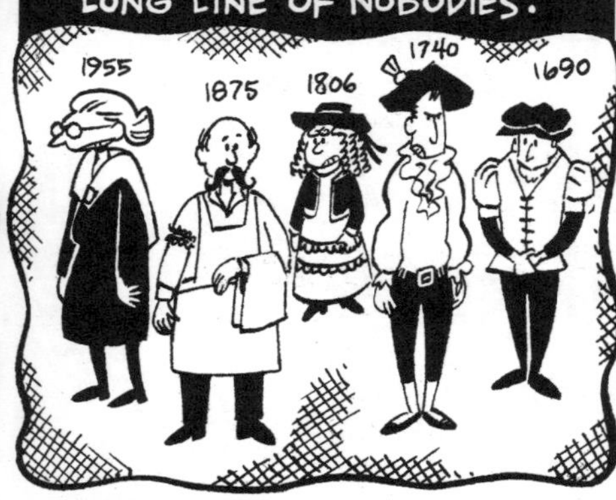


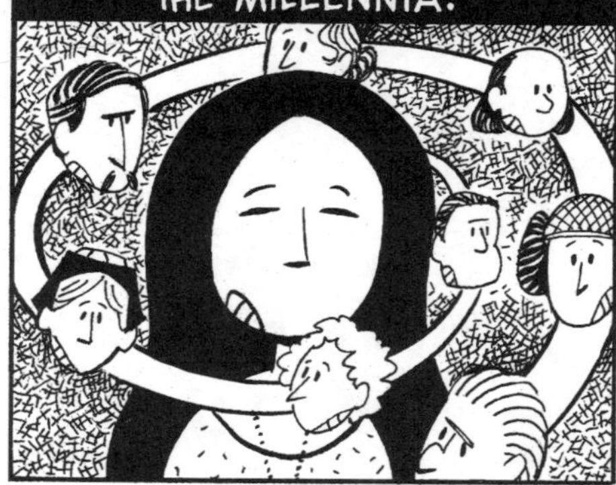


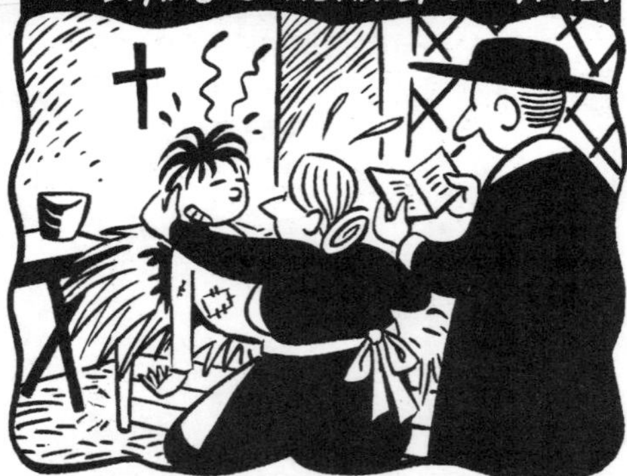


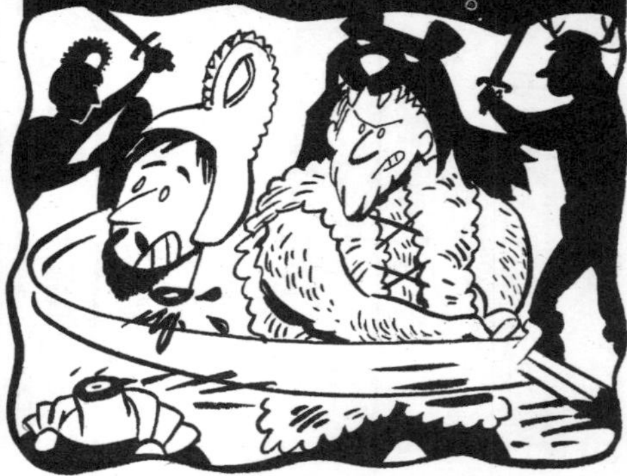


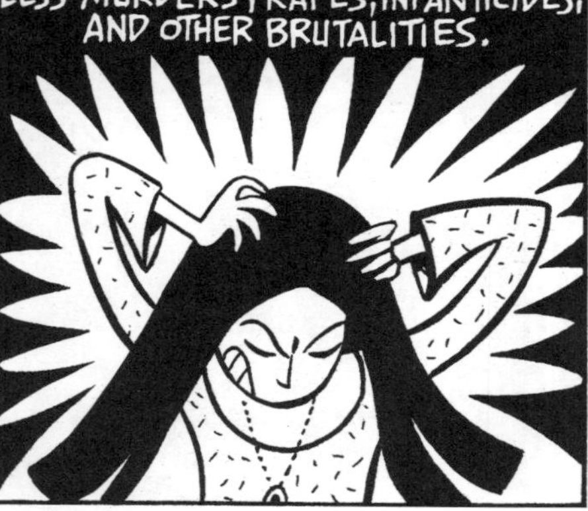


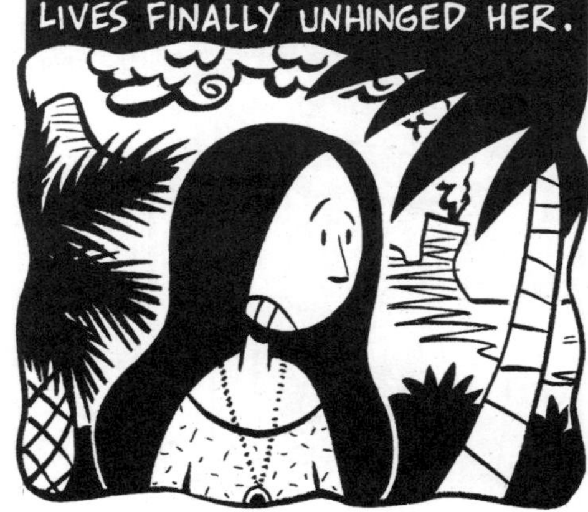


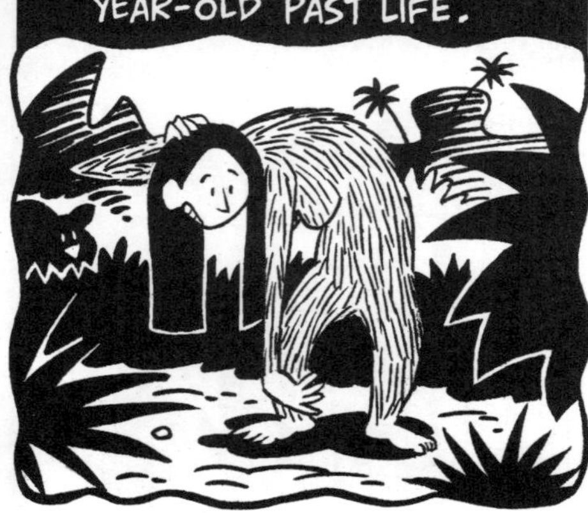


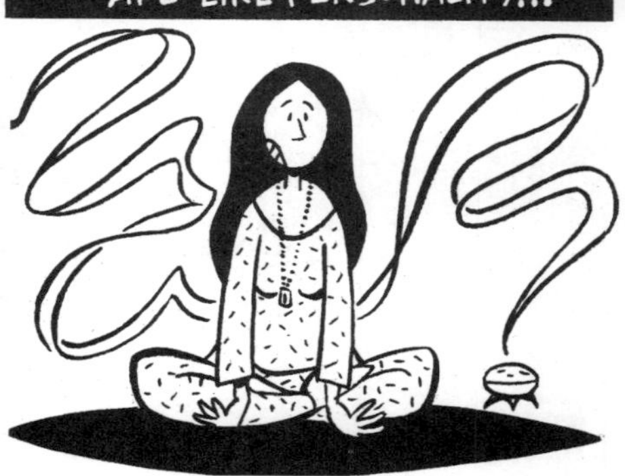


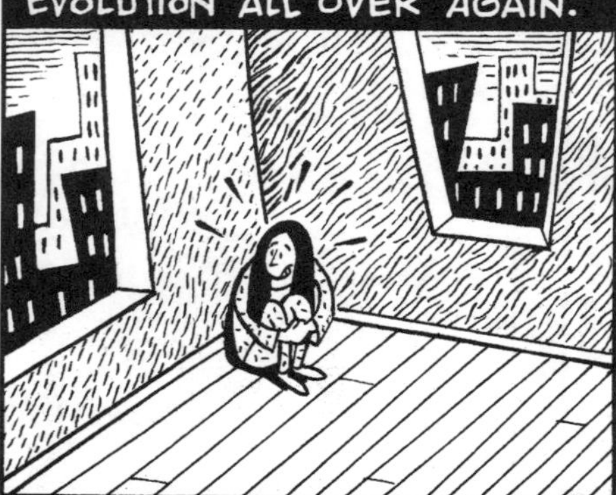

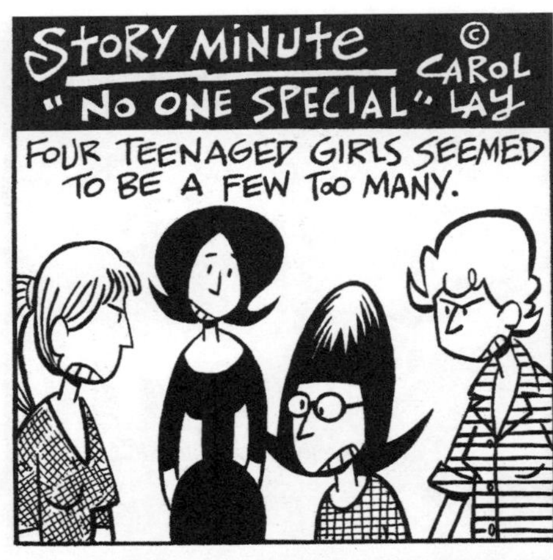

STORY MINUTE
© CAROL LAY
"NO ONE SPECIAL"
FOUR TEENAGED GIRLS SEEMED TO BE A FEW TOO MANY.


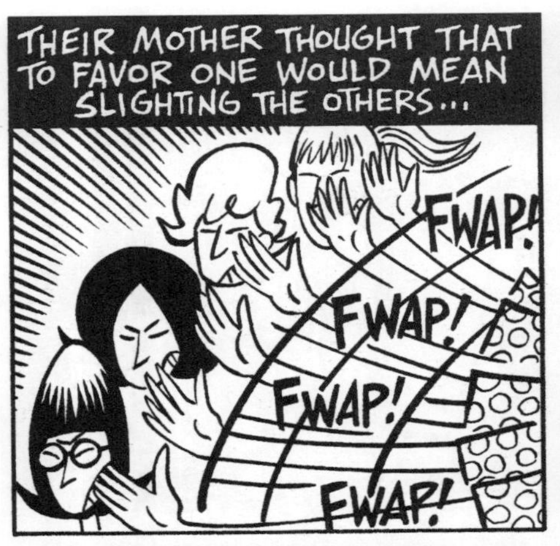

THEIR MOTHER THOUGHT THAT TO FAVOR ONE WOULD MEAN SLIGHTING THE OTHERS...
FWAP!
FWAP!
FWAP!
FWAP!


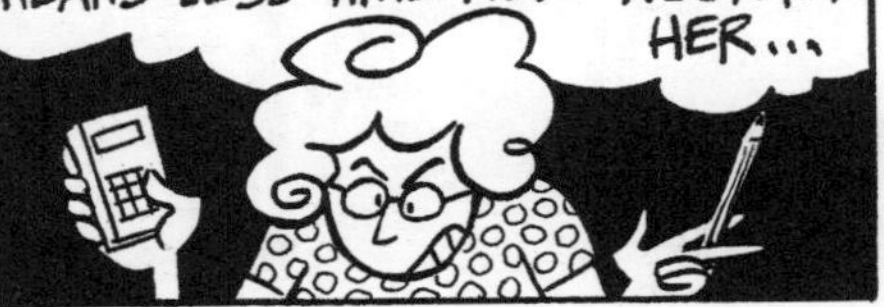

...SO THEY ALL GOT EQUAL TIME AND TREATMENT—AND VERY LITTLE OF THAT.
LET'S SEE...15 MINUTES AND A TRIP TO THE DENTIST FOR EMMA, 25 MINUTES AND A RIDE TO A PARTY FOR AMY, 10 MINUTES AND A CONFERENCE WITH HER TEACHER FOR LIZ, AND AN HOUR WITH CONNIE WHICH MEANS LESS TIME NEXT WEEK FOR HER...


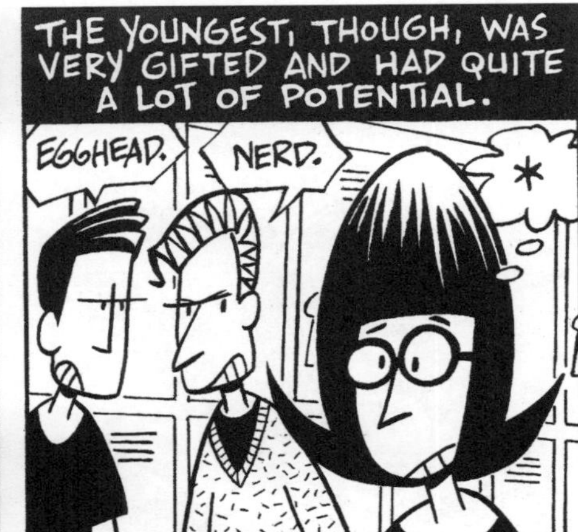

THE YOUNGEST, THOUGH, WAS VERY GIFTED AND HAD QUITE A LOT OF POTENTIAL.
EGGHEAD.
NERD.
*


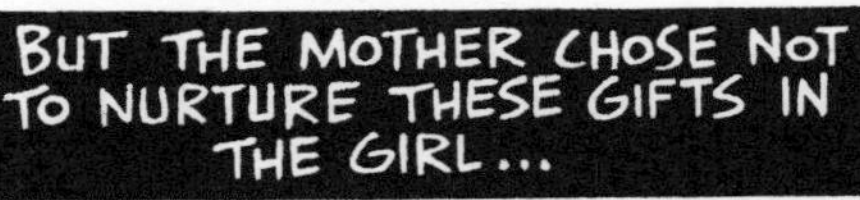

BUT THE MOTHER CHOSE NOT TO NURTURE THESE GIFTS IN THE GIRL...


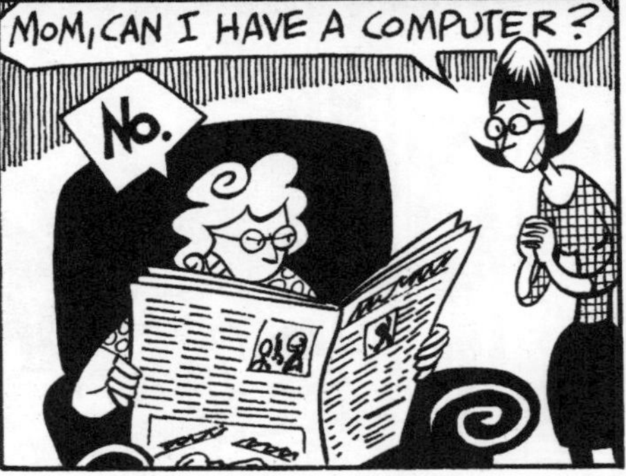

MOM, CAN I HAVE A COMPUTER?
NO.


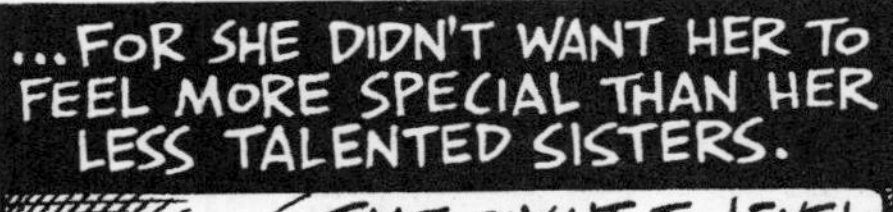

...FOR SHE DIDN'T WANT HER TO FEEL MORE SPECIAL THAN HER LESS TALENTED SISTERS.


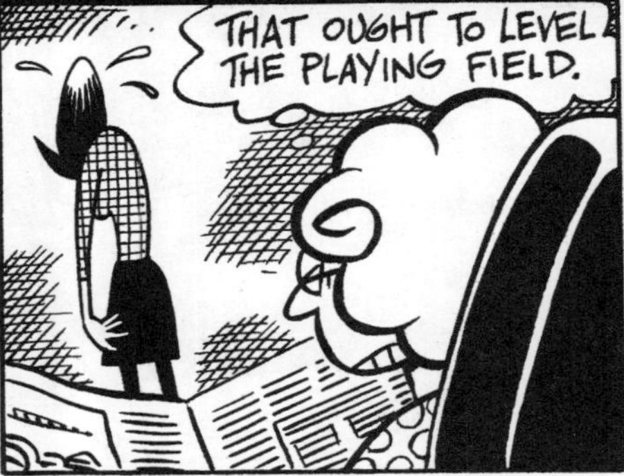

THAT OUGHT TO LEVEL THE PLAYING FIELD.


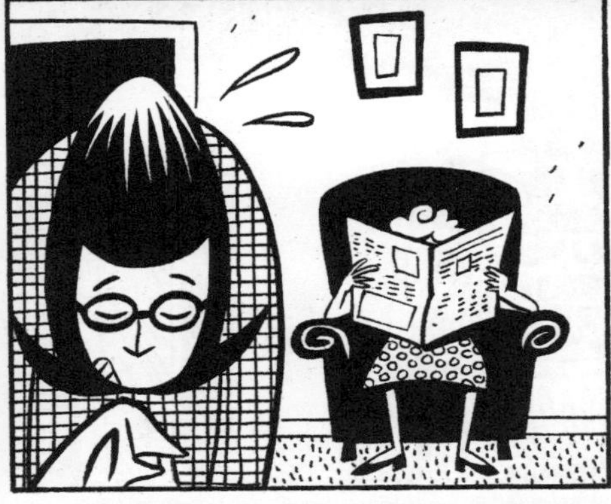

BUT HER MOTHER'S GOOD INTENTIONS BACKFIRED...


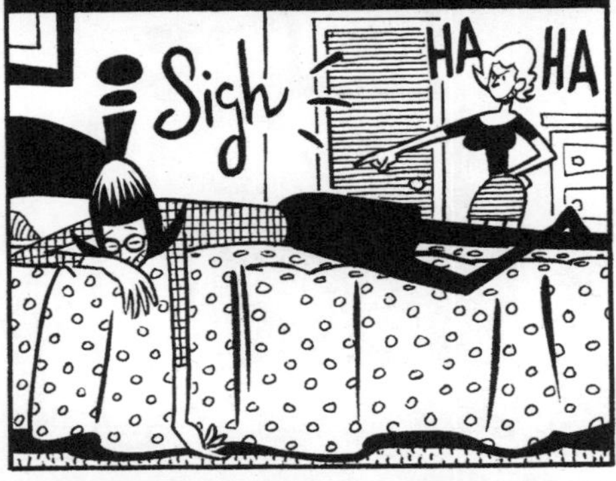

...AND INSTEAD OF FEELING SPECIAL, THE GIRL JUST FELT WORTHLESS.
Sigh
HA HA


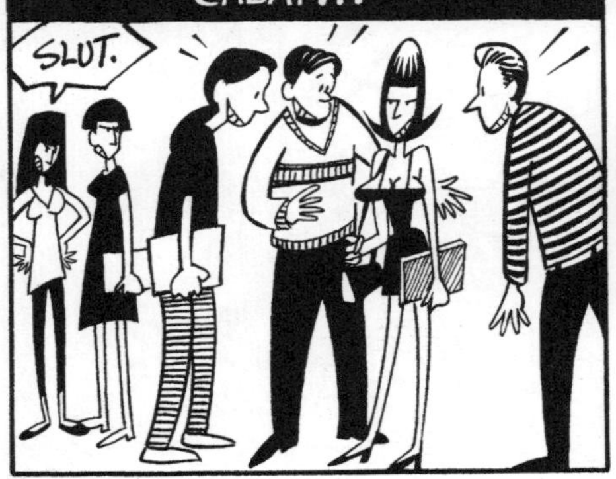

EVENTUALLY SHE WENT FROM FEELING WORTHLESS TO BEING CHEAP...
SLUT.


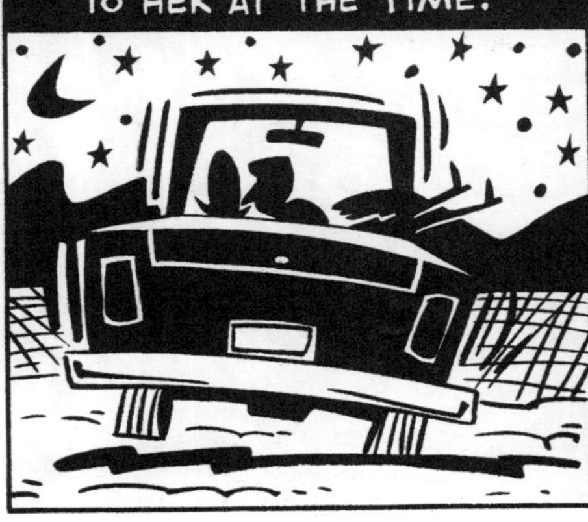

...WHICH SEEMED A STEP UP TO HER AT THE TIME.


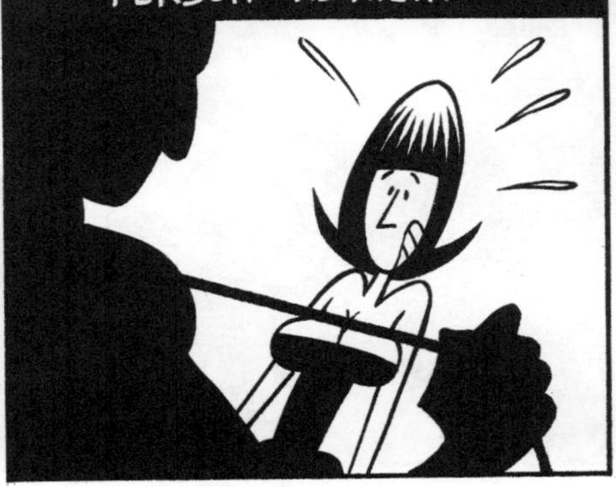

UNFORTUNATELY, SHE TRIED TO GET ATTENTION FROM THE WRONG PERSON ONE NIGHT...


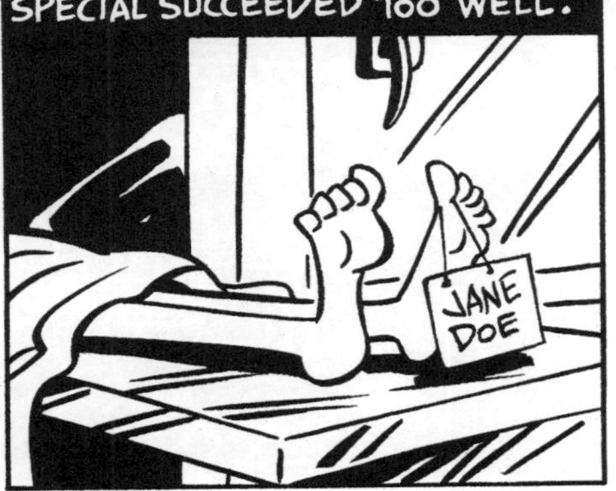

...AND HER MOTHER'S EFFORTS TO KEEP HER FROM FEELING SPECIAL SUCCEEDED TOO WELL.
JANE DOE

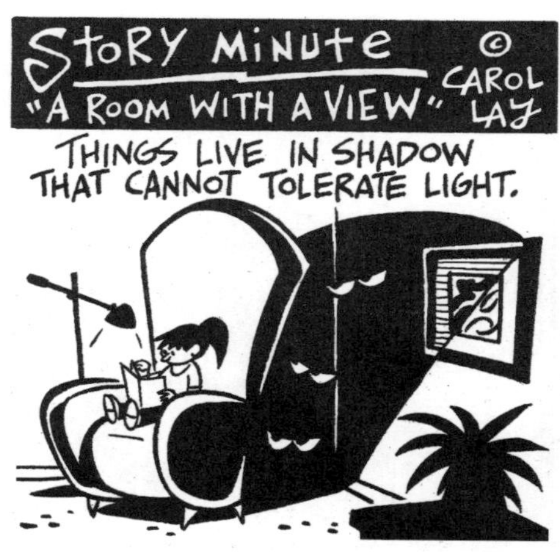
STORY MINUTE © CAROL LAY
"A ROOM WITH A VIEW"
THINGS LIVE IN SHADOW THAT CANNOT TOLERATE LIGHT.

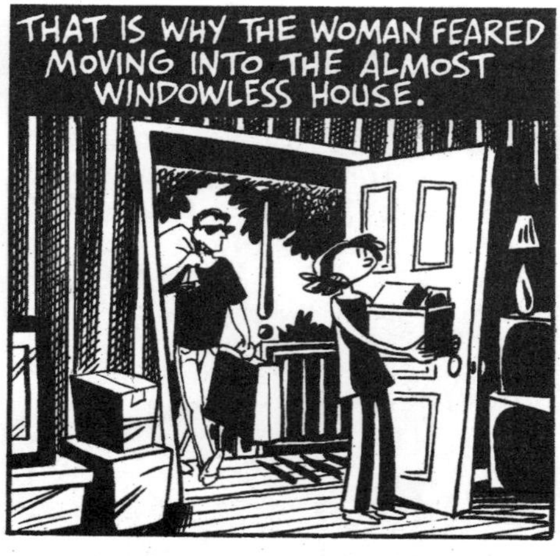
THAT IS WHY THE WOMAN FEARED MOVING INTO THE ALMOST WINDOWLESS HOUSE.

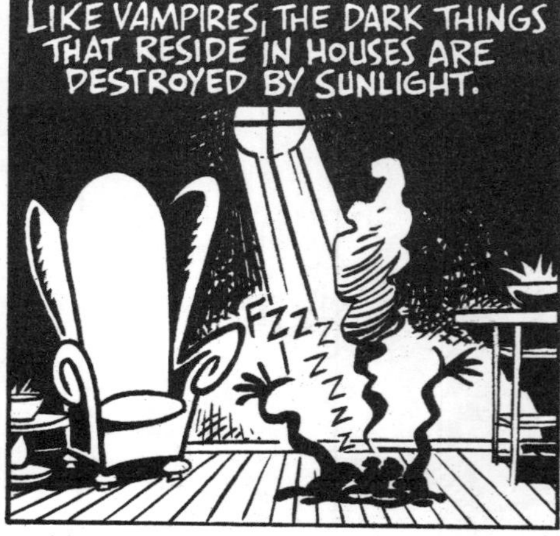
LIKE VAMPIRES, THE DARK THINGS THAT RESIDE IN HOUSES ARE DESTROYED BY SUNLIGHT.
FZZZZZZZ

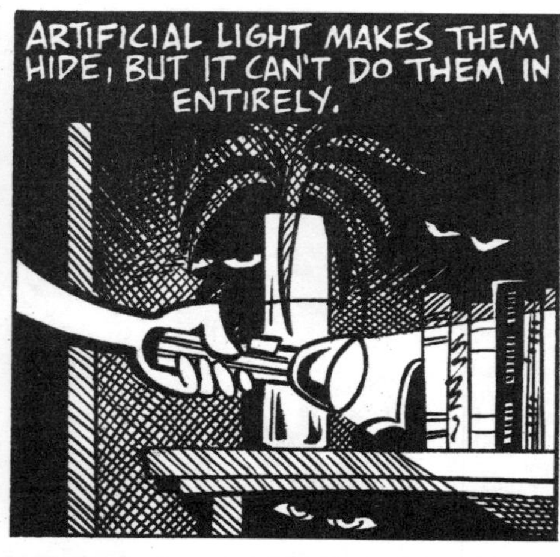
ARTIFICIAL LIGHT MAKES THEM HIDE, BUT IT CAN'T DO THEM IN ENTIRELY.

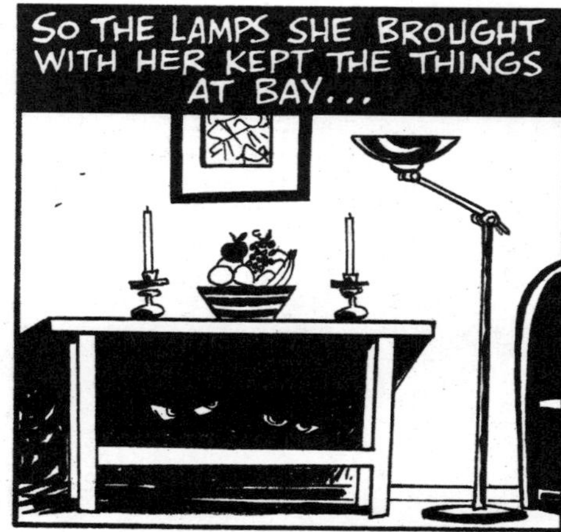
SO THE LAMPS SHE BROUGHT WITH HER KEPT THE THINGS AT BAY...

...BUT UNINTERRUPTED BY SUNLIGHT, THE DARK THINGS GREW STRONGER.

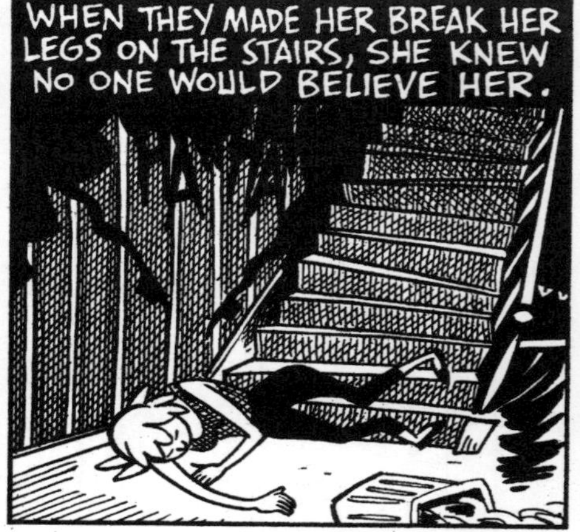
WHEN THEY MADE HER BREAK HER LEGS ON THE STAIRS, SHE KNEW NO ONE WOULD BELIEVE HER.

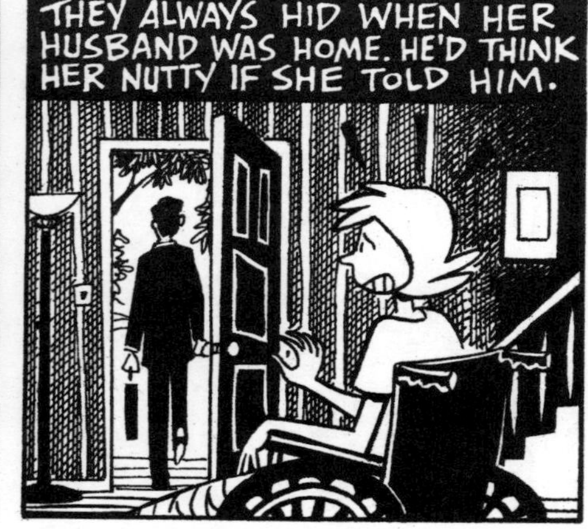
THEY ALWAYS HID WHEN HER HUSBAND WAS HOME. HE'D THINK HER NUTTY IF SHE TOLD HIM.

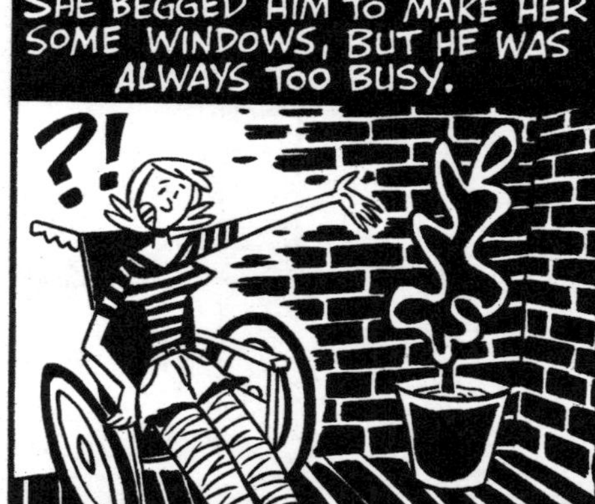
SHE BEGGED HIM TO MAKE HER SOME WINDOWS, BUT HE WAS ALWAYS TOO BUSY.
?!

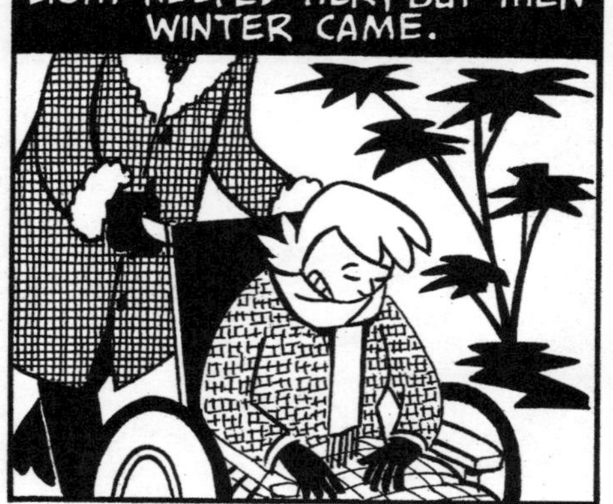
HER BRIEF OUTINGS IN THE DAY-LIGHT HELPED HER, BUT THEN WINTER CAME.

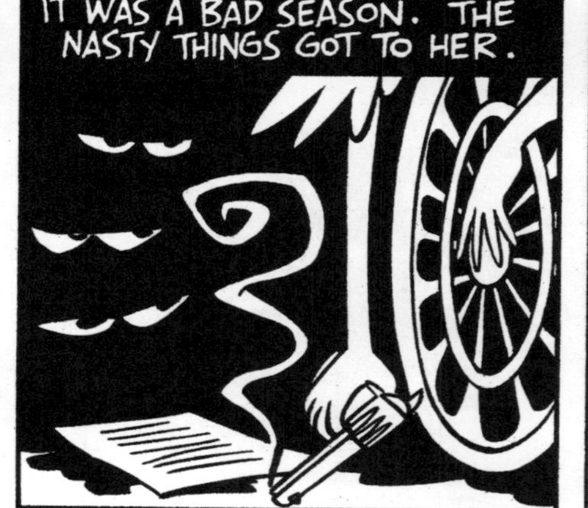
IT WAS A BAD SEASON. THE NASTY THINGS GOT TO HER.

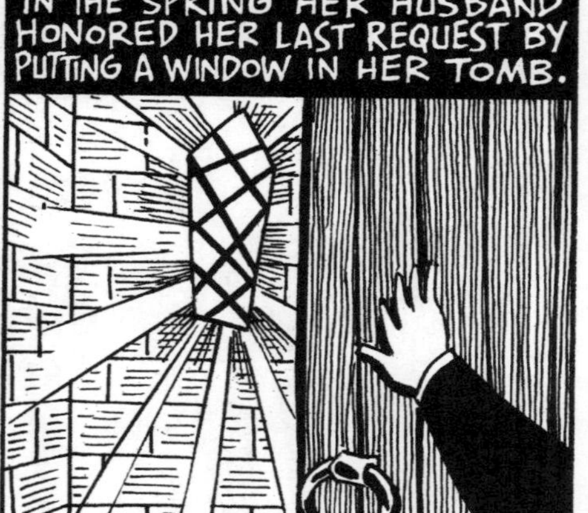
IN THE SPRING HER HUSBAND HONORED HER LAST REQUEST BY PUTTING A WINDOW IN HER TOMB.

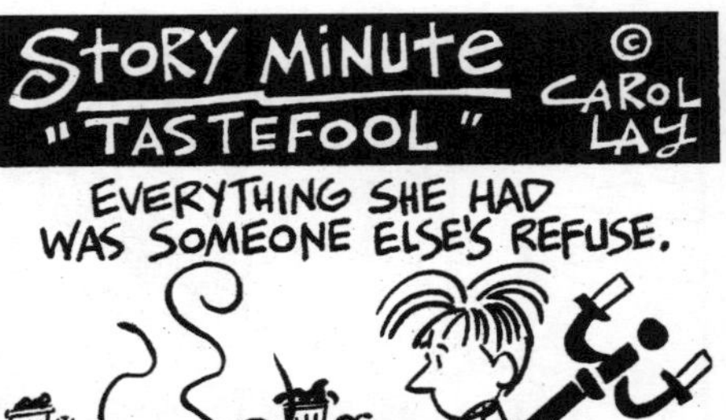
STORY MINUTE
"TASTEFOOL"
© CAROL LAY
EVERYTHING SHE HAD WAS SOMEONE ELSE'S REFUSE.
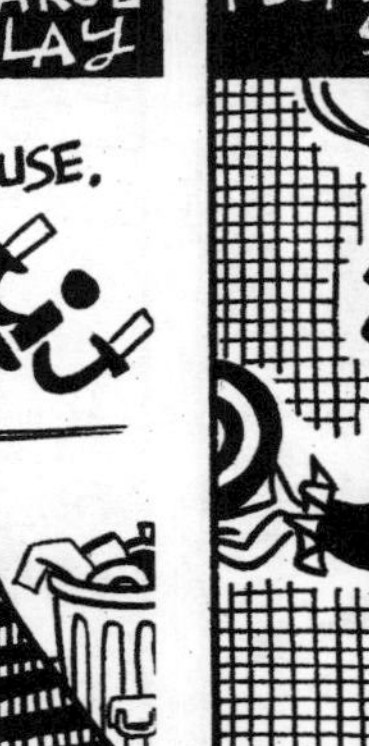
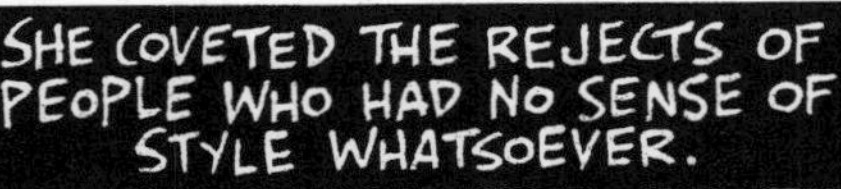
SHE COVETED THE REJECTS OF PEOPLE WHO HAD NO SENSE OF STYLE WHATSOEVER.
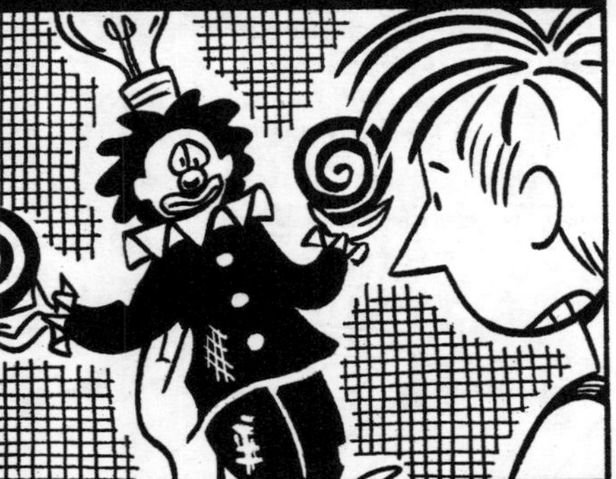
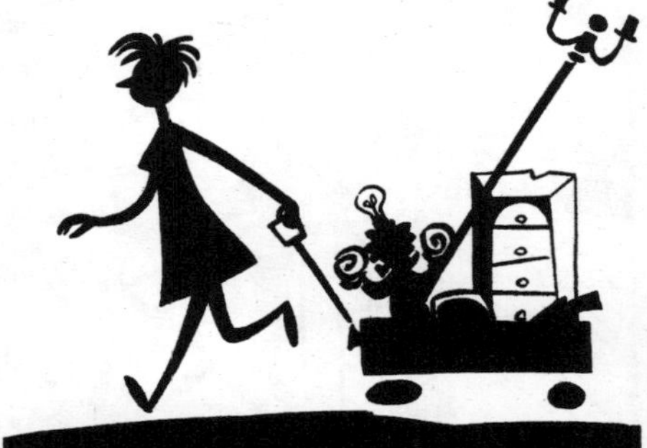
SHE FIGURED IF AN OBJECT WAS THROWN OUT BY SOMEONE WHO HAD ABSOLUTELY NO TASTE...
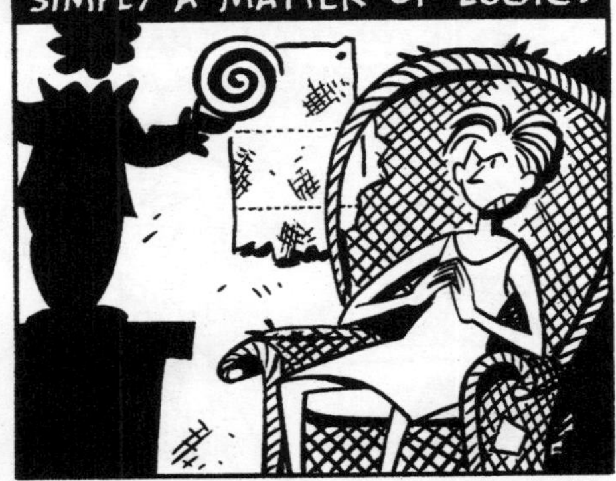
...THEN IT MUST BE A THING OF SUPERLATIVE BEAUTY. THIS WAS SIMPLY A MATTER OF LOGIC.
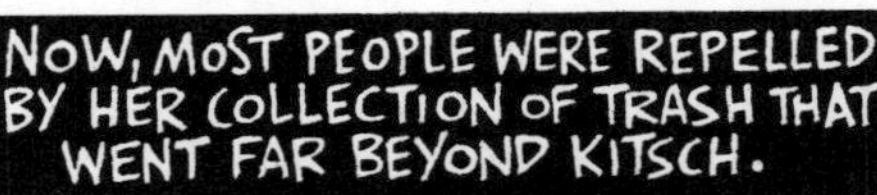
NOW, MOST PEOPLE WERE REPELLED BY HER COLLECTION OF TRASH THAT WENT FAR BEYOND KITSCH.
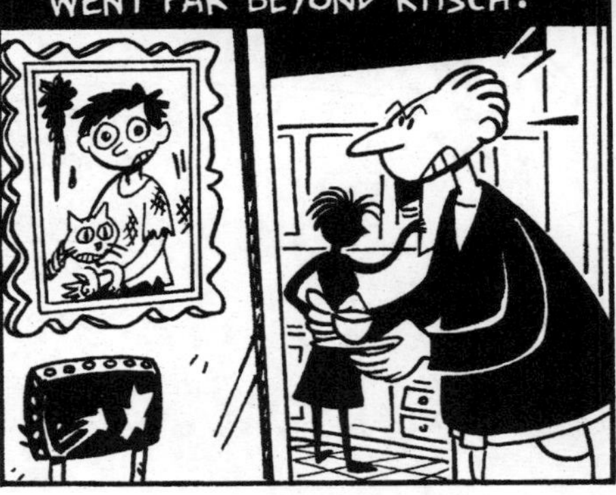
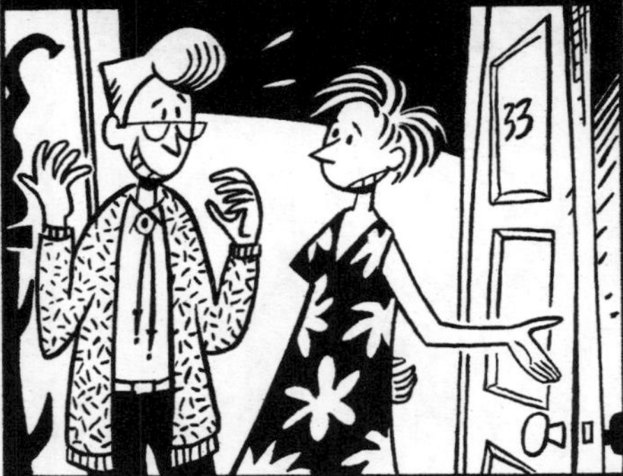
BUT ONE PERSON HAPPENED ALONG WHO FINALLY RECOGNIZED THE GENIUS OF HER STYLE.
33
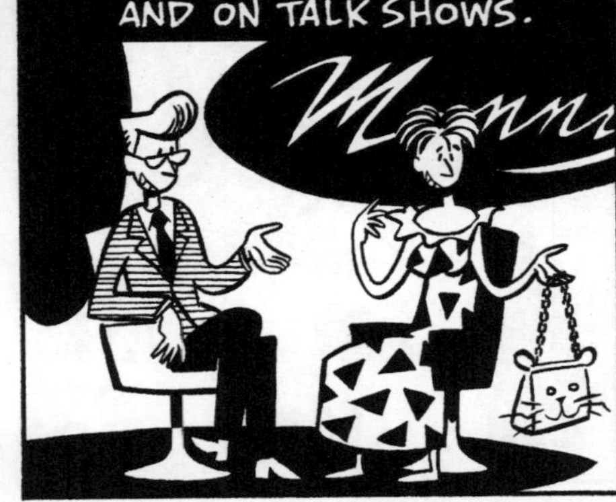
HE CELEBRATED HER "ANTI-ESTHETICISM" IN MAGAZINES AND ON TALK SHOWS.
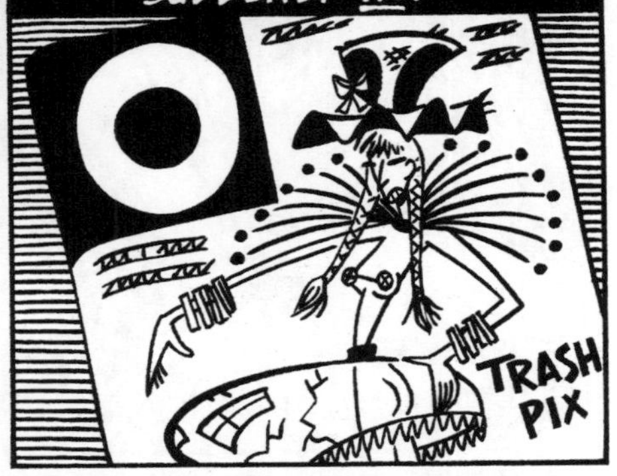
THE TIME WAS RIGHT FOR SUCH A REVERSAL OF STYLE. UGLY WAS SUDDENLY IN.
TRASH PIX
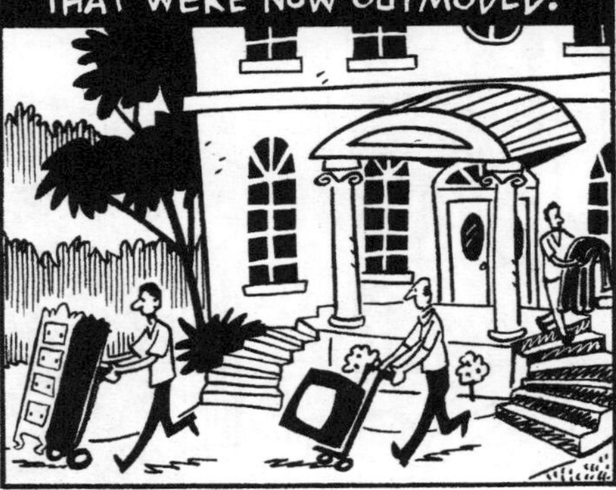
EVERYONE THREW OUT THEIR EXPENSIVE AND BEAUTIFUL THINGS THAT WERE NOW OUTMODED.
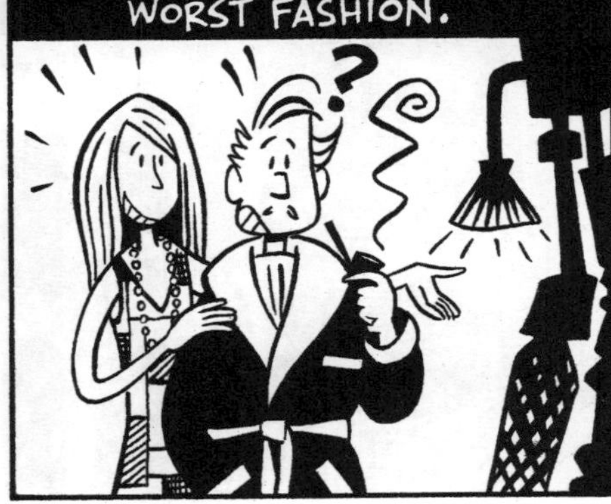
THEY HAD THEIR DECORATORS REDO THEIR PLACES IN THE WORST FASHION.
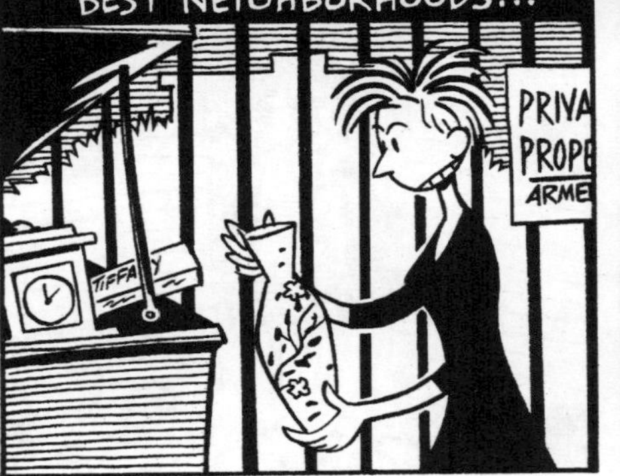
THE TREND-SETTER, THOUGH, NOW WENT TRASH-PICKING IN THE BEST NEIGHBORHOODS...
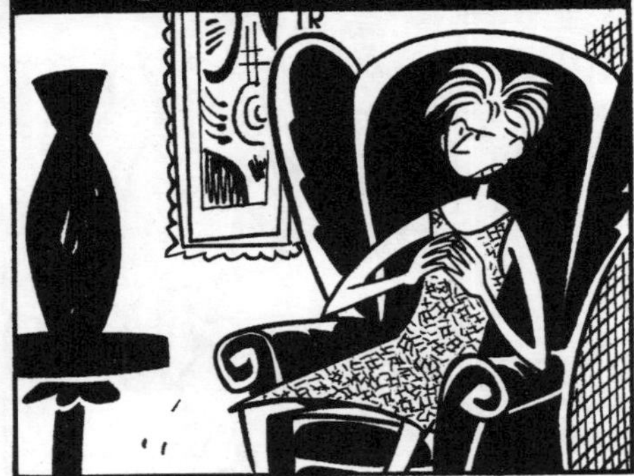
...BECAUSE NOW THEY, TOO, SHOWED SIGNS OF HAVING NO REAL SENSE OF STYLE.

STORY MINUTE
"BLACK CAT"
© CAROL LAY

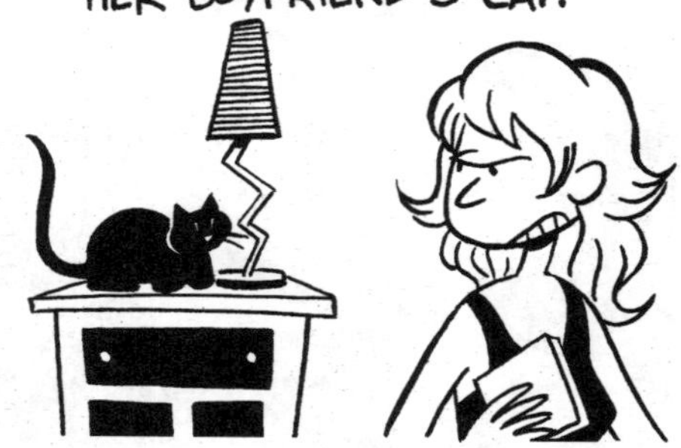
SHE FEARED AND HATED HER BOYFRIEND'S CAT.

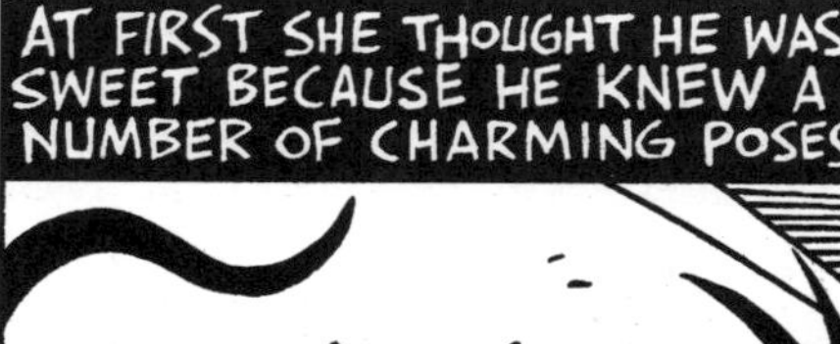
AT FIRST SHE THOUGHT HE WAS SWEET BECAUSE HE KNEW A NUMBER OF CHARMING POSES.

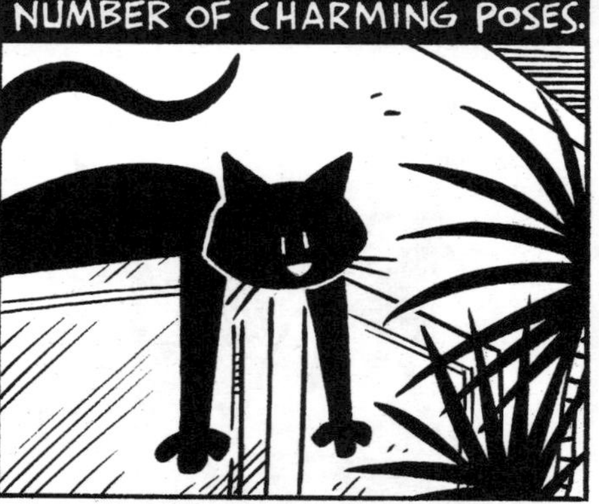

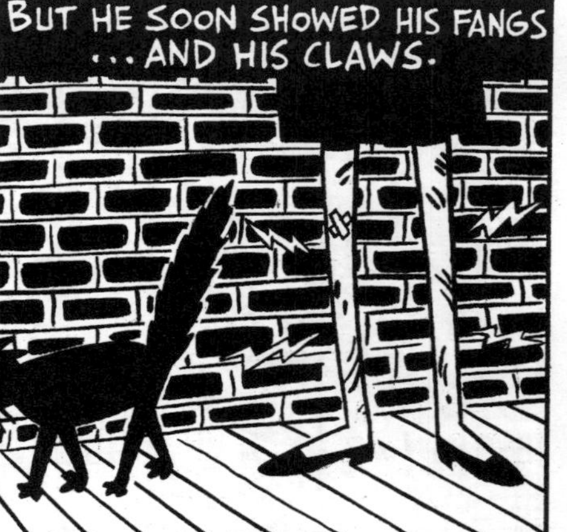
BUT HE SOON SHOWED HIS FANGS ...AND HIS CLAWS.

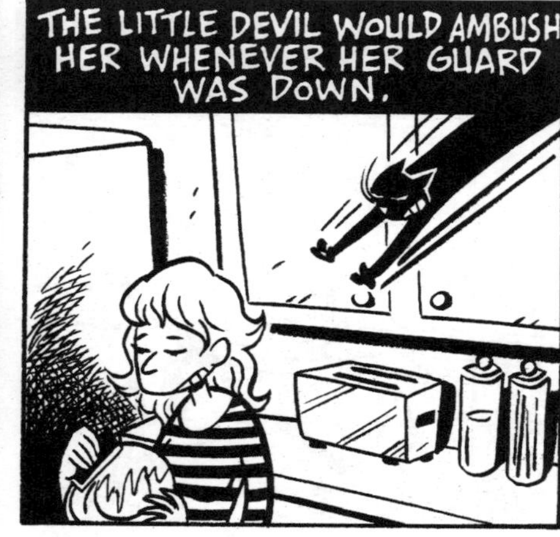
THE LITTLE DEVIL WOULD AMBUSH HER WHENEVER HER GUARD WAS DOWN.

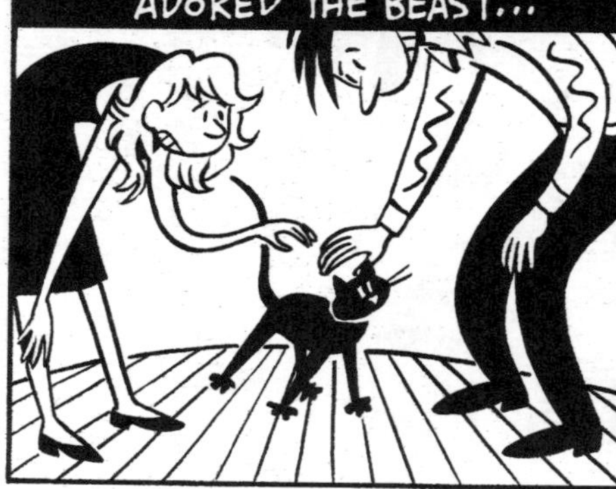
SHE HAD TO PRETEND TO LIKE HIM BECAUSE HER BOYFRIEND ADORED THE BEAST...

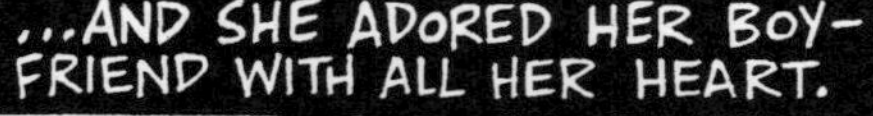
...AND SHE ADORED HER BOY-FRIEND WITH ALL HER HEART.

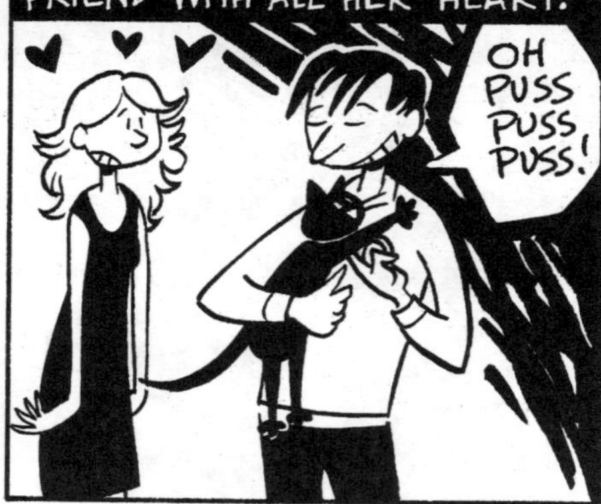
OH PUSS PUSS PUSS!

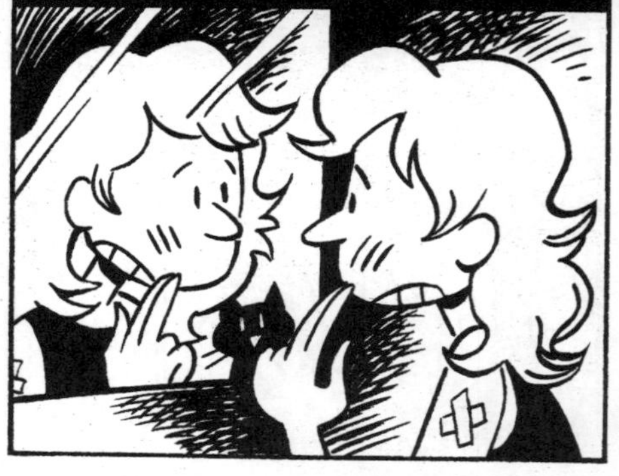
BUT SHE GREW VERY NERVOUS AS SHE COLLECTED MORE BITES AND SCRATCHES DAILY.

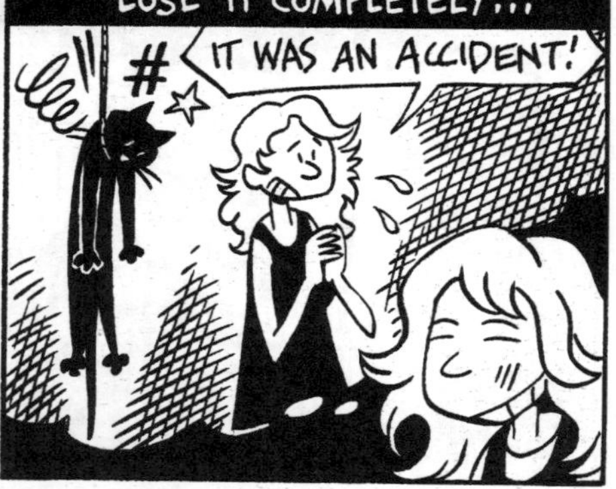
SHE COULDN'T CONTINUE LIVING WITH IT OR SHE MIGHT FINALLY LOSE IT COMPLETELY...
#
IT WAS AN ACCIDENT!

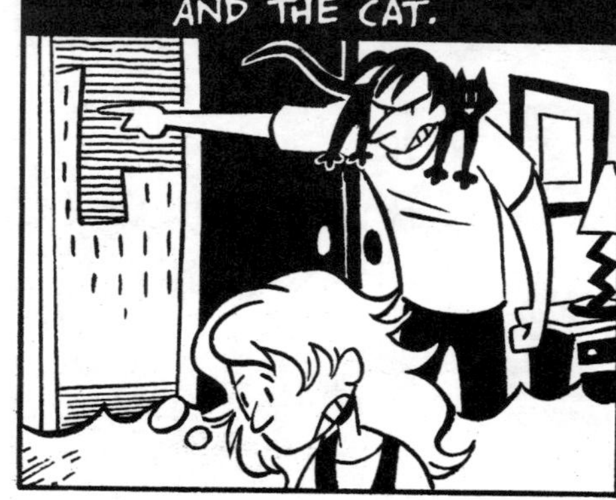
...AND SHE WAS AFRAID TO ASK HIM TO CHOOSE BETWEEN HER AND THE CAT.

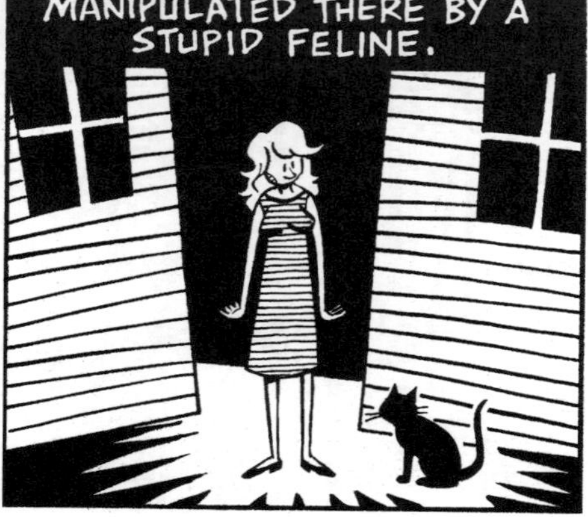
SHE WAS IN A NO-WIN SITUATION, MANIPULATED THERE BY A STUPID FELINE.

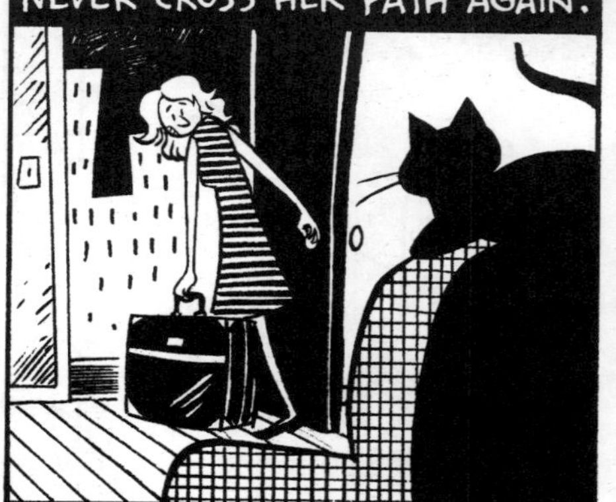
SO SHE LEFT. THE CAT WOULD NEVER CROSS HER PATH AGAIN.

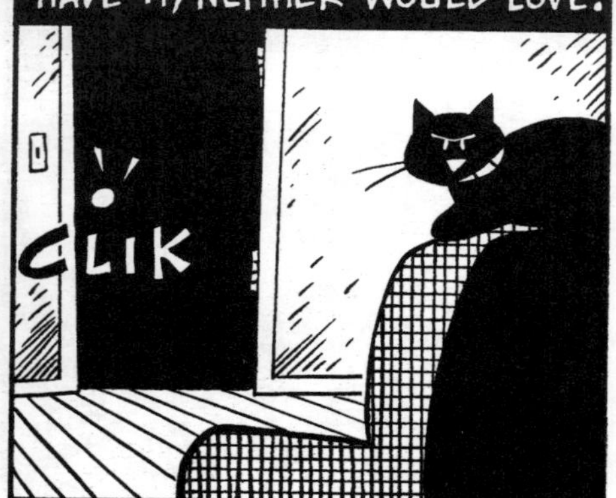
BUT, AS THE BAD LUCK CAT WOULD HAVE IT, NEITHER WOULD LOVE.
CLIK

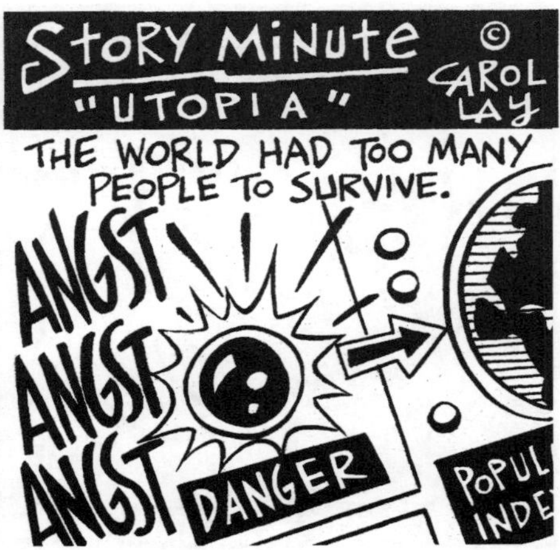
Story Minute
"UTOPIA"
© CAROL LAY
THE WORLD HAD TOO MANY PEOPLE TO SURVIVE.
ANGST ANGST ANGST
DANGER
POPUL INDE

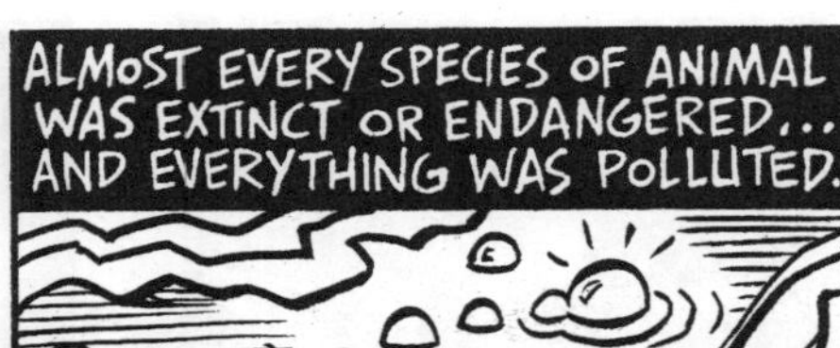
ALMOST EVERY SPECIES OF ANIMAL WAS EXTINCT OR ENDANGERED... AND EVERYTHING WAS POLLUTED.

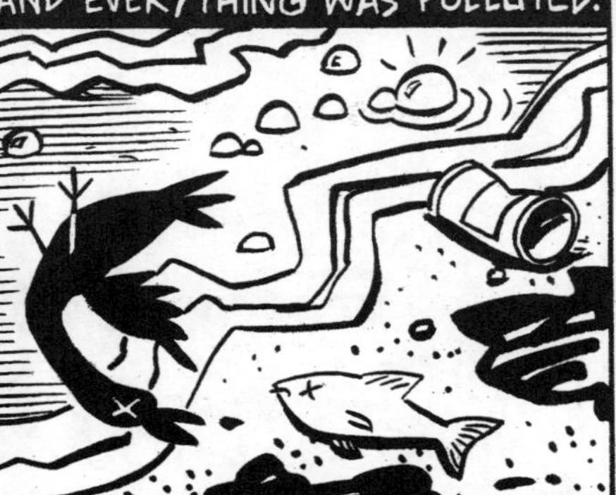

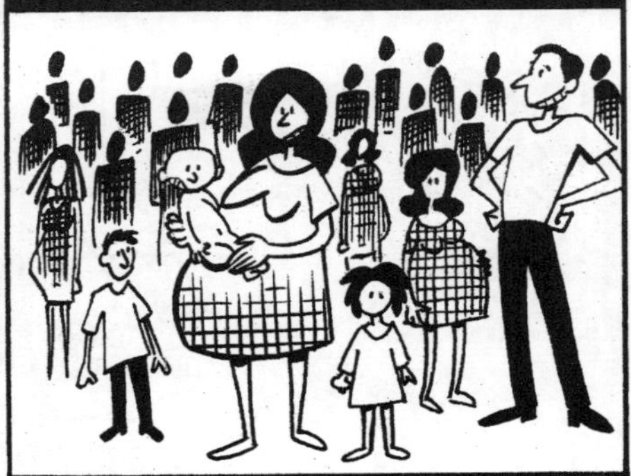
YET PEOPLE KEPT BREEDING LIKE THERE WAS NO TOMORROW — WHICH MIGHT HAVE BEEN THE CASE.

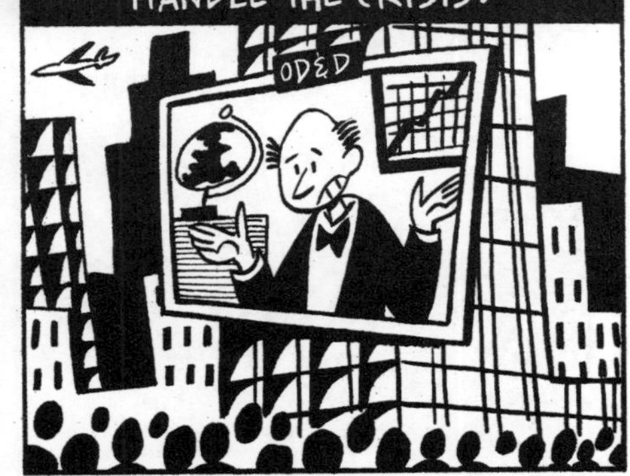
BUT A WORLD-WIDE EMERGENCY GOVERNMENT WAS INSTALLED TO HANDLE THE CRISIS.
OD&D

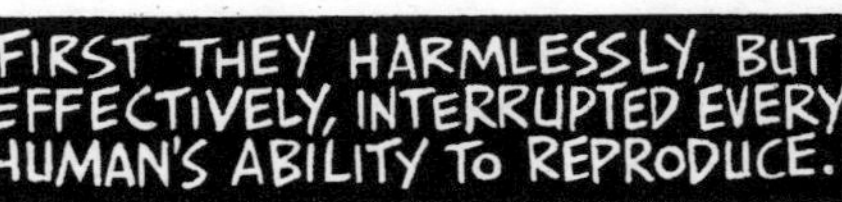
FIRST THEY HARMLESSLY, BUT EFFECTIVELY, INTERRUPTED EVERY HUMAN'S ABILITY TO REPRODUCE.

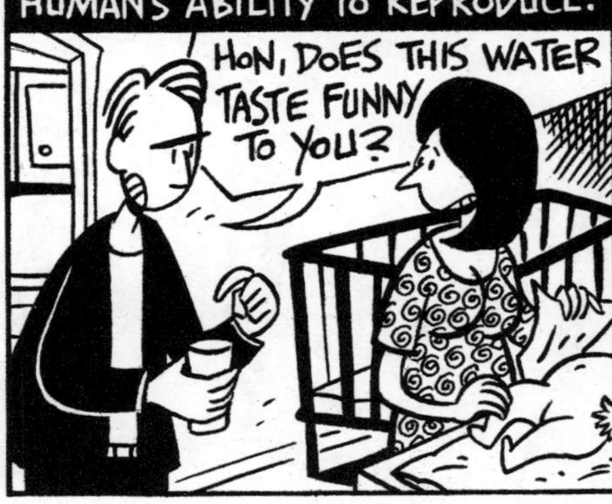
HON, DOES THIS WATER TASTE FUNNY TO YOU?

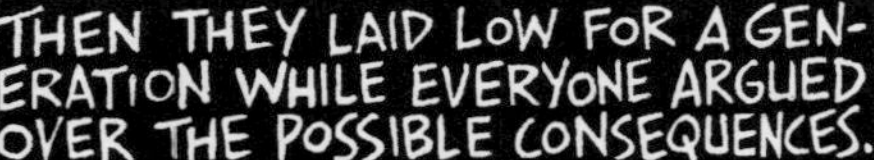
THEN THEY LAID LOW FOR A GENERATION WHILE EVERYONE ARGUED OVER THE POSSIBLE CONSEQUENCES.

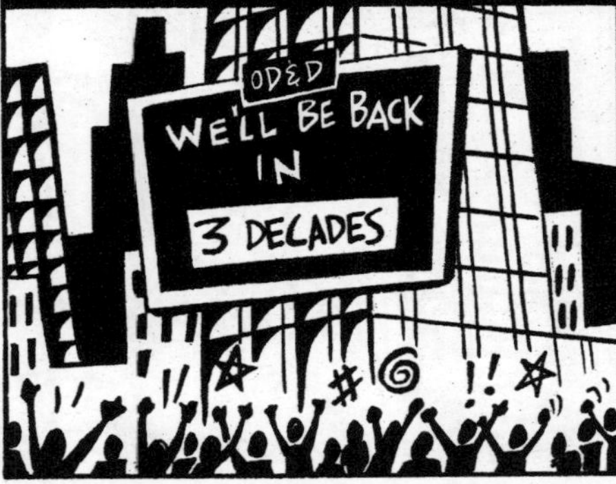
OD&D
WE'LL BE BACK IN
3 DECADES

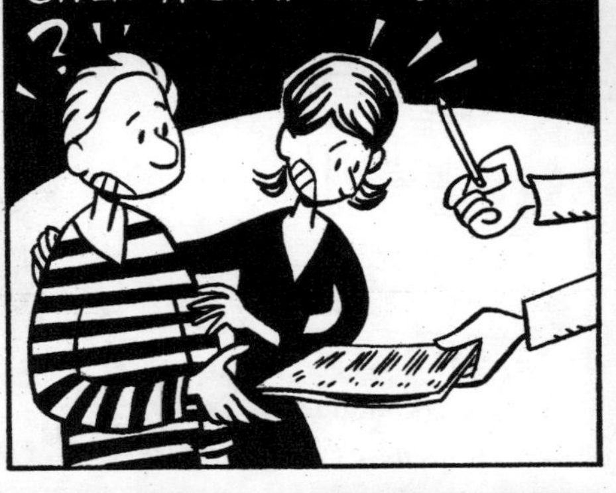
THIRTY YEARS LATER, COUPLES OF CHILD-BEARING YEARS WERE GIVEN A COMPREHENSIVE TEST.

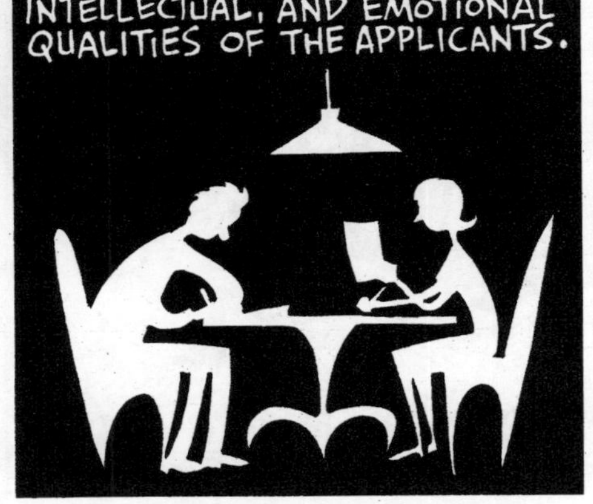
THE TEST EXAMINED THE ETHICAL, INTELLECTUAL, AND EMOTIONAL QUALITIES OF THE APPLICANTS.

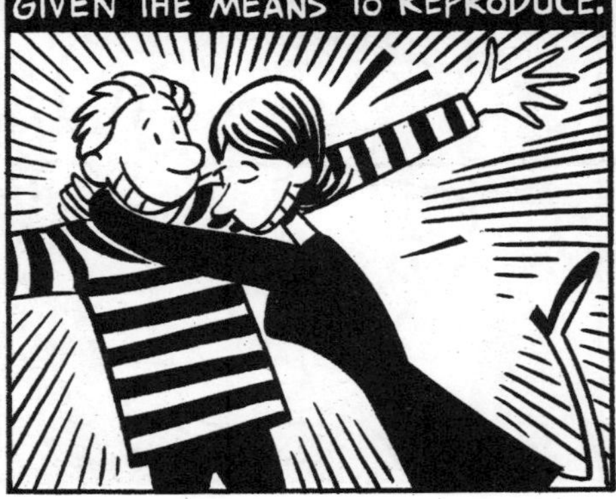
THOSE WHO WOULD MAKE EXCELLENT, LOVING PARENTS WERE GIVEN THE MEANS TO REPRODUCE.

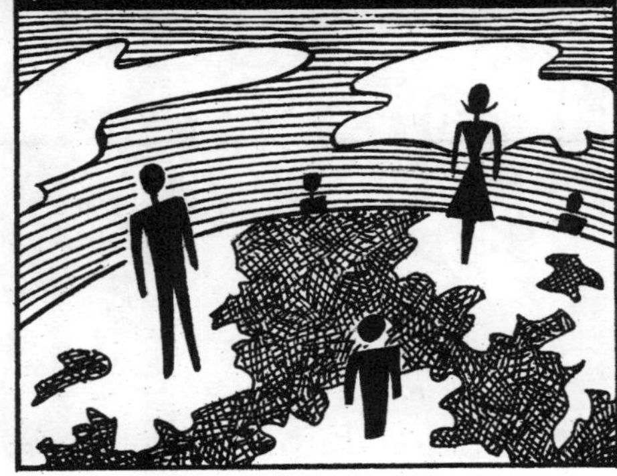
SINCE THESE WERE SURPRISINGLY FEW IN NUMBER, THE EARTH'S POPULATION QUICKLY STABILIZED.

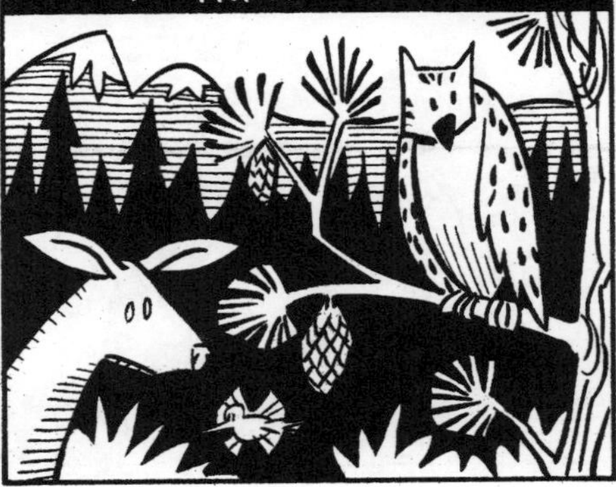
THE REMAINING FLORA AND FAUNA WERE REINTRODUCED AND ALLOWED TO THRIVE AGAIN.

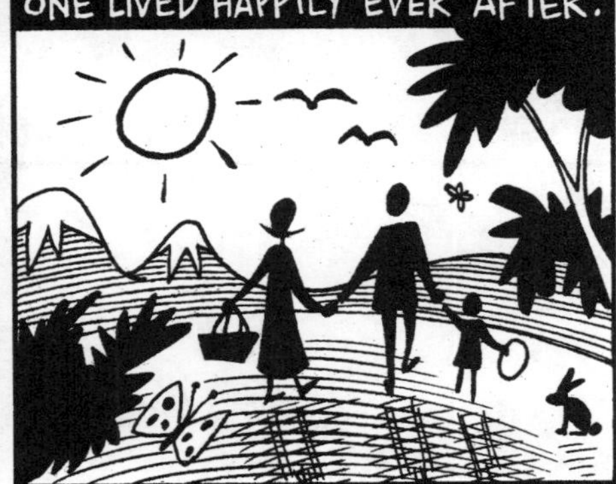
AND, TRUE TO THE IMPOSSIBLE NATURE OF FAIRY TALES, EVERYONE LIVED HAPPILY EVER AFTER.

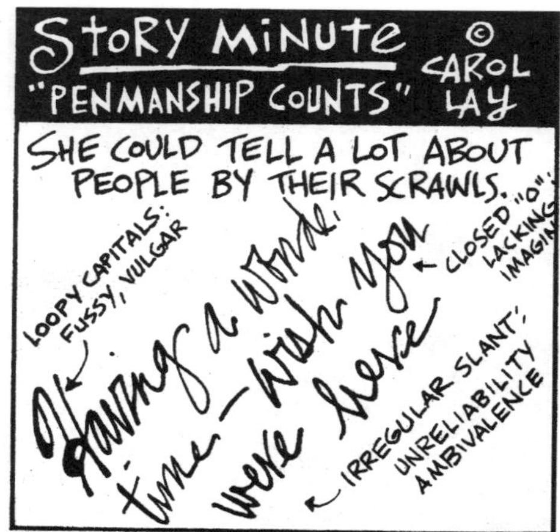
STORY MINUTE
© CAROL LAY
"PENMANSHIP COUNTS"
SHE COULD TELL A LOT ABOUT PEOPLE BY THEIR SCRAWLS.
LOOPY CAPITALS: FUSSY, VULGAR
CLOSED "O": LACKING IMAGIN
IRREGULAR SLANT: UNRELIABILITY AMBIVALENCE

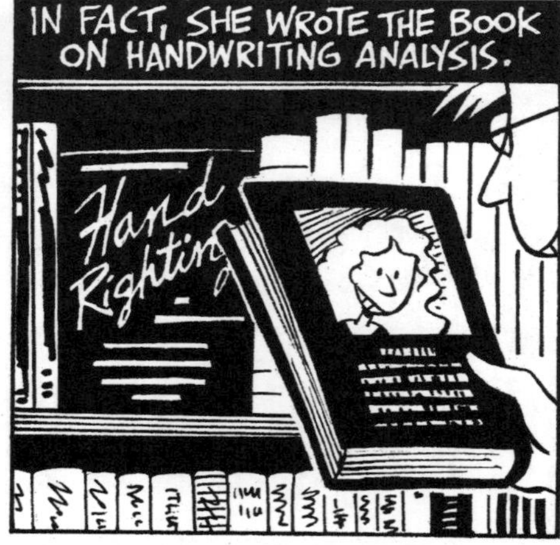
IN FACT, SHE WROTE THE BOOK ON HANDWRITING ANALYSIS.
Hand Righting

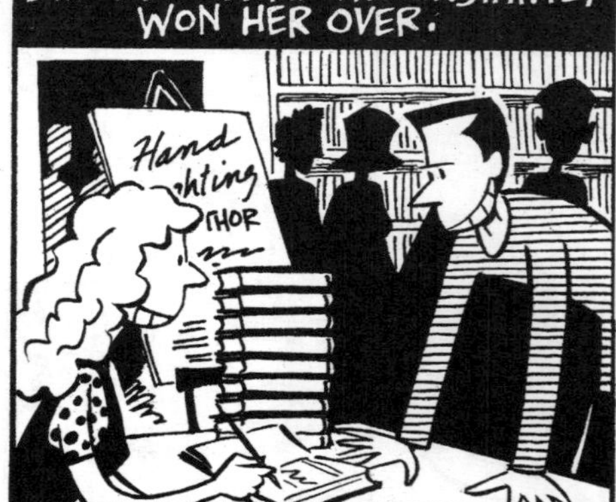
WHILE PROMOTING HER BOOK, SHE MET A MAN WHO INSTANTLY WON HER OVER.

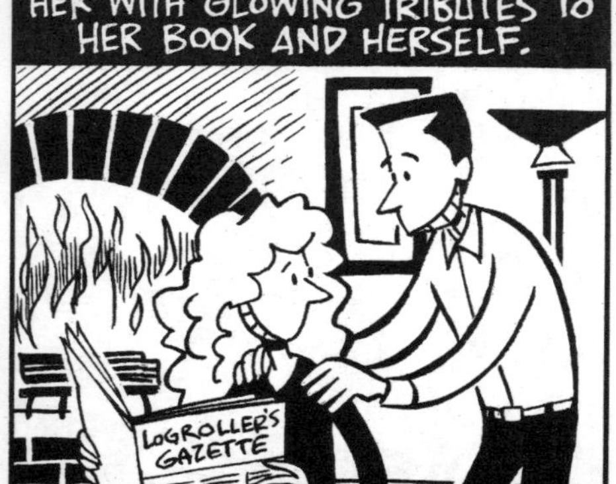
ANOTHER WRITER, HE FLATTERED HER WITH GLOWING TRIBUTES TO HER BOOK AND HERSELF.
LOGROLLER'S GAZETTE

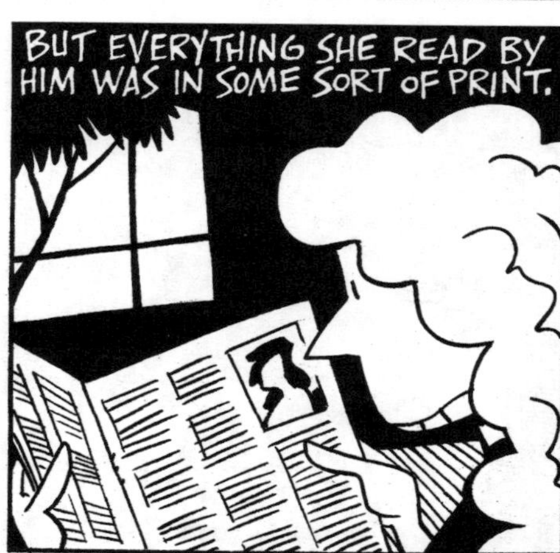
BUT EVERYTHING SHE READ BY HIM WAS IN SOME SORT OF PRINT.

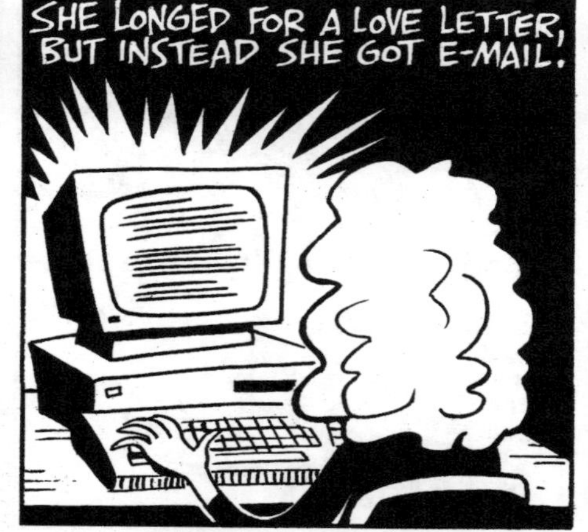
SHE LONGED FOR A LOVE LETTER, BUT INSTEAD SHE GOT E-MAIL.

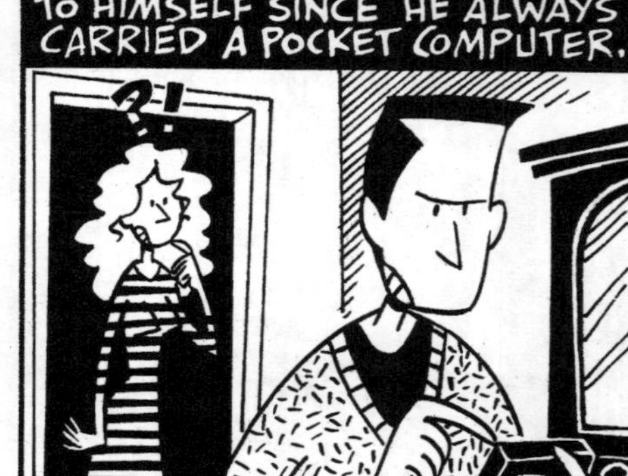
AND HE NEVER WROTE NOTES TO HIMSELF SINCE HE ALWAYS CARRIED A POCKET COMPUTER.
?!

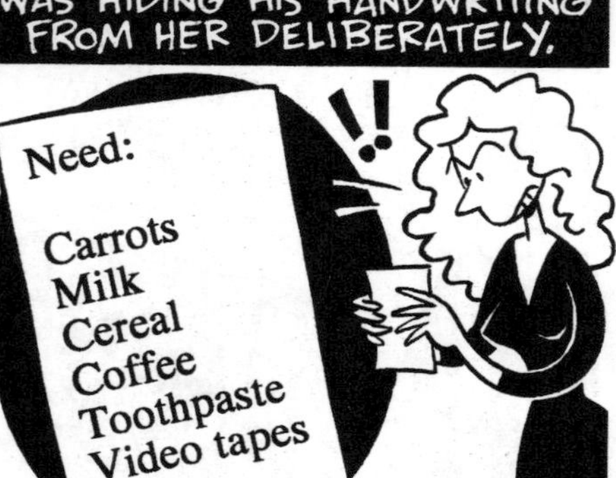
SHE BEGAN TO SUSPECT THAT HE WAS HIDING HIS HANDWRITING FROM HER DELIBERATELY.
!!
Need:
Carrots
Milk
Cereal
Coffee
Toothpaste
Video tapes

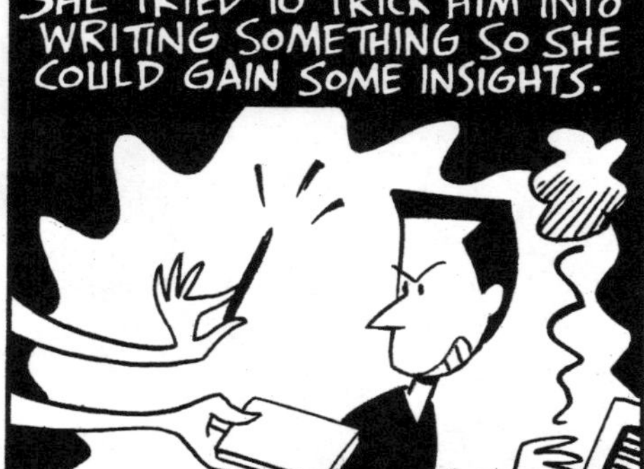
SHE TRIED TO TRICK HIM INTO WRITING SOMETHING SO SHE COULD GAIN SOME INSIGHTS.

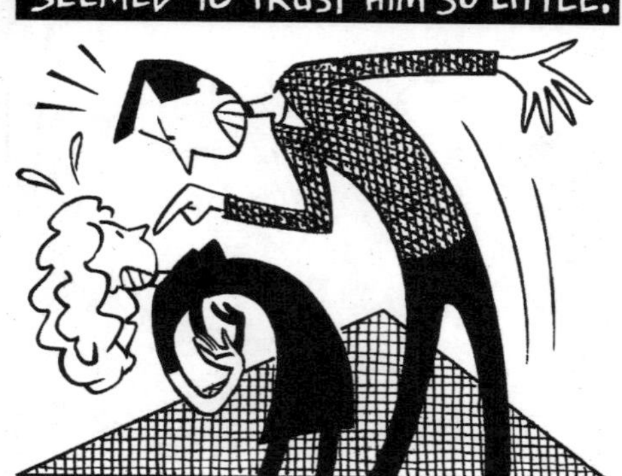
HE FIGURED OUT HER GAME AND WAS OUTRAGED THAT SHE SEEMED TO TRUST HIM SO LITTLE.

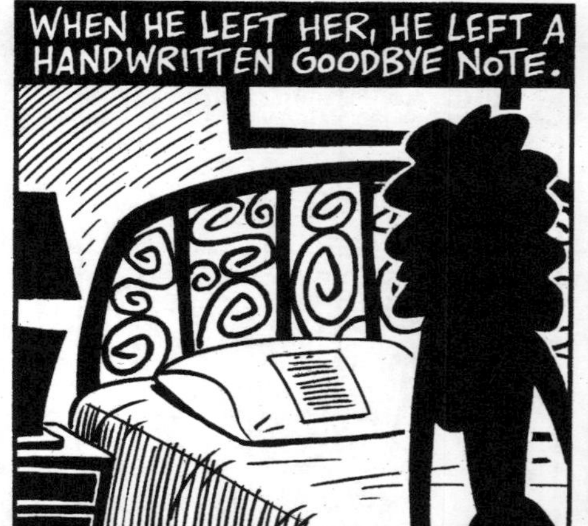
WHEN HE LEFT HER, HE LEFT A HANDWRITTEN GOODBYE NOTE.

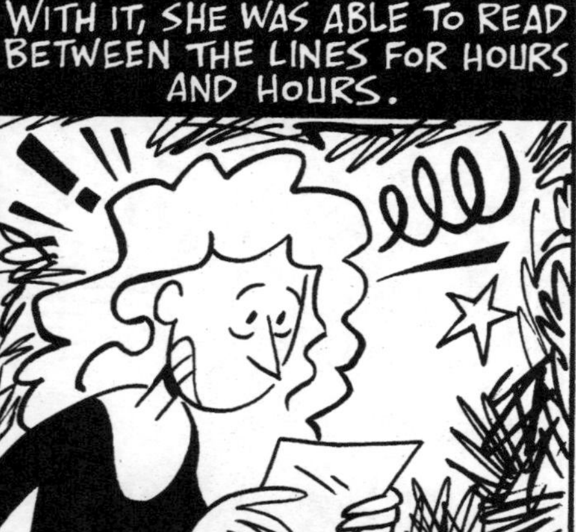
WITH IT, SHE WAS ABLE TO READ BETWEEN THE LINES FOR HOURS AND HOURS.
!

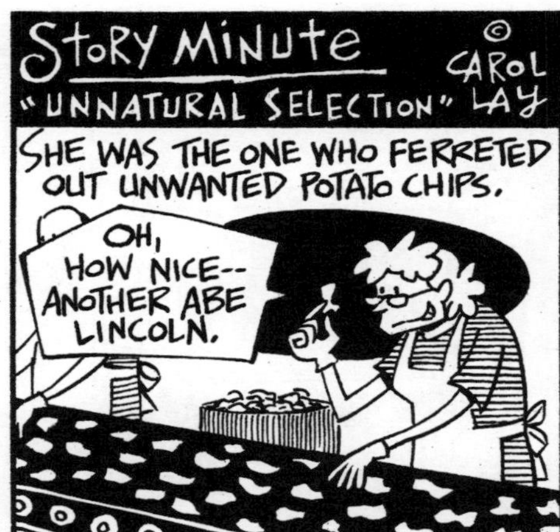
Story Minute
© CAROL LAY
"UNNATURAL SELECTION"
SHE WAS THE ONE WHO FERRETED OUT UNWANTED POTATO CHIPS.
OH, HOW NICE-- ANOTHER ABE LINCOLN.

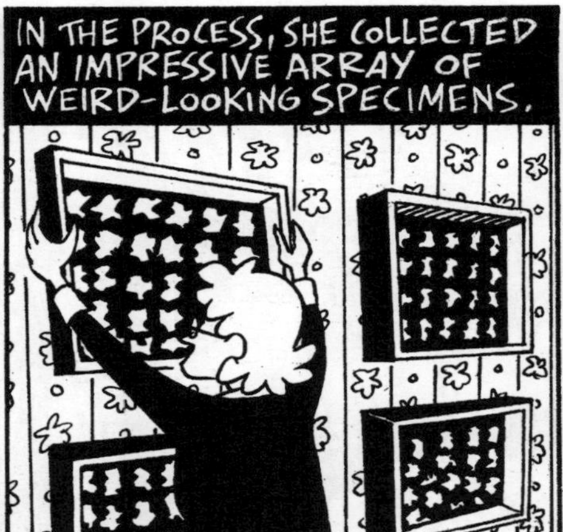
IN THE PROCESS, SHE COLLECTED AN IMPRESSIVE ARRAY OF WEIRD-LOOKING SPECIMENS.

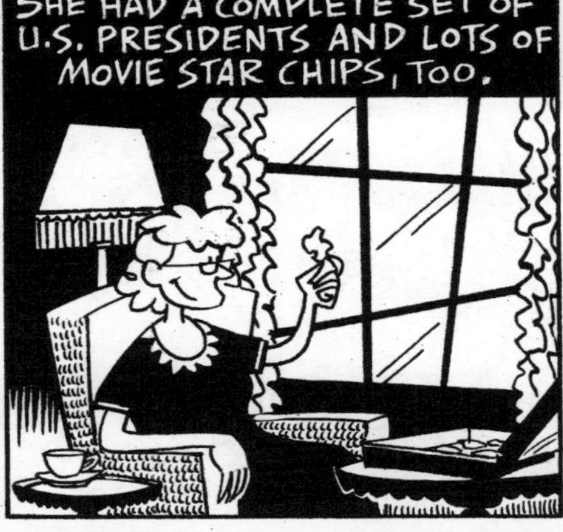
SHE HAD A COMPLETE SET OF U.S. PRESIDENTS AND LOTS OF MOVIE STAR CHIPS, TOO.

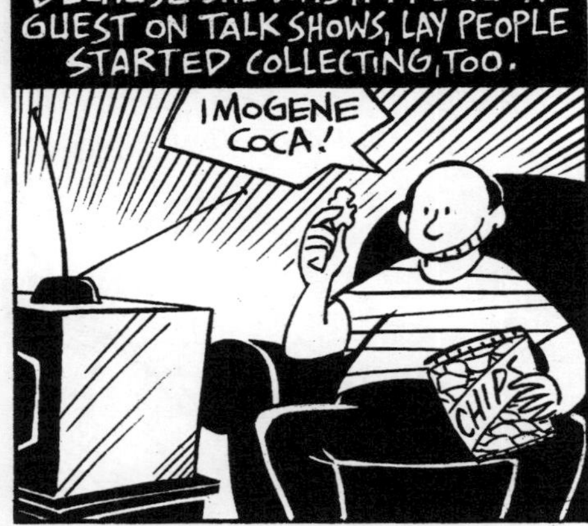
BECAUSE SHE WAS A FREQUENT GUEST ON TALK SHOWS, LAY PEOPLE STARTED COLLECTING, TOO.
IMOGENE COCA!
CHIPS

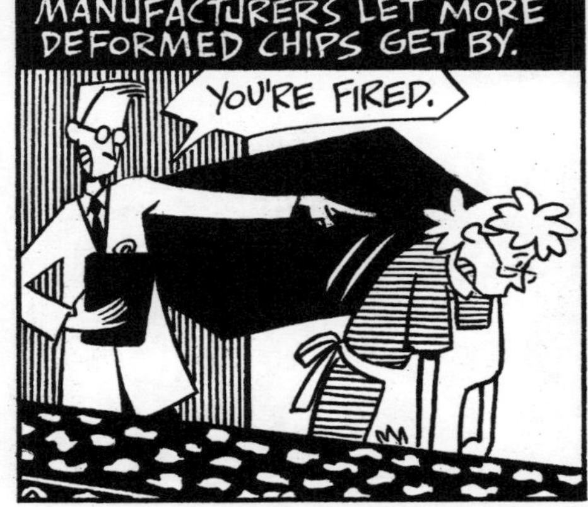
TO ENCOURAGE THE FAD, CHIP MANUFACTURERS LET MORE DEFORMED CHIPS GET BY.
YOU'RE FIRED.

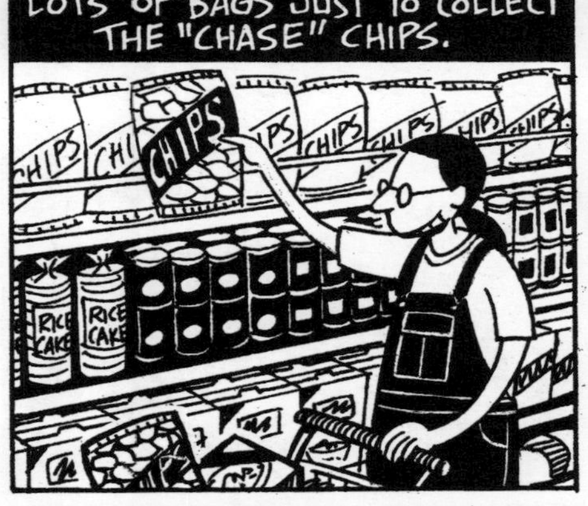
EVEN HEALTH NUTS BOUGHT LOTS OF BAGS JUST TO COLLECT THE "CHASE" CHIPS.
CHIPS
RICE CAKE
RICE CAKE

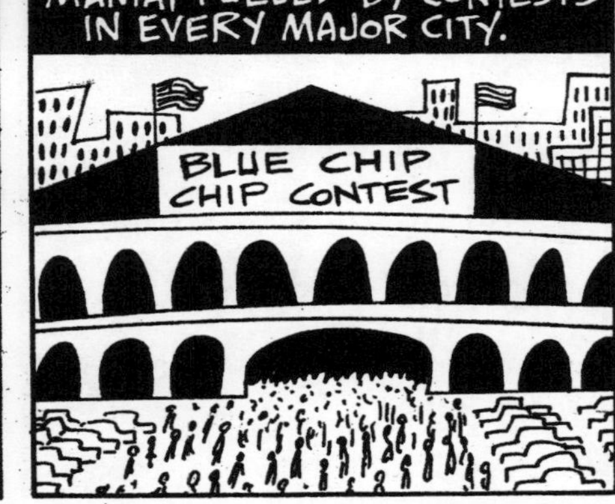
THE FAD BECAME A NATIONAL MANIA, FUELED BY CONTESTS IN EVERY MAJOR CITY.
BLUE CHIP CHIP CONTEST

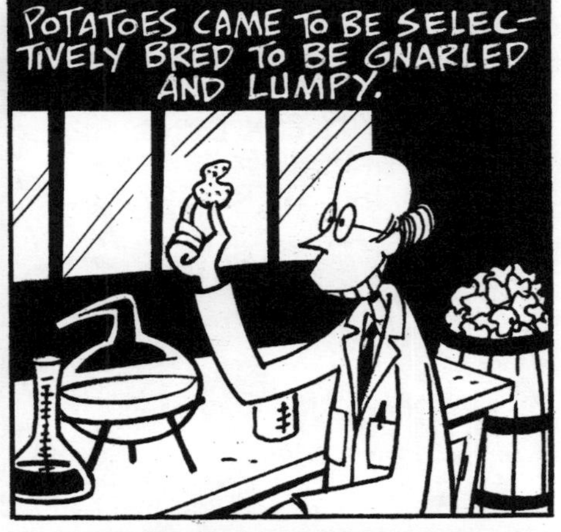
POTATOES CAME TO BE SELECTIVELY BRED TO BE GNARLED AND LUMPY.

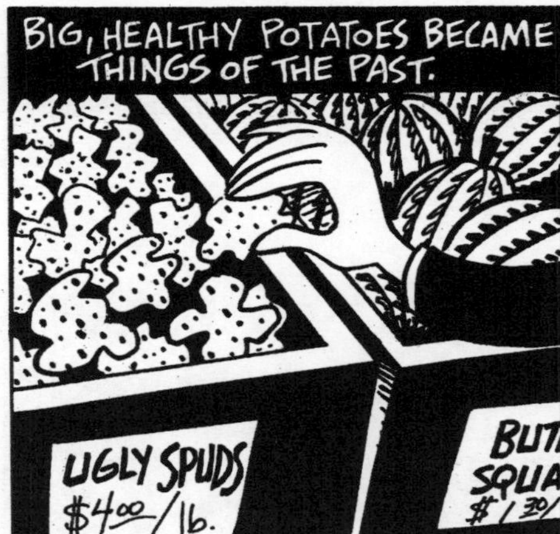
BIG, HEALTHY POTATOES BECAME THINGS OF THE PAST.
UGLY SPUDS $4.00/lb.

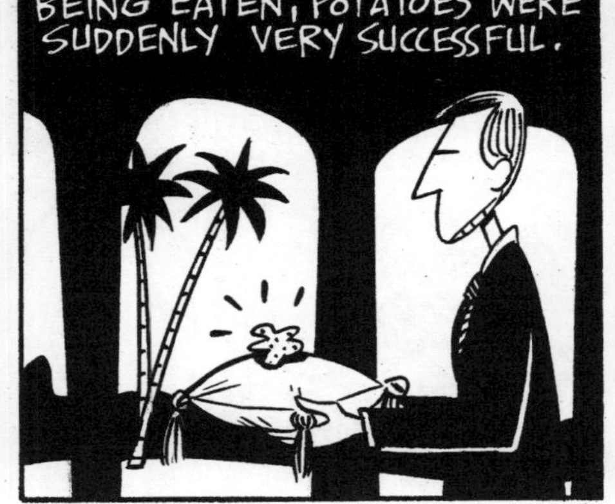
SO, IF SURVIVAL MEANS NOT BEING EATEN, POTATOES WERE SUDDENLY VERY SUCCESSFUL.

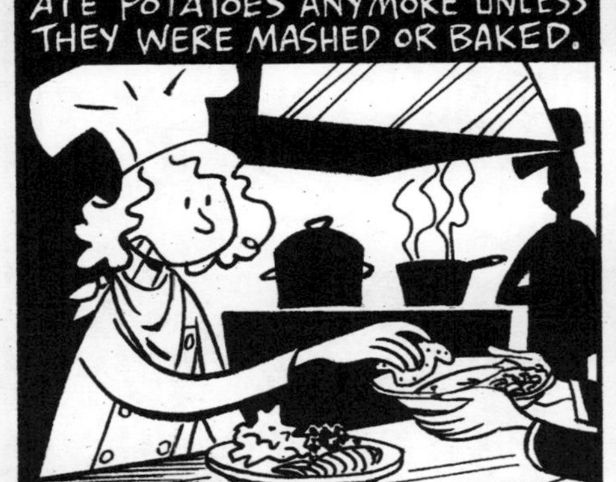
AFTER ALL, NO ONE ACTUALLY ATE POTATOES ANYMORE UNLESS THEY WERE MASHED OR BAKED.

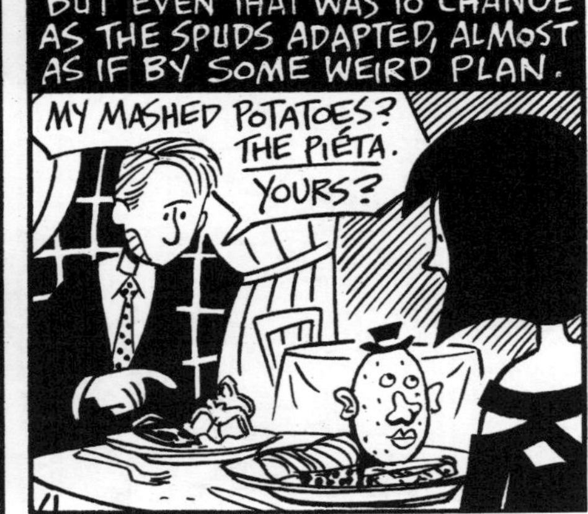
BUT EVEN THAT WAS TO CHANGE AS THE SPUDS ADAPTED, ALMOST AS IF BY SOME WEIRD PLAN.
MY MASHED POTATOES? THE PIÉTA.
YOURS?

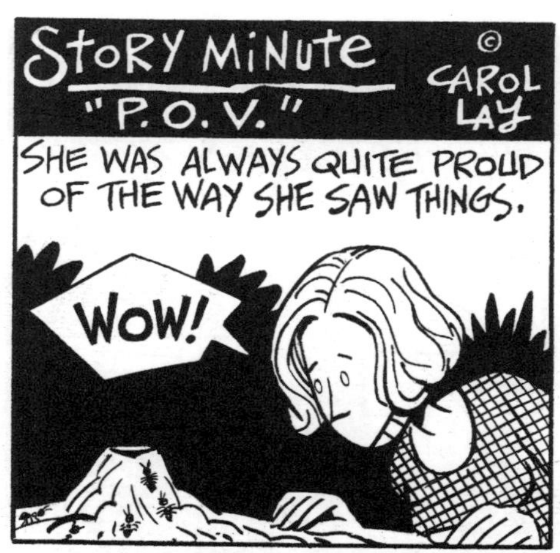
Story Minute
"P.O.V."
© Carol Lay
She was always quite proud of the way she saw things.
WOW!

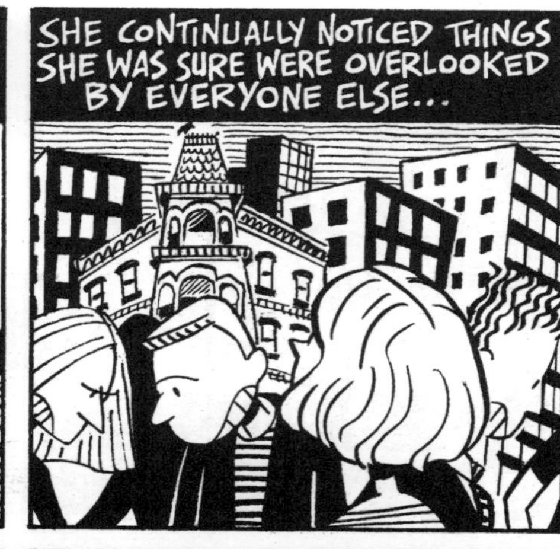
She continually noticed things she was sure were overlooked by everyone else...

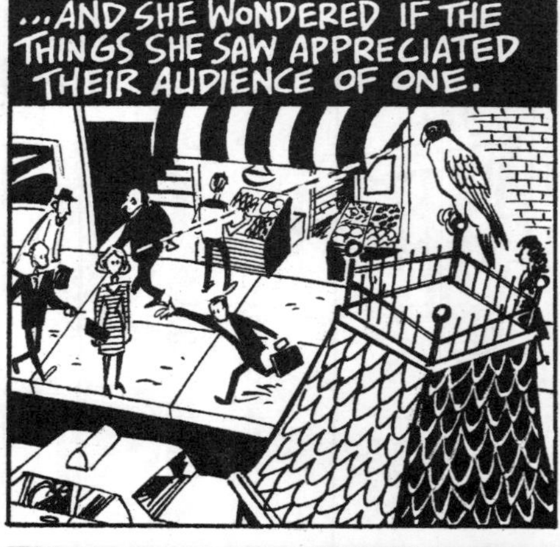
...And she wondered if the things she saw appreciated their audience of one.

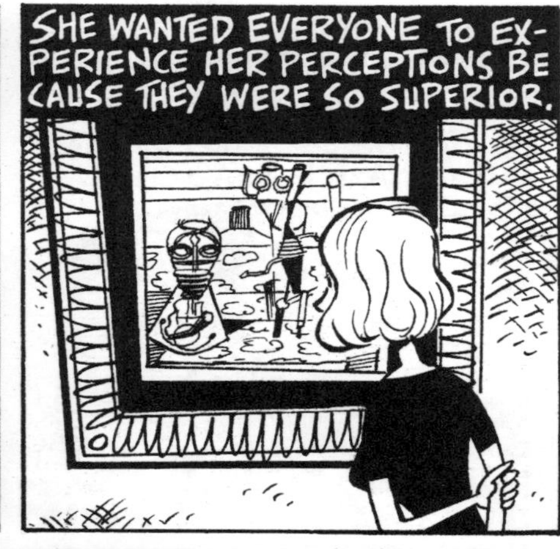
She wanted everyone to experience her perceptions because they were so superior.

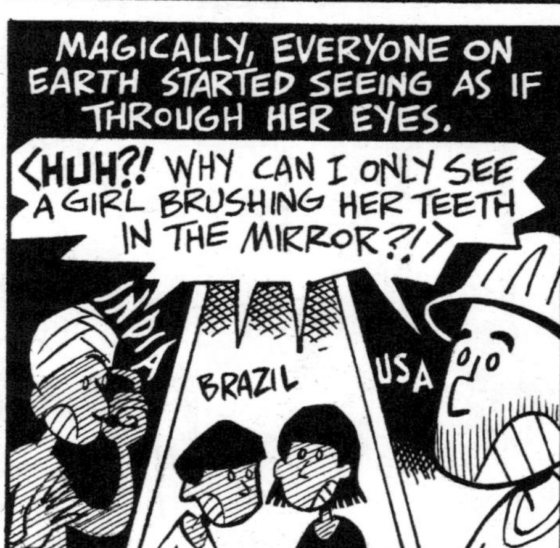
Magically, everyone on earth started seeing as if through her eyes.
<Huh?! Why can I only see a girl brushing her teeth in the mirror?!>
India
Brazil
USA

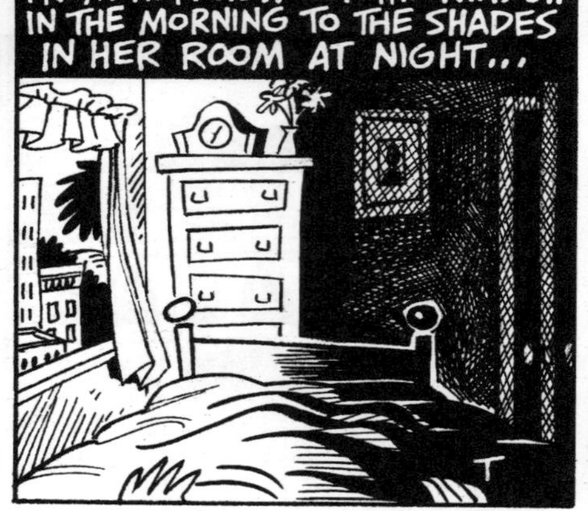
From her view out the window in the morning to the shades in her room at night...

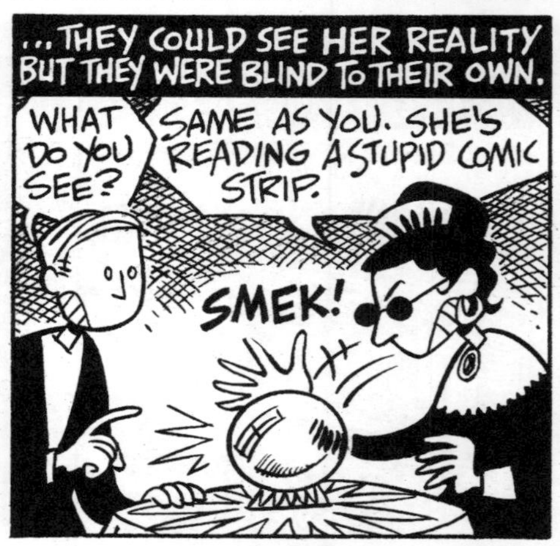
...They could see her reality but they were blind to their own.
What do you see?
Same as you. She's reading a stupid comic strip.
SMEK!

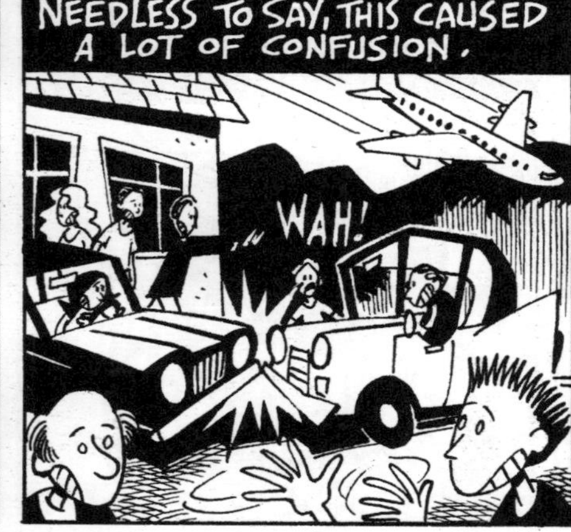
Needless to say, this caused a lot of confusion.
WAH!

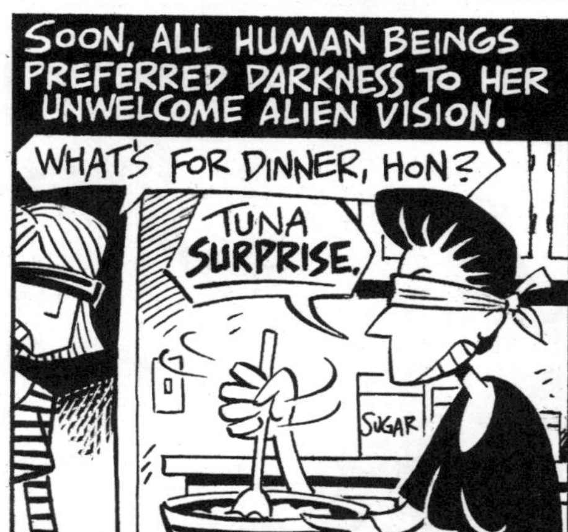
Soon, all human beings preferred darkness to her unwelcome alien vision.
What's for dinner, hon?
Tuna SURPRISE.
SUGAR

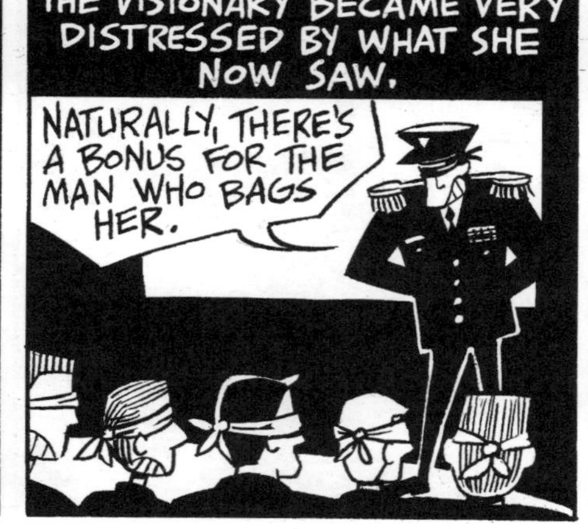
The visionary became very distressed by what she now saw.
Naturally, there's a bonus for the man who bags her.

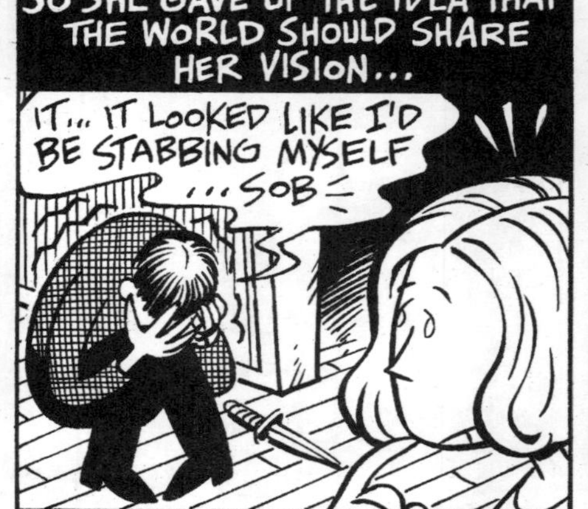
So she gave up the idea that the world should share her vision...
It... it looked like I'd be stabbing myself ...sob

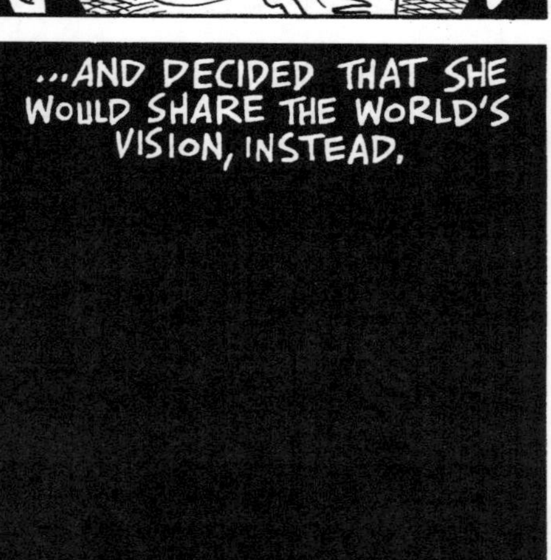
...And decided that she would share the world's vision, instead.

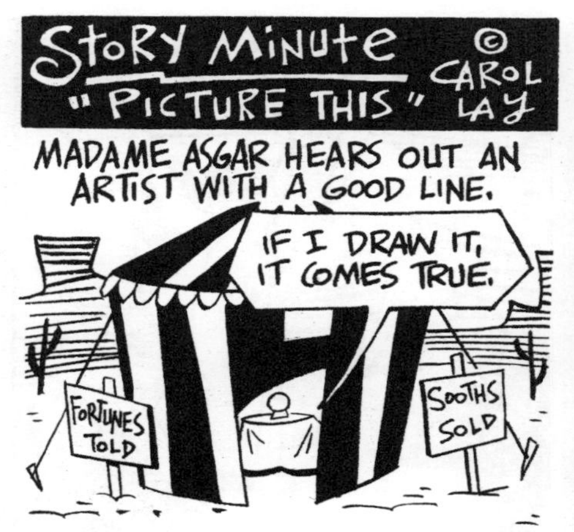
STORY MINUTE
"PICTURE THIS"
© CAROL LAY
MADAME ASGAR HEARS OUT AN ARTIST WITH A GOOD LINE.
IF I DRAW IT, IT COMES TRUE.
FORTUNES TOLD
SOOTHS SOLD

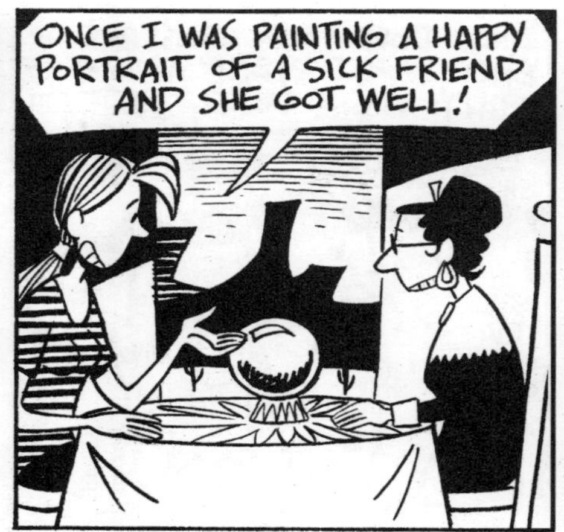
ONCE I WAS PAINTING A HAPPY PORTRAIT OF A SICK FRIEND AND SHE GOT WELL!

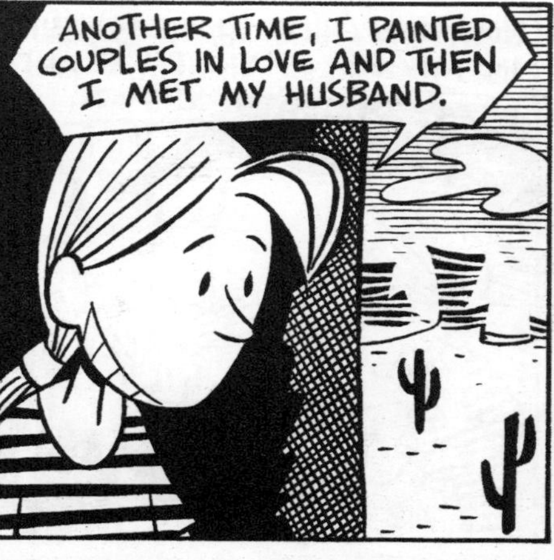
ANOTHER TIME, I PAINTED COUPLES IN LOVE AND THEN I MET MY HUSBAND.

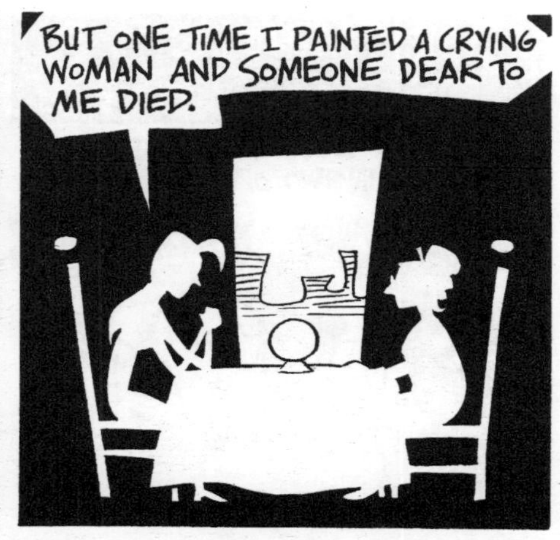
BUT ONE TIME I PAINTED A CRYING WOMAN AND SOMEONE DEAR TO ME DIED.

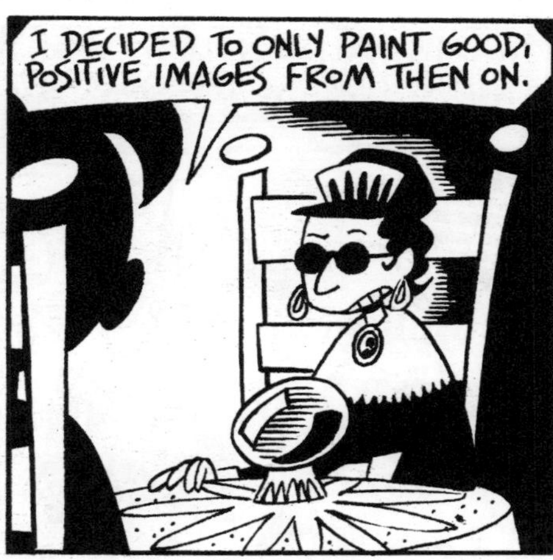
I DECIDED TO ONLY PAINT GOOD, POSITIVE IMAGES FROM THEN ON.

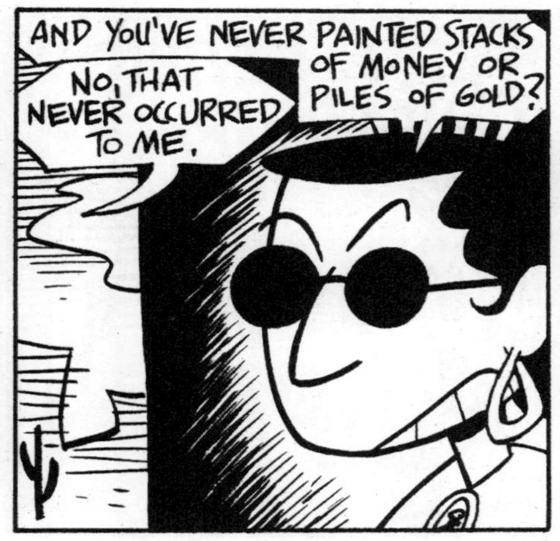
AND YOU'VE NEVER PAINTED STACKS OF MONEY OR PILES OF GOLD?
NO, THAT NEVER OCCURRED TO ME.

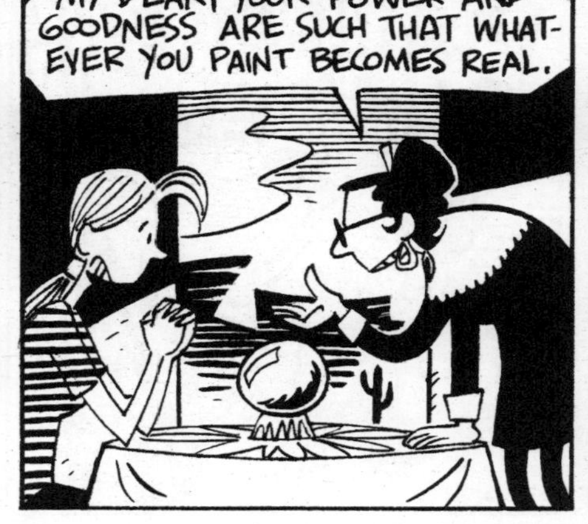
MY DEAR, YOUR POWER AND GOODNESS ARE SUCH THAT WHATEVER YOU PAINT BECOMES REAL.

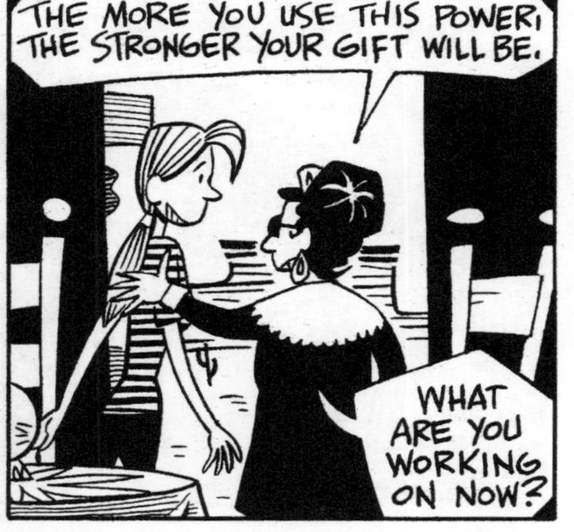
THE MORE YOU USE THIS POWER, THE STRONGER YOUR GIFT WILL BE.
WHAT ARE YOU WORKING ON NOW?

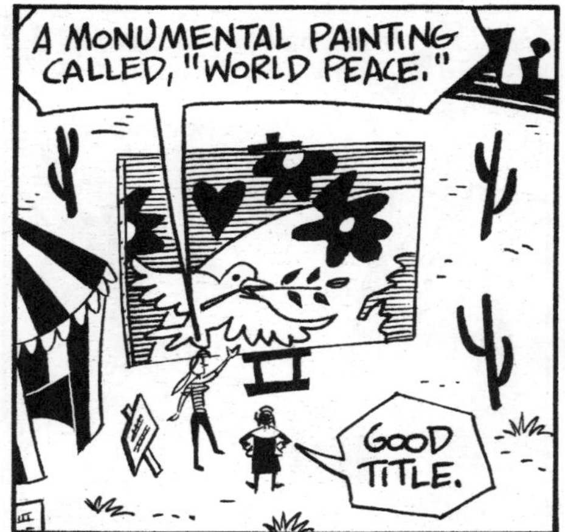
A MONUMENTAL PAINTING CALLED, "WORLD PEACE."
GOOD TITLE.

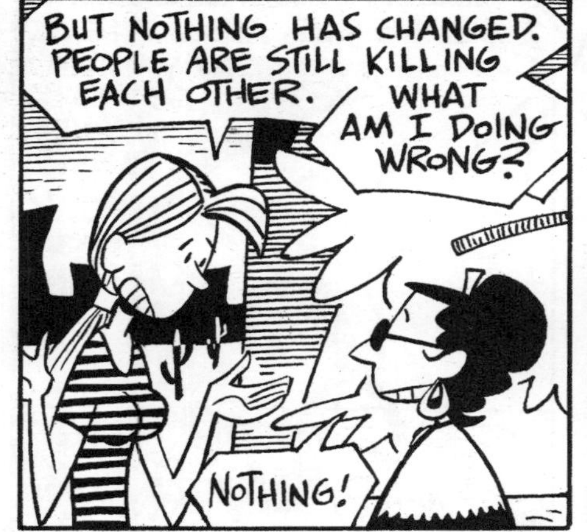
BUT NOTHING HAS CHANGED. PEOPLE ARE STILL KILLING EACH OTHER.
WHAT AM I DOING WRONG?
NOTHING!

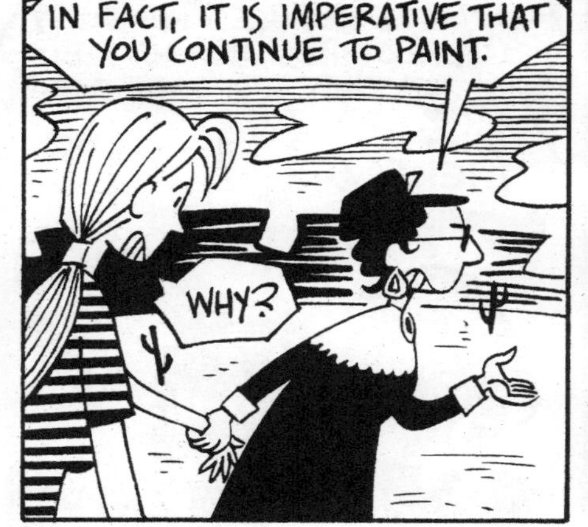
IN FACT, IT IS IMPERATIVE THAT YOU CONTINUE TO PAINT.
WHY?

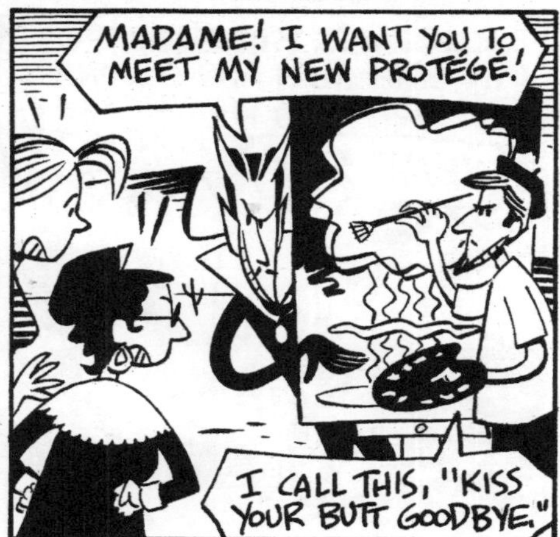
MADAME! I WANT YOU TO MEET MY NEW PROTÉGÉ!
I CALL THIS, "KISS YOUR BUTT GOODBYE."

STORY MINUTE
"DAUB JOB"
© CAROL LAY

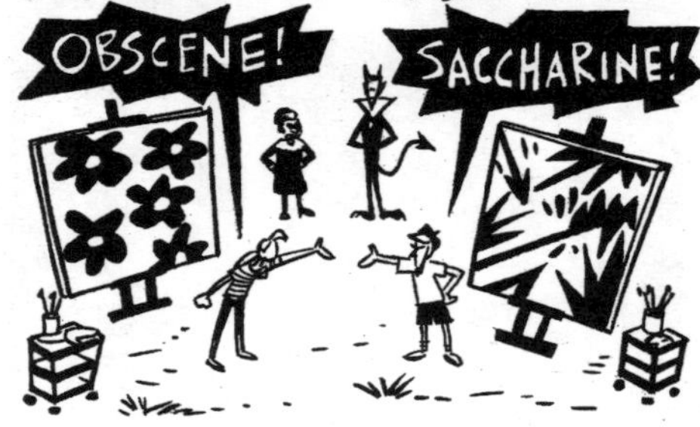
GOOD AND EVIL HAVE BECOME EMBODIED IN TWO OPPOSING ARTISTS.
OBSCENE!
SACCHARINE!

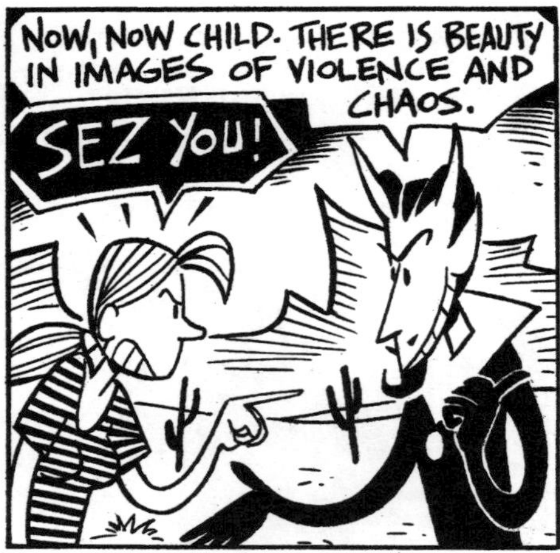
NOW, NOW CHILD. THERE IS BEAUTY IN IMAGES OF VIOLENCE AND CHAOS.
SEZ YOU!

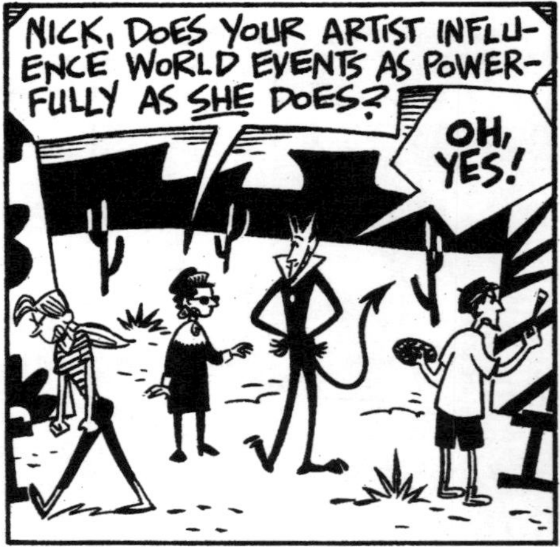
NICK, DOES YOUR ARTIST INFLUENCE WORLD EVENTS AS POWERFULLY AS SHE DOES?
OH, YES!

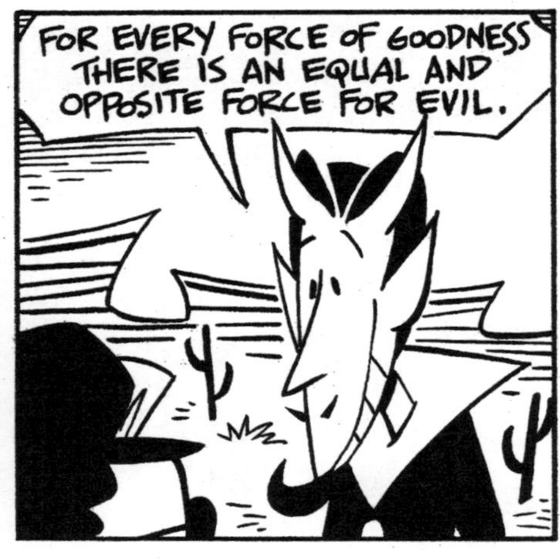
FOR EVERY FORCE OF GOODNESS THERE IS AN EQUAL AND OPPOSITE FORCE FOR EVIL.

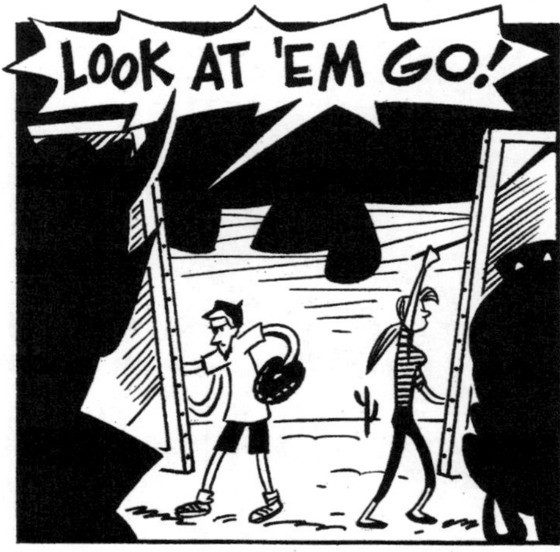
LOOK AT 'EM GO!

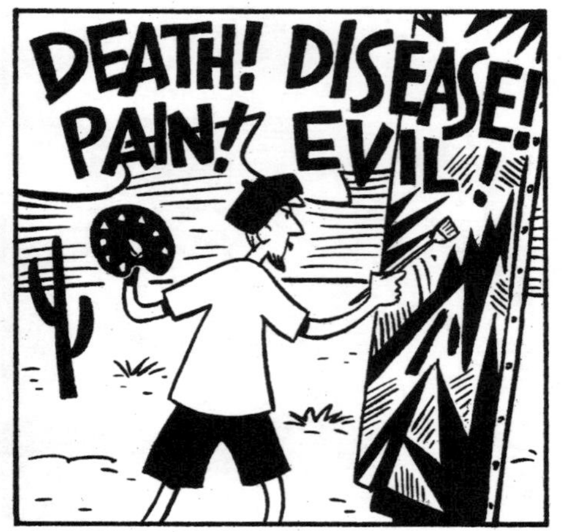
DEATH! DISEASE! PAIN! EVIL!

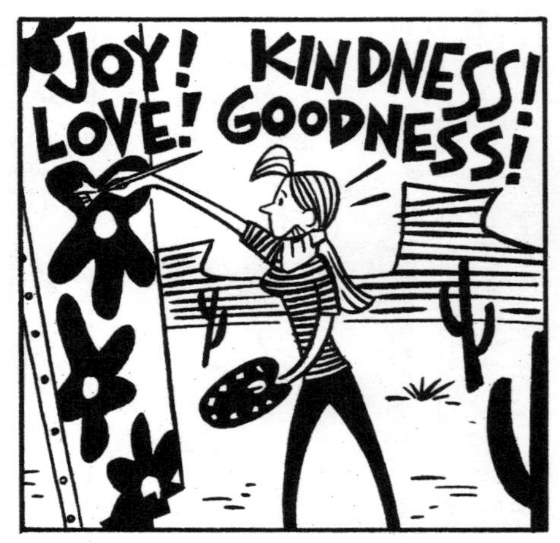
JOY! LOVE! KINDNESS! GOODNESS!

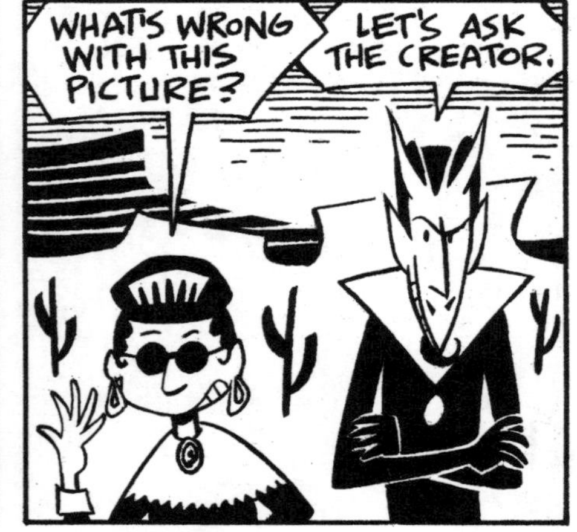
WHAT'S WRONG WITH THIS PICTURE?
LET'S ASK THE CREATOR.

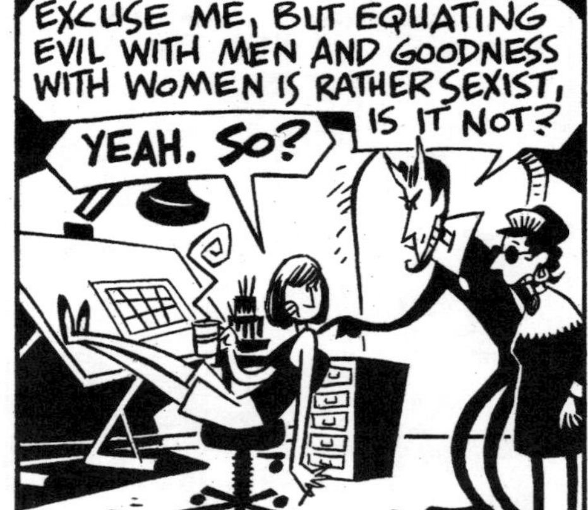
EXCUSE ME, BUT EQUATING EVIL WITH MEN AND GOODNESS WITH WOMEN IS RATHER SEXIST, IS IT NOT?
YEAH. SO?

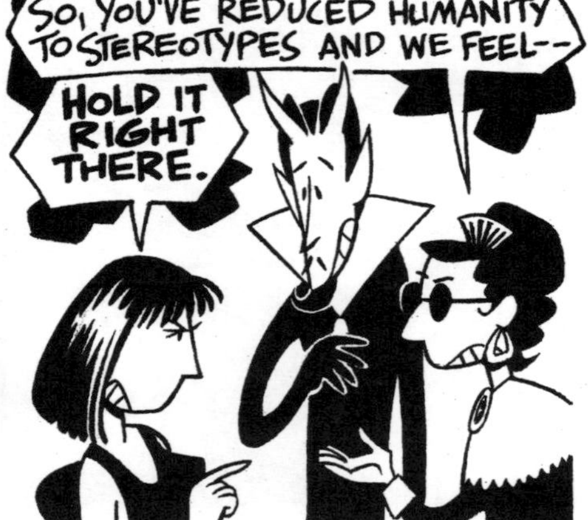
SO, YOU'VE REDUCED HUMANITY TO STEREOTYPES AND WE FEEL--
HOLD IT RIGHT THERE.

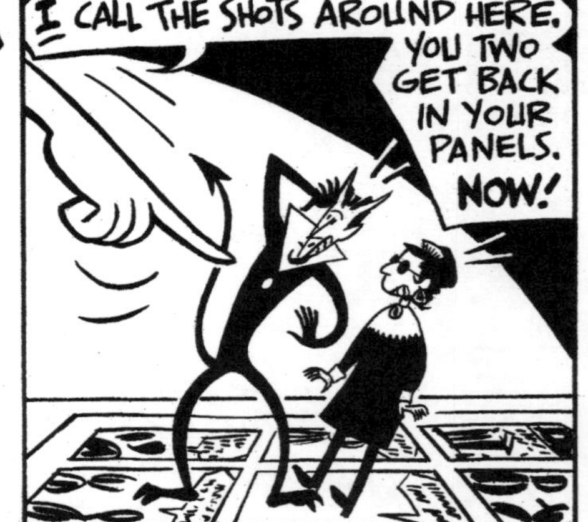
I CALL THE SHOTS AROUND HERE. YOU TWO GET BACK IN YOUR PANELS. NOW!

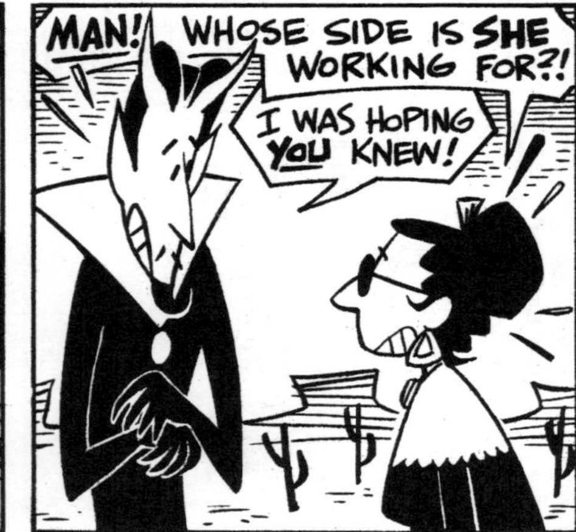
MAN!
WHOSE SIDE IS SHE WORKING FOR?!
I WAS HOPING YOU KNEW!

STORY MINUTE © CAROL LAY
"THE BRUSH-OFF"

THE ARTISTS WHO REPRESENT GOOD AND EVIL ARE IN HOT COMPETITION.

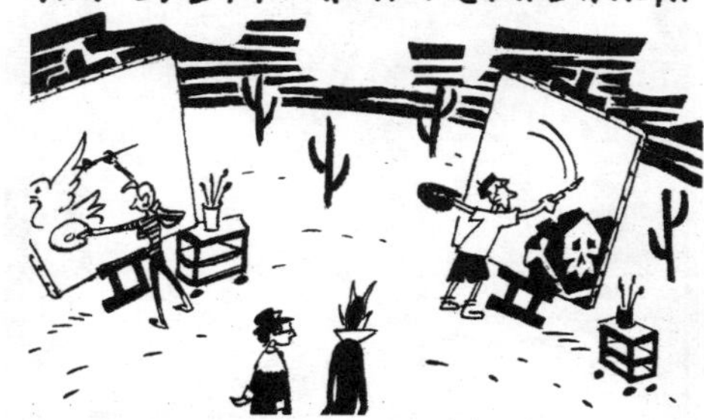

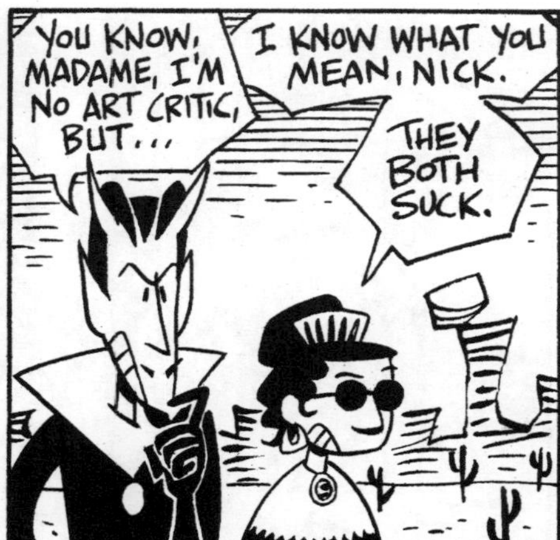


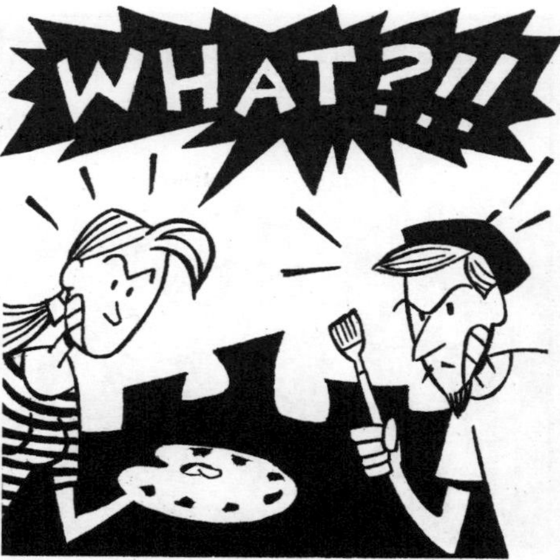


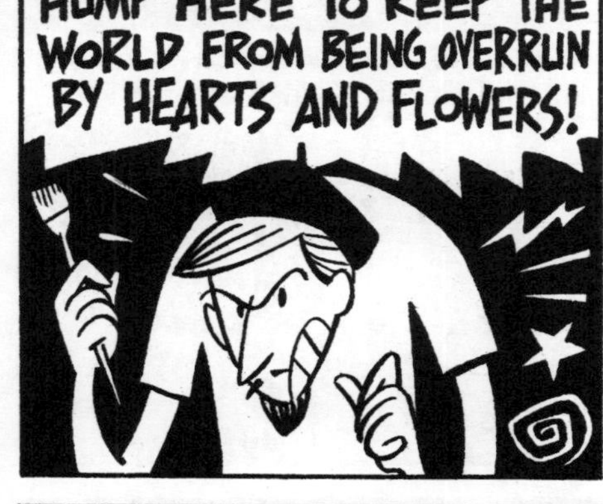

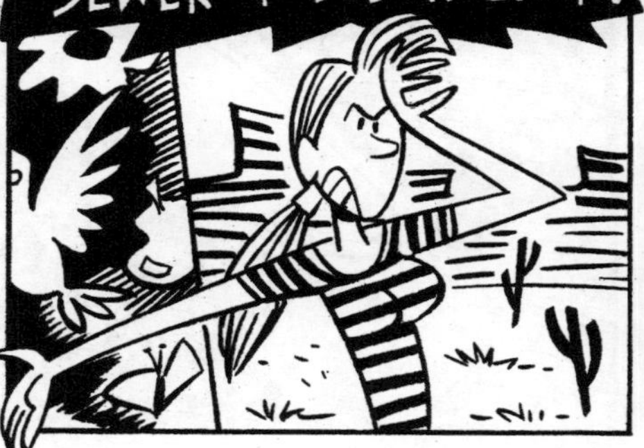

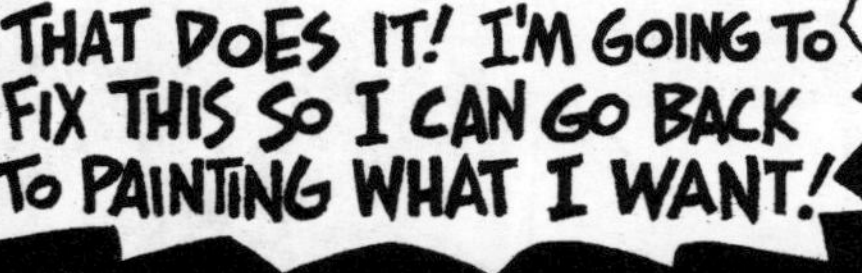


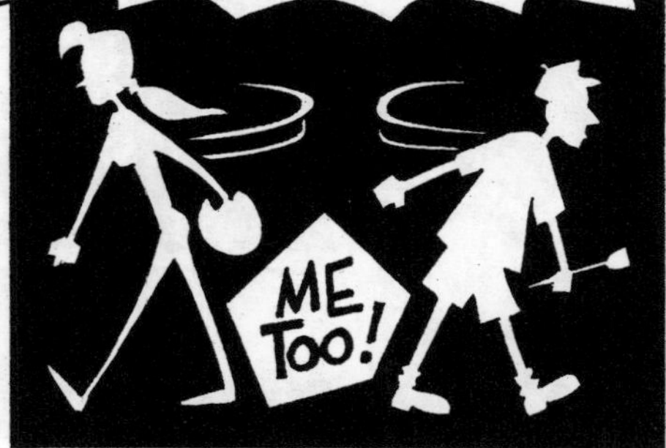


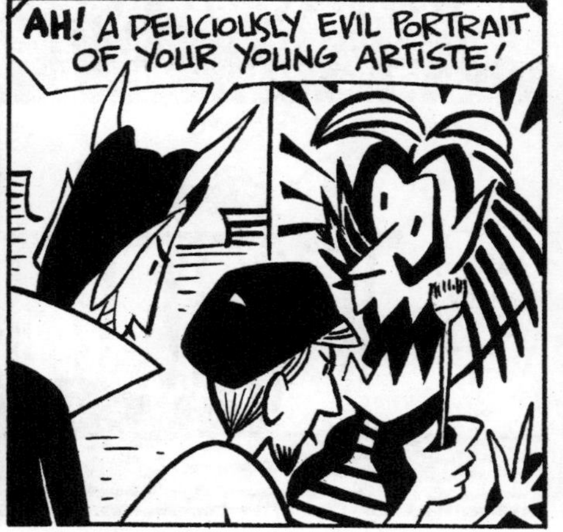


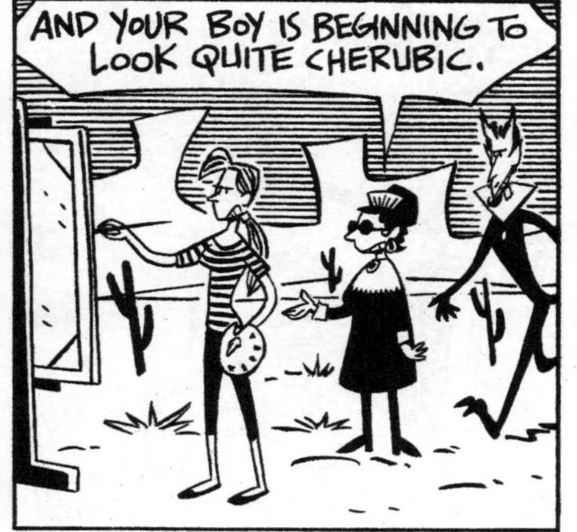


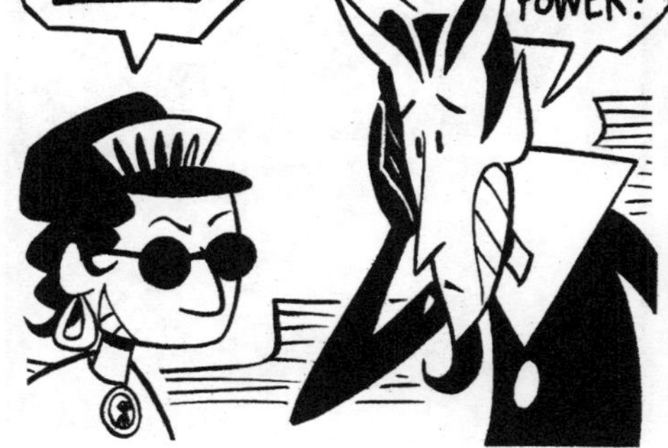


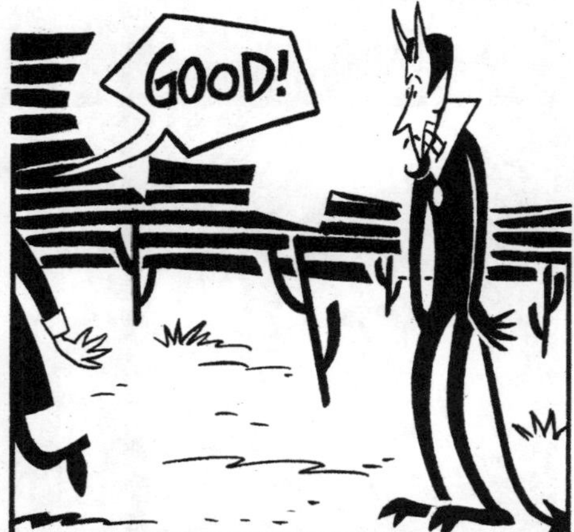


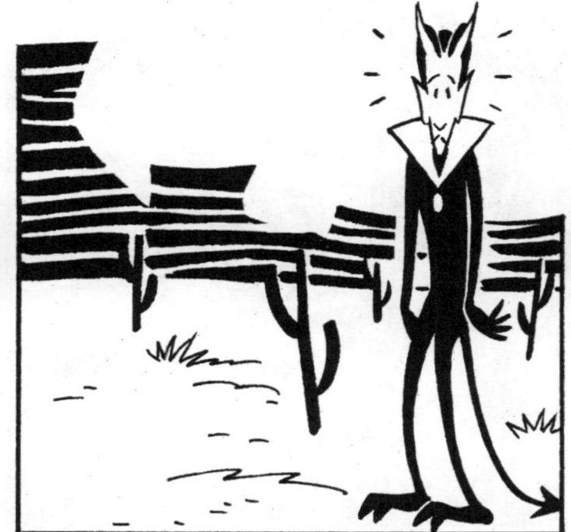

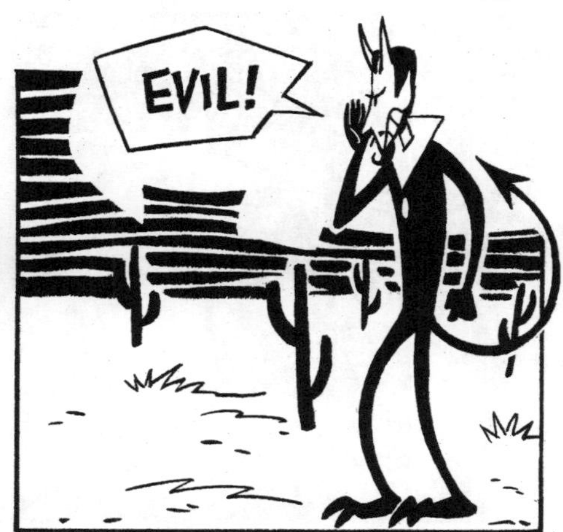

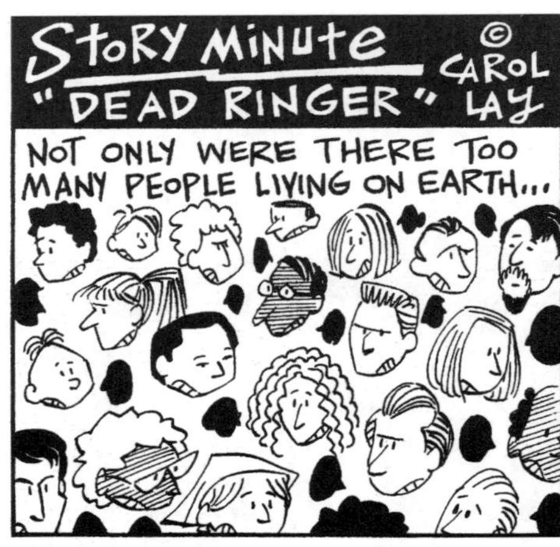
Story Minute
© CAROL LAY
"DEAD RINGER"
NOT ONLY WERE THERE TOO MANY PEOPLE LIVING ON EARTH...

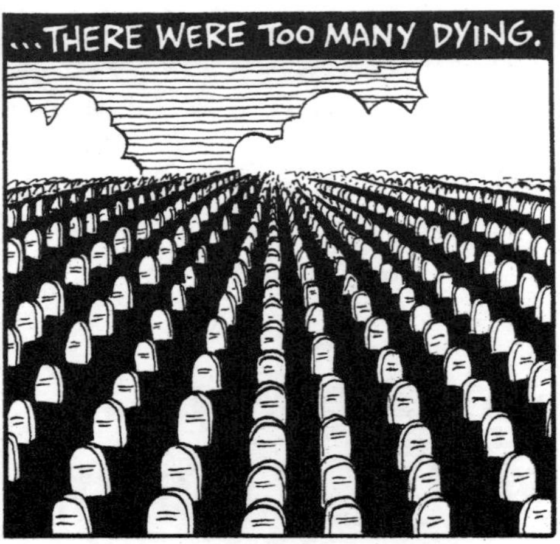
...THERE WERE TOO MANY DYING.

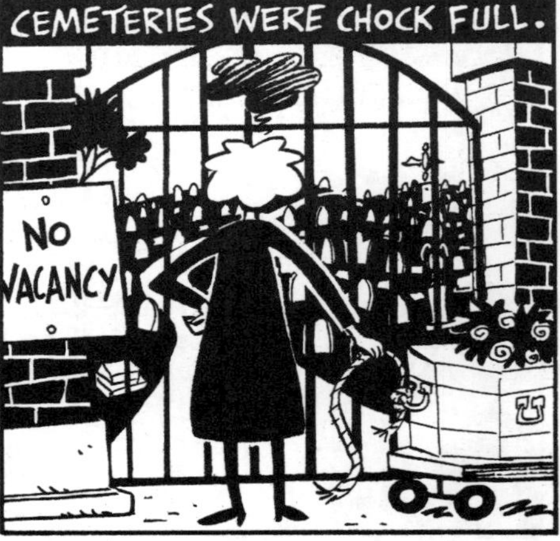
CEMETERIES WERE CHOCK FULL.
NO VACANCY

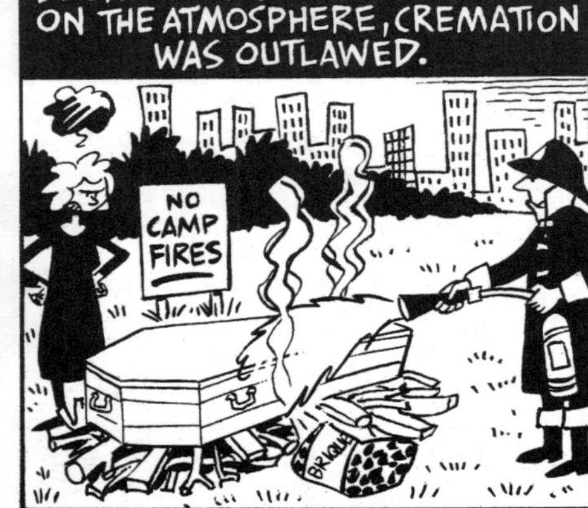
BECAUSE OF POLLUTING EFFECTS ON THE ATMOSPHERE, CREMATION WAS OUTLAWED.
NO CAMP FIRES

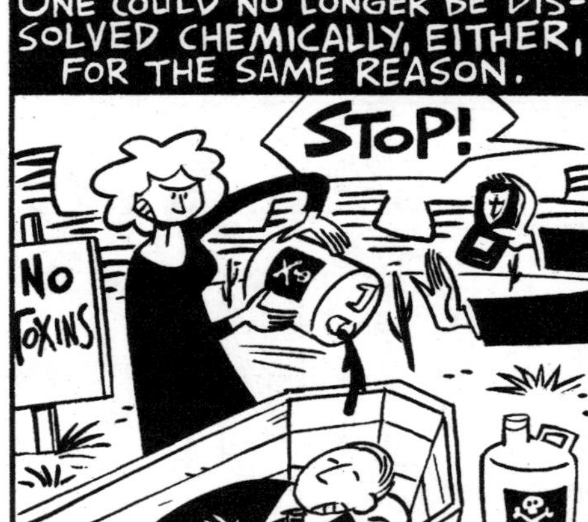
ONE COULD NO LONGER BE DIS-SOLVED CHEMICALLY, EITHER, FOR THE SAME REASON.
STOP!
NO TOXINS

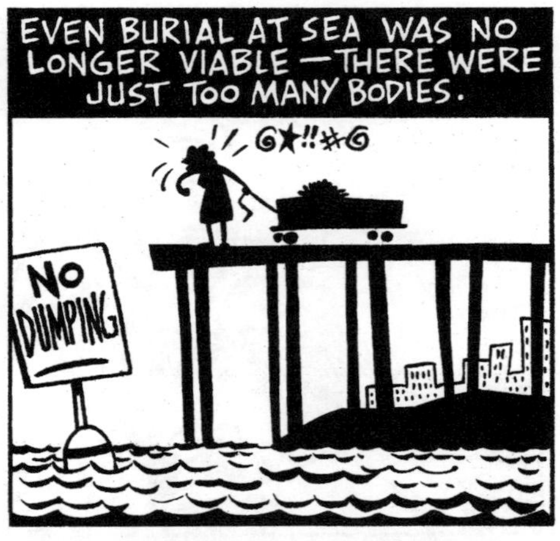
EVEN BURIAL AT SEA WAS NO LONGER VIABLE—THERE WERE JUST TOO MANY BODIES.
NO DUMPING

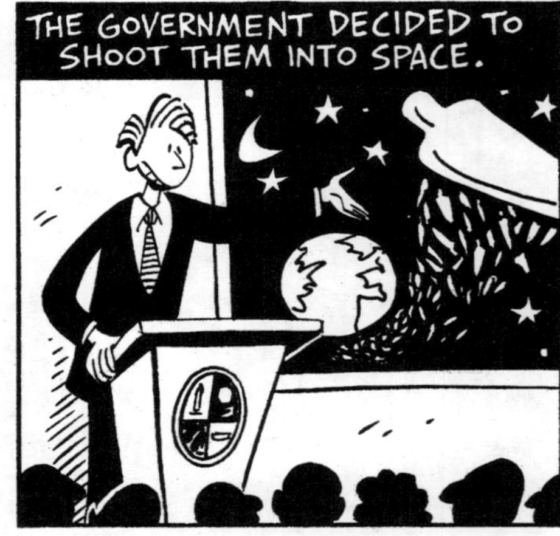
THE GOVERNMENT DECIDED TO SHOOT THEM INTO SPACE.

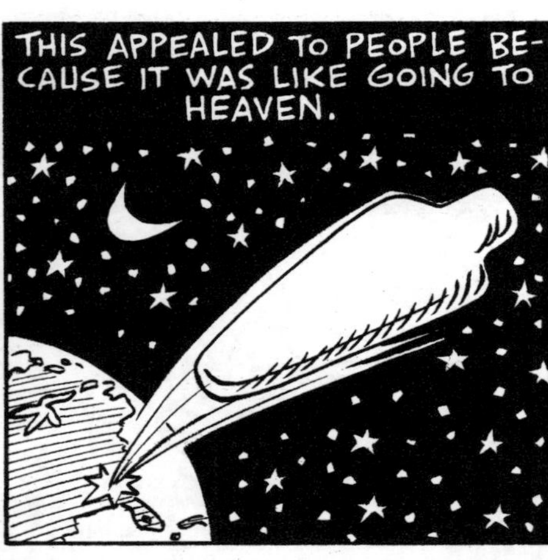
THIS APPEALED TO PEOPLE BE-CAUSE IT WAS LIKE GOING TO HEAVEN.

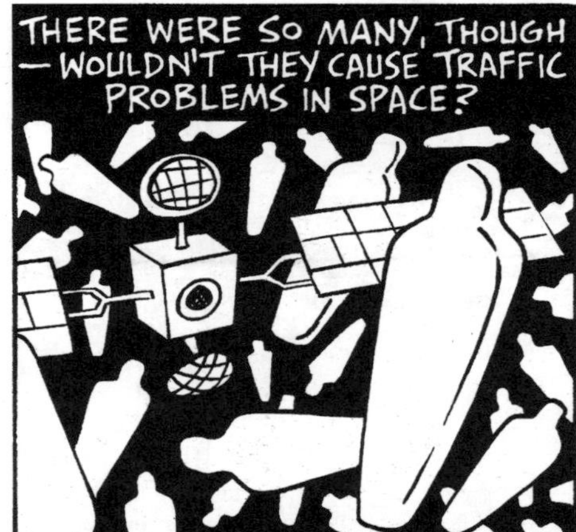
THERE WERE SO MANY, THOUGH —WOULDN'T THEY CAUSE TRAFFIC PROBLEMS IN SPACE?

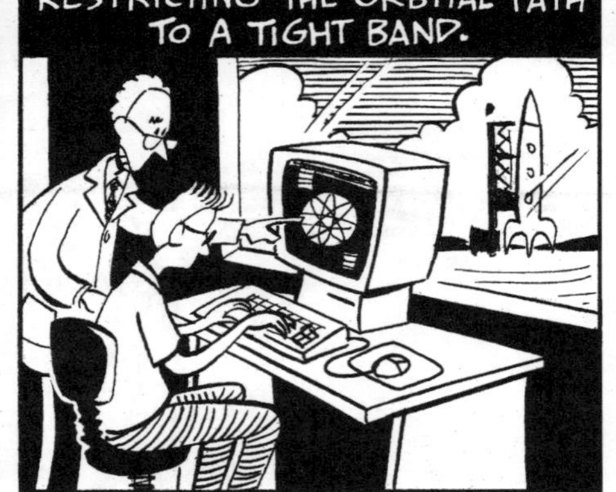
THEY SOLVED THE PROBLEM BY RESTRICTING THE ORBITAL PATH TO A TIGHT BAND.

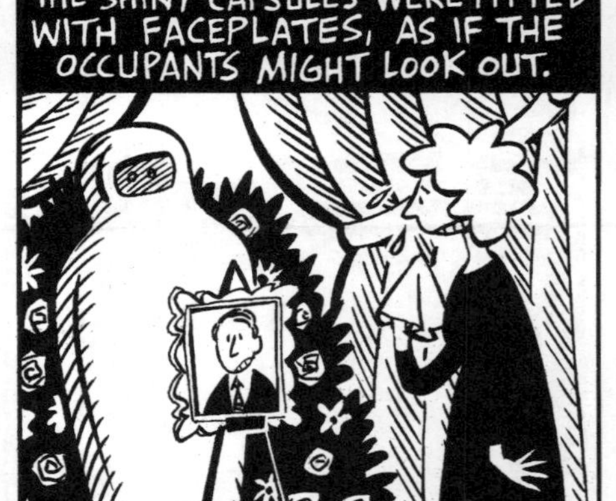
THE SHINY CAPSULES WERE FITTED WITH FACEPLATES, AS IF THE OCCUPANTS MIGHT LOOK OUT.

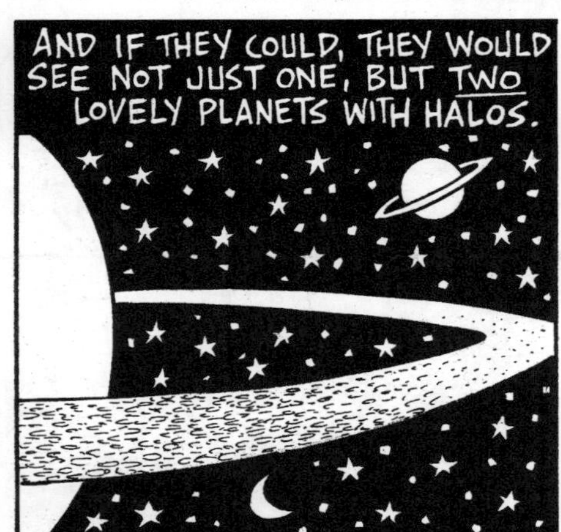
AND IF THEY COULD, THEY WOULD SEE NOT JUST ONE, BUT TWO LOVELY PLANETS WITH HALOS.

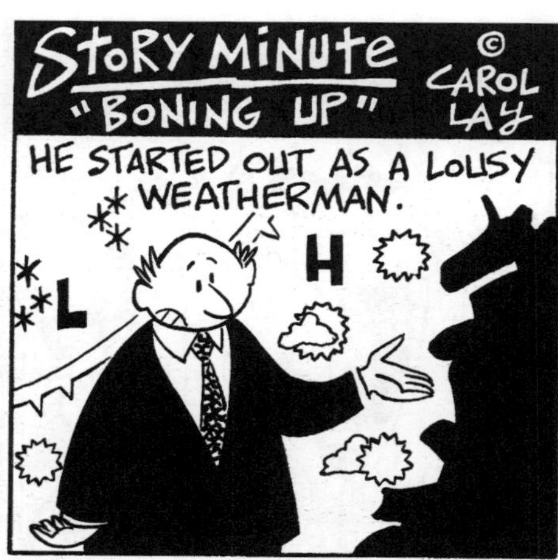

STORY MINUTE
"BONING UP"
© CAROL LAY
HE STARTED OUT AS A LOUSY WEATHERMAN.
L
H


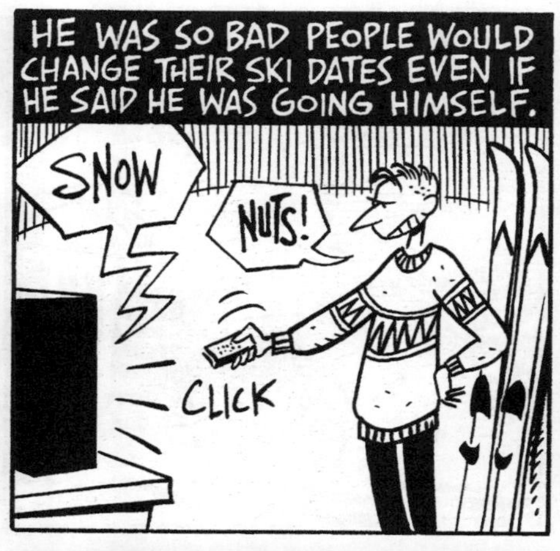

HE WAS SO BAD PEOPLE WOULD CHANGE THEIR SKI DATES EVEN IF HE SAID HE WAS GOING HIMSELF.
SNOW
NUTS!
CLICK


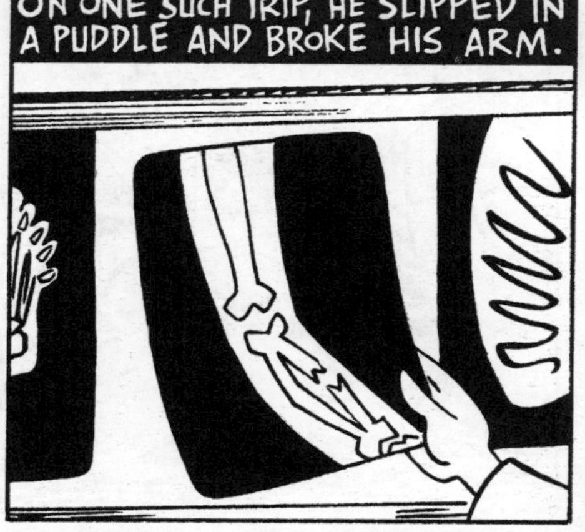

ON ONE SUCH TRIP, HE SLIPPED IN A PUDDLE AND BROKE HIS ARM.


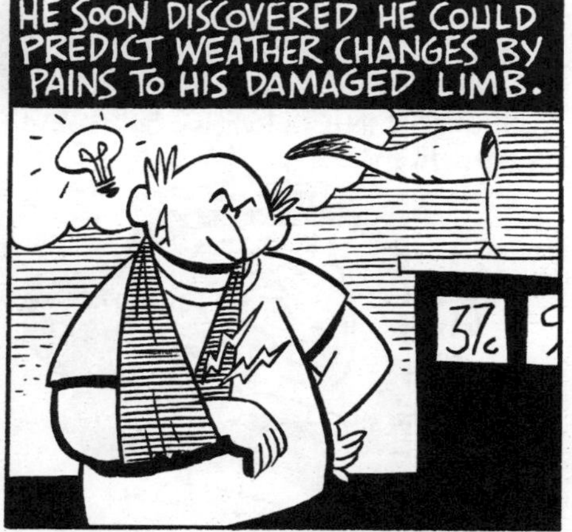

HE SOON DISCOVERED HE COULD PREDICT WEATHER CHANGES BY PAINS TO HIS DAMAGED LIMB.
37c


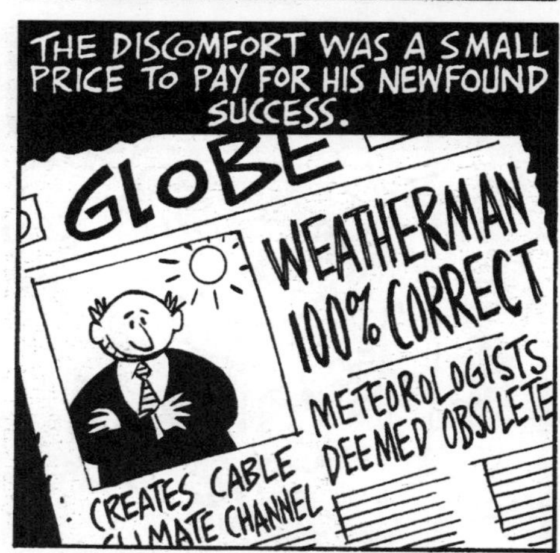

THE DISCOMFORT WAS A SMALL PRICE TO PAY FOR HIS NEWFOUND SUCCESS.
GLOBE
WEATHERMAN 100% CORRECT
METEOROLOGISTS DEEMED OBSOLETE
CREATES CABLE CLIMATE CHANNEL


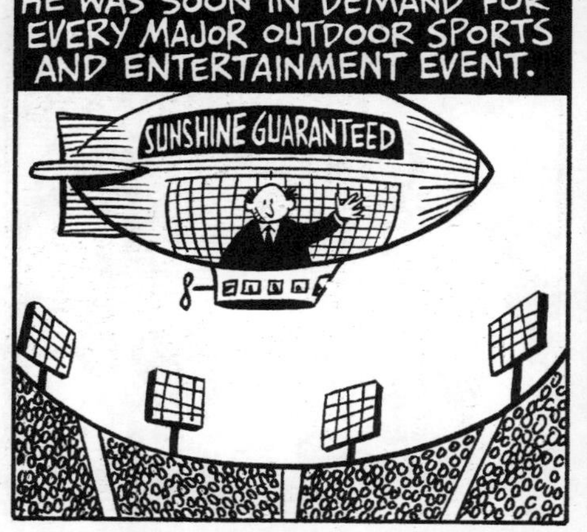

HE WAS SOON IN DEMAND FOR EVERY MAJOR OUTDOOR SPORTS AND ENTERTAINMENT EVENT.
SUNSHINE GUARANTEED


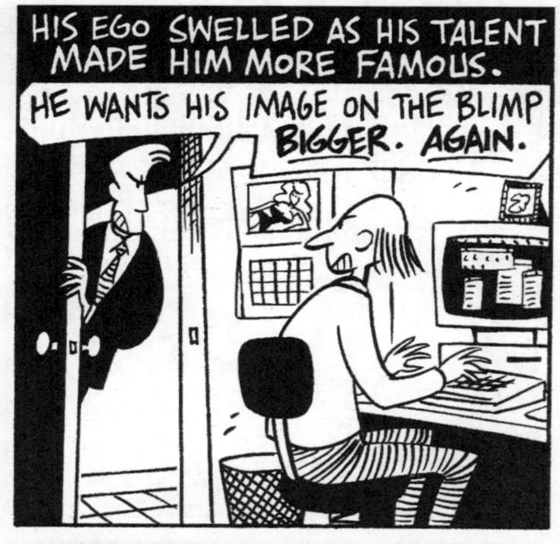

HIS EGO SWELLED AS HIS TALENT MADE HIM MORE FAMOUS.
HE WANTS HIS IMAGE ON THE BLIMP BIGGER. AGAIN.


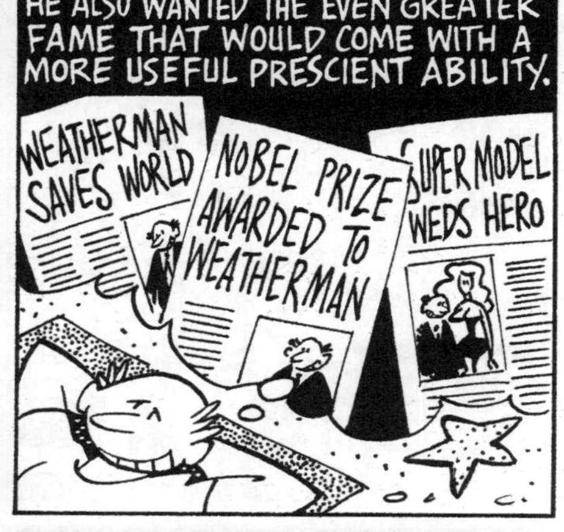

HE ALSO WANTED THE EVEN GREATER FAME THAT WOULD COME WITH A MORE USEFUL PRESCIENT ABILITY.
WEATHERMAN SAVES WORLD
NOBEL PRIZE AWARDED TO WEATHERMAN
SUPER MODEL WEDS HERO


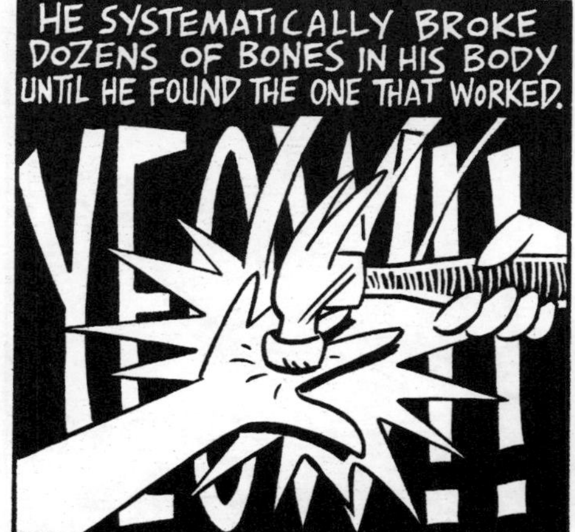

HE SYSTEMATICALLY BROKE DOZENS OF BONES IN HIS BODY UNTIL HE FOUND THE ONE THAT WORKED.


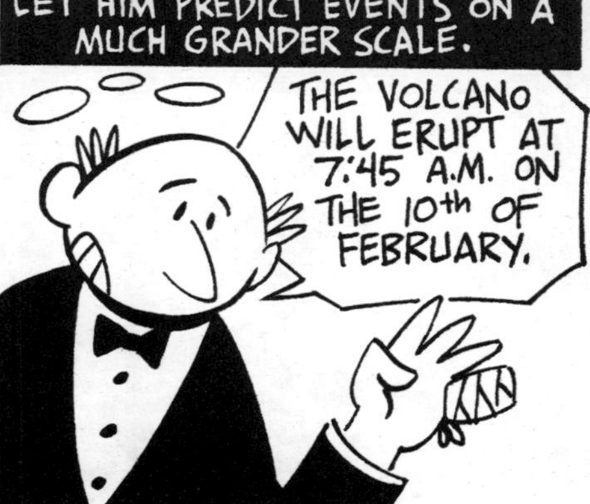

ONCE BROKEN, THIS TINY BONE LET HIM PREDICT EVENTS ON A MUCH GRANDER SCALE.
THE VOLCANO WILL ERUPT AT 7:45 A.M. ON THE 10th OF FEBRUARY.


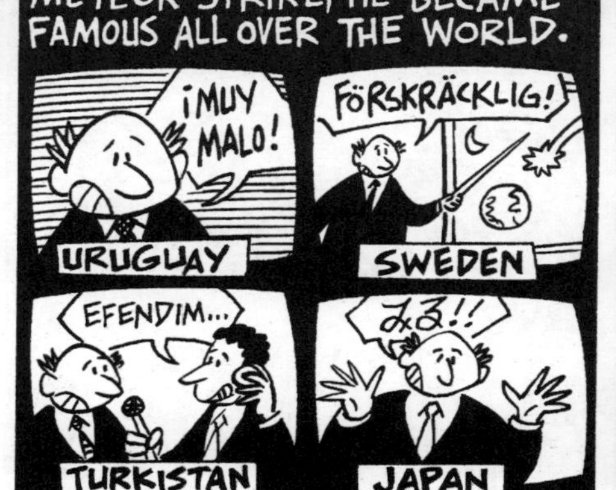

WHEN HE FORECAST THE GIANT METEOR STRIKE, HE BECAME FAMOUS ALL OVER THE WORLD.
¡MUY MALO!
URUGUAY
FÖRSKRÄCKLIG!
SWEDEN
EFENDIM...
TURKISTAN
JAPAN


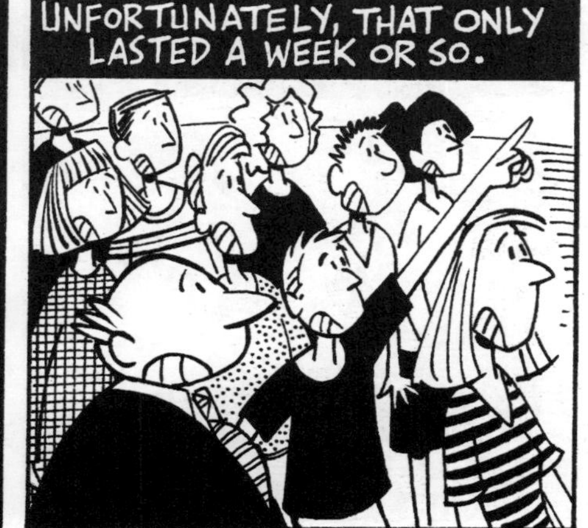

UNFORTUNATELY, THAT ONLY LASTED A WEEK OR SO.

Story Minute
"Dumb Animals"
© Carol Lay
Superior intelligence supposedly made humans' lives sacred...

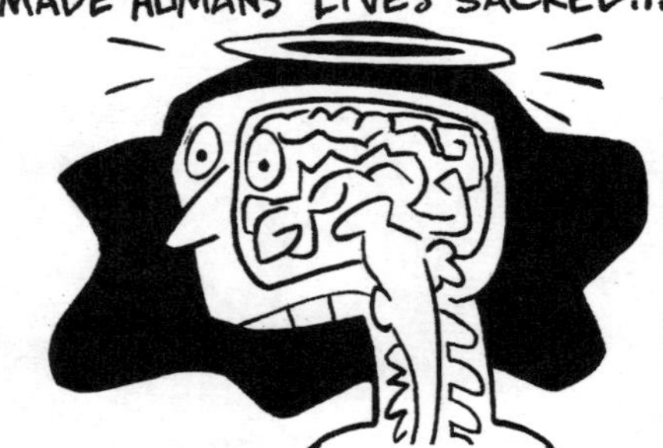

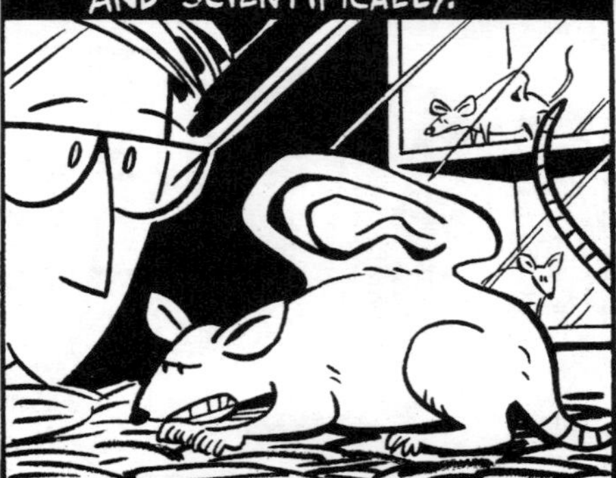
...While the lives of animals were up for grabs commercially and scientifically.

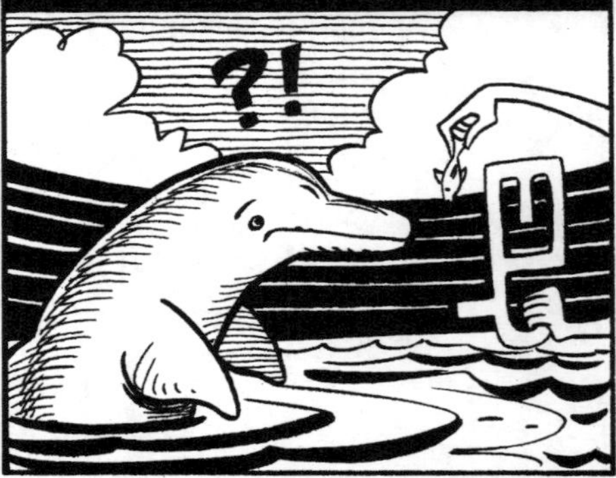
Sometimes animals were imprisoned to see how their brains might operate...
?!

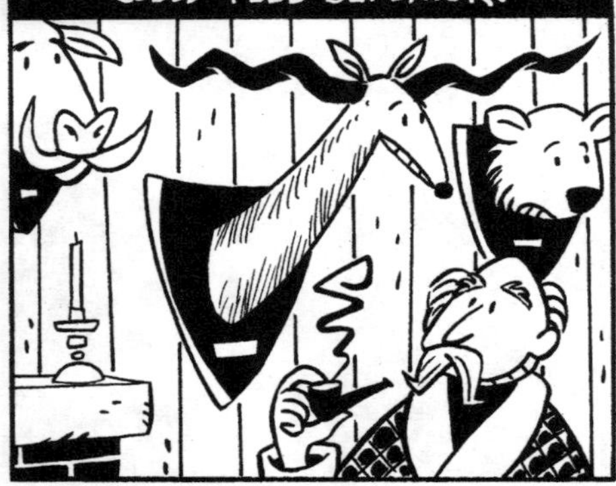
...But often their lives were forfeited just so some human could feel superior.

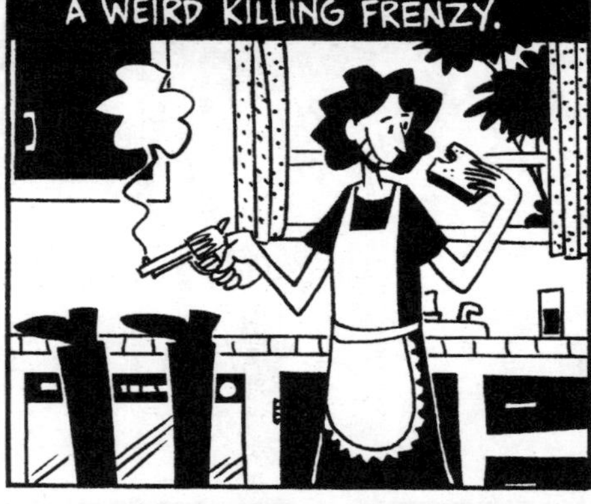
One day, though, humans turned on each other exclusively in a weird killing frenzy.

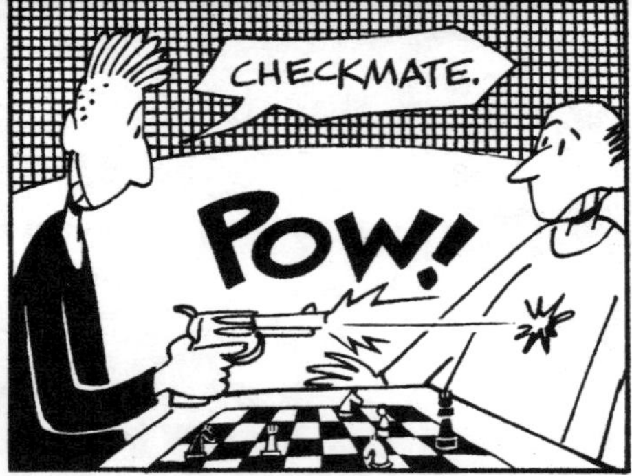
They used the same justifications for killing their own, i.e. intellectual superiority.
Checkmate.
POW!

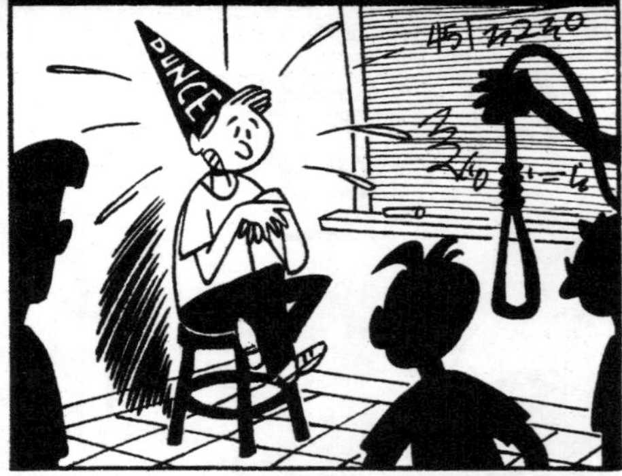
People were picked off pretty much according to what their individual I.Q. was.
DUNCE

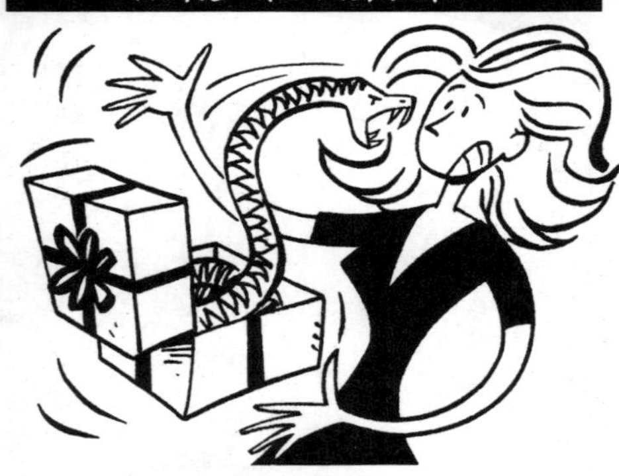
The smarter and smaller the field became, the more clever were the murders.

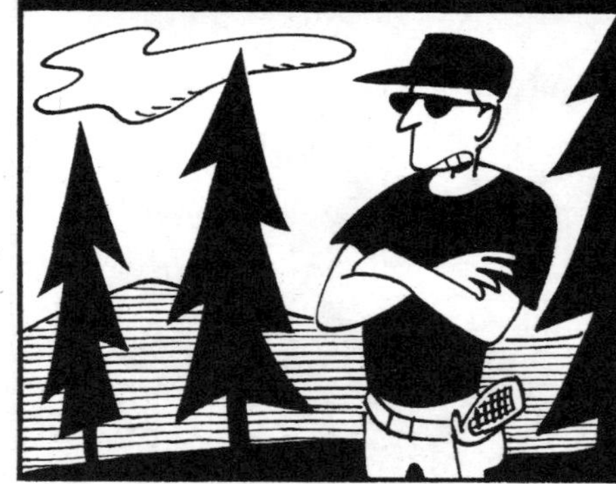
Finally, there was only one person left — the smartest homo sapien on the planet.

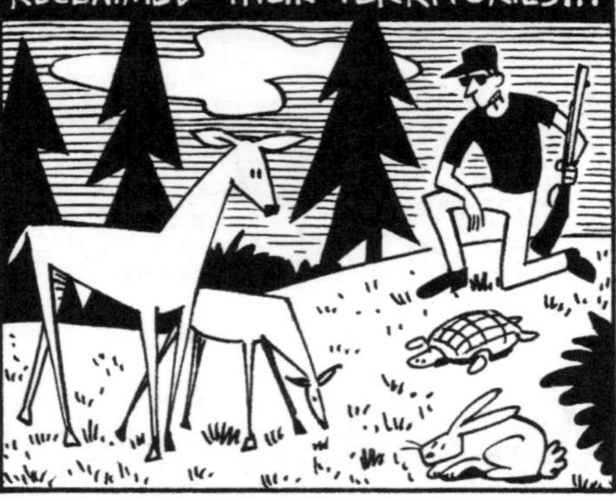
He had to admire the speed with which the flora and fauna reclaimed their territories...

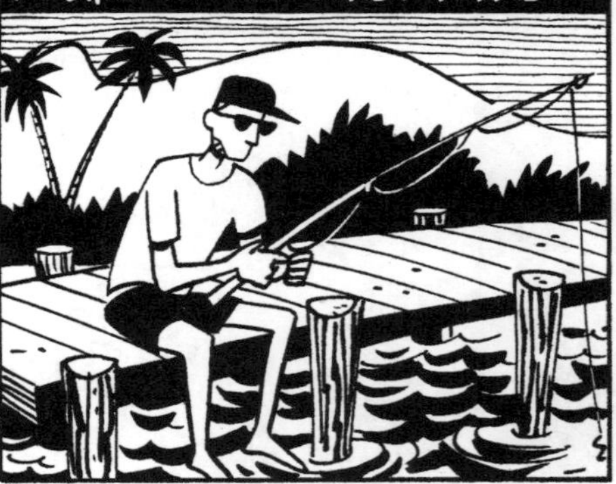
...But even he didn't know what had started all the killing in the first place...

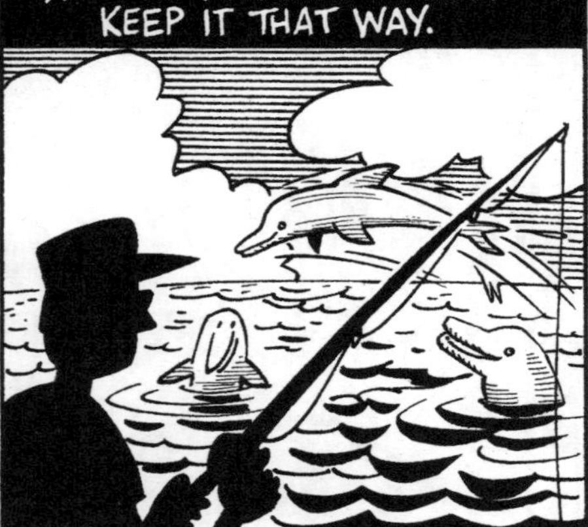
...And the dolphins decided to keep it that way.

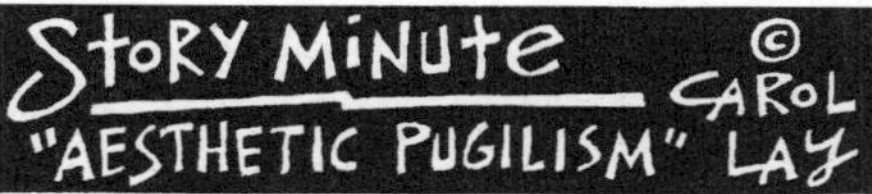
STORY MINUTE © CAROL LAY
"AESTHETIC PUGILISM"

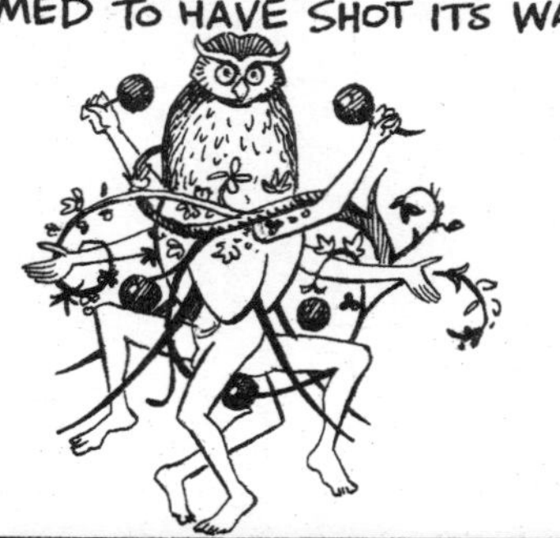
BY THE MILLENNIUM'S END, ART SEEMED TO HAVE SHOT ITS WAD.

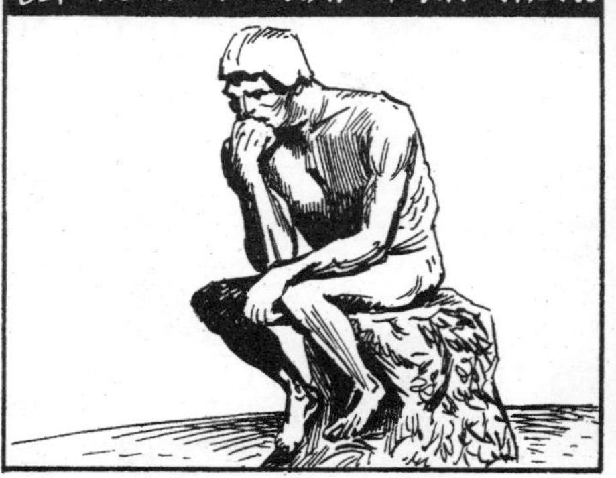
MOVEMENTS DISSIPATED QUICKLY BECAUSE IT HAD ALL BEEN DONE BEFORE IN ONE WAY OR ANOTHER.

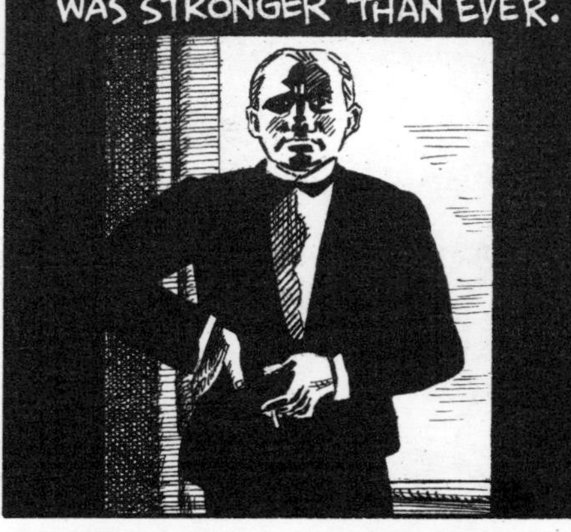
THE ARTISTIC EGO, HOWEVER, WAS STRONGER THAN EVER.

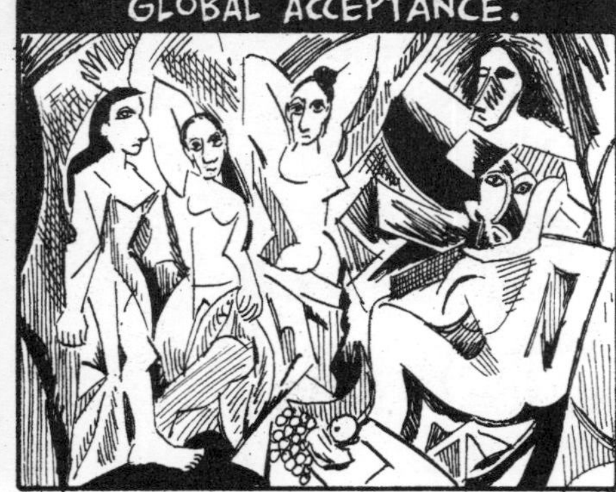
WHEN "BEST ARTISTISM" APPEARED, THE TIME WAS RIGHT FOR ITS GLOBAL ACCEPTANCE.

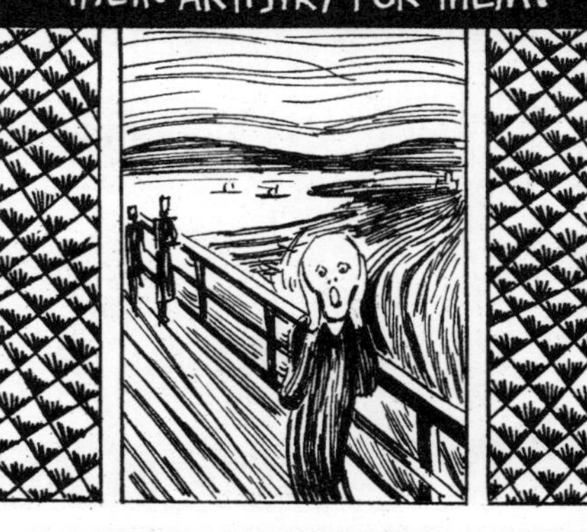
THE MOST AMBITIOUS ARTISTS RECRUITED FANS TO CHAMPION THEIR ARTISTRY FOR THEM.

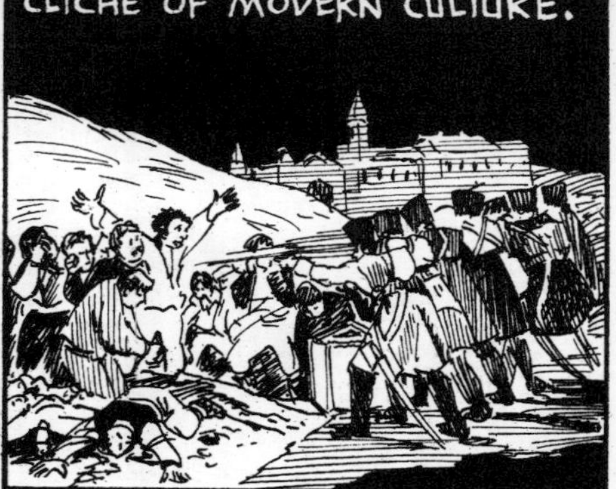
THE MOVEMENT QUICKLY EMBRACED GANGSTER FORMS, ALREADY A CLICHÉ OF MODERN CULTURE.

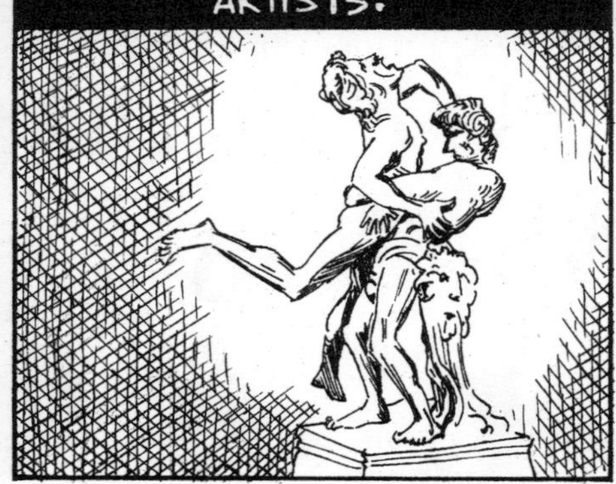
THE GANGS FOUGHT TO THE DEATH IN THE NAME OF THEIR PATRON ARTISTS.

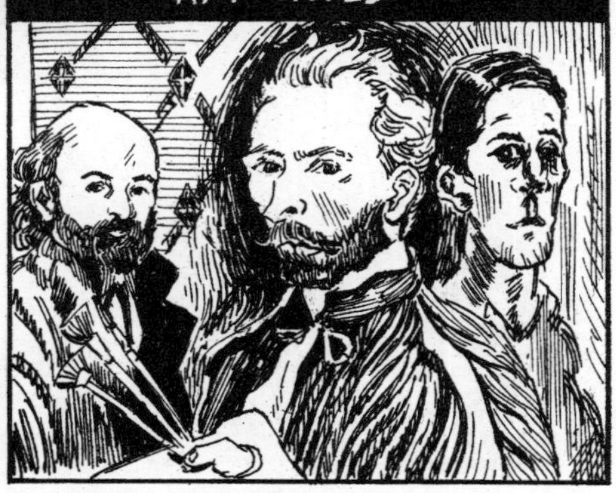
EVEN A FEW LONG-DEAD PAINTERS ATTRACTED LEGIONS OF LOYAL ADVOCATES.

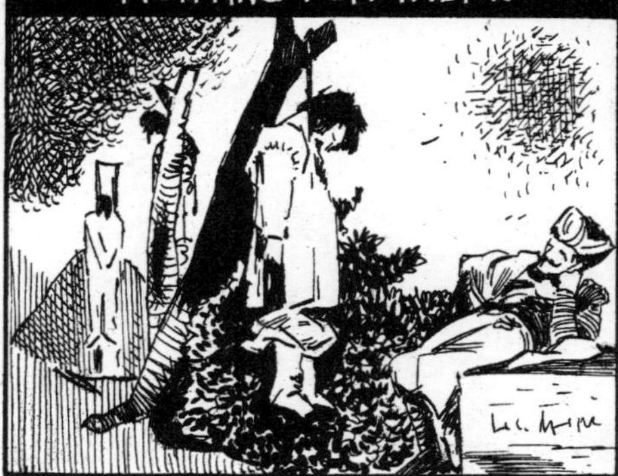
ONE CHICKEN OUTFIT, THE KOSTABIS, HIRED OTHER GANGS TO DO THEIR FIGHTING FOR THEM.

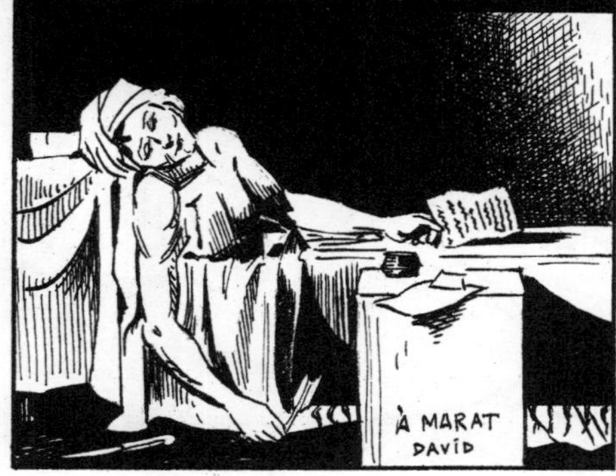
ASSASSINATIONS GREW COMMON AND MOST OF THE WORLD'S ART WAS DESTROYED BY ARSON.
À MARAT
DAVID

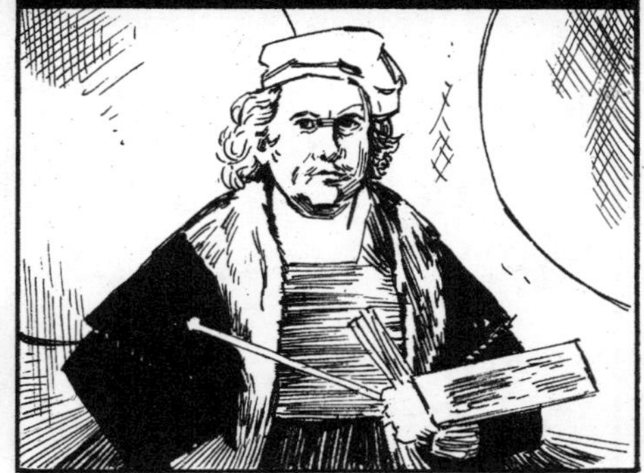
WHEN THE DUST CLEARED, THE SURVIVING ARTISTS RETURNED TO WORK WITH RENEWED VIGOR...

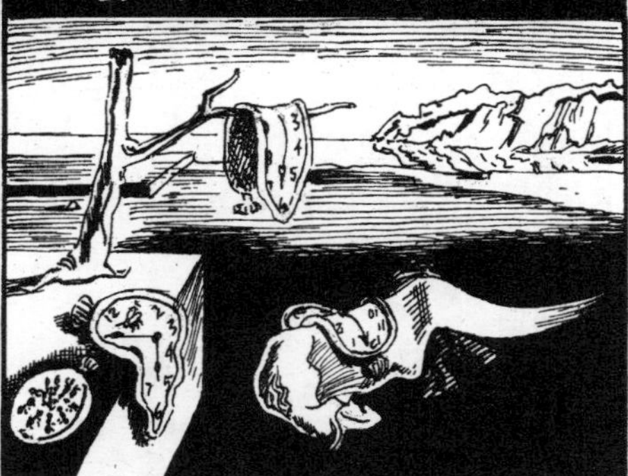
...FOR NOW THEY HAD A CHANCE TO REPLACE ART INSTEAD OF MERELY REPEATING IT.

STORY MINUTE © CAROL LAY

"DIVINING INTERVENTION"

SHE DOWSED EVERYTHING WITH WHICH SHE CAME IN CONTACT.

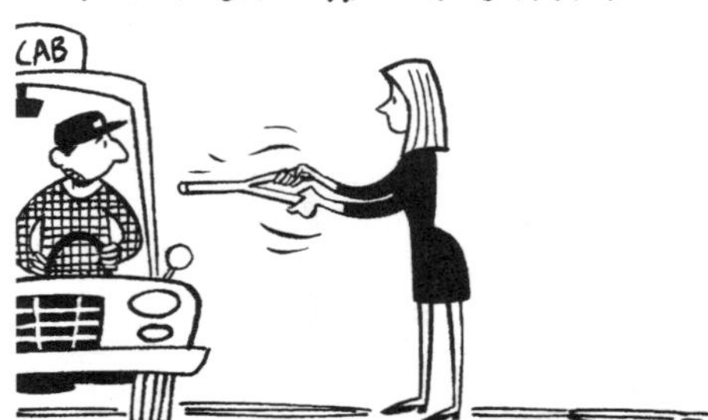


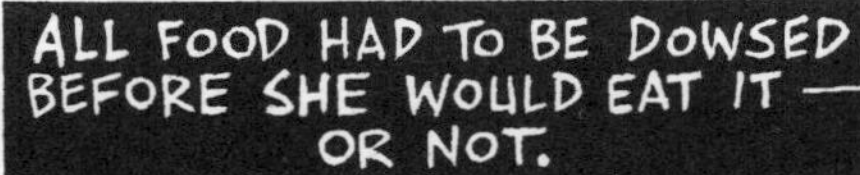


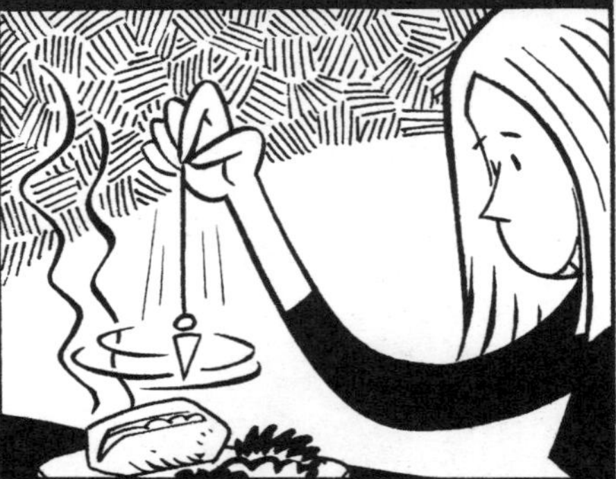

SHE ASKED ABOUT THE EDIFYING AND ENTERTAINING QUALITIES OF VIDEOTAPES AND BOOKS.

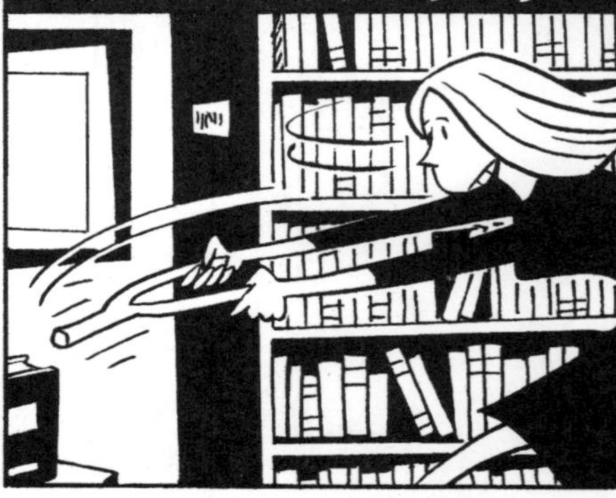

EVERYTHING IN HER DOWSED HOUSE HAD BEEN GIVEN THE OK IN THIS MANNER.

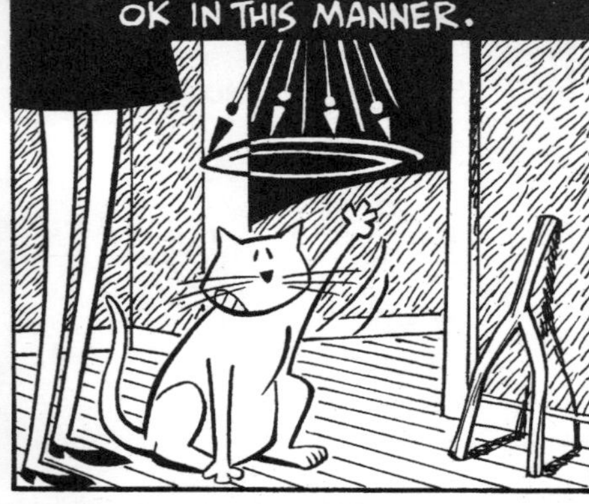

NOW, PRACTICING THIS RITUAL IN PUBLIC WAS NOT CONDUCIVE TO MEETING MEN.

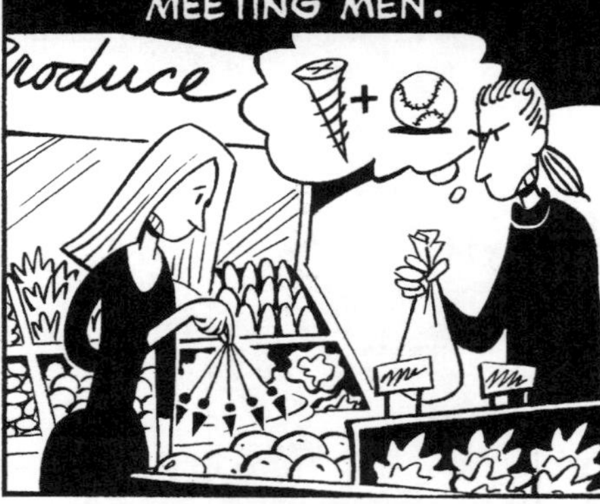

SHE MADE FRIENDS OF LIKE-MINDED PEOPLE AT DOWSING CONVENTIONS...

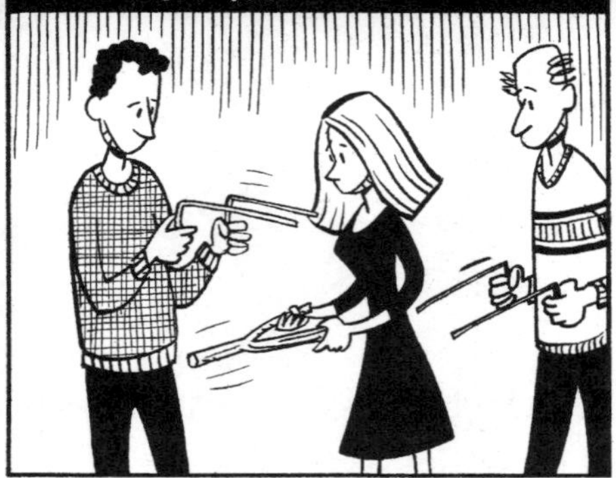

...BUT NONE OF THOSE MEN WERE DEEMED TO BE GOOD FOR HER BY HER WITCHING STICK.

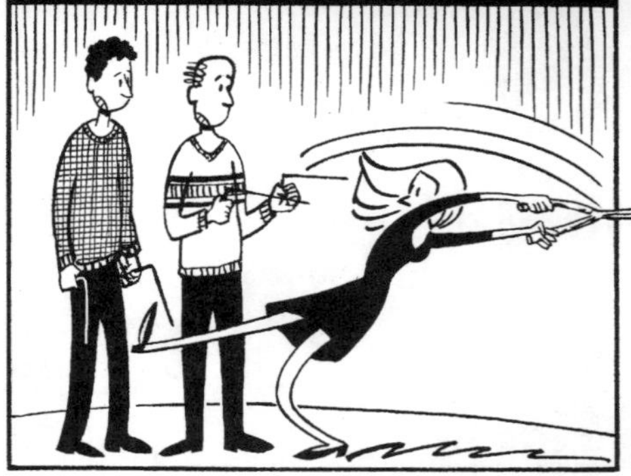

IT TOLD HER THAT, FOR TRUE BALANCE, SHE NEEDED A MAN WHO DID NOT BELIEVE IN DOWSING.

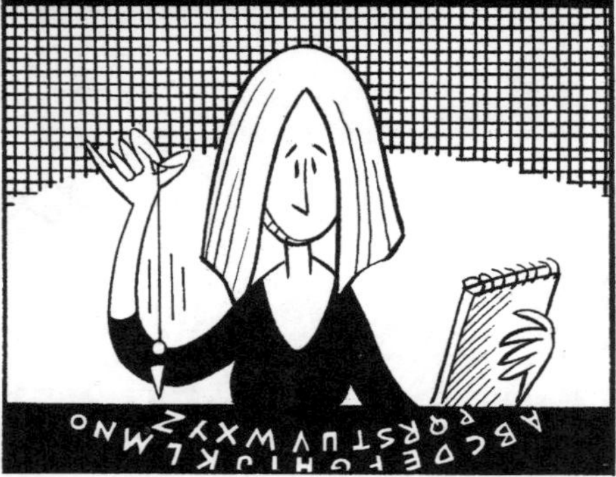

THE STICK FINALLY FOUND A MAN IT APPROVED OF, BUT THE MAN DID NOT APPROVE OF THE STICK.

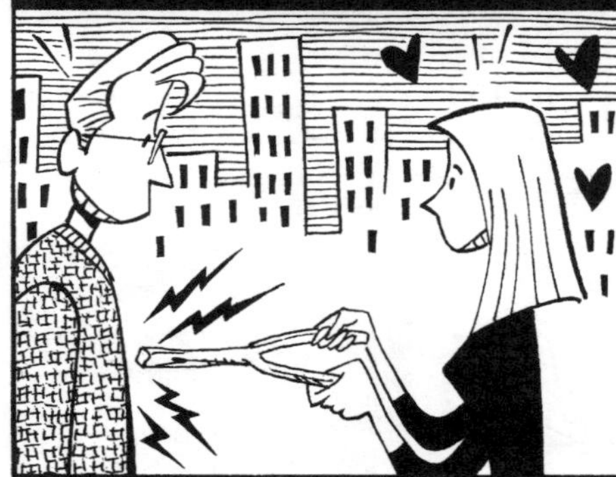

WHEN HE ASKED HER TO CHOOSE BETWEEN HIM AND THE DIVINING ROD, SHE CONSULTED IT AGAIN.

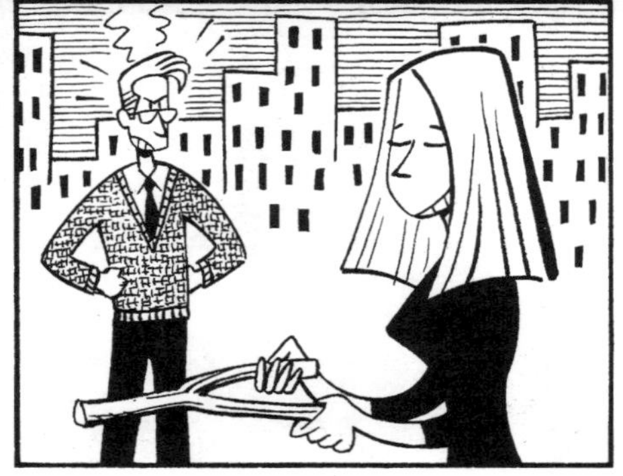

IT TOLD HER TO CHOOSE THE MAN BUT, OF COURSE, HE HAD SEEN HER ACTION AND HE WAS GONE.

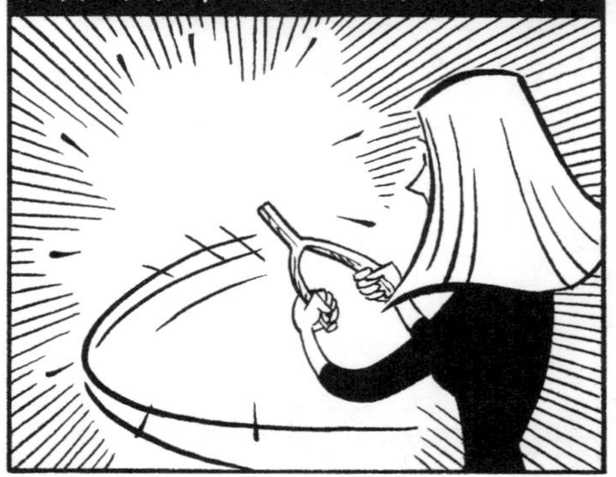

AND THE STICK HAD ADVISED HER SO EXCELLENTLY, SHE KNEW SHE COULD NEVER GIVE IT UP.

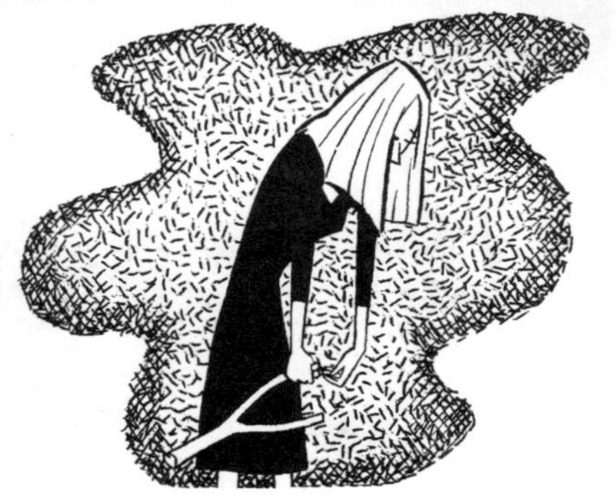

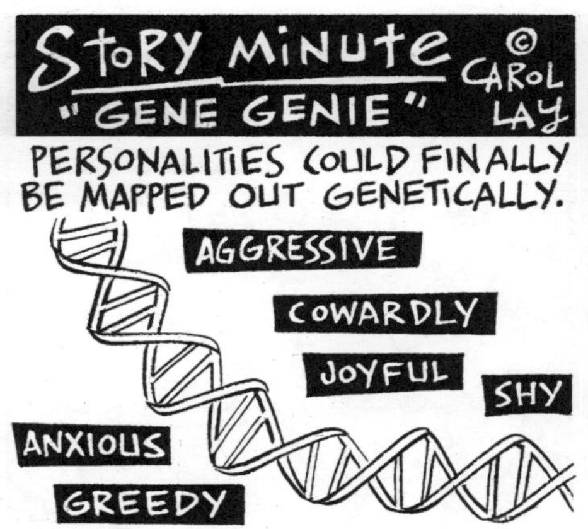
STORY MINUTE
"GENE GENIE"
© CAROL LAY
PERSONALITIES COULD FINALLY BE MAPPED OUT GENETICALLY.
AGGRESSIVE
COWARDLY
JOYFUL
SHY
ANXIOUS
GREEDY

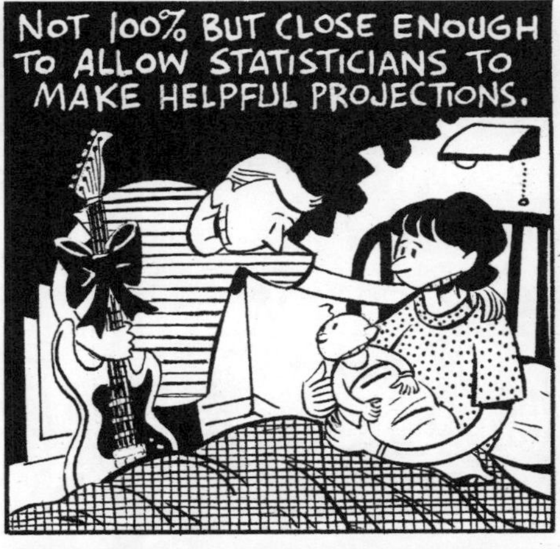
NOT 100% BUT CLOSE ENOUGH TO ALLOW STATISTICIANS TO MAKE HELPFUL PROJECTIONS.

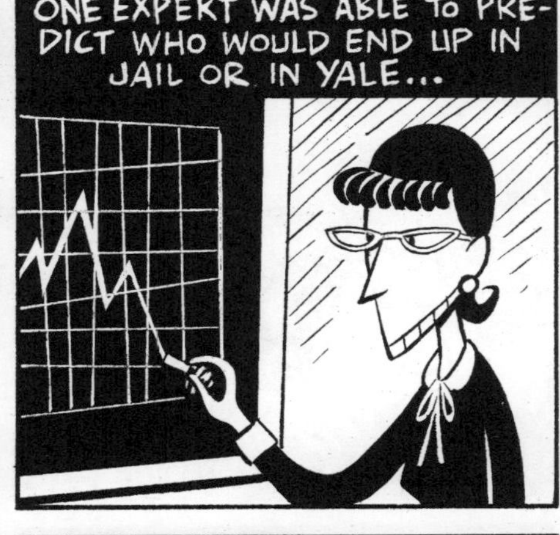
ONE EXPERT WAS ABLE TO PREDICT WHO WOULD END UP IN JAIL OR IN YALE...

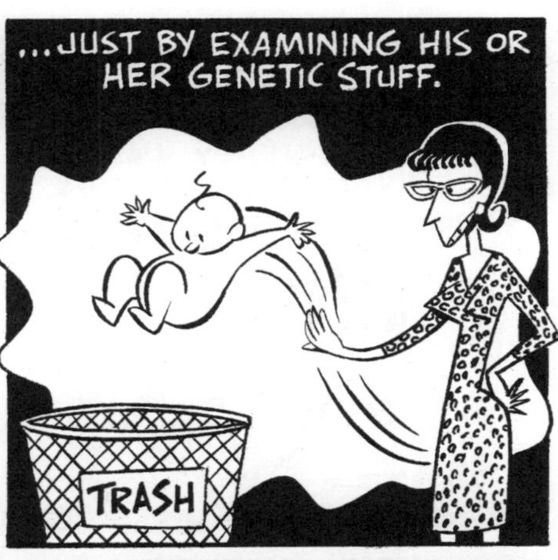
...JUST BY EXAMINING HIS OR HER GENETIC STUFF.
TRASH

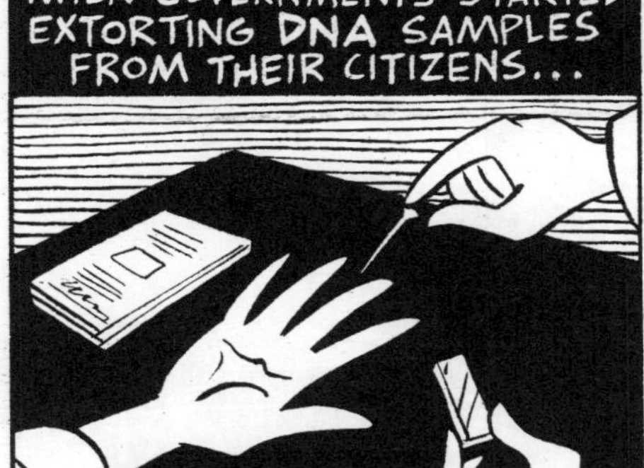
WHEN GOVERNMENTS STARTED EXTORTING DNA SAMPLES FROM THEIR CITIZENS...

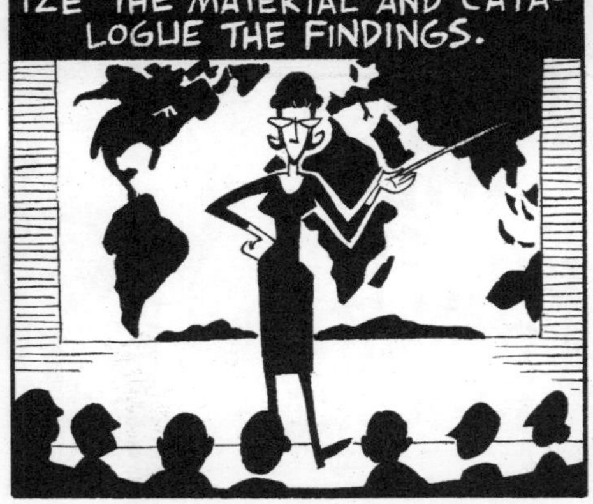
...THEY HIRED HER TO ORGANIZE THE MATERIAL AND CATALOGUE THE FINDINGS.

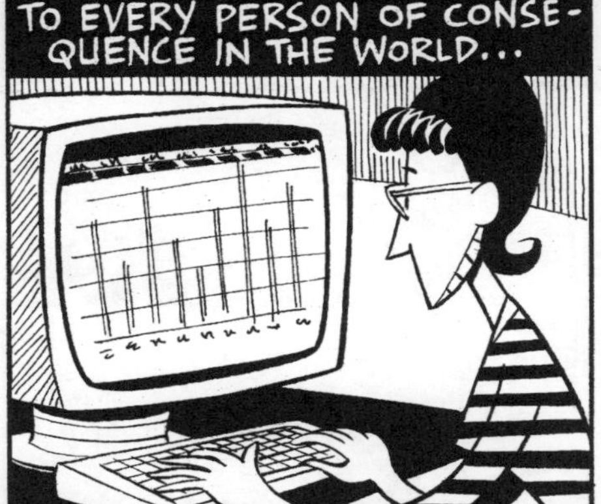
NOW SHE NOT ONLY HAD A KEY TO EVERY PERSON OF CONSEQUENCE IN THE WORLD...

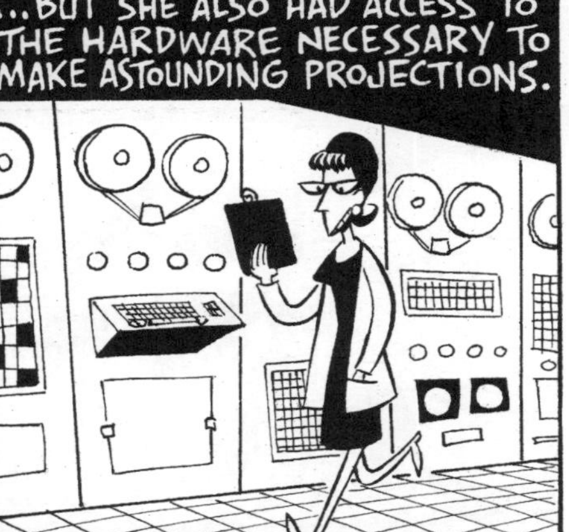
...BUT SHE ALSO HAD ACCESS TO THE HARDWARE NECESSARY TO MAKE ASTOUNDING PROJECTIONS.

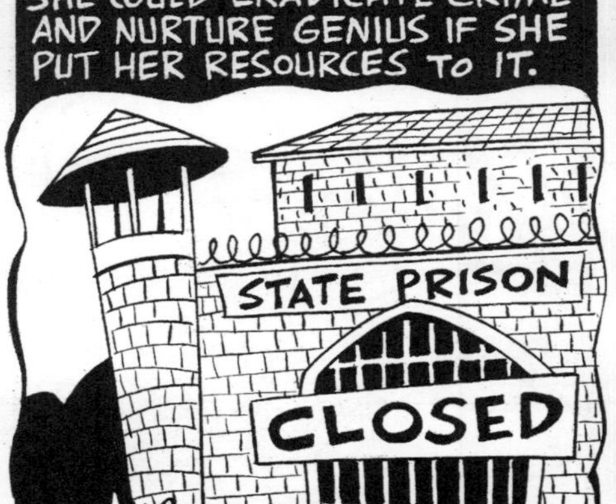
SHE COULD ERADICATE CRIME AND NURTURE GENIUS IF SHE PUT HER RESOURCES TO IT.
STATE PRISON
CLOSED

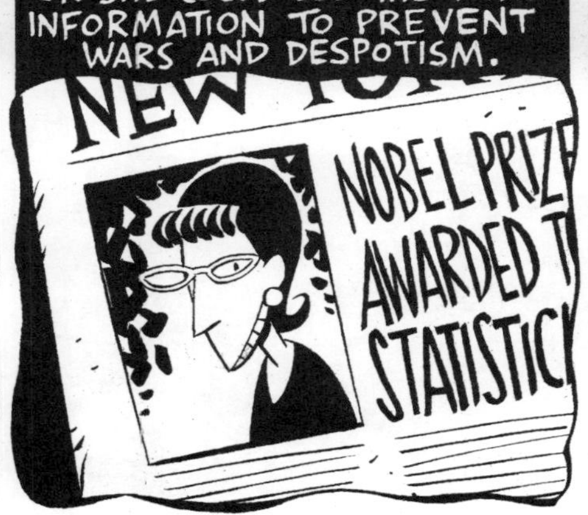
OR SHE COULD USE THE VITAL INFORMATION TO PREVENT WARS AND DESPOTISM.
NOBEL PRIZ
AWARDED T
STATISTIC

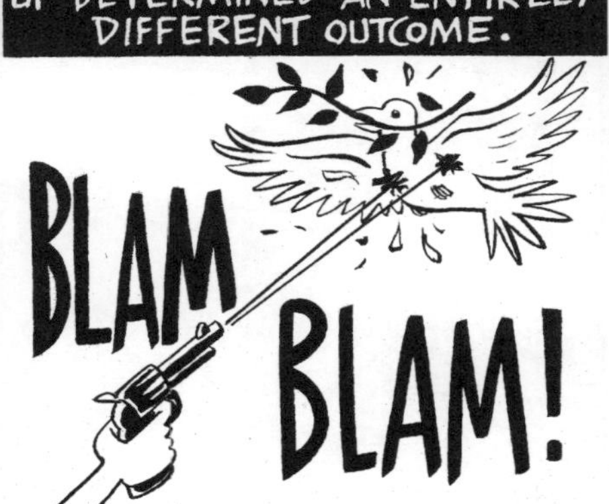
BUT HER OWN GENETIC MAKEUP DETERMINED AN ENTIRELY DIFFERENT OUTCOME.
BLAM
BLAM!

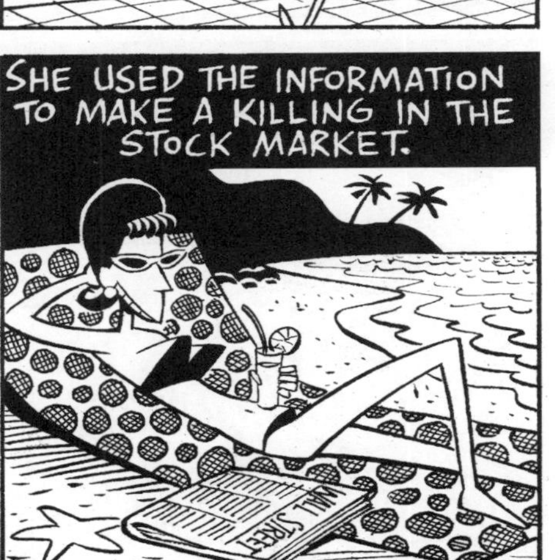
SHE USED THE INFORMATION TO MAKE A KILLING IN THE STOCK MARKET.
WALL STREET

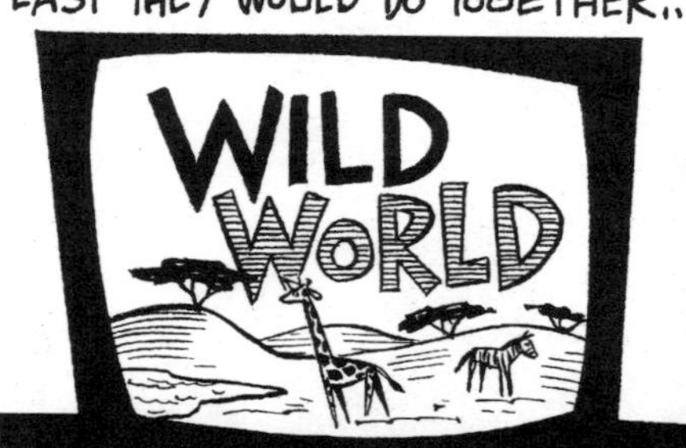
STORY MINUTE
"INTERFERING NATURE"
© CAROL LAY
THIS DOCUMENTARY WAS THE LAST THEY WOULD DO TOGETHER...
WILD WORLD

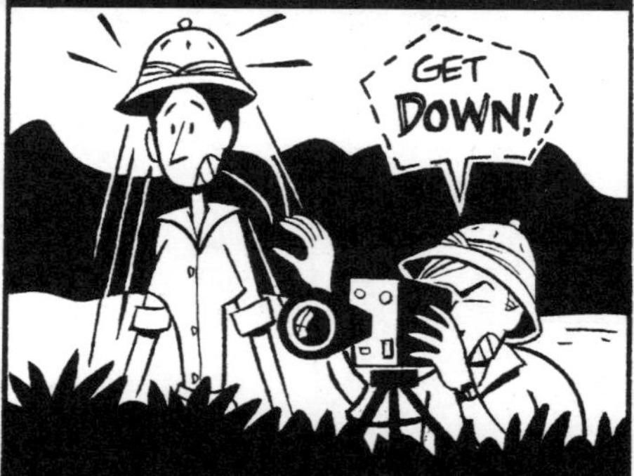
...BECAUSE THE WOMAN COULD NO LONGER JUST STAND BY AS ONE ANIMAL KILLED AND ATE ANOTHER.
GET DOWN!

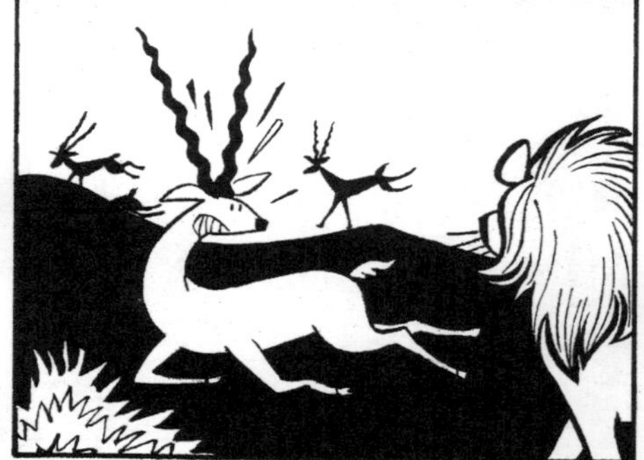
TRUE, IT WAS NATURE'S WAY THAT THE WEAK SHOULD FALL VICTIM TO THE STRONG...

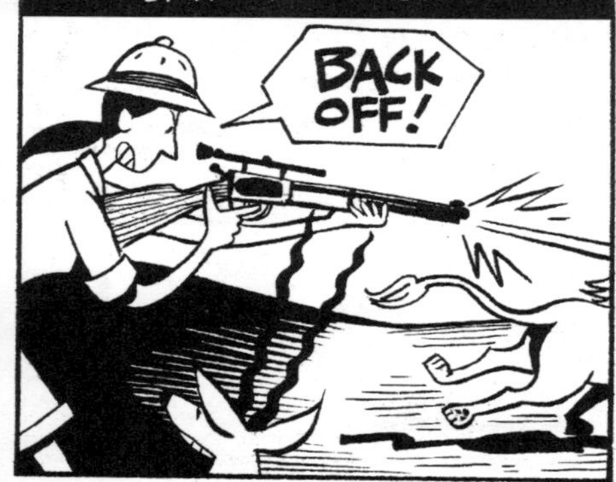
...BUT SHE BELIEVED THE NATURAL ORDER COULD SUFFER A FEW SMALL RESCUES.
BACK OFF!

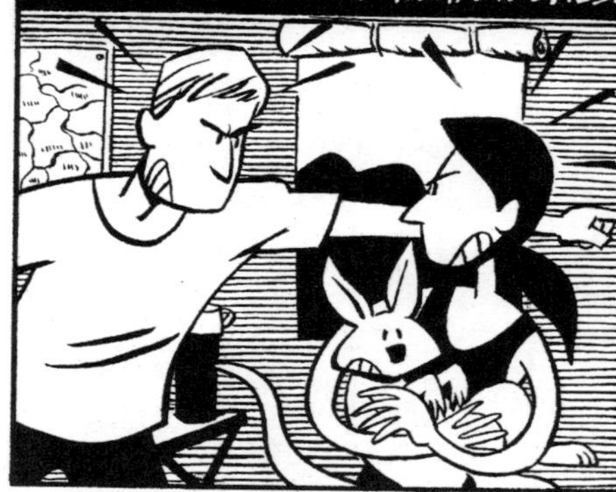
HER HUSBAND WAS OUTRAGED BY HER LACK OF PROFESSIONALISM AND THE BETRAYAL OF THEIR IDEALS.

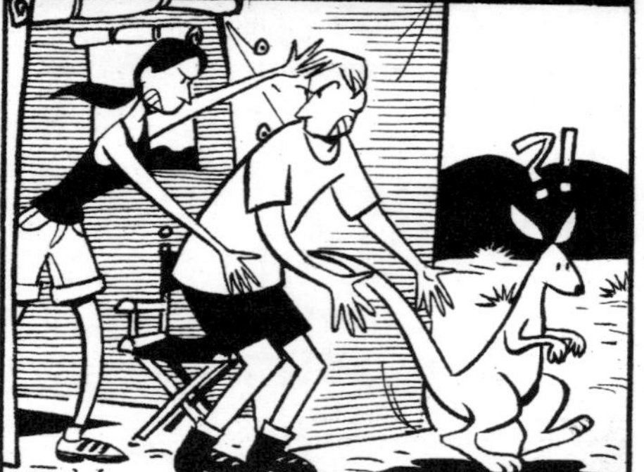
HE BELIEVED THEY SHOULD BE OBSERVERS OF NATURE, NOT PARTICIPANTS IN IT.
?!

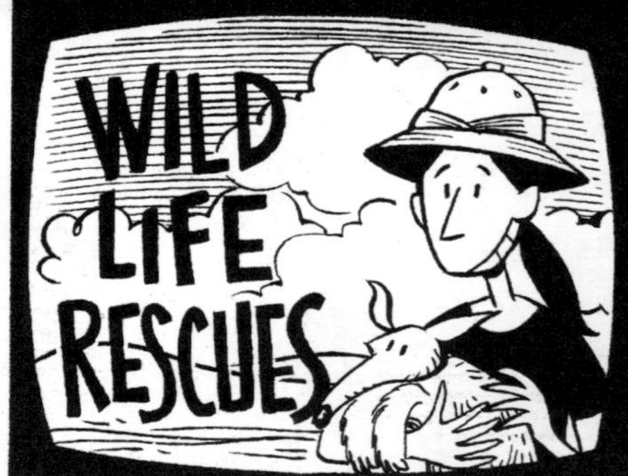
SHE SET OFF AND MADE IMMENSELY POPULAR FILMS OF WILDLIFE RESCUE OPERATIONS.
WILD LIFE RESCUES

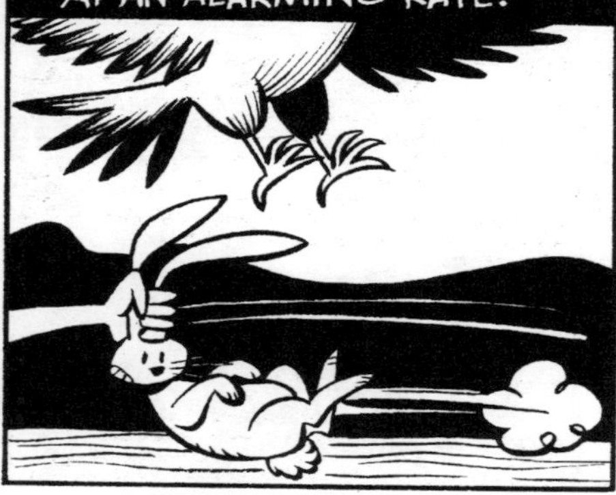
BUT DISCIPLES OF HER SHOW INTERFERED WITH NATURAL SELECTION AT AN ALARMING RATE.

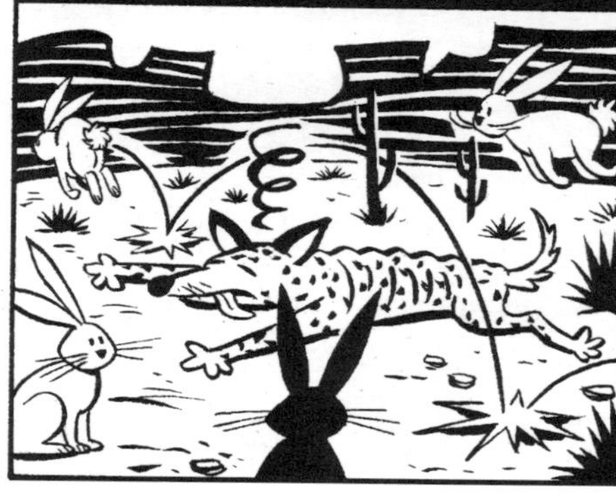
PREDATORS DIED OF STARVATION WHILE THE WEAK THREATENED TO INHERIT THE EARTH.

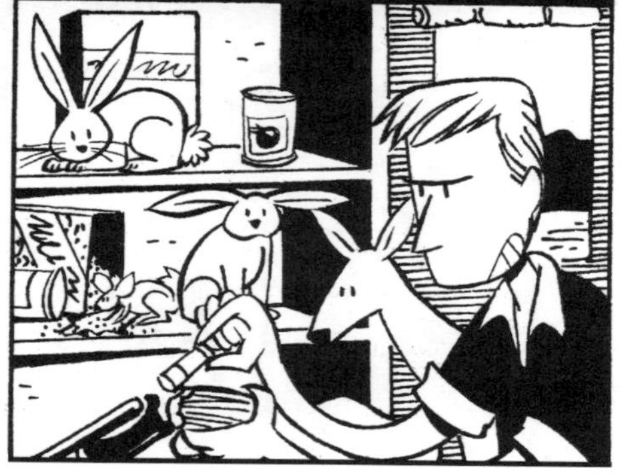
IN ORDER TO RESTORE BALANCE, HER HUSBAND HAD TO TAKE DOWN THEIR LEADER, HIS FORMER WIFE.

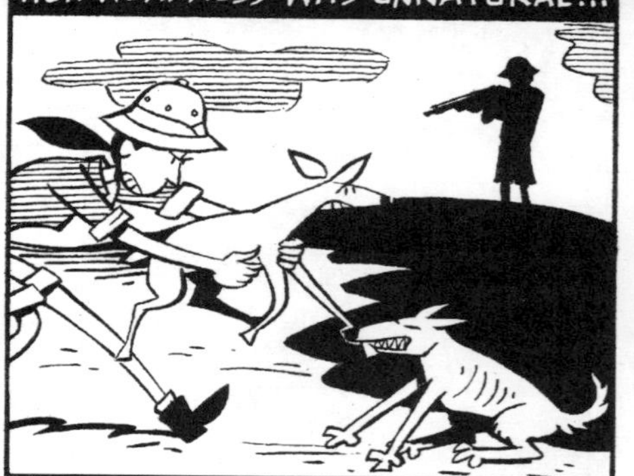
HE DIDN'T SEE THE ACT AS INTERFERING WITH NATURE BECAUSE HER WEAKNESS WAS UNNATURAL...

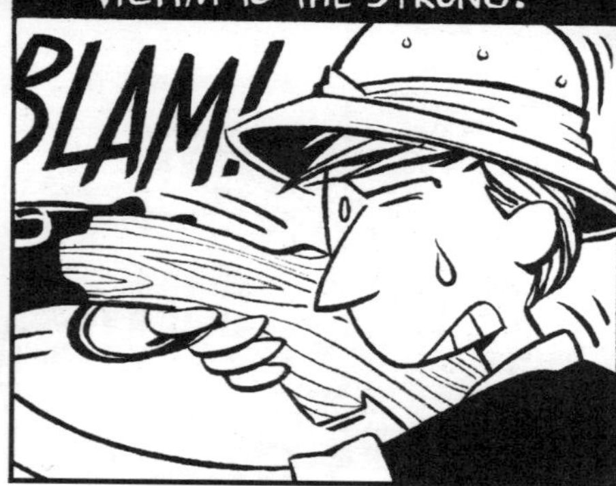
...AND, IN NATURE, HE KNEW THAT THE WEAK SHOULD ALWAYS FALL VICTIM TO THE STRONG.
BLAM!

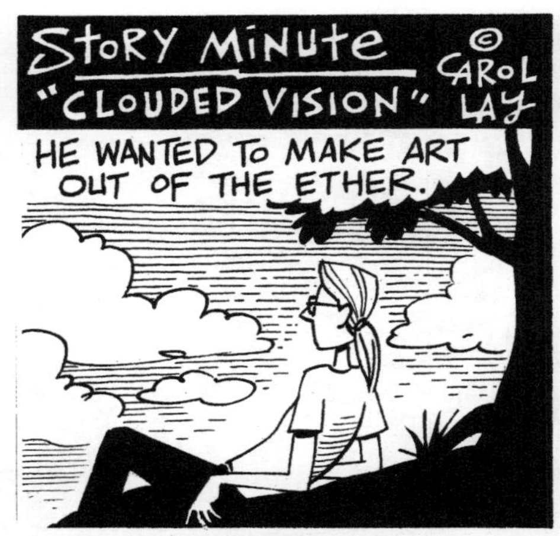
STORY MINUTE
"CLOUDED VISION"
© CAROL LAY
HE WANTED TO MAKE ART OUT OF THE ETHER.

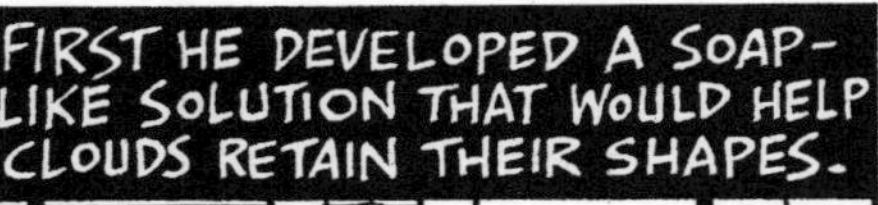
FIRST HE DEVELOPED A SOAP-LIKE SOLUTION THAT WOULD HELP CLOUDS RETAIN THEIR SHAPES.

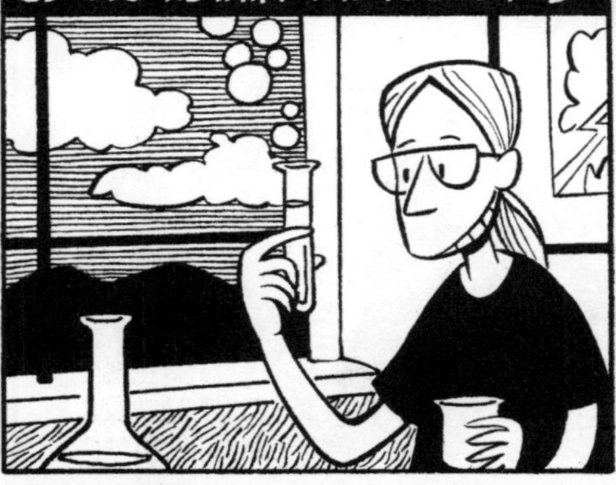

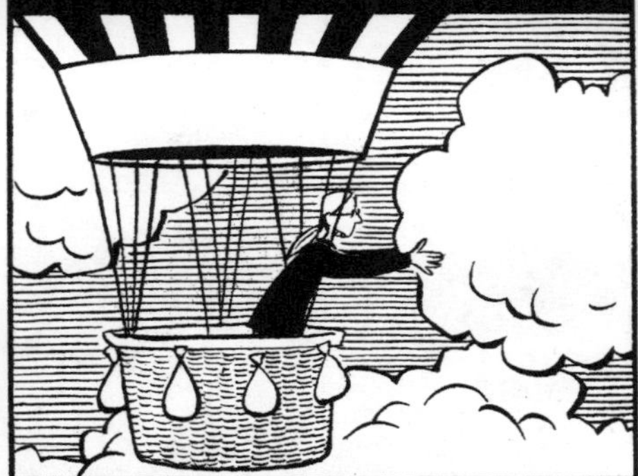
THEN HE SAILED UP IN A BALLOON TO SCULPT IMAGES WITH THE VAPOROUS MATERIAL.

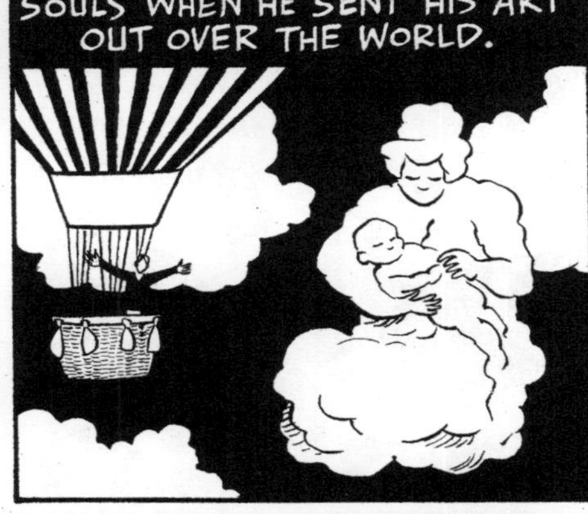
HE HOPED TO TOUCH PEOPLE'S SOULS WHEN HE SENT HIS ART OUT OVER THE WORLD.

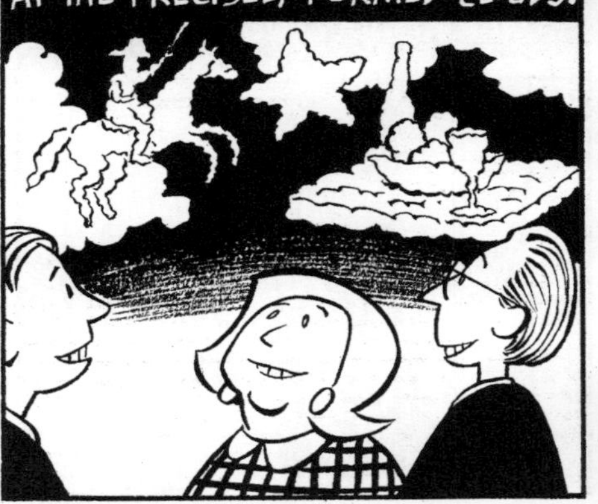
AT FIRST PEOPLE MARVELLED AT THE PRECISELY-FORMED CLOUDS.

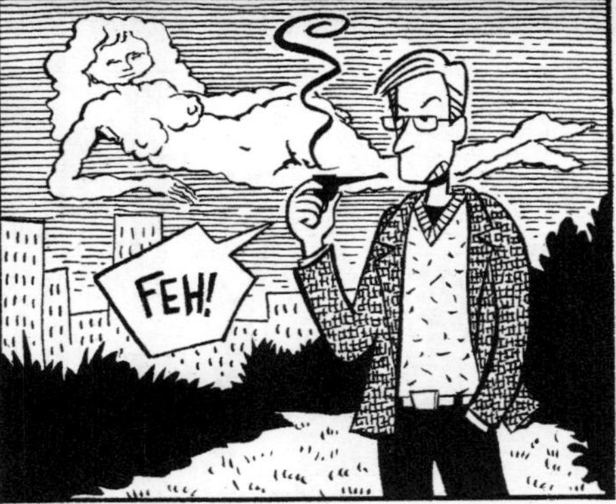
BUT THEY SOON GREW SCORNFUL OF THE GIMMICKY CARTOON CLUTTER.
FEH!

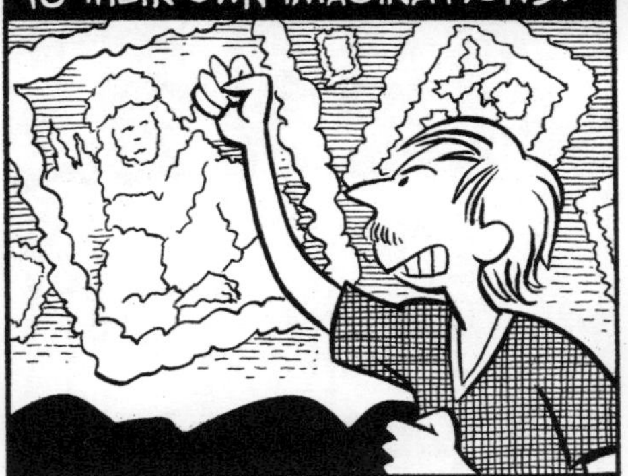
THEY WERE ALSO NO LONGER FREE TO INTERPRET CLOUDS ACCORDING TO THEIR OWN IMAGINATIONS.

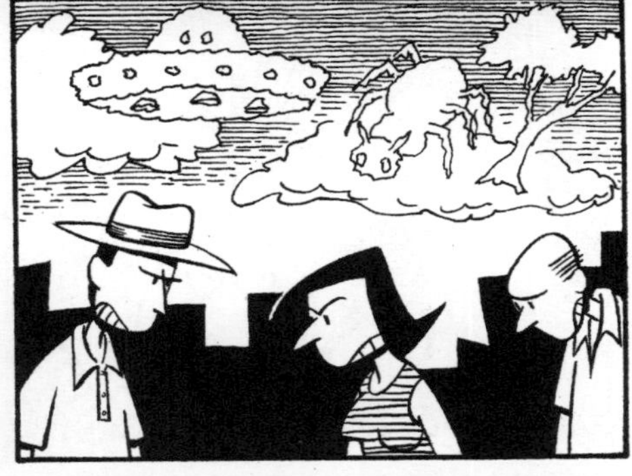
WHATEVER EMOTIONAL INVOLVEMENT THE ARTIST HAD WANTED TO GENERATE JUST WASN'T THERE.

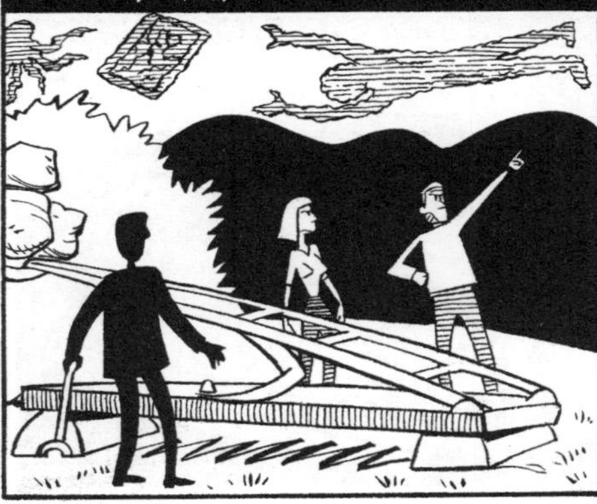
SOME FOLKS SHOT OBJECTS AT THE FLUFFY WHITE CONFECTIONS.

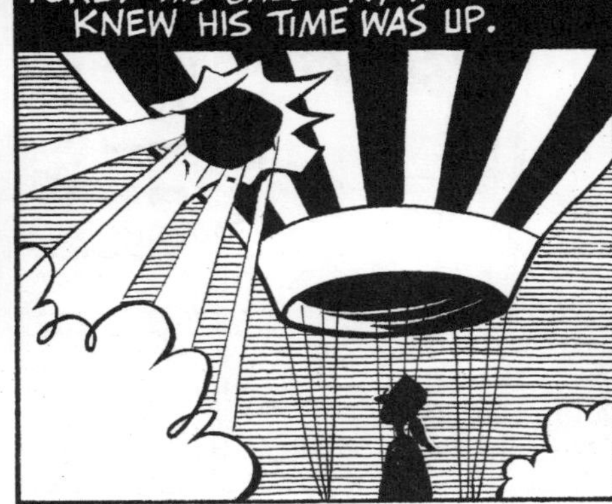
WHEN ONE OF THE MISSILES PUNCTURED HIS BALLOON, THE ARTIST KNEW HIS TIME WAS UP.

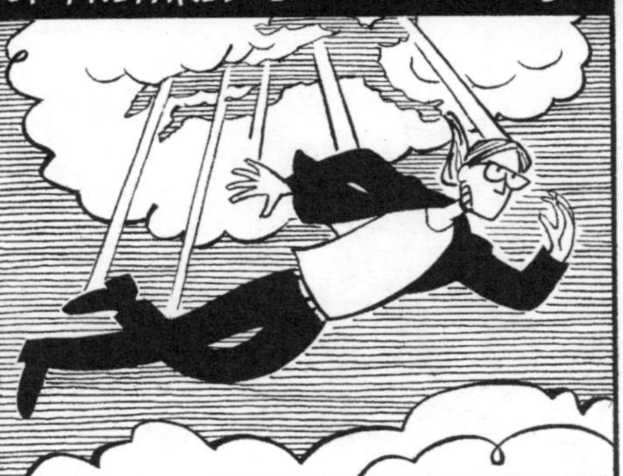
BUT HE WAS PROUD WHEN HE PLUNGED THROUGH THE LAYERS OF PREPARED CLOUD CANVASES...

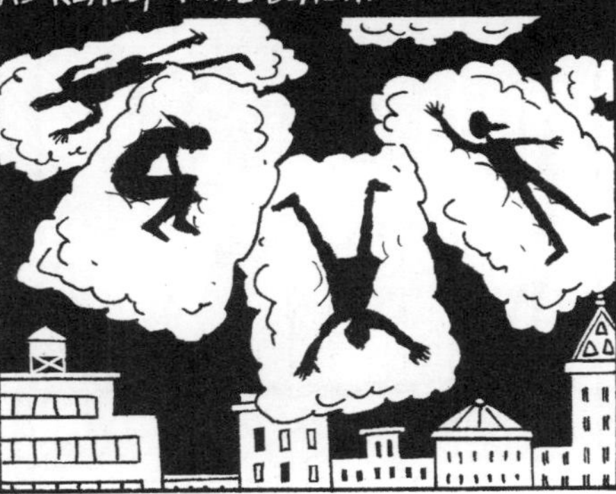
BECAUSE HE KNEW THESE FINAL PIECES OF ART WOULD STRIKE PEOPLE AS REALLY QUITE BEAUTIFUL AND SAD.

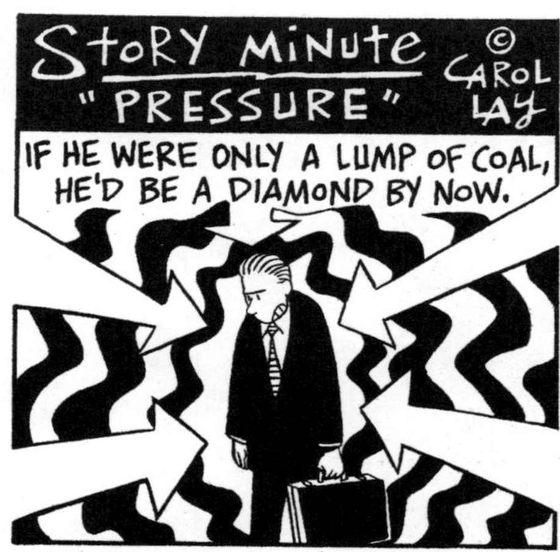
Story Minute
"PRESSURE"
© CAROL LAY
IF HE WERE ONLY A LUMP OF COAL, HE'D BE A DIAMOND BY NOW.

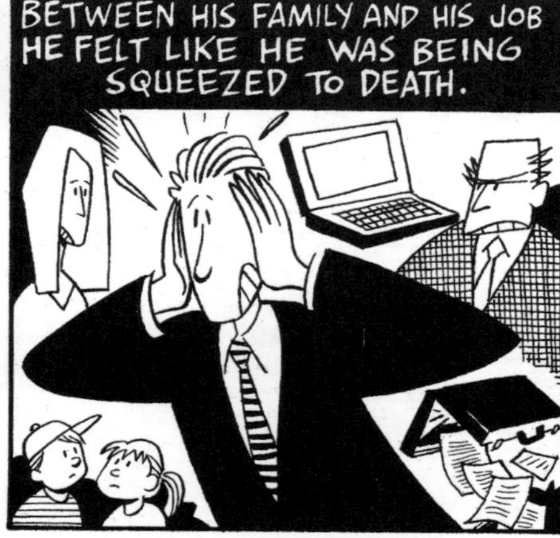
BETWEEN HIS FAMILY AND HIS JOB HE FELT LIKE HE WAS BEING SQUEEZED TO DEATH.

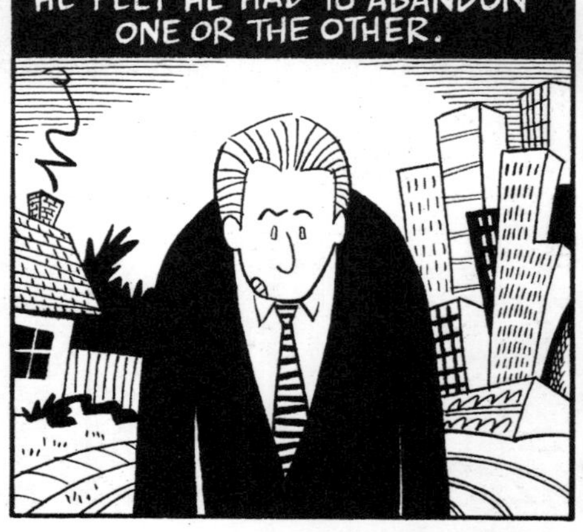
HE FELT HE HAD TO ABANDON ONE OR THE OTHER.

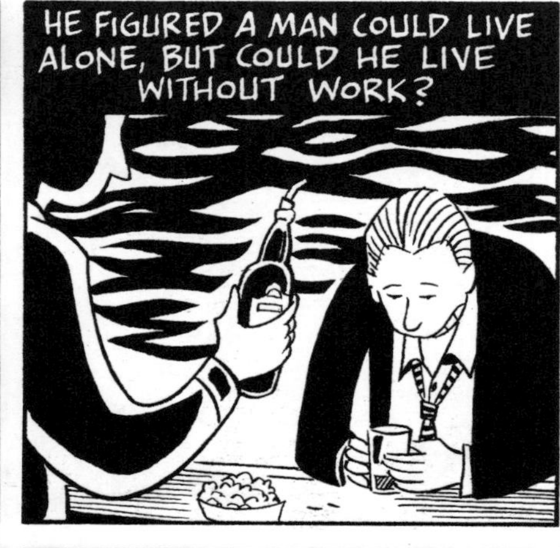
HE FIGURED A MAN COULD LIVE ALONE, BUT COULD HE LIVE WITHOUT WORK?

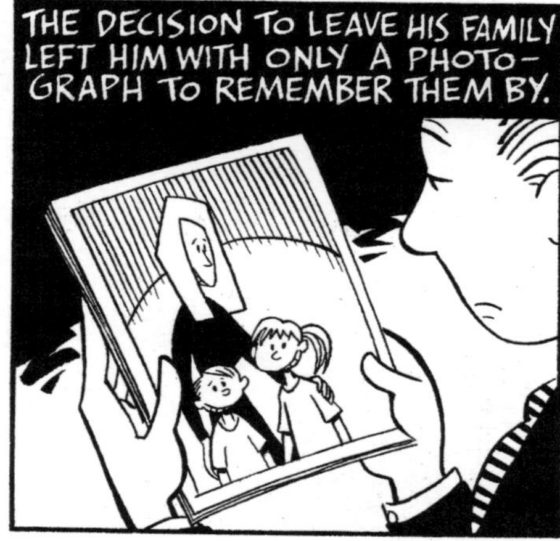
THE DECISION TO LEAVE HIS FAMILY LEFT HIM WITH ONLY A PHOTOGRAPH TO REMEMBER THEM BY.

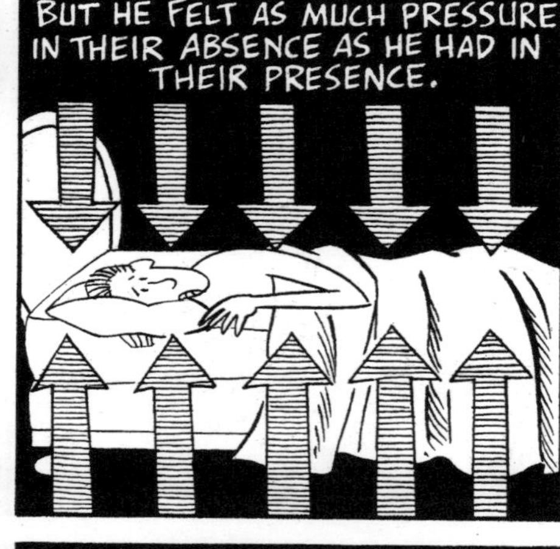
BUT HE FELT AS MUCH PRESSURE IN THEIR ABSENCE AS HE HAD IN THEIR PRESENCE.

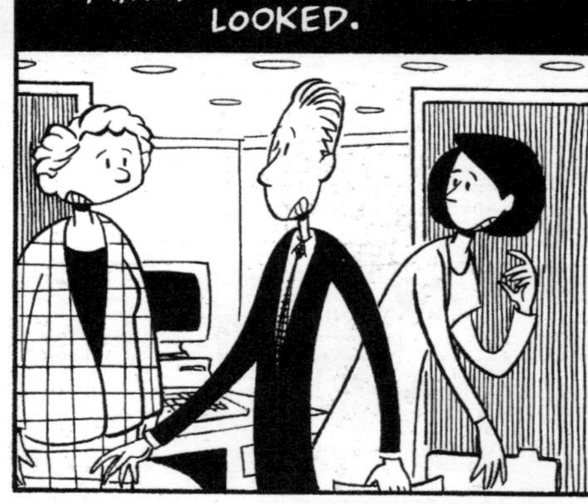
COWORKERS BEGAN TO COMMENT ON HOW THIN HE LOOKED.

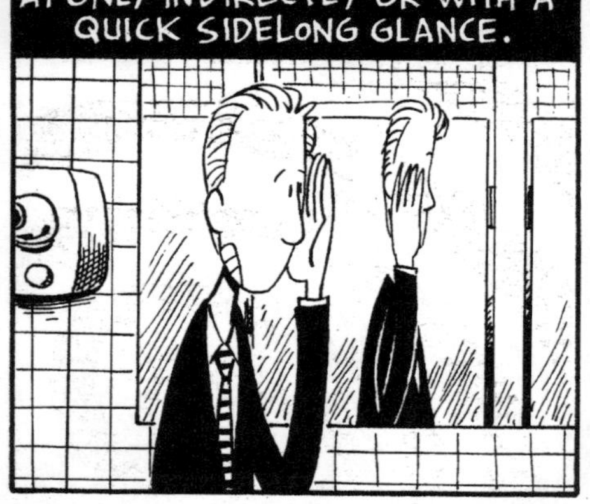
MIRRORS WERE TO BE LOOKED AT ONLY INDIRECTLY OR WITH A QUICK SIDELONG GLANCE.

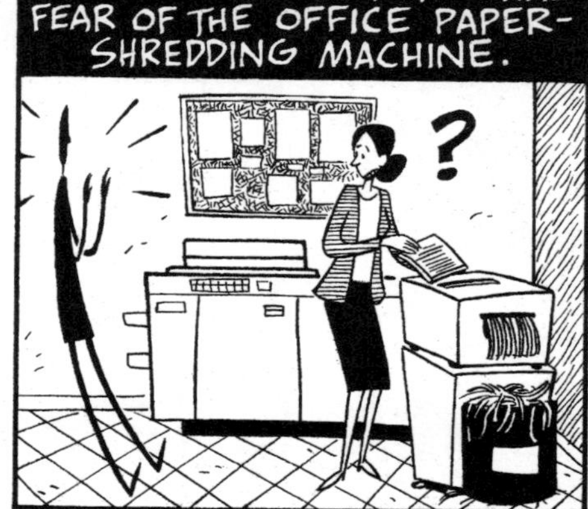
HE DEVELOPED AN IRRATIONAL FEAR OF THE OFFICE PAPER-SHREDDING MACHINE.
?

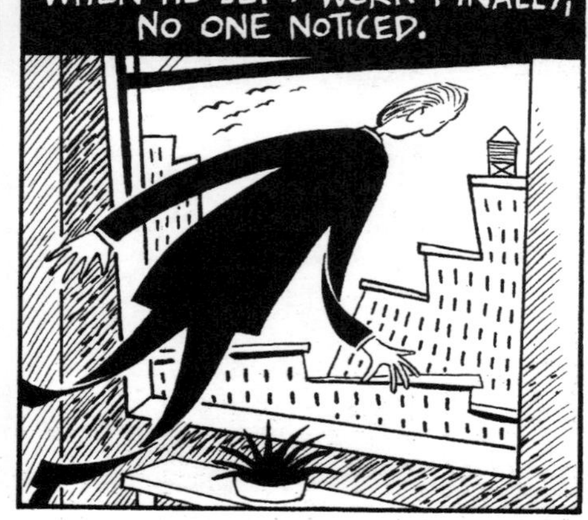
WHEN HE LEFT WORK FINALLY, NO ONE NOTICED.

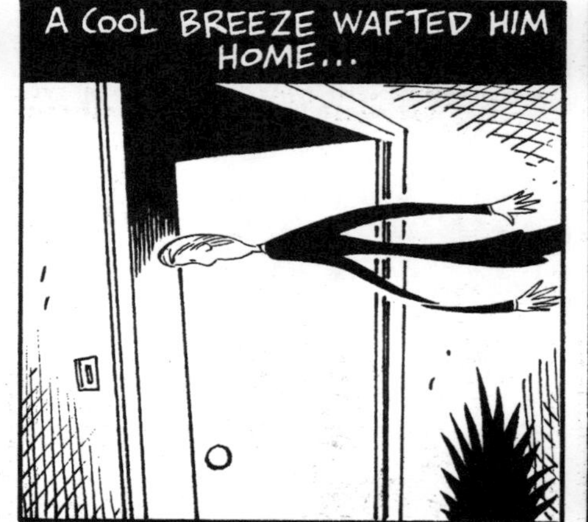
A COOL BREEZE WAFTED HIM HOME...

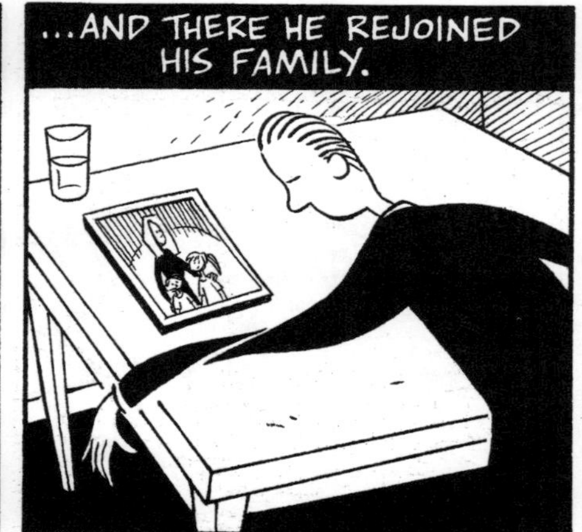
...AND THERE HE REJOINED HIS FAMILY.

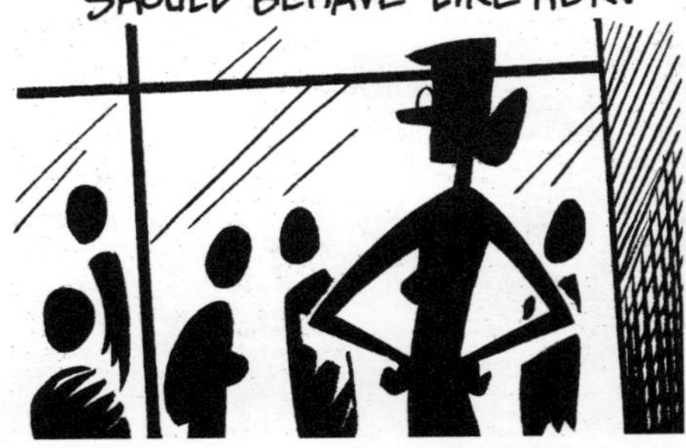
STORY MINUTE
"ROLE MODEL"
© CAROL LAY
SHE THOUGHT THAT EVERYONE SHOULD BEHAVE LIKE HER.

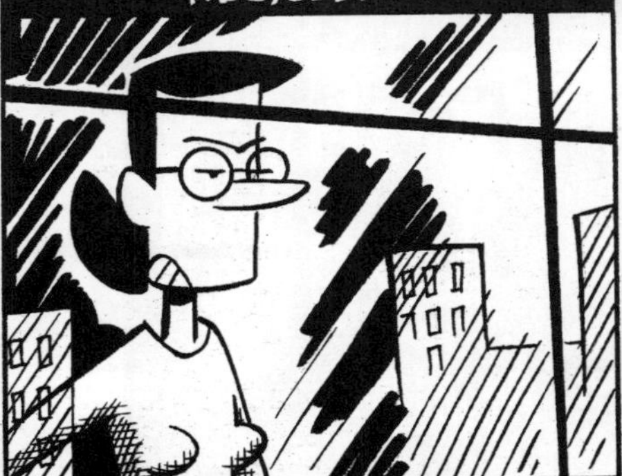
AFTERALL, SHE WAS RESPONSIBLE, HONEST, AND A CONSIDERATE RECYCLER.

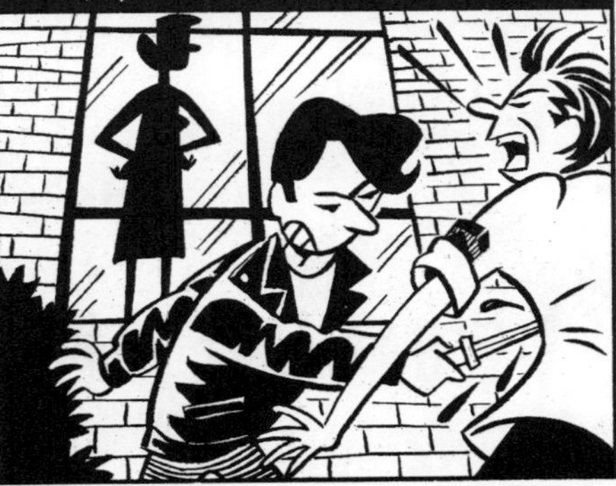
OBSERVATION SHOWED HER THAT MOST PEOPLE WERE THOUGHTLESS — IF NOT DOWNRIGHT RUDE.

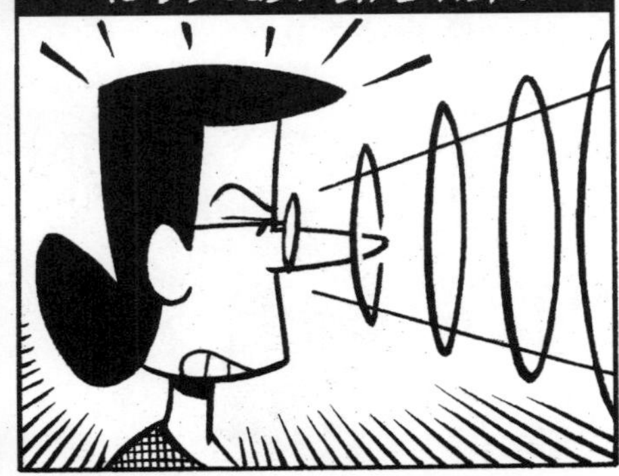
SHE PUT A LOT OF MENTAL ENERGY INTO IMAGINING THEM TO BE JUST LIKE HER.

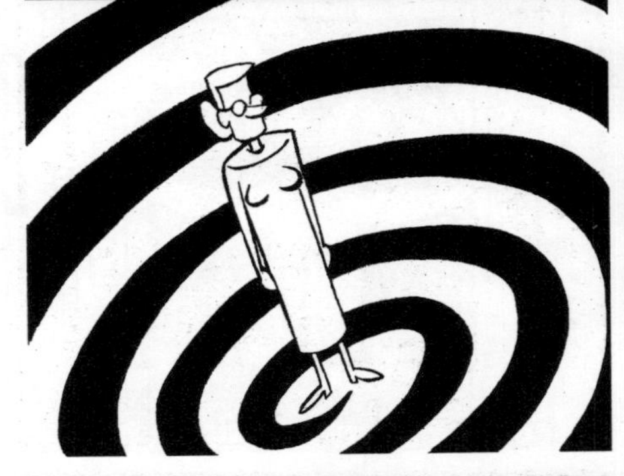
SHE THOUGHT IF SHE CONCENTRATED ENOUGH, HER WILL WOULD SPREAD TO EVERYONE.

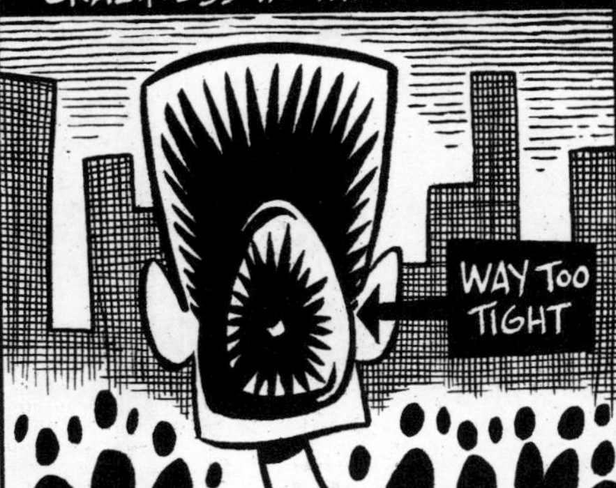
SUCH A SENSIBLE MORAL STANDARD COULD SURELY RIGHT THE CRAZINESS IN THE WORLD.
WAY TOO TIGHT

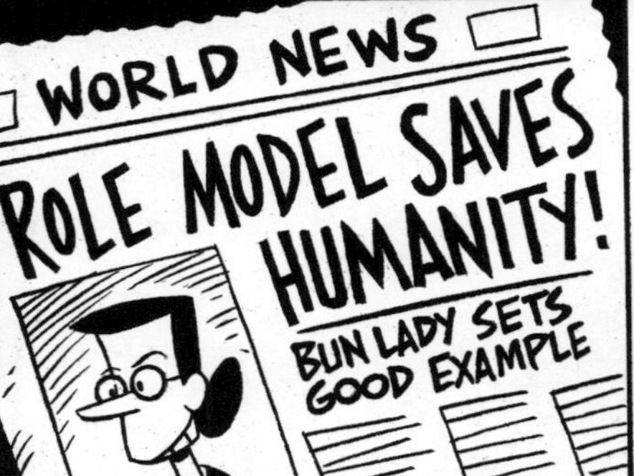
HER THOUGHTS WOULD BE INSTRUMENTAL IN ENDING WAR, POVERTY, AND OVERPOPULATION.
WORLD NEWS
ROLE MODEL SAVES HUMANITY!
BUN LADY SETS GOOD EXAMPLE

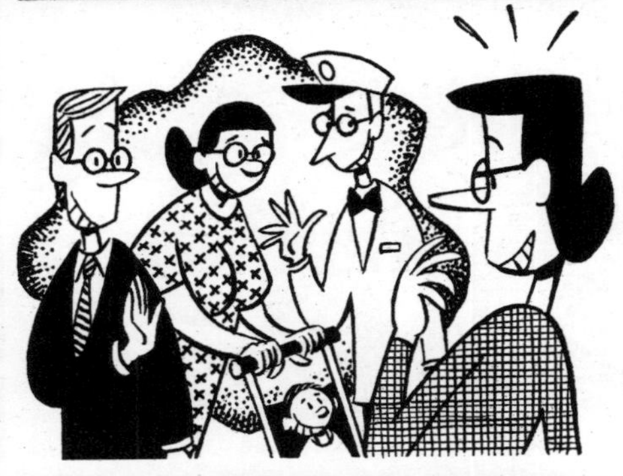
BUT ONE DAY SHE NO LONGER HAD TO IMAGINE IT— EVERYONE BEHAVED JUST LIKE HER.

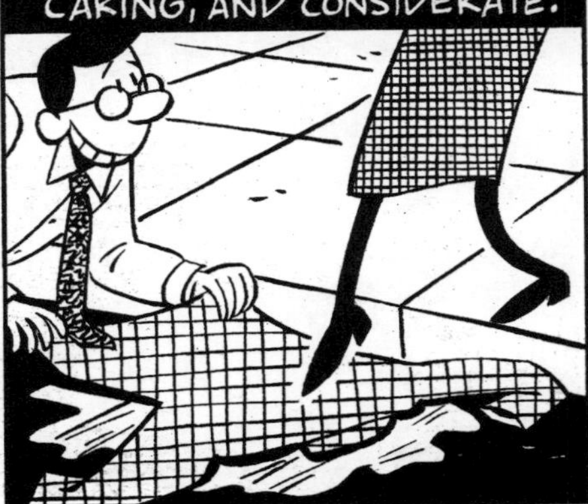
THEY WERE ALL VERY POLITE, CARING, AND CONSIDERATE.

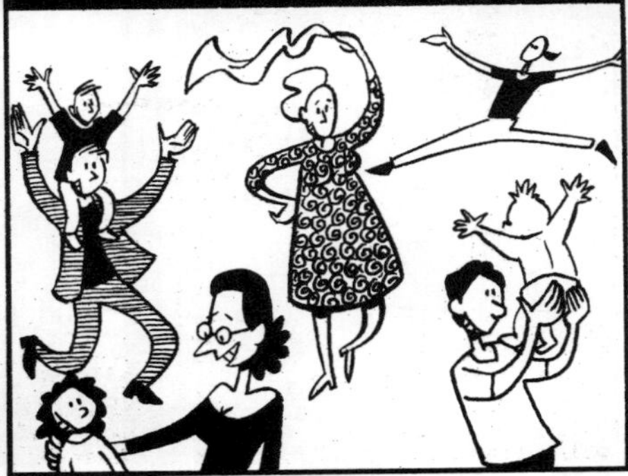
WAR, POVERTY, AND ALL OTHER PROBLEMS FADED TO NOTHINGNESS.

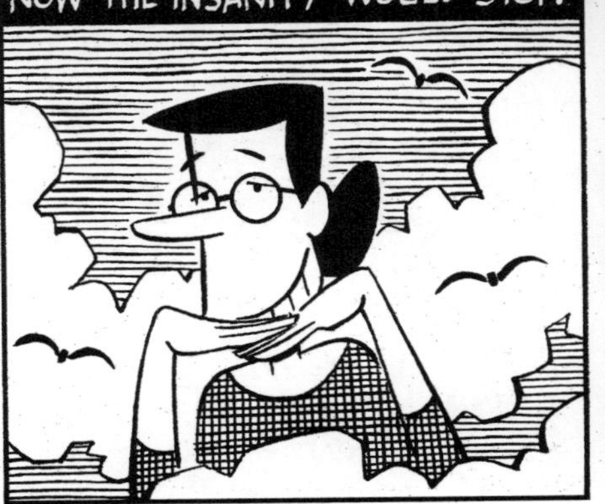
SHE HAD BEEN SUCCESSFUL. NOW THE INSANITY WOULD STOP.

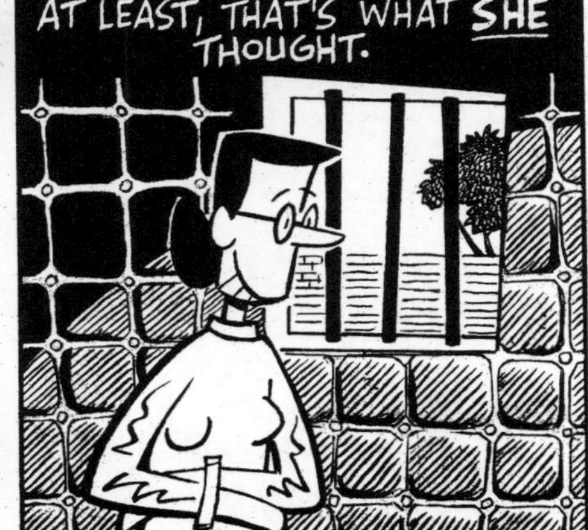
AT LEAST, THAT'S WHAT SHE THOUGHT.

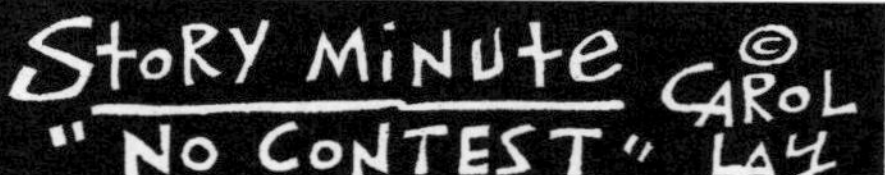

Story Minute
"No Contest"
© Carol Lay

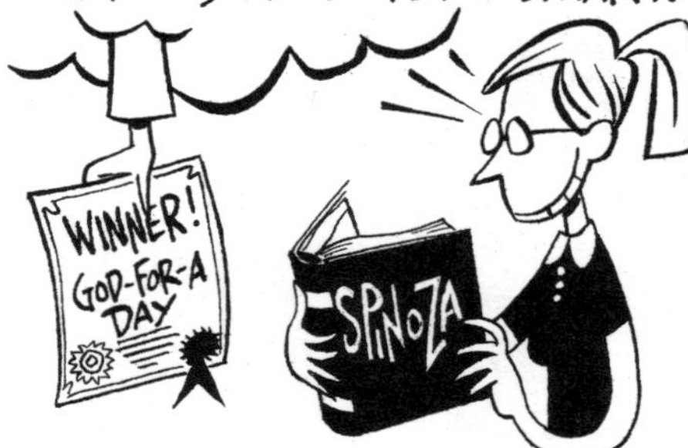

THE "GOD-FOR-A-DAY" WINNERS WERE USUALLY VERY SMART.
WINNER! GOD-FOR-A DAY
SPINOZA

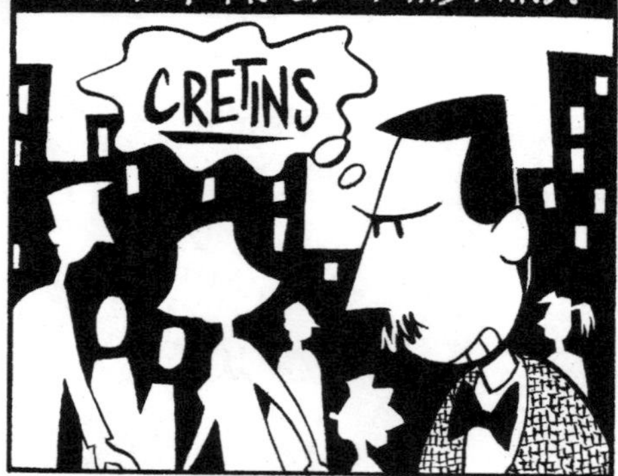

THIS WEEK'S WINNER WAS NO EXCEPTION, ALTHOUGH HE WAS OVERLY PROUD OF HIS MIND.
CRETINS

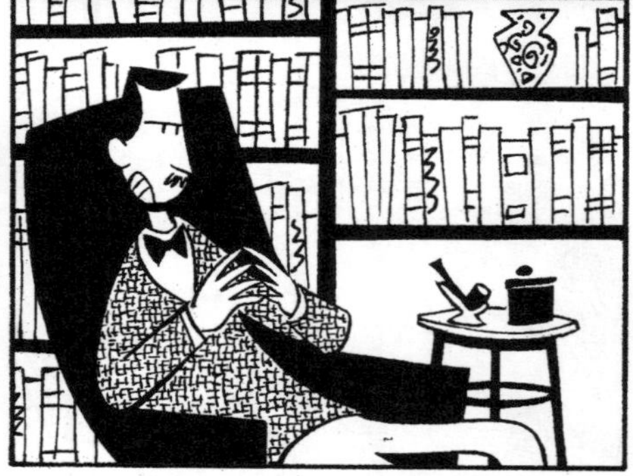

SO—WHAT COULD HE DO IN A DAY THAT WOULD MAKE A POSITIVE DIFFERENCE?

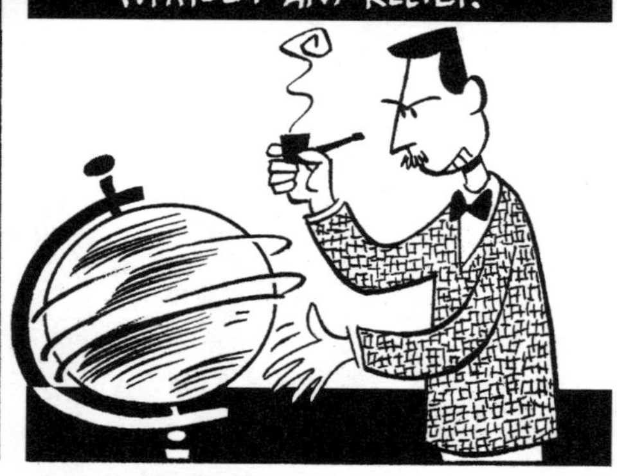

HE KNEW THE EARTH WAS TOO CROWDED AND WOULD BE DOOMED WITHOUT ANY RELIEF.

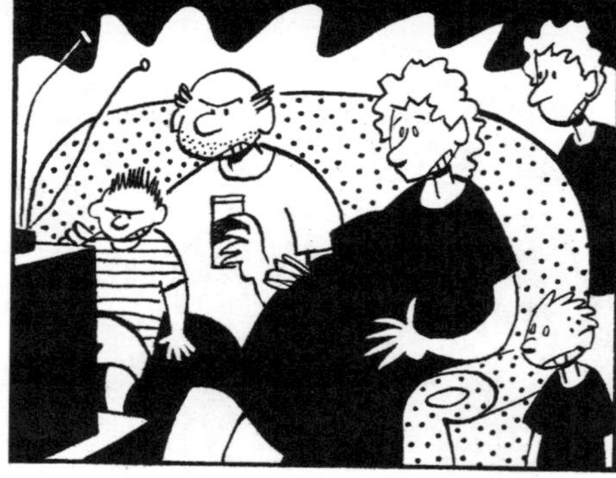

HE ALSO THOUGHT HE HAD NO USE FOR UNINTELLIGENT TYPES WHO WERE FAR TOO FERTILE.

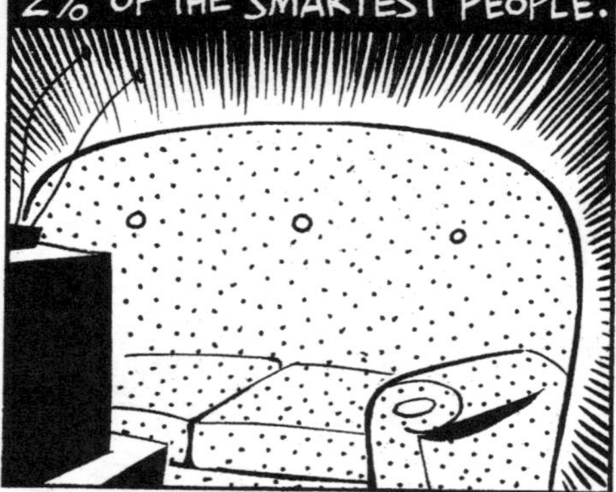

HIS FIRST ACT AS GOD WAS TO ELIMINATE ALL BUT THE TOP 2% OF THE SMARTEST PEOPLE.

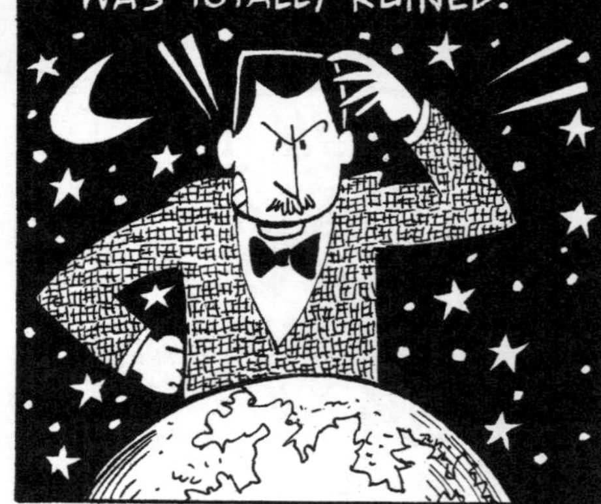

WELL, AFTER THAT HIS DAY WAS TOTALLY RUINED.

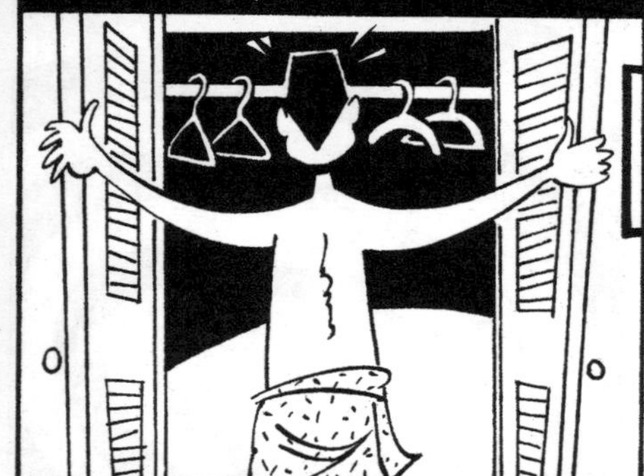

HIS DRY CLEANING WASN'T DONE AND HE COULDN'T ORDER IN A MEAL.

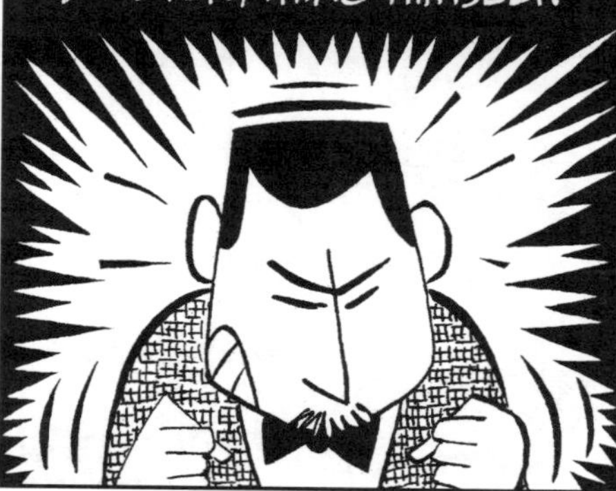

THERE WAS NO PHONE, MAIL, OR MAID SERVICE. HE HAD TO DO EVERYTHING HIMSELF.

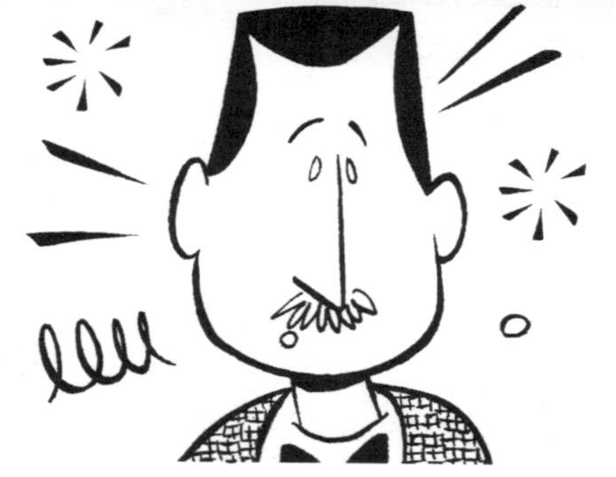

BUT HIS OMNIPOTENCE WOULD END WITH THE DAY AND THEN WHAT WOULD HE DO?

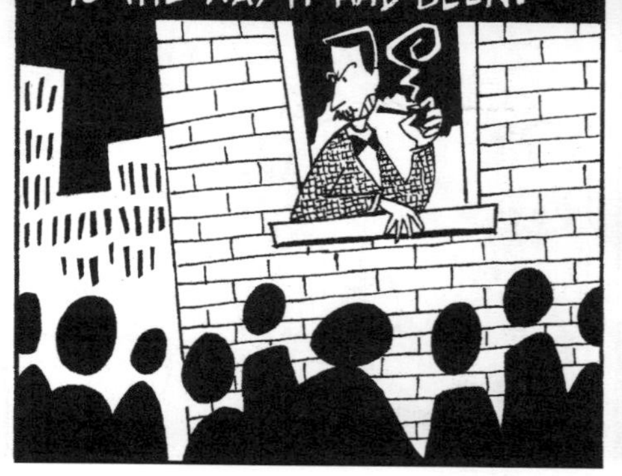

AT THE END OF HIS 24 HOURS HE TURNED EVERYTHING BACK TO THE WAY IT HAD BEEN.

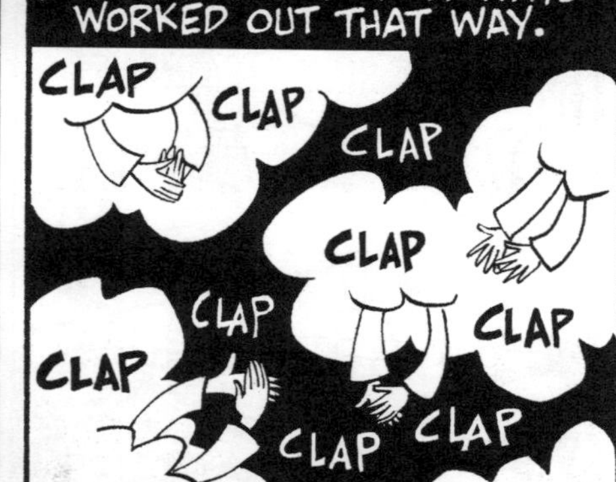

THE REAL GODS GOT A BIG KICK OUT OF HOW IT ALWAYS WORKED OUT THAT WAY.
CLAP
CLAP
CLAP
CLAP
CLAP
CLAP
CLAP
CLAP
CLAP

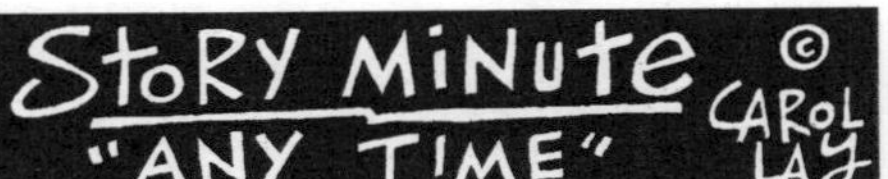
STORY MINUTE
"ANY TIME"
© CAROL LAY

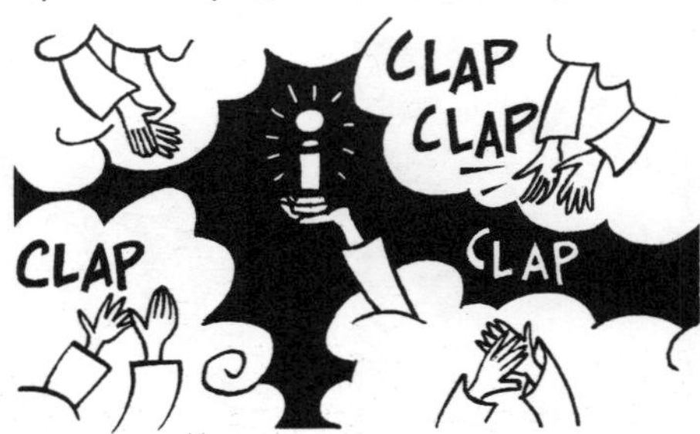
THE GOD-FOR-A-DAY CONTEST HAD A RUNNER-UP PRIZE.
CLAP
CLAP
CLAP
CLAP

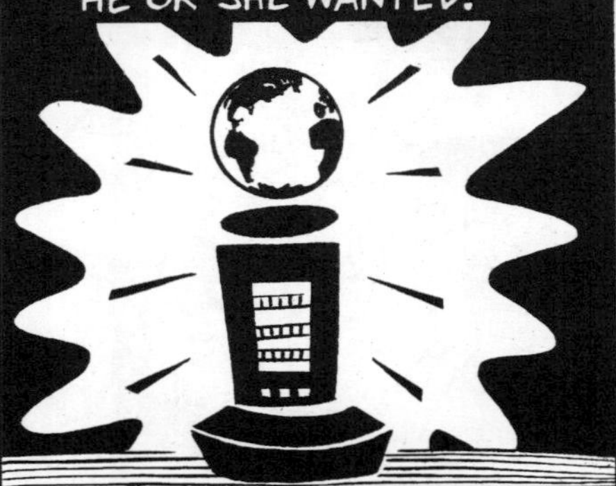
WHOEVER WON IT COULD CHOOSE TO LIVE IN ANY PLACE OR TIME HE OR SHE WANTED.

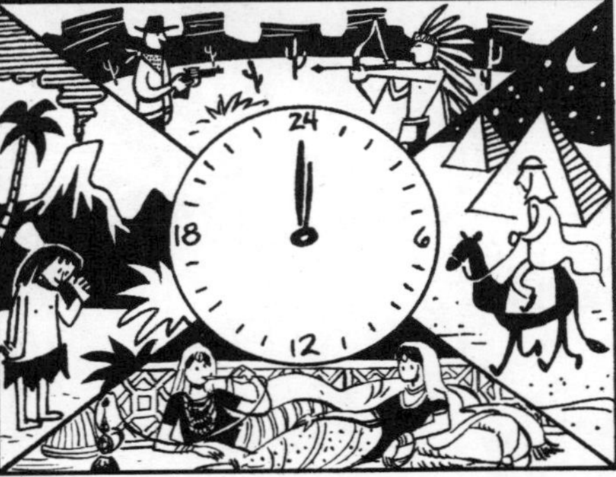
THE LUCKY WINNER COULD SAMPLE DIFFERENT ERAS OVER A PERIOD OF 24 HOURS.
24
6
12
18

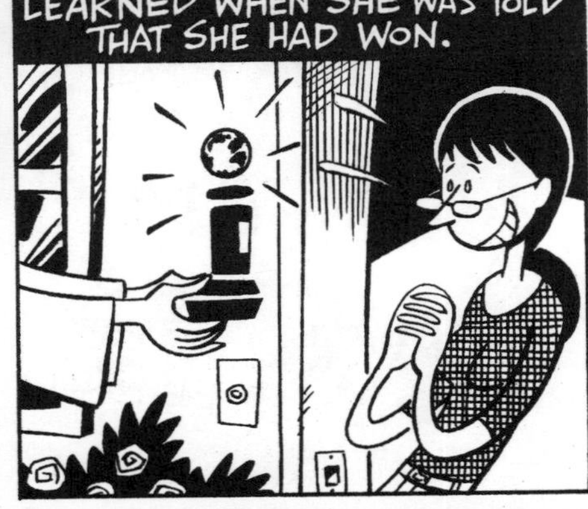
THAT IS WHAT ONE WOMAN LEARNED WHEN SHE WAS TOLD THAT SHE HAD WON.

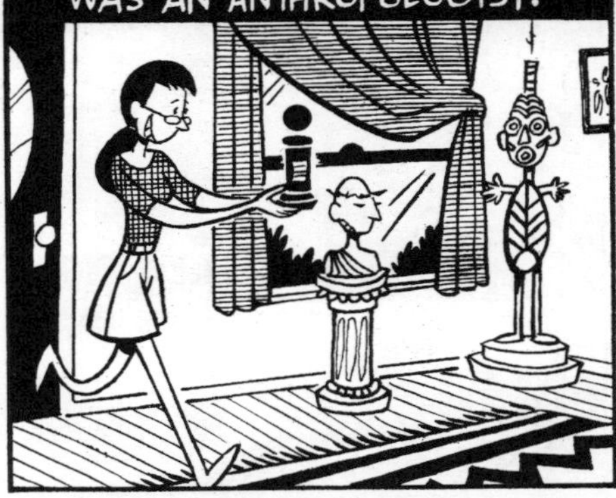
THE PRIZE COULD NOT HAVE BEEN MORE APPROPRIATE — SHE WAS AN ANTHROPOLOGIST.

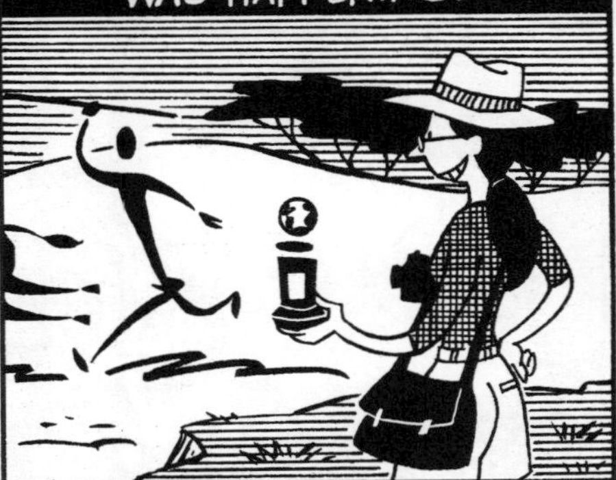
NOW SHE COULD PICK A FAVORITE CULTURE AND STUDY IT AS IT WAS HAPPENING.

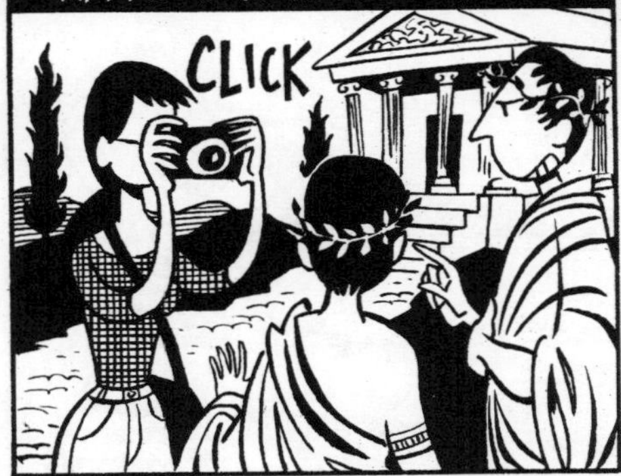
BUT SHE WOULD BE LONG GONE BY THE TIME ANYONE COULD APPRECIATE HER WORK.
CLICK

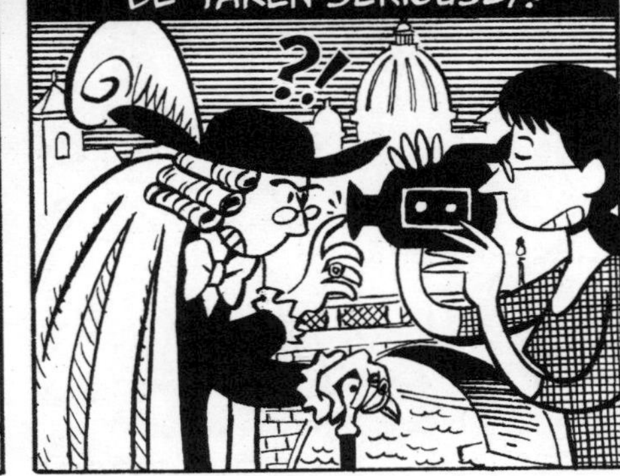
AND WOULD HER STUDIES EVEN SURVIVE THROUGH TIME — OR BE TAKEN SERIOUSLY?
?!

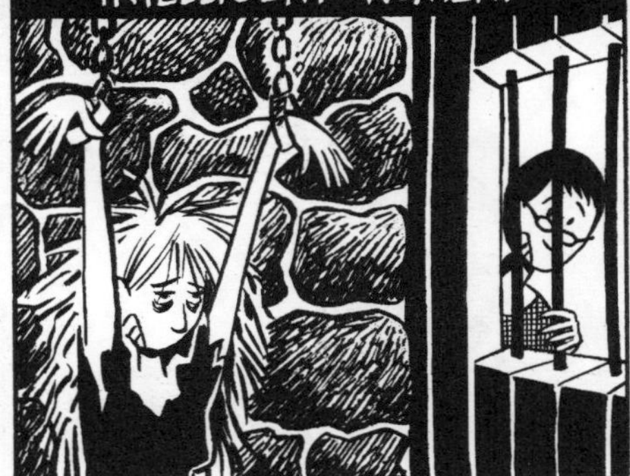
ALSO, MOST EXTINCT CULTURES WERE NOT FRIENDLY TO INTELLIGENT WOMEN.

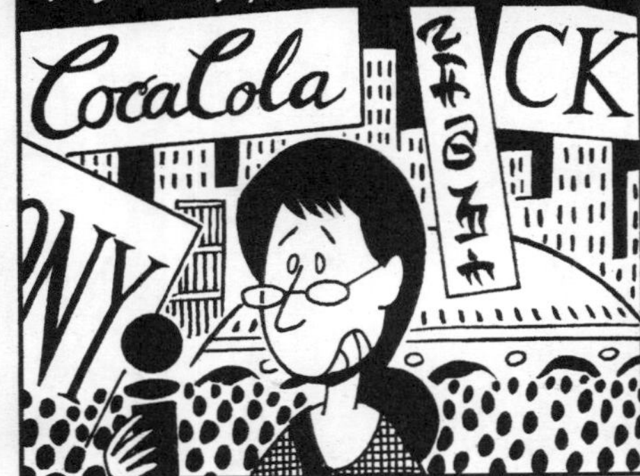
SHE SAMPLED THE FUTURE BUT FOUND THE HOMOGENOUS WORLD TO BE UGLY AND OVERCROWDED.
CocaCola
CK

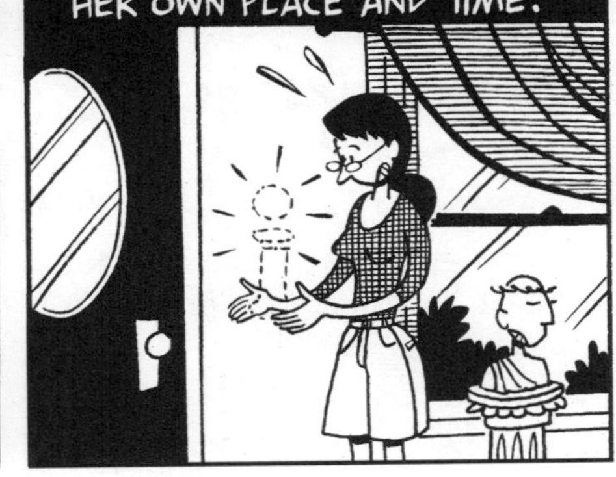
AT THE END OF HER 24 HOURS SHE CHOSE TO KEEP LIVING IN HER OWN PLACE AND TIME.

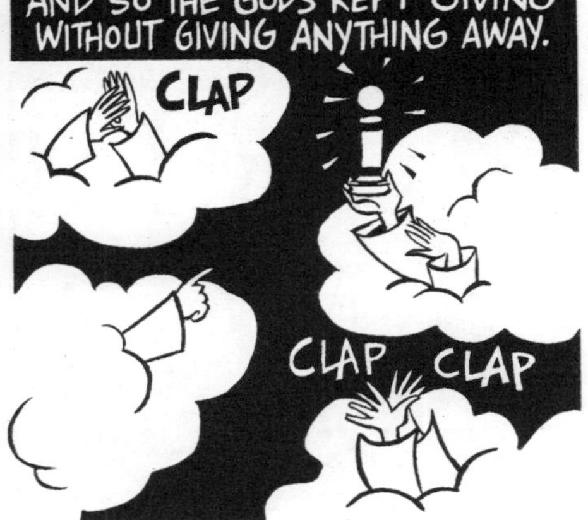
AND SO THE GODS KEPT GIVING WITHOUT GIVING ANYTHING AWAY.
CLAP
CLAP
CLAP

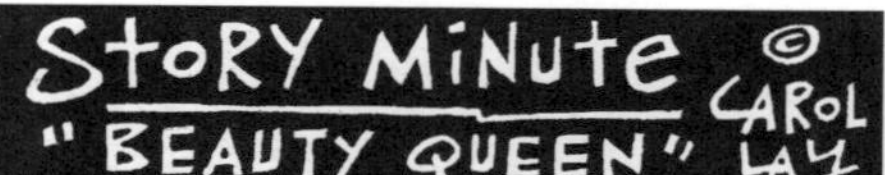


SHE WAS IN HER FIRST BEAUTY CONTEST BEFORE SHE WAS EVEN BORN.

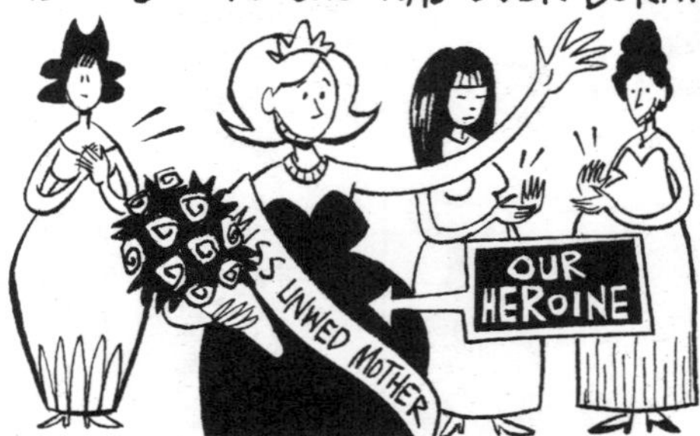


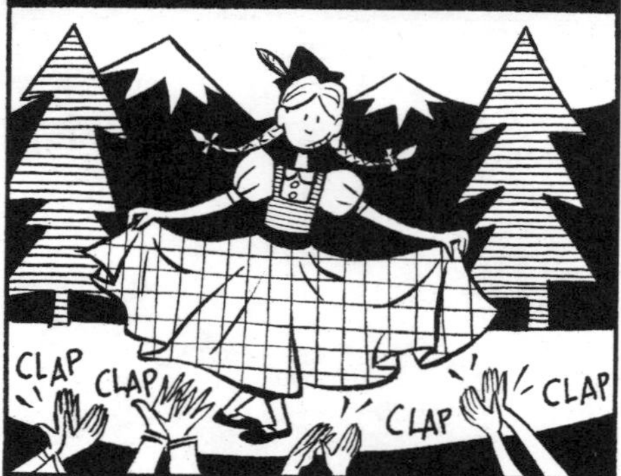


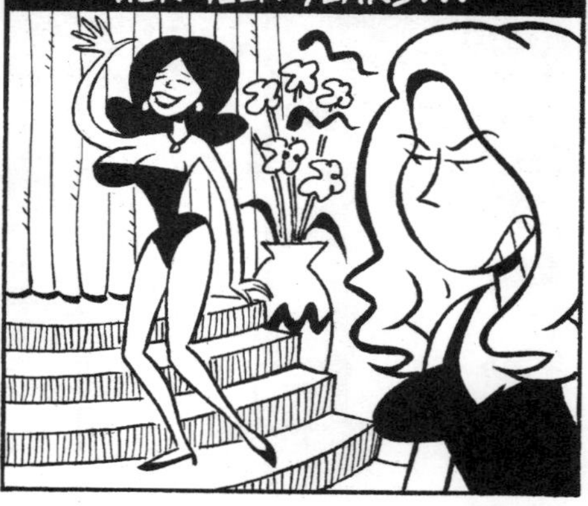


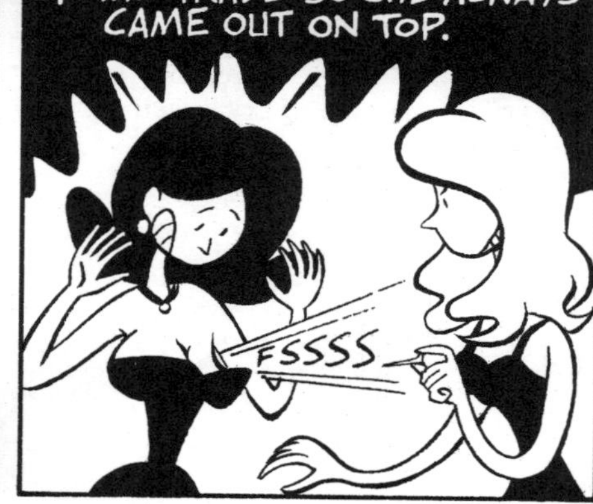


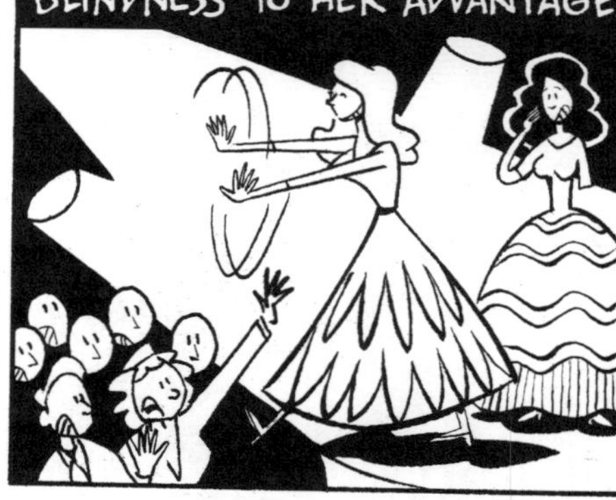


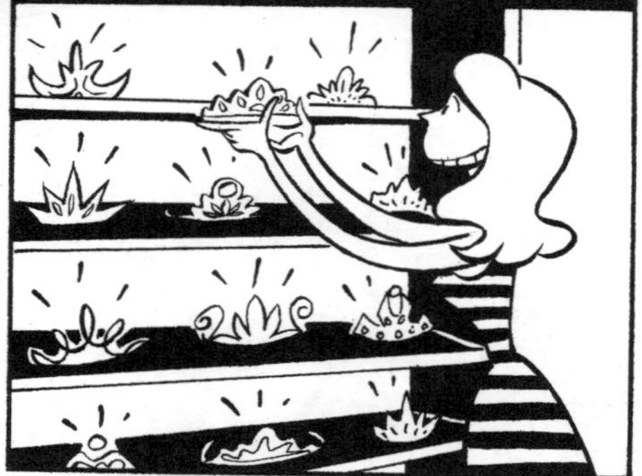


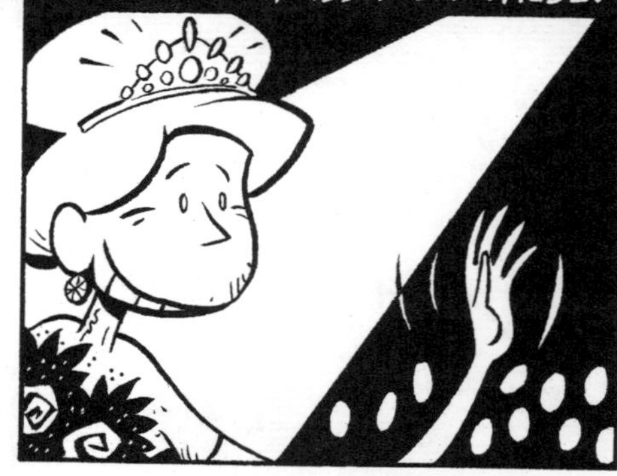


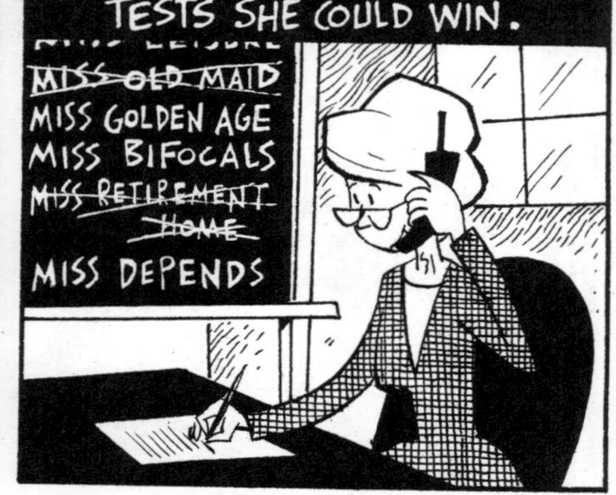


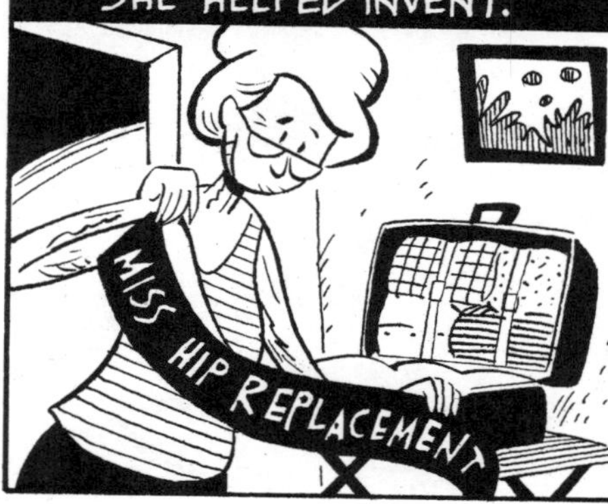


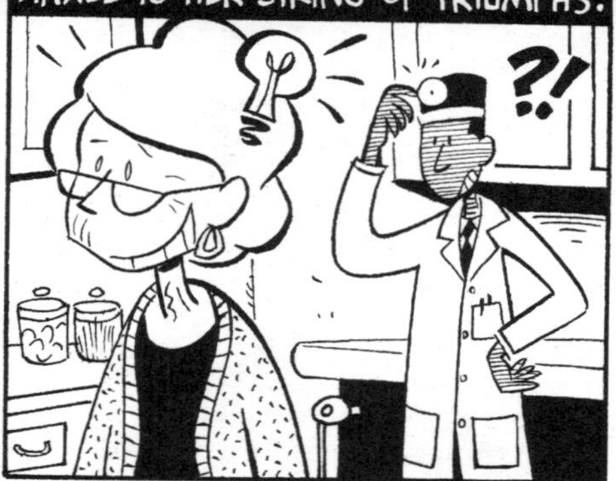


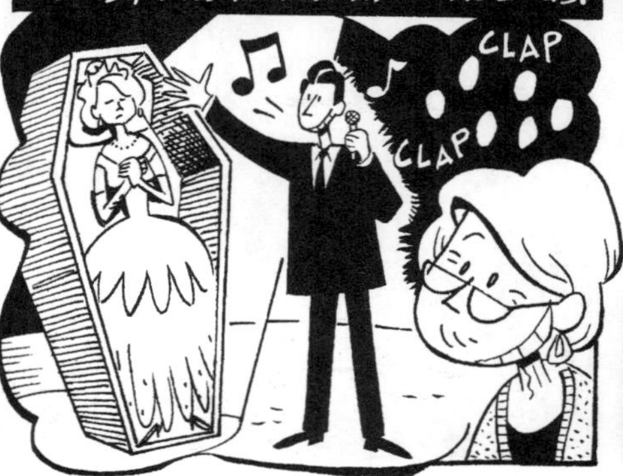


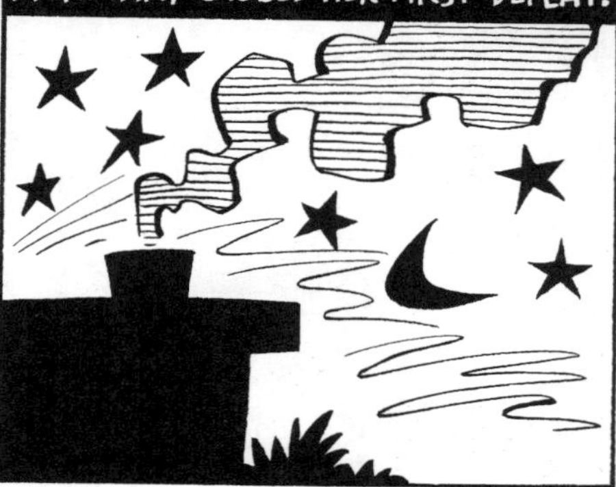

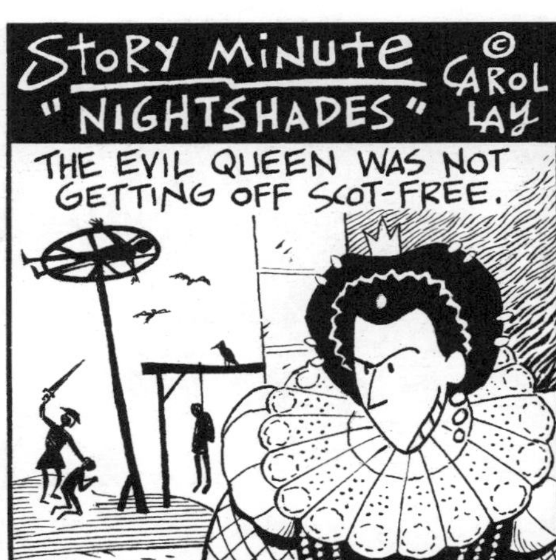
STORY MINUTE
"NIGHTSHADES"
© CAROL LAY
THE EVIL QUEEN WAS NOT GETTING OFF SCOT-FREE.

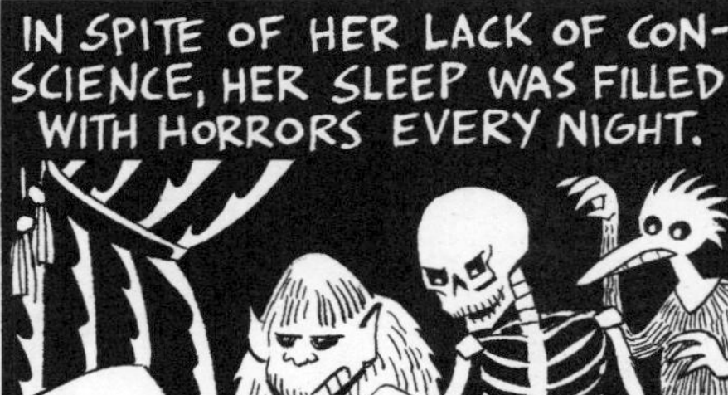
IN SPITE OF HER LACK OF CONSCIENCE, HER SLEEP WAS FILLED WITH HORRORS EVERY NIGHT.

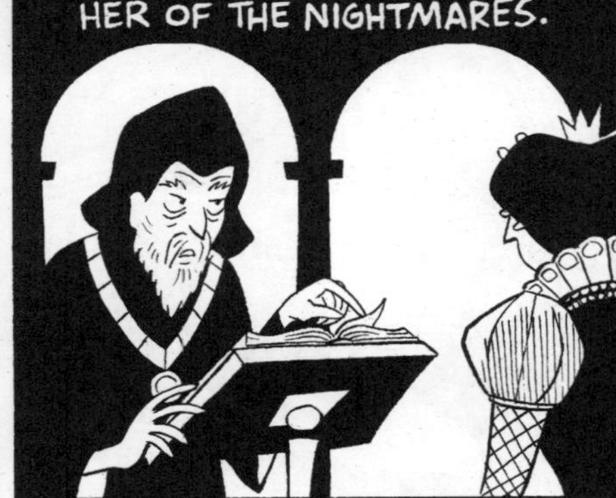
SHE CONSULTED HER SORCERER WHO PRESCRIBED A WAY TO RID HER OF THE NIGHTMARES.

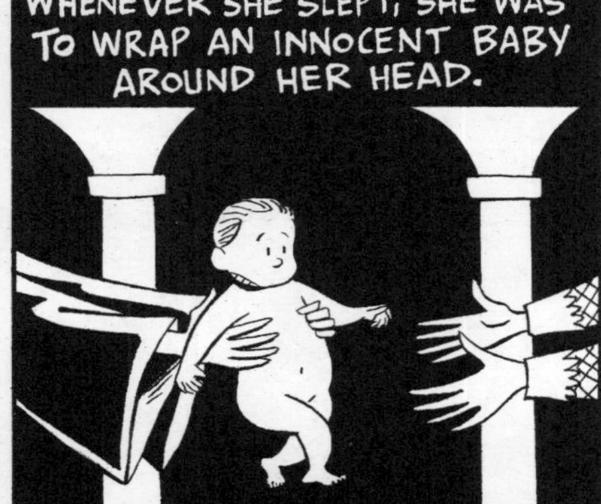
WHENEVER SHE SLEPT, SHE WAS TO WRAP AN INNOCENT BABY AROUND HER HEAD.

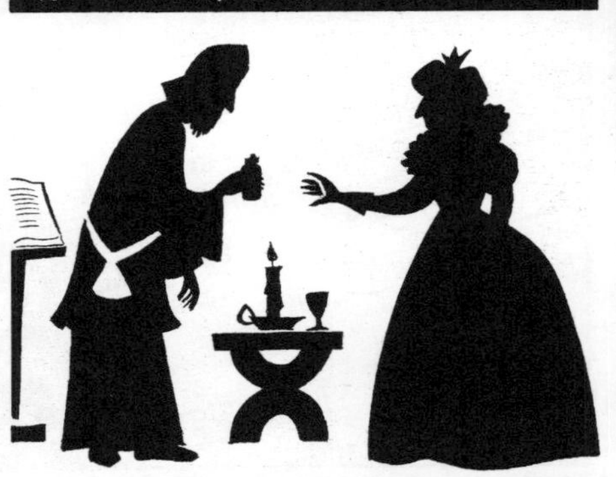
THAT, AND A POTION, WOULD CAUSE THE CHILD TO DREAM THE NIGHTMARES FOR HER.

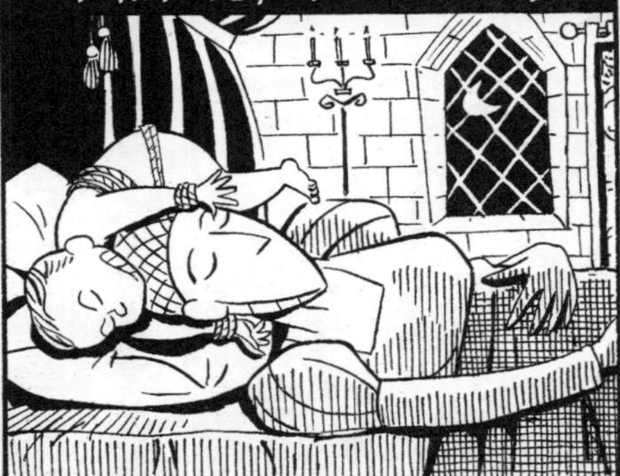
SHE FOLLOWED HIS DIRECTIONS AND WAS IMMEDIATELY RELIEVED OF HER PSYCHIC BURDENS.

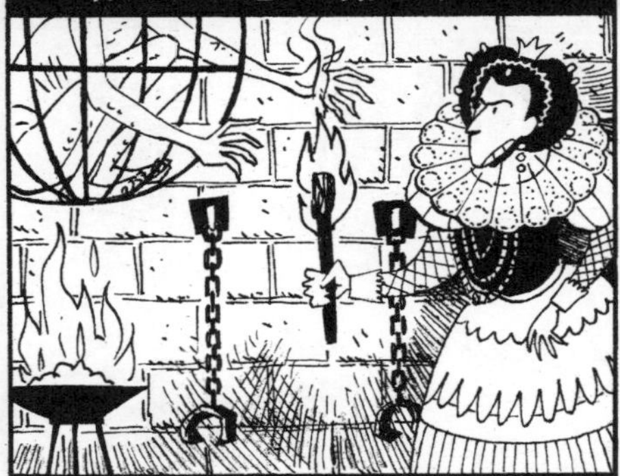
BUT, INSTEAD OF ADDING BLISS TO HER LIFE, SHE BECAME MORE RUTHLESS THAN EVER.

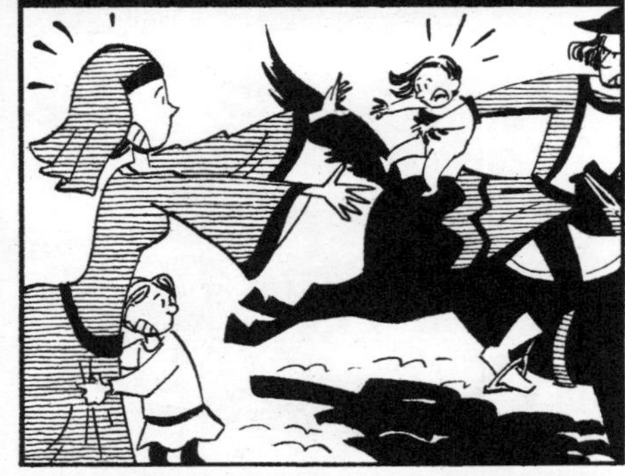
A NEW CHILD HAD TO BE BROUGHT TO HER EACH NIGHT TO FREE HER MIND OF GUILTY AFTERTHOUGHTS.

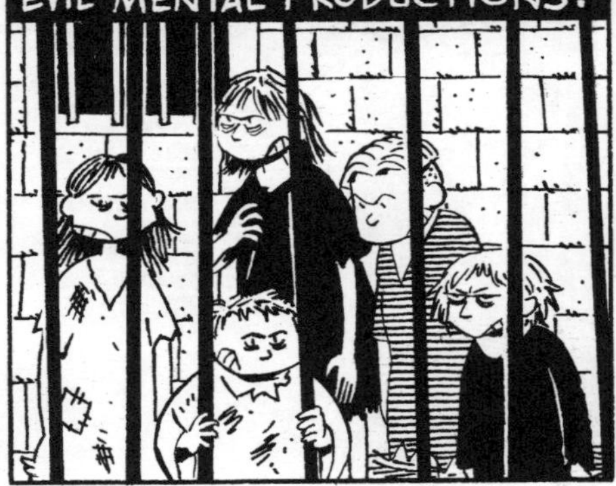
BUT THE CHILDREN BECAME DAMAGED — CORRUPTED BY HER EVIL MENTAL PRODUCTIONS.

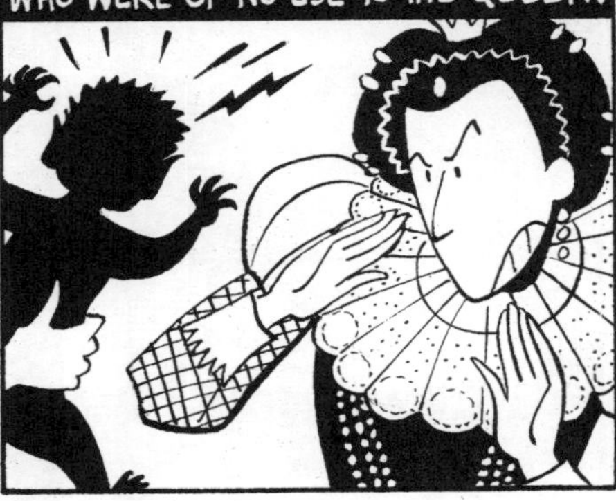
THEY GREW UP TWISTED AND HAD THEIR OWN EVIL OFFSPRING WHO WERE OF NO USE TO THE QUEEN.

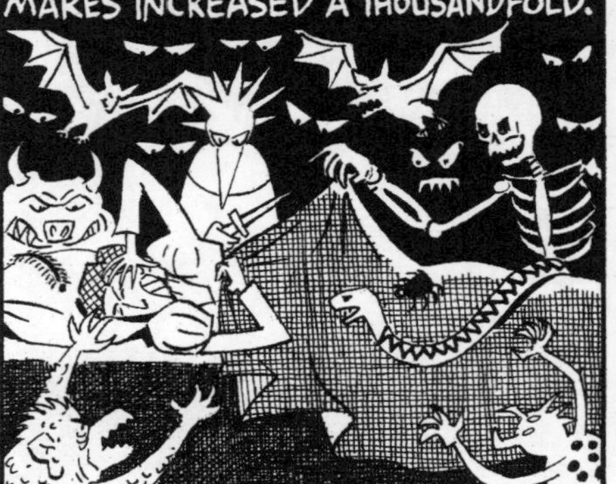
WITH NO PURE SOUL IN THE KINGDOM TO RELIEVE HER, THE NIGHTMARES INCREASED A THOUSANDFOLD.

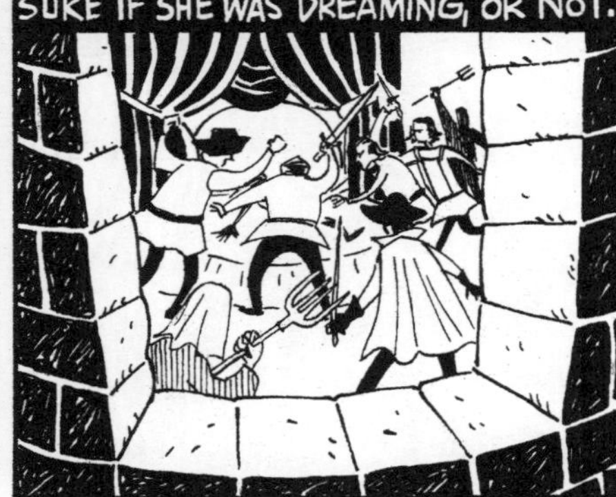
WHEN HER SUBJECTS FINALLY TORE HER LIMB FROM LIMB, SHE WASN'T SURE IF SHE WAS DREAMING, OR NOT.

Story Minute
© Carol Lay
"Address Book"
THERE ARE PRACTICAL THINGS TO CONSIDER WHEN A LOVED ONE DIES.

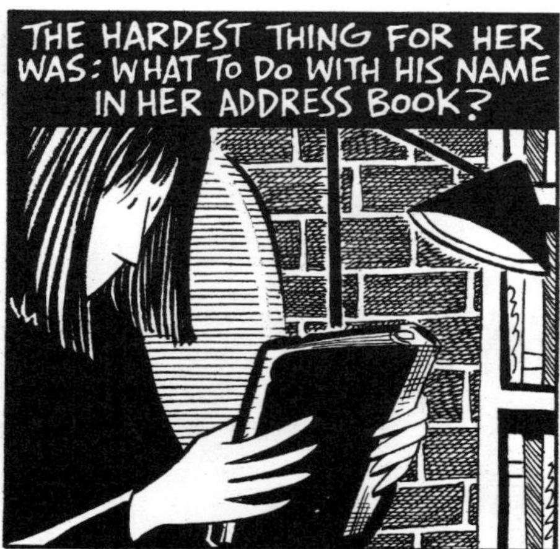
THE HARDEST THING FOR HER WAS: WHAT TO DO WITH HIS NAME IN HER ADDRESS BOOK?

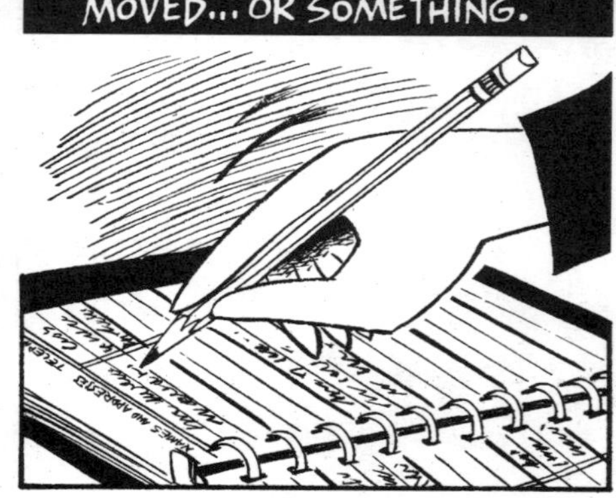
IT WAS WRITTEN IN PENCIL, AS WAS EVERYONE'S IN CASE THEY MOVED... OR SOMETHING.

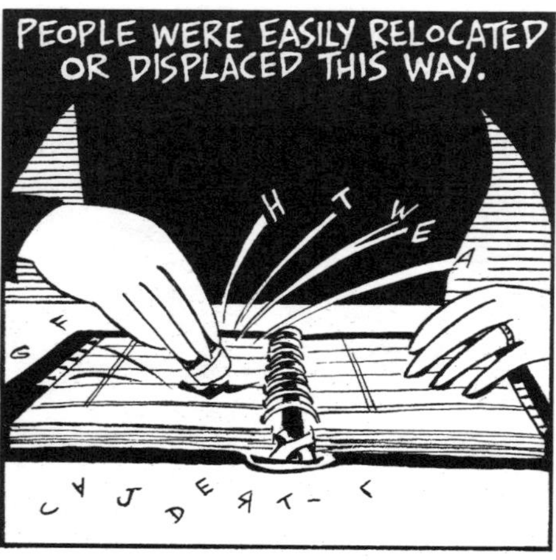
PEOPLE WERE EASILY RELOCATED OR DISPLACED THIS WAY.

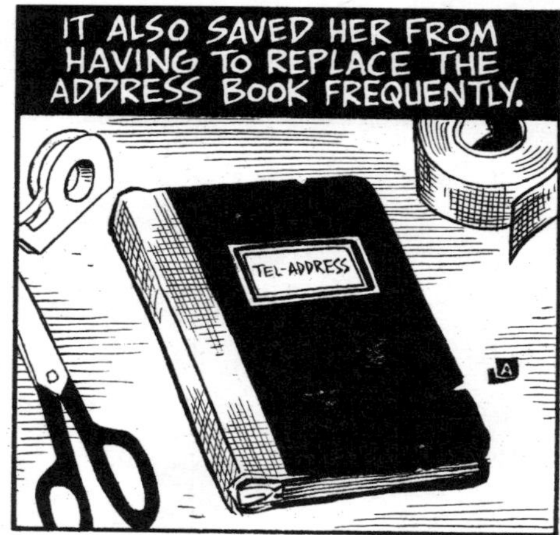
IT ALSO SAVED HER FROM HAVING TO REPLACE THE ADDRESS BOOK FREQUENTLY.
TEL-ADDRESS

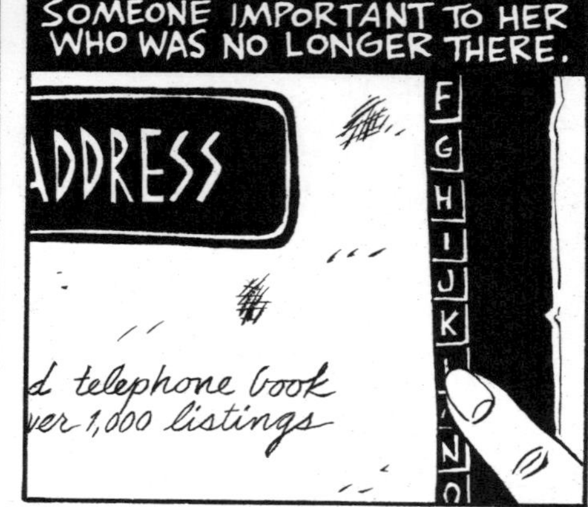
BUT THIS NAME REPRESENTED SOMEONE IMPORTANT TO HER WHO WAS NO LONGER THERE.
ADDRESS
d telephone book
ver 1,000 listings

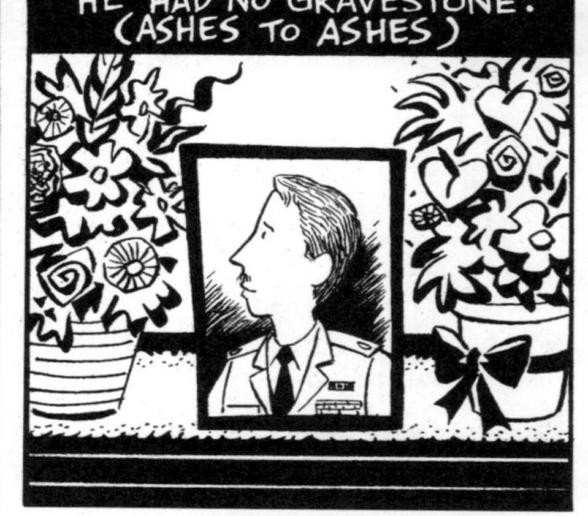
HE HAD NO GRAVESTONE. (ASHES TO ASHES)

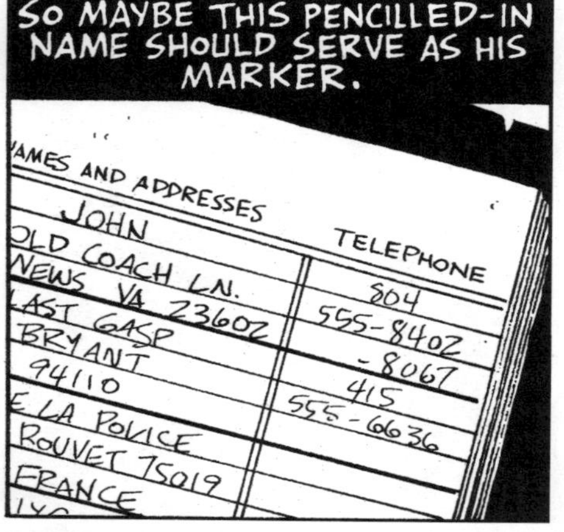
SO MAYBE THIS PENCILLED-IN NAME SHOULD SERVE AS HIS MARKER.
AMES AND ADDRESSES
TELEPHONE
JOHN
OLD COACH LN.
NEWS VA 23602
804
555-8402
LAST GASP
BRYANT
94110
-8067
415
555-6636
E LA POLICE
ROUVET 75019
FRANCE

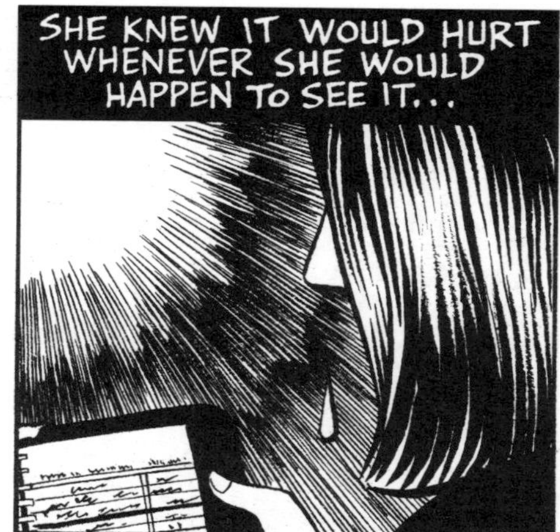
SHE KNEW IT WOULD HURT WHENEVER SHE WOULD HAPPEN TO SEE IT...

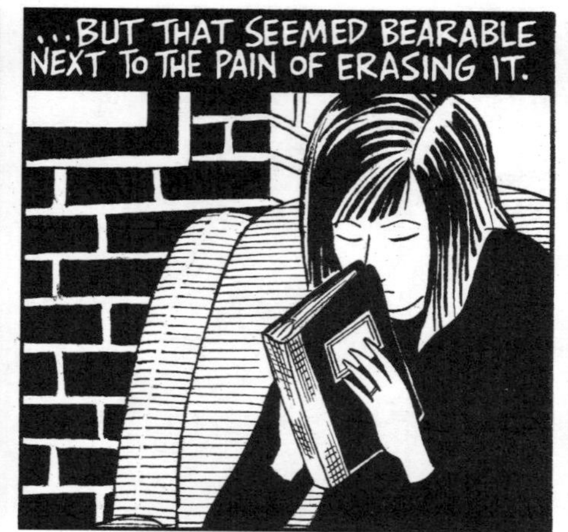
...BUT THAT SEEMED BEARABLE NEXT TO THE PAIN OF ERASING IT.

SO SHE KEPT HIS MEMORY IN HER DOG-EARED ADDRESS BOOK...

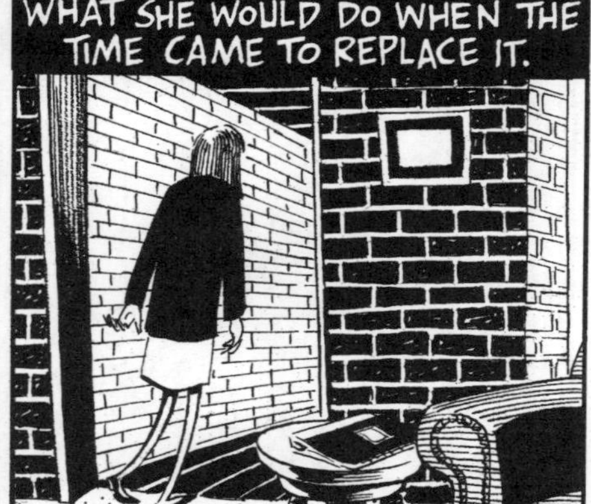
...AND TRIED NOT TO THINK OF WHAT SHE WOULD DO WHEN THE TIME CAME TO REPLACE IT.

STORY MINUTE © CAROL LAY
"LIVING HELL"

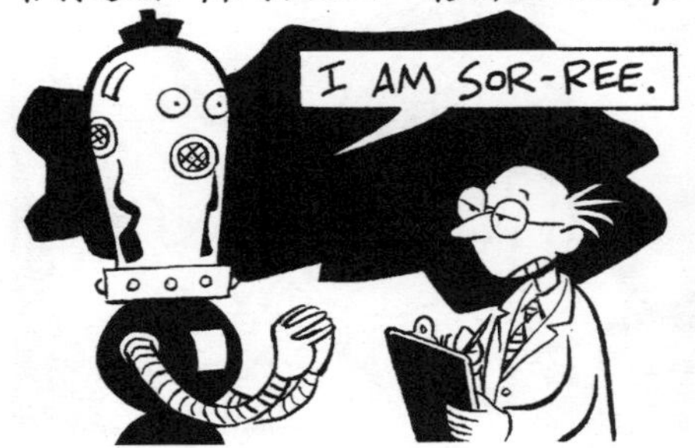


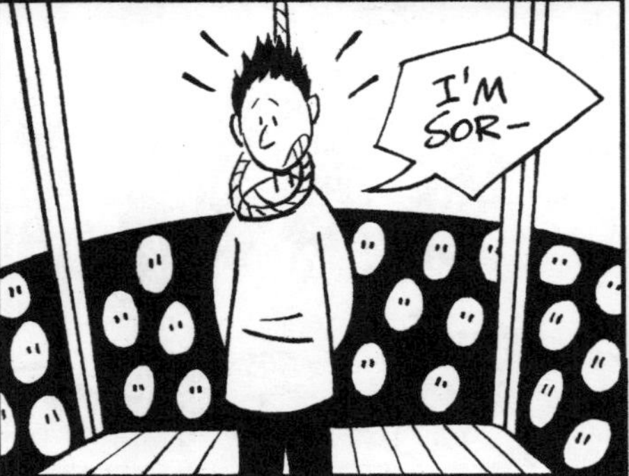


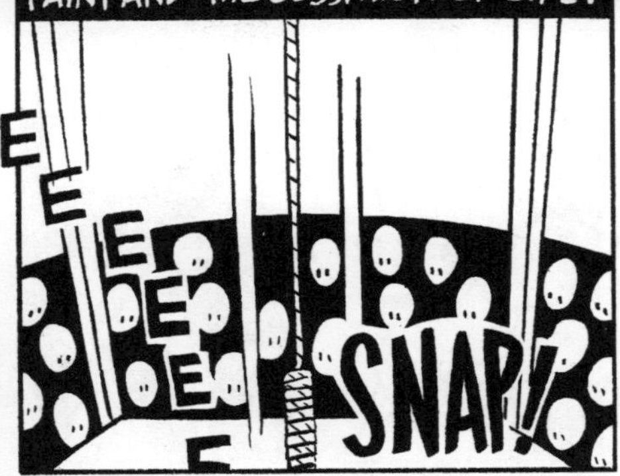


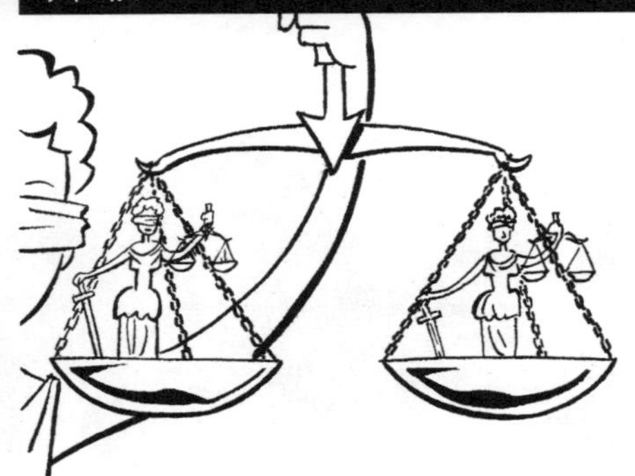


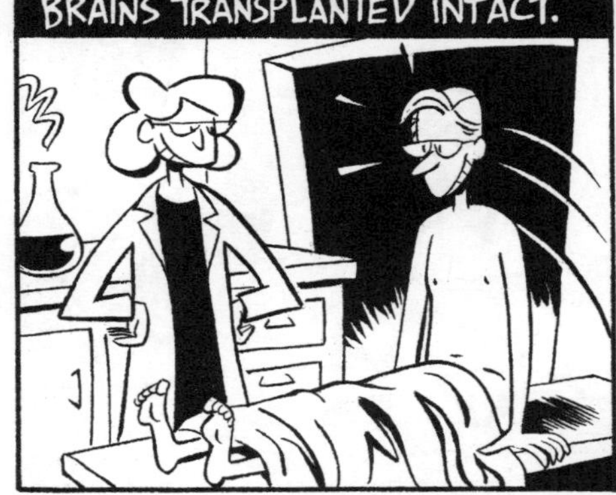


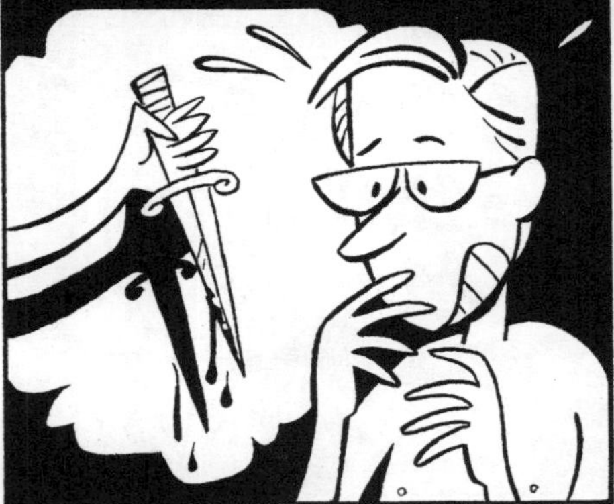


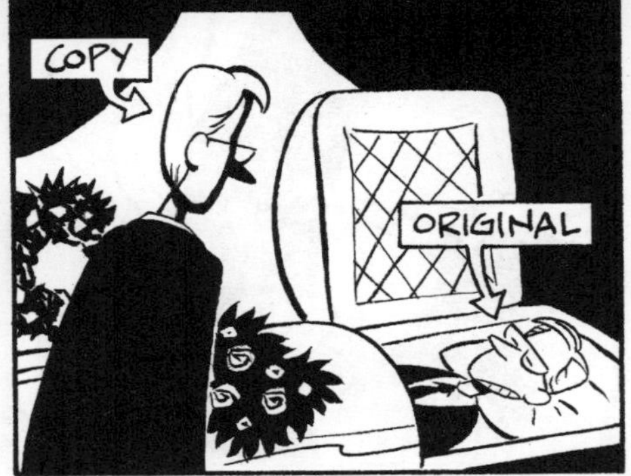


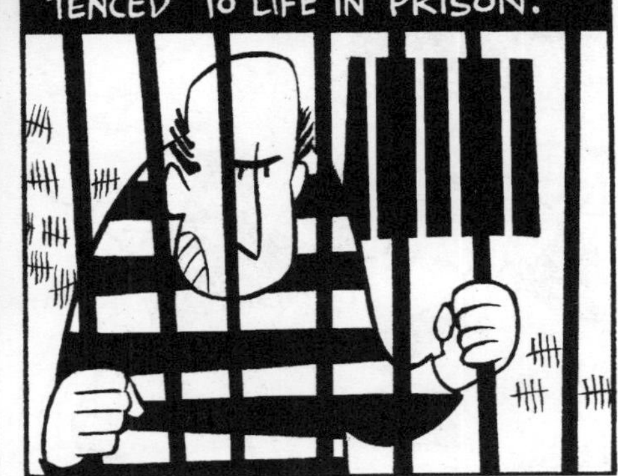

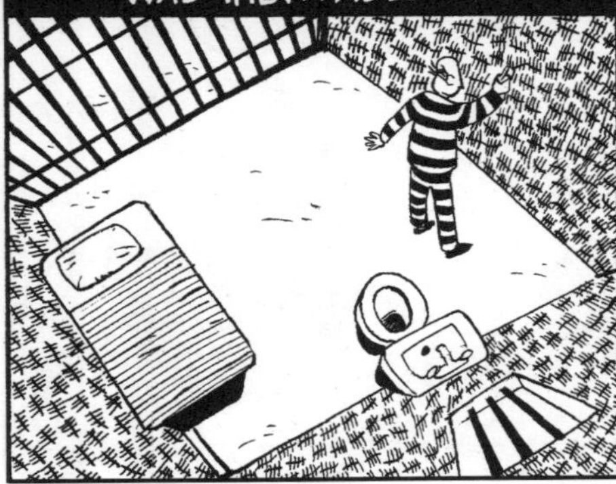


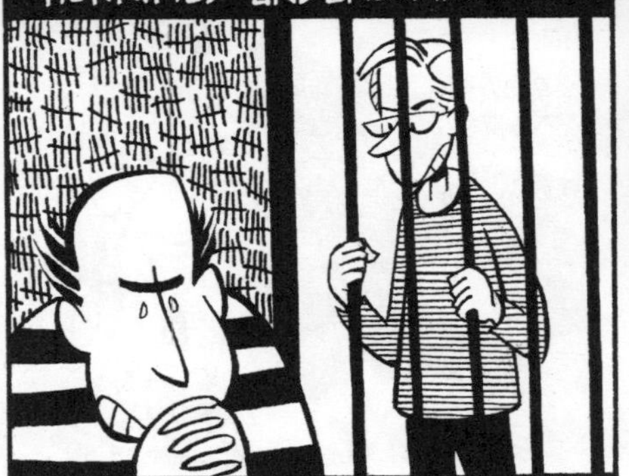

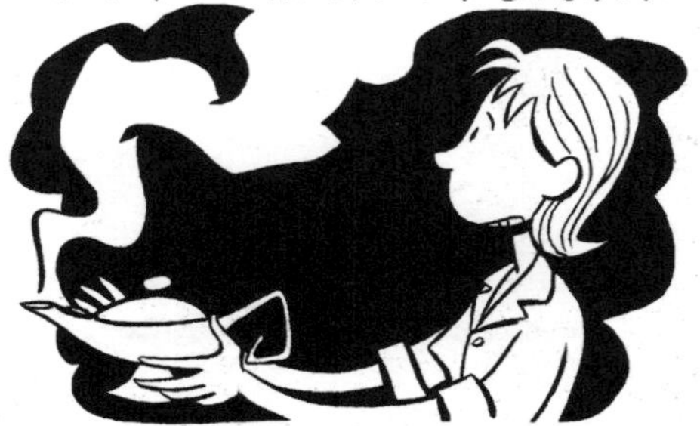
STORY MINUTE © CAROL LAY
"WISH FULFILLMENT"
WHEN THE GENIE APPEARED, THE WOMAN HAD A LOT TO CONSIDER.

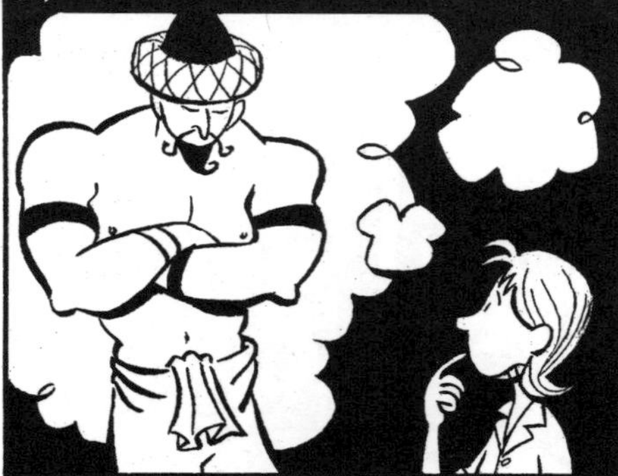
SHE'D HEARD TOO MANY STORIES OF PEOPLE GETTING BURNED BY THEIR OWN SELFISH WISHES.

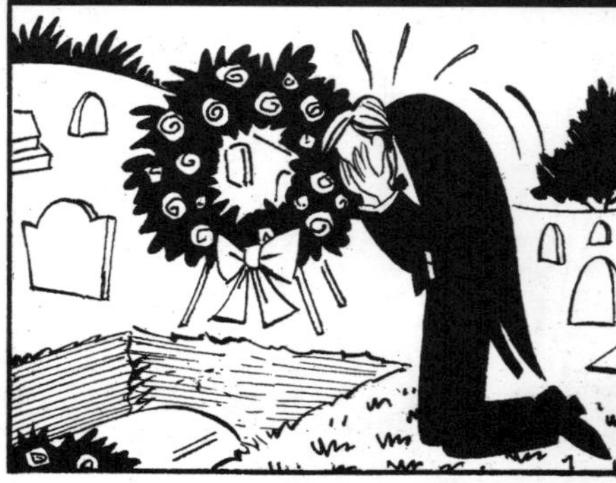
LIKE THE MAN WHO RECEIVED A FORTUNE AT THE COST OF LOSING HIS BELOVED RICH UNCLE.

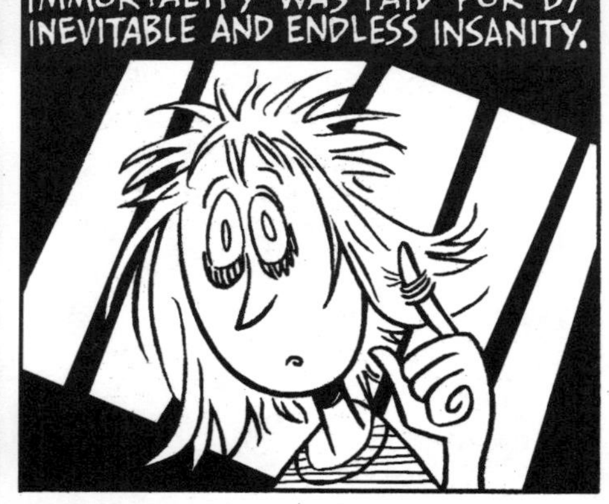
OR THE WOMAN WHOSE DESIRED IMMORTALITY WAS PAID FOR BY INEVITABLE AND ENDLESS INSANITY.

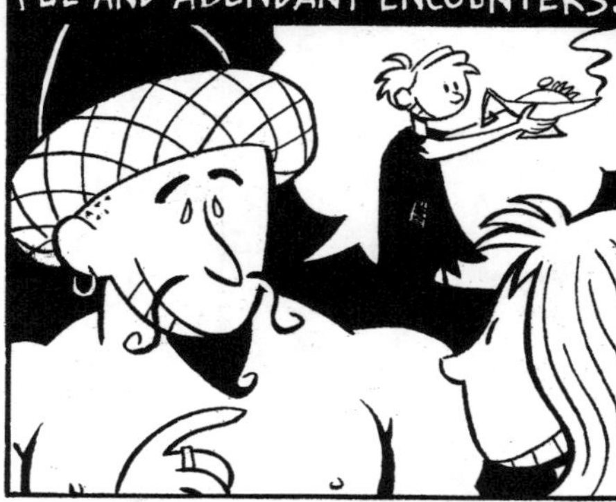
THE GENIE RECOUNTED MANY OTHER STORIES FROM HIS COLORFUL AND ABUNDANT ENCOUNTERS.

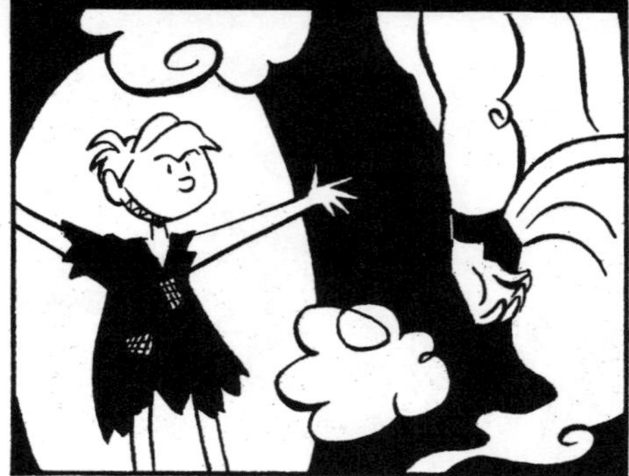
SHE COULD DO AS ONE LAD DID WHO WISHED FOR ALL OF HIS SUBSEQUENT WISHES TO COME TRUE.

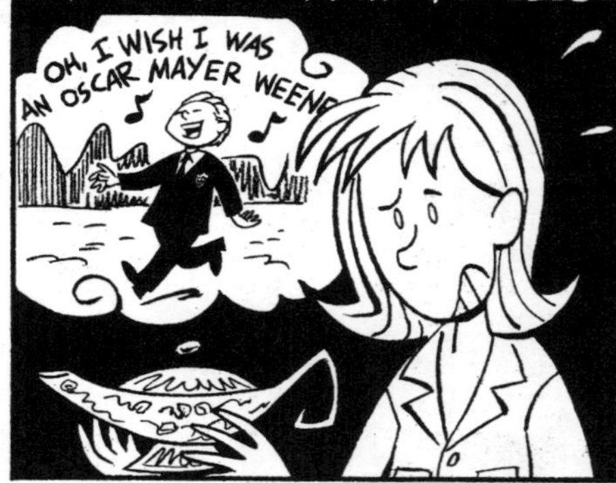
BUT COUNTLESS WISHES WOULD JUST INCREASE THE HAZARDS THAT WERE INHERENT IN THE PROCESS.
OH, I WISH I WAS AN OSCAR MAYER WEENE

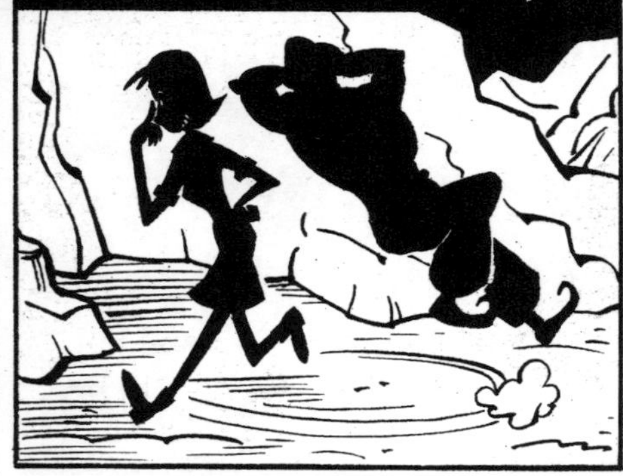
WANTING TO IMPROVE HER DRAB LIFE, SHE CONTEMPLATED OPTIONS TO THE BEST OF HER ABILITY...

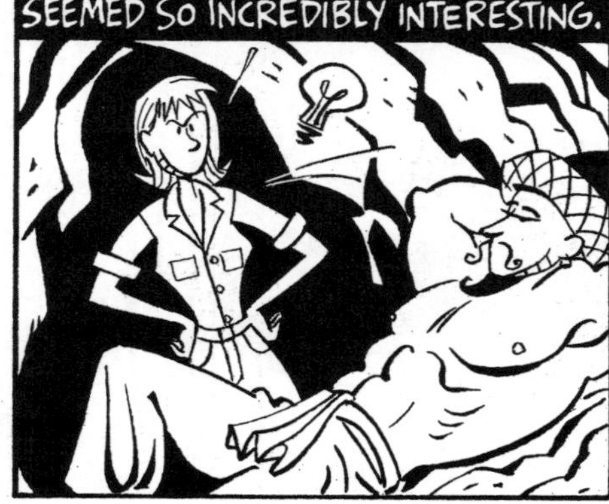
...WHEREUPON SHE REALIZED THAT SHE ENVIED THE GENIE WHOSE JOB SEEMED SO INCREDIBLY INTERESTING.

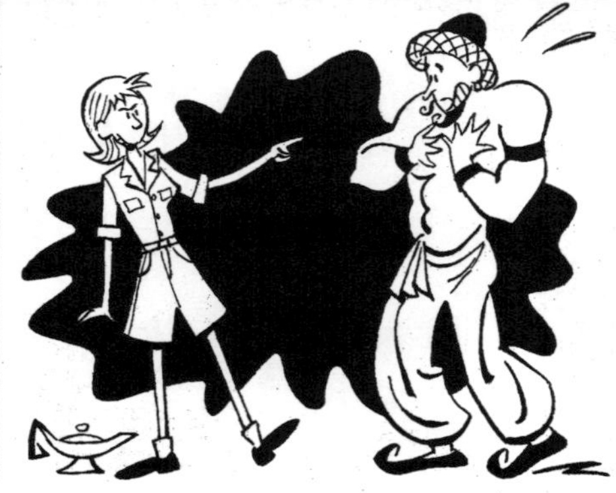
SHE WISHED TO CHANGE LIVES WITH HIM AND IT WAS DONE.

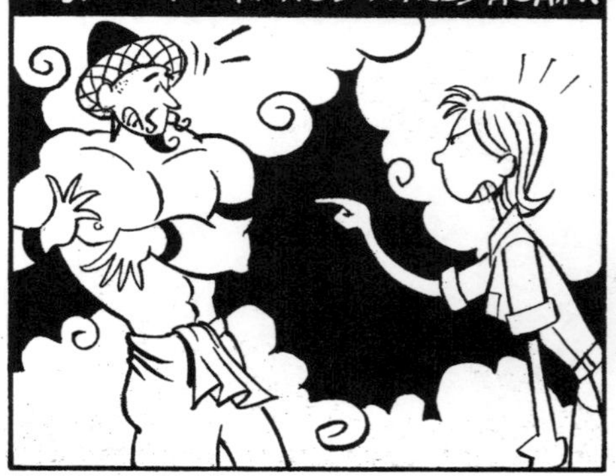
BUT NOW THE FORMER GENIE WAS ENTITLED TO A WISH AND HE WISHED TO CHANGE PLACES AGAIN.

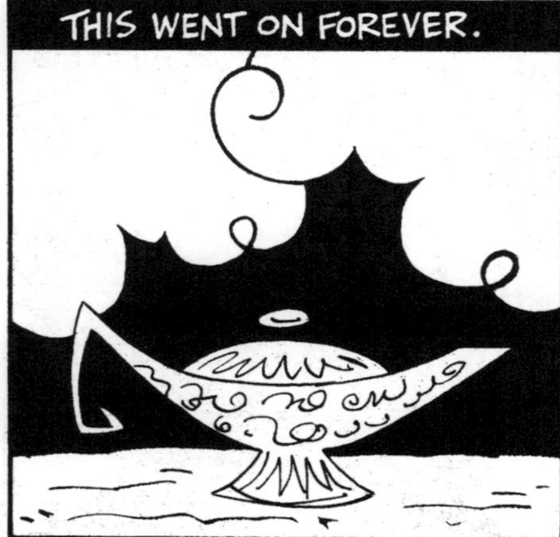
THIS WENT ON FOREVER.

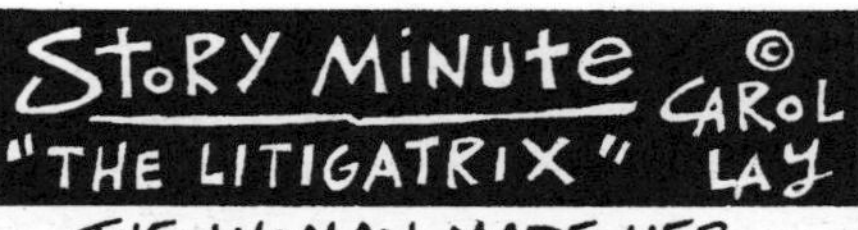
STORY MINUTE © CAROL LAY
"THE LITIGATRIX"

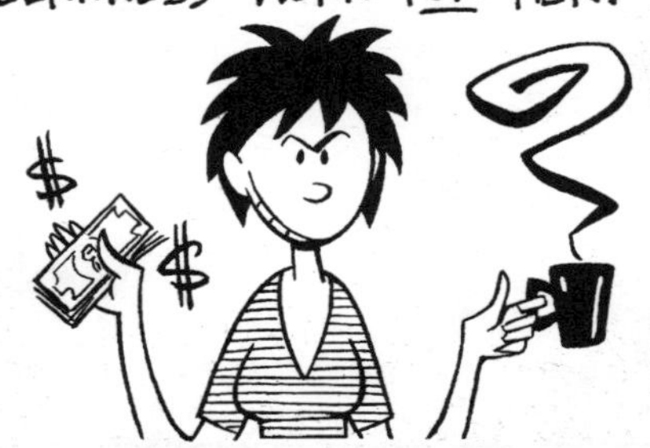
THE WOMAN MADE HER JERKNESS WORK FOR HER.
$
$

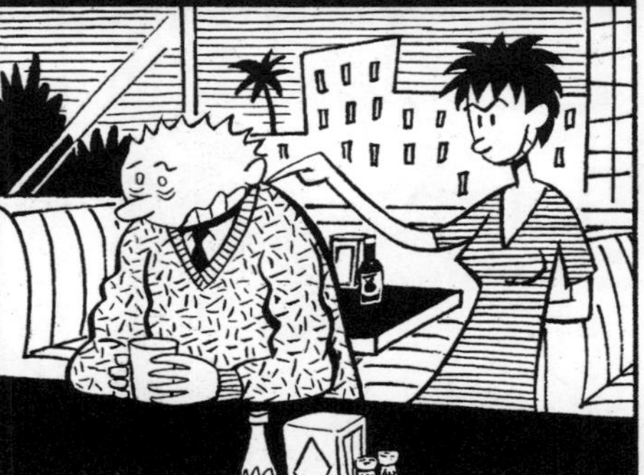
FIRST SHE WOULD GO INTO A COFFEE SHOP AND FIND SOMEONE WHO HAD HAD TOO MUCH CAFFEINE.

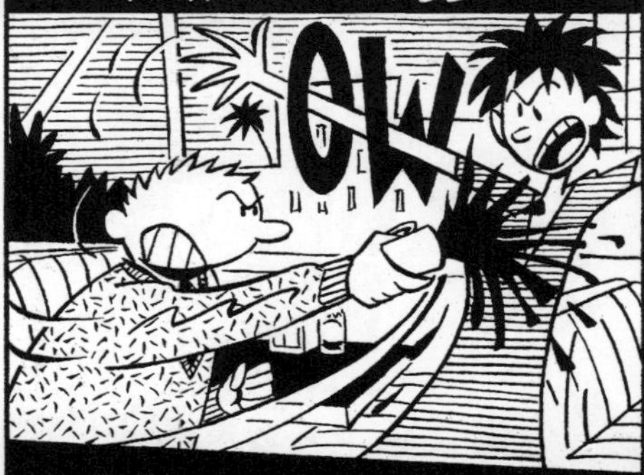
SHE WOULD AGGRAVATE THAT PERSON UNTIL HE DOUSED HER WITH HOT COFFEE.
OW

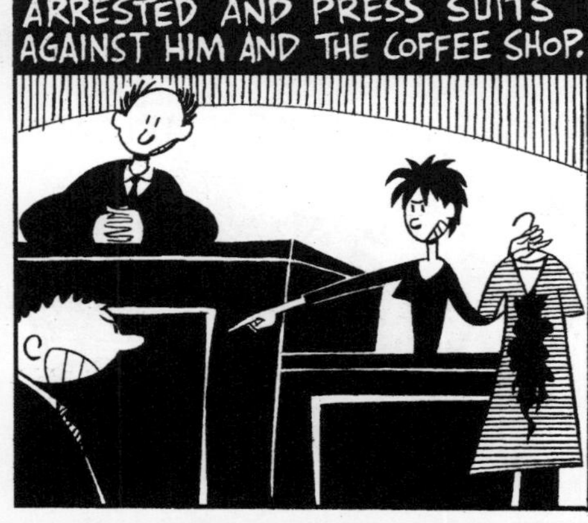
THEN SHE WOULD HAVE HIM ARRESTED AND PRESS SUITS AGAINST HIM AND THE COFFEE SHOP.

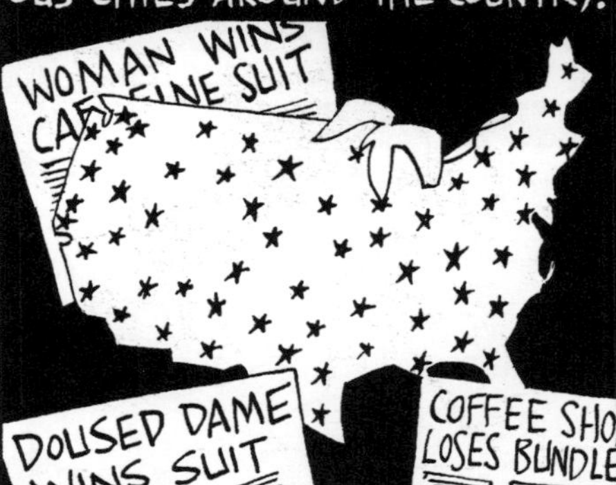
SHE MADE A GOOD LIVING AT THIS FOR MANY YEARS IN VARIOUS CITIES AROUND THE COUNTRY.
WOMAN WINS
DOUSED DAME
COFFEE SHO
LOSES BUNDLE

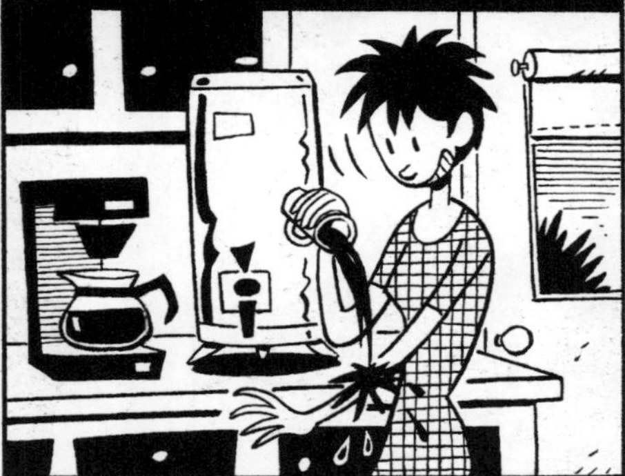
BUT SHE BECAME ADDICTED TO CAFFEINE AND STARTED TO NEED IT ON HER SKIN CONSTANTLY.

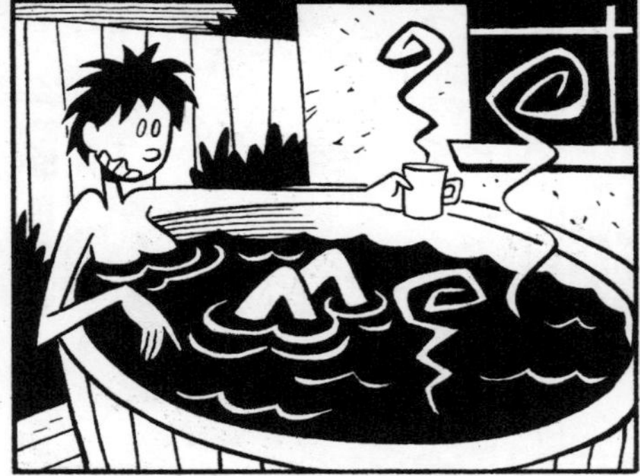
SHE FILLED A HOT TUB WITH COFFEE AND SOAKED IN IT UNTIL SHE WAS TOTALLY WIRED, NEVER SLEEPING.

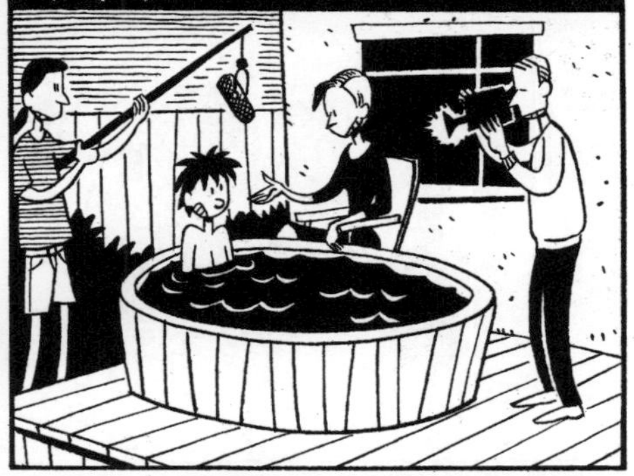
A TABLOID NEWS SHOW GOT WIND OF THIS AND AIRED A PIECE ON HER SLEEPLESS LIFESTYLE.

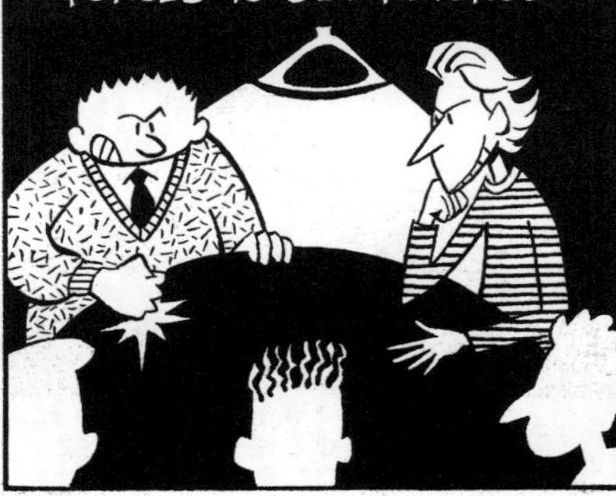
SEVERAL OF HER LAWSUIT VICTIMS SAW THE SHOW AND JOINED FORCES TO GET REVENGE.

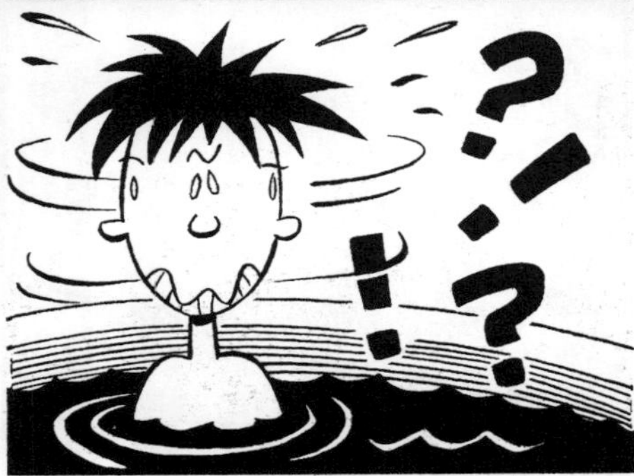
BUT HOW COULD THEY TAKE HER UNAWARES WHEN SHE WAS ALWAYS WIRED TO THE GILLS?
?!
!?

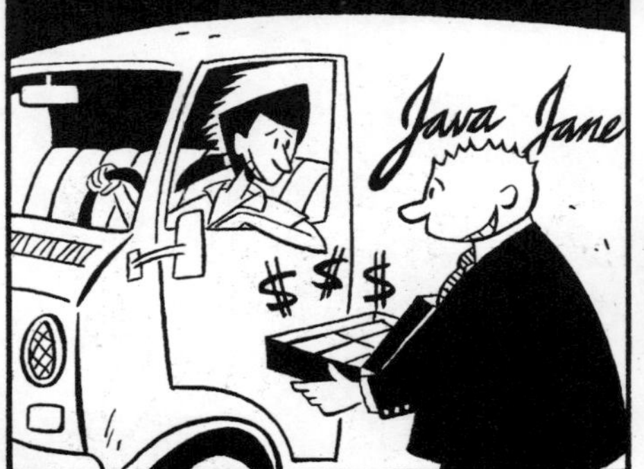
THEY BRIBED HER COFFEE DELIVERY PERSON INTO SWITCHING DECAF FOR THE REGULAR.
Java Jane
$ $ $

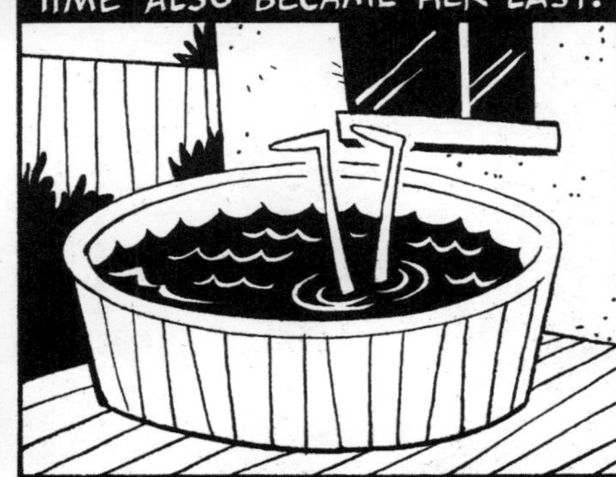
SO IT HAPPENED THAT HER FIRST GOOD NIGHT OF SLEEP IN A LONG TIME ALSO BECAME HER LAST.

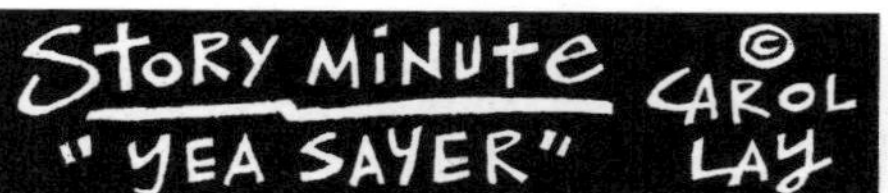
Story Minute
"Yea Sayer"
© Carol Lay

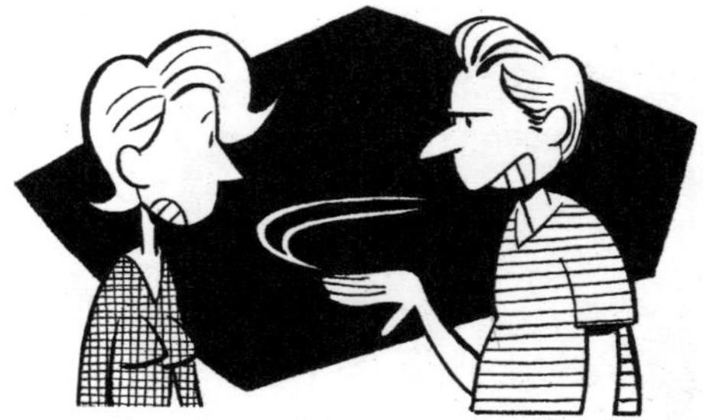
According to others, goals were almost impossible to attain.

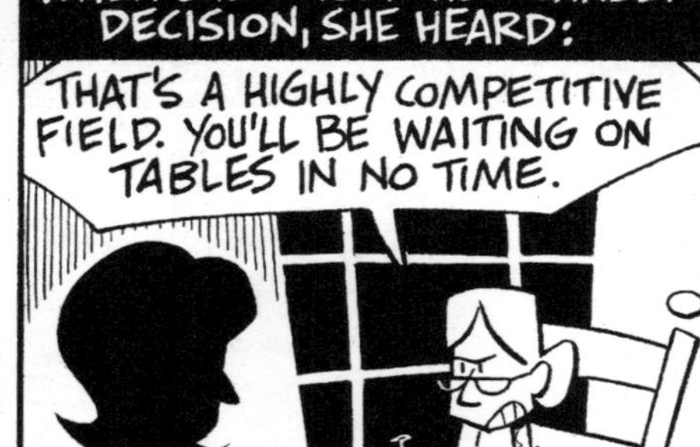
When she voiced her career decision, she heard:
That's a highly competitive field. You'll be waiting on tables in no time.

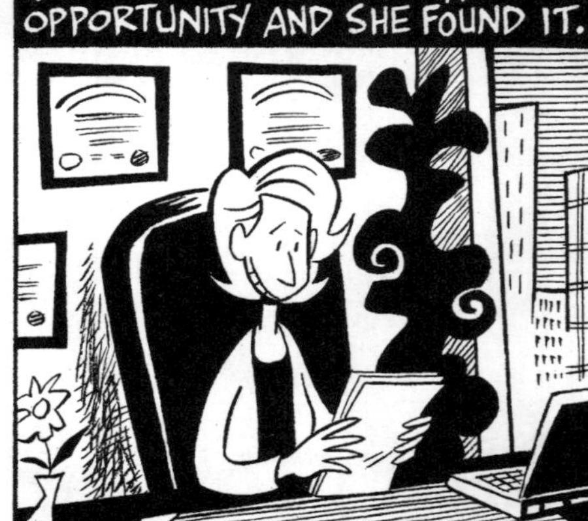
But all she needed was one opportunity and she found it.

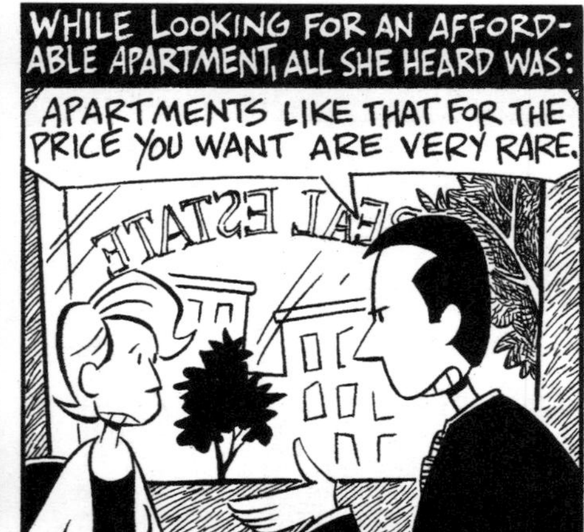
While looking for an affordable apartment, all she heard was:
Apartments like that for the price you want are very rare.
Real Estate

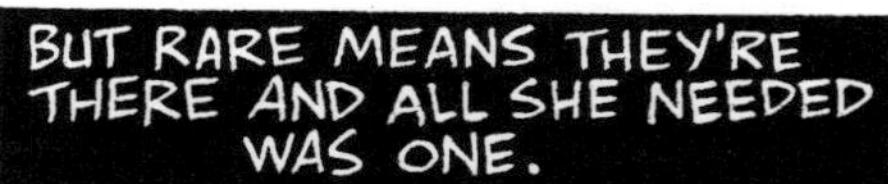
But rare means they're there and all she needed was one.

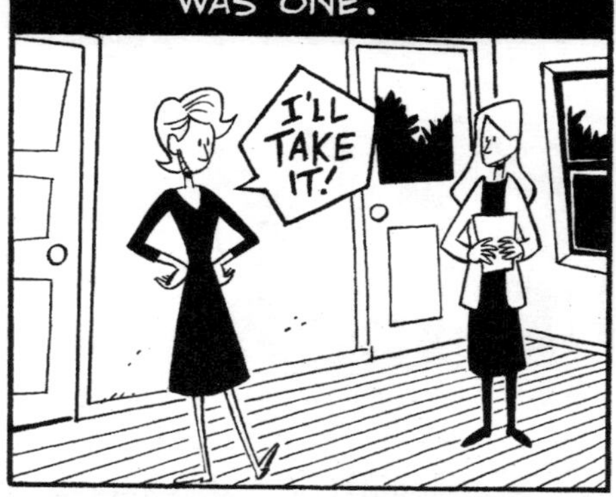
I'll take it!

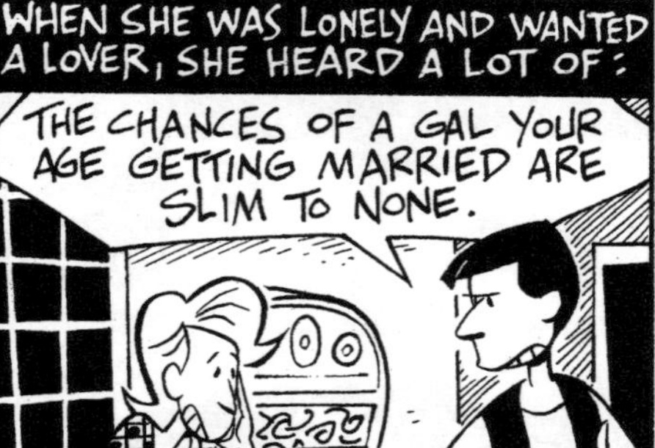
When she was lonely and wanted a lover, she heard a lot of:
The chances of a gal your age getting married are slim to none.

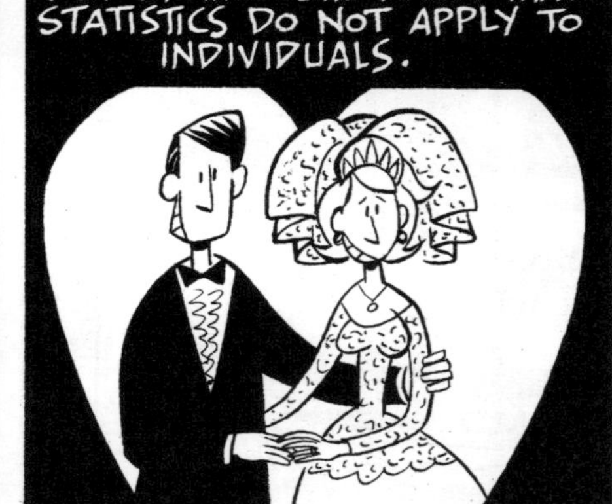
But by then she knew that statistics do not apply to individuals.

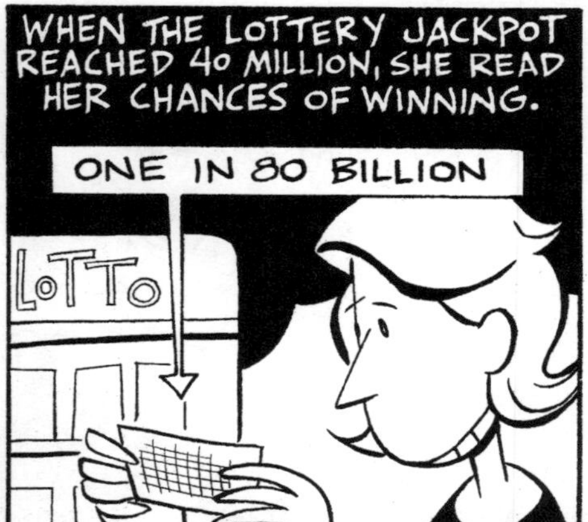
When the lottery jackpot reached 40 million, she read her chances of winning.
One in 80 billion
Lotto

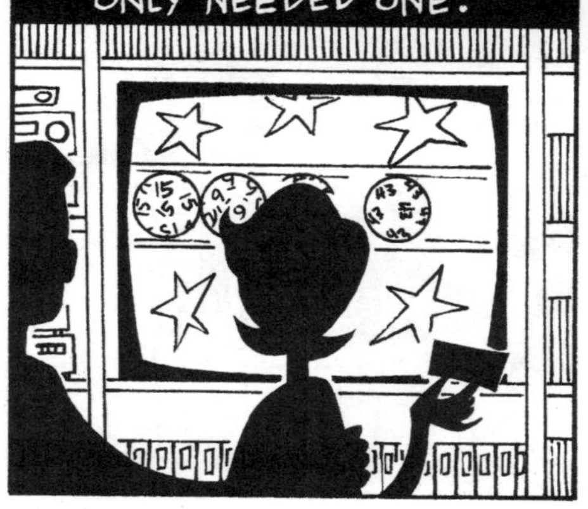
Again, she knew that she only needed one.

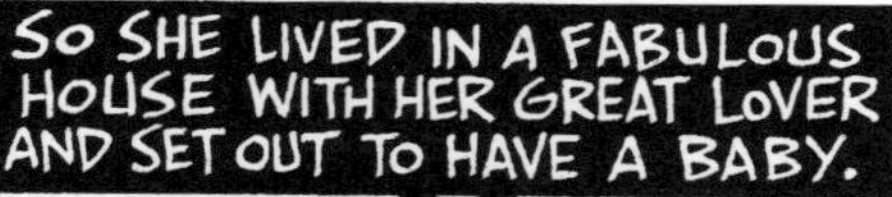
So she lived in a fabulous house with her great lover and set out to have a baby.

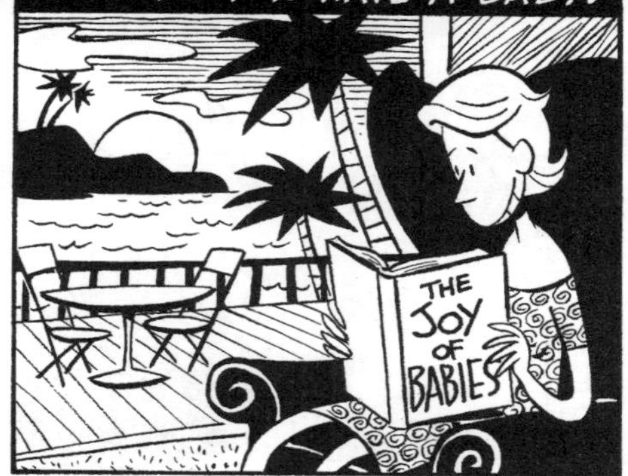
The Joy of Babies

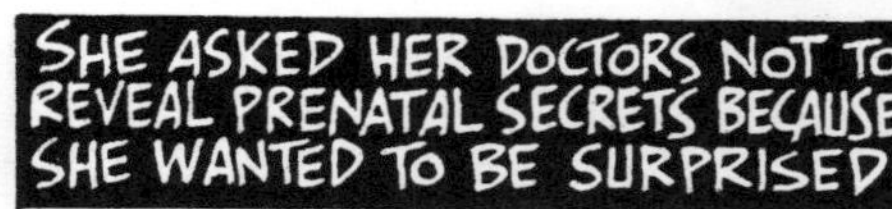
She asked her doctors not to reveal prenatal secrets because she wanted to be surprised

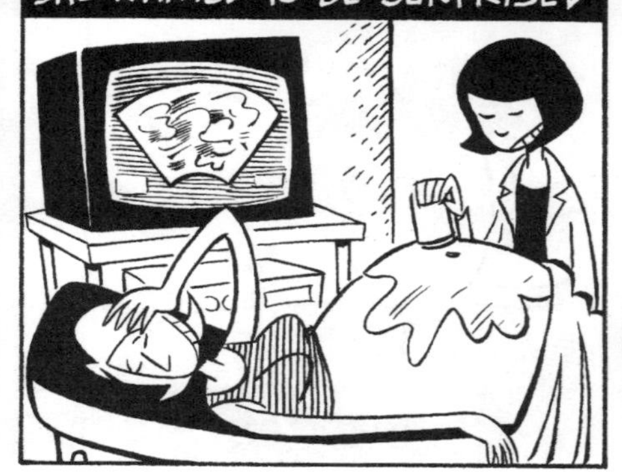

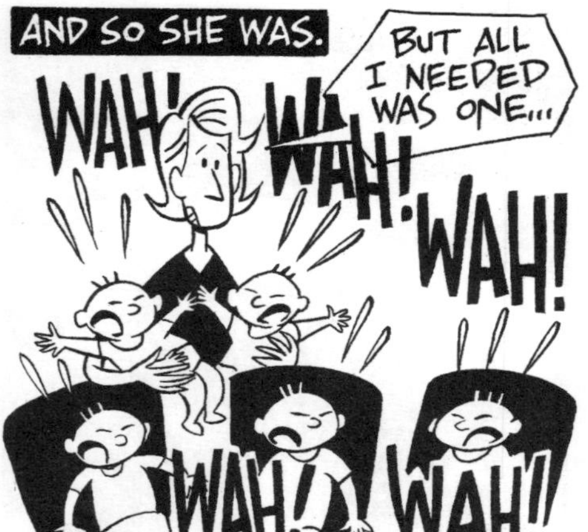
And so she was.
But all I needed was one...
Wah!
Wah!
Wah!
Wah!
Wah!

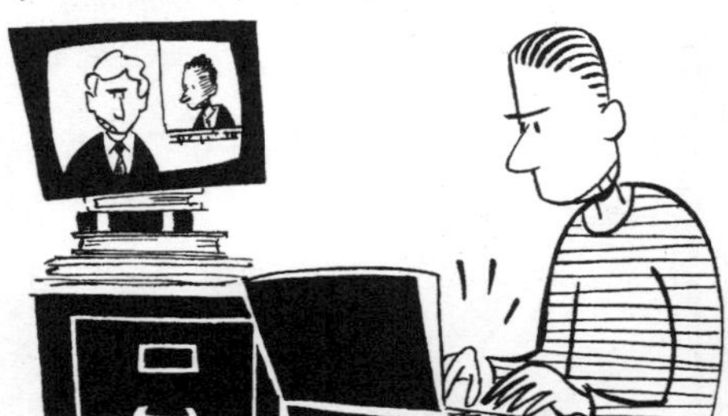
STORY MINUTE
"DEATH SENTENCES"
© CAROL LAY
THE NETWORK NEWS OBITUARY WRITER WAS A PERFECTIONIST.

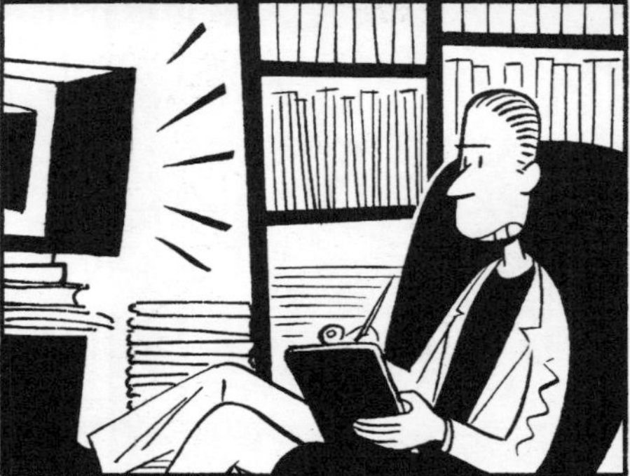
HIS JOB WAS SUCH THAT HE COMPILED THE INFORMATION WHILE HIS SUBJECTS WERE STILL ALIVE.

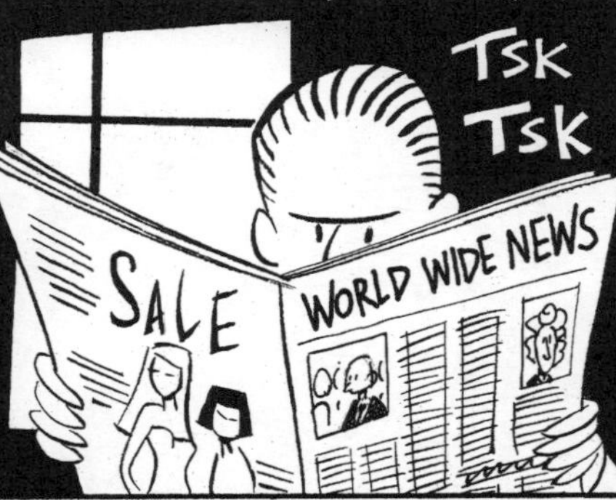
HE COULDN'T HELP BUT BECOME OBSESSED WITH THESE CELEBRITIES AND POLITICIANS...
TSK
TSK
SALE
WORLD WIDE NEWS

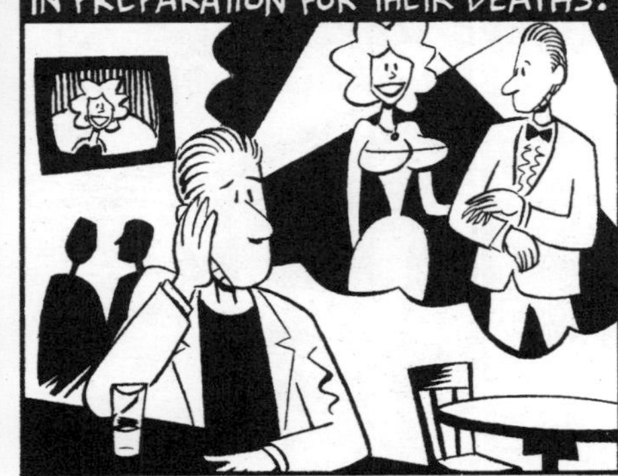
...FOR HE WAS CONTINUALLY REVIEWING AND EDITING THEIR LIVES IN PREPARATION FOR THEIR DEATHS.

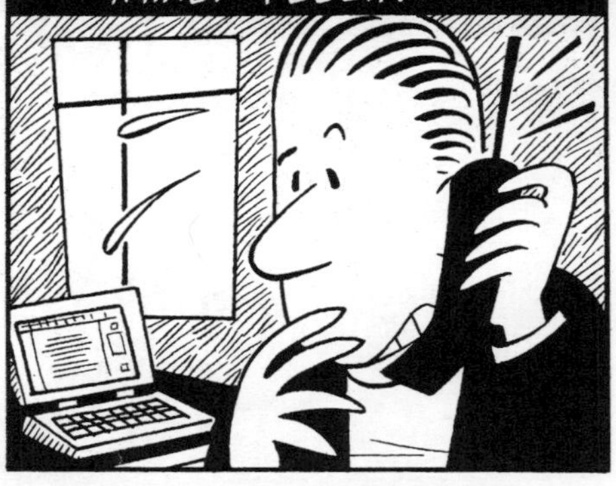
THE FIRST TIME ONE OF HIS SUBJECTS DIED HE HAD MIXED FEELINGS.

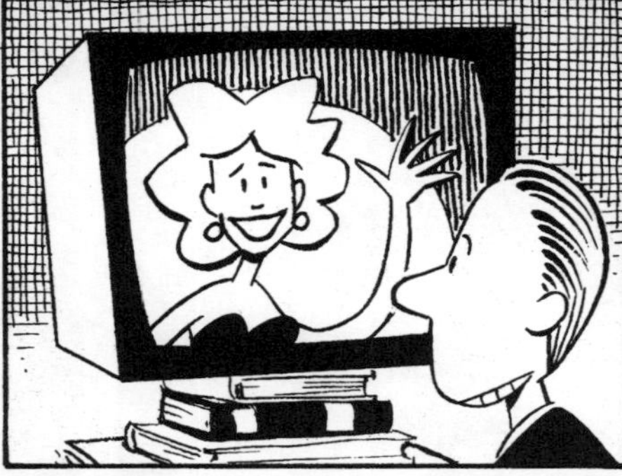
HE FELT GENUINE GRIEF FOR HER PASSING, BUT OVERWHELMING PRIDE WHEN HIS OBIT AIRED.

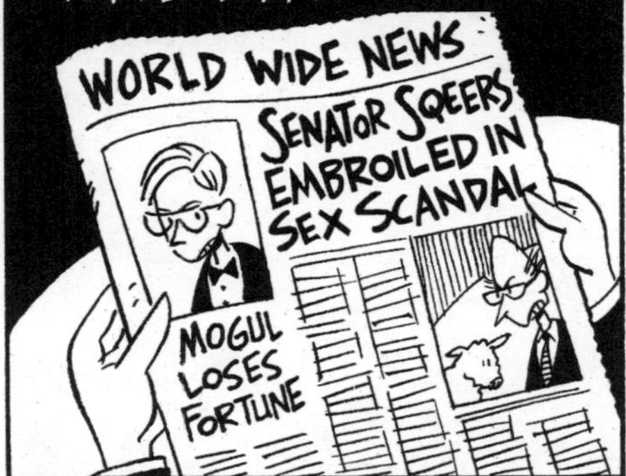
OFTEN, THOUGH, A SUBJECT DID SOMETHING TO RUIN HIS OR HER PERFECT PRE-OBITUARY.
WORLD WIDE NEWS
SENATOR SQEERS EMBROILED IN SEX SCANDAL
MOGUL LOSES FORTUNE

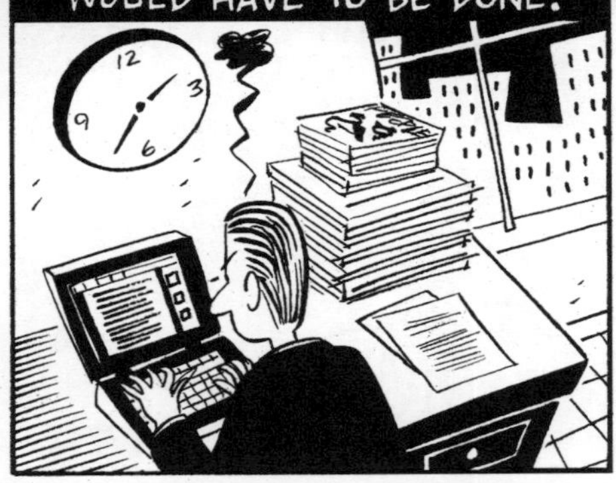
THESE EVENTS OUTRAGED HIM BECAUSE A LOT OF REWRITING WOULD HAVE TO BE DONE.
12
3
6
9

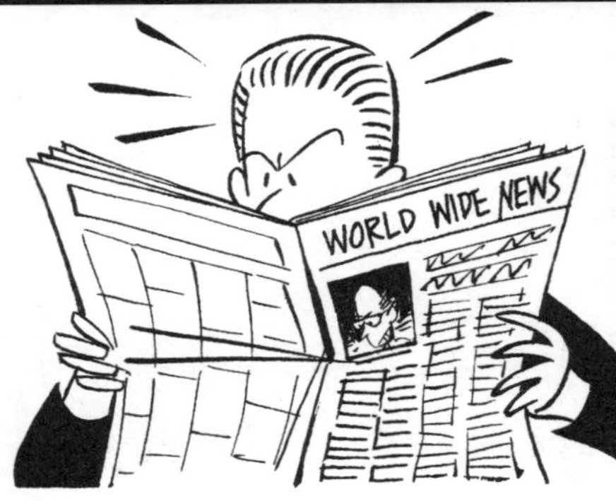
AT ONE POINT, HE SWORE HE'D NEVER LET ANYONE MESS WITH HIS WORK LIKE THAT AGAIN.
WORLD WIDE NEWS

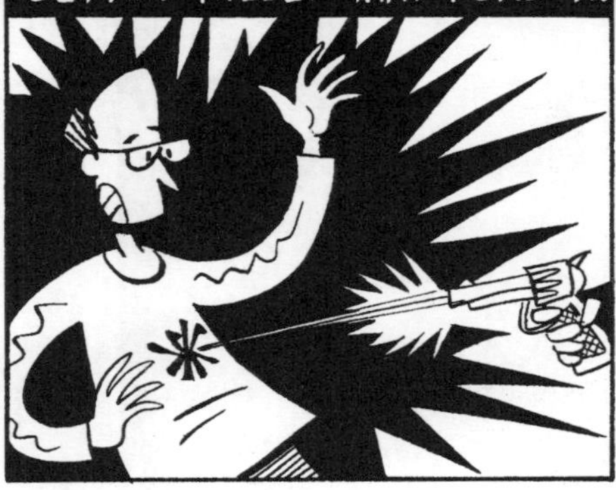
AS SOON AS HE PERFECTED A SUBJECT'S OBITUARY, HE WENT OUT AND KILLED THAT PERSON.

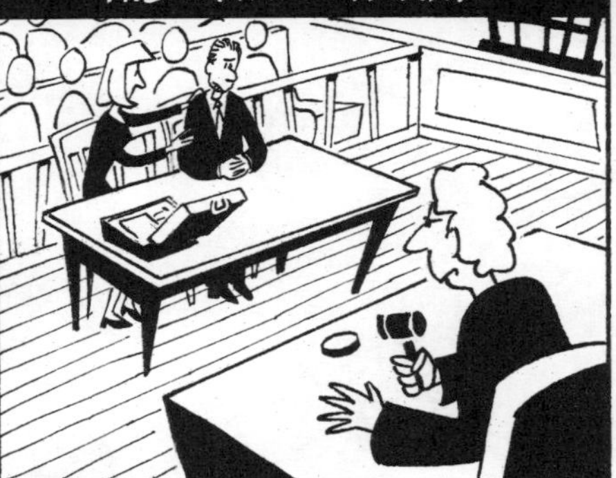
WHEN HE WAS FINALLY CONVICTED HE ASKED IF HE COULD WRITE HIS OWN OBITUARY.

HE EVEN KNEW THE DAY HE WOULD DIE SO NO ONE WOULD HAVE TO REWRITE A WORD OF IT.

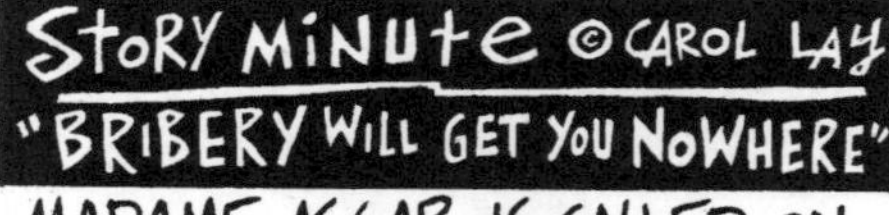


MADAME ASGAR IS CALLED ON BY A REAL WHEELER-DEALER.

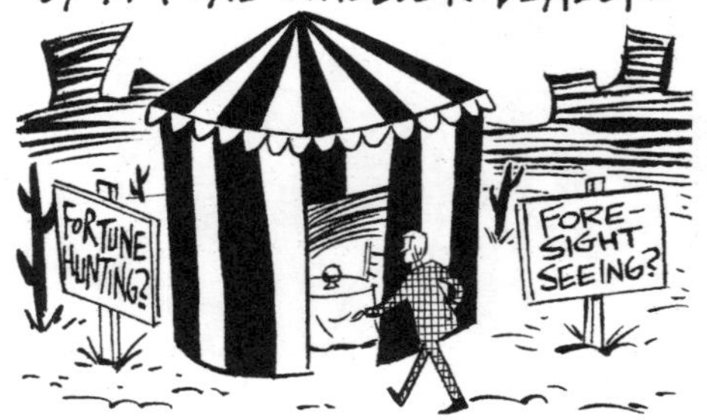


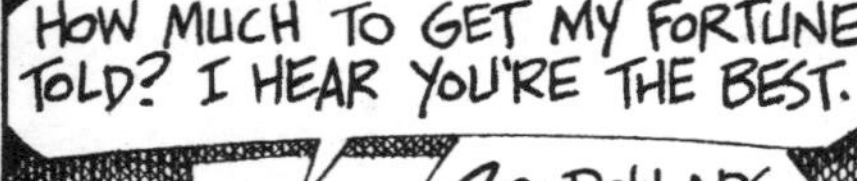


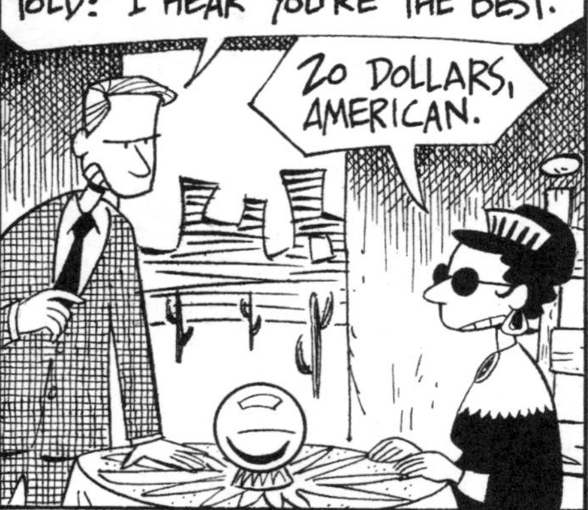


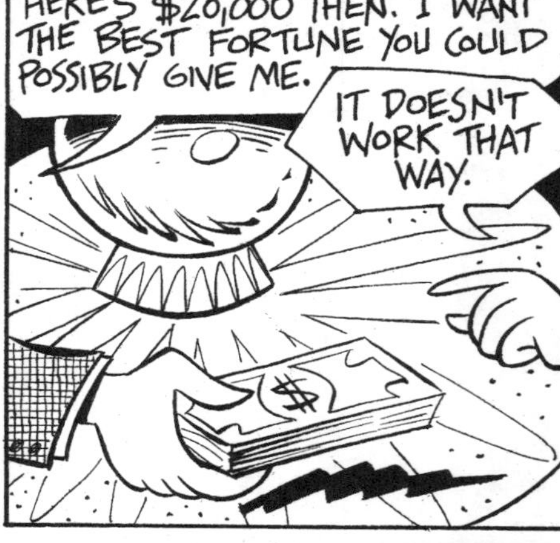


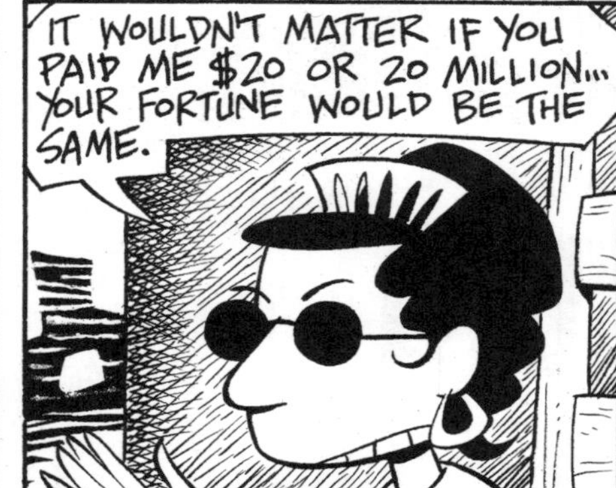


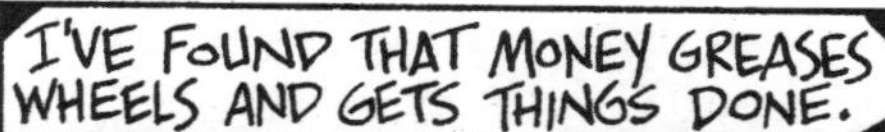


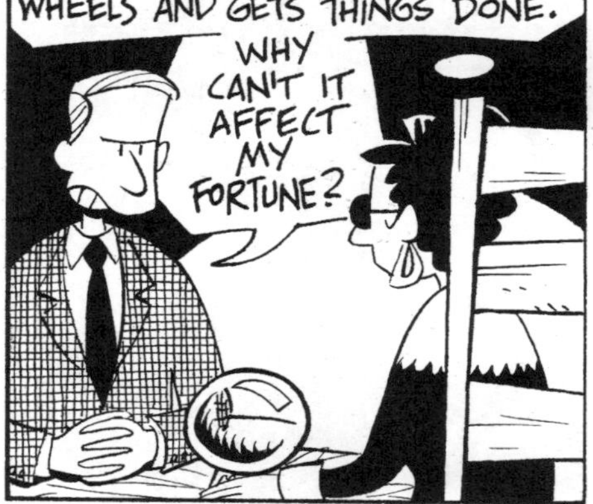


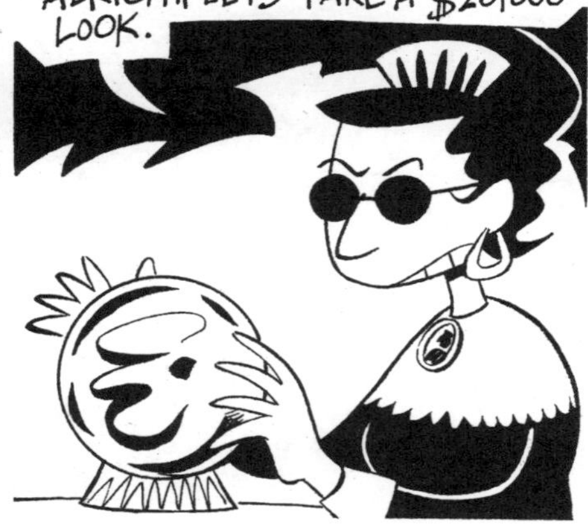

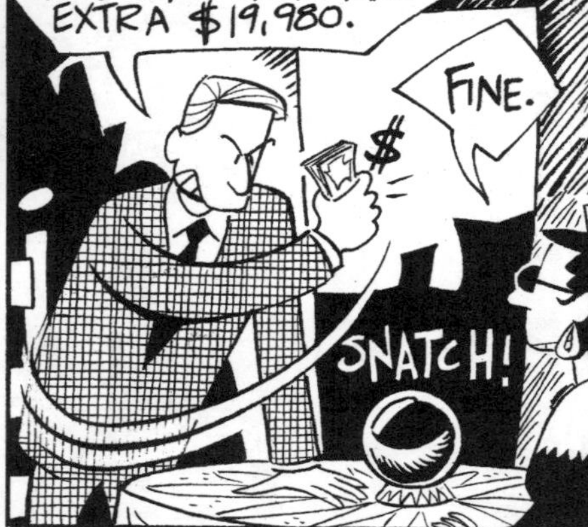


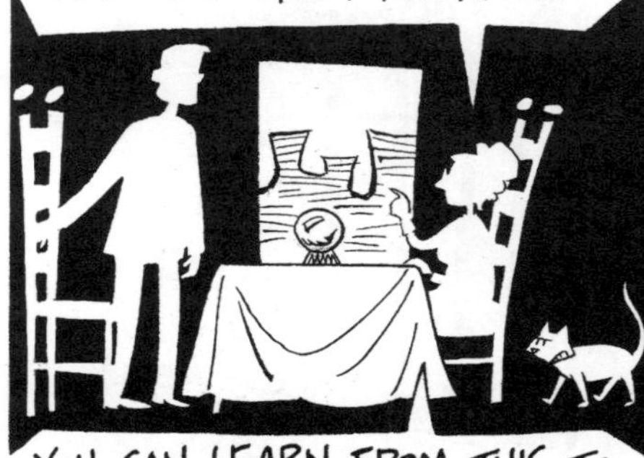


YOU'RE **RIGHT**! I'LL JUST ADD **THIS** TO THE JUDGE'S BRIBE AND HE'LL BE **SURE** TO ACCEPT IT!

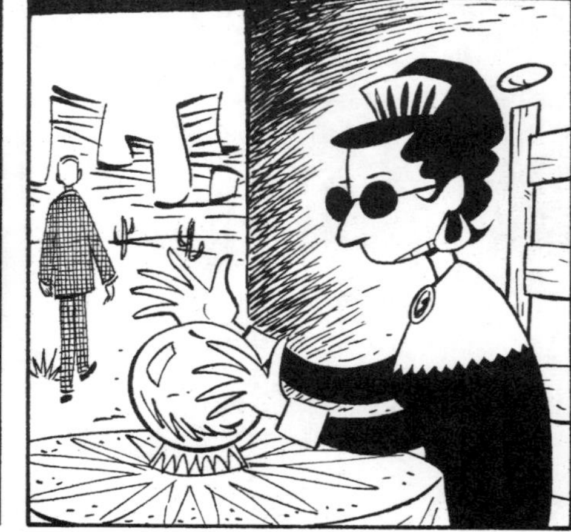

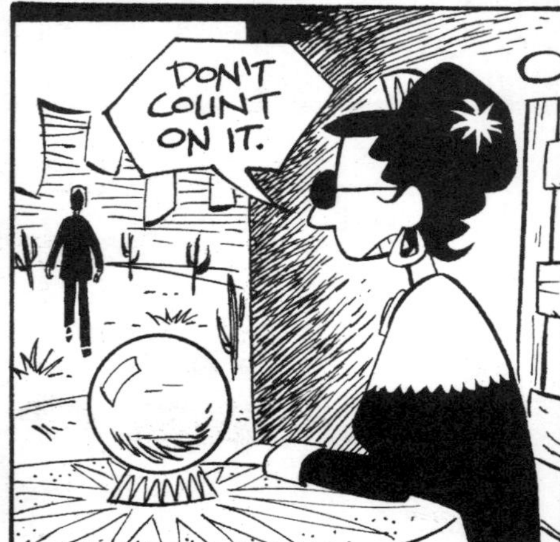

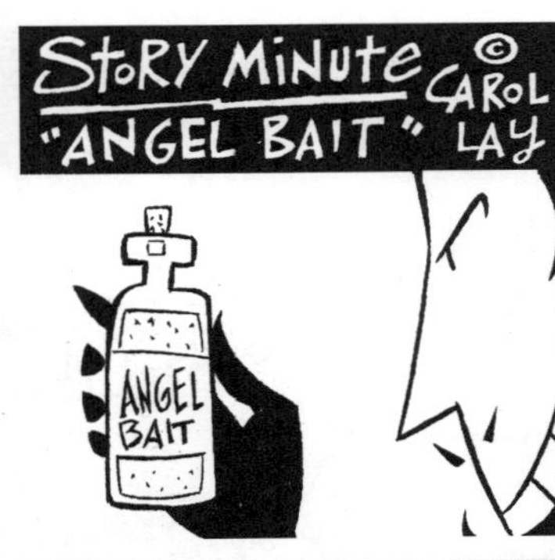
STORY MINUTE
"ANGEL BAIT"
© CAROL LAY
ANGEL BAIT
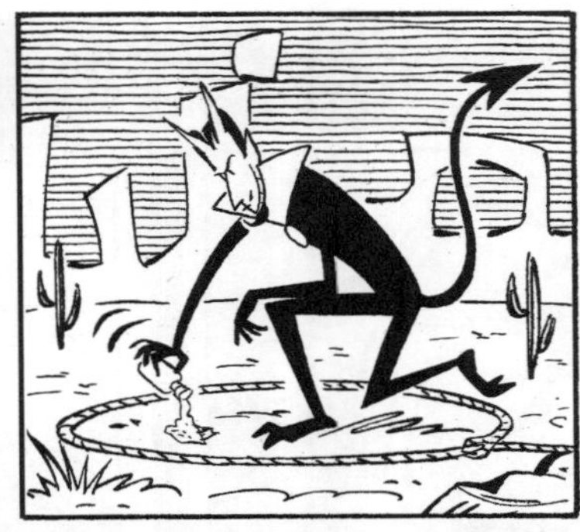
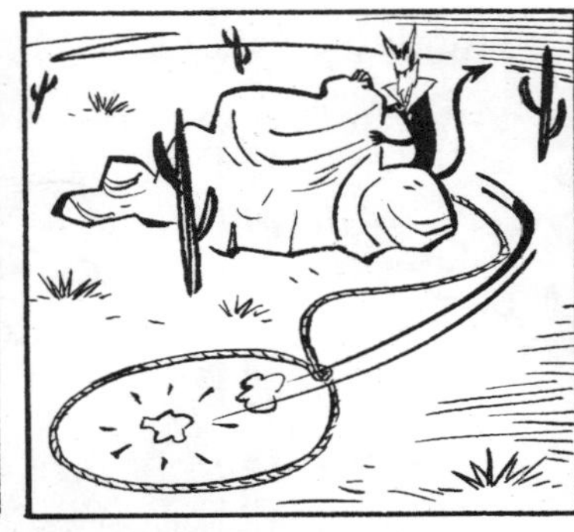
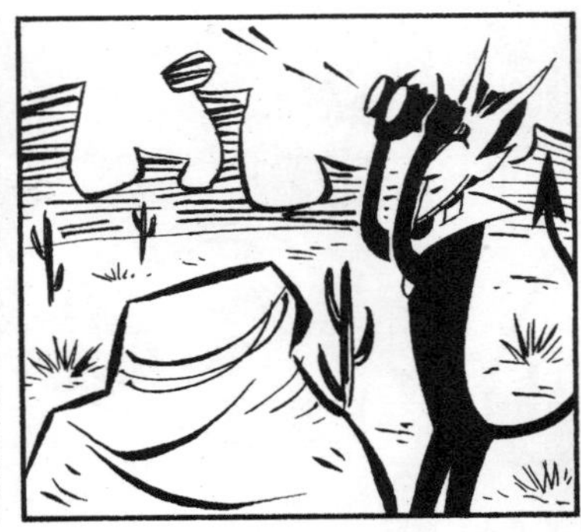
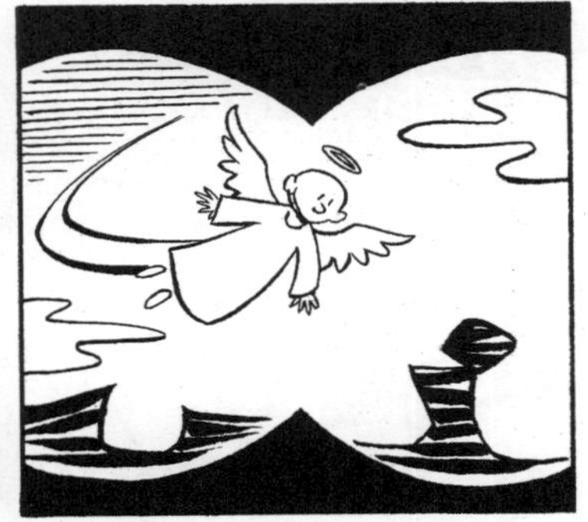
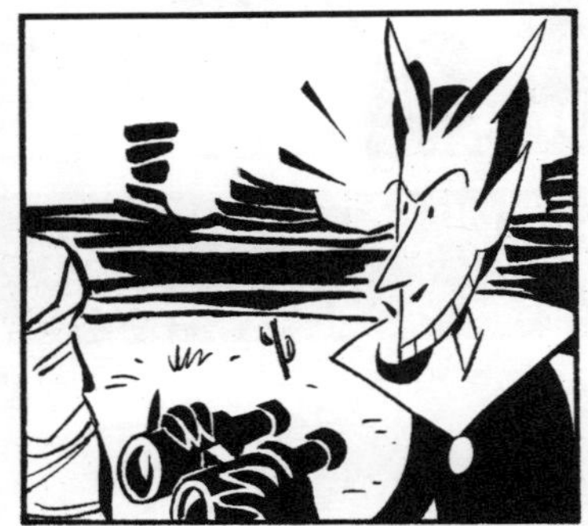
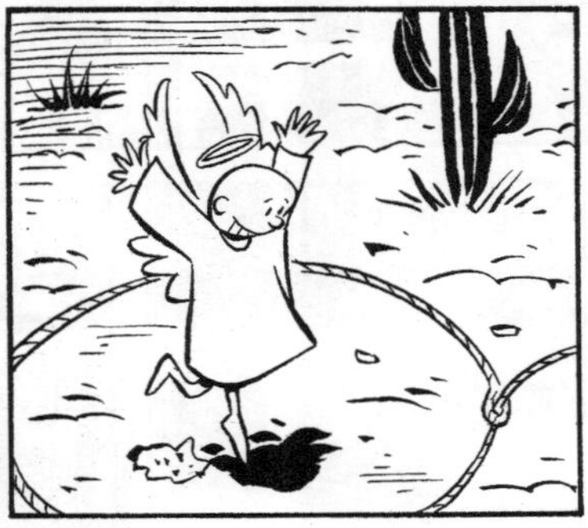
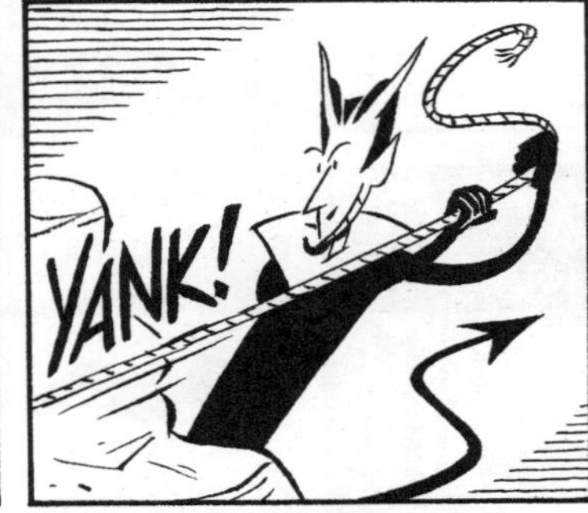
YANK!
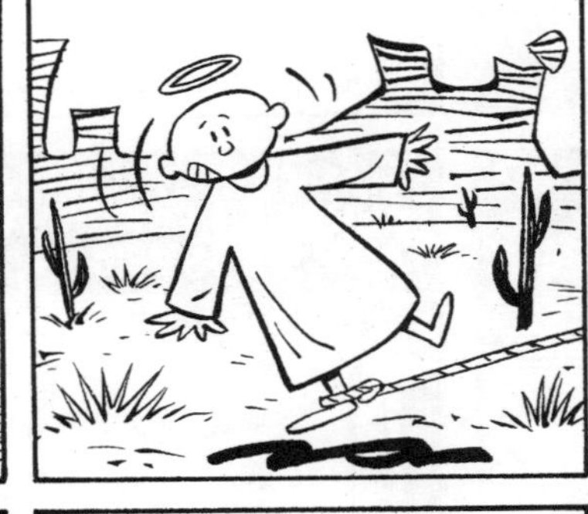
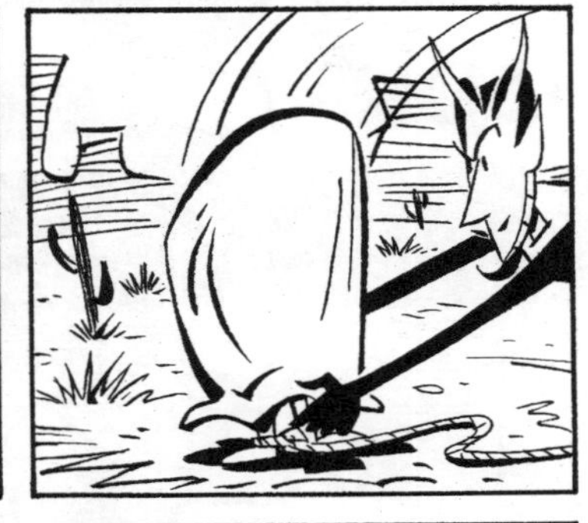
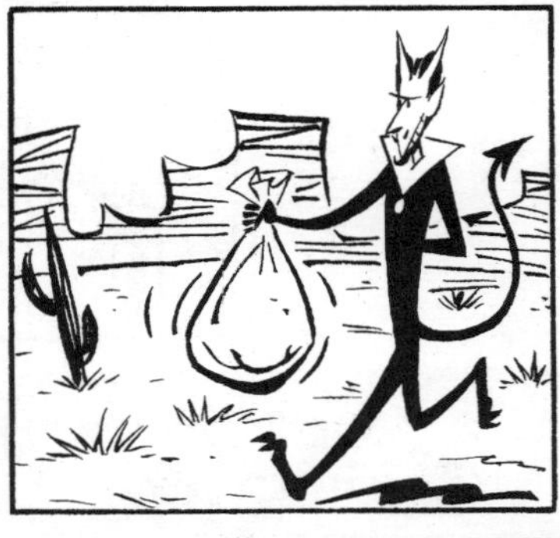
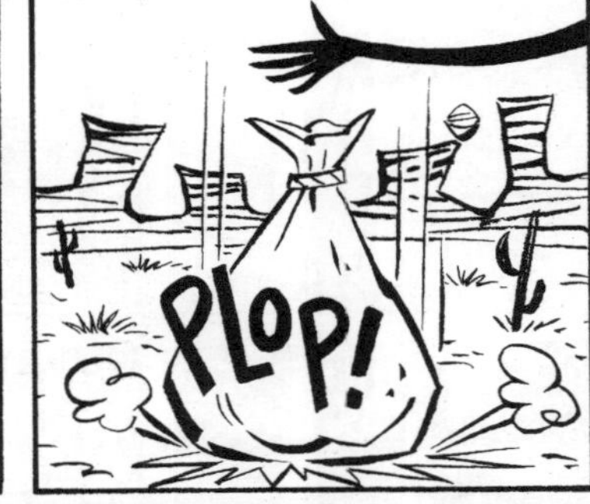
PLOP!
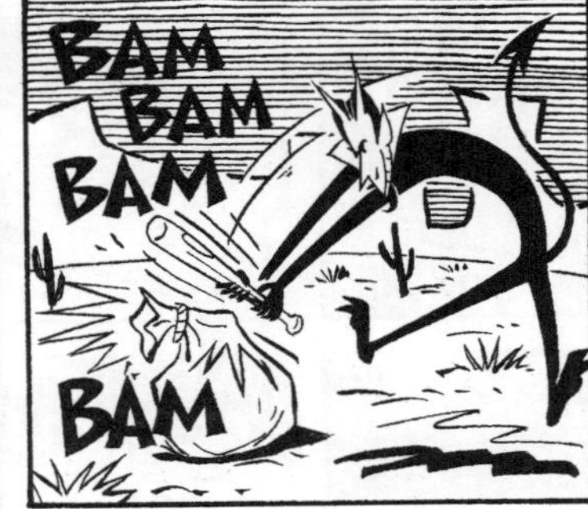
BAM
BAM
BAM
BAM
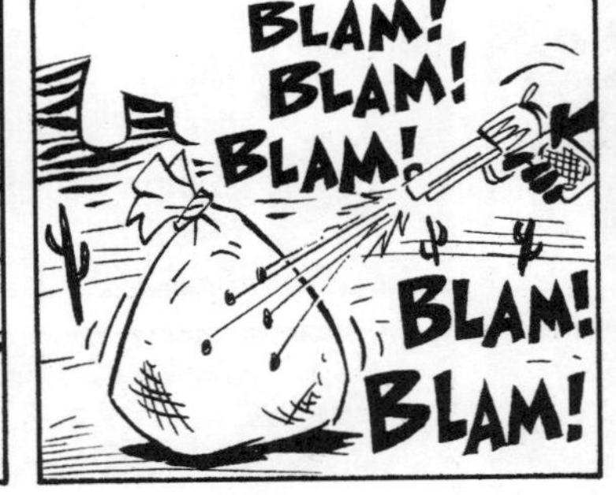
BLAM!
BLAM!
BLAM!
BLAM!
BLAM!

FSSSSSSSSS
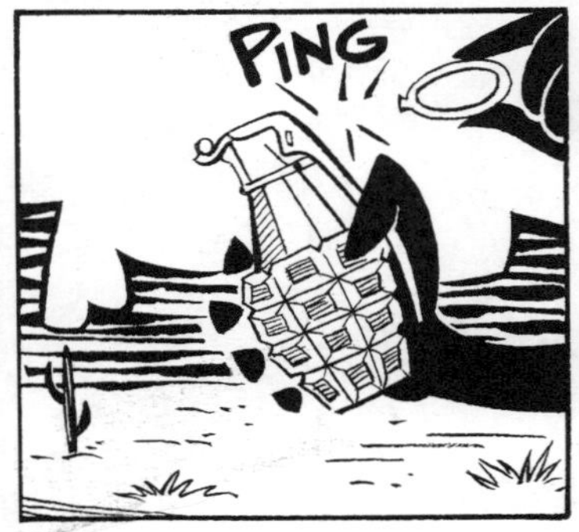
PING
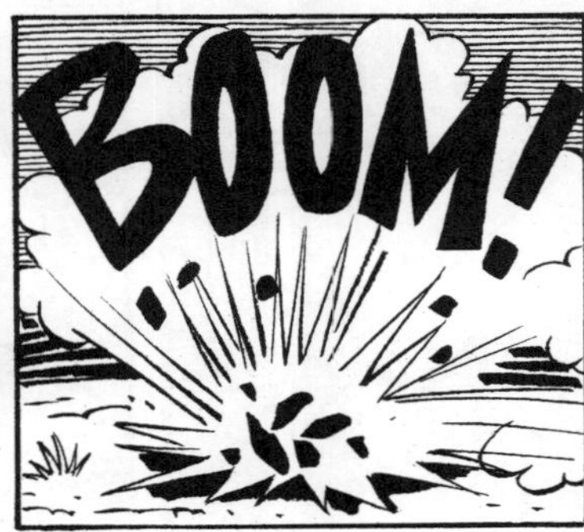
BOOM!
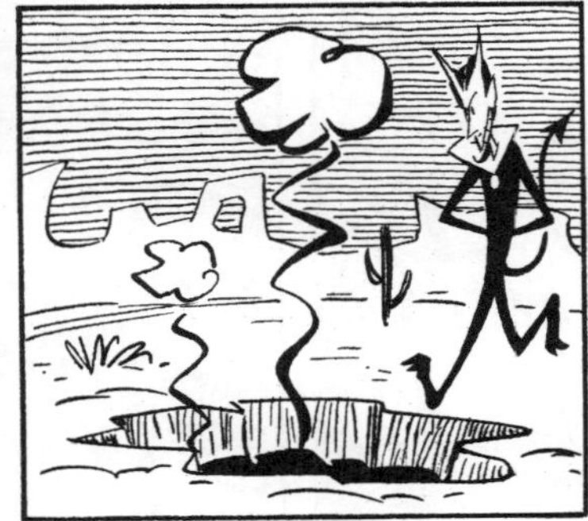
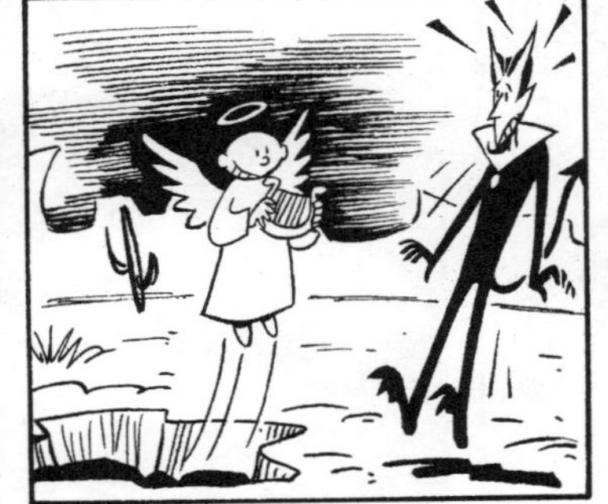
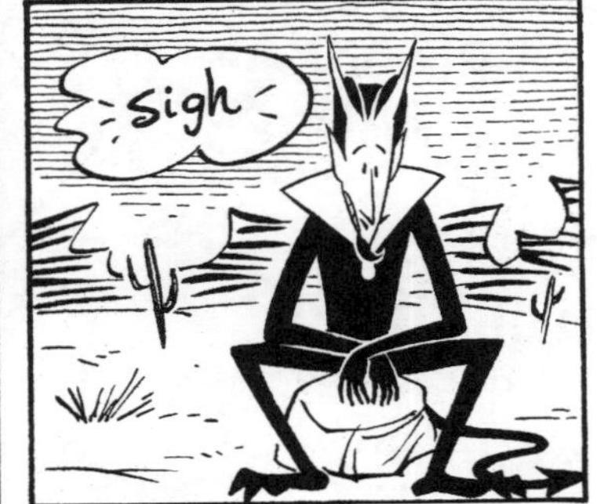
sigh

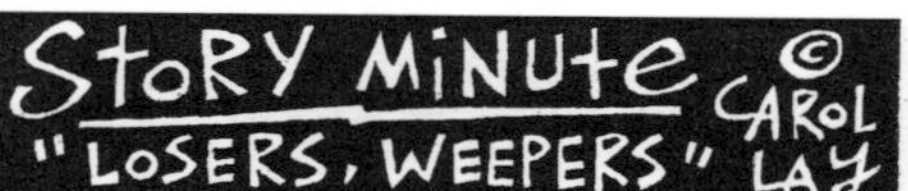


IT WAS NOT IMPOSSIBLE TO FIND THE LAND OF LOST THINGS.

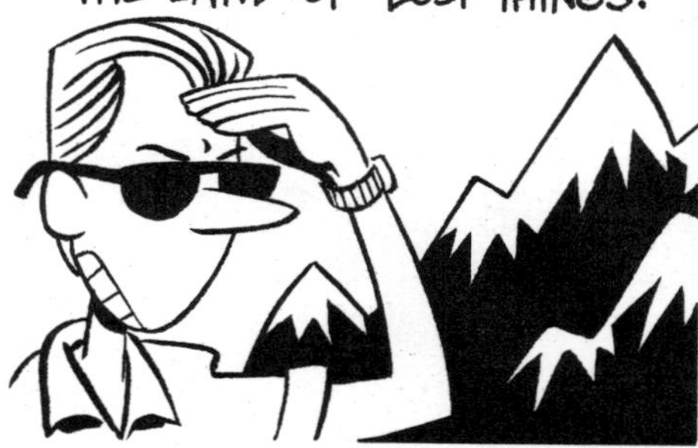

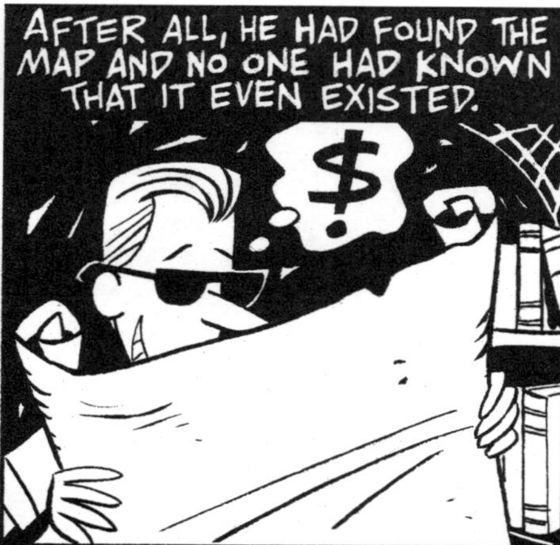


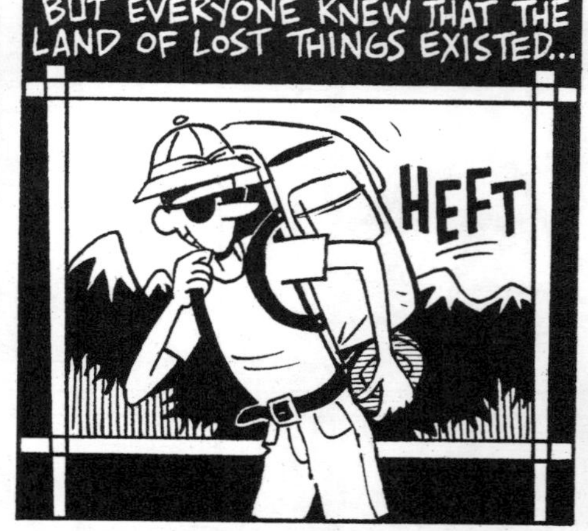


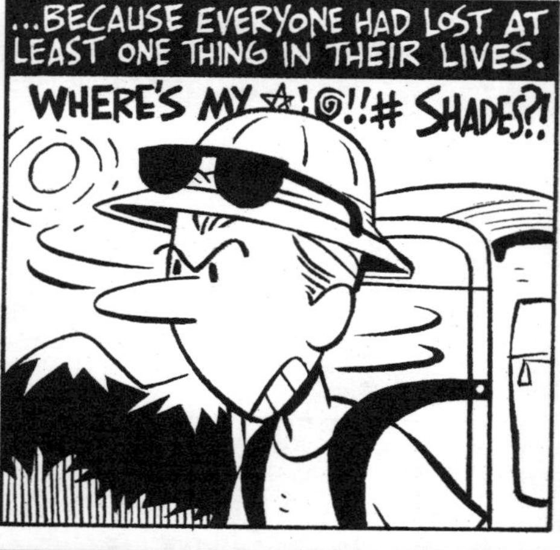


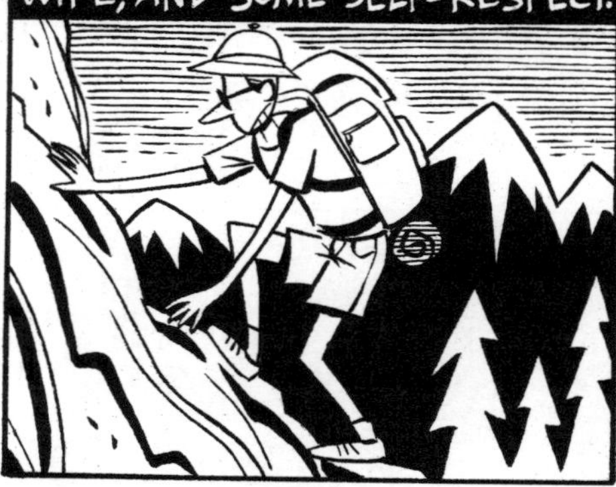


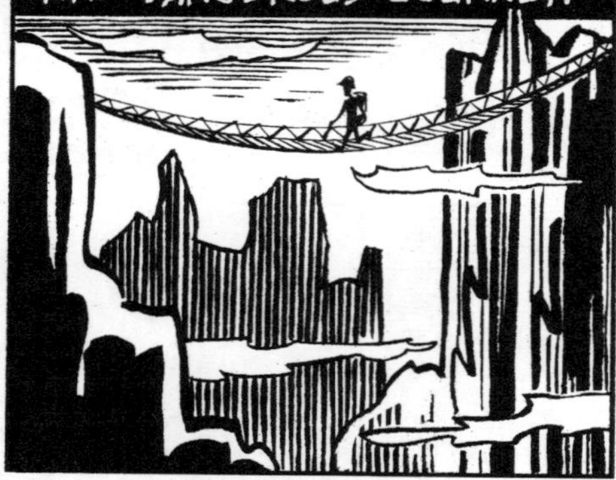


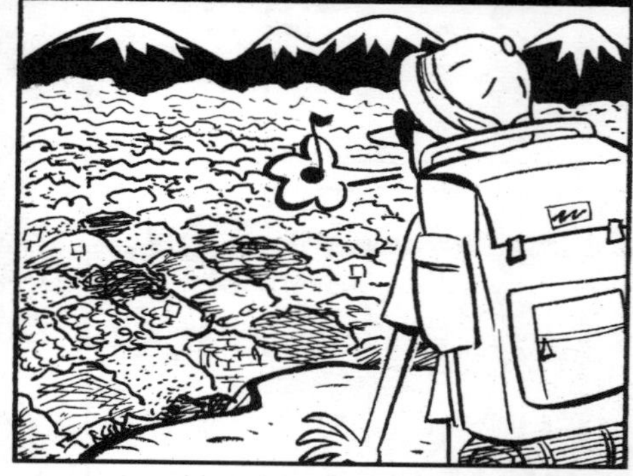


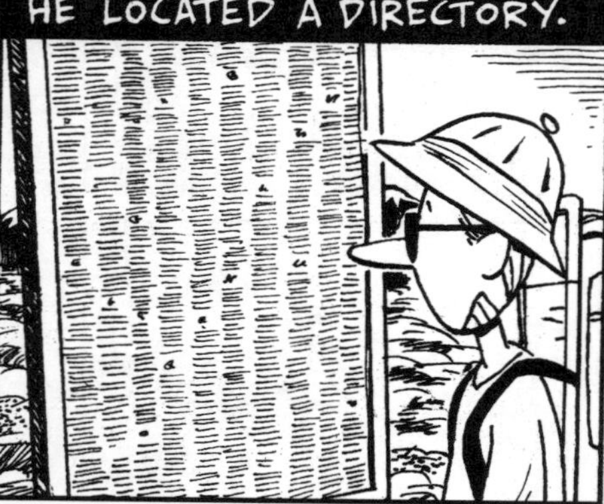


IN LOOKING UP HIS OWN LOST THINGS HE SPOTTED OTHER ITEMS OF INTEREST.

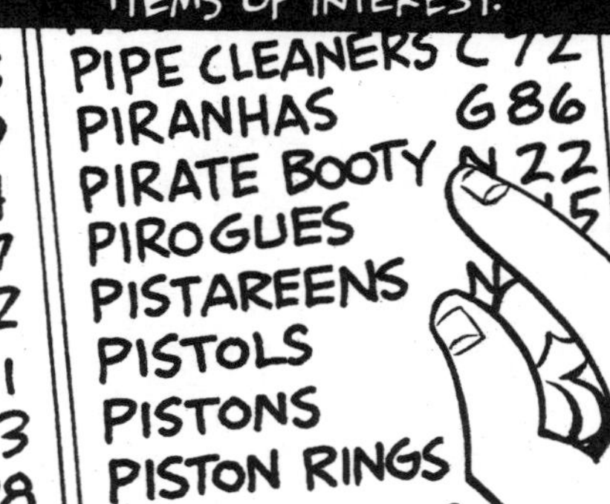


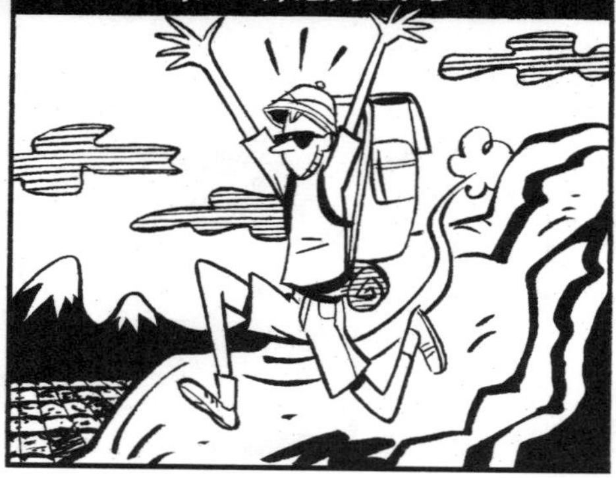


WHEN HE FINALLY FOUND IT, HE REALIZED HE WAS LOST.

N22

?

HIS NAME WAS ADDED TO THE DIRECTORY AT THE INSTANT HE SET OUT TO FIND IT.

UHN!

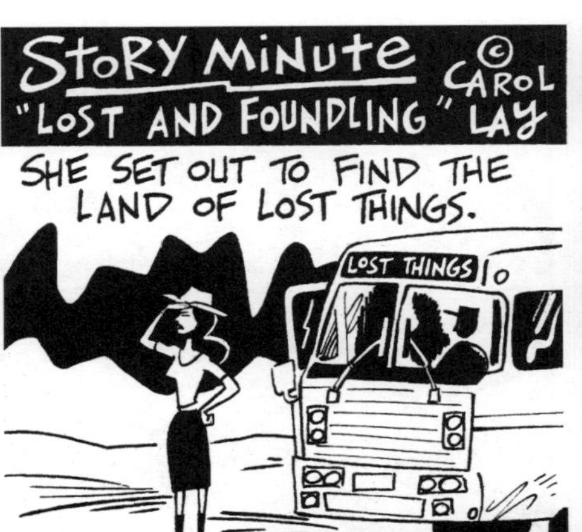
STORY MINUTE
© CAROL LAY
"LOST AND FOUNDLING"
SHE SET OUT TO FIND THE LAND OF LOST THINGS.
LOST THINGS

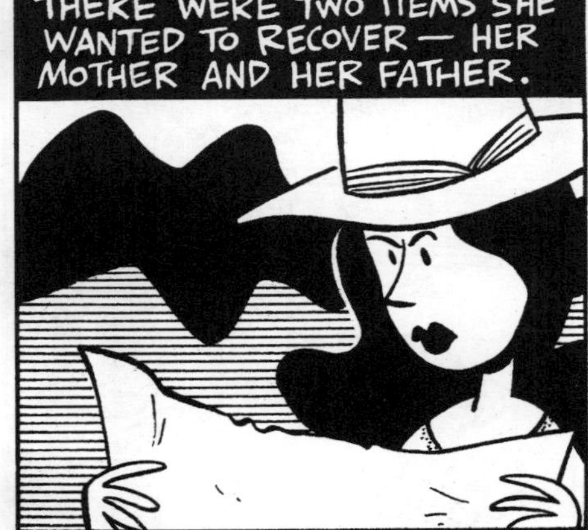
THERE WERE TWO ITEMS SHE WANTED TO RECOVER— HER MOTHER AND HER FATHER.

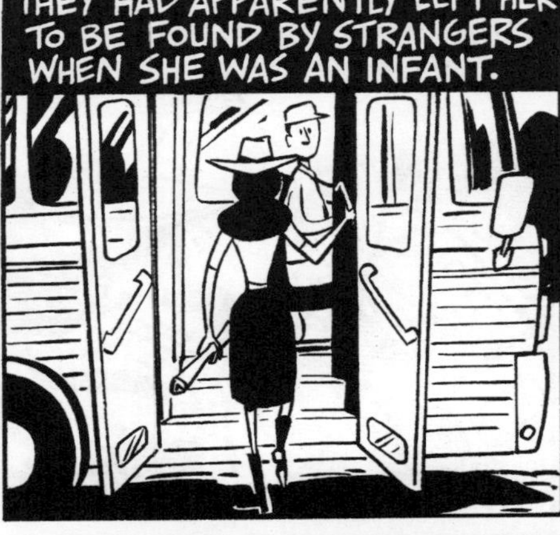
THEY HAD APPARENTLY LEFT HER TO BE FOUND BY STRANGERS WHEN SHE WAS AN INFANT.

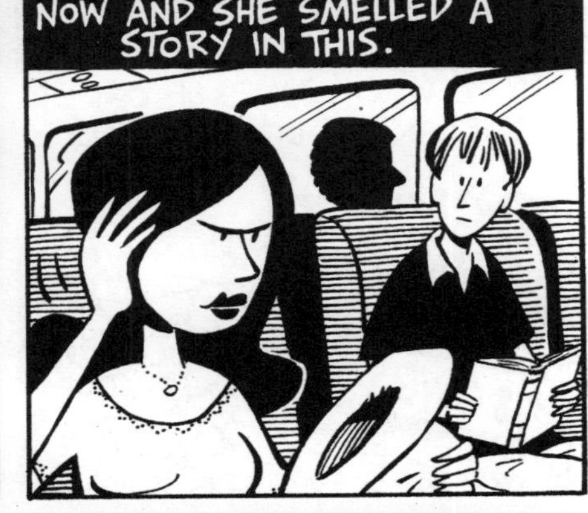
BUT SHE WAS A TALK SHOW HOST NOW AND SHE SMELLED A STORY IN THIS.

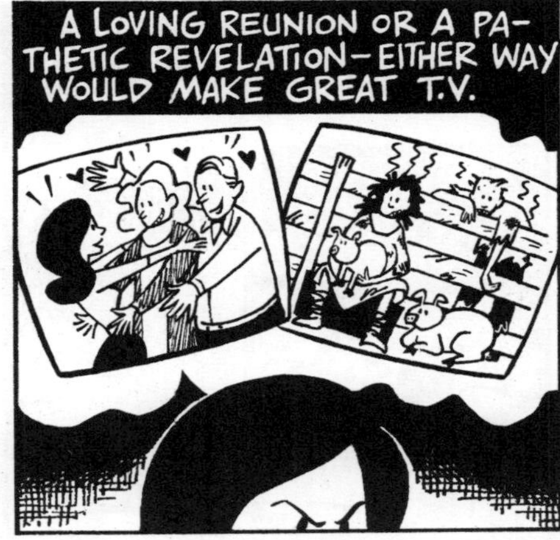
A LOVING REUNION OR A PATHETIC REVELATION– EITHER WAY WOULD MAKE GREAT T.V.

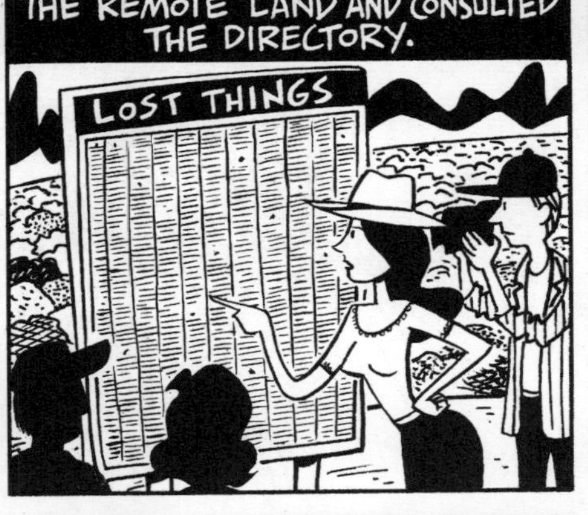
SHE AND HER CREW FINALLY FOUND THE REMOTE LAND AND CONSULTED THE DIRECTORY.
LOST THINGS

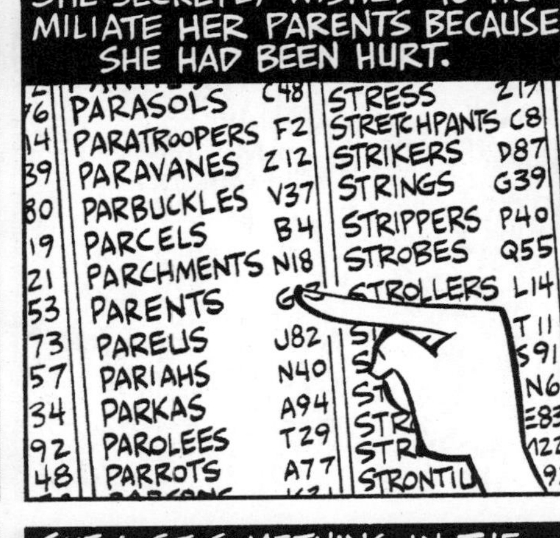
SHE SECRETLY WISHED TO HUMILIATE HER PARENTS BECAUSE SHE HAD BEEN HURT.
PARASOLS C48
PARATROOPERS F2
PARAVANES Z12
PARBUCKLES V37
PARCELS B4
PARCHMENTS N18
PARENTS
PAREUS J82
PARIAHS N40
PARKAS A94
PAROLEES T29
PARROTS A77
STRESS
STRETCHPANTS C8
STRIKERS D87
STRINGS G39
STRIPPERS P40
STROBES Q55
STROLLERS L14

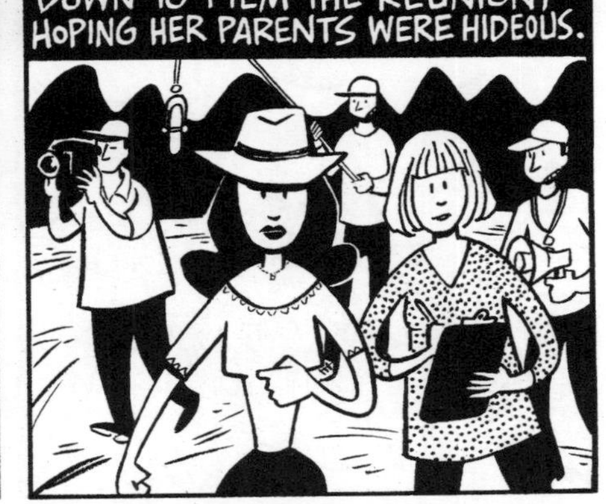
THE T.V. STAR LED HER PEOPLE DOWN TO FILM THE REUNION, HOPING HER PARENTS WERE HIDEOUS.

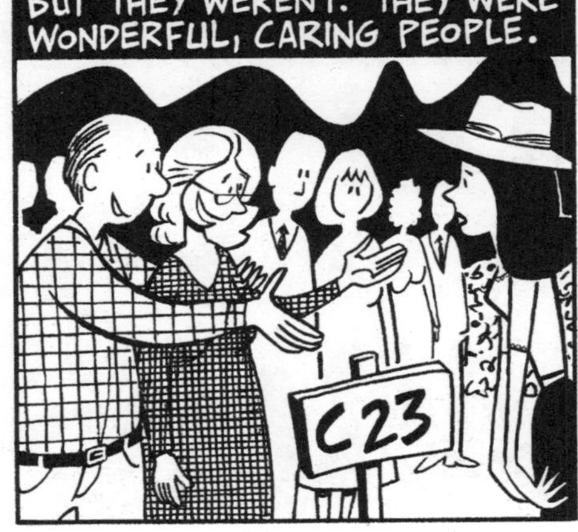
BUT THEY WEREN'T. THEY WERE WONDERFUL, CARING PEOPLE.
C23

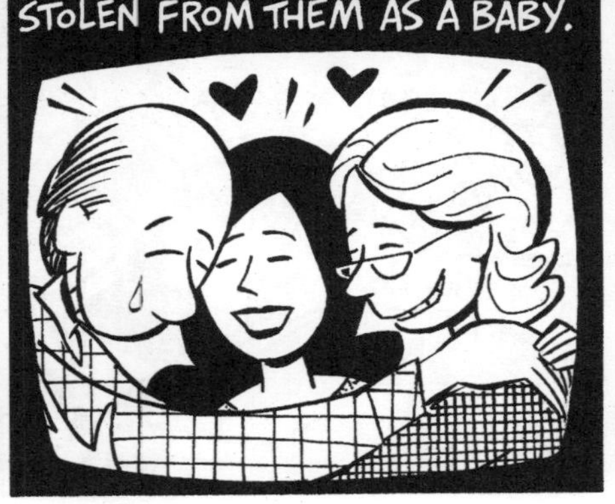
THEY HAD BEEN SEARCHING FOR HER EVER SINCE SHE HAD BEEN STOLEN FROM THEM AS A BABY.

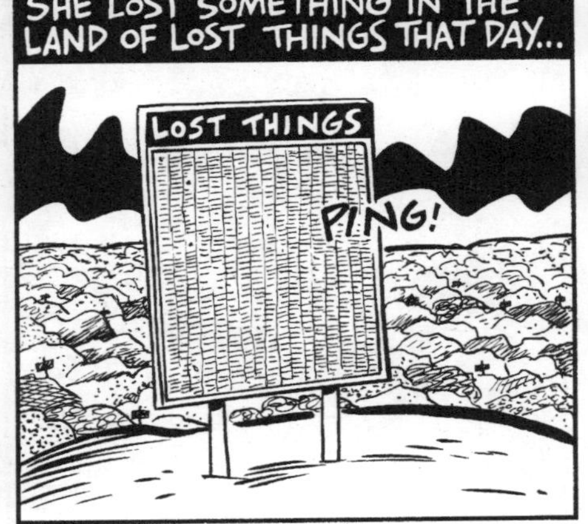
SHE LOST SOMETHING IN THE LAND OF LOST THINGS THAT DAY...
LOST THINGS
PING!

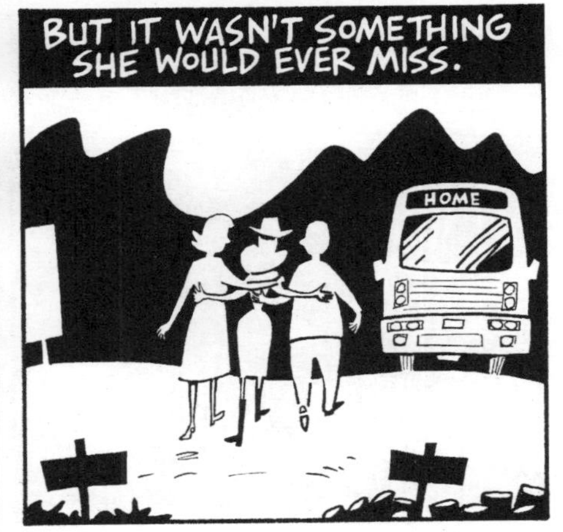
BUT IT WASN'T SOMETHING SHE WOULD EVER MISS.
HOME

THERE WERE RULES OF ORDER IN THE LAND OF LOST THINGS.

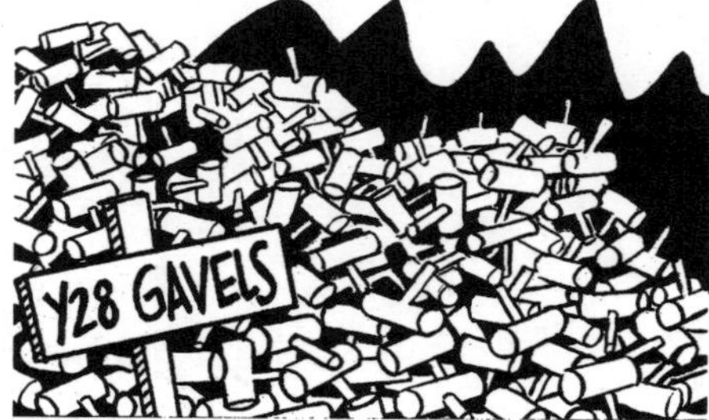


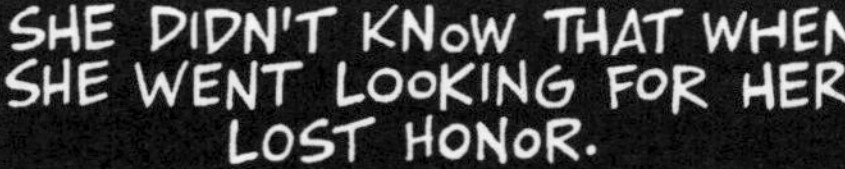


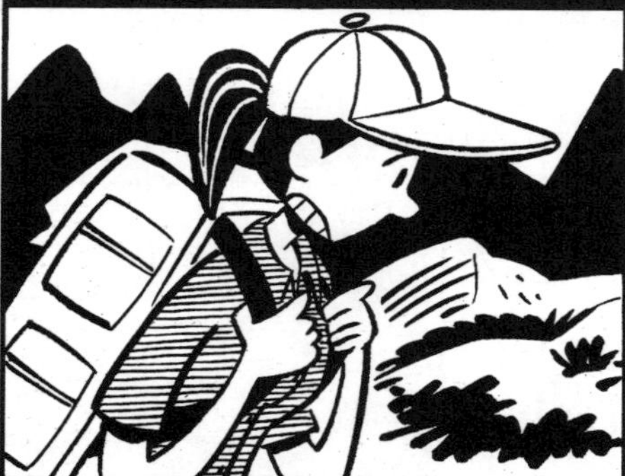

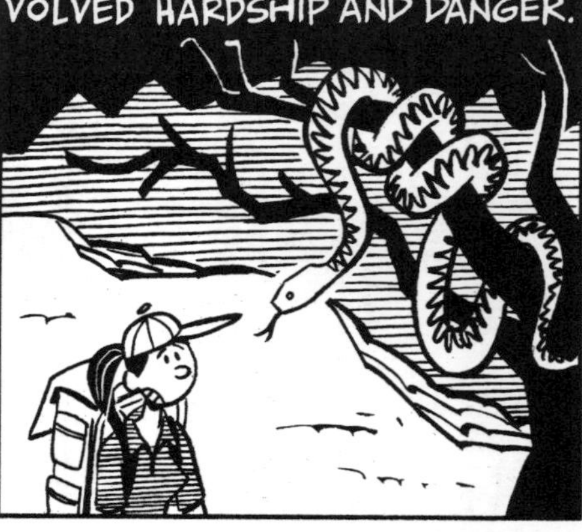


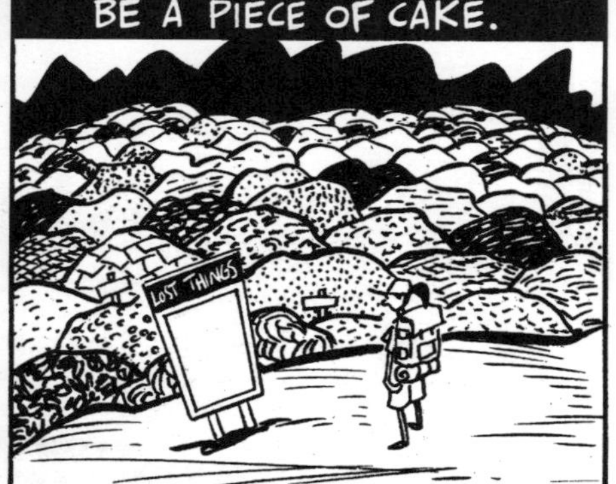


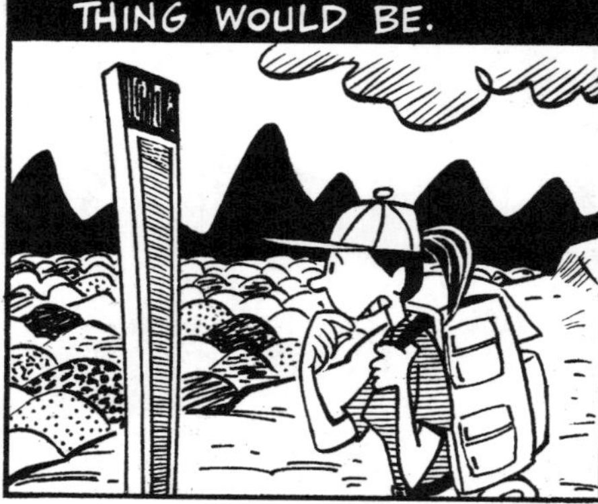


THE DIRECTORY ALSO LISTED OTHER PEOPLE'S THINGS THAT SHE WANTED TO GO AFTER.

| | | | |
|---|---|---|---|
| HONOR | Z23 | MODESTY | |
| HONORARIUMS | B14 | MOHAIRS | D28 |
| HOODS | D92 | MOHURS | R72 |
| HOOKS | A87 | MOLARS | W6 |
| HOOPS | A20 | MOLLS | H1 |
| HOOPSKIRTS | B67 | MONEY | P3 |
| HORIZONS | Q15 | MONEY BELTS | I8 |
| HORNS | A44 | MONEY ORDERS | |
| HOROSCOPES | C56 | MONGOOSES | |
| HORSES | M8 | MONKS | |
| HOSE | J43 | MONKEYS | |
| | S27 | M. WRENCHES | |

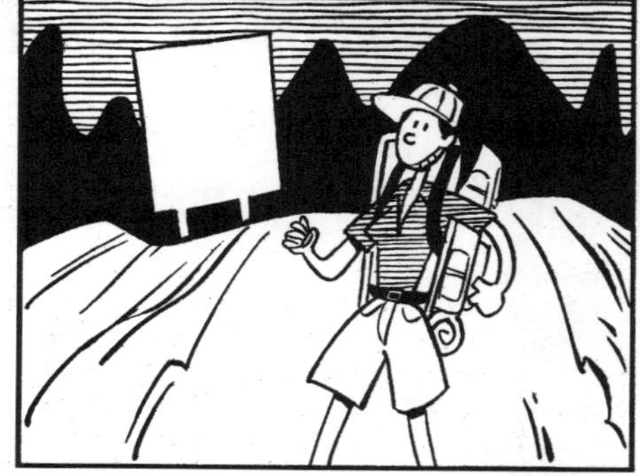


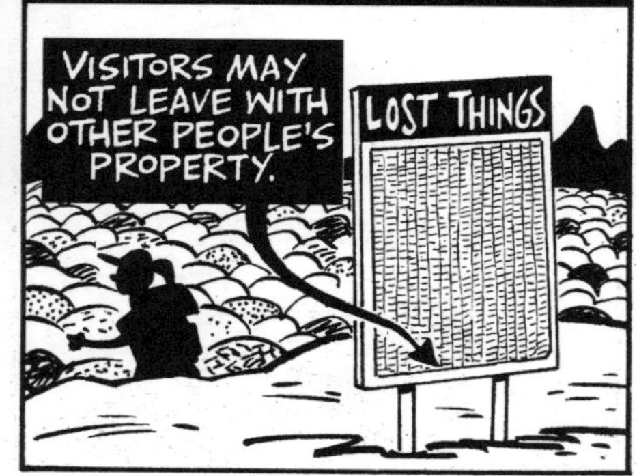


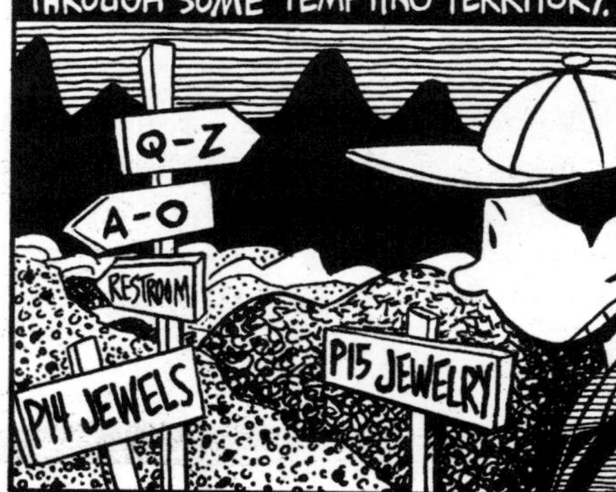


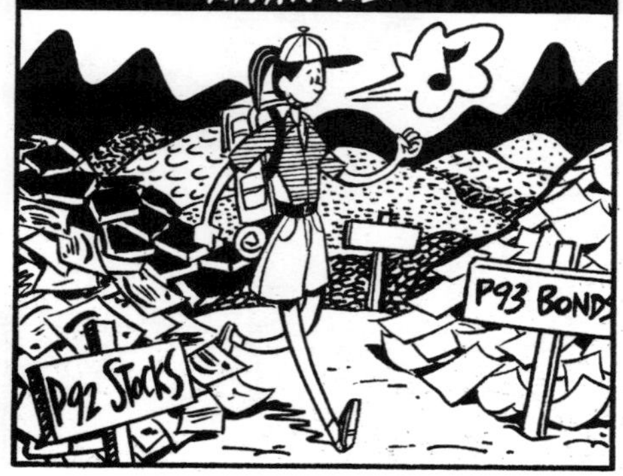


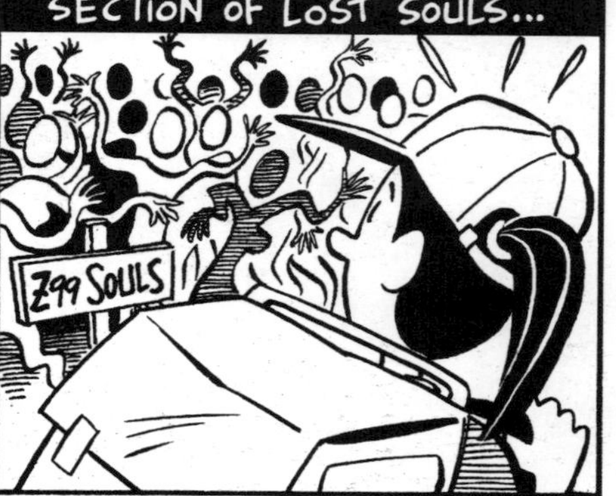


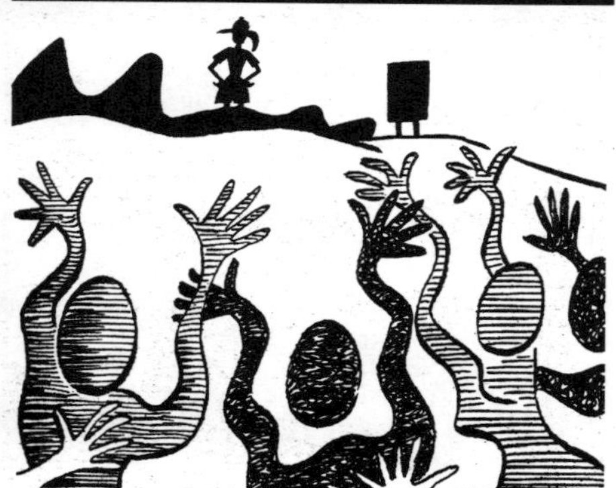

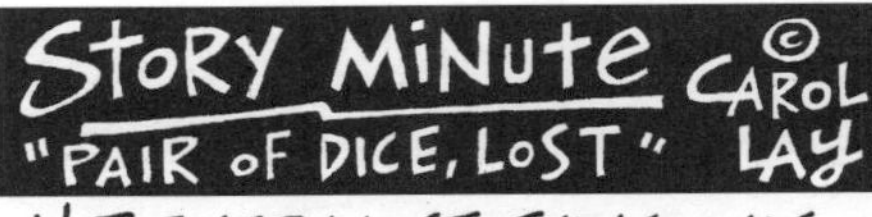
STORY MINUTE © CAROL LAY
"PAIR OF DICE, LOST"

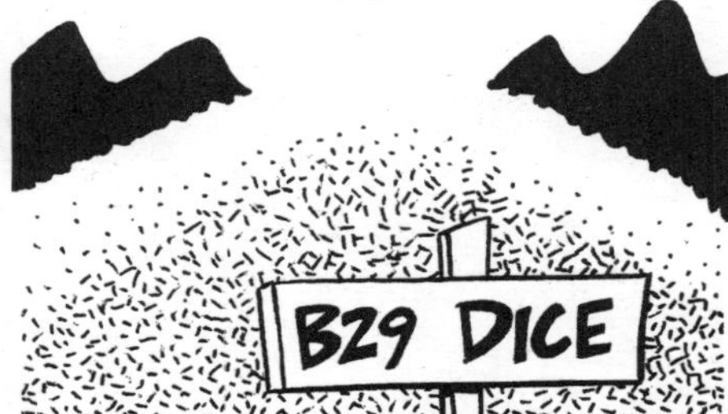
NOT EVERY LOST THING WAS WORTH LOOKING FOR.
B29 DICE

LOST SOCKS, LIBRARY CARDS, NAIL FILES, AND THE LIKE WERE NEVER WORTH THE TRIP.

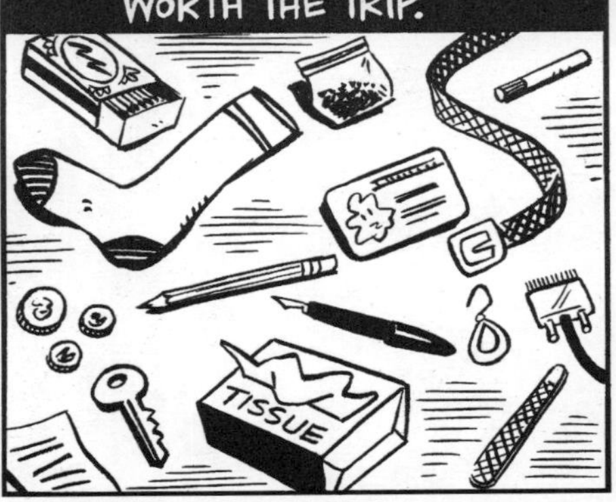
TISSUE

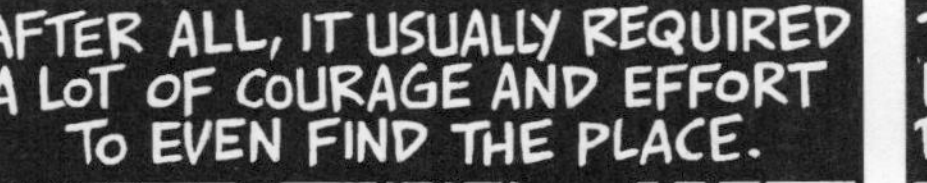
AFTER ALL, IT USUALLY REQUIRED A LOT OF COURAGE AND EFFORT TO EVEN FIND THE PLACE.

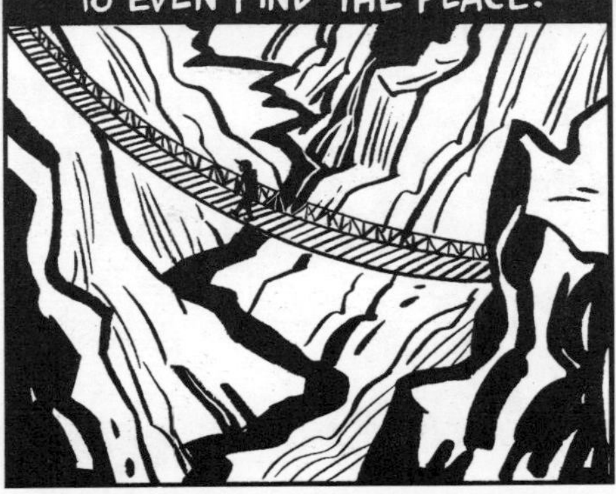

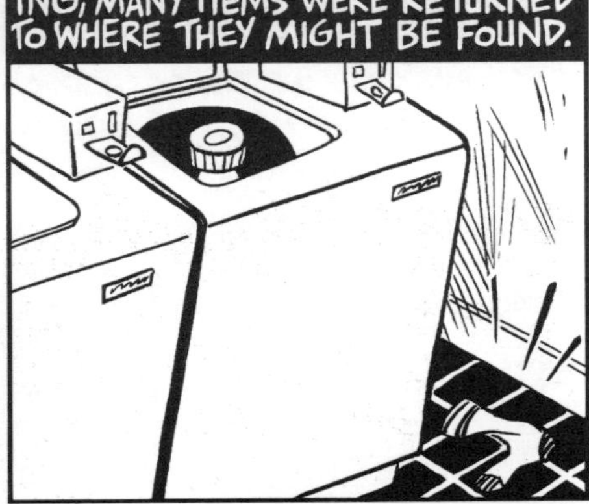
TO PREVENT IT FROM OVERFLOWING, MANY ITEMS WERE RETURNED TO WHERE THEY MIGHT BE FOUND.

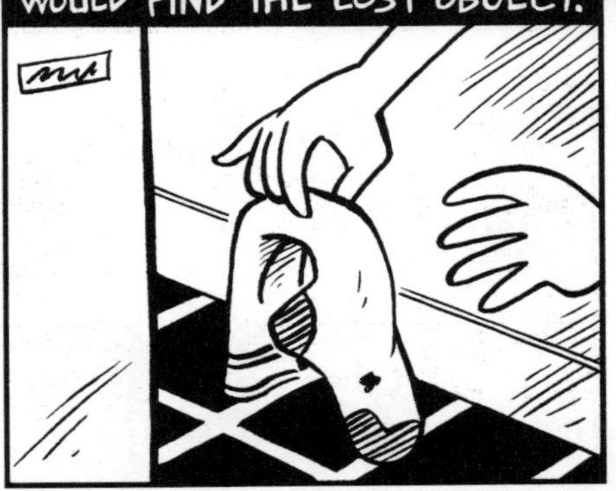
NOW, IT WOULD NOT NECESSARILY BE THE RIGHTFUL OWNER WHO WOULD FIND THE LOST OBJECT.

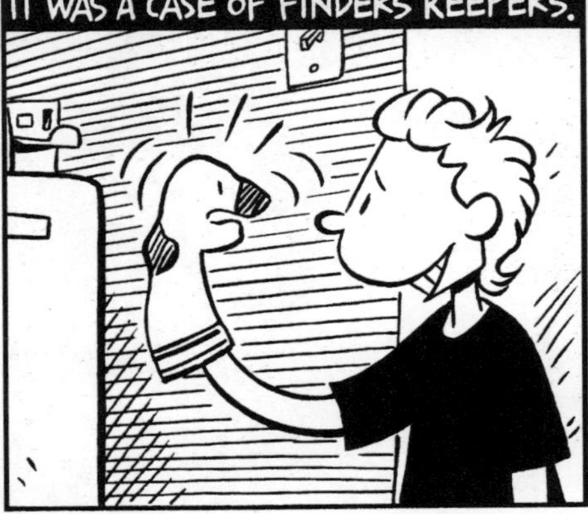
IF THE THING HAD LITTLE VALUE IT WAS A CASE OF FINDERS KEEPERS.

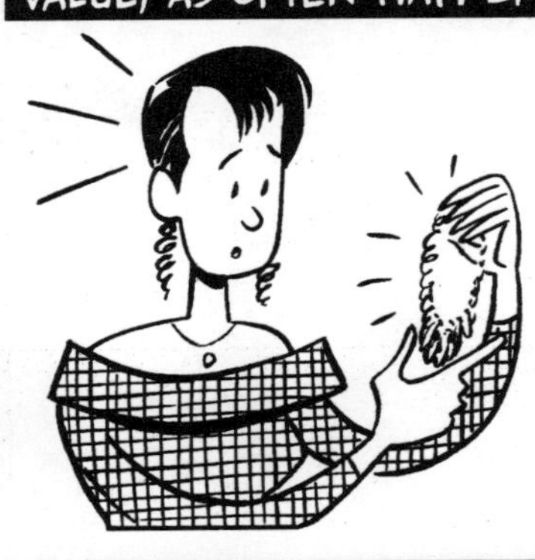
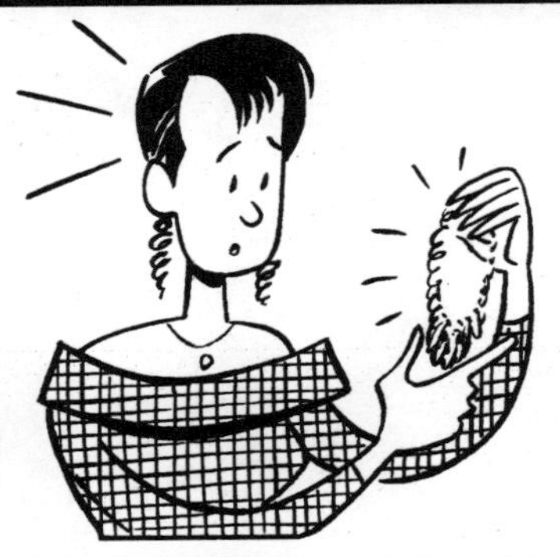
IF, HOWEVER, THE OBJECT WAS OF MODERATE OR EVEN GREATER VALUE, AS OFTEN HAPPENED...

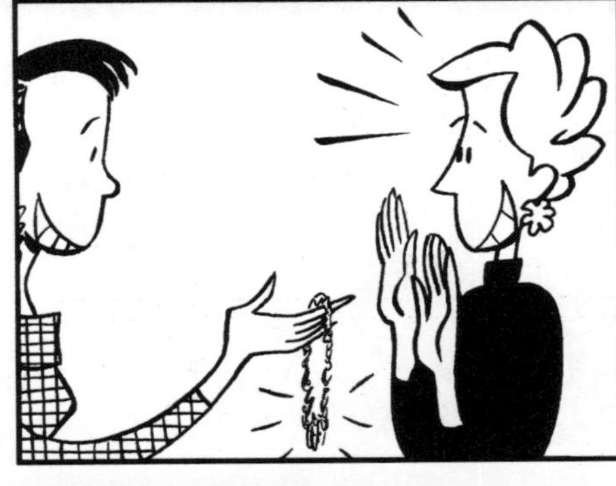
...IT WAS HOPED THAT THE FINDER WOULD BE HONEST ENOUGH TO RETURN IT TO ITS OWNER.

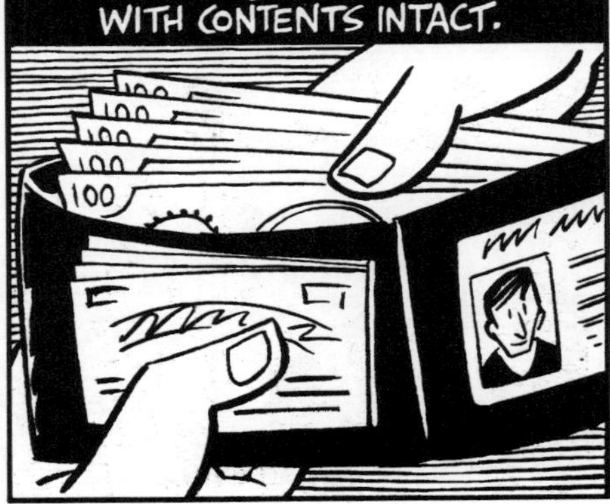
SO, MANY FINDERS RETURNED LOST WALLETS TO THEIR OWNERS WITH CONTENTS INTACT.

MANY OTHERS, THOUGH, DID NOT.

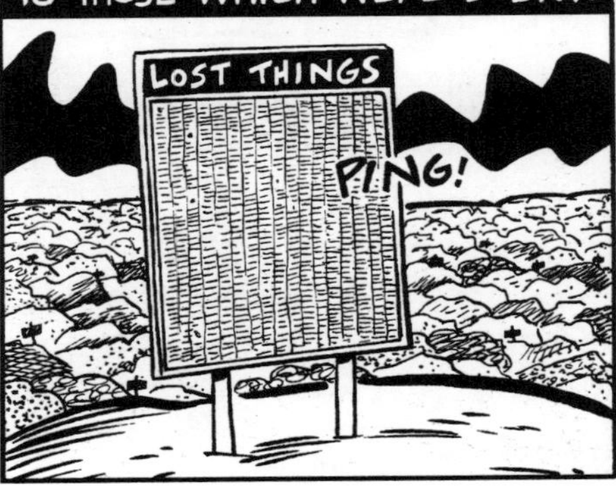
THE LATTER WOULD REGRET IT LATER AS THEIR SOULS WERE ADDED TO THOSE WHICH WERE LOST...
LOST THINGS
PING!

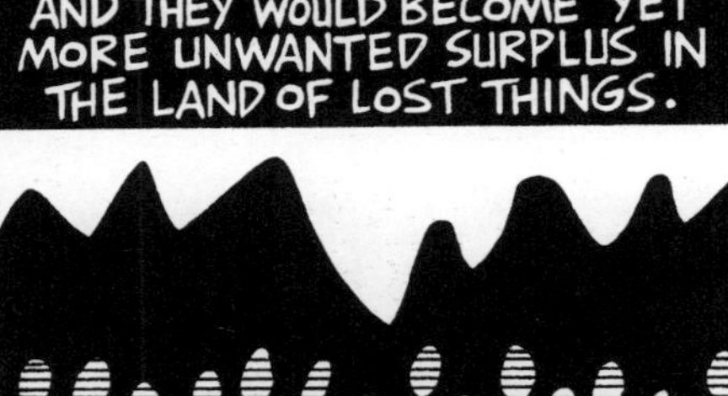
AND THEY WOULD BECOME YET MORE UNWANTED SURPLUS IN THE LAND OF LOST THINGS.
Z99 SOULS

**STORY MINUTE** © CAROL LAY

**"SOUL SEARCHING"**

THE LAND OF LOST THINGS HAD A SPECIAL SECTION FOR LOST SOULS.

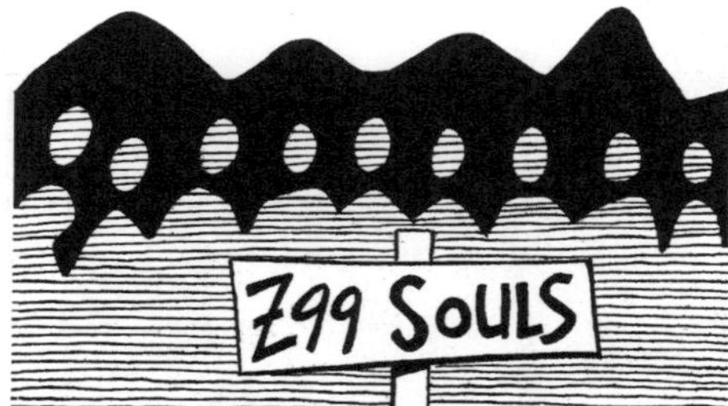


IRONICALLY, THEY WERE EASY TO RECLAIM ONCE ONE MADE THE EFFORT.

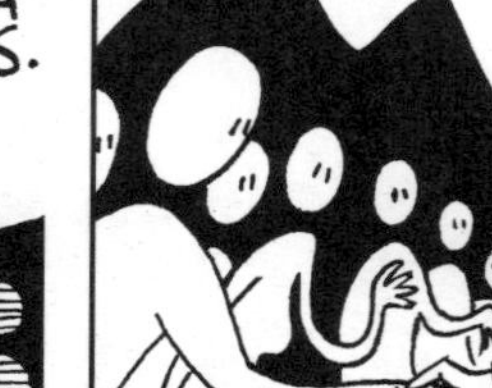

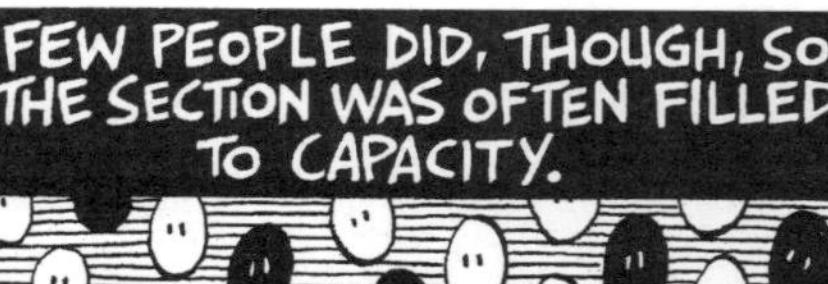


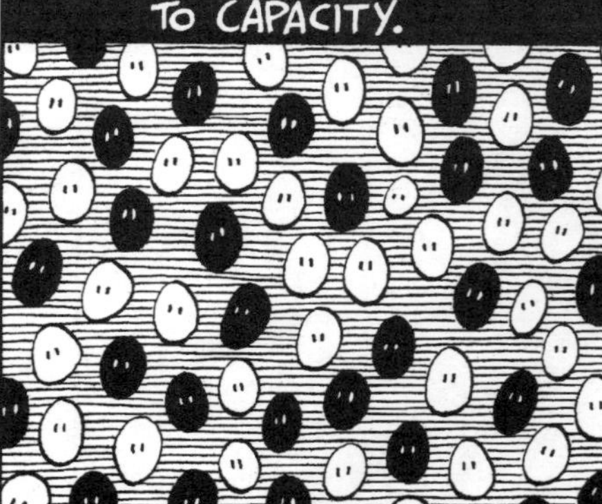

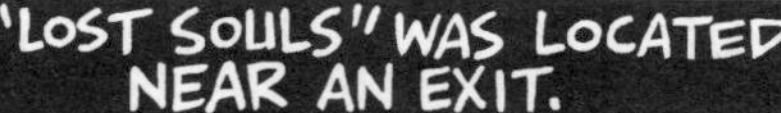


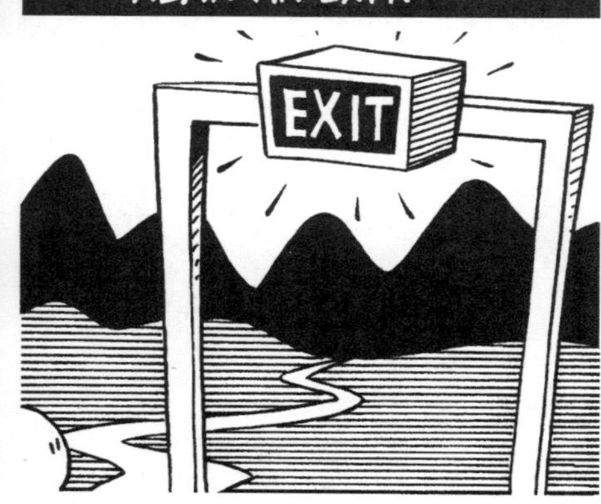


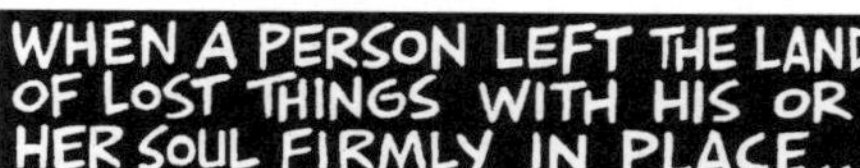


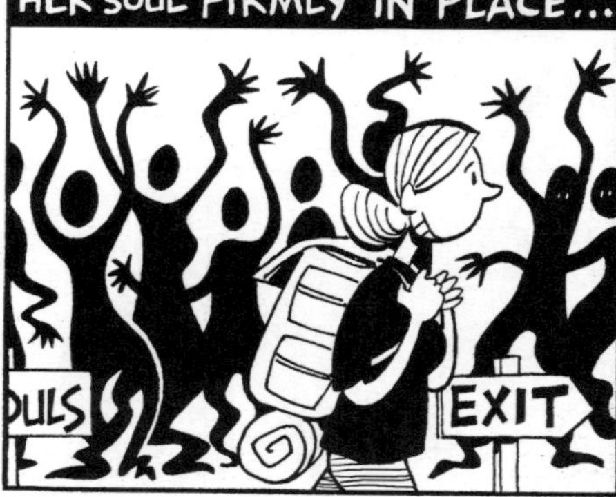


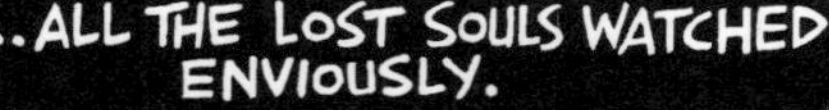


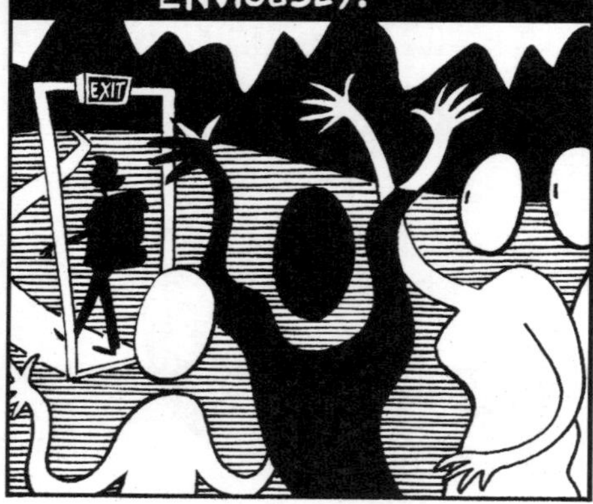


OCCASIONALLY ONE WOULD TRY TO PASS ALONG AN ENTREATY TO BE CLAIMED...

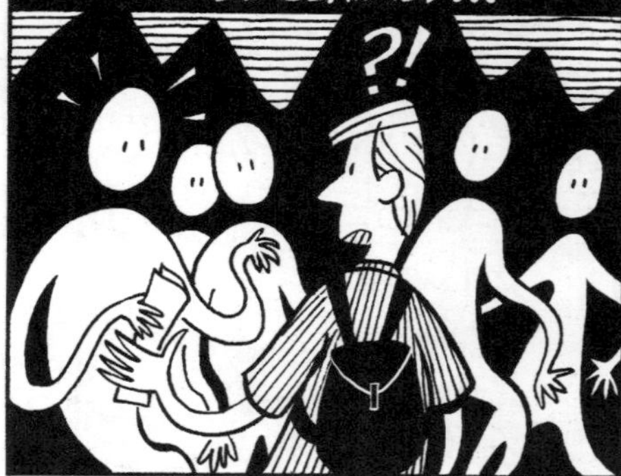


...BUT FEW PEOPLE WOULD MAKE THE HARD JOURNEY TO TAKE BACK THEIR OWN SOULS.

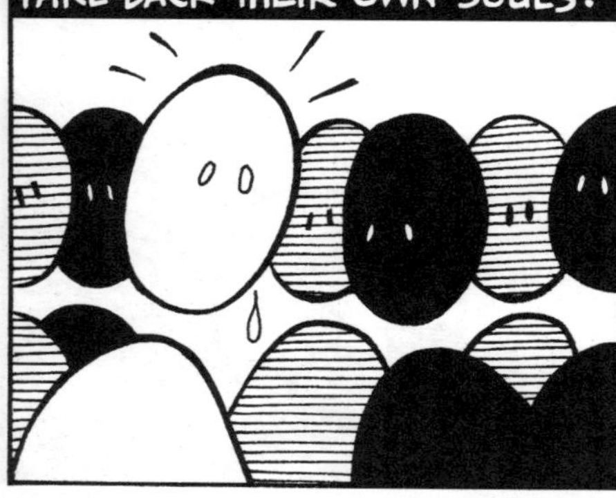

OFTEN A SOUL WOULD ESCAPE AND FIND ITS WAY BACK TO ITS HOME.

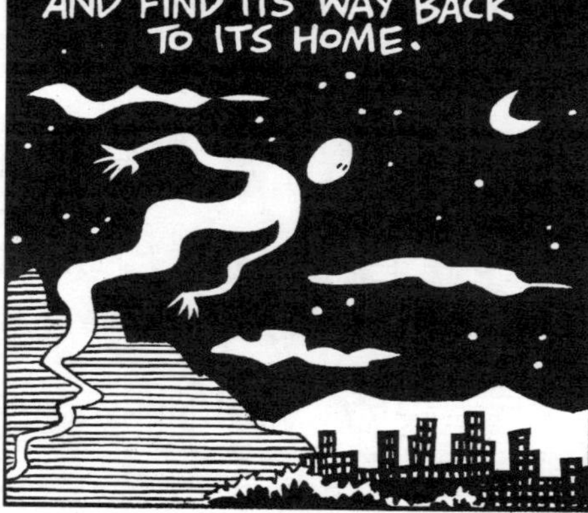

BUT BY NOT HAVING BEEN STRONG ENOUGH TO PURSUE THE SOUL...

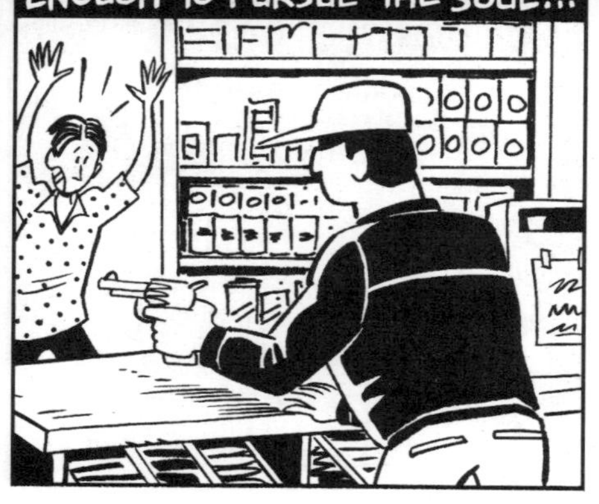

...A PERSON COULD NOT HOLD ONTO IT FOR LONG.

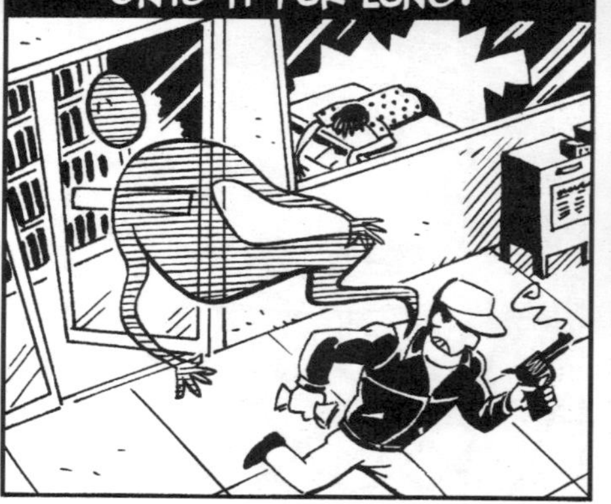

EVERY SO OFTEN THE DEVIL CAME BY AND BOUGHT UNCLAIMED SOULS BY THE POUND.

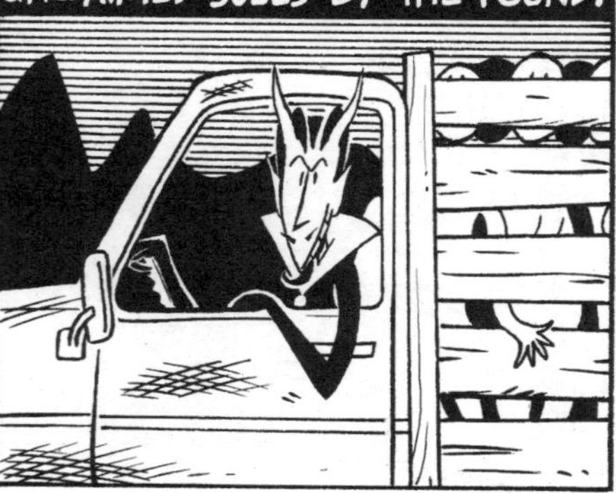

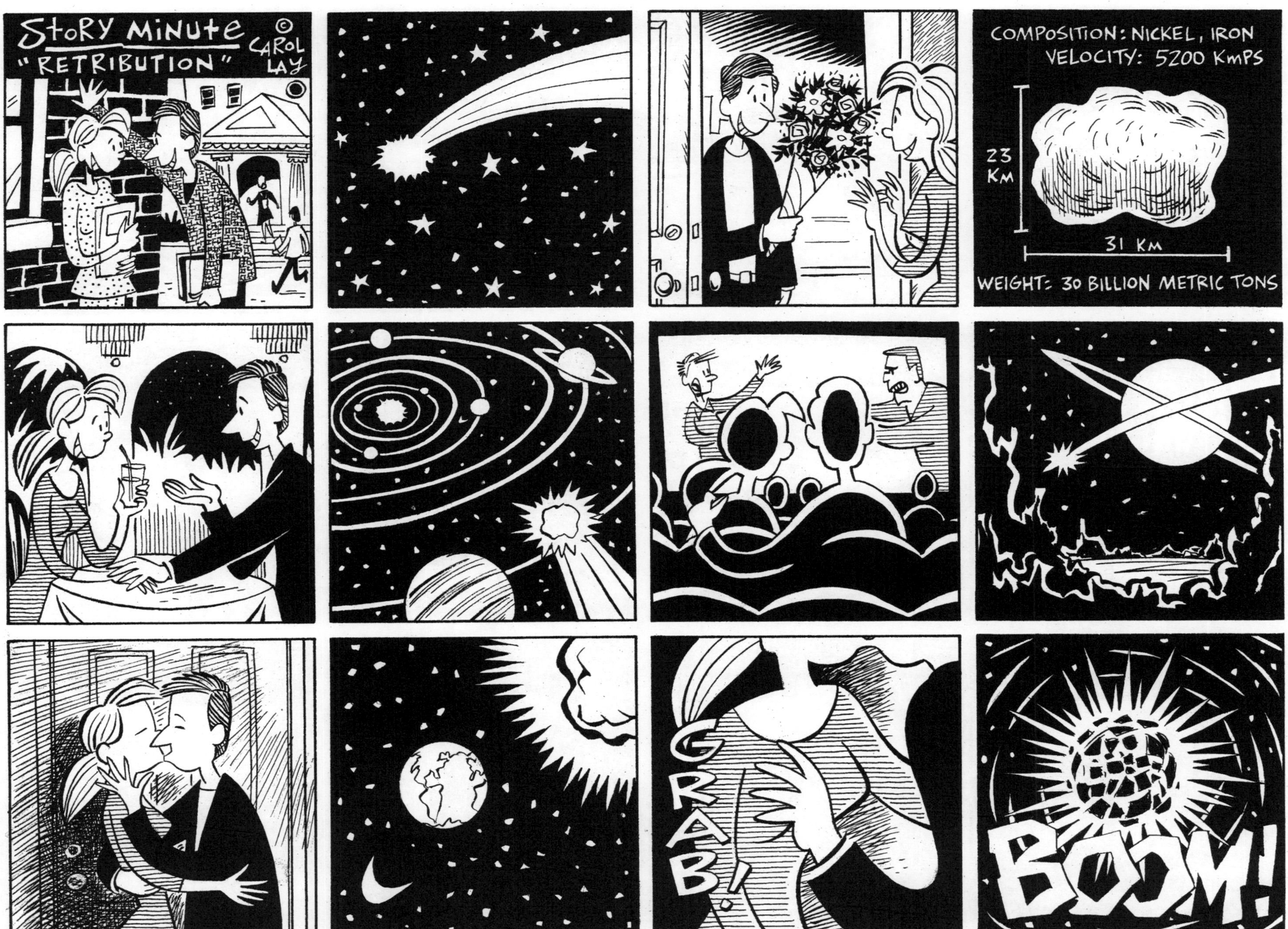
STORY MINUTE
"RETRIBUTION"
© CAROL LAY
COMPOSITION: NICKEL, IRON
VELOCITY: 5200 KmPS
23 KM
31 KM
WEIGHT: 30 BILLION METRIC TONS
GRAB!
BOOM!

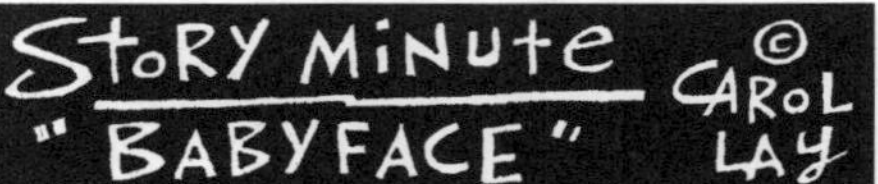

STORY MINUTE
"BABYFACE"
© CAROL LAY


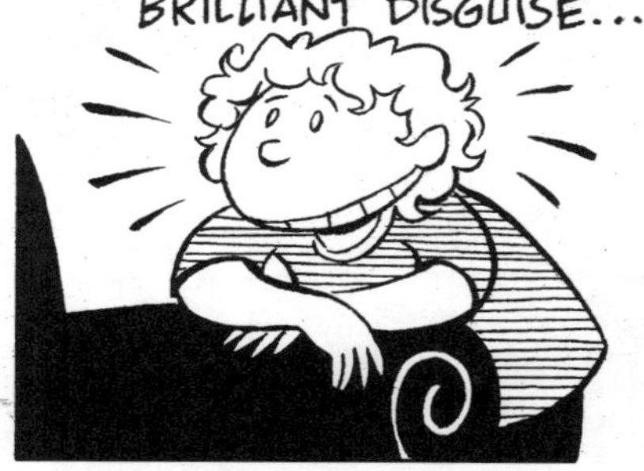

THE BOY'S CHERUBIC FACE WAS A BRILLIANT DISGUISE...


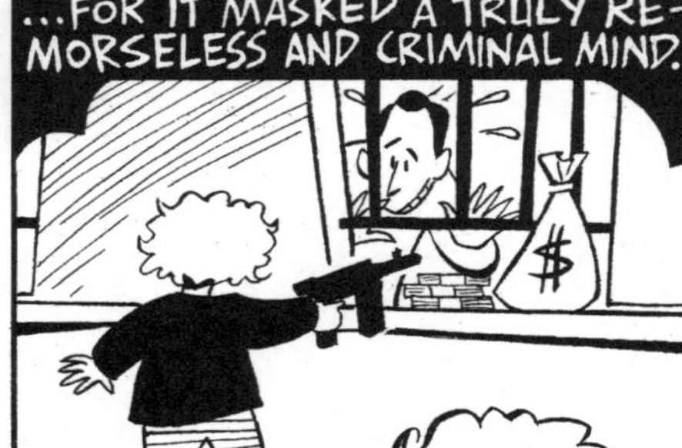

...FOR IT MASKED A TRULY RE-MORSELESS AND CRIMINAL MIND.
$


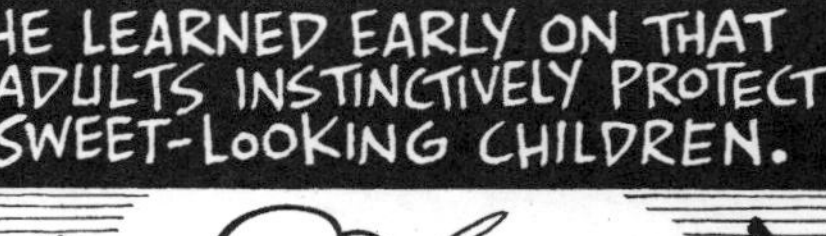

HE LEARNED EARLY ON THAT ADULTS INSTINCTIVELY PROTECT SWEET-LOOKING CHILDREN.


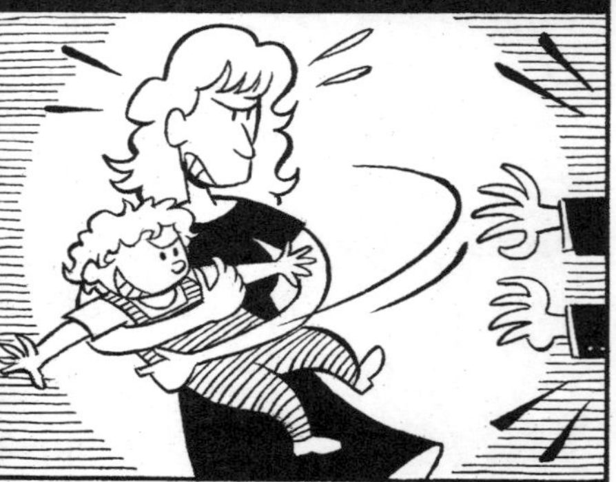

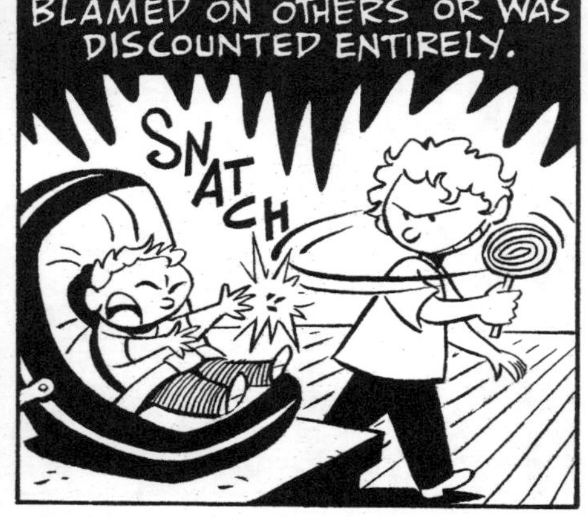

SO EVERY WRONG HE DID WAS BLAMED ON OTHERS OR WAS DISCOUNTED ENTIRELY.
SNATCH


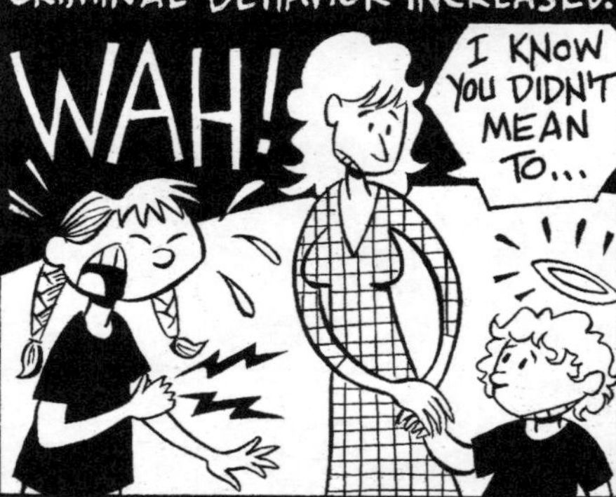

HE BECAME MORE CONVINCED OF HIS INVINCIBILITY AS HIS CRIMINAL BEHAVIOR INCREASED.
WAH!
I KNOW YOU DIDN'T MEAN TO...


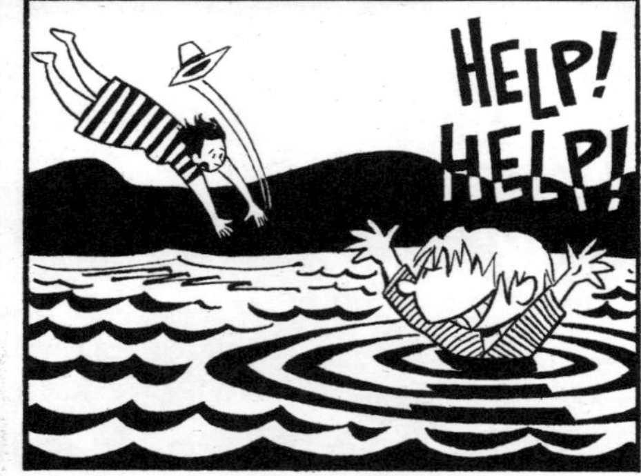

MOTHERS WOULD RUIN THEIR SUNDAY BEST TO SAVE HIM FROM APPARENT HARM.
HELP! HELP!


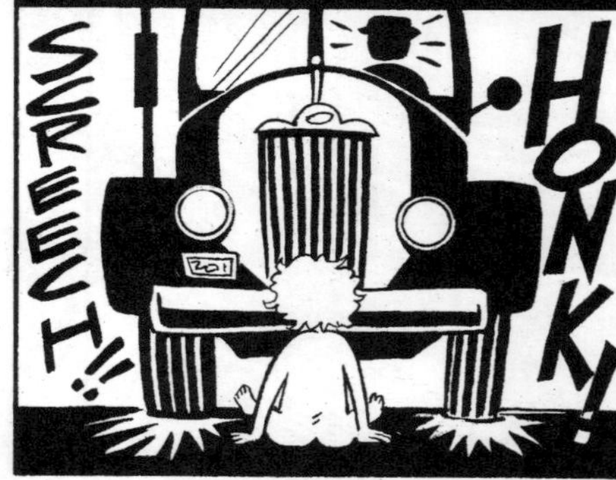

FOUR-TON TRUCKS STOPPED ON A DIME BECAUSE OF HIS INNOCENT GOOD LOOKS.
SCREECH!!
HONK!


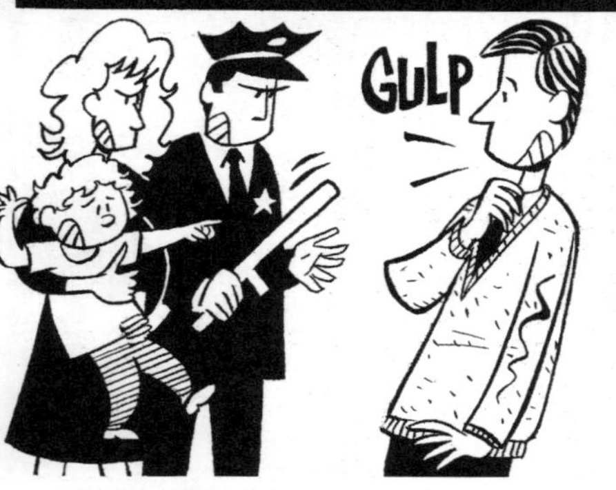

STRICT TEACHERS COULD BE JAILED ON THE STRENGTH OF A FEW SOBBING ACCUSATIONS.
GULP


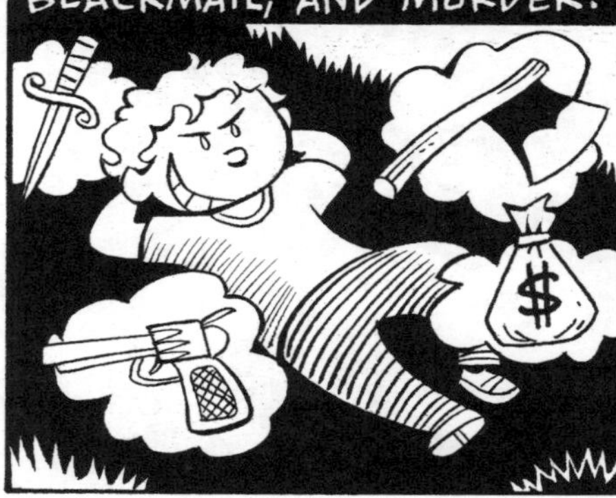

HE MADE BIG PLANS THAT INCLUDED ROBBERY, FRAUD, BLACKMAIL, AND MURDER.
$


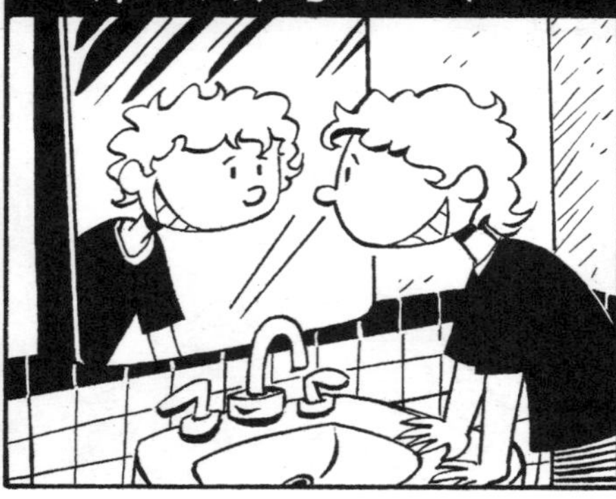

AS LONG AS HIS CUPID'S FACE HELD OUT, HE WOULD BE FREE FROM PROSECUTION.


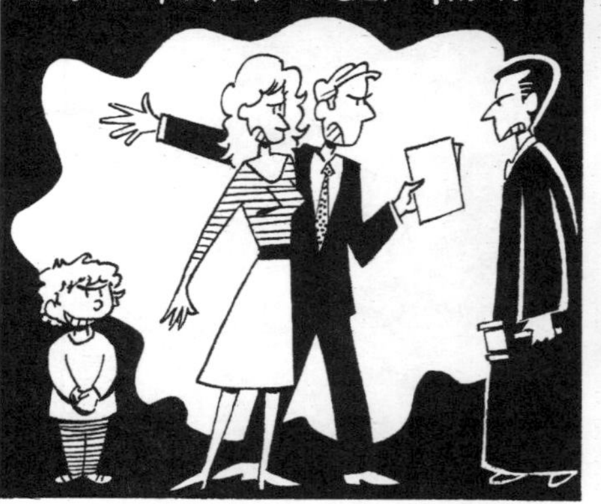

HE WAS IMPERVIOUS. ADULTS COULD NEVER TOUCH HIM.


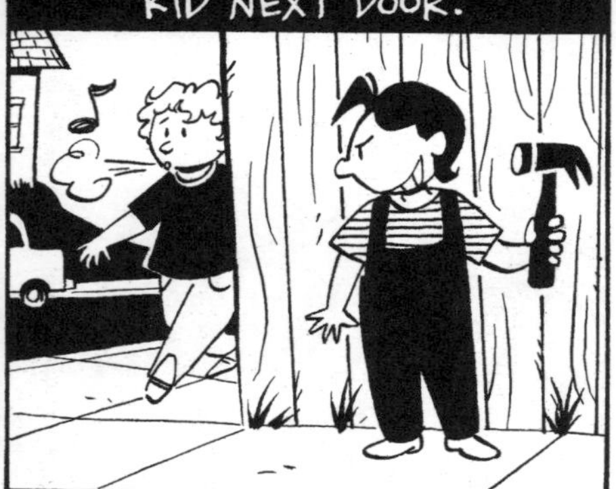

BUT HE FORGOT TO FACTOR IN THE ABSOLUTELY ANGELIC KID NEXT DOOR.

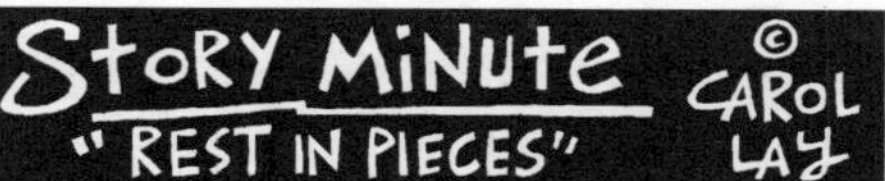


THE PSYCHIATRIST BOUGHT THE OLD GHOST-INFESTED MANSION.

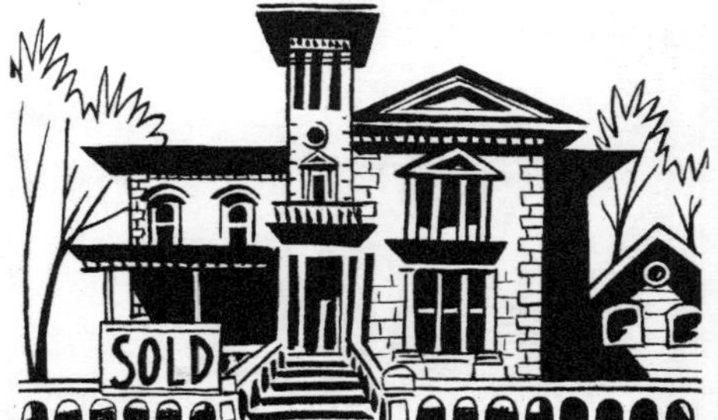


ITS PREVIOUS OCCUPANT, DISSATISFIED IN LIFE, HAD SUFFERED FROM MULTIPLE PERSONALITIES.

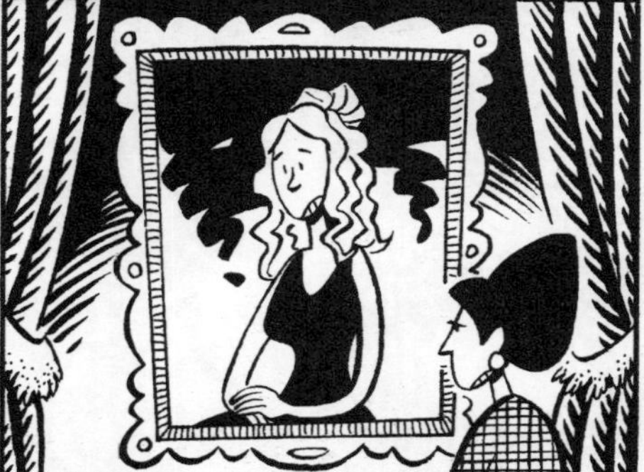

THE GHOST OF EACH PERSONALITY WAS MANIFESTED IN A DIFFERENT ROOM OF THE MANSION.

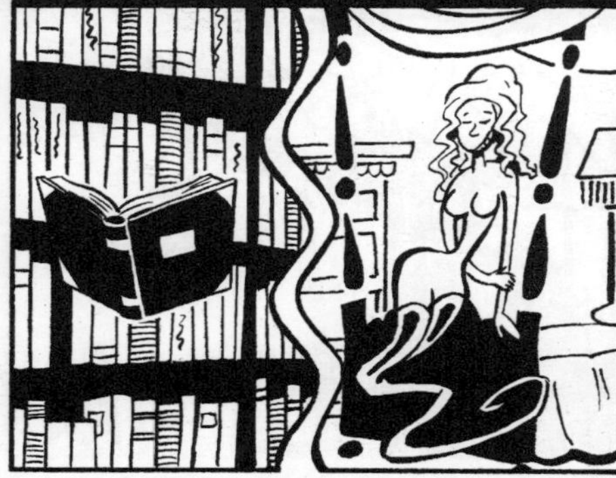

THE ONLY TRULY ANNOYING ONE FANCIED HERSELF TO BE A PROFESSIONAL KNIFE THROWER.

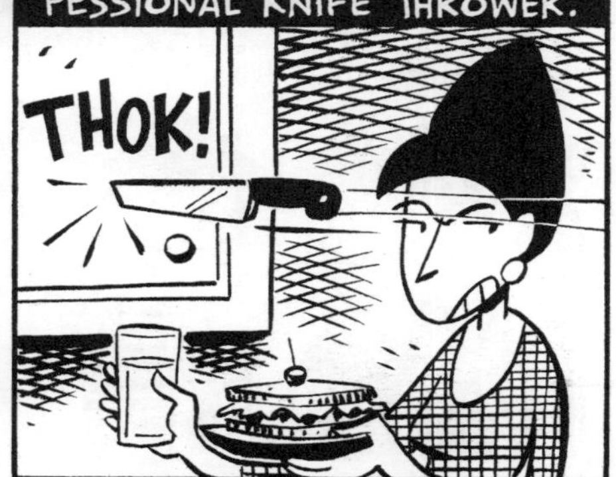


BUT THE GHOSTS HAD TO GO BEFORE SHE COULD SET UP HER PRACTICE.

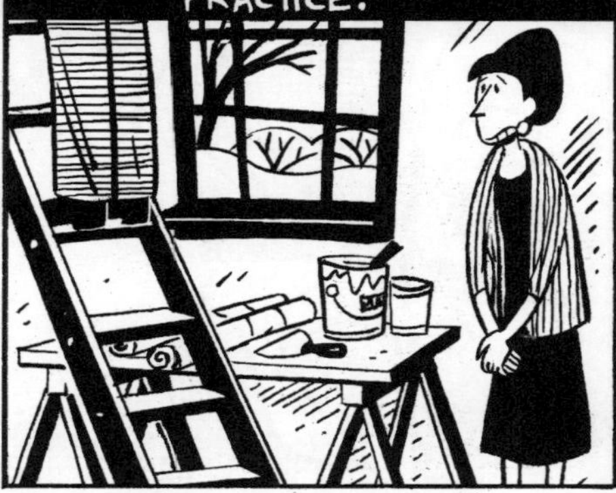

THE DOCTOR KNEW HOW TO TREAT LIVING PATIENTS, BUT GHOSTS WERE DIFFERENT.

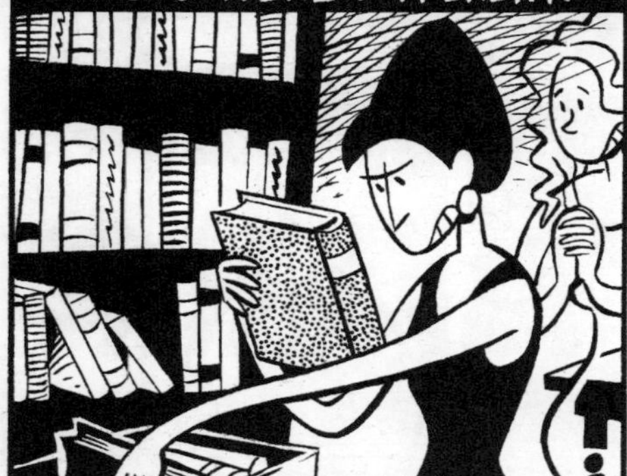

FOR ONE THING, THEY LIKED THE FREEDOM OF OCCUPYING THEIR OWN SEPARATE FORMS.

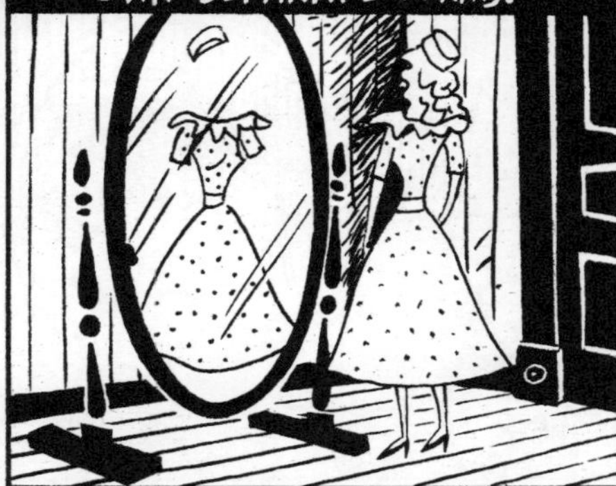

SHE TRIED COUNSELING THEM INDIVIDUALLY, BUT THAT ONLY ENHANCED EACH PERSONALITY.

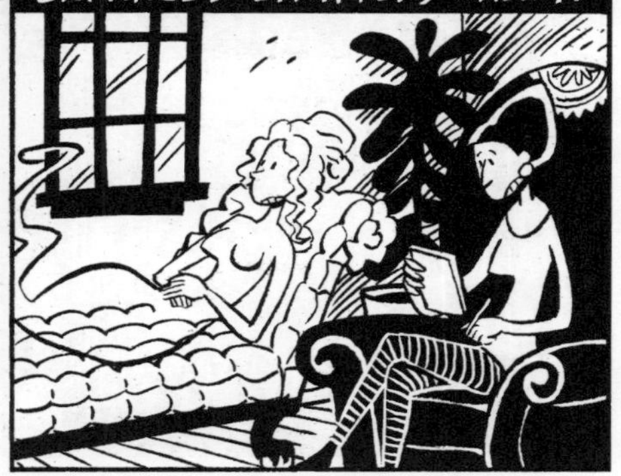

SHE KNEW THEN THAT SHE WOULD HAVE TO GET THEM TO FRAGMENT EXPONENTIALLY.

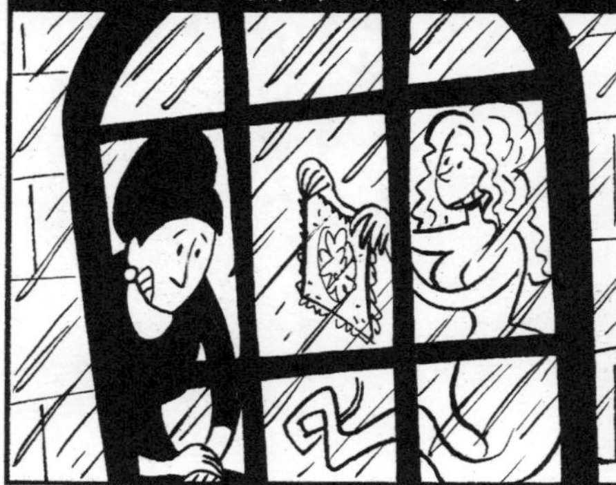

THE POOR SOULS' STRENGTH DISSIPATED WITH EACH NEW PERSONALITY FOUND OUT...

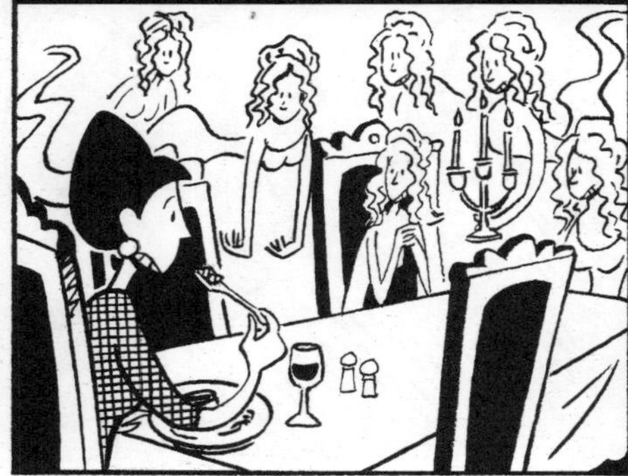

...UNTIL THEY ALL LOST THEIR TENUOUS GRASP ON THE MORTAL WORLD.

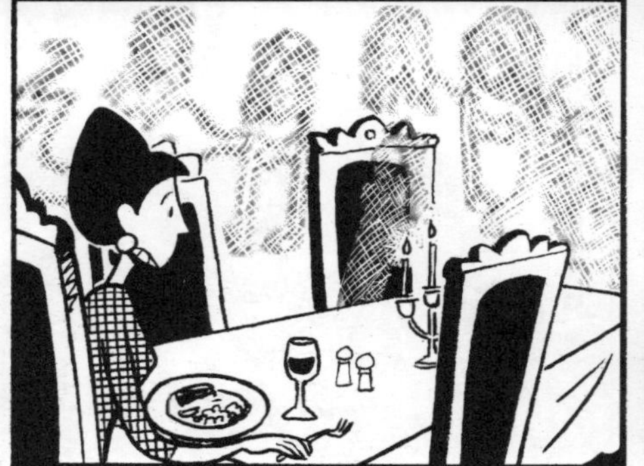

WHEN SHE WAS DONE SHE KNEW THEY WERE ALL SLEEPING PEACEFULLY TOGETHER AT LAST.

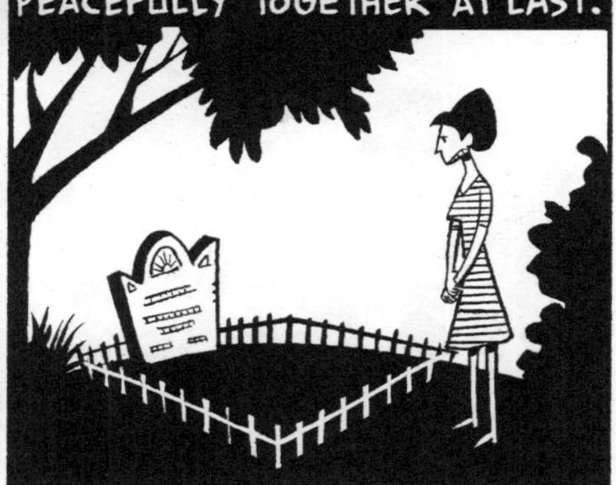

STORY MINUTE ©C. LAY

"FRANKENSTEIN'S DAUGHTER"

A CLASSIC UGLY DUCKLING, SHE WAS VERY UNHAPPY.

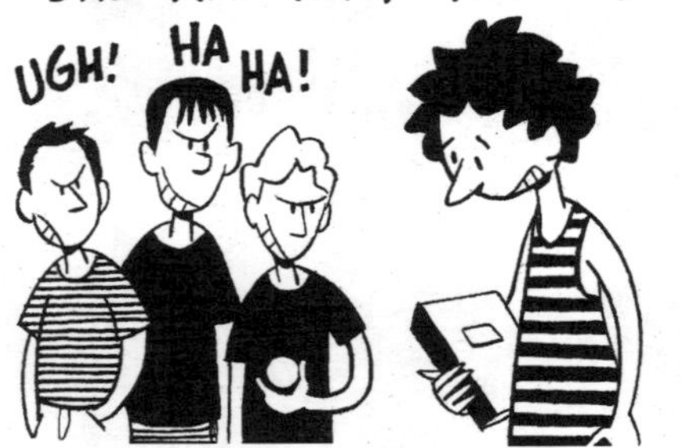


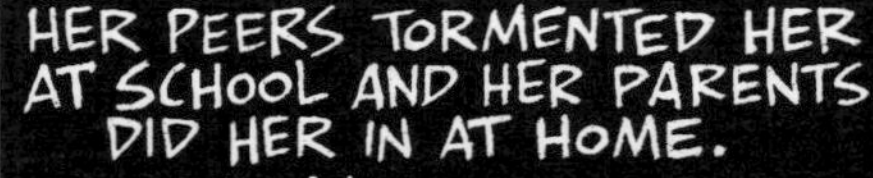


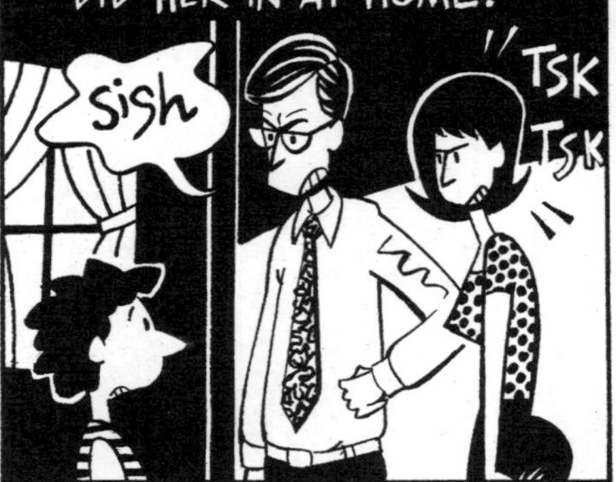


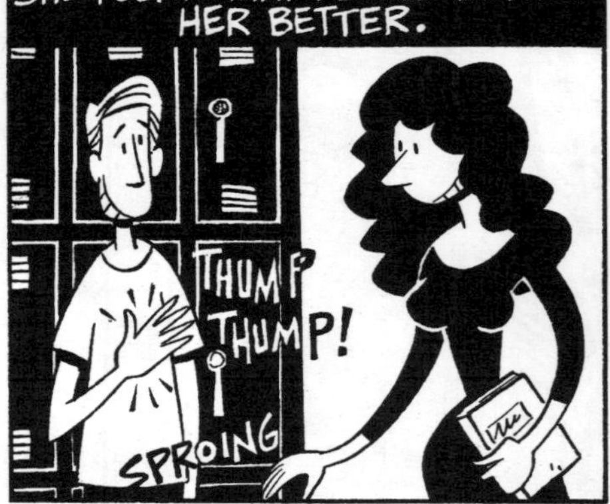


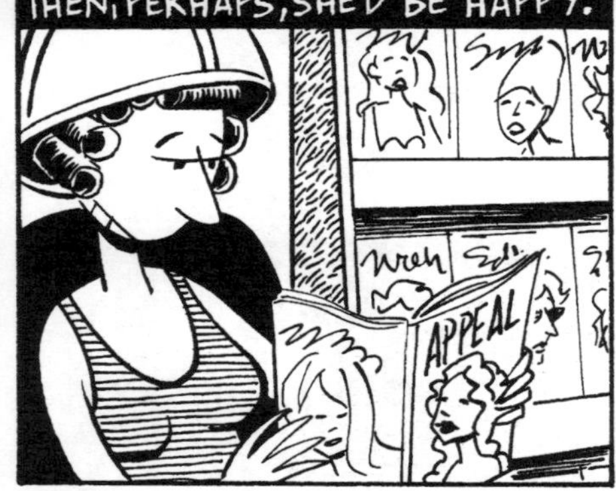


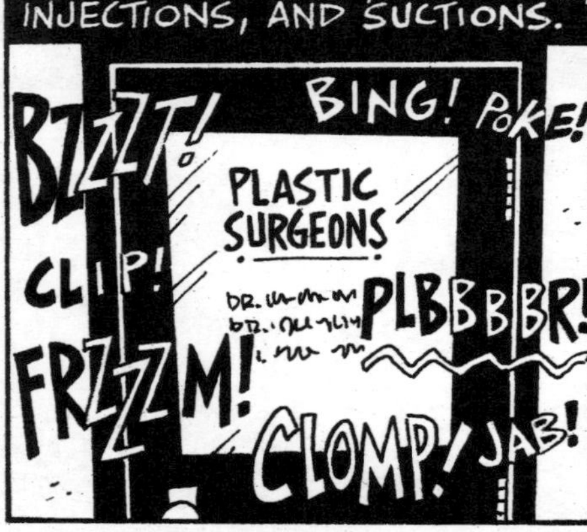


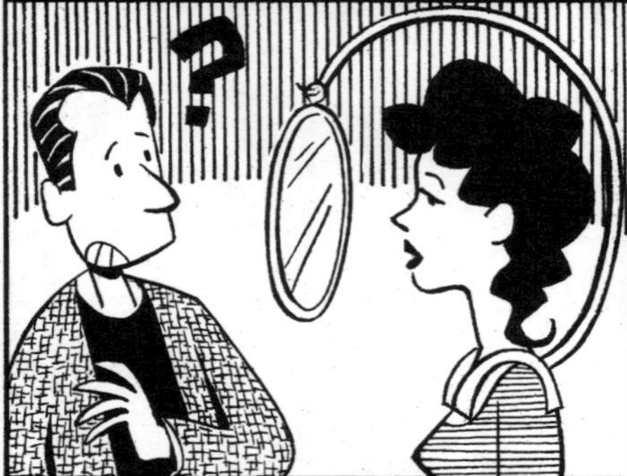


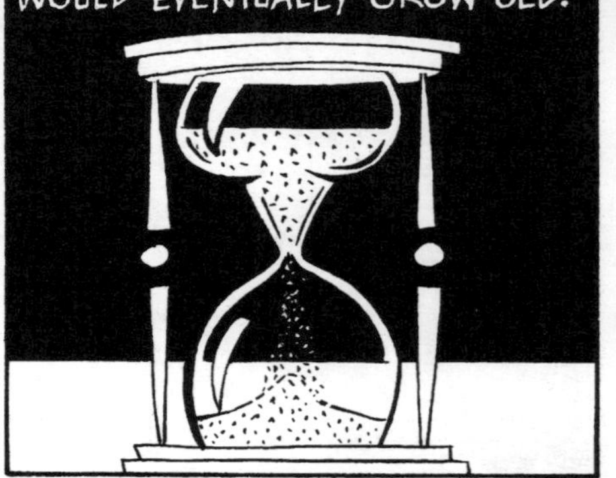


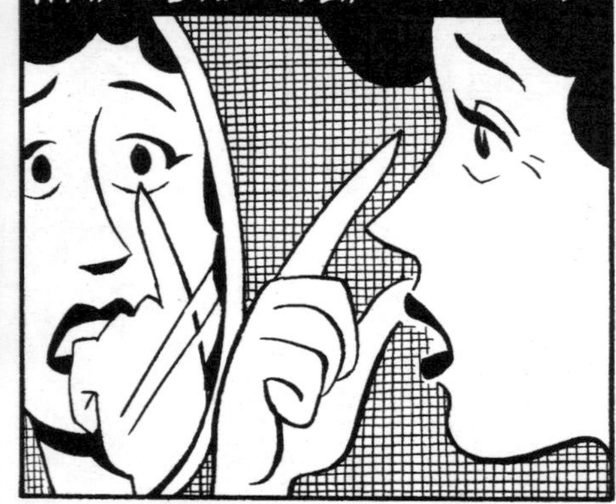


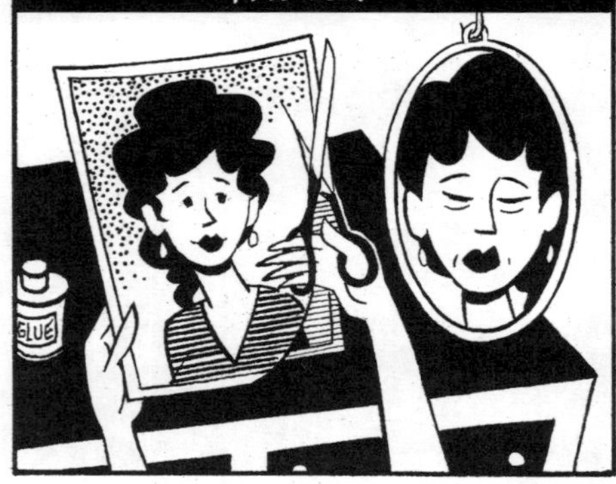


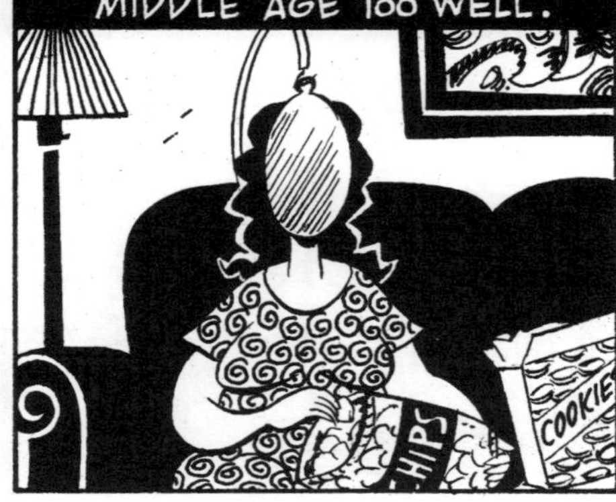


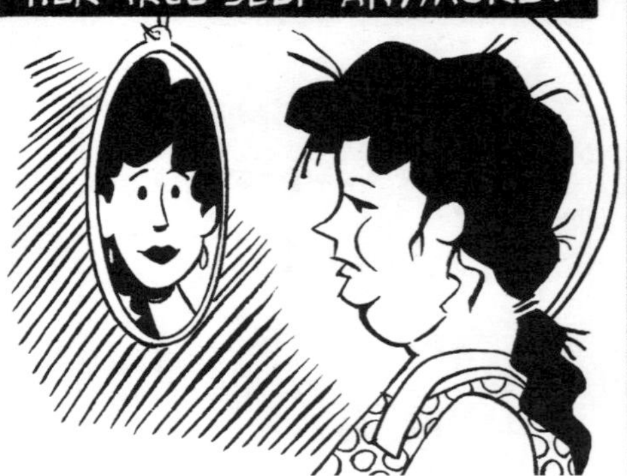


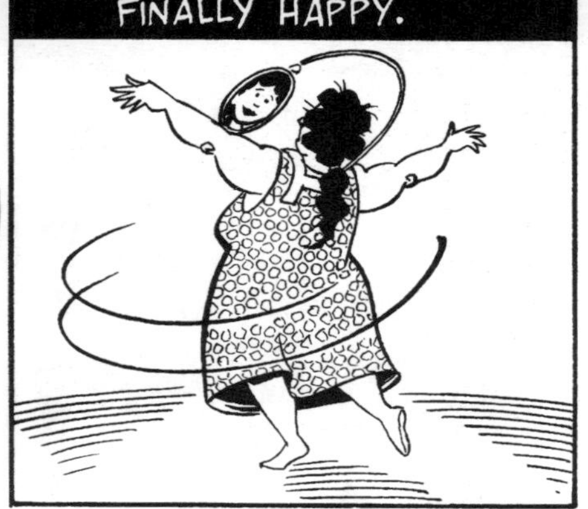

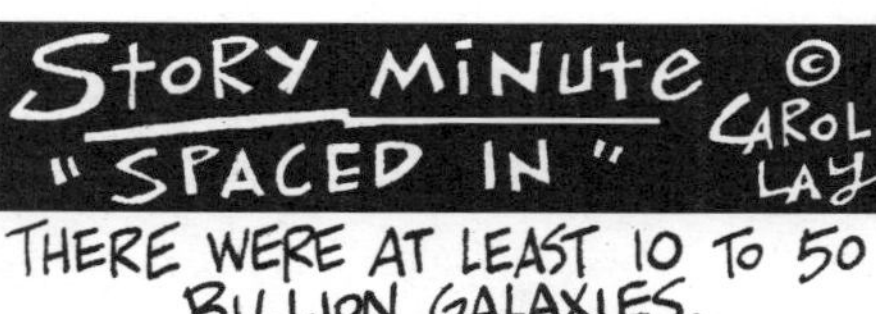
STORY MINUTE
"SPACED IN"
© CAROL LAY
THERE WERE AT LEAST 10 TO 50 BILLION GALAXIES.

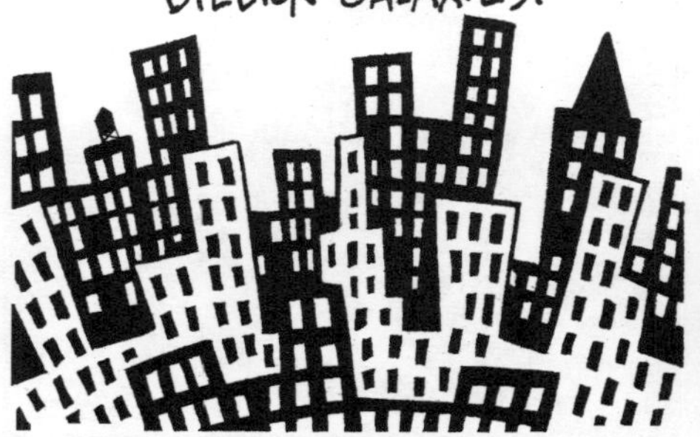

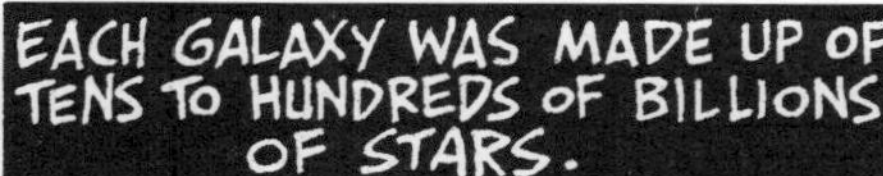
EACH GALAXY WAS MADE UP OF TENS TO HUNDREDS OF BILLIONS OF STARS.

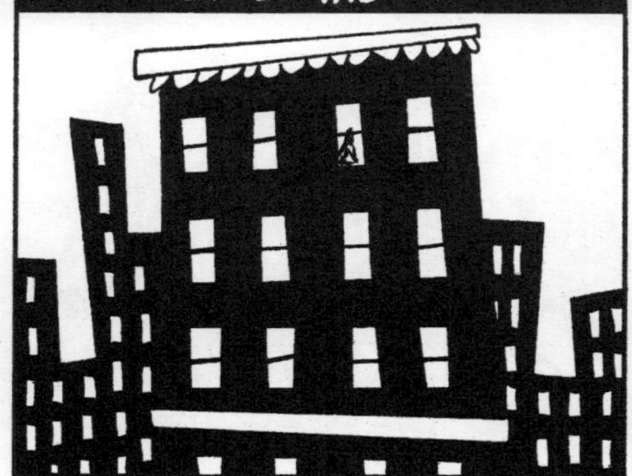

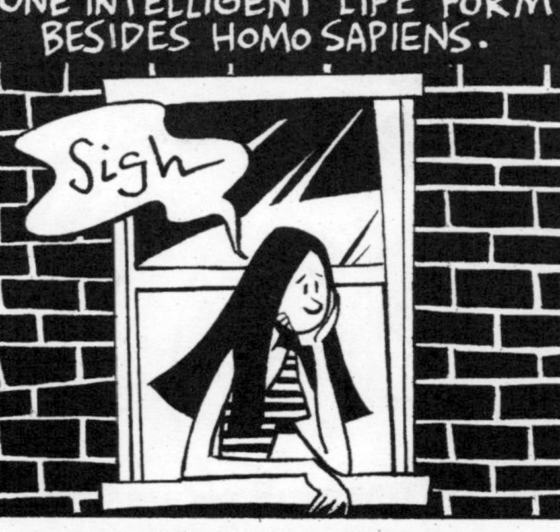
SURELY, THERE WAS AT LEAST ONE INTELLIGENT LIFE FORM BESIDES HOMO SAPIENS.
Sigh

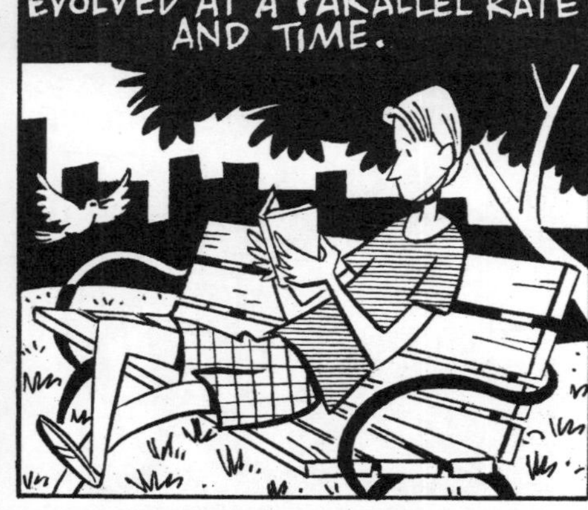
AND THERE WAS. THEY EVEN EVOLVED AT A PARALLEL RATE AND TIME.

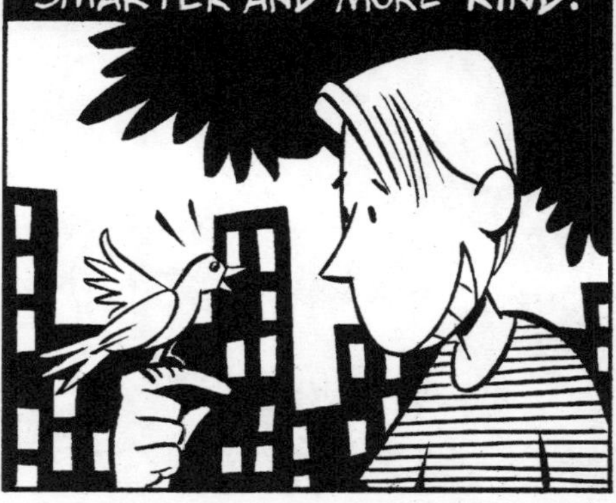
THEY WERE VERY MUCH LIKE HUMANS EXCEPT THEY WERE SMARTER AND MORE KIND.

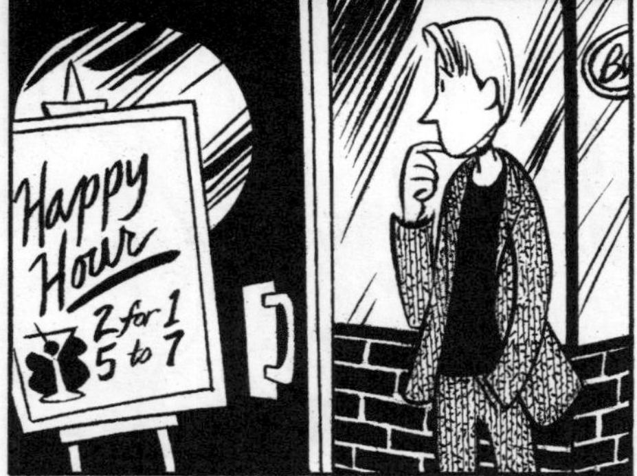
THEY SPECULATED THAT OTHERS MIGHT EXIST AND MADE SIMILAR ATTEMPTS AT EXPLORATION.
Happy Hour
2 for 1
5 to 7

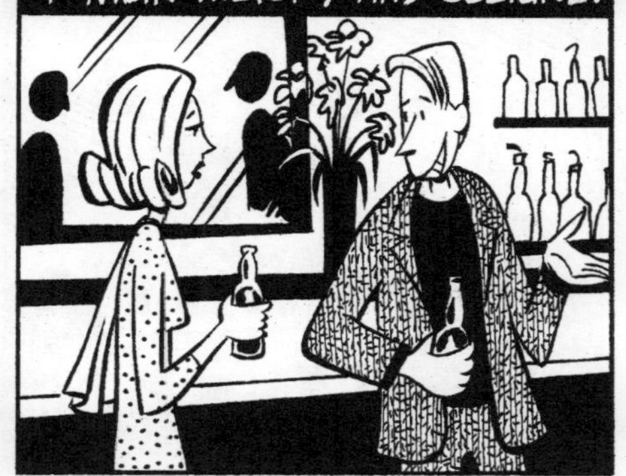
LIKE HUMANS, THEY SENT OUT PROBES THAT CARRIED PIECES OF THEIR HISTORY AND CULTURE.

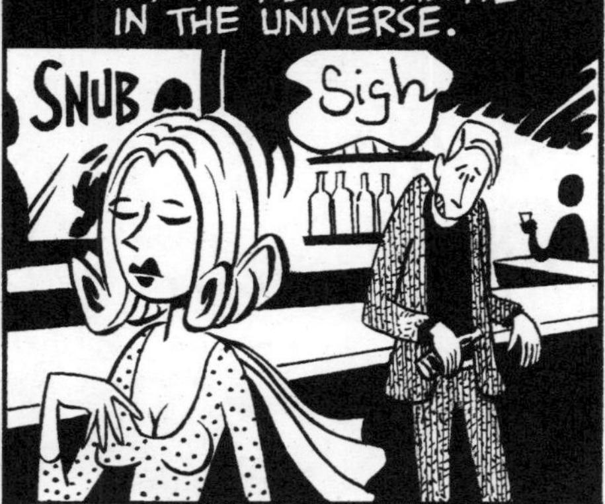
THEY WANTED PROOF THAT THEY WERE NOT ALONE IN THE UNIVERSE.
SNUB
Sigh

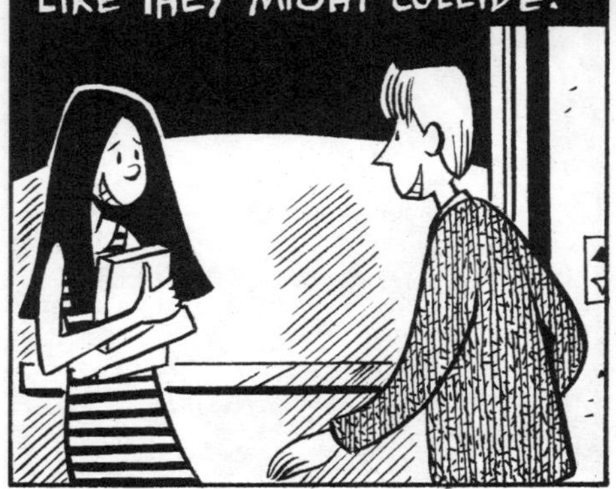
CENTURIES AFTER THE PROBES WERE LAUNCHED IT LOOKED LIKE THEY MIGHT COLLIDE.

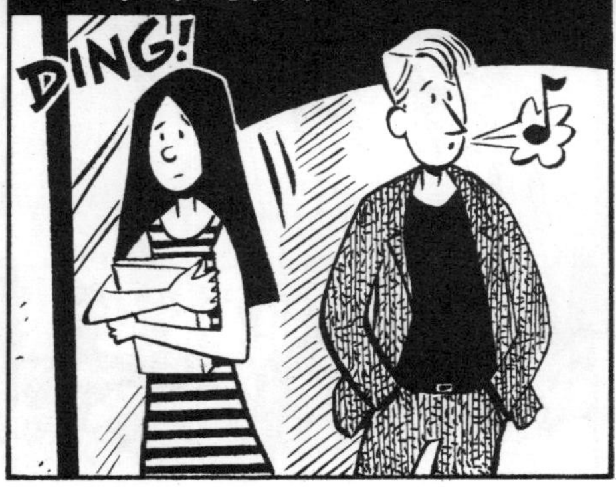
BUT THEY JUST SAILED PAST EACH OTHER ON THEIR WAYS TO DEEPER SPACE.
DING!

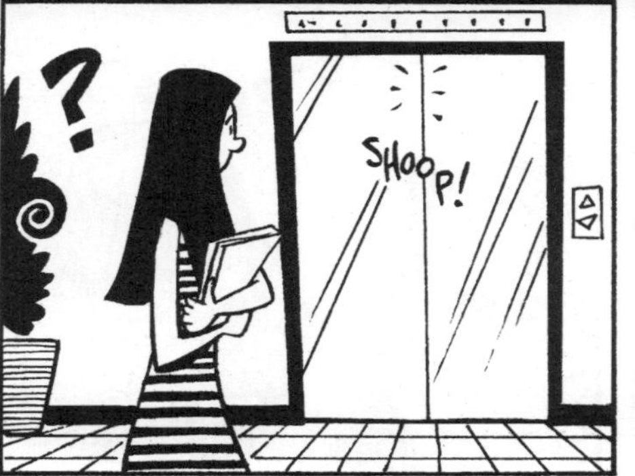
EVEN WITH GREAT ADVANCES IN SCIENCE, THEY MIGHT NEVER MANAGE TO FIND EACH OTHER.
?
SHOOP!

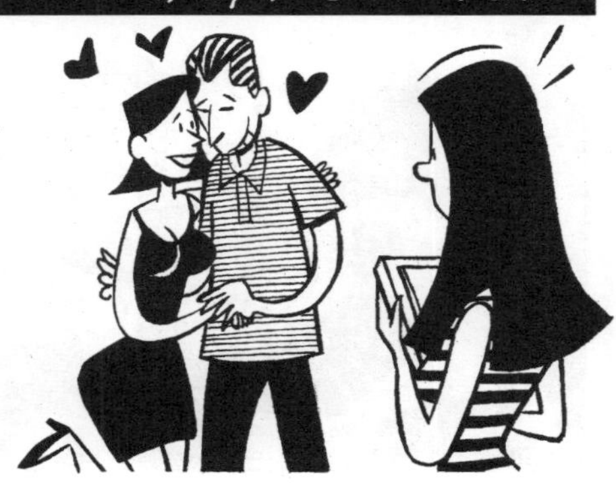
BUT IT WAS A BIG PLACE. IT WAS BOUND TO HAPPEN SOMEWHERE, SOMETIME, TO SOMEONE.

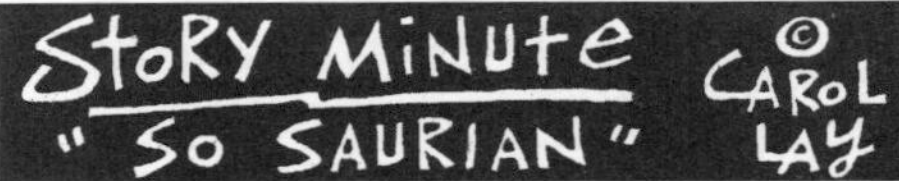
Story Minute © Carol Lay
"So Saurian"

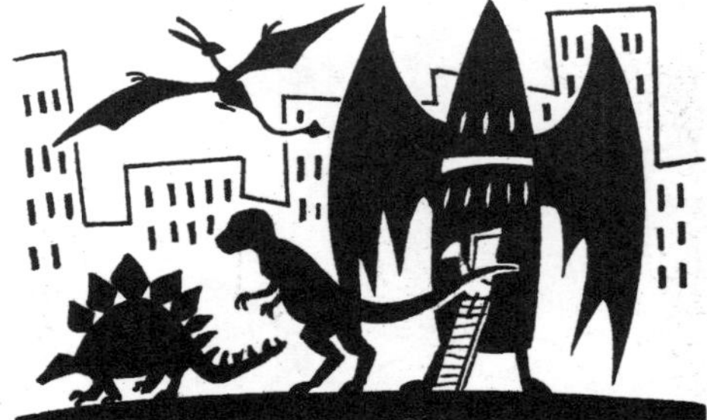
THE DINOSAURS CAME BACK TO SET THE RECORD STRAIGHT.

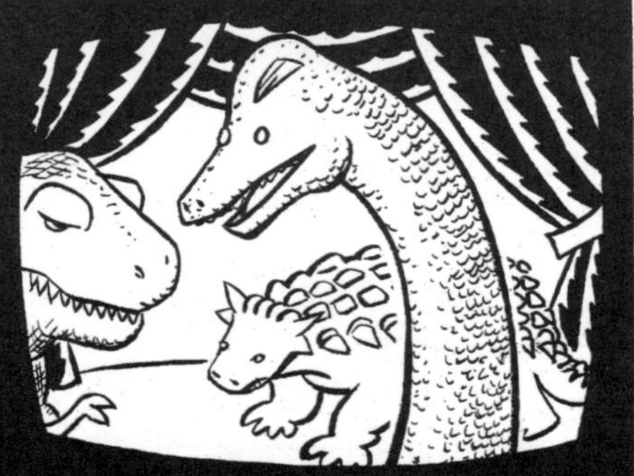
IN THEIR PRESS CONFERENCE, THEY VOICED EXPLANATIONS AND SOME VALID COMPLAINTS.

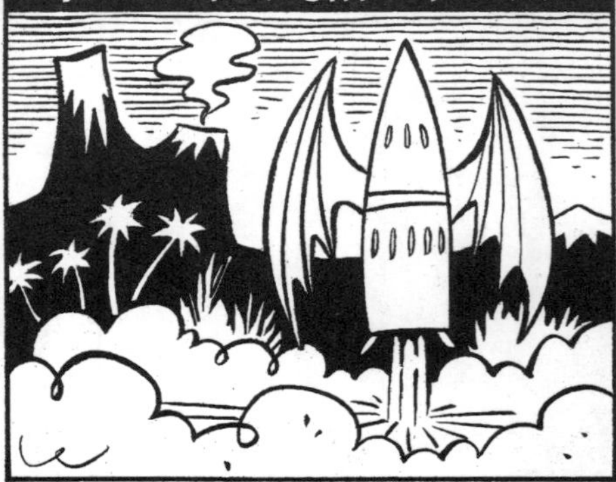
FIRST, THEY DID NOT PERISH AS HUMANS BELIEVED—THEY JUST DEVELOPED SPACE FLIGHT.

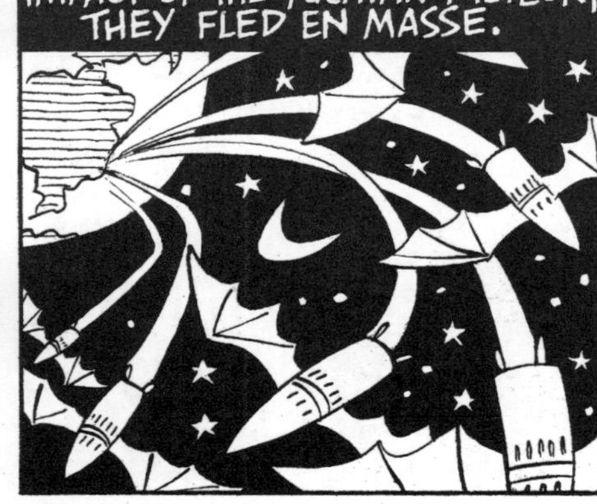
AWARE OF THE IMMINENT IMPACT OF THE YUCATAN METEOR, THEY FLED EN MASSE.

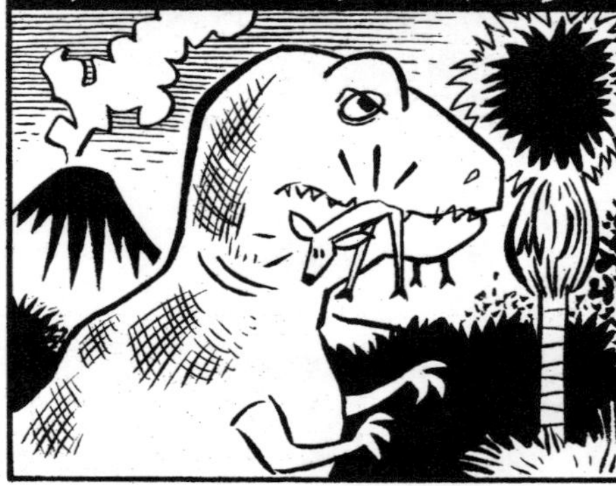
THEY SETTLED ON A NICE PLANET WITH LOTS OF GREENS AND CRUNCHY MAMMALS.

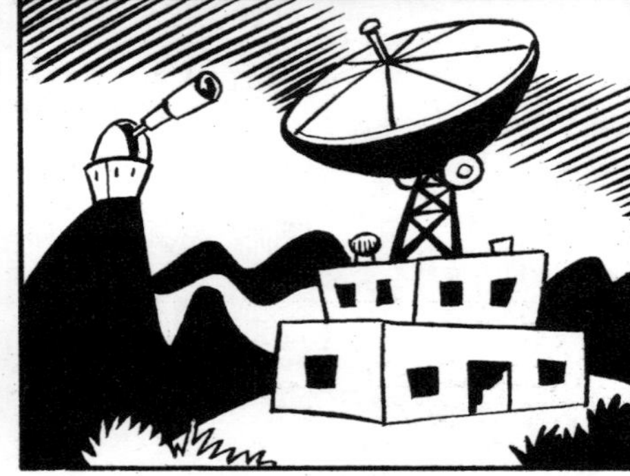
BUT EVENTUALLY, BROADCAST NOISE FROM EARTH CAME TO THEIR ATTENTION.

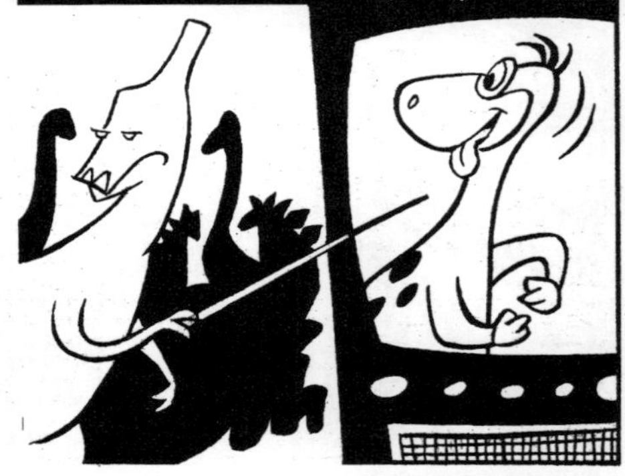
THEY FOUND THE MEDIA'S PORTRAYAL OF THEIR KIND UNINFORMED AND HIGHLY OFFENSIVE.

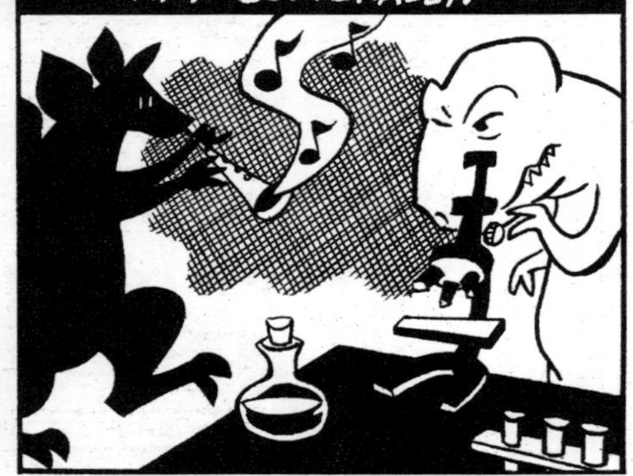
THEY WERE ACTUALLY QUITE ADVANCED BOTH TECHNOLOGICALLY AND CULTURALLY.

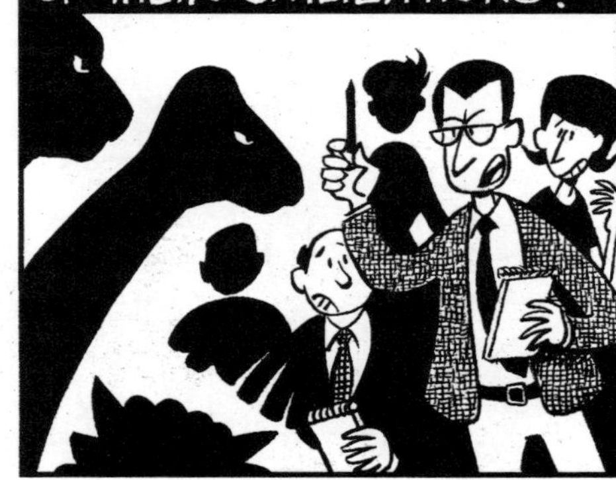
BUT WHERE, WONDERED THE PRESS, WERE THE REMAINS OF THEIR CIVILIZATIONS?

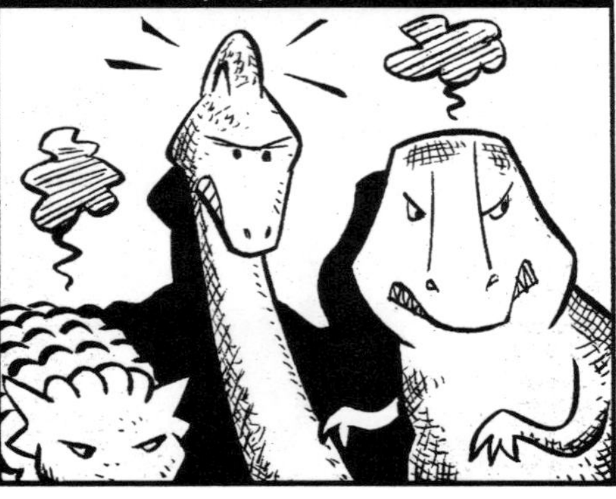
THE ECOLOGICALLY-CORRECT BEINGS REPLIED THAT THEY HAD CLEANED UP AFTER THEMSELVES.

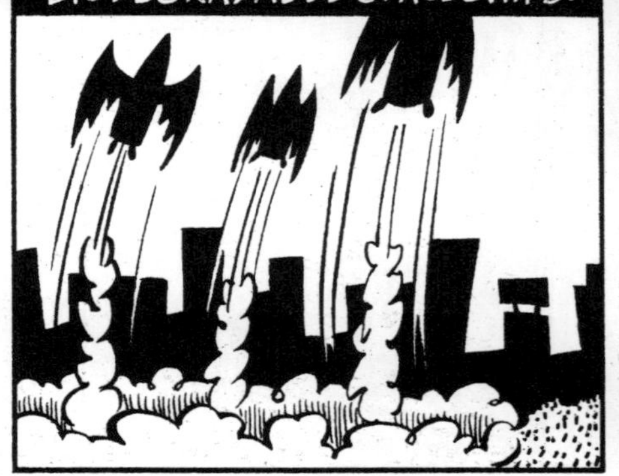
WHEN THE EARTHLINGS SCOFFED THE DINOSAURS LEFT IN THEIR BIODEGRADABLE SPACESHIPS.

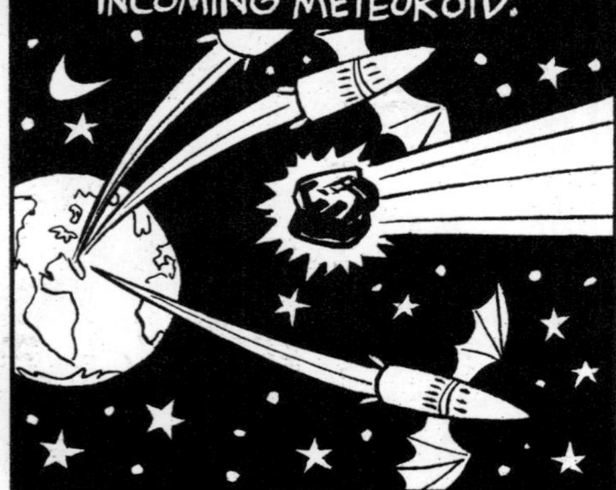
AND, IN THEIR PIQUE, THEY FORGOT TO MENTION YET ANOTHER INCOMING METEOROID.

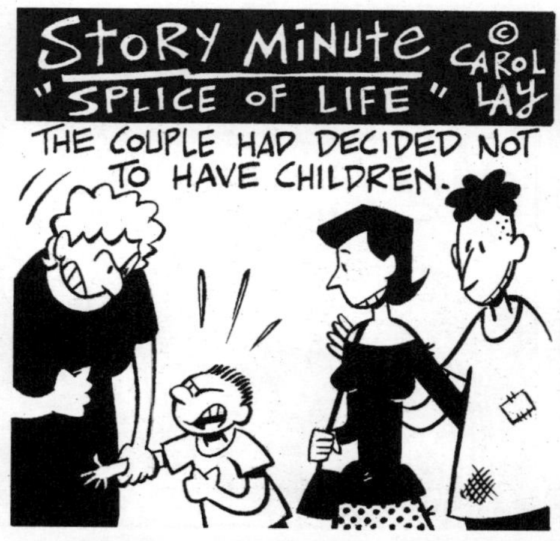
Story Minute © Carol Lay
"Splice of Life"
THE COUPLE HAD DECIDED NOT TO HAVE CHILDREN.

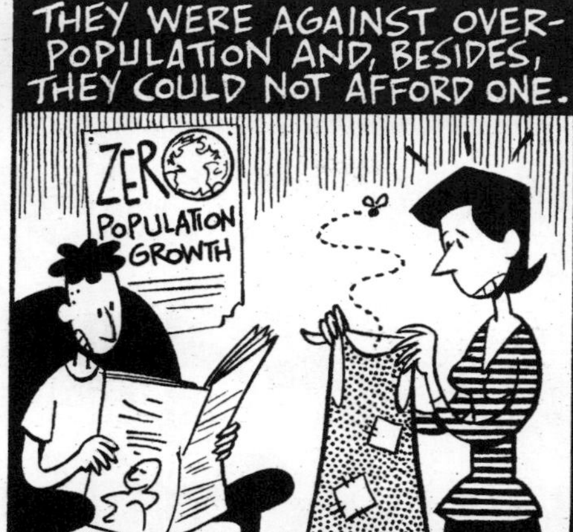
THEY WERE AGAINST OVER-POPULATION AND, BESIDES, THEY COULD NOT AFFORD ONE.
ZERO POPULATION GROWTH

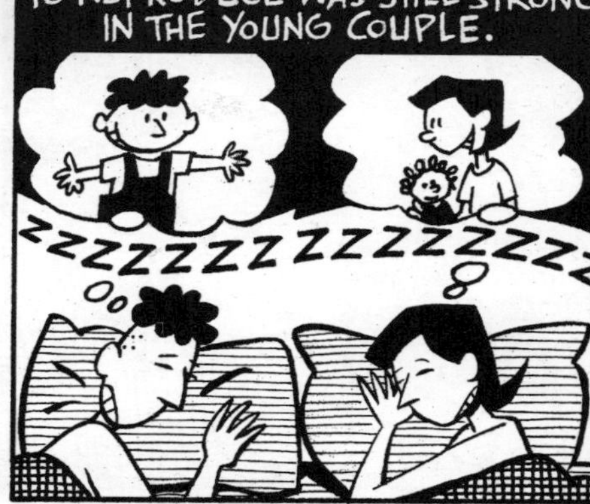
BUT THE BIOLOGICAL IMPERATIVE TO REPRODUCE WAS STILL STRONG IN THE YOUNG COUPLE.
ZZZZZZZZZZZZZZZZ

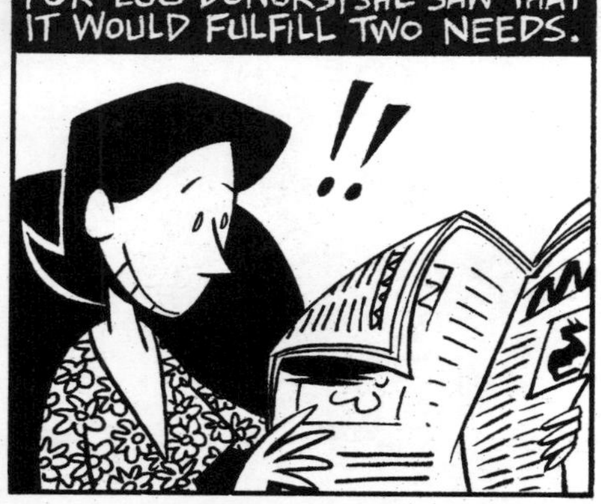
WHEN THE WOMAN SAW AN AD FOR EGG DONORS, SHE SAW THAT IT WOULD FULFILL TWO NEEDS.
!!

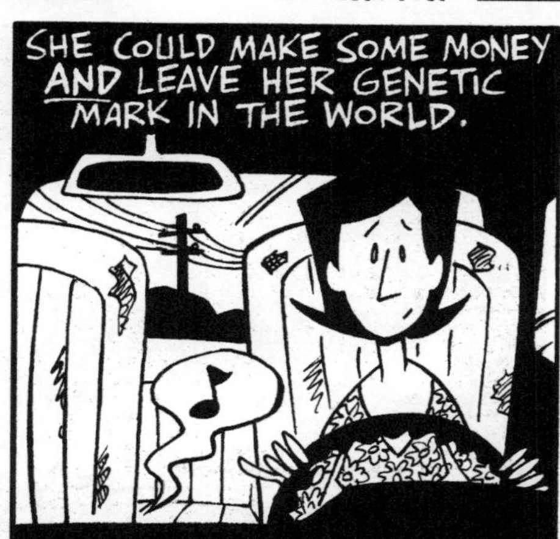
SHE COULD MAKE SOME MONEY AND LEAVE HER GENETIC MARK IN THE WORLD.

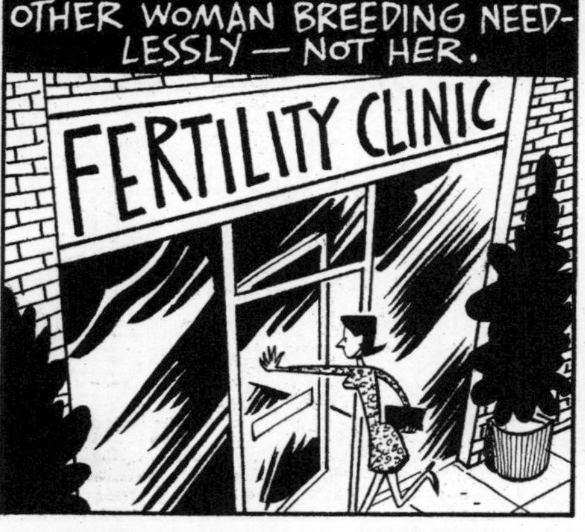
AFTER ALL, IT WOULD BE SOME OTHER WOMAN BREEDING NEED-LESSLY — NOT HER.
FERTILITY CLINIC

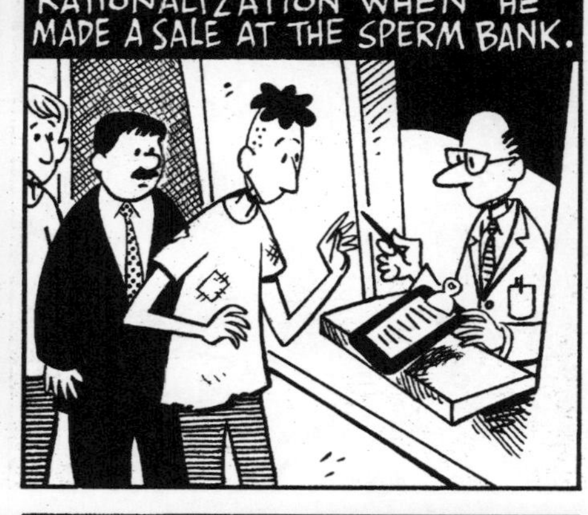
HER HUSBAND MADE THE SAME RATIONALIZATION WHEN HE MADE A SALE AT THE SPERM BANK.

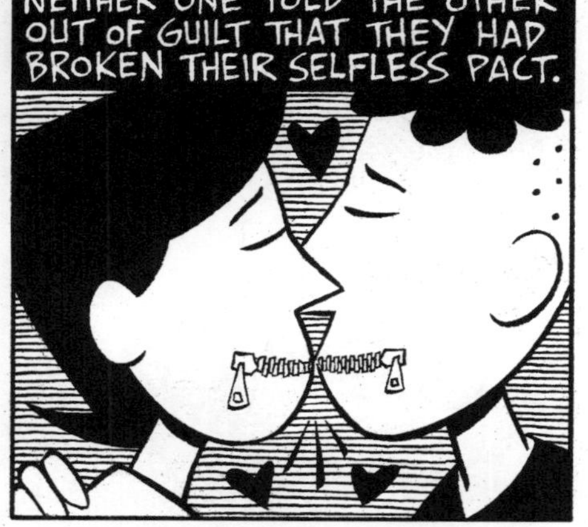
NEITHER ONE TOLD THE OTHER OUT OF GUILT THAT THEY HAD BROKEN THEIR SELFLESS PACT.

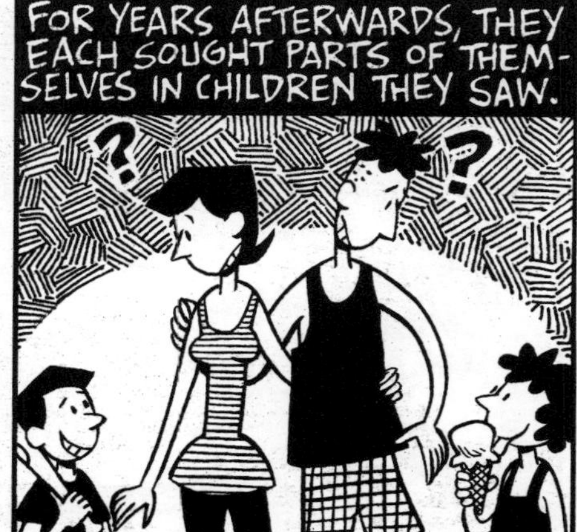
FOR YEARS AFTERWARDS, THEY EACH SOUGHT PARTS OF THEM-SELVES IN CHILDREN THEY SAW.
?
?

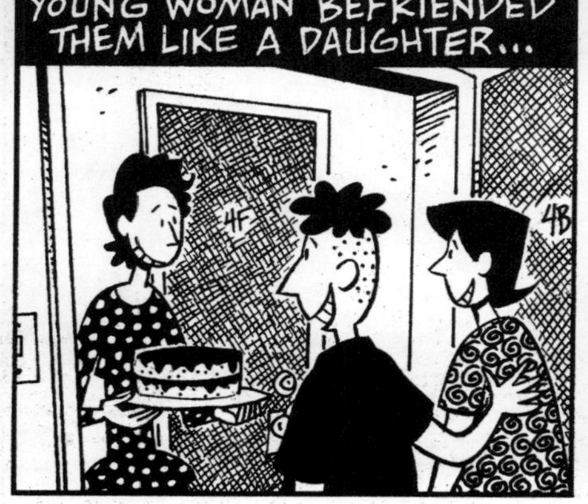
WHEN, MANY YEARS LATER, A YOUNG WOMAN BEFRIENDED THEM LIKE A DAUGHTER...
4F
4B

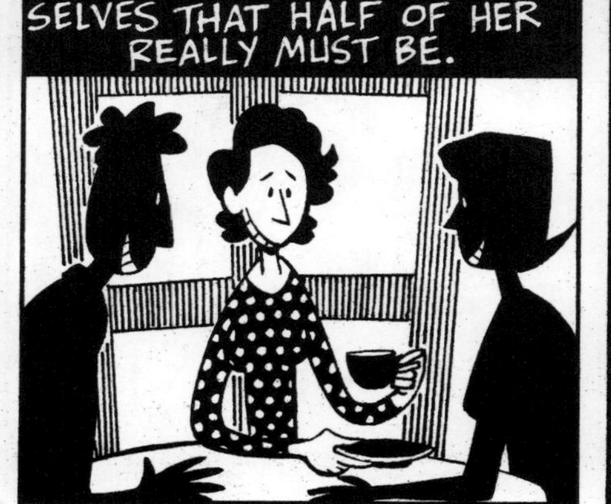
...THEY BOTH THOUGHT TO THEM-SELVES THAT HALF OF HER REALLY MUST BE.

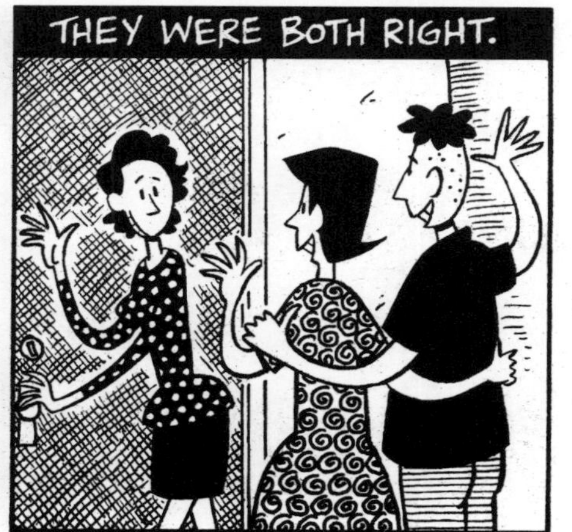
THEY WERE BOTH RIGHT.

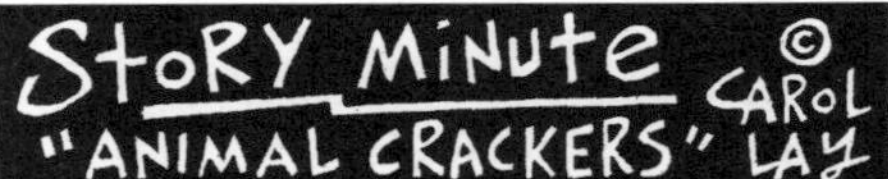


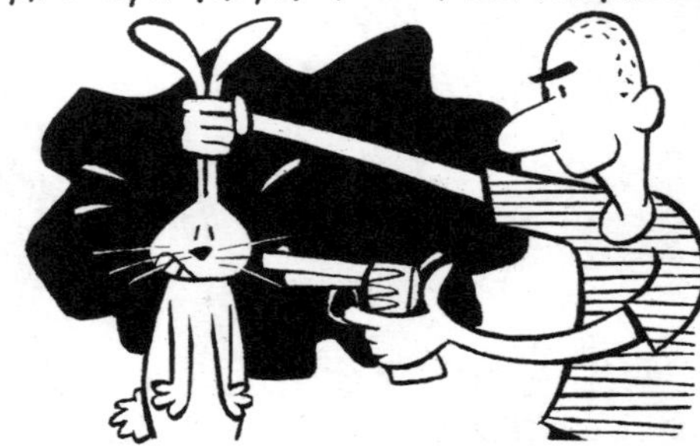


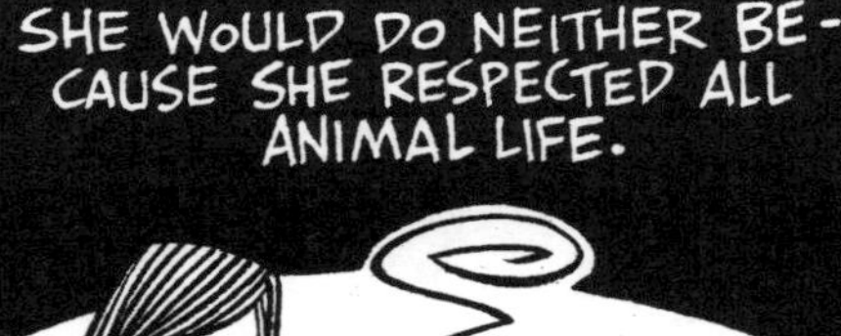


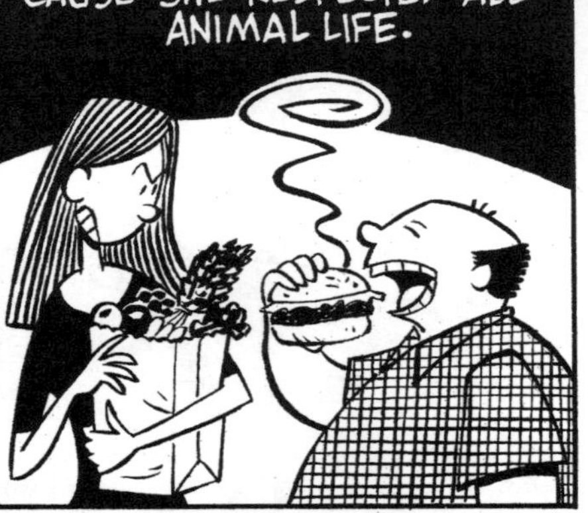

She even wore plastic shoes and cloth coats.

TSK!

?

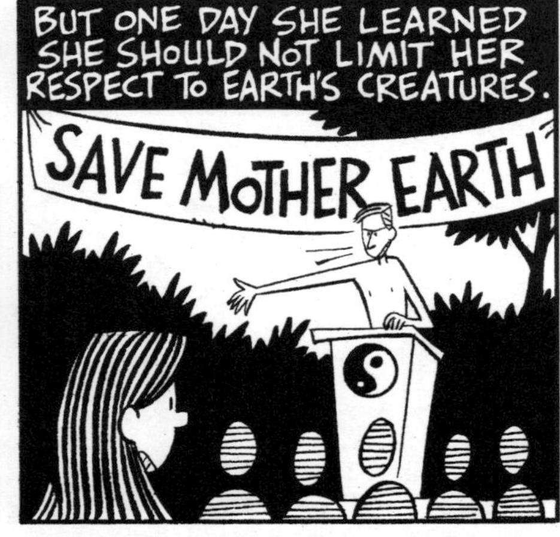


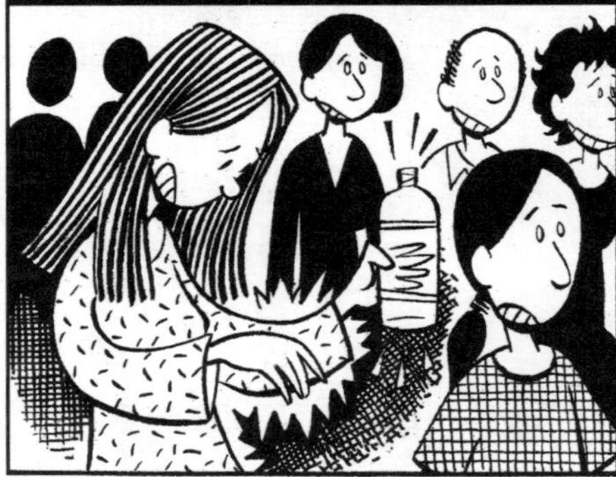


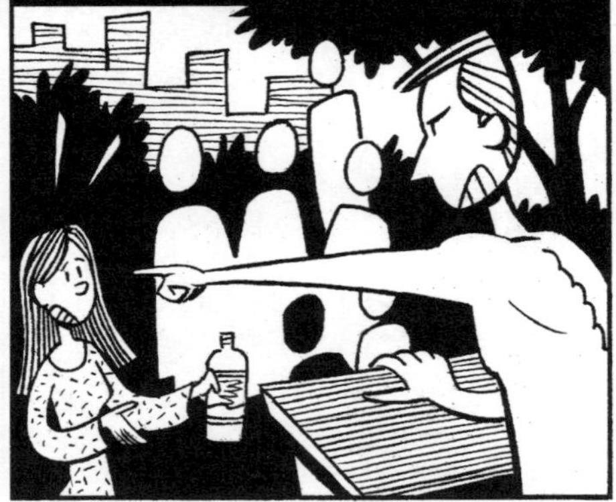


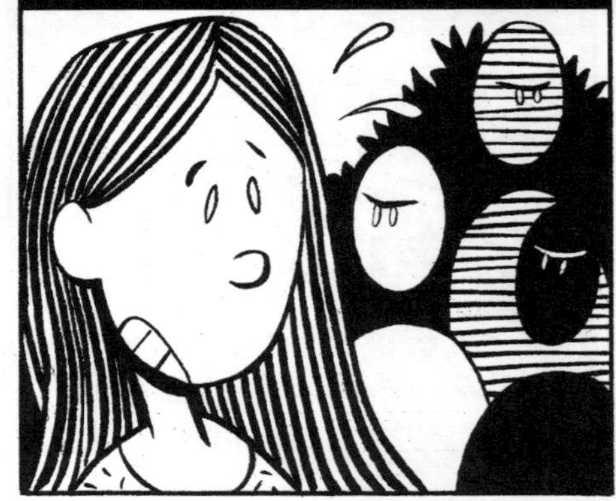


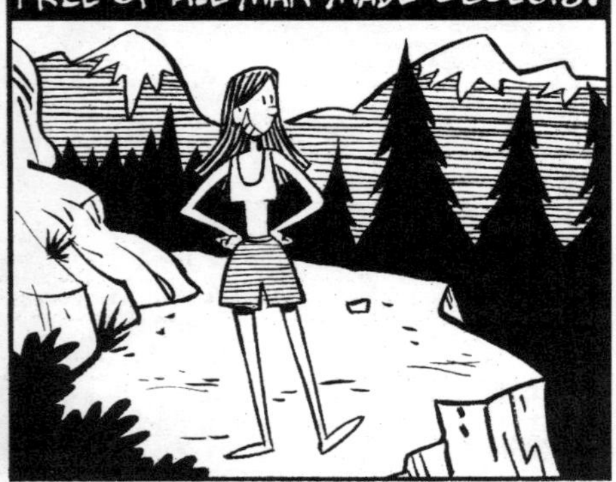


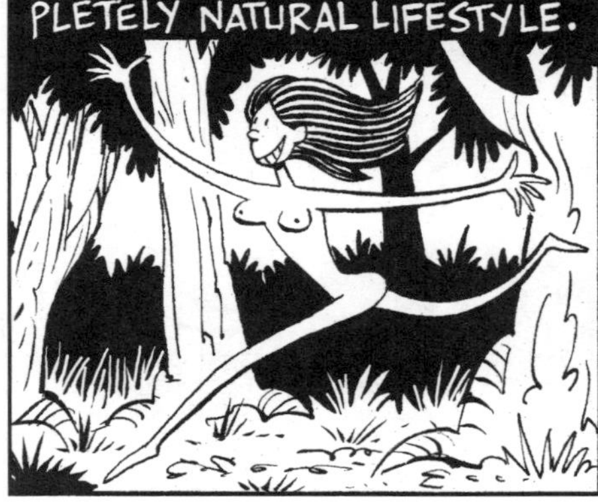


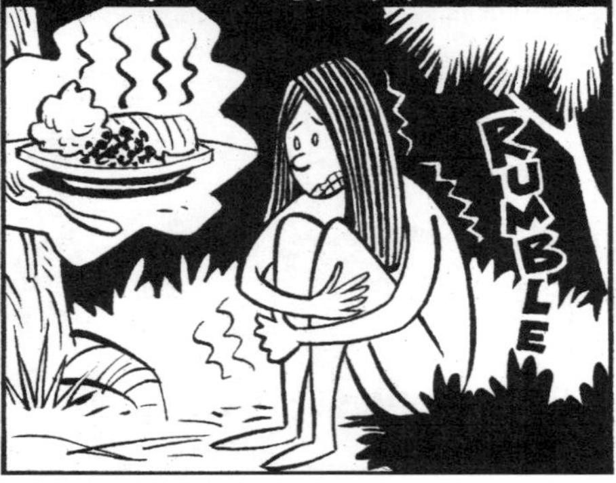


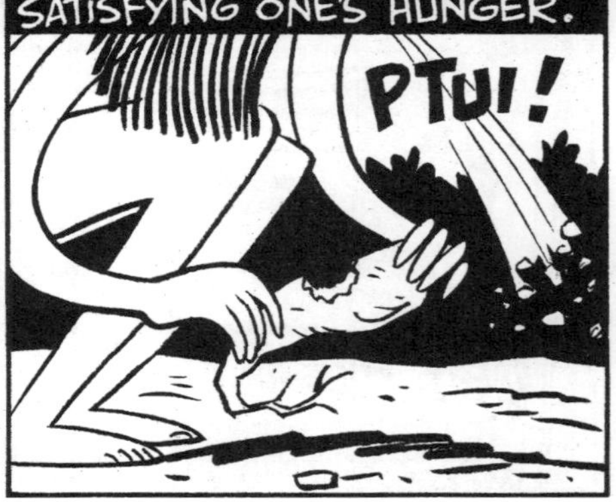


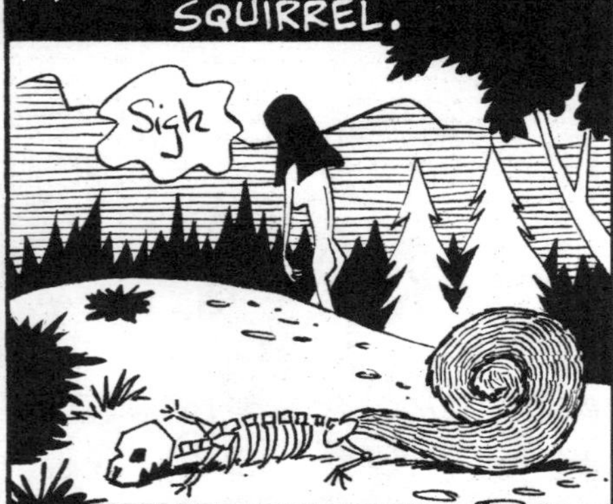

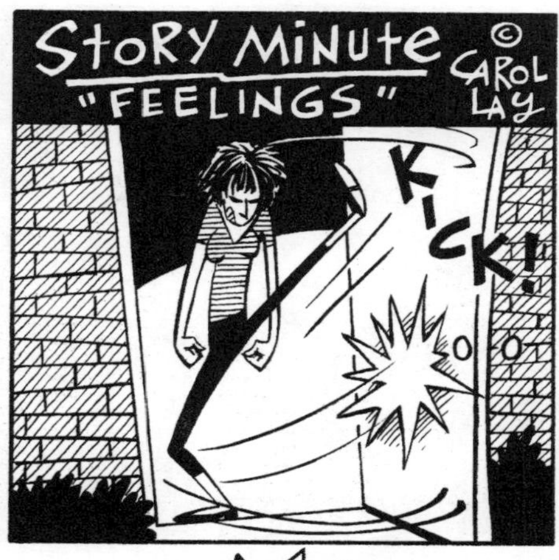
STORY MINUTE
"FEELINGS"
© CAROL LAY
KICK!

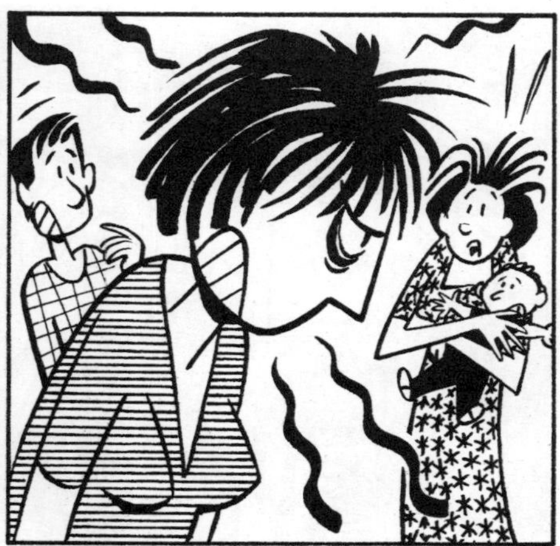

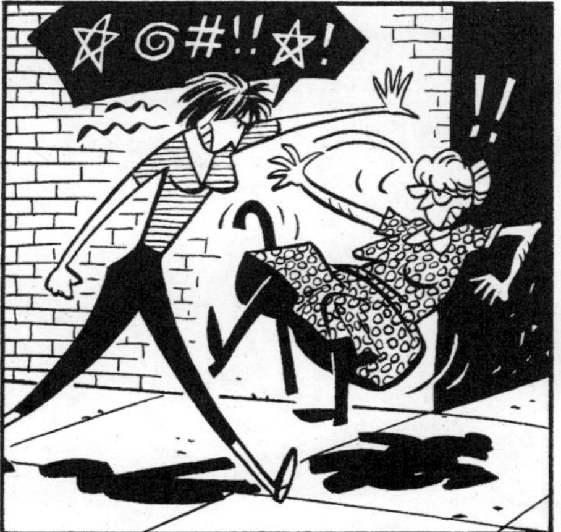
!!

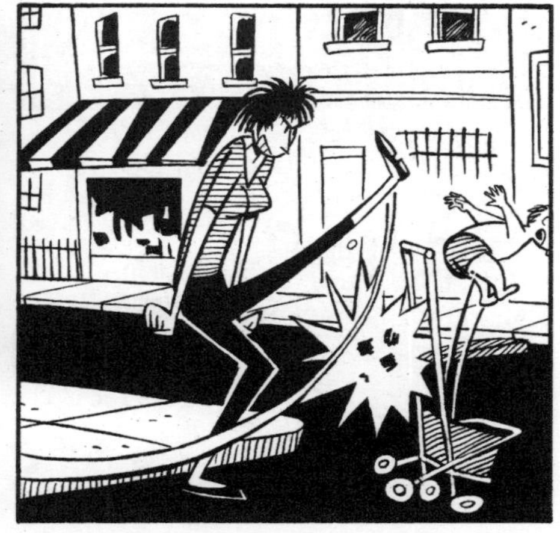

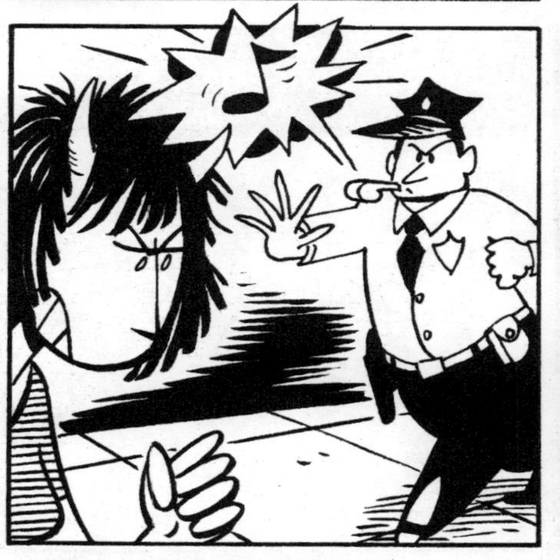

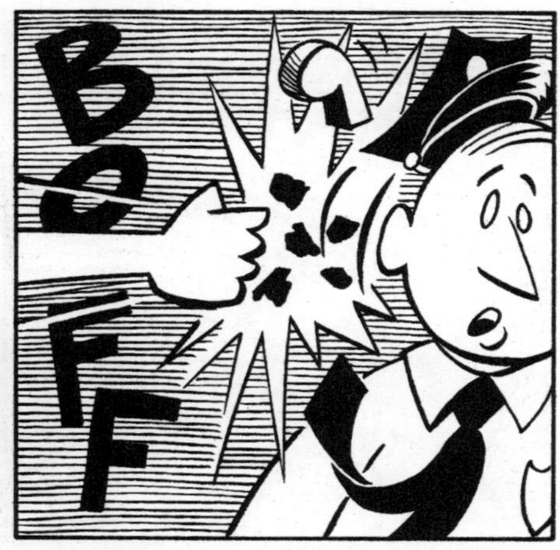
BOFF

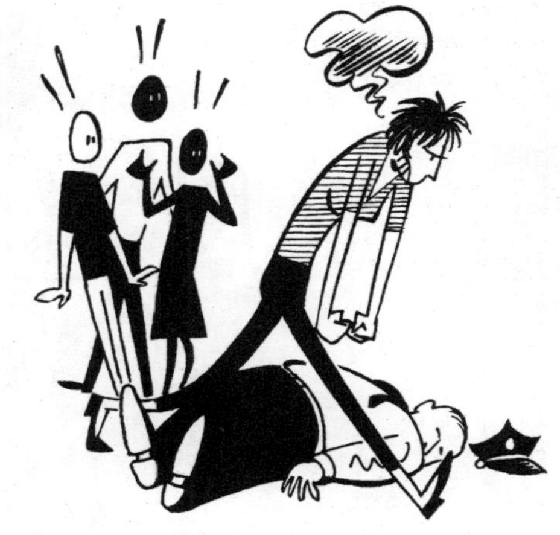

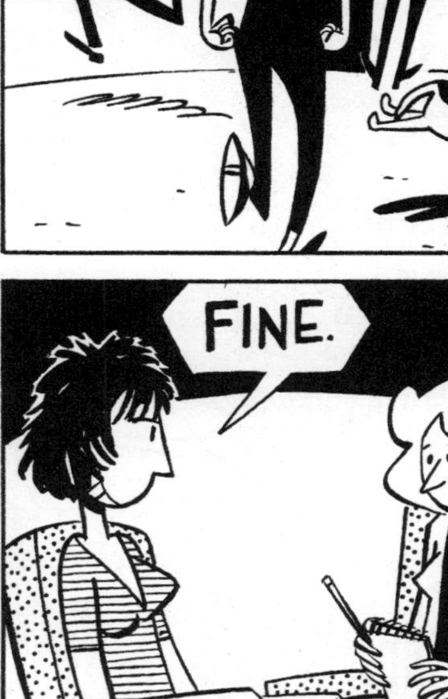
FINE.

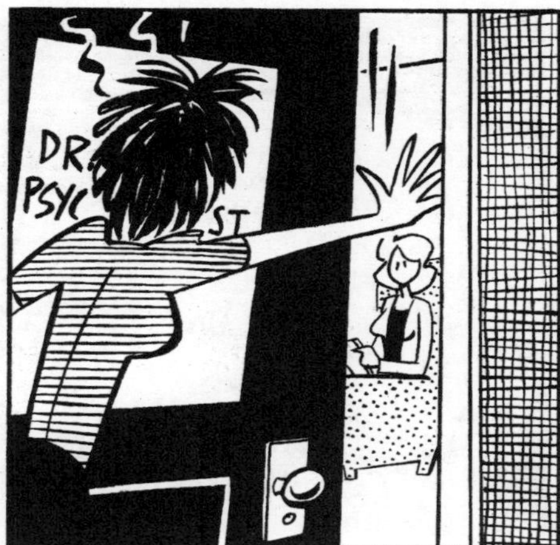
DR
PSYC
ST

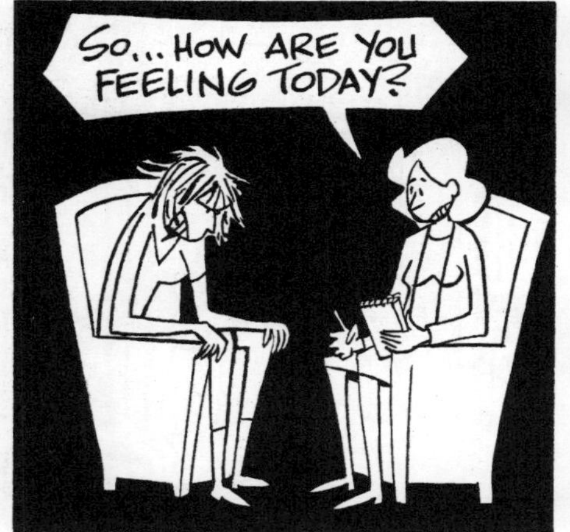
SO... HOW ARE YOU FEELING TODAY?

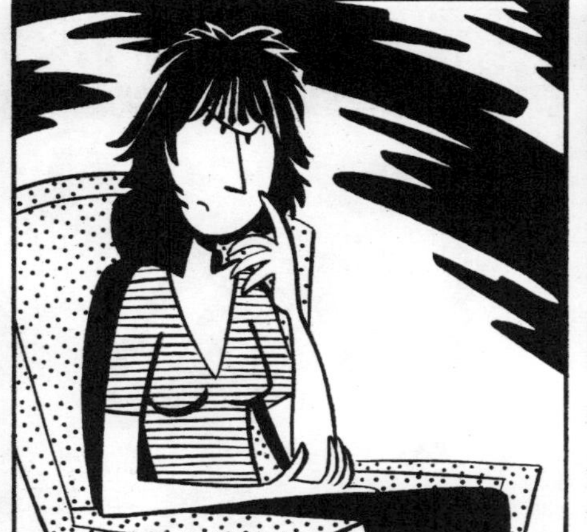

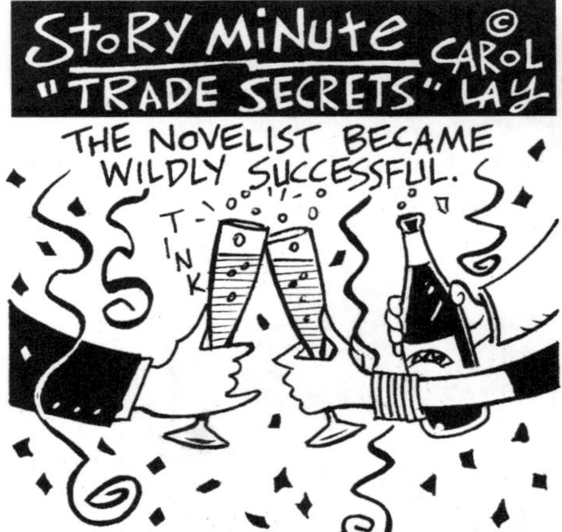
STORY MINUTE
"TRADE SECRETS"
© CAROL LAY
THE NOVELIST BECAME WILDLY SUCCESSFUL.
TINK

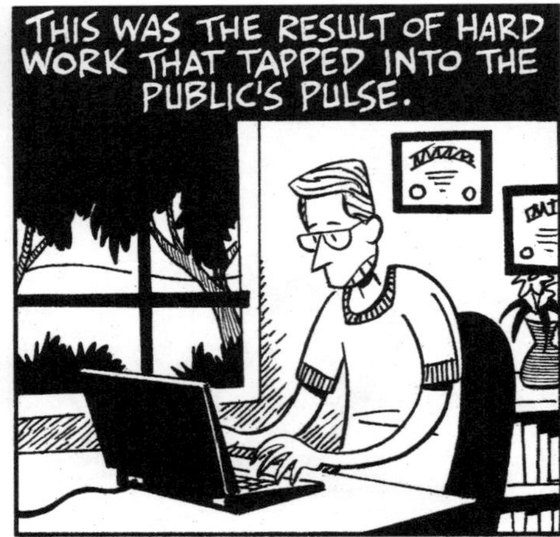
THIS WAS THE RESULT OF HARD WORK THAT TAPPED INTO THE PUBLIC'S PULSE.

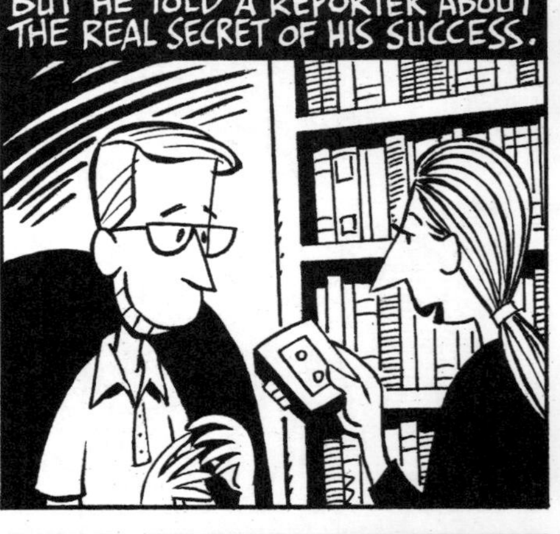
BUT HE TOLD A REPORTER ABOUT THE REAL SECRET OF HIS SUCCESS.

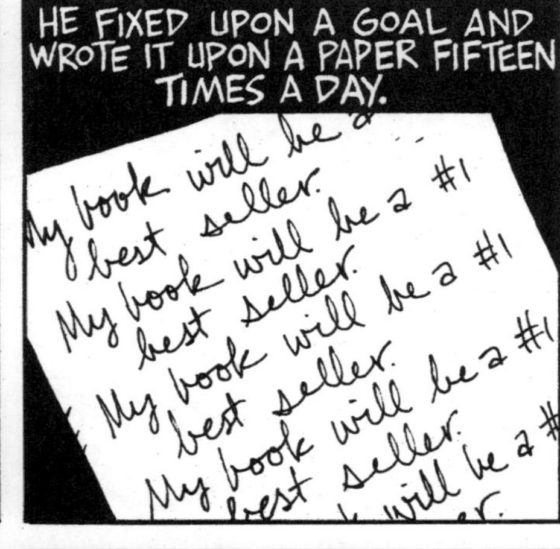
HE FIXED UPON A GOAL AND WROTE IT UPON A PAPER FIFTEEN TIMES A DAY.
best seller.
My book will be a #1
best seller.
My book will be a #1
best seller.
My book will be a #1
best seller.

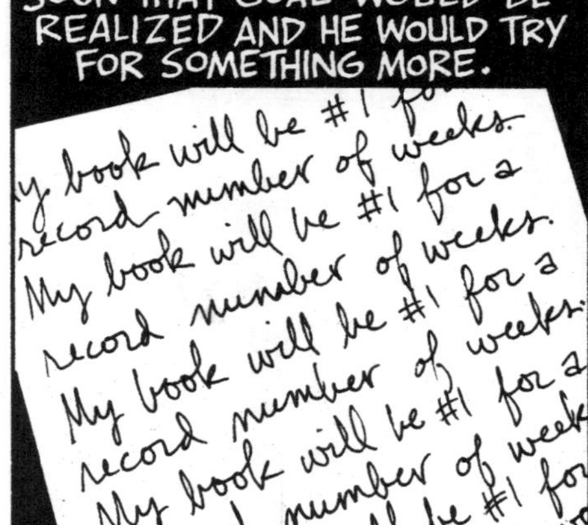
SOON THAT GOAL WOULD BE REALIZED AND HE WOULD TRY FOR SOMETHING MORE.
record number of weeks.
My book will be #1 for a
record number of weeks.
My book will be #1 for a
record number of weeks.
My book will be #1 for a

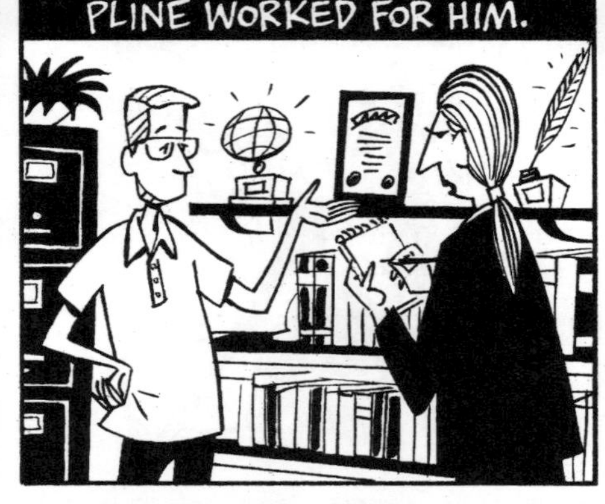
HE GAVE THE REPORTER SEVERAL EXAMPLES OF HOW THIS DISCIPLINE WORKED FOR HIM.

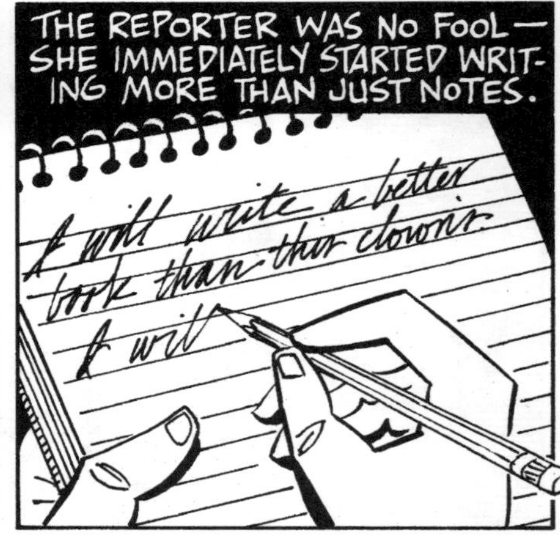
THE REPORTER WAS NO FOOL— SHE IMMEDIATELY STARTED WRITING MORE THAN JUST NOTES.
I will write a better
book than this clown's
I wil

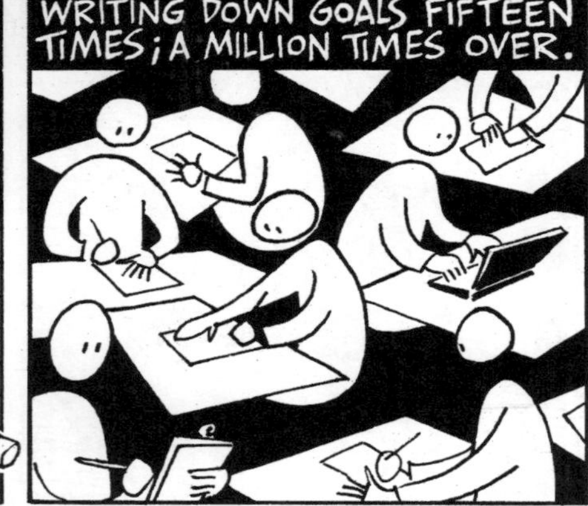
HER READERS DID LIKEWISE, WRITING DOWN GOALS FIFTEEN TIMES; A MILLION TIMES OVER.

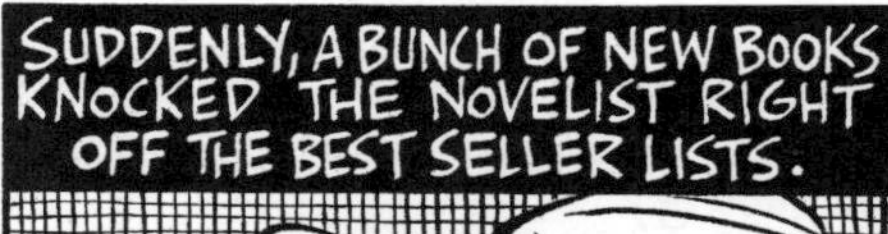
SUDDENLY, A BUNCH OF NEW BOOKS KNOCKED THE NOVELIST RIGHT OFF THE BEST SELLER LISTS.

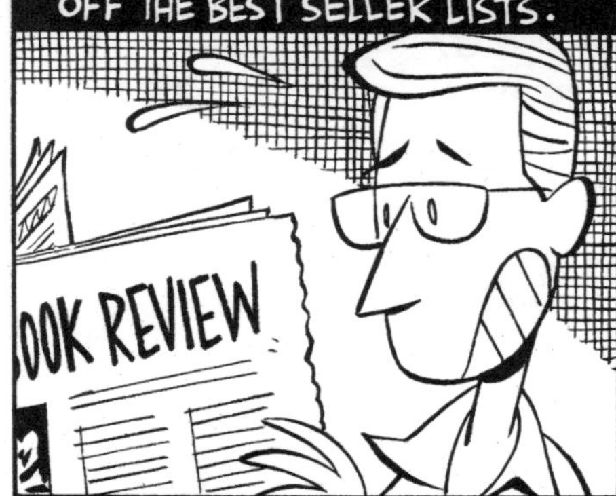
OOK REVIEW

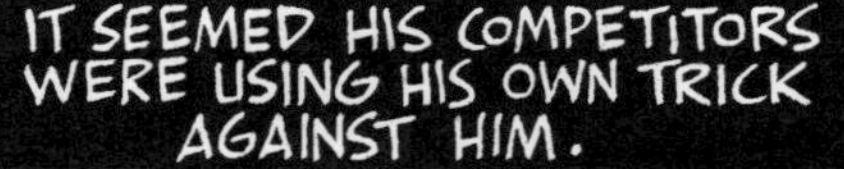
IT SEEMED HIS COMPETITORS WERE USING HIS OWN TRICK AGAINST HIM.

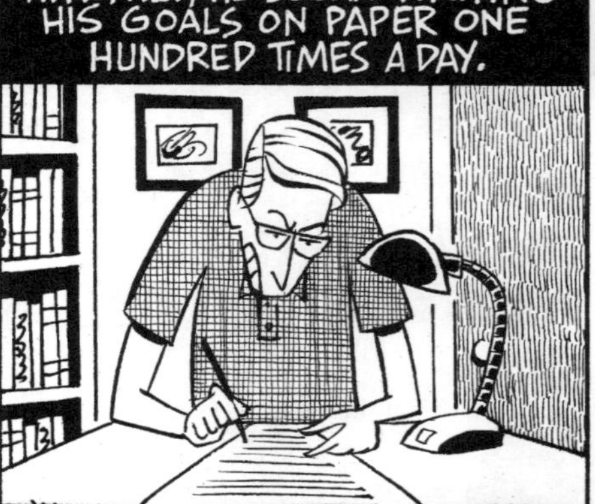
UNDAUNTED, HE BEGAN WRITING HIS GOALS ON PAPER ONE HUNDRED TIMES A DAY.

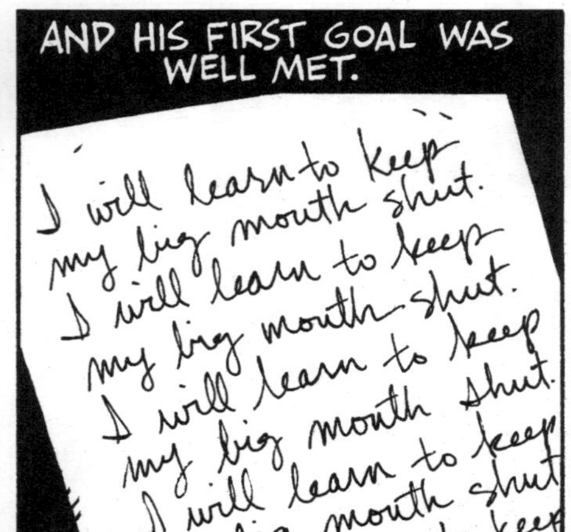
AND HIS FIRST GOAL WAS WELL MET.
I will learn to keep
my big mouth shut.
I will learn to keep
my big mouth shut.
I will learn to keep
my big mouth shut.
I will learn to keep

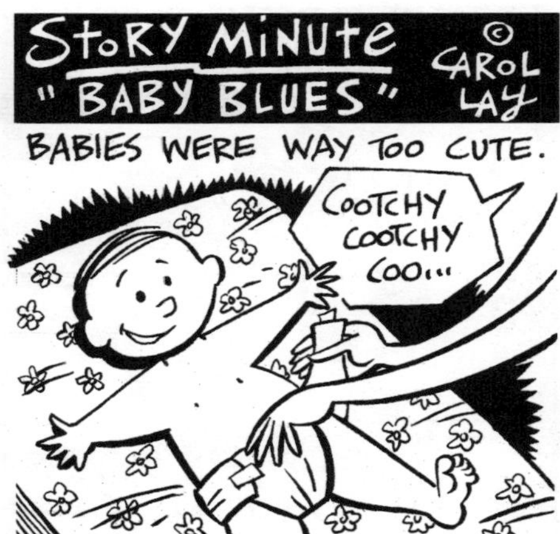
STORY MINUTE
"BABY BLUES"
© CAROL LAY
BABIES WERE WAY TOO CUTE.
COOTCHY COOTCHY COO...

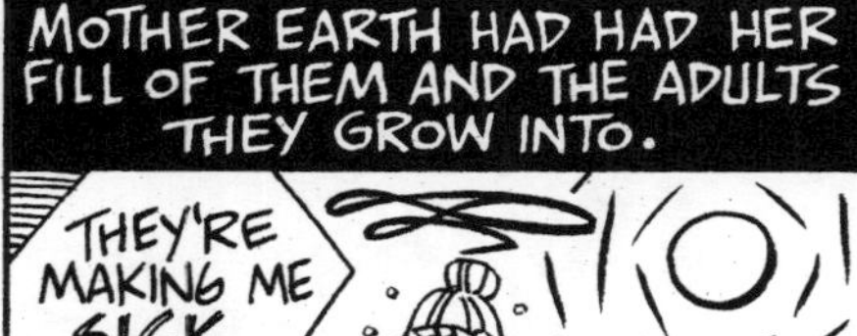
MOTHER EARTH HAD HAD HER FILL OF THEM AND THE ADULTS THEY GROW INTO.

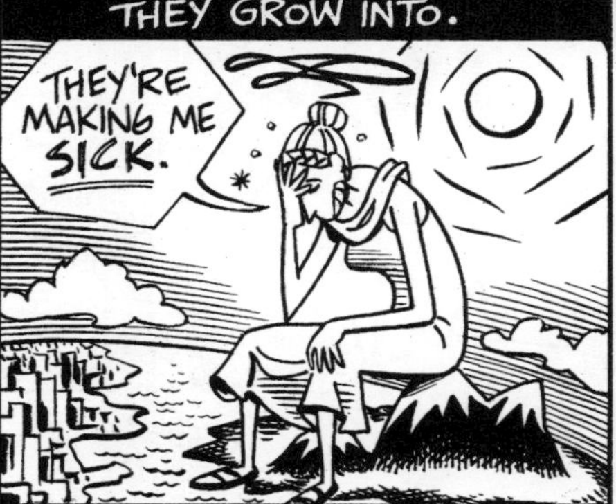
THEY'RE MAKING ME SICK.

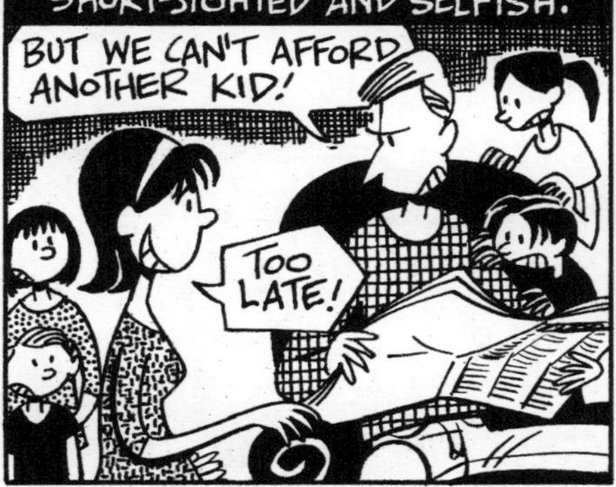
THE ADULTS KEPT BREEDING BECAUSE THEY WERE EXTREMELY SHORT-SIGHTED AND SELFISH.
BUT WE CAN'T AFFORD ANOTHER KID!
TOO LATE!

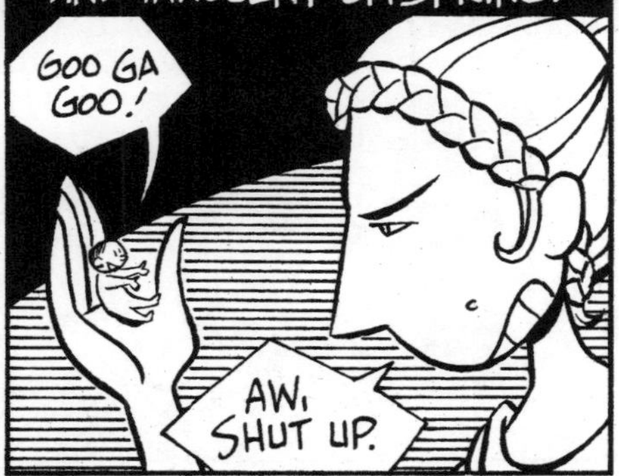
MS. NATURE DECIDED TO ATTACK THEM THROUGH THEIR CUTE AND INNOCENT OFFSPRING.
GOO GA GOO!
AW, SHUT UP.

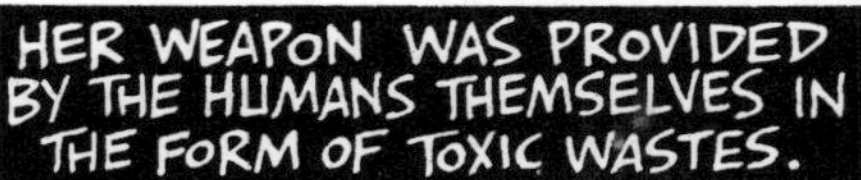
HER WEAPON WAS PROVIDED BY THE HUMANS THEMSELVES IN THE FORM OF TOXIC WASTES.

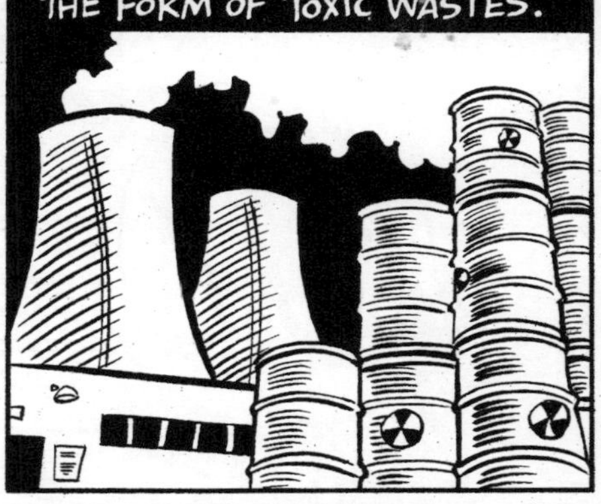

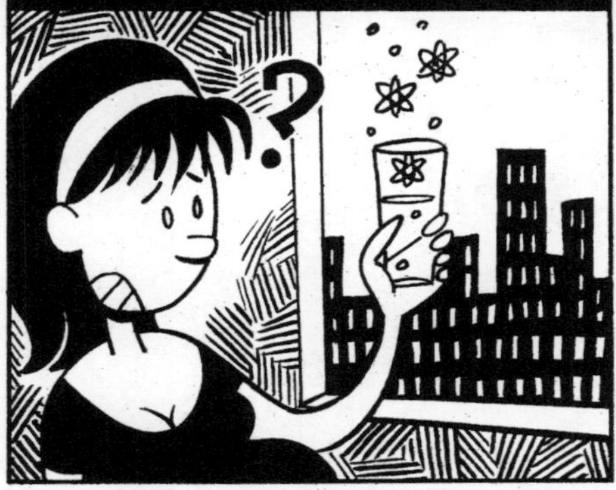
SHE MANEUVERED THEM THROUGH EARTH, AIR, AND WATER TO ALL OF HER TWO-LEGGED TARGETS.
?

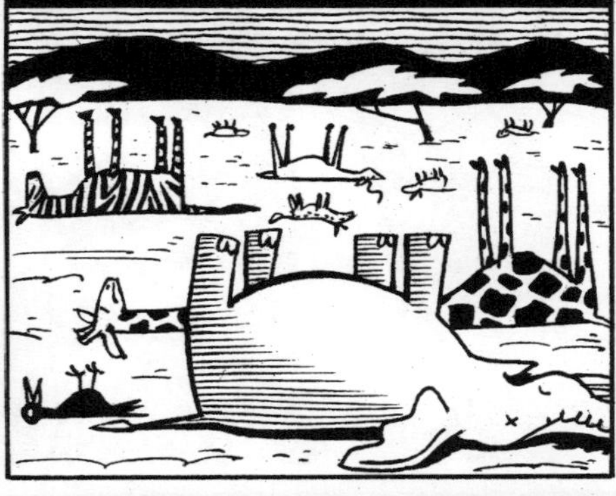
OTHER SPECIES DIED IN THE PROCESS, BUT THEY WERE NEC-ESSARY CASUALTIES OF WAR.

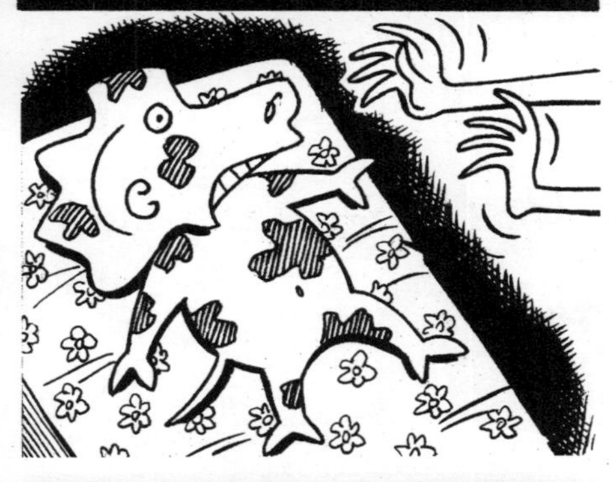
BABIES WERE SOON BORN AS MONSTERS — WHICH SHOULD HAVE STOPPED THEM.

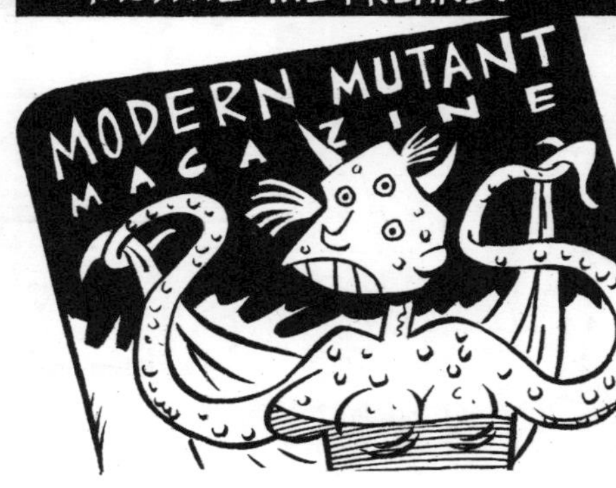
BUT STANDARDS OF BEAUTY MERELY CHANGED TO ACCOM-MODATE THE FREAKS.
MODERN MUTANT MAGAZINE

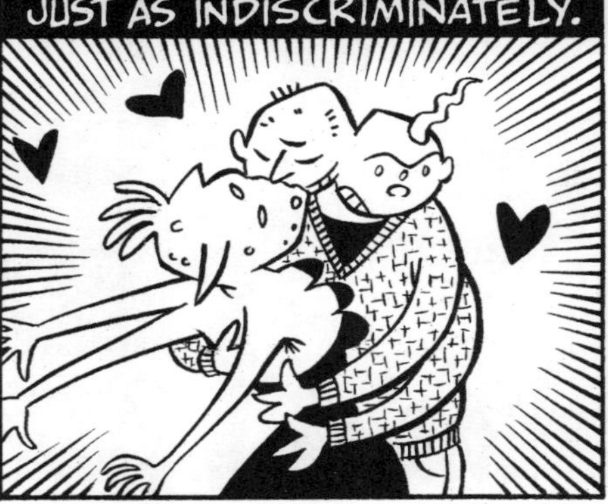
A NEW GENERATION OF MON-STER TEENS TRIED TO BREED, JUST AS INDISCRIMINATELY.

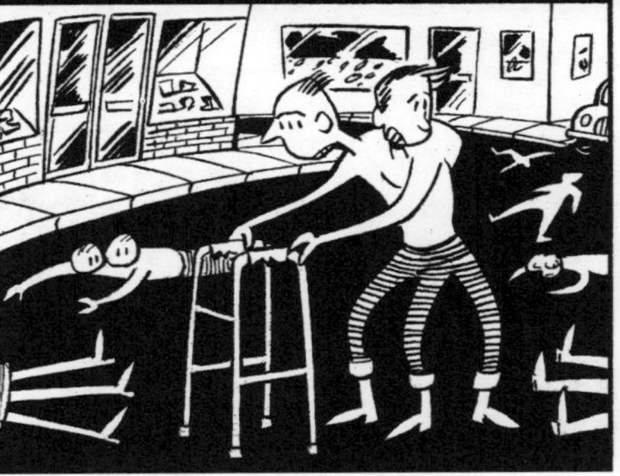
BUT THE TOXINS THEY HAD GIVEN TO NATURE HAD STERILIZED THEM SO HUMANS EVENTUALLY DIED OUT.

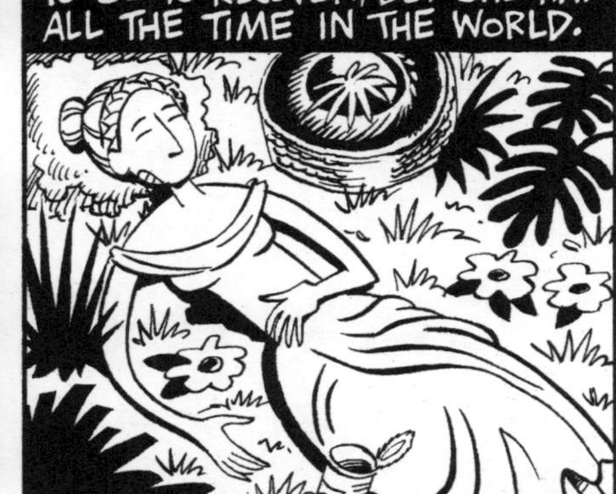
THE EARTH HAD A LONG WAY TO GO TO RECOVER, BUT SHE HAD ALL THE TIME IN THE WORLD.

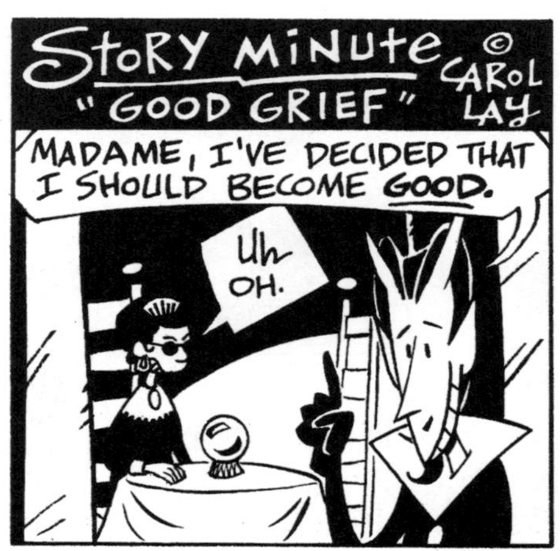
STORY MINUTE © CAROL LAY
"GOOD GRIEF"
MADAME, I'VE DECIDED THAT I SHOULD BECOME GOOD.
Uh OH.

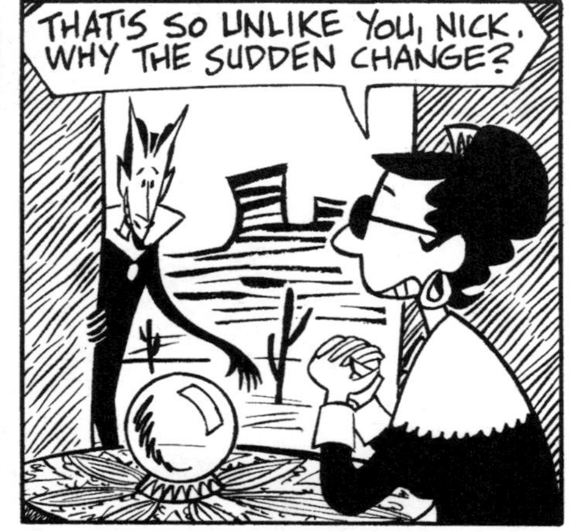
THAT'S SO UNLIKE YOU, NICK. WHY THE SUDDEN CHANGE?

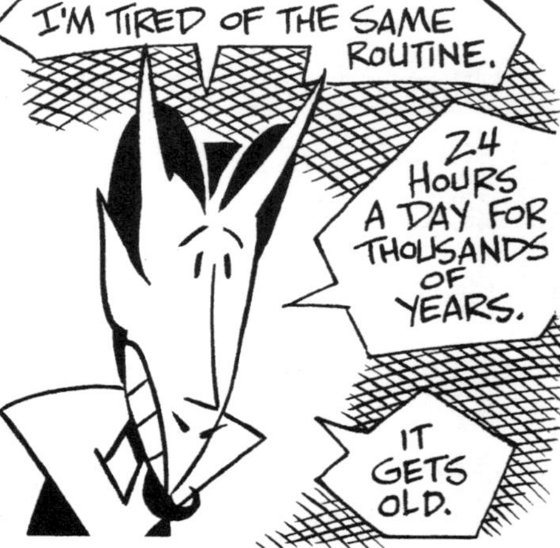
I'M TIRED OF THE SAME ROUTINE.
24 HOURS A DAY FOR THOUSANDS OF YEARS.
IT GETS OLD.

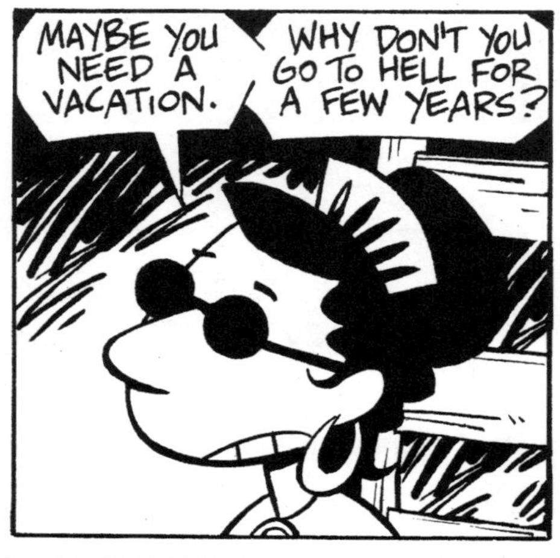
MAYBE YOU NEED A VACATION.
WHY DON'T YOU GO TO HELL FOR A FEW YEARS?

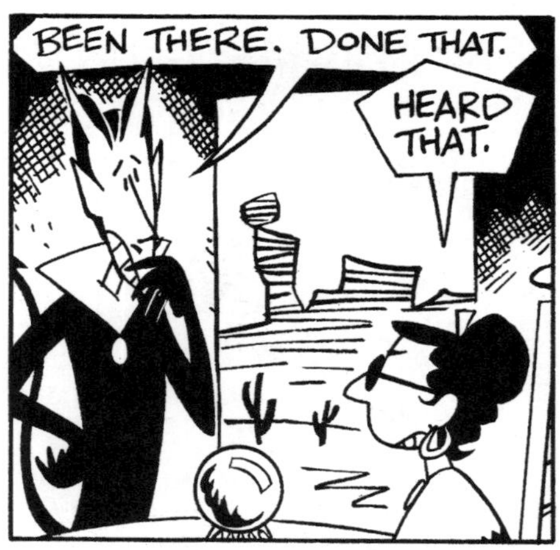
BEEN THERE. DONE THAT.
HEARD THAT.

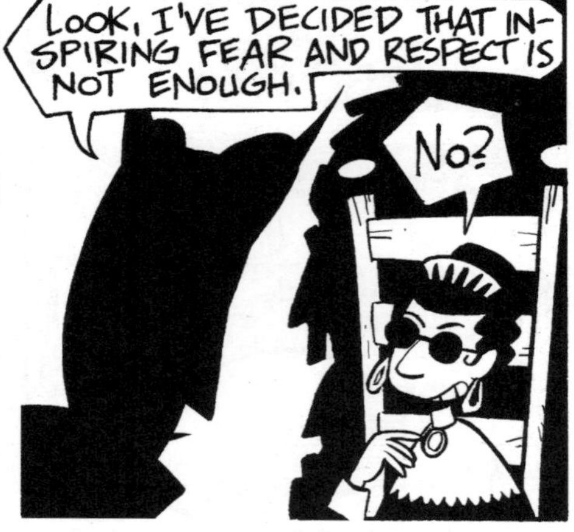
LOOK, I'VE DECIDED THAT INSPIRING FEAR AND RESPECT IS NOT ENOUGH.
No?

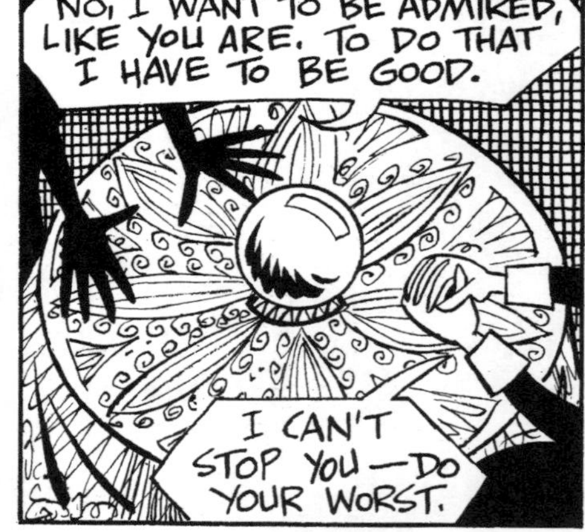
NO, I WANT TO BE ADMIRED, LIKE YOU ARE. TO DO THAT I HAVE TO BE GOOD.
I CAN'T STOP YOU—DO YOUR WORST.

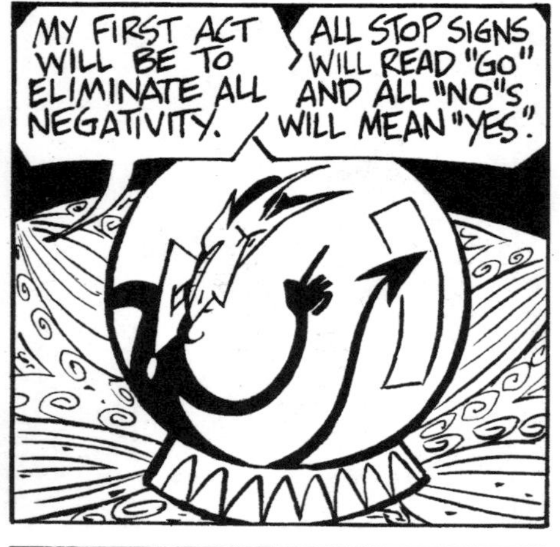
MY FIRST ACT WILL BE TO ELIMINATE ALL NEGATIVITY.
ALL STOP SIGNS WILL READ "GO" AND ALL "NO"S WILL MEAN "YES".

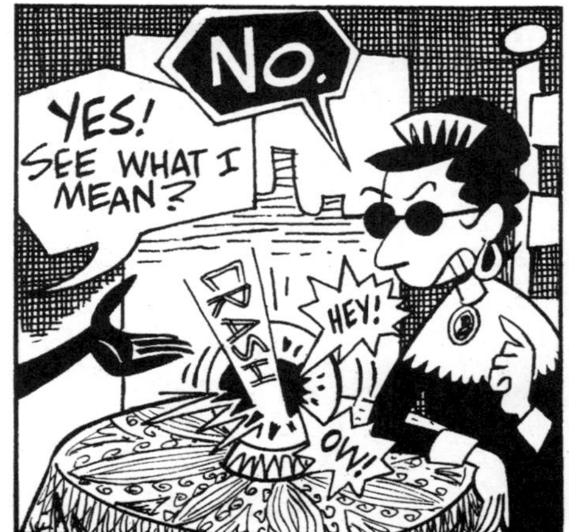
NO.
YES! SEE WHAT I MEAN?
CRASH
HEY!
OW!

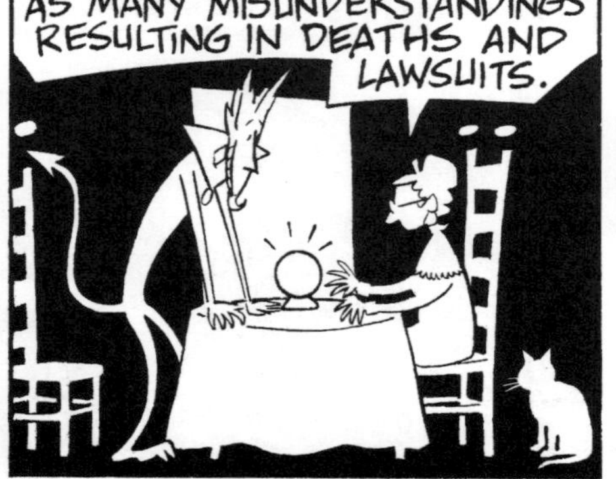
YOU'VE JUST CAUSED 582,643 TRAFFIC ACCIDENTS AND TWICE AS MANY MISUNDERSTANDINGS RESULTING IN DEATHS AND LAWSUITS.

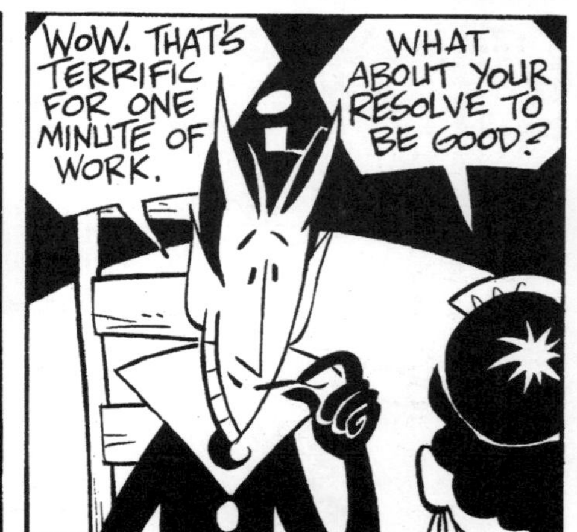
WOW. THAT'S TERRIFIC FOR ONE MINUTE OF WORK.
WHAT ABOUT YOUR RESOLVE TO BE GOOD?

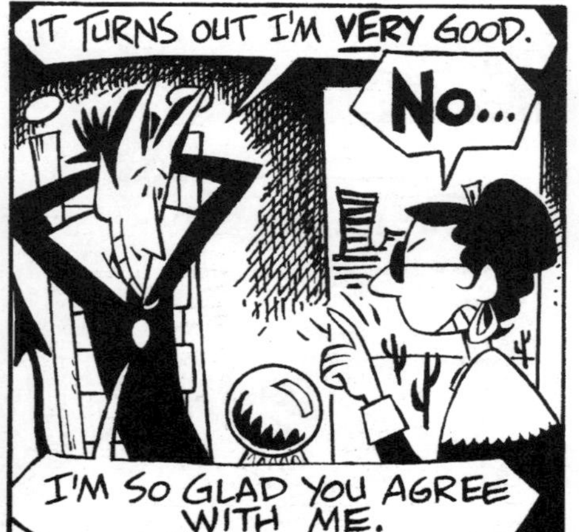
IT TURNS OUT I'M VERY GOOD.
NO...
I'M SO GLAD YOU AGREE WITH ME.

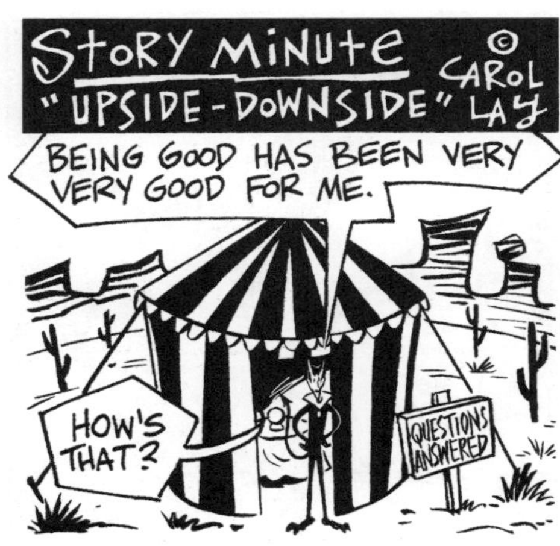
STORY MINUTE © CAROL LAY
"UPSIDE-DOWNSIDE"
BEING GOOD HAS BEEN VERY VERY GOOD FOR ME.
HOW'S THAT?
QUESTIONS ANSWERED

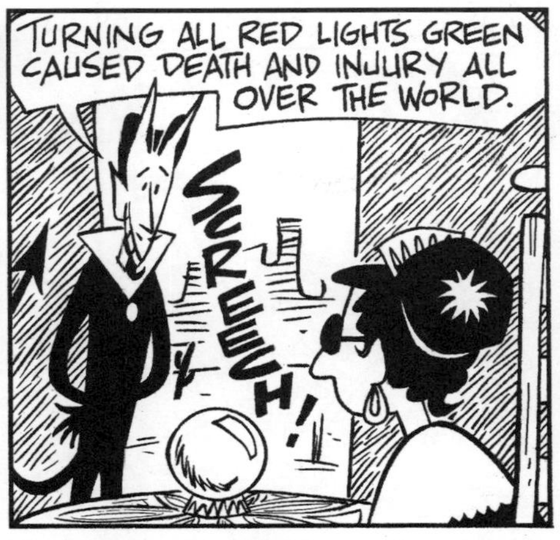
TURNING ALL RED LIGHTS GREEN CAUSED DEATH AND INJURY ALL OVER THE WORLD.
SCREECH!

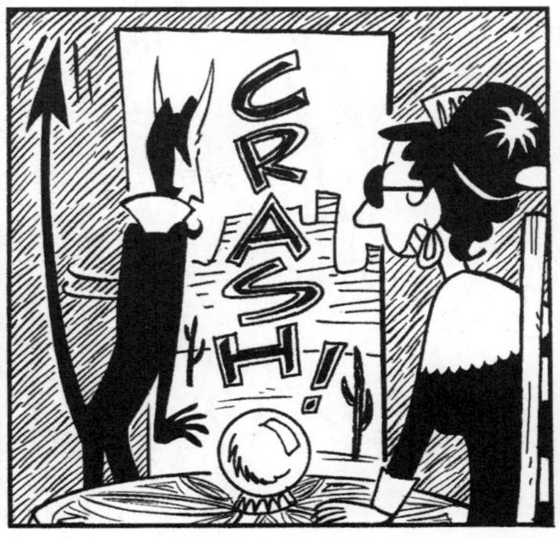
CRASH!

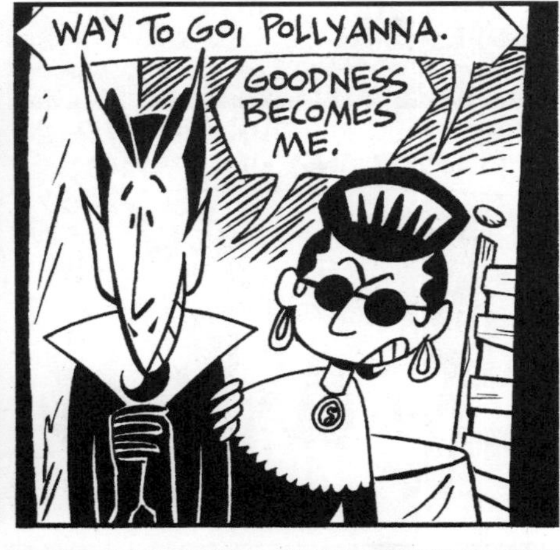
WAY TO GO, POLLYANNA.
GOODNESS BECOMES ME.

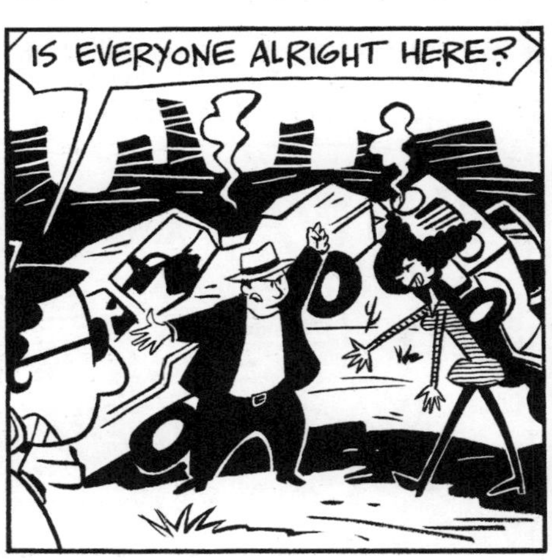
IS EVERYONE ALRIGHT HERE?

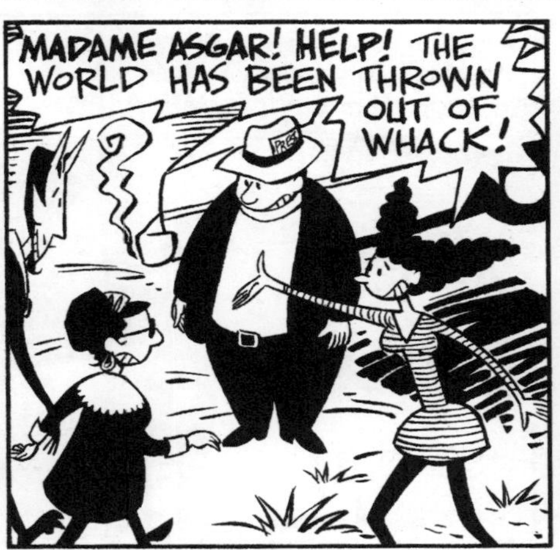
MADAME ASGAR! HELP! THE WORLD HAS BEEN THROWN OUT OF WHACK!
PRESS

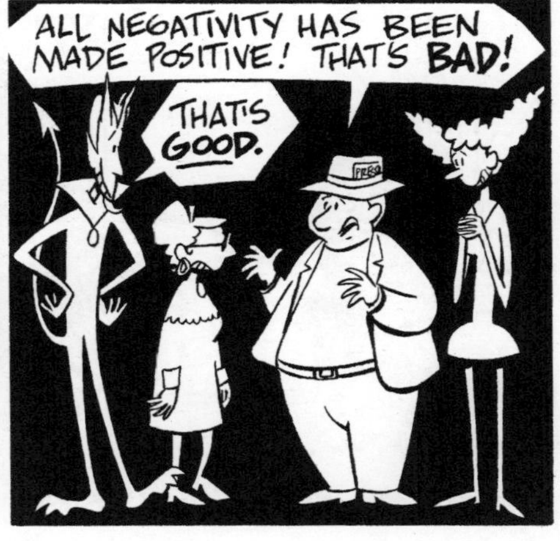
ALL NEGATIVITY HAS BEEN MADE POSITIVE! THAT'S BAD!
THAT'S GOOD.

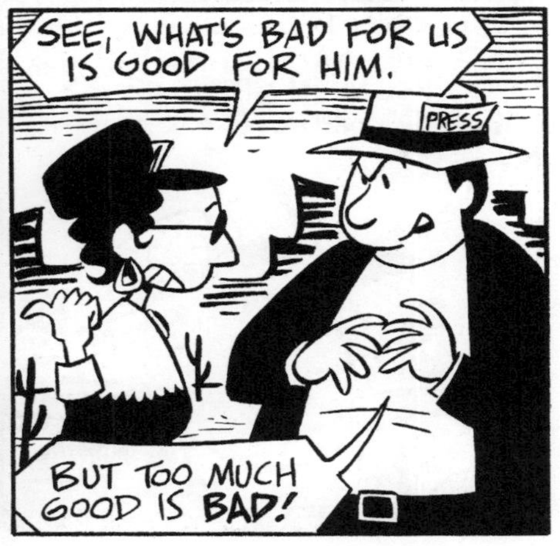
SEE, WHAT'S BAD FOR US IS GOOD FOR HIM.
PRESS
BUT TOO MUCH GOOD IS BAD!

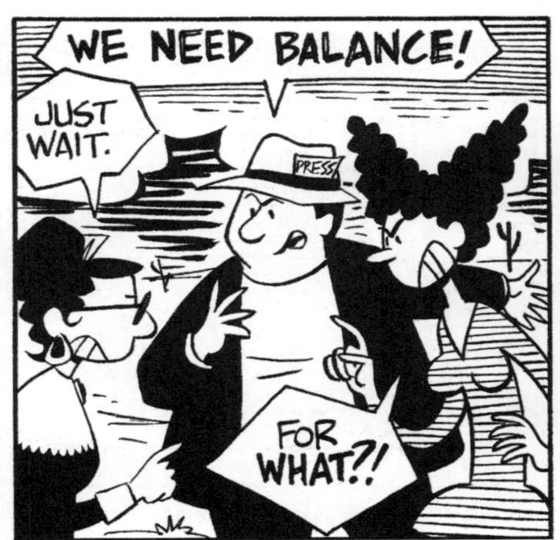
WE NEED BALANCE!
JUST WAIT.
PRESS
FOR WHAT?!

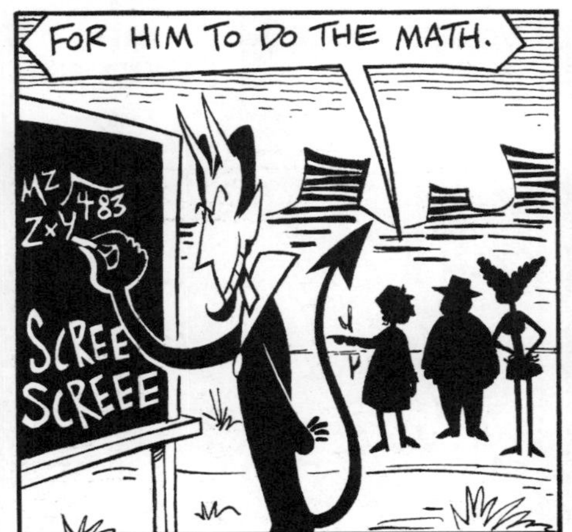
FOR HIM TO DO THE MATH.
SCREE SCREEE

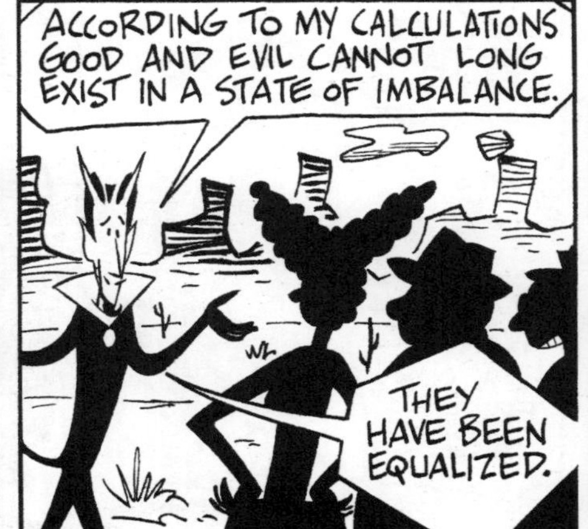
ACCORDING TO MY CALCULATIONS GOOD AND EVIL CANNOT LONG EXIST IN A STATE OF IMBALANCE.
THEY HAVE BEEN EQUALIZED.

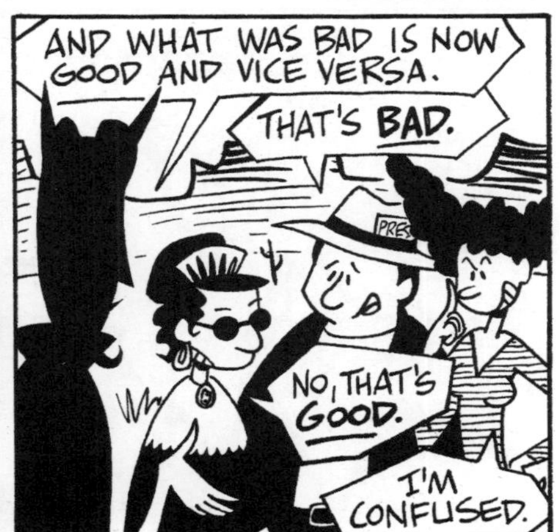
AND WHAT WAS BAD IS NOW GOOD AND VICE VERSA.
THAT'S BAD.
NO, THAT'S GOOD.
I'M CONFUSED.

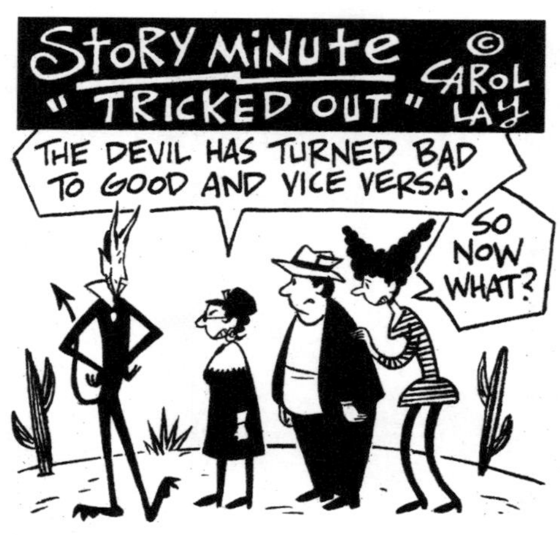
STORY MINUTE © CAROL LAY
"TRICKED OUT"
THE DEVIL HAS TURNED BAD TO GOOD AND VICE VERSA.
SO NOW WHAT?

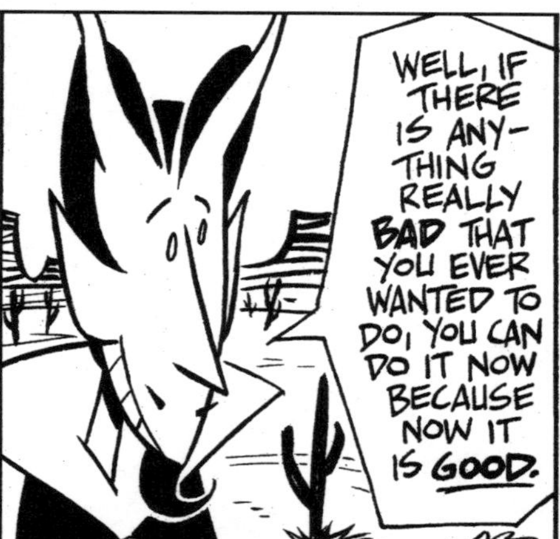
WELL, IF THERE IS ANY-THING REALLY BAD THAT YOU EVER WANTED TO DO, YOU CAN DO IT NOW BECAUSE NOW IT IS GOOD.

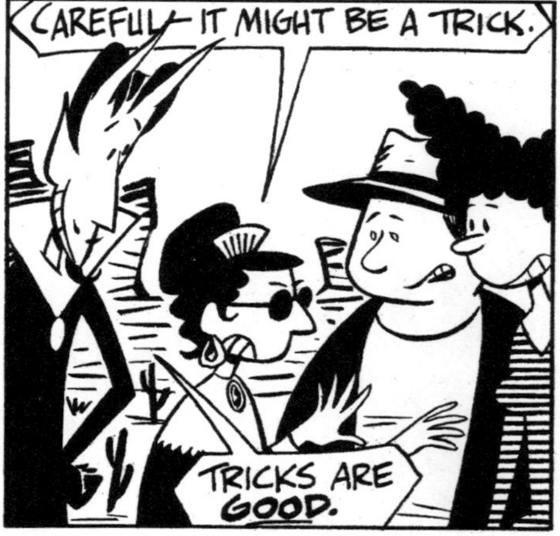
CAREFUL-- IT MIGHT BE A TRICK.
TRICKS ARE GOOD.

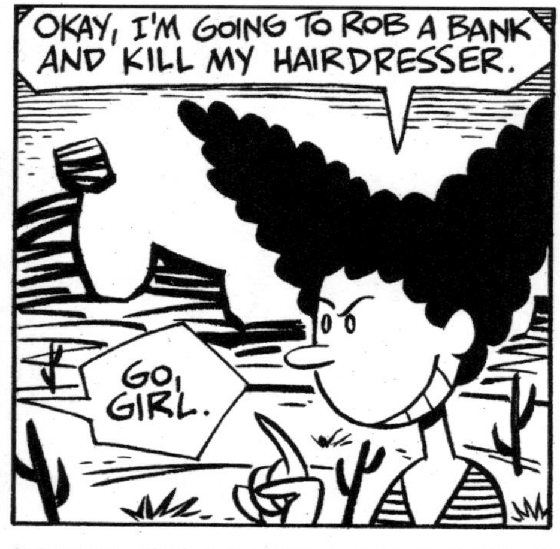
OKAY, I'M GOING TO ROB A BANK AND KILL MY HAIRDRESSER.
GO, GIRL.

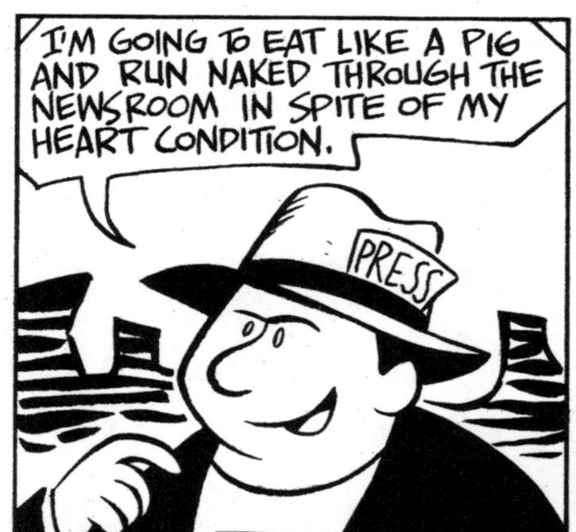
I'M GOING TO EAT LIKE A PIG AND RUN NAKED THROUGH THE NEWSROOM IN SPITE OF MY HEART CONDITION.
PRESS

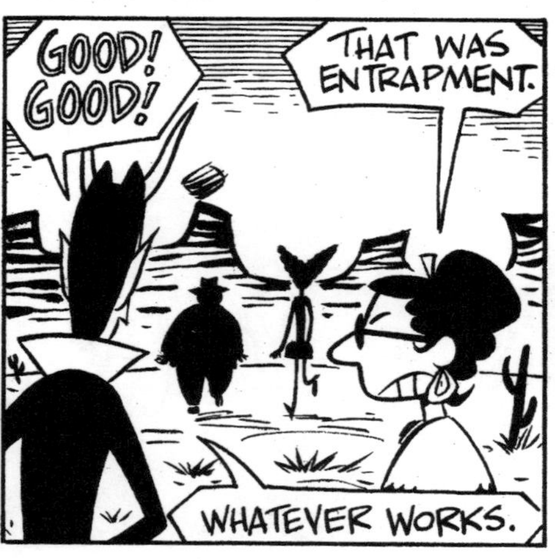
GOOD! GOOD!
THAT WAS ENTRAPMENT.
WHATEVER WORKS.

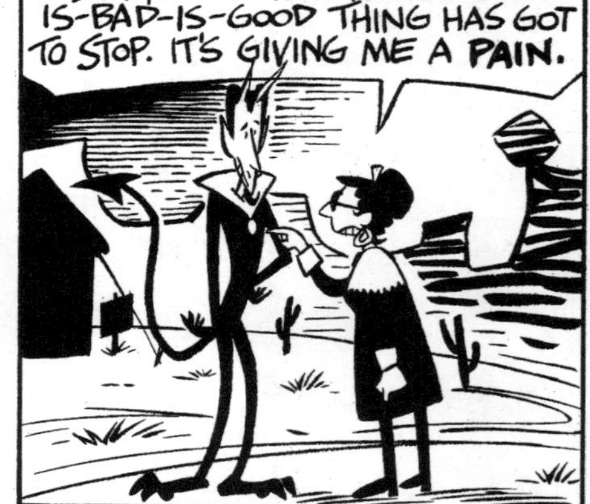
LISTEN, NICK. THIS WHOLE GOOD-IS-BAD-IS-GOOD THING HAS GOT TO STOP. IT'S GIVING ME A PAIN.

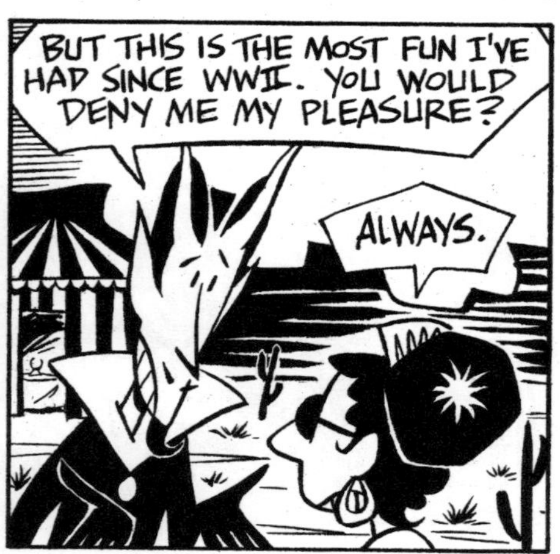
BUT THIS IS THE MOST FUN I'VE HAD SINCE WWII. YOU WOULD DENY ME MY PLEASURE?
ALWAYS.

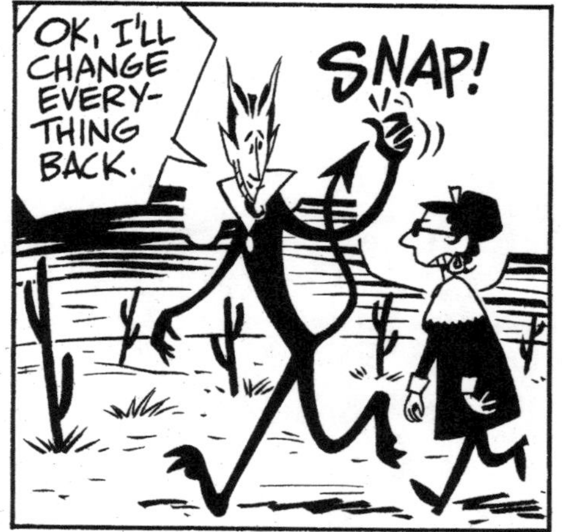
OK, I'LL CHANGE EVERY-THING BACK.
SNAP!

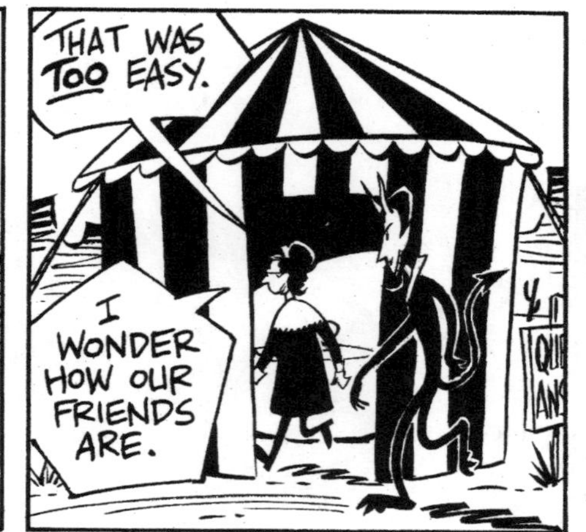
THAT WAS TOO EASY.
I WONDER HOW OUR FRIENDS ARE.

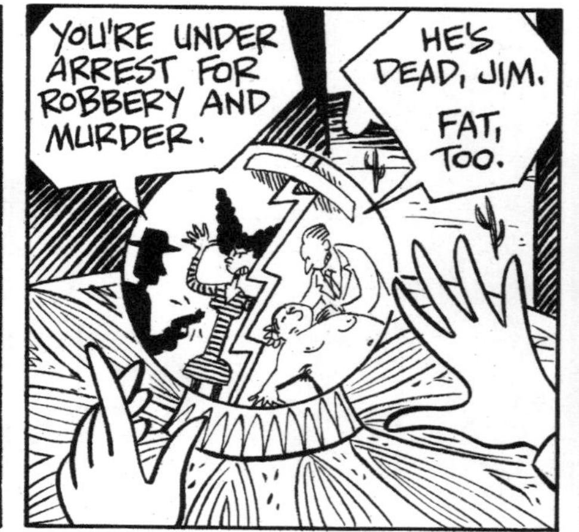
YOU'RE UNDER ARREST FOR ROBBERY AND MURDER.
HE'S DEAD, JIM.
FAT, TOO.

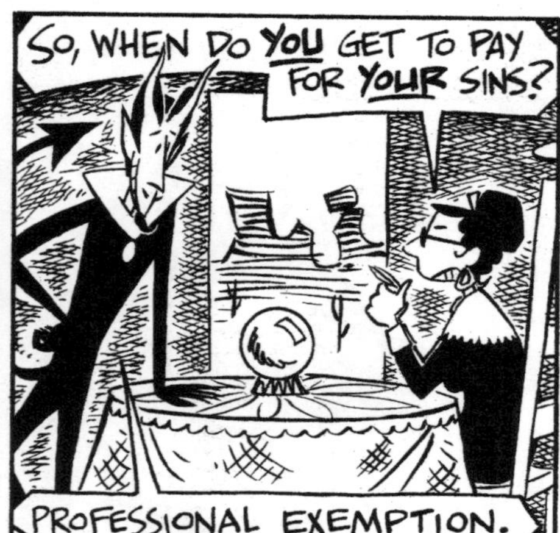
SO, WHEN DO YOU GET TO PAY FOR YOUR SINS?
PROFESSIONAL EXEMPTION.

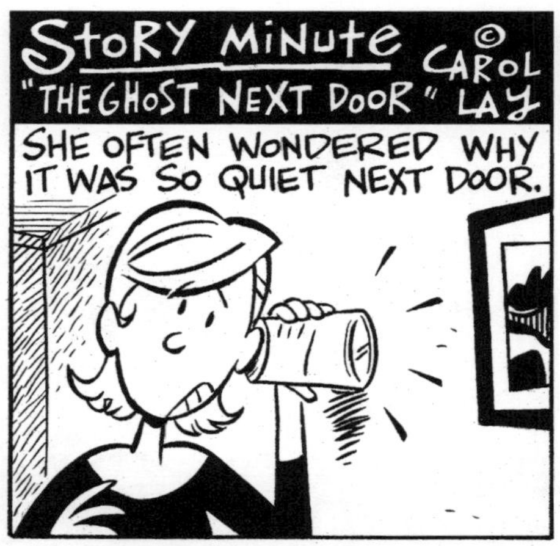
STORY MINUTE
© CAROL LAY
"THE GHOST NEXT DOOR"
SHE OFTEN WONDERED WHY IT WAS SO QUIET NEXT DOOR.

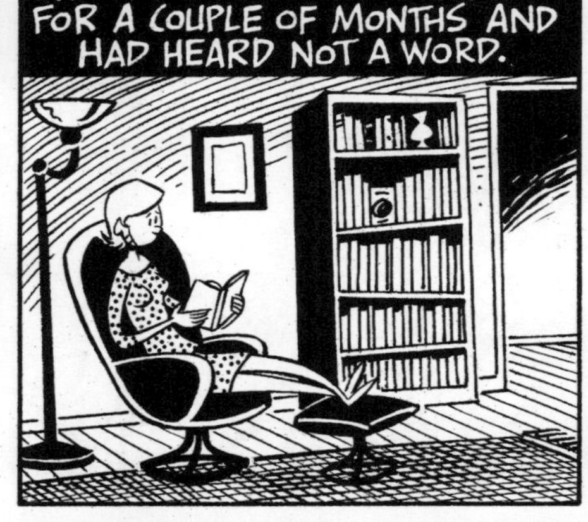
SHE'D LIVED IN THE BUILDING FOR A COUPLE OF MONTHS AND HAD HEARD NOT A WORD.

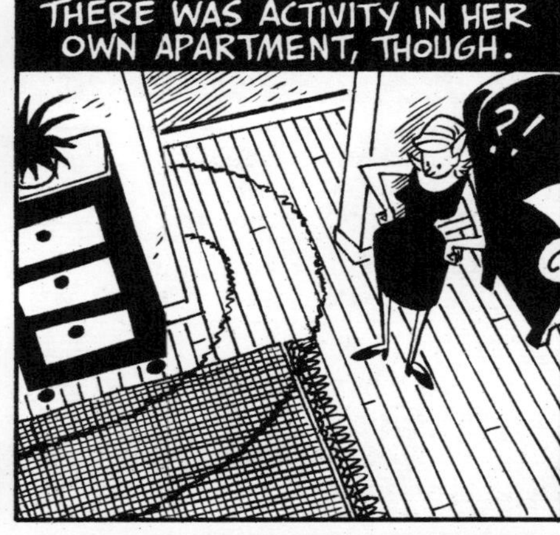
THERE WAS ACTIVITY IN HER OWN APARTMENT, THOUGH.
?!

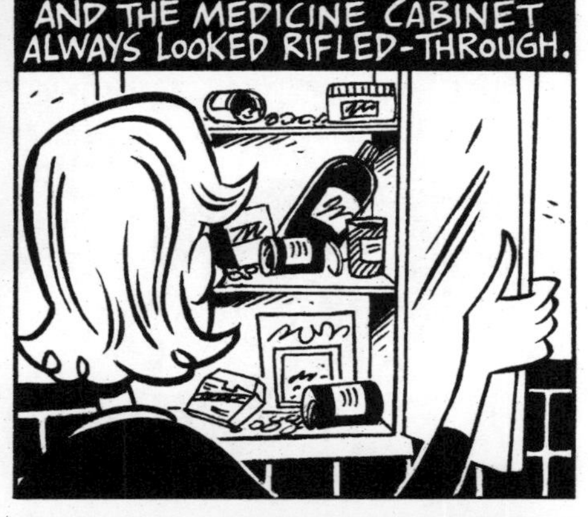
DOORS OPENED FOR NO REASON AND THE MEDICINE CABINET ALWAYS LOOKED RIFLED-THROUGH.

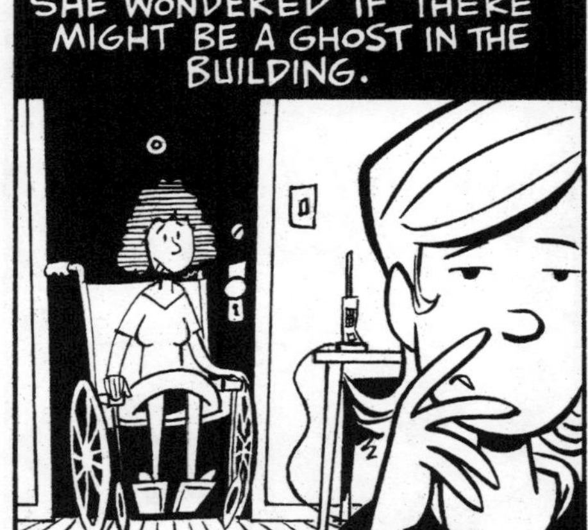
SHE WONDERED IF THERE MIGHT BE A GHOST IN THE BUILDING.

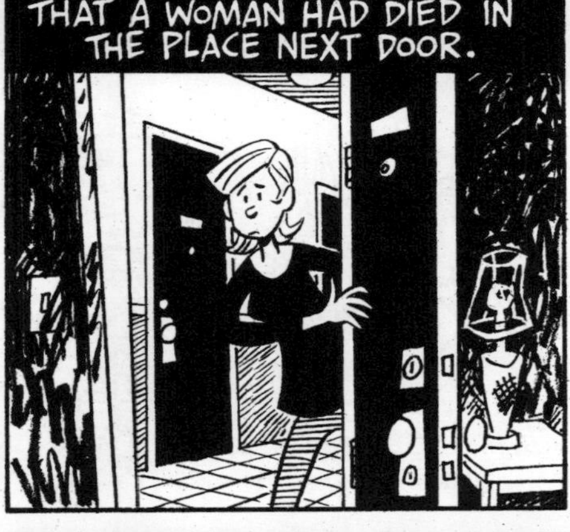
THE NEXT DAY SHE LEARNED THAT A WOMAN HAD DIED IN THE PLACE NEXT DOOR.

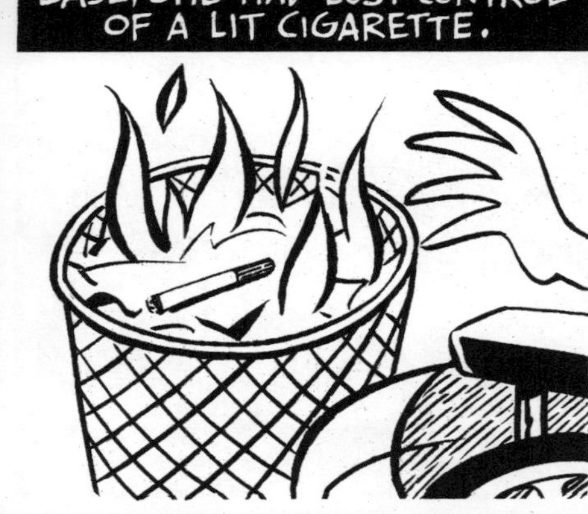
A VICTIM OF A MUSCULAR DIS-EASE, SHE HAD LOST CONTROL OF A LIT CIGARETTE.

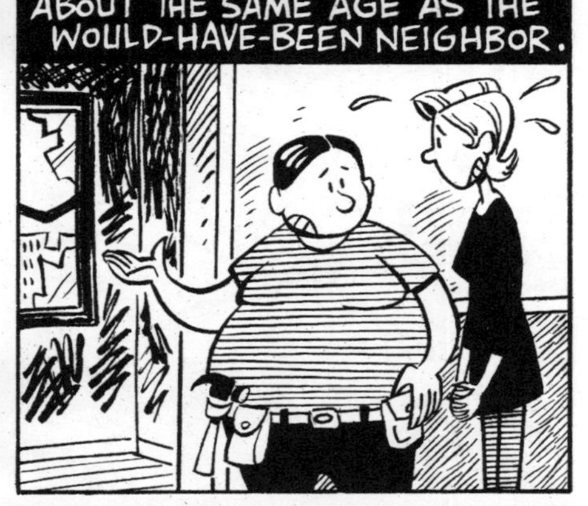
SHE HAD BEEN A PROFESSIONAL, ABOUT THE SAME AGE AS THE WOULD-HAVE-BEEN NEIGHBOR.

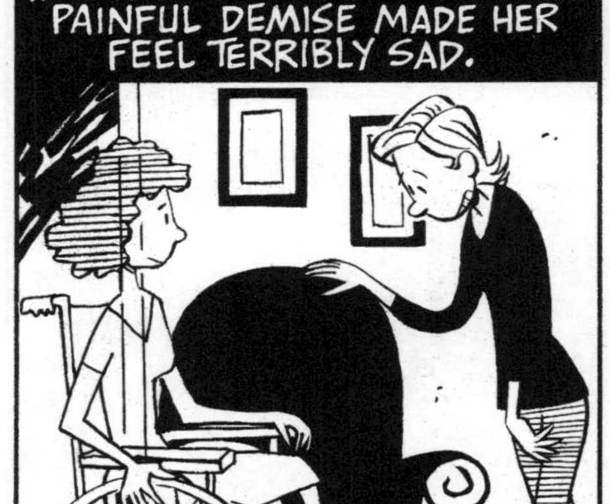
IMAGINING THE POOR WOMAN'S PAINFUL DEMISE MADE HER FEEL TERRIBLY SAD.

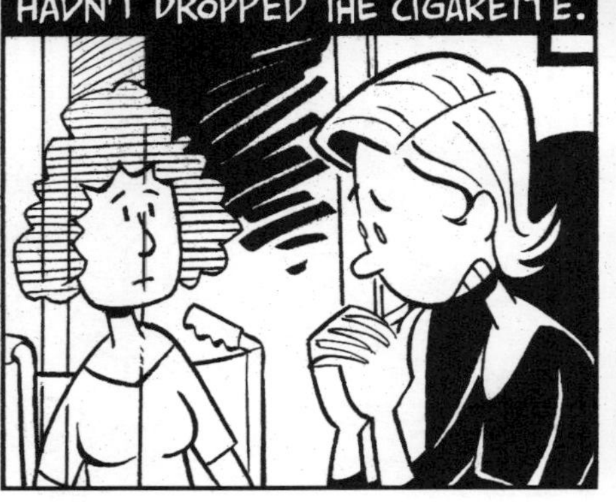
AFTER ALL, THEY MIGHT HAVE BECOME FRIENDS IF THE WOMAN HADN'T DROPPED THE CIGARETTE.

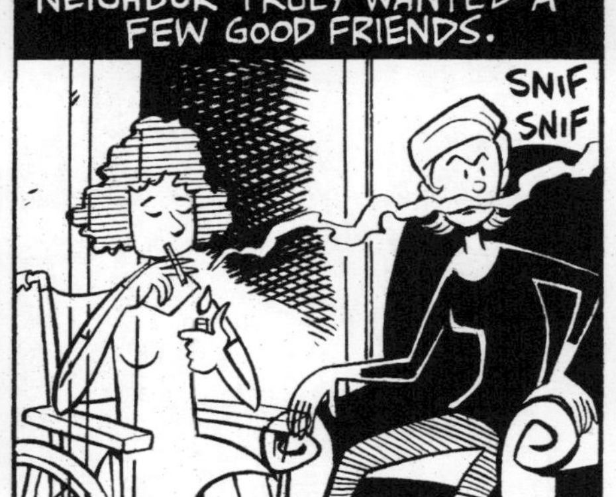
AND, NEW IN TOWN, THE ALMOST-NEIGHBOR TRULY WANTED A FEW GOOD FRIENDS.
SNIF
SNIF

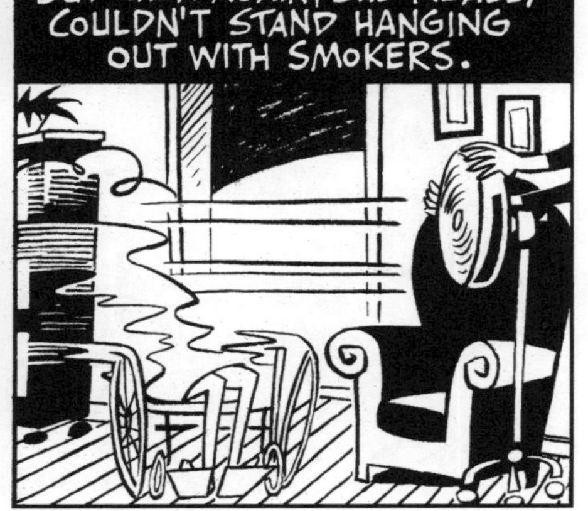
BUT THEN AGAIN, SHE REALLY COULDN'T STAND HANGING OUT WITH SMOKERS.

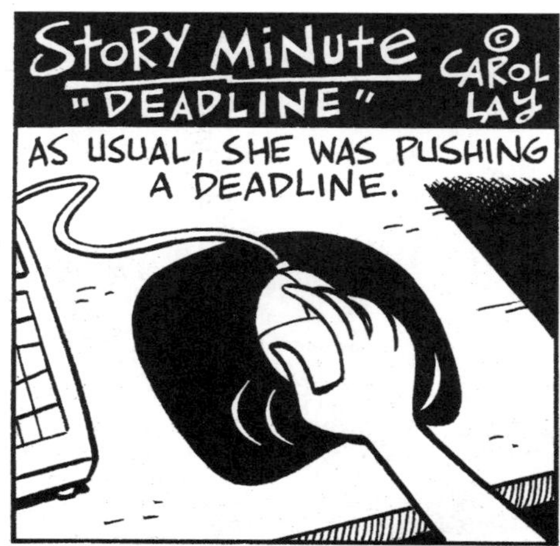
STORY MINUTE © CAROL LAY
"DEADLINE"
AS USUAL, SHE WAS PUSHING A DEADLINE.

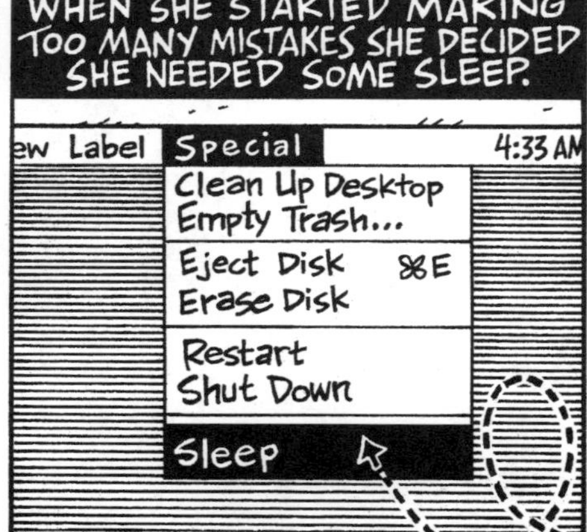
WHEN SHE STARTED MAKING TOO MANY MISTAKES SHE DECIDED SHE NEEDED SOME SLEEP.
ew Label
Special
4:33 AM
Clean Up Desktop
Empty Trash...
Eject Disk ⌘E
Erase Disk
Restart
Shut Down
Sleep

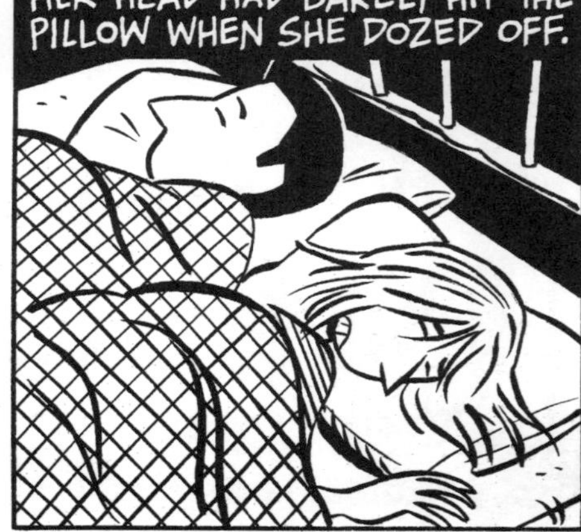
HER HEAD HAD BARELY HIT THE PILLOW WHEN SHE DOZED OFF.

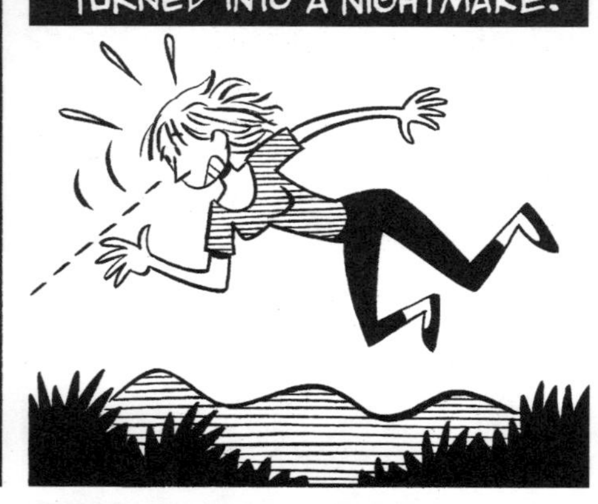
SOON, A PLEASANT DREAM TURNED INTO A NIGHTMARE.

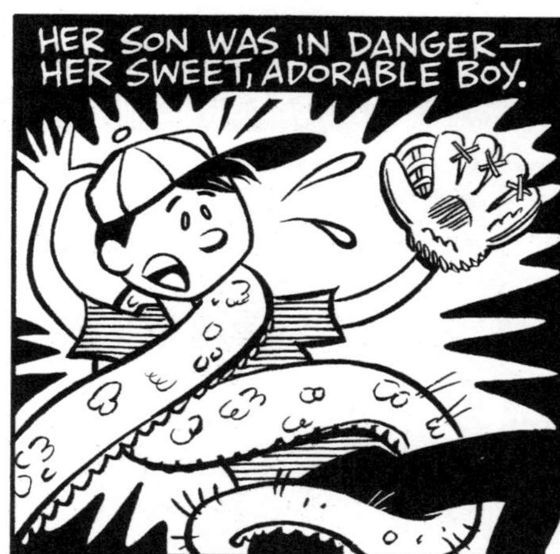
HER SON WAS IN DANGER— HER SWEET, ADORABLE BOY.

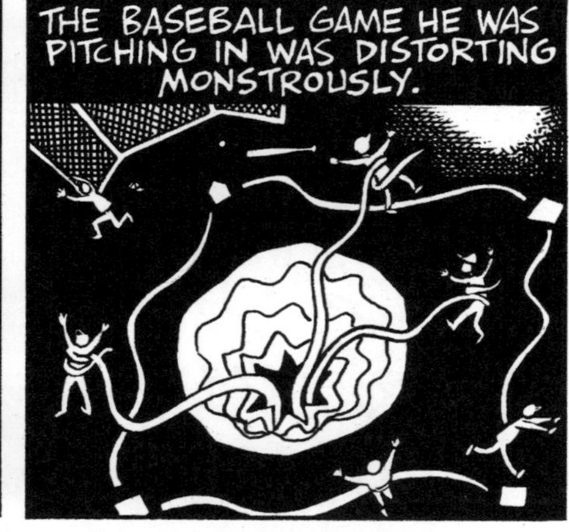
THE BASEBALL GAME HE WAS PITCHING IN WAS DISTORTING MONSTROUSLY.

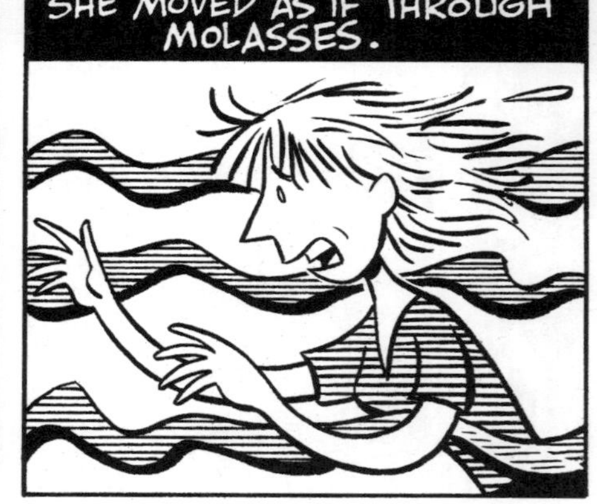
SHE TRIED TO SAVE HIM BUT SHE MOVED AS IF THROUGH MOLASSES.

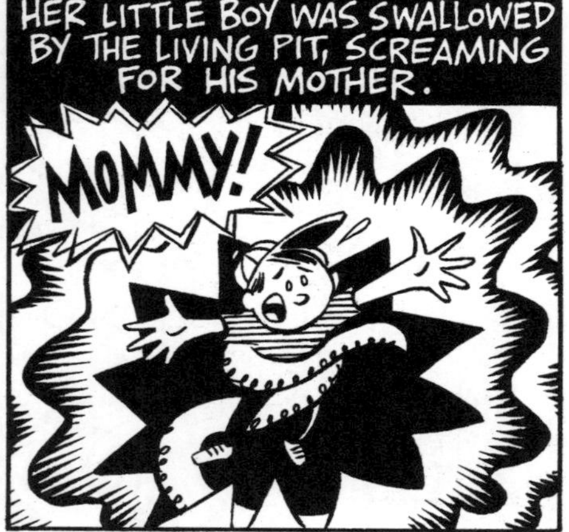
HER LITTLE BOY WAS SWALLOWED BY THE LIVING PIT, SCREAMING FOR HIS MOTHER.
MOMMY!

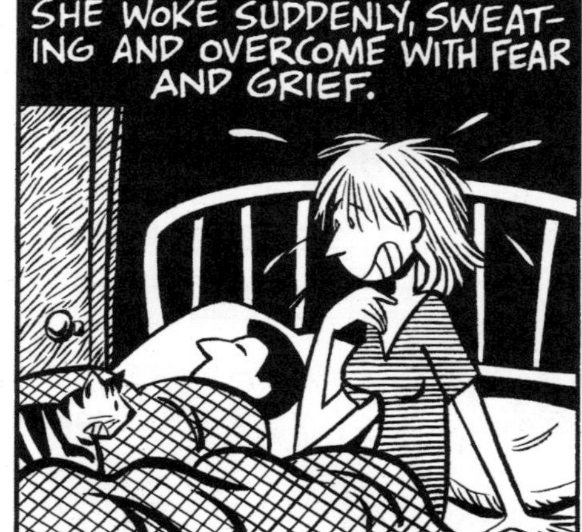
SHE WOKE SUDDENLY, SWEATING AND OVERCOME WITH FEAR AND GRIEF.

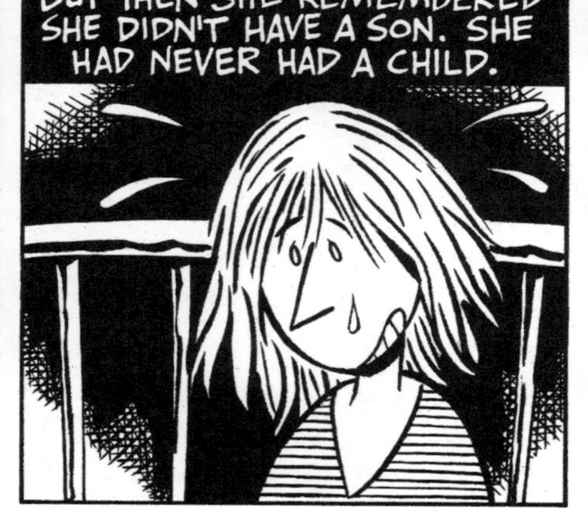
BUT THEN SHE REMEMBERED SHE DIDN'T HAVE A SON. SHE HAD NEVER HAD A CHILD.

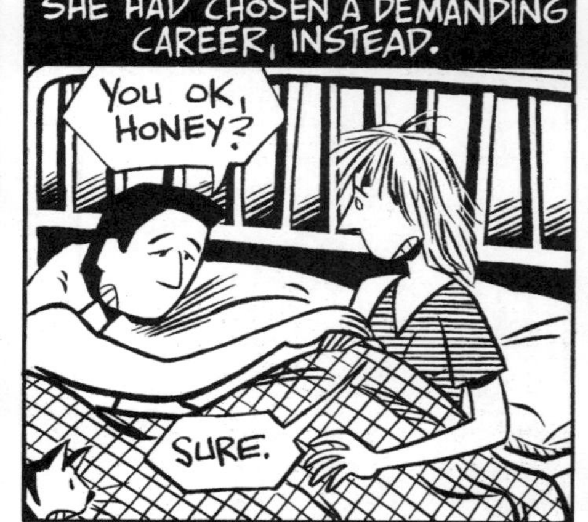
SHE HAD CHOSEN A DEMANDING CAREER, INSTEAD.
YOU OK, HONEY?
SURE.

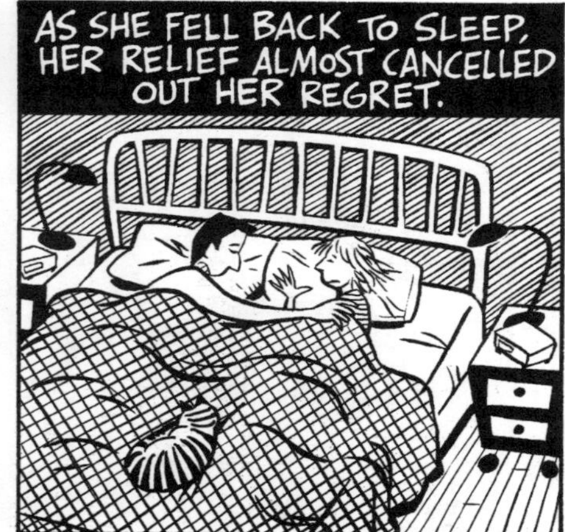
AS SHE FELL BACK TO SLEEP, HER RELIEF ALMOST CANCELLED OUT HER REGRET.

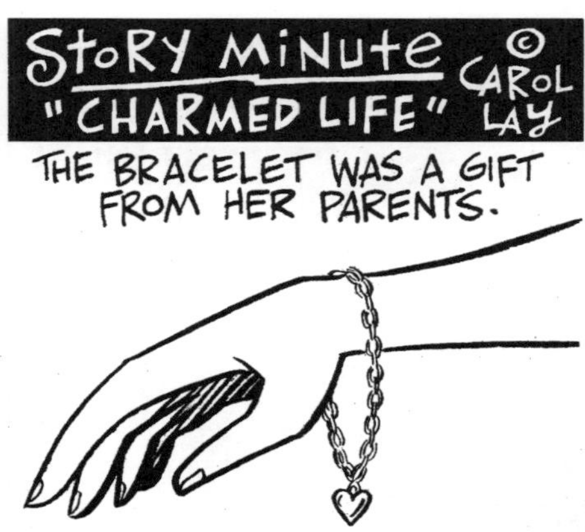
STORY MINUTE © CAROL LAY
"CHARMED LIFE"
THE BRACELET WAS A GIFT FROM HER PARENTS.

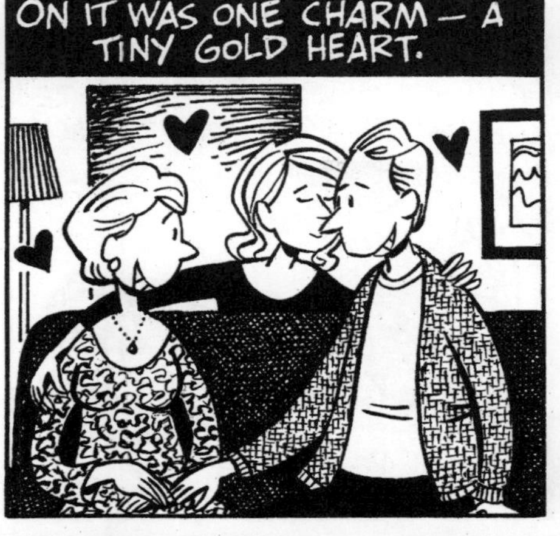
ON IT WAS ONE CHARM — A TINY GOLD HEART.

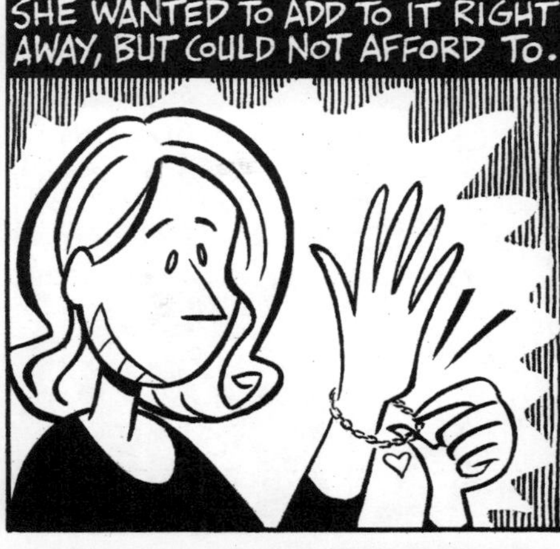
SHE WANTED TO ADD TO IT RIGHT AWAY, BUT COULD NOT AFFORD TO.

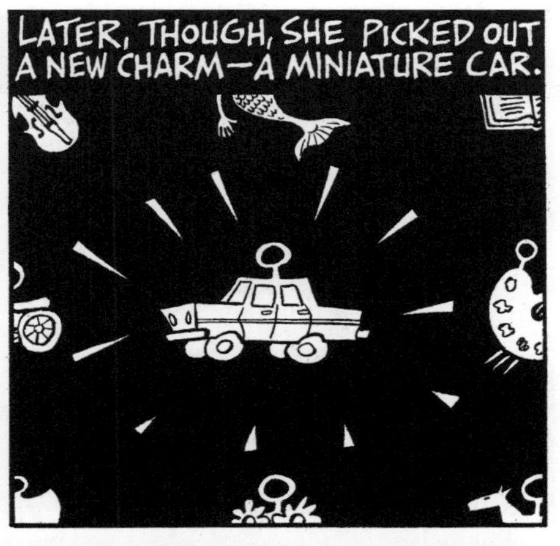
LATER, THOUGH, SHE PICKED OUT A NEW CHARM—A MINIATURE CAR.

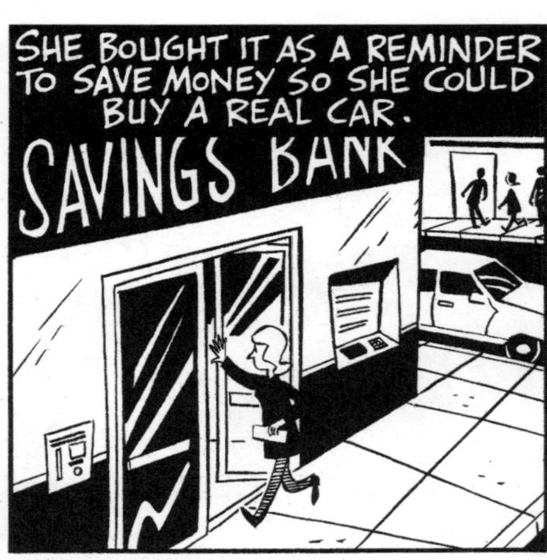
SHE BOUGHT IT AS A REMINDER TO SAVE MONEY SO SHE COULD BUY A REAL CAR.
SAVINGS BANK

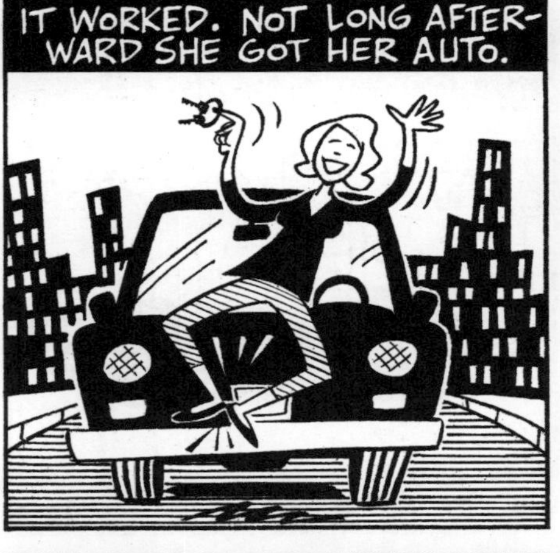
IT WORKED. NOT LONG AFTER-WARD SHE GOT HER AUTO.

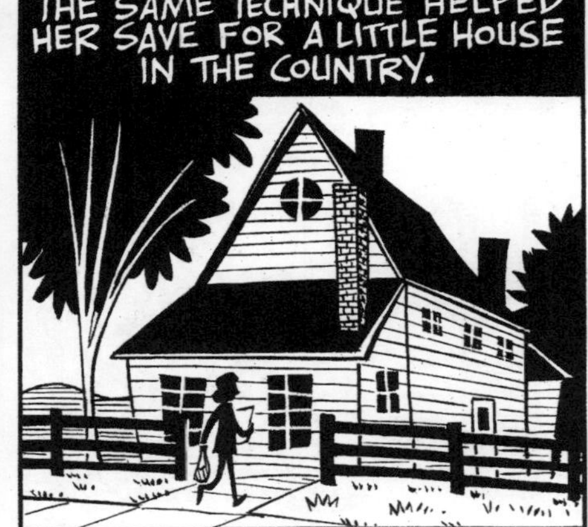
THE SAME TECHNIQUE HELPED HER SAVE FOR A LITTLE HOUSE IN THE COUNTRY.

SKILLS IN VARIOUS PURSUITS WERE ENHANCED WHEN SHE FOCUSED ON SELECTED TOKENS.

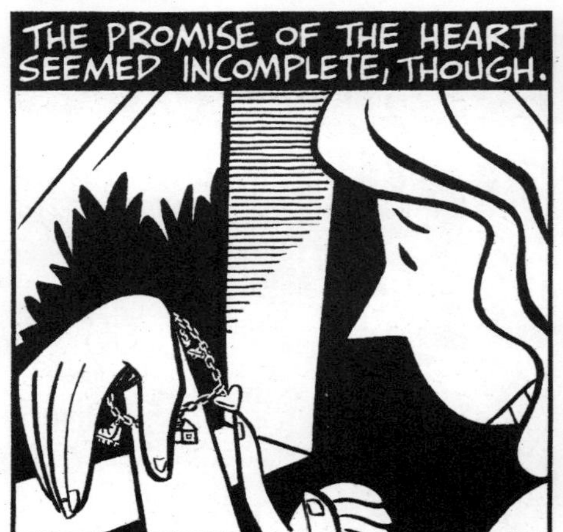
THE PROMISE OF THE HEART SEEMED INCOMPLETE, THOUGH.

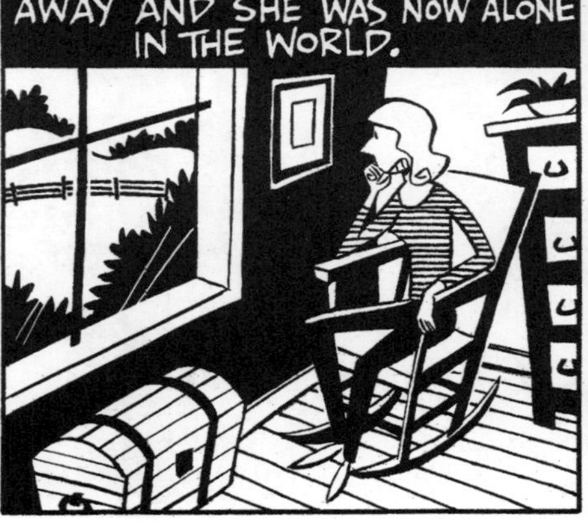
HER PARENTS HAD PASSED AWAY AND SHE WAS NOW ALONE IN THE WORLD.

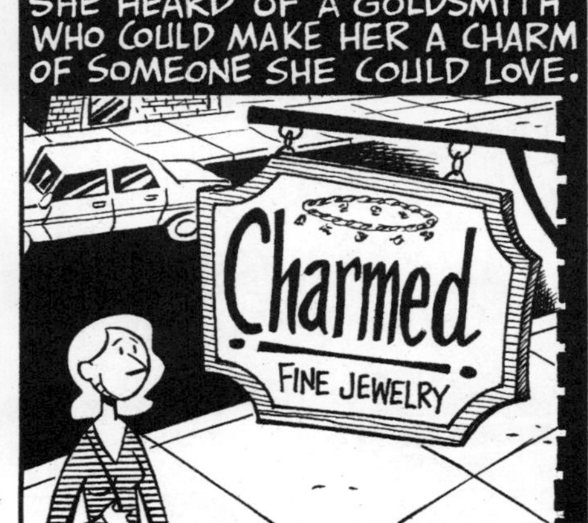
SHE HEARD OF A GOLDSMITH WHO COULD MAKE HER A CHARM OF SOMEONE SHE COULD LOVE.
Charmed
FINE JEWELRY

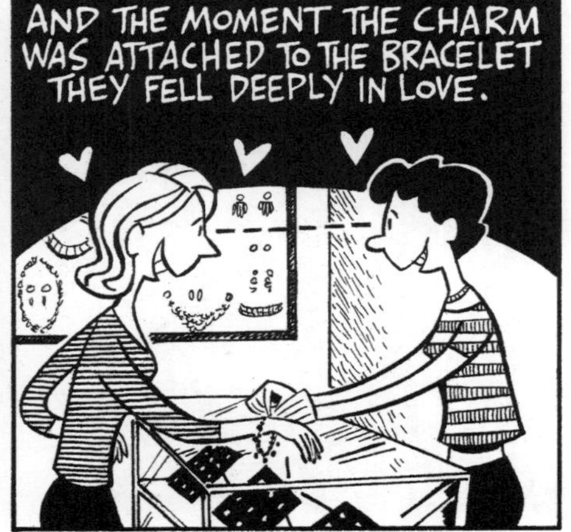
AND THE MOMENT THE CHARM WAS ATTACHED TO THE BRACELET THEY FELL DEEPLY IN LOVE.

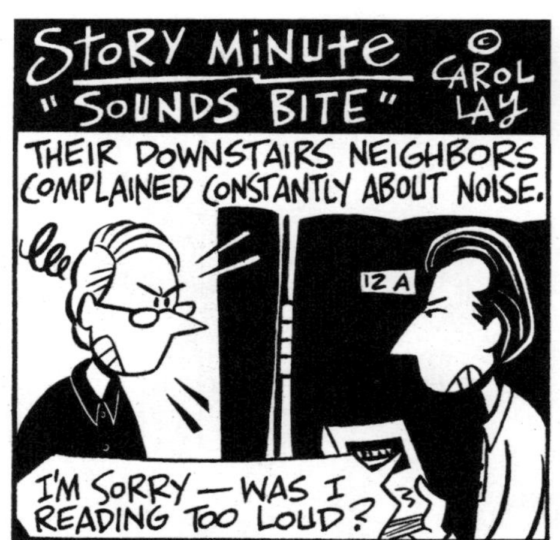
STORY MINUTE
"SOUNDS BITE"
© CAROL LAY
THEIR DOWNSTAIRS NEIGHBORS COMPLAINED CONSTANTLY ABOUT NOISE.
12 A
I'M SORRY — WAS I READING TOO LOUD?

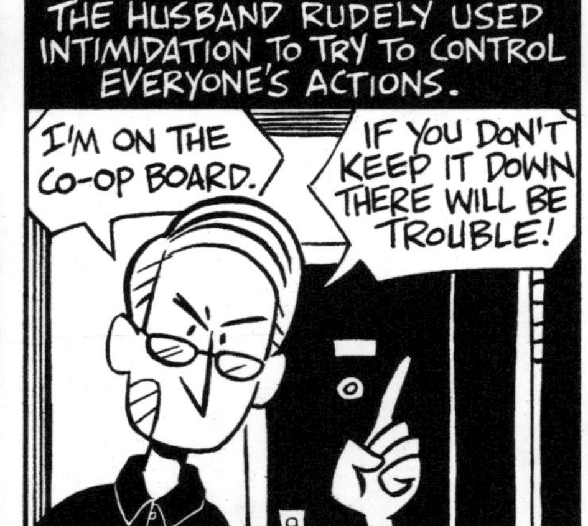
THE HUSBAND RUDELY USED INTIMIDATION TO TRY TO CONTROL EVERYONE'S ACTIONS.
I'M ON THE CO-OP BOARD.
IF YOU DON'T KEEP IT DOWN THERE WILL BE TROUBLE!

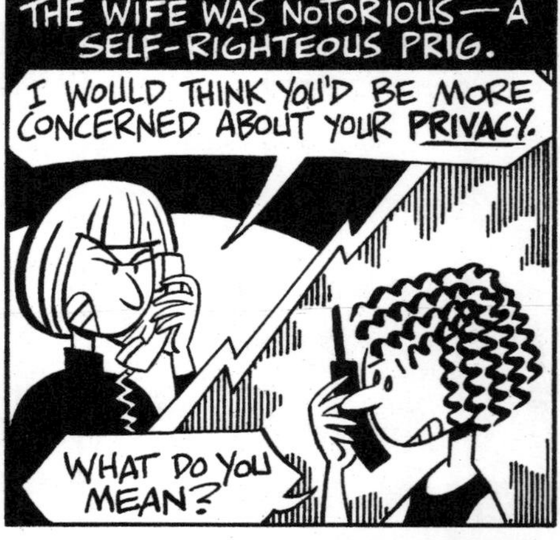
THE WIFE WAS NOTORIOUS — A SELF-RIGHTEOUS PRIG.
I WOULD THINK YOU'D BE MORE CONCERNED ABOUT YOUR PRIVACY.
WHAT DO YOU MEAN?

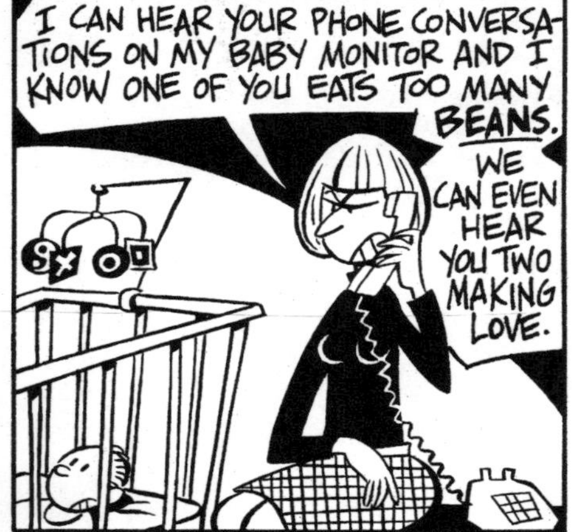
I CAN HEAR YOUR PHONE CONVERSATIONS ON MY BABY MONITOR AND I KNOW ONE OF YOU EATS TOO MANY BEANS.
WE CAN EVEN HEAR YOU TWO MAKING LOVE.

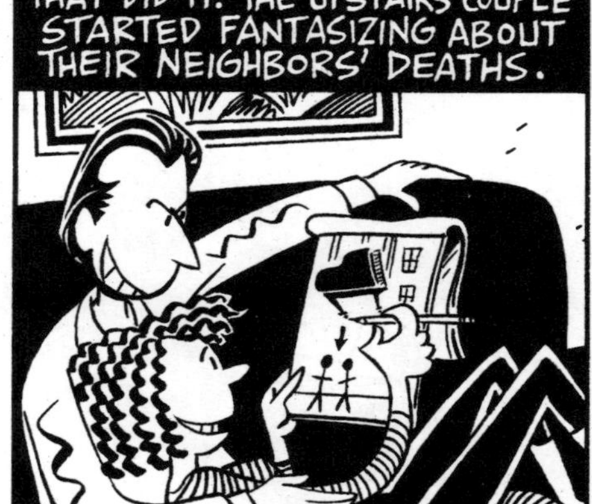
THAT DID IT. THE UPSTAIRS COUPLE STARTED FANTASIZING ABOUT THEIR NEIGHBORS' DEATHS.

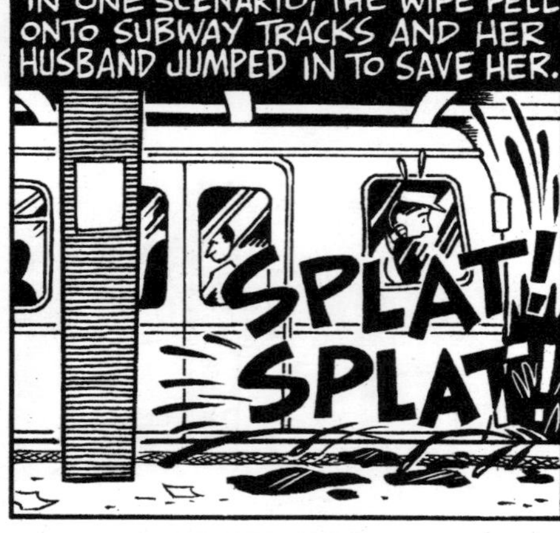
IN ONE SCENARIO, THE WIFE FELL ONTO SUBWAY TRACKS AND HER HUSBAND JUMPED IN TO SAVE HER.
SPLAT!
SPLAT!

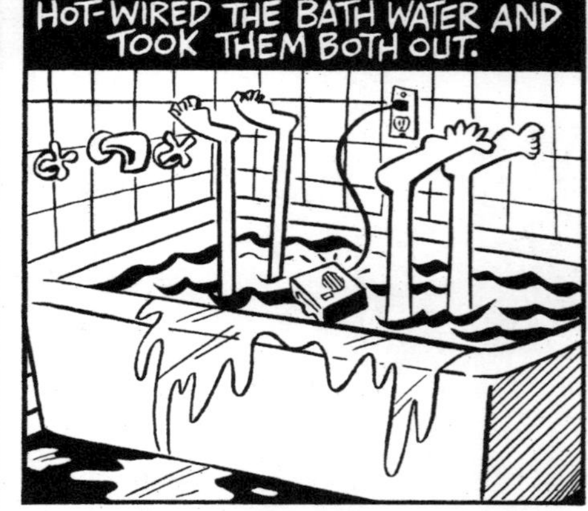
IN ANOTHER, THE BABY MONITOR HOT-WIRED THE BATH WATER AND TOOK THEM BOTH OUT.

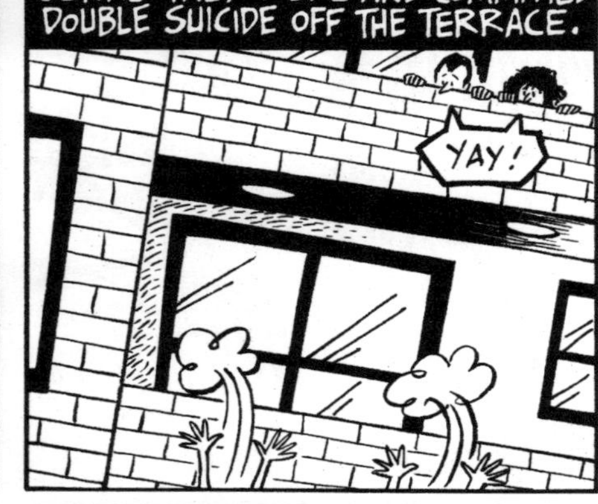
OR THEY JUST REALIZED WHAT JERKS THEY WERE AND COMMITTED DOUBLE SUICIDE OFF THE TERRACE.
YAY!

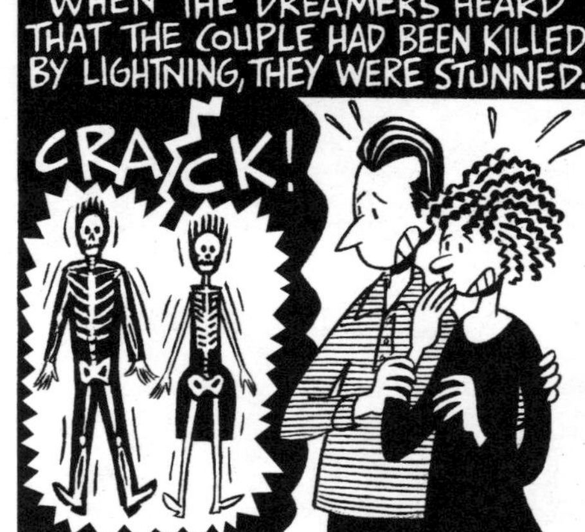
WHEN THE DREAMERS HEARD THAT THE COUPLE HAD BEEN KILLED BY LIGHTNING, THEY WERE STUNNED.
CRACK!

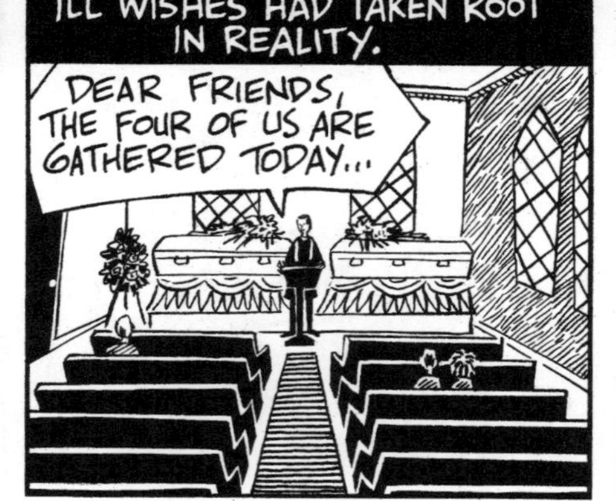
THEY ALMOST FELT LIKE THEIR ILL WISHES HAD TAKEN ROOT IN REALITY.
DEAR FRIENDS, THE FOUR OF US ARE GATHERED TODAY...

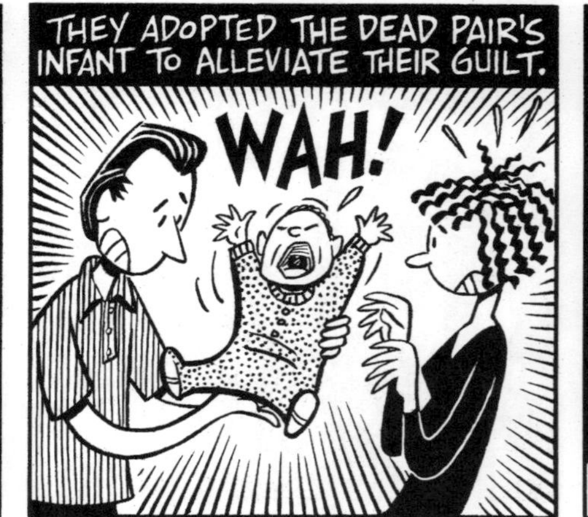
THEY ADOPTED THE DEAD PAIR'S INFANT TO ALLEVIATE THEIR GUILT.
WAH!

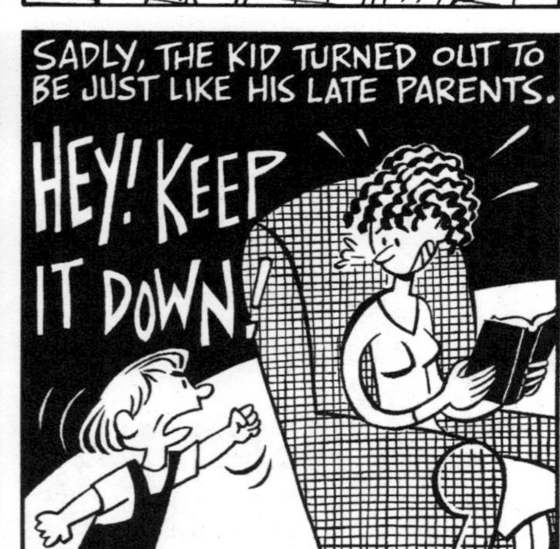
SADLY, THE KID TURNED OUT TO BE JUST LIKE HIS LATE PARENTS.
HEY! KEEP IT DOWN!

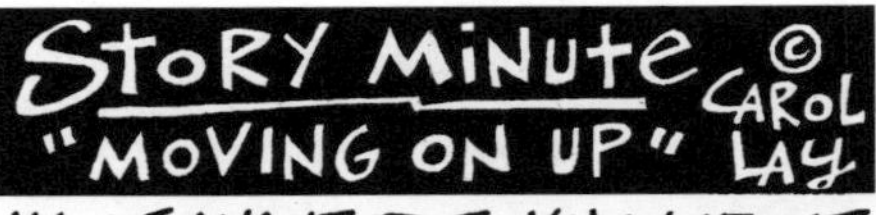


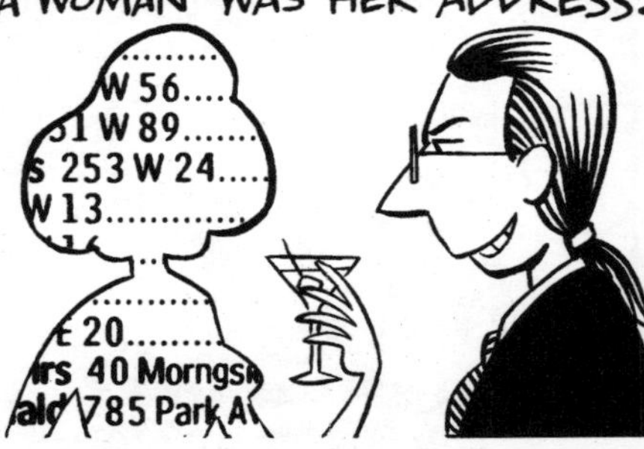


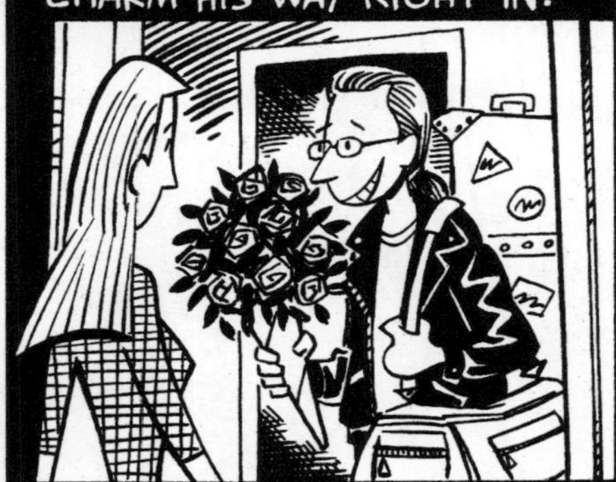


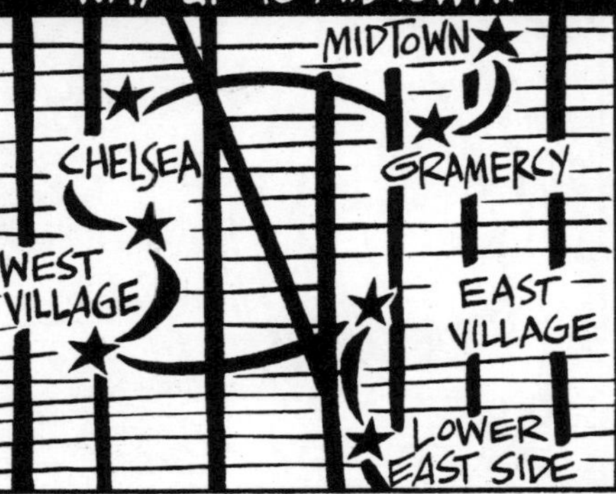


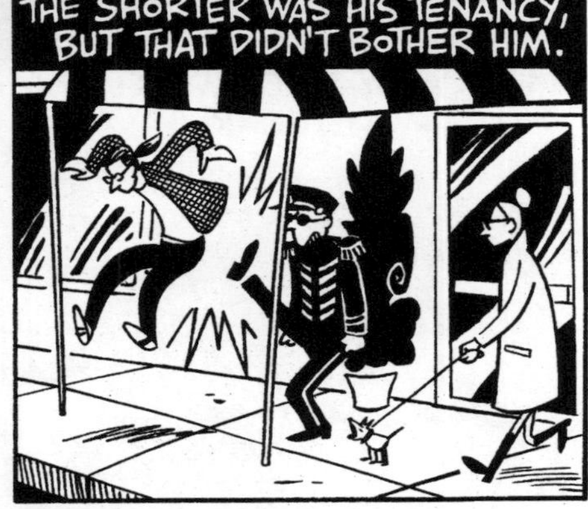


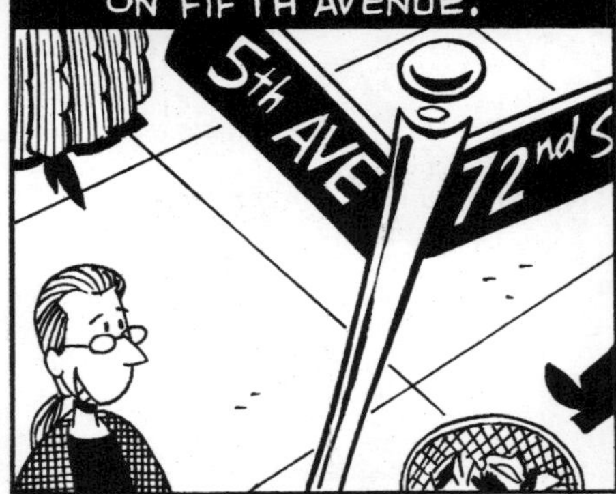


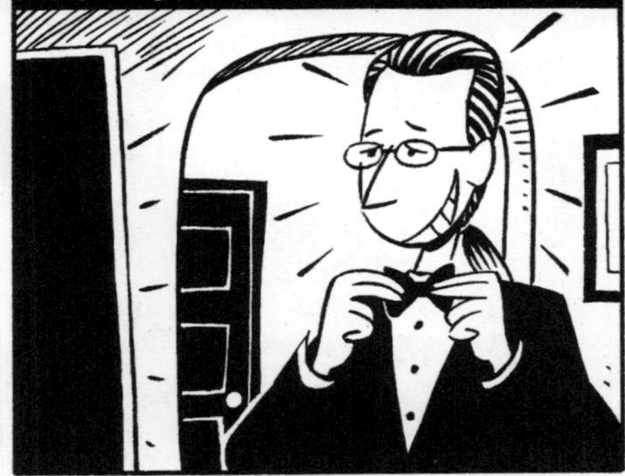


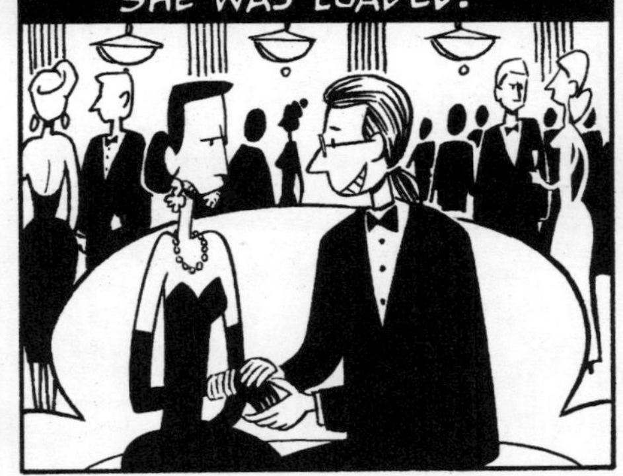


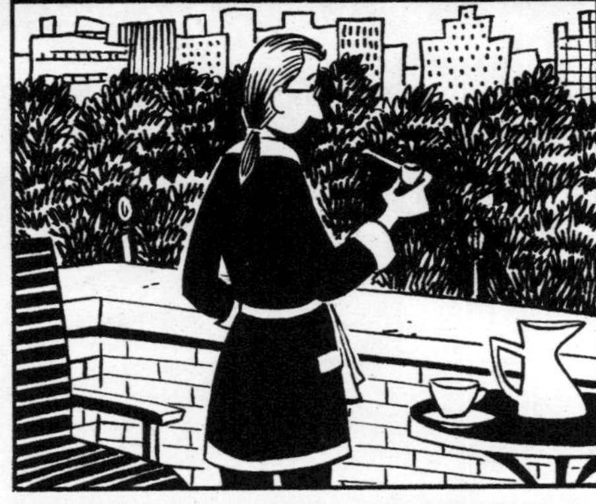


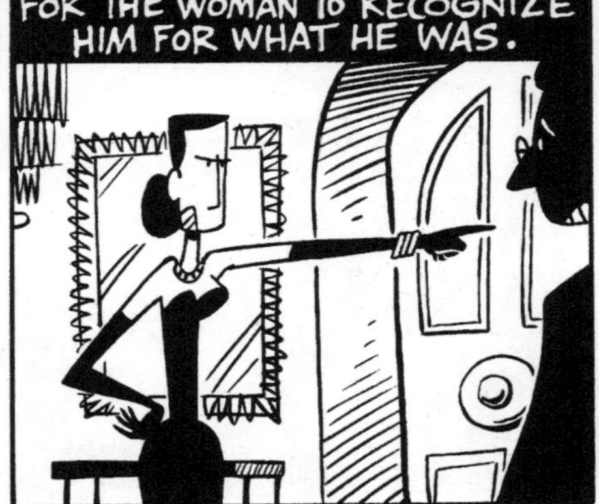


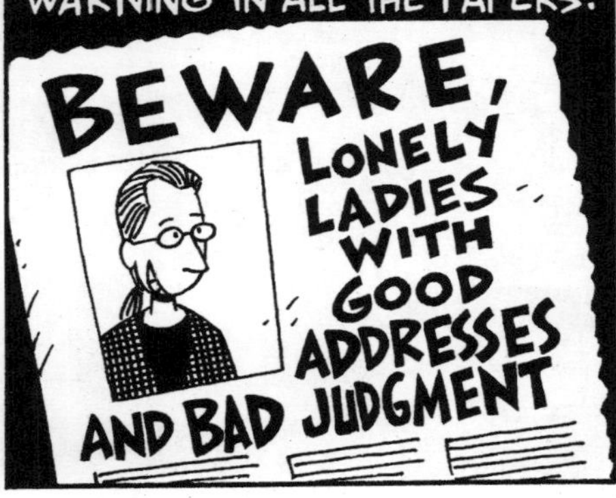


NO WOMAN WHO SAW THAT AD WOULD EVER FALL PREY TO HIS GAME AGAIN.

?

!

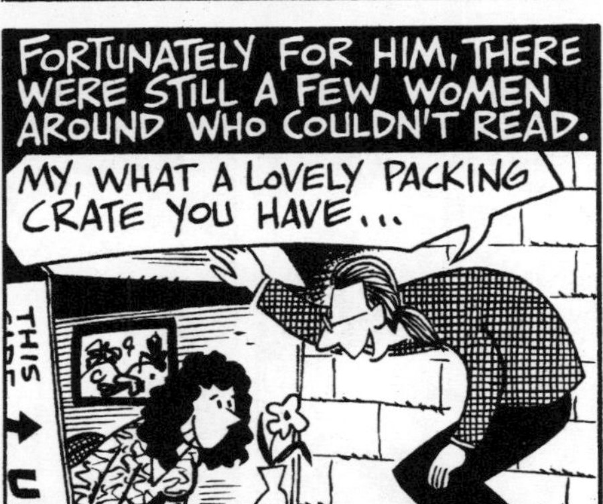

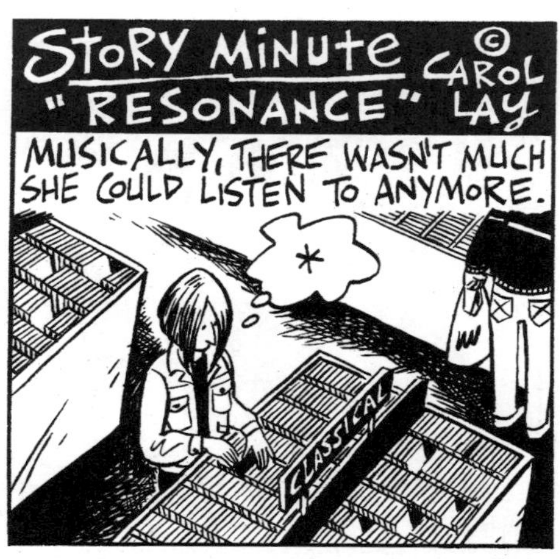
STORY MINUTE © CAROL LAY
"RESONANCE"
MUSICALLY, THERE WASN'T MUCH SHE COULD LISTEN TO ANYMORE.
*
CLASSICAL

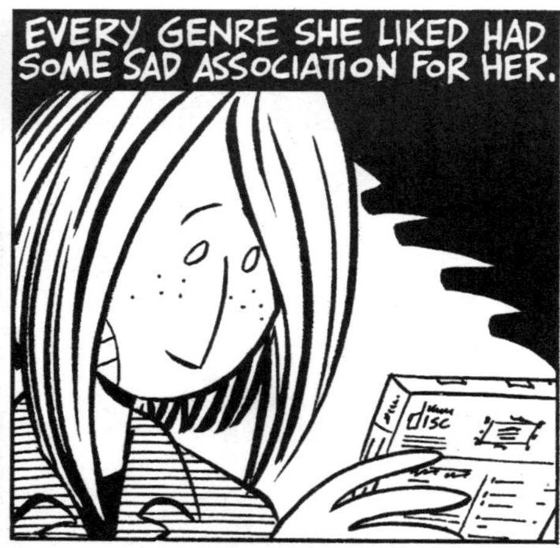
EVERY GENRE SHE LIKED HAD SOME SAD ASSOCIATION FOR HER.
DISC

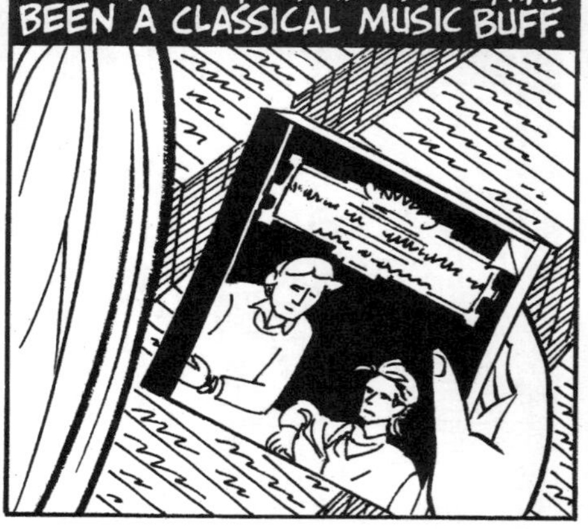
HER FATHER, FOR INSTANCE, HAD BEEN A CLASSICAL MUSIC BUFF.

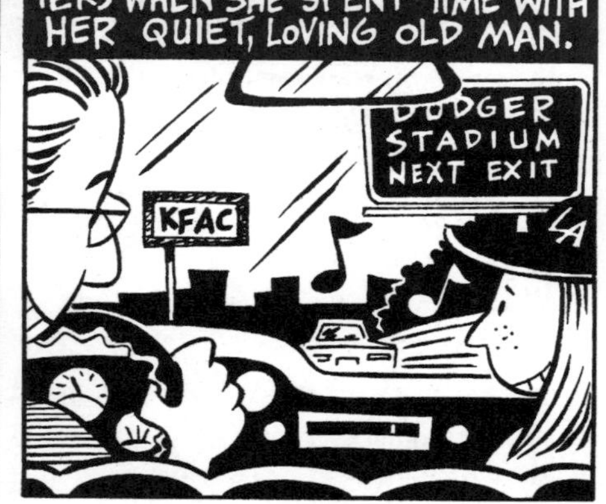
SHE HAD SOAKED UP THE OLD MASTERS WHEN SHE SPENT TIME WITH HER QUIET, LOVING OLD MAN.
DODGER STADIUM NEXT EXIT
KFAC
LA

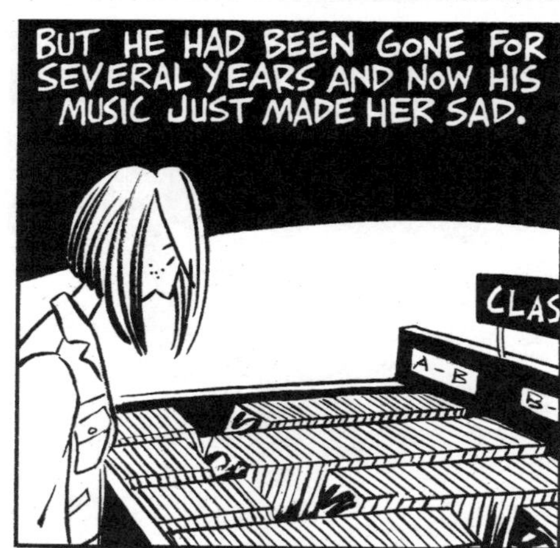
BUT HE HAD BEEN GONE FOR SEVERAL YEARS AND NOW HIS MUSIC JUST MADE HER SAD.
CLAS
A-B

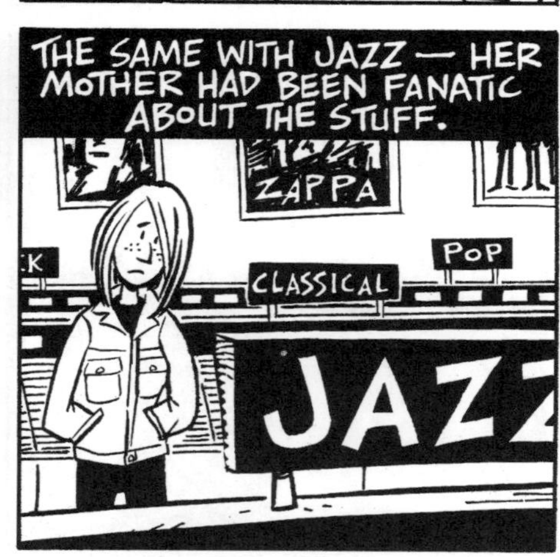
THE SAME WITH JAZZ — HER MOTHER HAD BEEN FANATIC ABOUT THE STUFF.
ZAPPA
POP
CLASSICAL
JAZZ

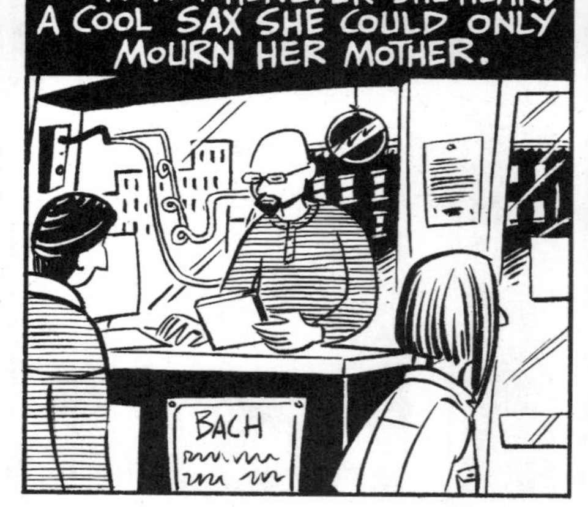
SO NOW WHENEVER SHE HEARD A COOL SAX SHE COULD ONLY MOURN HER MOTHER.
BACH

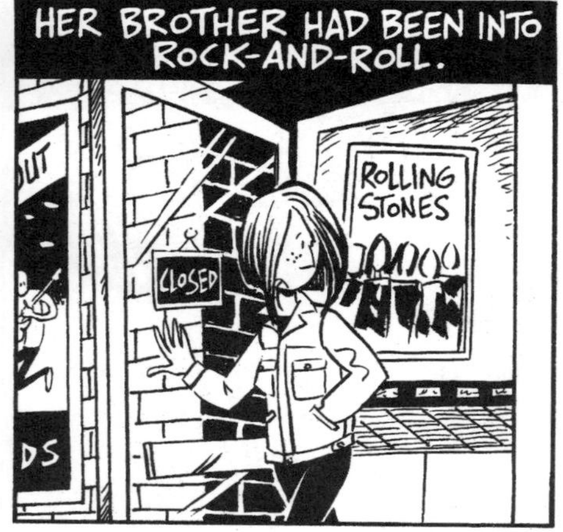
HER BROTHER HAD BEEN INTO ROCK-AND-ROLL.
ROLLING STONES
CLOSED

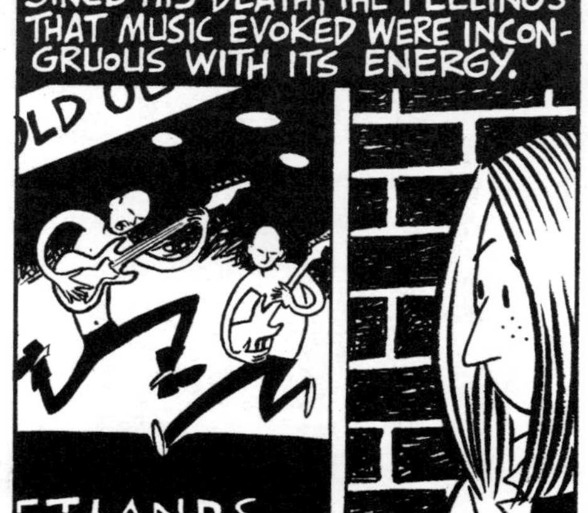
SINCE HIS DEATH, THE FEELINGS THAT MUSIC EVOKED WERE INCONGRUOUS WITH ITS ENERGY.

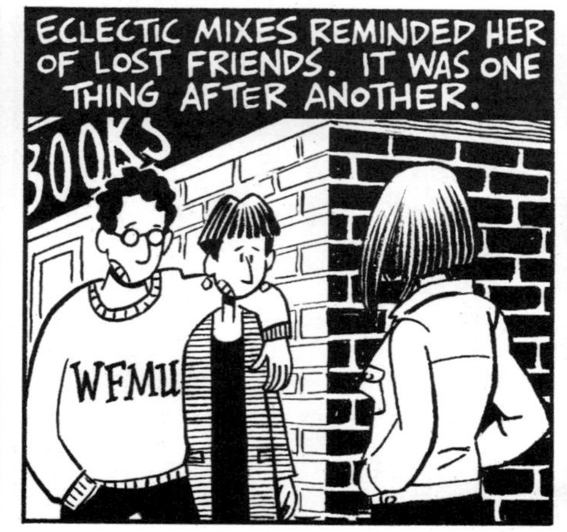
ECLECTIC MIXES REMINDED HER OF LOST FRIENDS. IT WAS ONE THING AFTER ANOTHER.
BOOKS
WFMU

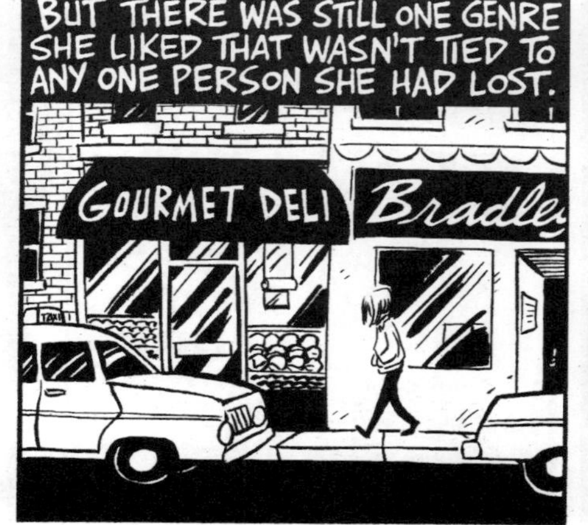
BUT THERE WAS STILL ONE GENRE SHE LIKED THAT WASN'T TIED TO ANY ONE PERSON SHE HAD LOST.
GOURMET DELI

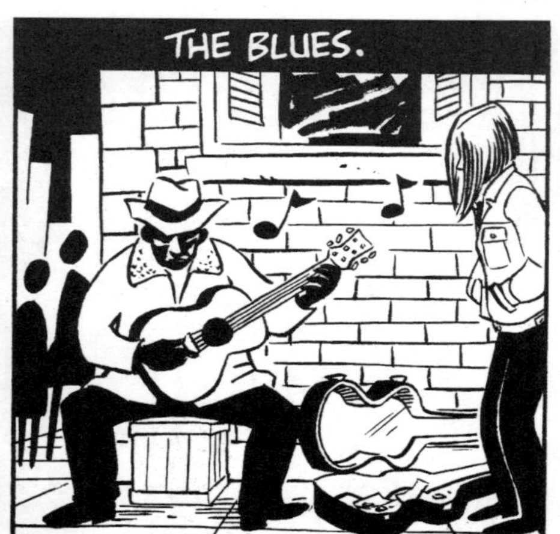
THE BLUES.

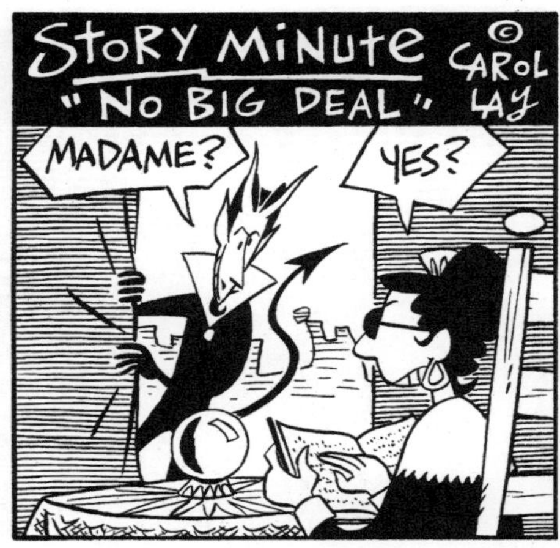
STORY MINUTE © CAROL LAY
"NO BIG DEAL"
MADAME?
YES?
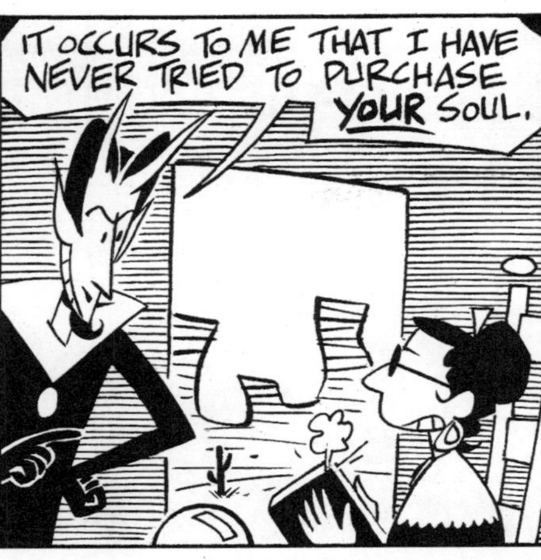
IT OCCURS TO ME THAT I HAVE NEVER TRIED TO PURCHASE YOUR SOUL.
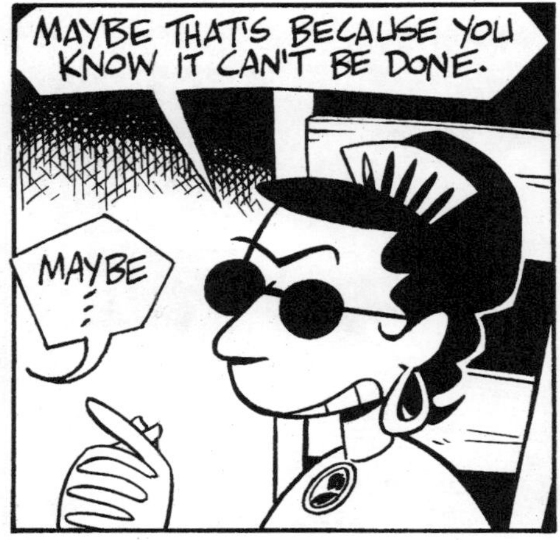
MAYBE THAT'S BECAUSE YOU KNOW IT CAN'T BE DONE.
MAYBE
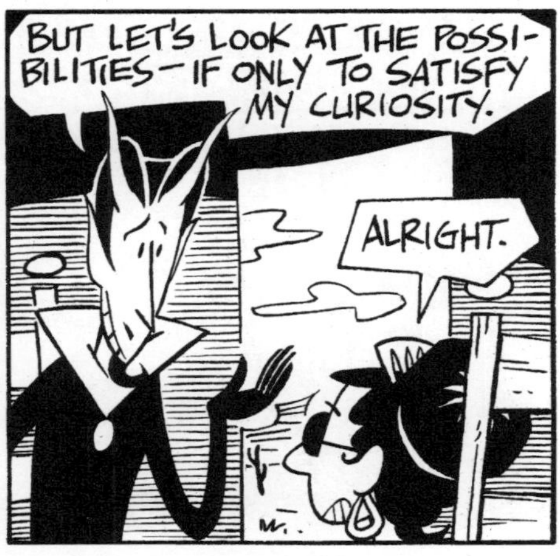
BUT LET'S LOOK AT THE POSSIBILITIES—IF ONLY TO SATISFY MY CURIOSITY.
ALRIGHT.
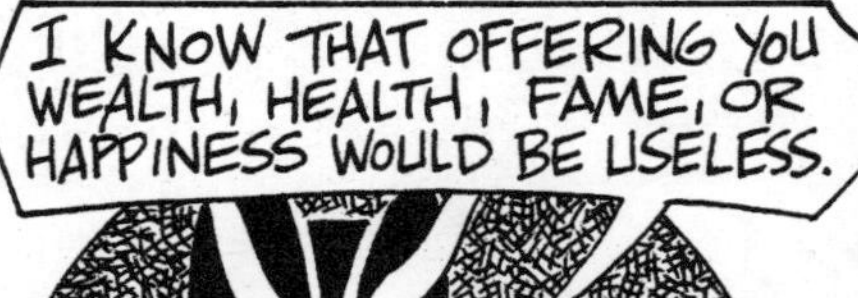
I KNOW THAT OFFERING YOU WEALTH, HEALTH, FAME, OR HAPPINESS WOULD BE USELESS.
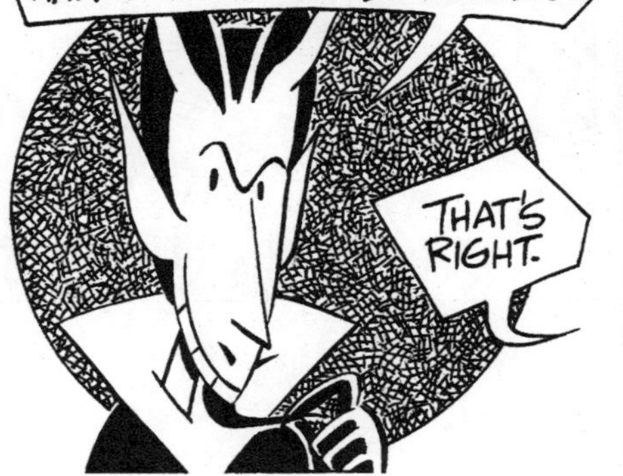
THAT'S RIGHT.
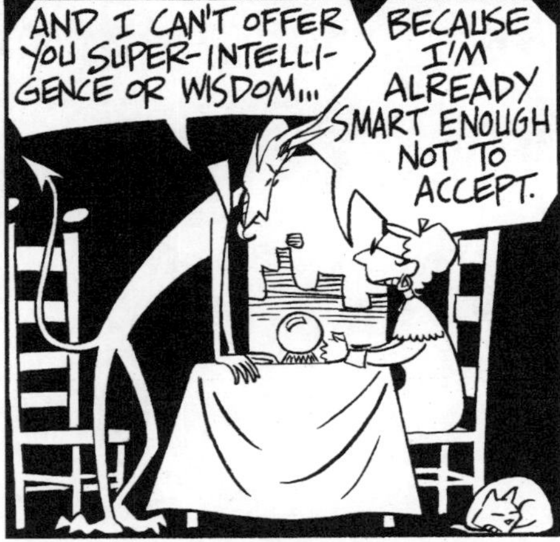
AND I CAN'T OFFER YOU SUPER-INTELLIGENCE OR WISDOM...
BECAUSE I'M ALREADY SMART ENOUGH NOT TO ACCEPT.
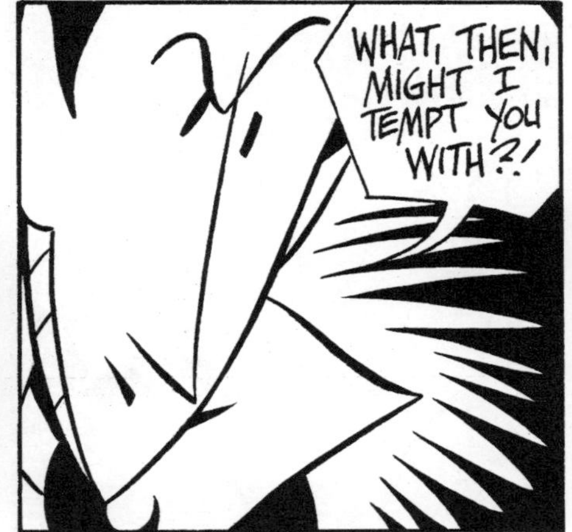
WHAT, THEN, MIGHT I TEMPT YOU WITH?!
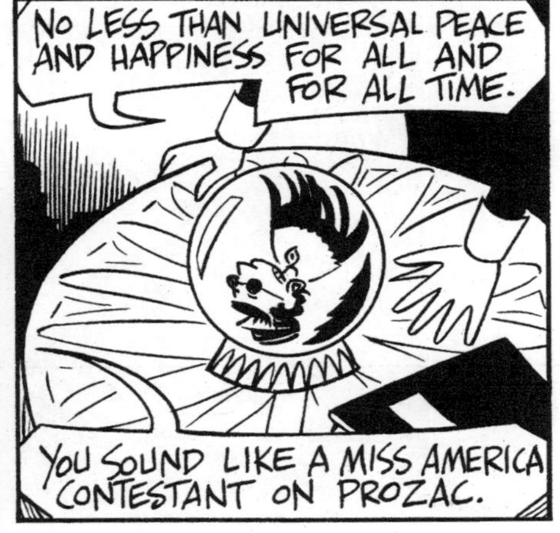
NO LESS THAN UNIVERSAL PEACE AND HAPPINESS FOR ALL AND FOR ALL TIME.
YOU SOUND LIKE A MISS AMERICA CONTESTANT ON PROZAC.
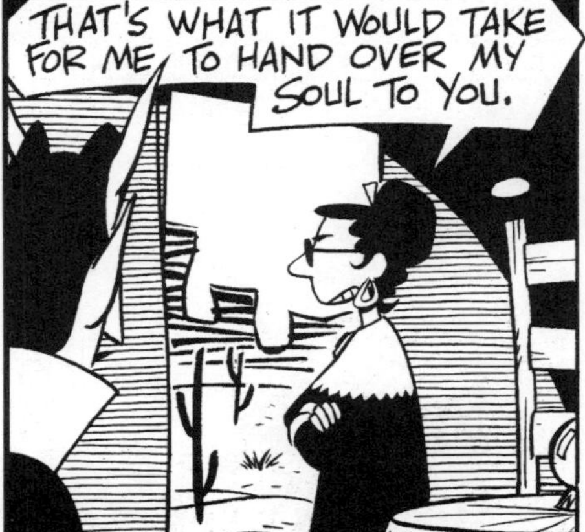
THAT'S WHAT IT WOULD TAKE FOR ME TO HAND OVER MY SOUL TO YOU.
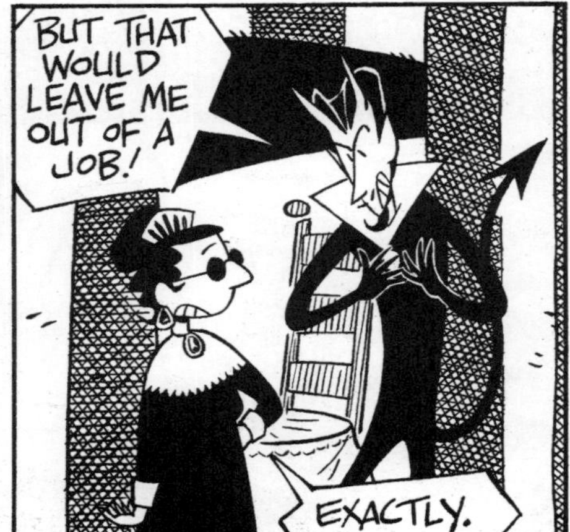
BUT THAT WOULD LEAVE ME OUT OF A JOB!
EXACTLY.
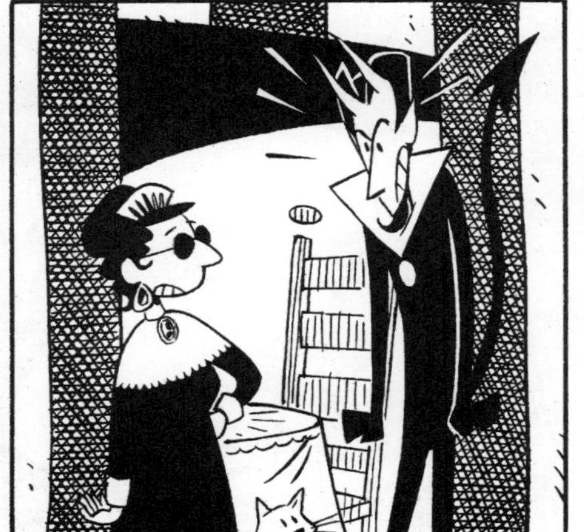
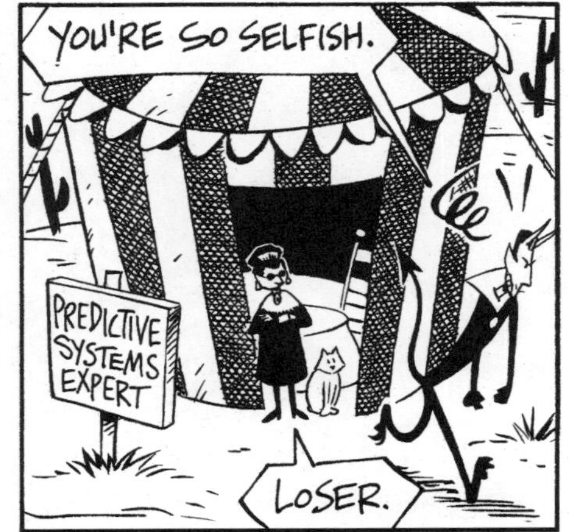
YOU'RE SO SELFISH.
PREDICTIVE SYSTEMS EXPERT
LOSER.

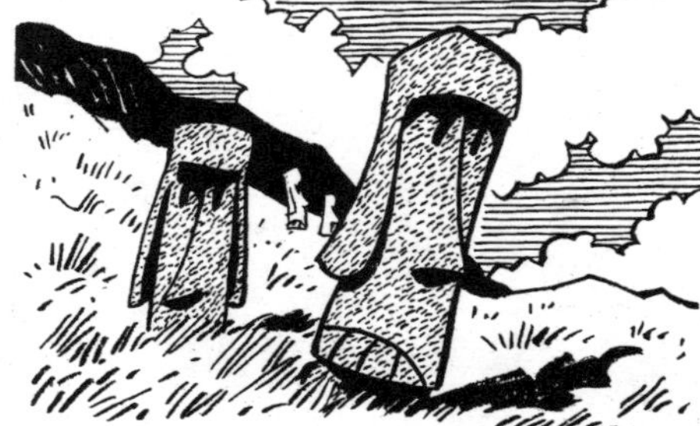
STORY MINUTE © CAROL LAY
"THE 2000 PARTY"
THEY HAD CHOSEN THE PLACE FOR ITS AUSTERE SPOOKINESS.

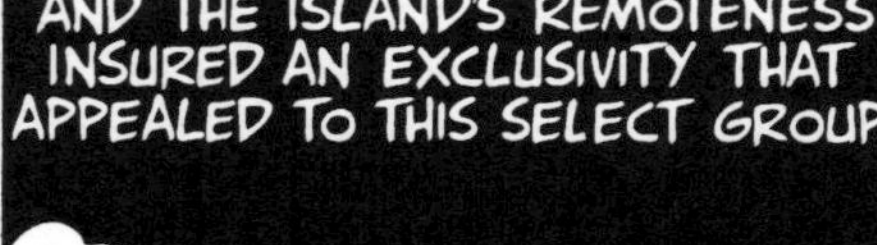
AND THE ISLAND'S REMOTENESS INSURED AN EXCLUSIVITY THAT APPEALED TO THIS SELECT GROUP.

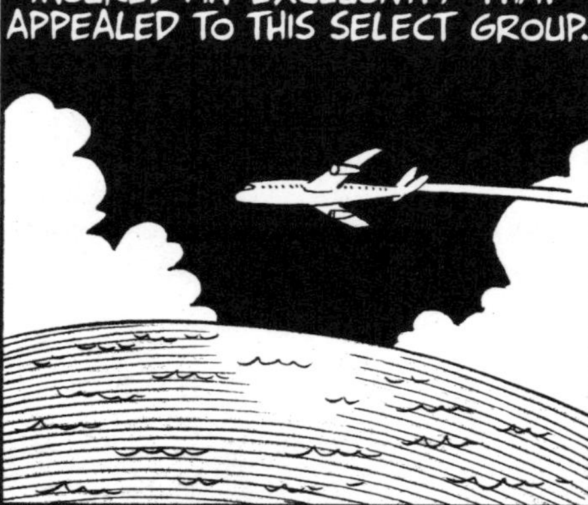

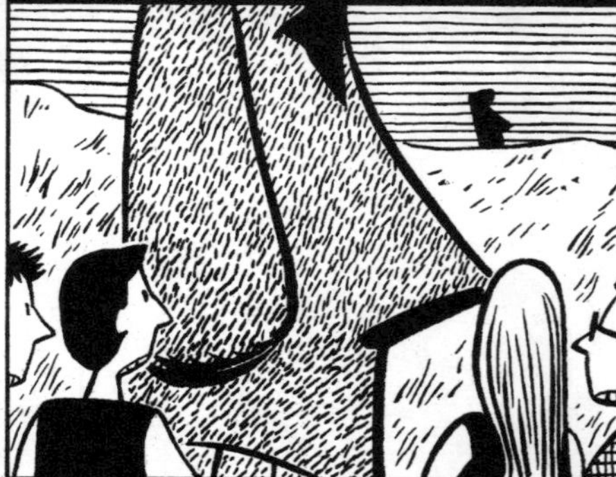
THE HUGE STONE HEADS STOOD IN MUTE TESTIMONY TO THE GRANDEUR OF HUMAN STUPIDITY.

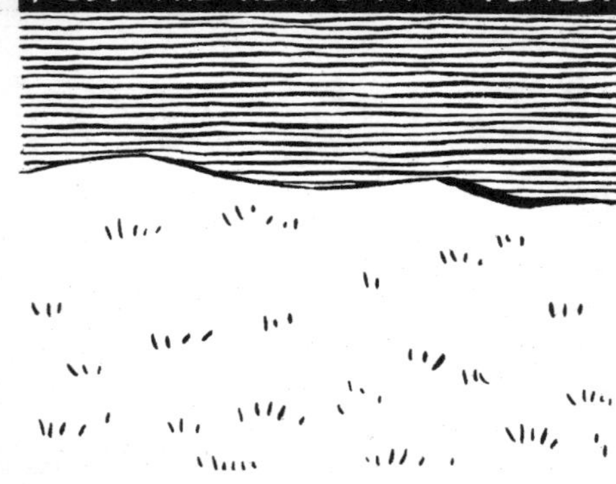
THE FORMER INHABITANTS HAD CUT DOWN ALL THEIR TREES TO ROLL THE HEADS INTO PLACE.

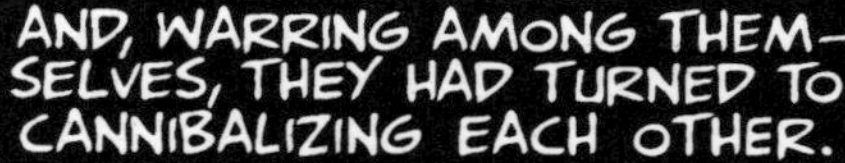
AND, WARRING AMONG THEMSELVES, THEY HAD TURNED TO CANNIBALIZING EACH OTHER.

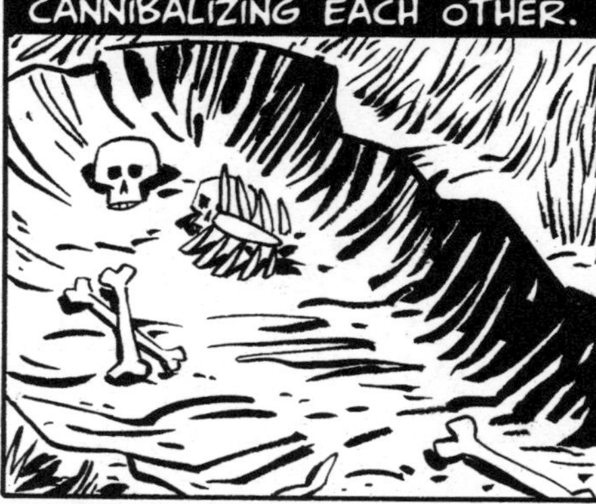

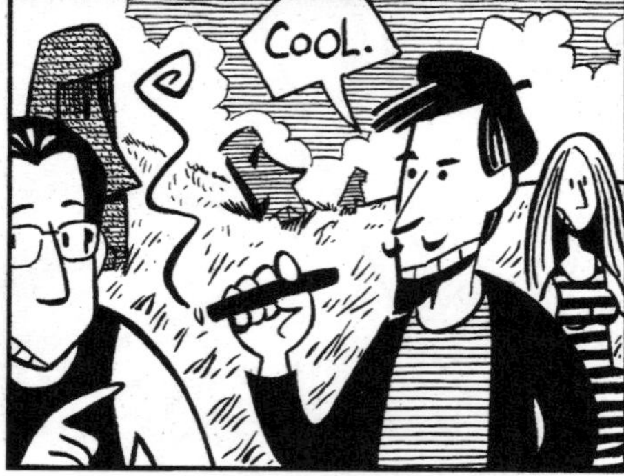
SO, WHAT BETTER PLACE COULD THERE BE FOR CELEBRATING THE COMING NEW MILLENNIUM?
COOL.

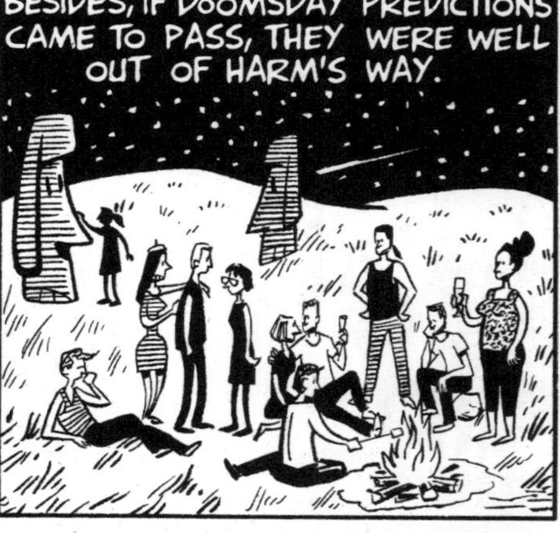
BESIDES, IF DOOMSDAY PREDICTIONS CAME TO PASS, THEY WERE WELL OUT OF HARM'S WAY.

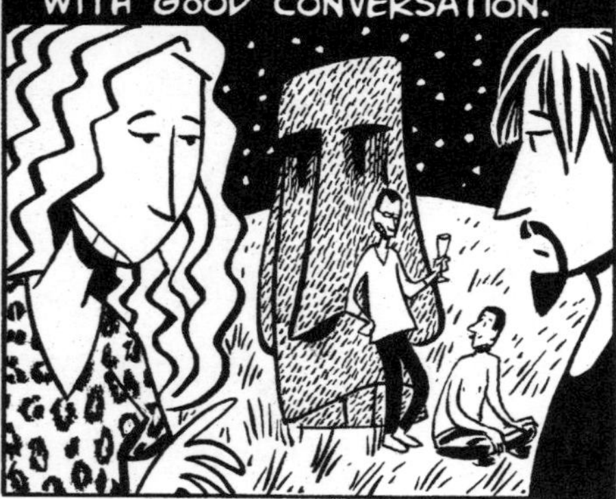
THEY SUPPLIED THEIR OWN ENTERTAINMENT IN THE DESOLATE PLACE WITH GOOD CONVERSATION.

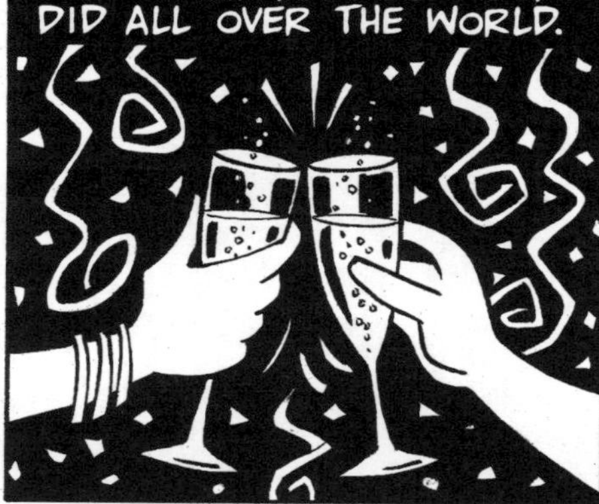
AND THEY TOASTED THE NEW YEAR AT MIDNIGHT AS OTHERS DID ALL OVER THE WORLD.

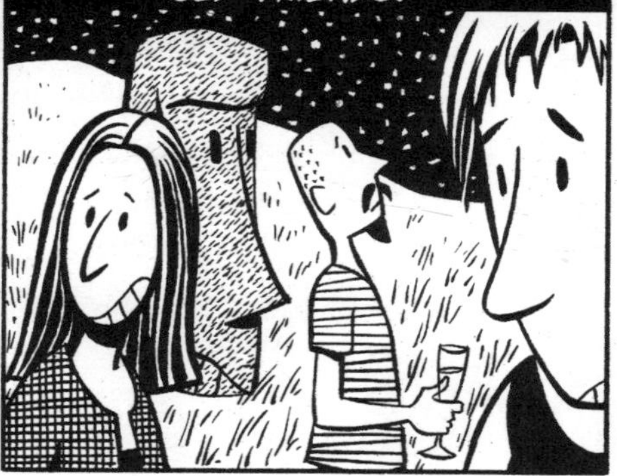
BUT A PECULIAR SENSE OF FOREBODING CIRCULATED AMONG THE OLD FRIENDS.

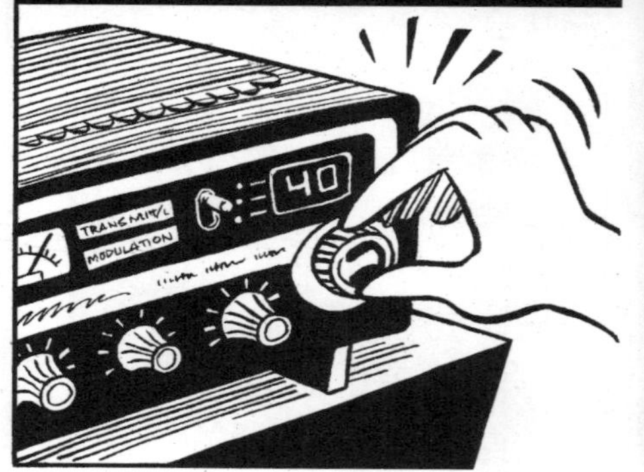
THEY SOON FOUND OUT THEY HAD NO HOMES TO RETURN TO. THE UNTHINKABLE HAD HAPPENED.
40
MODULATION

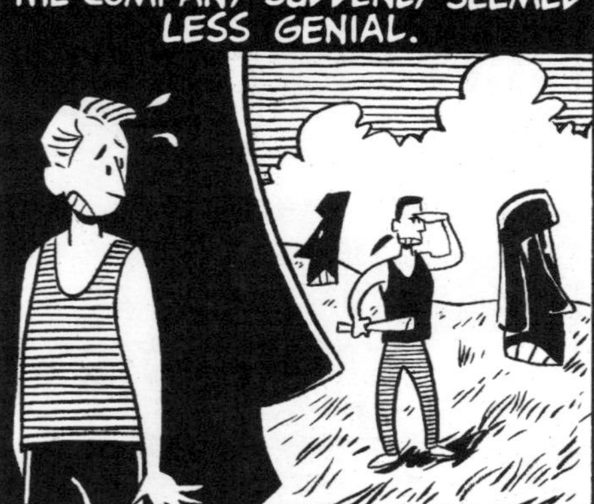
AS THE FOOD SUPPLY RAN LOW THE COMPANY SUDDENLY SEEMED LESS GENIAL.

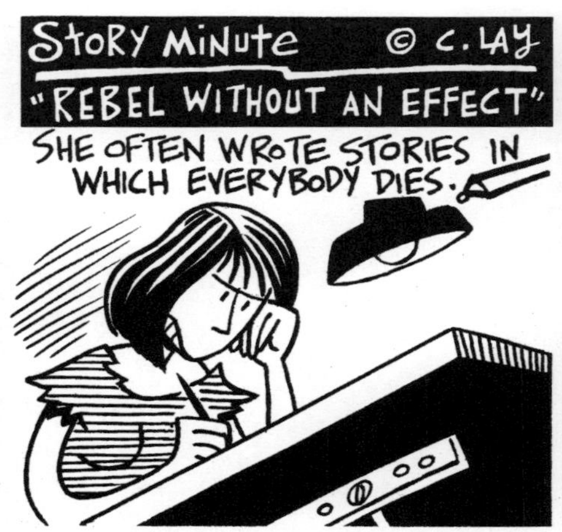

STORY MINUTE © C. LAY
"REBEL WITHOUT AN EFFECT"
SHE OFTEN WROTE STORIES IN WHICH EVERYBODY DIES.


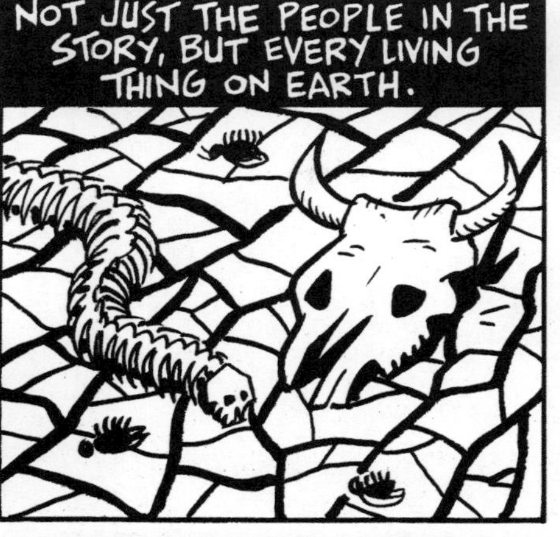

NOT JUST THE PEOPLE IN THE STORY, BUT EVERY LIVING THING ON EARTH.


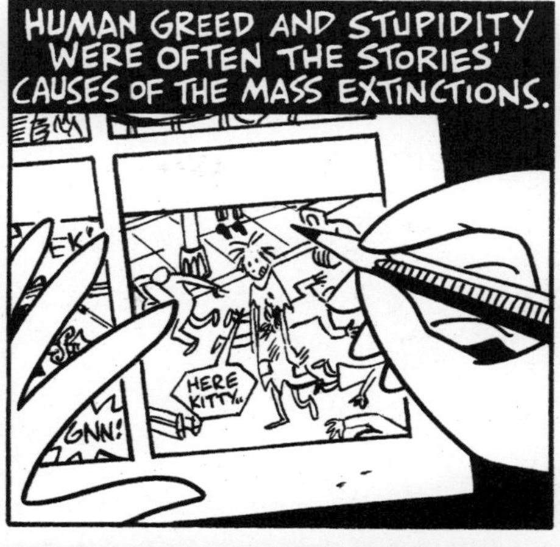

HUMAN GREED AND STUPIDITY WERE OFTEN THE STORIES' CAUSES OF THE MASS EXTINCTIONS.
EEK!
HERE KITTY..
GNN!


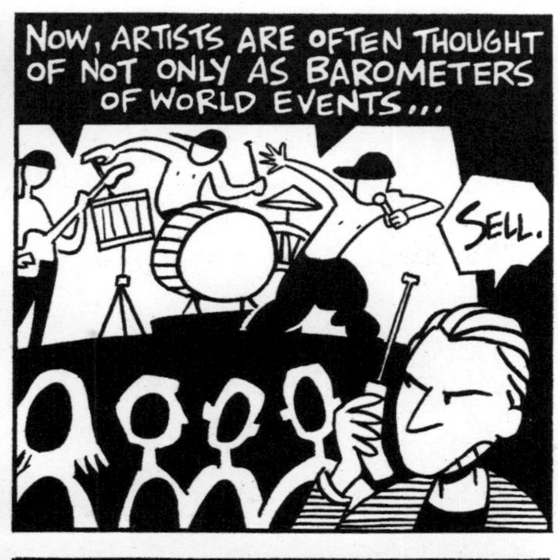

NOW, ARTISTS ARE OFTEN THOUGHT OF NOT ONLY AS BAROMETERS OF WORLD EVENTS...
SELL.


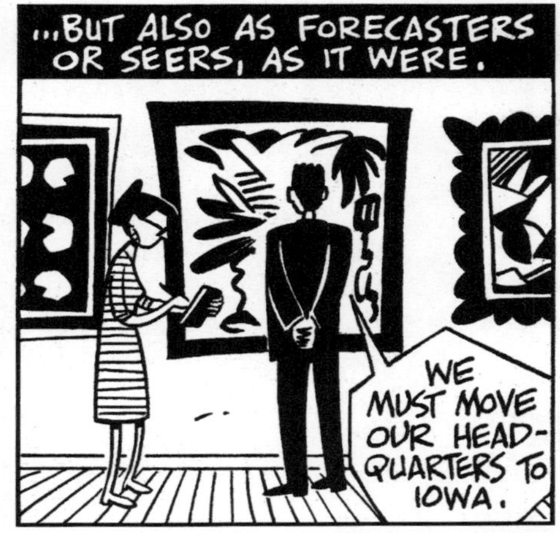

...BUT ALSO AS FORECASTERS OR SEERS, AS IT WERE.
WE MUST MOVE OUR HEAD-QUARTERS TO IOWA.


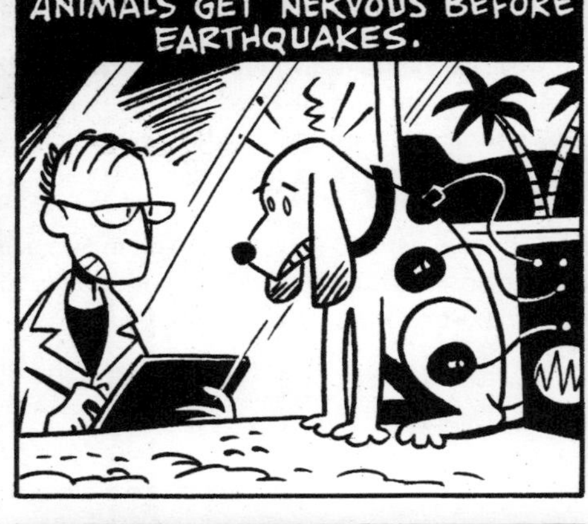

MAYBE IT'S SOMETHING LIKE HOW ANIMALS GET NERVOUS BEFORE EARTHQUAKES.


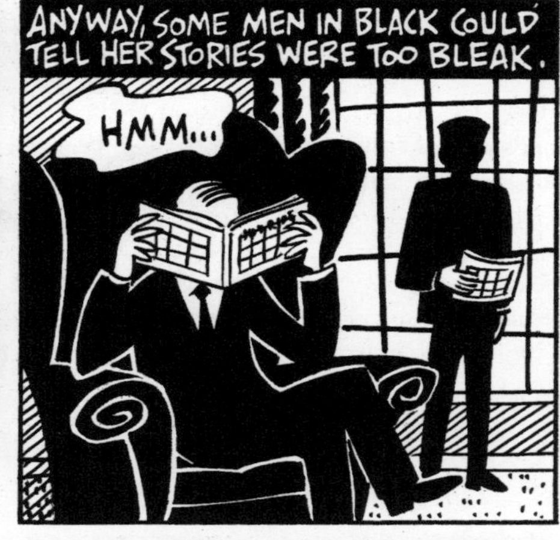

ANYWAY, SOME MEN IN BLACK COULD TELL HER STORIES WERE TOO BLEAK.
HMM...


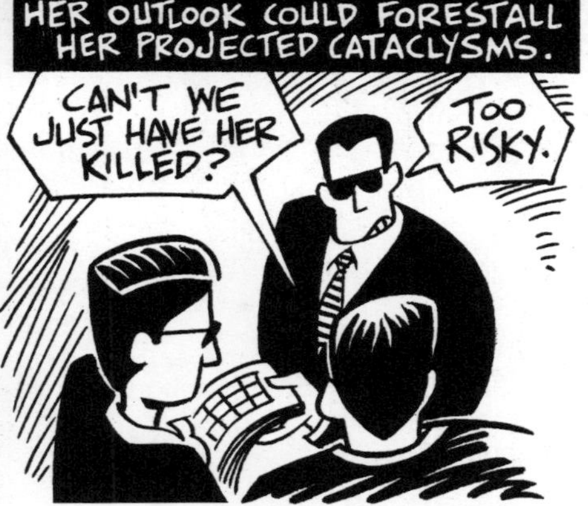

THEY WANTED TO KNOW IF CHANGING HER OUTLOOK COULD FORESTALL HER PROJECTED CATACLYSMS.
CAN'T WE JUST HAVE HER KILLED?
TOO RISKY.


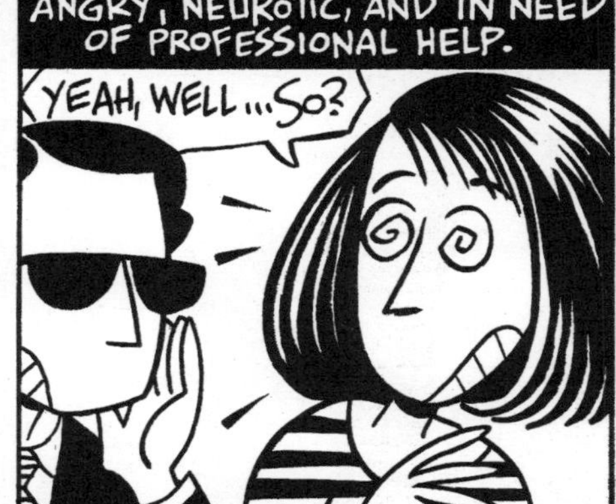

THEY CONVINCED HER SHE WAS ANGRY, NEUROTIC, AND IN NEED OF PROFESSIONAL HELP.
YEAH, WELL...SO?


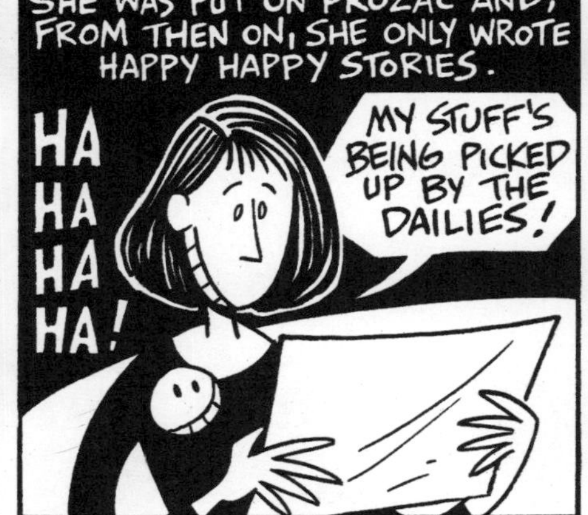

SHE WAS PUT ON PROZAC AND, FROM THEN ON, SHE ONLY WROTE HAPPY HAPPY STORIES.
HA HA HA HA HA!
MY STUFF'S BEING PICKED UP BY THE DAILIES!


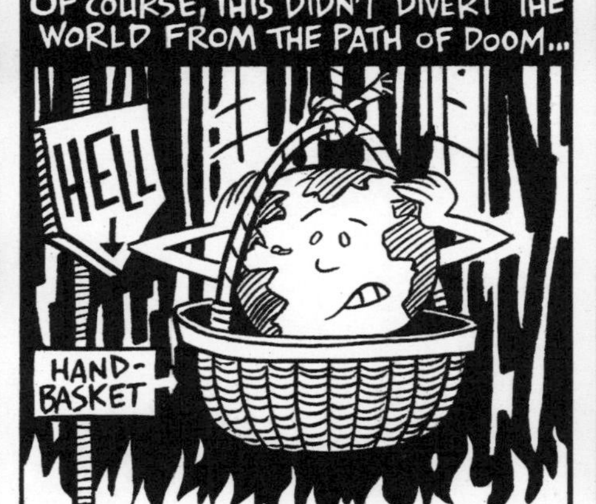

OF COURSE, THIS DIDN'T DIVERT THE WORLD FROM THE PATH OF DOOM...
HELL
HAND-BASKET


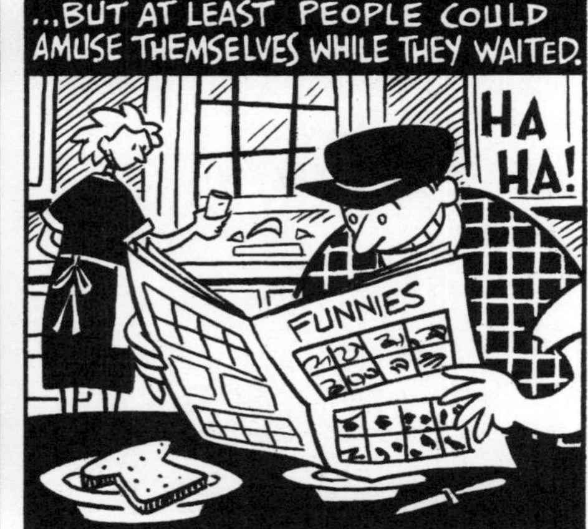

...BUT AT LEAST PEOPLE COULD AMUSE THEMSELVES WHILE THEY WAITED.
HA HA!
FUNNIES

## "Story of Minutes"

Early in 1995, two years before daily strip creators did likewise, cartoonist Tony Millionaire suggested that our local weekly paper's regular comix contributors swap strips for April Fool's Day. Tony, of *Maakies* fame, sent up Mark Beyer's *Amy and Jordan* strip. Mark did an excellent parody of Kaz's *Underworld* comic, Kaz nailed Doug Allen's *Steven,* Doug tackled Takeshi Tadatsu's *Tokyo New York,* Takeshi was stuck with doing my strip, and I did Millionaire's. The readers loved it.

Poor Takeshi got the raw end of the deal, though. He is more comfortable with the Japanese language, and *Story Minute* is usually well-stocked with captions or dialogue. Or, as he observed while working on his piece, "You have a lot of English." He overcame that obstacle, though, and produced the most excellent "Story of Minutes."

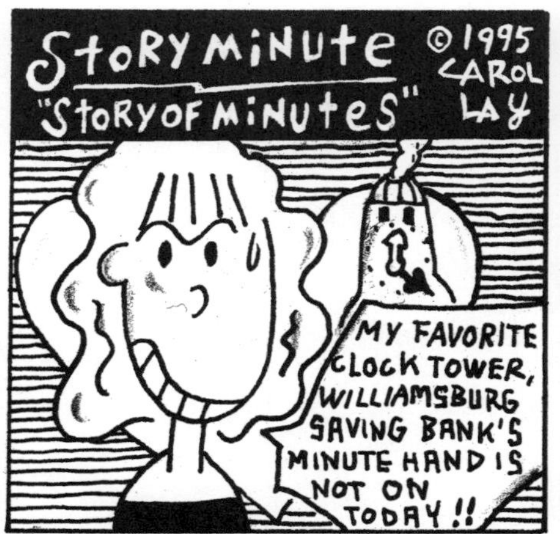
STORY MINUTE "STORY OF MINUTES"
©1995 CAROL LAY
MY FAVORITE CLOCK TOWER, WILLIAMSBURG SAVING BANK'S MINUTE HAND IS NOT ON TODAY!!

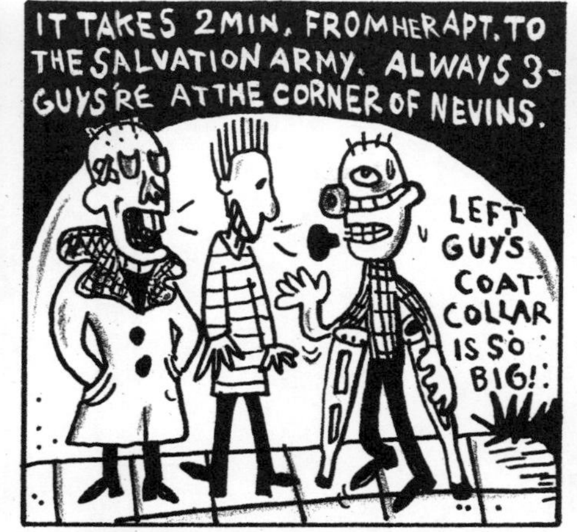
IT TAKES 2MIN. FROM HER APT. TO THE SALVATION ARMY. ALWAYS 3-GUYS'RE AT THE CORNER OF NEVINS.
LEFT GUY'S COAT COLLAR IS SO BIG!

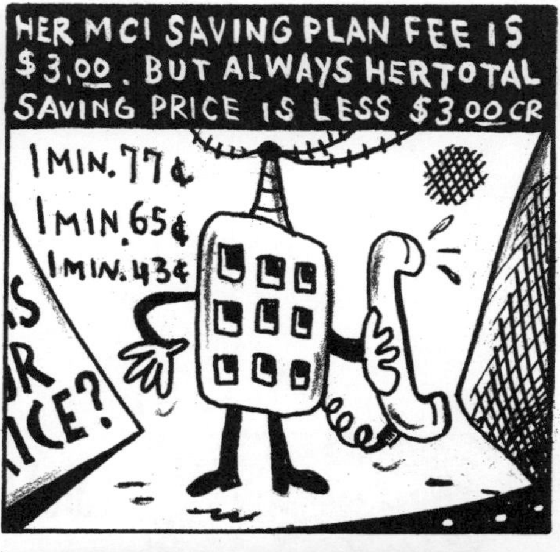
HER MCI SAVING PLAN FEE IS $3.00. BUT ALWAYS HER TOTAL SAVING PRICE IS LESS $3.00 CR
1MIN. 77¢
1MIN. 65¢
1MIN. 43¢

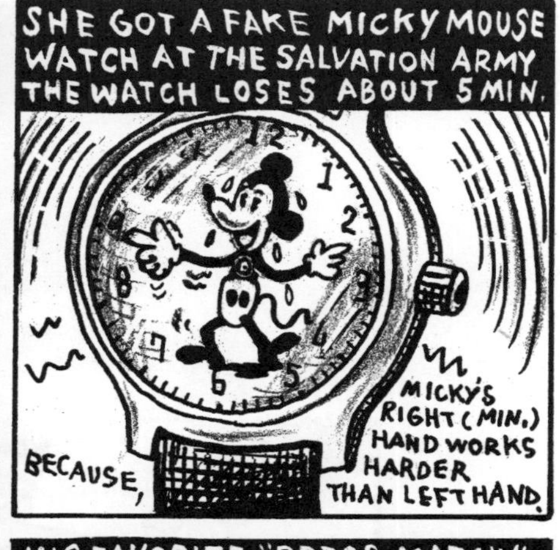
SHE GOT A FAKE MICKY MOUSE WATCH AT THE SALVATION ARMY THE WATCH LOSES ABOUT 5MIN.
BECAUSE,
MICKY'S RIGHT (MIN.) HAND WORKS HARDER THAN LEFT HAND.

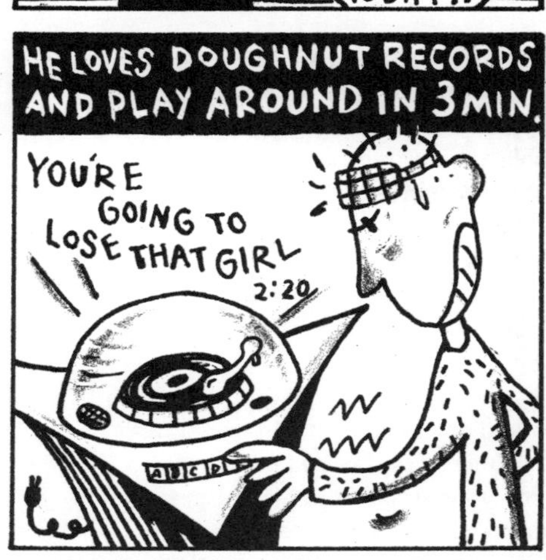
HE LOVES DOUGHNUT RECORDS AND PLAY AROUND IN 3MIN.
YOU'RE GOING TO LOSE THAT GIRL
2:20

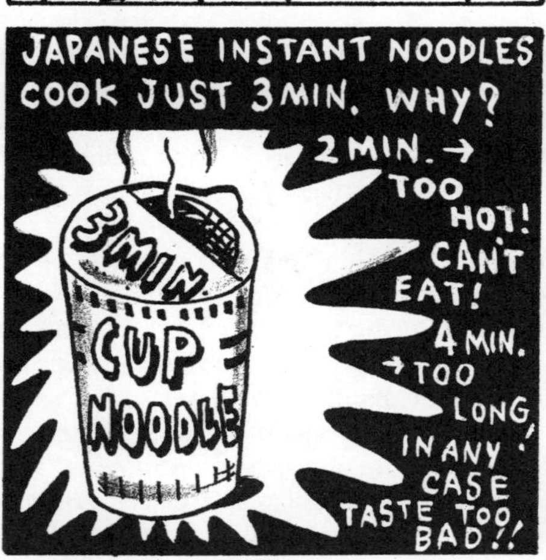
JAPANESE INSTANT NOODLES COOK JUST 3MIN. WHY?
3MIN
CUP NOODLE
2MIN. → TOO HOT! CAN'T EAT!
4MIN. → TOO LONG,
IN ANY CASE TASTE TOO BAD!!

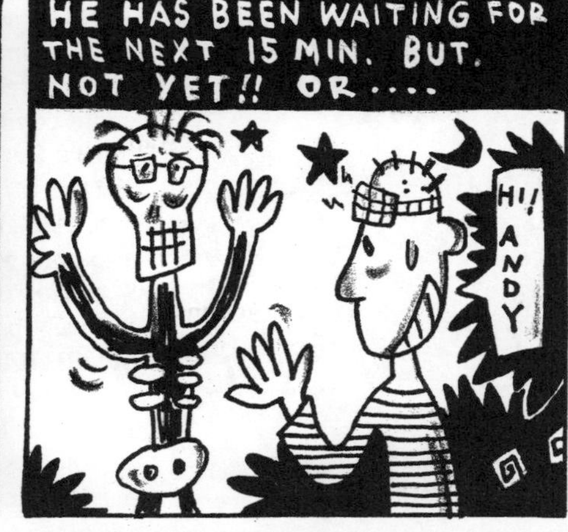
HE HAS BEEN WAITING FOR THE NEXT 15 MIN. BUT. NOT YET!! OR....
HI! ANDY

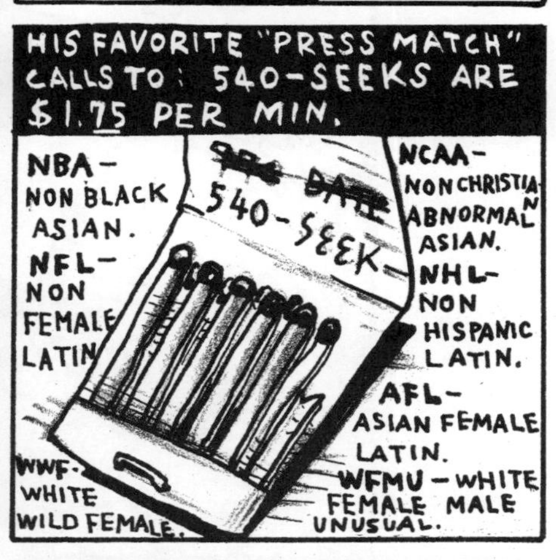
HIS FAVORITE "PRESS MATCH" CALLS TO: 540-SEEKS ARE $1.75 PER MIN.
540-SEEK
NBA - NON BLACK ASIAN.
NFL - NON FEMALE LATIN
WWF - WHITE WILD FEMALE.
NCAA - NON CHRISTIAN ABNORMAL ASIAN.
NHL - NON HISPANIC LATIN.
AFL - ASIAN FEMALE LATIN.
WFMU - WHITE FEMALE MALE UNUSUAL.

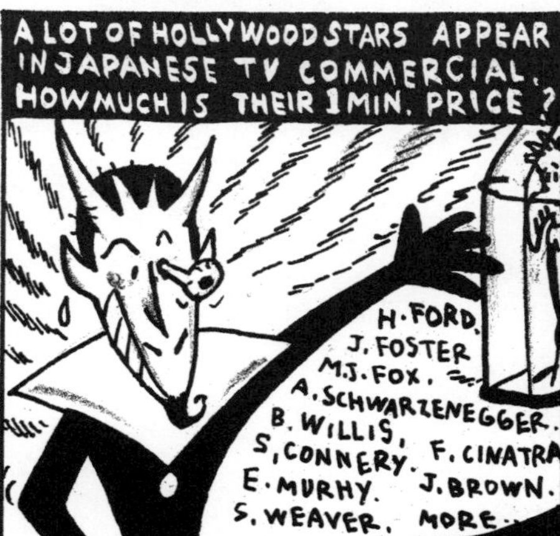
A LOT OF HOLLYWOOD STARS APPEAR IN JAPANESE TV COMMERCIAL. HOW MUCH IS THEIR 1MIN. PRICE?
H. FORD, J. FOSTER M.J. FOX, A. SCHWARZENEGGER. B. WILLIS, S. CONNERY. F. CINATRA E. MURHY. J. BROWN. S. WEAVER. MORE...

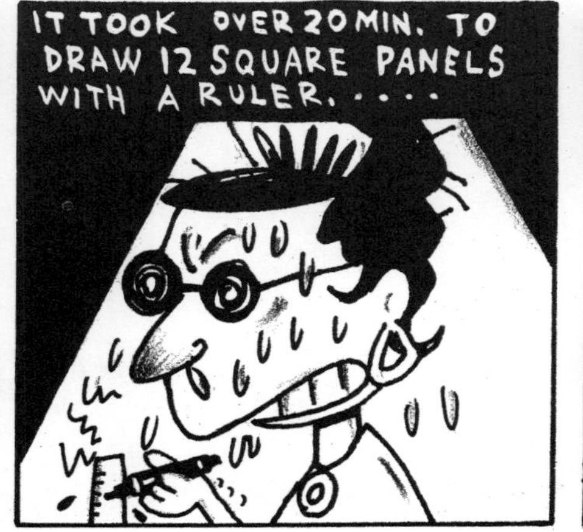
IT TOOK OVER 20MIN. TO DRAW 12 SQUARE PANELS WITH A RULER....

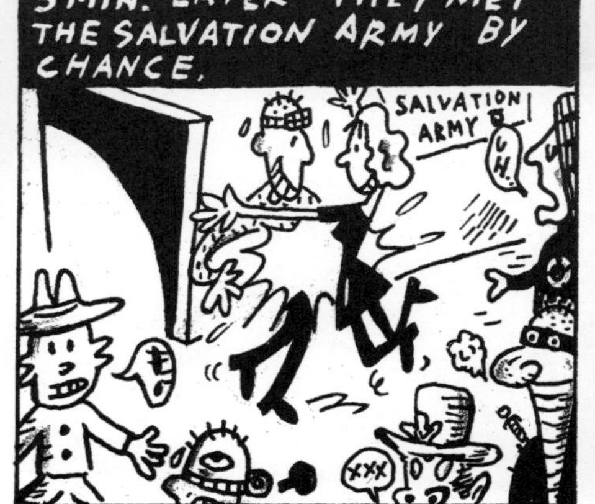
3MIN. LATER THEY MET THE SALVATION ARMY BY CHANCE.
SALVATION ARMY
UH.

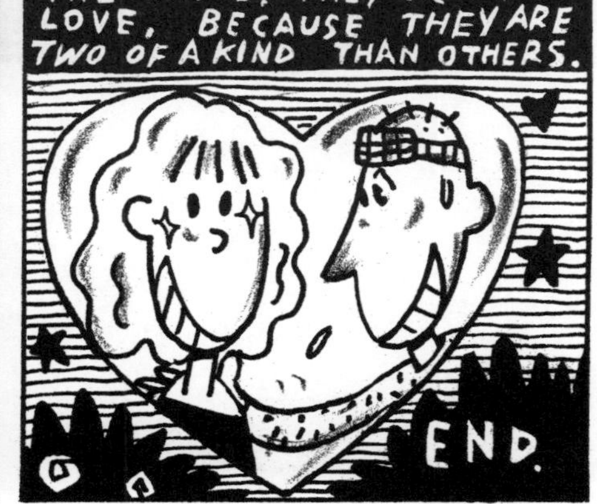
THE MINUTE, THEY'RE IN LOVE, BECAUSE THEY ARE TWO OF A KIND THAN OTHERS.
END.

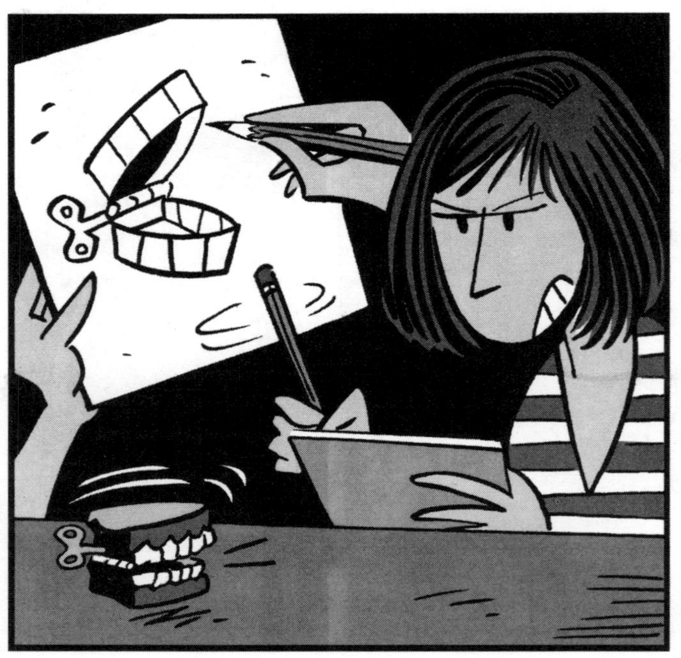

# Carol Lay

was born and raised in Orange County, California. She went to college at UCLA where she got her BFA in 1975. She then worked as a commercial artist for several years in Los Angeles, doing storyboards for feature films, commercials, rock videos, and animation. She also drew and wrote comics for various underground and mainstream publishers, worked on several Barbie comics for Mattel, and illustrated for publications such as *Entertainment Weekly, Newsweek,* and the *Village Voice.*

In 1993, Lay moved to New York to concentrate on her weekly comic strip and to do more magazine work. Her cartoon strip, *Story Minute,* now appears regularly in the *LA Weekly,* the *San Francisco Examiner,* the *Dallas Observer, Salon Magazine,* and numerous other weekly and daily papers. Her cartoons and illustrations have also appeared in the *Wall Street Journal, Details, MAD* magazine, and the *New Yorker.*

Previous collections of Lay's strips include *Now, Endsville* and *Joy Ride*—both from Kitchen Sink Press. Her stories have also appeared in *Twisted Sisters* Volumes I and II, and other comics anthologies. Several strips and stories have been translated into at least four other languages.

Lay currently resides in Brooklyn with her husband and three cats.

Web site: www.waylay.com
Email: lay@echonyc.com